GLOBALIZATION

Also available:

The Globalization Reader, 5th Edition
Edited by Frank J. Lechner, John Boli

Globalization: The Essentials
George Ritzer

Readings in Globalization: Key Concepts and Major Debates
Edited by George Ritzer and Zeynep Atalay

The Wiley-Blackwell Encyclopedia of Globalization
(www.globalizationencyclopedia.com)
Edited by George Ritzer

The Blackwell Companion to Globalization
Edited by George Ritzer

Introducing Globalization: Ties, Tensions, and Uneven Integration
Matthew Sparke

GLOBALIZATION | A BASIC TEXT

GEORGE RITZER AND
PAUL DEAN

Second Edition

WILEY Blackwell

This second edition first published 2015
© 2015 John Wiley & Sons, Ltd
Edition history: Blackwell Publishing Ltd (1e, 2010)

Registered Office
John Wiley & Sons, Ltd, The Atrium, Southern Gate, Chichester, West Sussex, PO19 8SQ, UK

Editorial Offices
350 Main Street, Malden, MA 02148-5020, USA
9600 Garsington Road, Oxford, OX4 2DQ, UK
The Atrium, Southern Gate, Chichester, West Sussex, PO19 8SQ, UK

For details of our global editorial offices, for customer services, and for information about
how to apply for permission to reuse the copyright material in this book please see our
website at www.wiley.com/wiley-blackwell.

The right of George Ritzer and Paul Dean to be identified as the authors of this work has been
asserted in accordance with the UK Copyright, Designs and Patents Act 1988.

Library of Congress Cataloging-in-Publication Data

Ritzer, George.
Globalization: a basic text / George Ritzer and Paul Dean. – Second edition.
    pages   cm
  Includes bibliographical references and index.
  ISBN 978-1-118-68712-3 (pbk.)
1. Globalization.   I. Title.
  JZ1318.R577 2015
  303.48′2–dc23
                                                              2014029766

A catalogue record for this book is available from the British Library.

Cover image: World map © Derrrek / iStockphoto,
Background dot patten © Maria Kazanova / Shutterstock

Set in 10/12.5pt Minion by SPi Publisher Services, Pondicherry, India
Printed in Singapore by C.O.S. Printers Pte Ltd

5   2016

To Bodhi Axel Ritzer, With Much Love and Great Hope
for a Better World in Your Future
(GR)

To Tia Shields Dean, My Wonderful and Caring Wife who has Helped to Make
this Book and so Much More Possible
(PD)

CONTENTS

ABOUT THE WEBSITE

The *Globalization: A Basic Text, Second Edition*, companion website includes a number of resources created by the author that you will find helpful.

www.wiley.com/go/ritzer/globalization

FOR STUDENTS

- Student Study Guide
- Chapter Summaries
- Additional Readings
- Website Links
- Discussion Questions
- Additional Questions

FOR INSTRUCTORS

- Teaching Notes
- Discussion Question Answer Frames
- Additional Question Answer Frames
- PowerPoint Teaching Slides

FIGURES

As we revise this preface in July, 2014, we are struck by how much the events of the day both reflect, and are profoundly changing, the process of globalization. For example, we write this only hours before watching Lionel Messi and Argentina take on the Netherlands in the World Cup – the most famous *global* sporting event. Football (or soccer, as it is known in the United States) is the most played and most watched sport around the world. Football fandom also reflects a global culture and, with FIFA as its governing body, it has a global organizational structure.

It has been particularly fascinating to watch global events unfold as we were writing the second edition of this book. For instance, the first edition was published in the midst of the Great Recession. The ways in which economic processes (e.g. mortgage failures, credit freezes, the failure of legendary financial firms and banks), largely originating in the US, flowed around the world in relatively short order was breathtaking. As the crisis deepened and widened, political unrest grew, and the future of the global economy was uncertain. As of this writing, the global economy has stabilized but it has not yet rebounded to its pre-recessionary levels for many Americans and for many others in most parts of the world. A great number of scholars and activists argued that it was neoliberal policy (see Chapter 4) that led to the Great Recession, and as the economic turmoil wore on, some predicted its demise. Now, having emerged from the Great Recession, it is clear that neoliberalism remains a strong force in both global politics and the global economy.

Numerous recent events have also profoundly changed the process of globalization. For example, global climate change is dramatically affecting economic processes and flows of people. Tens of thousands of people are losing their homes to rising sea levels, and are being displaced to other countries, and creating new conflicts. Environmental problems flow seamlessly across national borders and many of these problems, such as global warming and deforestation, have come to affect the entire planet. Many previous skeptics are finally acknowledging human-caused global warming, even though governments around the world continue dragging their feet on combatting the problem (current scientific evidence is even more definitive than it was when the first edition was published).

Another area that is experiencing rapid developments, and is dramatically shaping globalization, is the various global high-tech flows (see Chapter 9). This encompasses much more than the explosive growth of social networking sites (e.g. Facebook) and other social media (e.g. Twitter), but the ways in which technological flows are monitored, governed, and used to promote other types of change. Through the efforts of Edward Snowden and Wikileaks, we now know more about how governments and corporations are spying on their citizens and customers. Our understanding of this surveillance has also facilitated changes in how the Internet is governed, marking a shift from a US-dominated framework to a more global (and potentially fragmented) governance system. Such high-tech flows have also been used by activists promoting political change, as was seen in the so-called "Twitter Revolution" in much of the Arab world.

The changes noted above illustrate some ways in which this second edition has been revised, and suggest that such topics will continue to be further revisited as other global processes become more apparent. Nonetheless, the basic foci, perspectives, concepts, and theories offered here apply to whatever changes are occurring in, and are in store for, globalization. Change is nothing new to globalization, indeed it could be argued that change, including cataclysmic events and changes (the Spanish influenza epidemic of 1919, the Great Depression, WW II), is an integral part of it. More recently, we have seen a variety of economic crises in, for example, Asia, Russia, and Argentina, that are also part of the process of globalization. Any useful perspective on globalization must be able to help us better understand such occurrences.

Writing a general overview of globalization has been, to put it mildly, a daunting task. It is almost literally about everything – every place, every thing, everybody, and virtually every field of study. It also requires a sense of a wide expanse of history and of what it is about the present "global age" that differentiates it from epochs that came before it. We have been involved in textbooks before, including one that covers all of classical and contemporary sociological theory, but none has been more challenging than this one. Beyond the sheer magnitude of what needs to be covered, there is the fact that globalization, at least in its present form, is quite new, with the term itself entering the lexicon only three decades ago. As a relatively new phenomenon, it is constantly changing, as are conceptions of it. With few precedents to rely on, we have had to "invent" an approach to globalization (based on major theoretical sources), as well as create a structure for the book that encompasses most of the major topics and issues in globalization today. This is difficult enough, but it is made far more difficult by the fact that global changes (e.g. the price of that all-important commodity, oil; the landscape of global protests and conflict) occur constantly.

This is related to the issue of sources for this book, which include popular books (e.g. those of Thomas Friedman, although we are highly critical of his work), newspapers, magazines, and websites. These are atypical sources for a textbook designed to offer an overview of what we know about a field from a scholarly point of view. However, globalization occurs in the real world and continues apace in that world. Such occurrences either do not find their way into academic works or do not do so for years after they have happened. Thus, in order to be up to date – and it is important that a text on globalization be current – this book relies, in part, on a variety of popular sources. Popular sources also serve the function of providing down-to-earth, real-world examples and case studies of globalization. They serve to make globalization less abstract.

However, because it is an academic text, this book relies far more on scholarly work, especially journal articles and academic monographs of various types. It is heavily referenced and the many entries in the References section at the end of the book (as well as suggested readings at the end of each chapter) provide students with an important resource should they wish to learn more about the many topics covered in this book.

Another challenge has been to bring together these popular and academic sources in a coherent overview of globalization and what we know about it. A related challenge is the need to write a book that is not only accessible, useful, and of interest to undergraduates (the main audience for this book), but also of use to beginning graduate students and even scholars looking for a book that gives them an overview of the field, its major topics, and key works in the area. We have tried to deal with a good portion of the increasingly voluminous scholarly work on globalization, but in a student-friendly way. We have also sought to use many examples to make the discussion both more interesting and more relevant to the student reader.

We have sought to put together a coherent overview of globalization based on a theoretical orientation (increasing liquidity as the core of today's global world) and a conceptual apparatus ("flows," "barriers," etc.) developed in the first chapter. The rest of the book looks at globalization through the lens of that perspective and those concepts. Great emphasis has been placed throughout on key concepts and "thick" descriptions of important aspects of globalization. We have tried not to get bogged down in the text itself with data and statistics on globalization (which are highly fluid and often open to question), but we have included a number of maps designed to summarize, in a highly visual way, important aspects of the data related to globalization.

The focus here, as suggested above, is on the flows among and between areas of the world (as well as barriers to them). That means that the focus is not on the areas themselves – the global North and South, the nation-states of the world, regions, etc. – but rather that which flows among and between them. Nevertheless, all of those areas come up often in these pages, if for no other reason than that they are often the beginning or end-point of various flows. We have tried to cover many areas of the world and nation-states in these pages, but the US looms large in this discussion for several reasons. First, it is the world leader in being both the source of many global flows and the recipient these days of many more, and much heavier, flows (of goods from China, etc.). Second, we are led by both its historical dominance and contemporary importance to a focus on the role of the US in globalization (although recent significant declines lead to the notion that we are now entering the "post-American" age). Third, the predispositions, and the resources at the disposal, of two American authors lead to a focus on the US, albeit one that is at many points highly critical of it and its role in globalization. Although there is a great deal of attention on the US, the reader's focus should be on the flows and barriers which are found throughout the world and are of general importance globally.

Theory plays a prominent role in this analysis, not only in the framework developed in Chapter 1 and used throughout the book, but also in a number of specific chapters. These include theories of imperialism, colonialism, development, Americanization (and anti-Americanism) in Chapter 3, neoliberalism in Chapter 4, theories of cultural differentialism, convergence, and hybridization in Chapter 8, and global inequality in Chapters 13 and 14. We have worked hard to make these theories accessible and to relate them to more down-to-earth examples.

While this is a textbook on globalization, there are some key themes that run through the book. One relates, as mentioned above, to the increasing fluidity of the contemporary global age and how much more fluid it is than previous epochs. Related to this is the similarly metaphorical idea that virtually everything in the contemporary world (things, people, ideas, etc.) is "lighter" than it has ever been. In the past, all of those things were quite "heavy" and difficult to move, especially globally, but that is increasingly less the case. Because things are lighter, more fluid, they can move about the globe more easily and much more quickly. However, it is also the case that many past structural barriers remain in place and many others are being created all the time to stem various global flows (e.g. the wall between Israel and the West Bank and the more recently constructed border fence between Greece and Turkey). Thus, one of the perspectives we would like the reader to come away with after reading this book is of the ongoing relationship between flows and barriers in the global world.

Another key theme is that globalization does *not* equal economic globalization. All too often there is a tendency to reduce globalization to economic globalization. While economic globalization is important, perhaps even the most important aspect of globalization, there is much more to the latter than its economic aspects. While we devote two chapters (6 and 7) to economic globalization, attention is devoted to many other aspects of globalization (e.g. political, cultural, technological, demographic, environmental, criminal, inequalities, and so on) throughout the book. In their totality, these other topics receive far more attention than economics (although, to be fair, all of the other topics have economic aspects, causes, and consequences).

One of the reasons that the multidimensionality of globalization is accorded so much emphasis here is frustration over the near-exclusive focus on economic globalization by both scholars and laypeople. Another is our concern when we hear people say that globalization is not good for "us" and we need to stop, or at least contain, it. We always ask them *which* globalization they want to stop or contain. Do they want to limit or stop the flow of inexpensive imports from China and on offer at Wal-Mart? Of life-saving pharmaceuticals? Of illegal drugs? Of participation in, or the televising of, the Olympics? Of global prohibitions against the use of landmines? Of oil and water? Of online social networking? Of terrorists? Of tourism? Of pollutants? The point is that one might be opposed to some of these (and other) forms of globalization, but no one is, or could be, opposed to all the myriad forms of globalization.

A number of important concepts are introduced throughout this book. Definitions of those concepts in bold typeface are found not only in the text, but also in the glossary at the end of the book, as well as often more briefly in boxes in the margins of the text.

There are a number of people to thank for their help in the years of work involved in writing this book. First, we would like to thank a number of graduate assistants including Nathan Jurgenson, Jillet Sam, and Michelle Smirnova, who assisted on the first edition of the book. Michelle was especially helpful in the early stages of the writing of this book, while Nathan and Jillet were of great help in the later stages in assisting the first author in getting the manuscript to the publisher. Nathan ably handled the inclusion of the many maps and Jillet was invaluable in hunting down missing sources and information. We would also like to thank the graduate students in various seminars on globalization, especially those in the fall 2008 seminar who read a draft of the first edition and offered numerous ideas on improving it. Then there are the three anonymous reviewers who offered very useful comments on revising this book for its second edition. The people associated with Wiley-Blackwell, including Louise Spencely, developmental editor Claire Cameron, and especially Ben Thatcher, have been extraordinarily helpful. Ben assisted us throughout the entire revision for the second edition, including in the arduous process of securing copyrights. Finally, we would like to thank our long-time editor at Wiley-Blackwell, Justin Vaughan, who has been deeply involved in this project, as well as many others already published or in the works. We owe him much gratitude, including for taking the first author "punting" in Oxford – a truly global and unforgettable experience.

GLOBALIZATION I

LIQUIDS, FLOWS, AND STRUCTURES

Globalization: A Basic Text, Second Edition. George Ritzer and Paul Dean.
© 2015 John Wiley & Sons, Ltd. Published 2015 by John Wiley & Sons, Ltd.

Globalization[1] is increasingly omnipresent. We are living in *a* – or even *the* – "global age" (Albrow 1996). Globalization is clearly a very important change; it can even be argued (Bauman 2003) that it is *the most important change in human history*.[2] This is reflected in many domains, but particularly in social relationships and social structures,[3] especially those that are widely dispersed geographically. "In the era of globalization. . . shared humanity face[s] *the most fateful* of the many fateful steps" it has made in its long history (Bauman 2003: 156, italics added).

The following is the definition of globalization[4] to be used in this book (note that all of the italicized terms will be discussed in this chapter):

> **globalization** is a transplanetary *process* or set of *processes* involving increasing *liquidity* and the growing multidirectional *flows* of people, objects, places and information as well as the *structures* they encounter and create that are *barriers* to, or *expedite*, those flows . . .[5]

In contrast to many other definitions of globalization, this one does *not* assume that greater integration is an inevitable component of globalization. That is, globalization can bring with it greater integration (especially when things flow easily), but it can also serve to reduce the level of integration (when structures are erected that successfully block flows).

Globalization: Transplanetary process(es) involving increasing liquidity and growing multidirectional flows as well as the structures they encounter and create.

SOME OF THE BASICS

In spite of the focus in this book on globalization, there are many scholars who do not accept the idea that we live in a global age (see Chapter 2). Nevertheless, this book embraces, and operates from, a "globalist" perspective (Hirst and Thompson 1999) – globalization *is* a reality. In fact, globalization is of such great importance that the era in which we live should be labeled the "global age."

Debates about globalization are one of the reasons that there is undoubtedly no topic today more difficult to get one's head around, let alone to master, than globalization. However, of far greater importance are the sheer magnitude, diversity, and complexity of the process of globalization which involves almost everyone, everything, and every place and each in innumerable ways. (The concept of **globality** refers to the condition [in this case omnipresence] resulting from the process of globalization [Scholte 2004].)

Globality: Omnipresence of the process of globalization.

For example, this book is being written by two Americans; our editor and copy-editor are in England; the development editor was in Canada; reviewers are from four continents; the book is printed in Singapore and distributed by the publisher throughout much of the world; and you might be reading it today on a plane en route from Vladivostok to Shanghai. Further, if it follows the pattern of many of our other books, it may well be translated into Russian, Chinese, and many other languages. This book is also available for Amazon's wireless portable reading device, Kindle. This would make the book highly liquid since it would be possible for it to be downloaded anywhere in the world at any time.

Metaphors: Use of one term to help us better understand another.

Before proceeding to the next section, a note is needed on the use of **metaphors** (Brown 1989), which will occupy a prominent place in the ensuing discussion. A metaphor involves the use of one term to better help us understand another term. Thus in the next section, we will use the metaphor of a "solid" to describe epochs before the era of globalization.[6] Similarly, the global world will be described as being "liquid." The use of such metaphors is designed to give the reader a better and a more vivid sense of the global age and how it differs from prior epochs.

FROM SOLIDS TO LIQUIDS (TO GASES)

SOLIDS

Prior to the current epoch of globalization (and as we will see, to most observers there *was* a previous global epoch [see Chapter 2], if not many previous epochs, of globalization), it could be argued that one of the things that characterized people, things, information, places, and much else was their greater **solidity**. That is, all of them tended to be hard or to harden (metaphorically, figuratively, not literally, of course) over time and therefore, among other things, to remain largely in place. As a result, people either did not go anywhere or they did not venture very far from where they were born and raised; their social relationships were restricted to those who were nearby. Much the same could be said of most objects (tools, food, and so on) which tended to be used where they were produced. The solidity of most material manifestations of information – stone tablets, newspapers, magazines, books, and so on – also made them at least somewhat difficult to move very far. Furthermore, since people didn't move very far, neither did information. Places were not only quite solid and immoveable, but they tended to confront solid natural (mountains, rivers, oceans) and humanly constructed (walls, gates) barriers that made it difficult for people and things to exit or to enter.

> **Solidity:** People, things, information, and places "harden" over time and therefore have limited mobility.

Above all, solidity describes a world in which barriers exist and are erected to prevent the free movement of all sorts of things. It was the nation-state that was most likely to create these "solid" barriers (for example, walls [e.g. the Great Wall of China; the wall between Israel and the West Bank], border gates, and guards), and the state itself grew increasingly solid as it resisted change. For much of the twentieth century this was epitomized by the Soviet Union and its satellite states which sought to erect any number of barriers in order to keep all sorts of things out *and* in (especially a disaffected population). With the passage of time, the Soviet Union grew increasingly sclerotic. The best example of this solidity was the erection (beginning in 1961), and maintenance, of the Berlin Wall in order to keep East Berliners in and Western influences out. There was a more fluid relationship between East and West Berlin prior to the erection of the wall, but that fluidity was seen in the East as being disadvantageous, even dangerous. Once the Wall was erected, relations between West and East Berlin were virtually frozen in place – they solidified – and there was comparatively little movement of anything between them.

The Wall, to say nothing of East Germany and the Soviet Union, are long gone and with them many of the most extreme forms of solidity brought into existence by the Cold War. Nonetheless, solid structures remain – e.g. the nation-state and its border and customs controls – and there are ever-present calls for the creation of new, and new types, of solid structures. Thus, in many parts of Europe there are demands for more barriers to authorized and unauthorized immigration. This has reached an extreme in the US with concern over undocumented Mexican (and other Latin American) immigrants leading to the erection of an enormous fence between the two countries. Thus, solidity is far from dead in the contemporary world. It is very often the case that demands for new forms of solidity are the result of increased fluidity. However, a strong case can, and will, be made that it is fluidity that is more characteristic of today's world, especially in terms of globalization.

Of course, people were *never* so solid that they were totally immobile or stuck completely in a given place (a few people were able to escape East Berlin in spite of the Wall and many would still be able to enter the US without documentation even if a fence on the Mexican border were to be completed), and this was especially true of the elite members of any society. Elites were (and are) better able to move about and that ability increased with advances in transportation technology. Commodities, especially those created for elites, also could almost always be moved and they, too, grew more moveable as technologies advanced. Information (because it was not solid, although it could be solidified in the form of, for example, a book) could always travel more easily than goods or people (it could be spread by word of mouth over great distances even if the originator of the information could not move very far; it moved even faster as more advanced communication technologies emerged [telegraph, telephone, the Internet]). And as other technologies developed (ships, automobiles, airplanes), people, especially those with the resources, were better able to leave places and get to others. They could even literally move places (or at least parts of them) as, for example, when in the early 1800s Lord Elgin dismantled parts of the Parthenon in Greece and transported them to London, where to this day they can be found in the British Museum.[7]

LIQUIDS AND GASES

However, at an increasing rate over the last few centuries, and especially in the last several decades, that which once seemed so solid has tended to "melt" and become increasingly *liquid*. Instead of thinking of people, objects, information, and places as being like solid blocks of ice, they need to be seen as tending, in recent years, to melt and as becoming increasingly liquid. It is, needless to say, far more difficult to move blocks of ice than the water that is produced when those blocks melt. Of course, to extend the metaphor, blocks of ice, even glaciers, continue to exist (although, even these are now literally melting), in the contemporary world that have not melted, at least completely. Solid material realities (people, cargo, newspapers) continue to exist, but because of a wide range of technological developments (in transportation, communication, the Internet, and so on) they can move across the globe far more readily.

Everywhere we turn, more things, including ourselves, are becoming increasingly liquefied. Furthermore, as the process continues, those liquids, as is the case in the natural world (e.g. ice to water to water vapor), tend to turn into *gases* of various types. Gases are lighter than liquids and therefore they move even more easily than liquids. This is most easily seen literally in the case of the global flow of natural gas through lengthy pipelines. More metaphorically, much of the information now available virtually instantly around the world wafts through the air in the form of signals beamed off satellites. Such signals become news bulletins on our television screens, messages from our global positioning systems letting us know the best route to our destination, or conversations on our smart phones.

It should be noted, once again, that all of the terms used above – solids, liquids, gases – are metaphors – little of the global world is literally a solid, a liquid, or a gas. They are metaphors designed to communicate a sense of fundamental changes taking place as the process of globalization proceeds.

Karl Marx opened the door to this kind of analysis (and to the use of such metaphors) when he famously argued that because of the nature of capitalism[8] as an economic system "everything solid melts into air." That is, many of the solid, material realities that preceded capitalism (e.g. the structures of feudalism) were "melted" by it and were transformed into liquids. To continue the imagery farther than Marx took it, they were ultimately transformed into gases that diffused in the atmosphere. However, while Marx was describing a largely destructive process, the point here is that the new liquids and gases that are being created are inherent parts of the new world and are radically transforming it. In the process, they are having *both* constructive and destructive effects (Schumpeter 1976).

Marx's insight of over a century-and-a-half ago was not only highly prescient, but is far truer today than in Marx's day. In fact, it is far truer than he could have ever imagined. Furthermore, that melting, much like one of the great problems in the global world today – the melting of the ice on and near the North and South poles as a result of global warming (see Chapter 11) – is not only likely to continue in the coming years, but to increase at an exponential rate. Indeed, the melting of the polar icecaps can be seen as another metaphor for the increasing fluidity associated with globalization, especially its problematic aspects. And, make no mistake, the increasing fluidity associated with globalization presents *both* great opportunities *and* great dangers.

Thus, the perspective on globalization presented here, following the work of Zygmunt Bauman (2000, 2003, 2005, 2006, 2011), is that it involves, above all else, increasing **liquidity** (Lakoff 2008) (and **gaseousness**).[9] Several of Bauman's ideas on liquidity are highly relevant to the perspective on globalization employed here.

For example, liquid phenomena do not easily, or for long, hold their shape. Thus, the myriad liquid phenomena associated with globalization are hard-pressed to maintain any particular form and, even if they acquire a form, it is likely to change quite quickly.

Liquid phenomena fix neither space nor time. That which is liquid is, by definition, opposed to any kind of fixity, be it spatial or temporal. This means that the spatial and temporal aspects of globalization are in continuous flux. That which is liquid is forever ready to change whatever shape (space) it might take on momentarily. Time (however short) in a liquid world is more important than space. Perhaps the best example of this is global finance where little or nothing (dollars, gold) actually changes its place (at least immediately), but time is of the essence in that the symbolic representations of money move instantaneously and great profits can be made or lost in split-second decisions on financial transactions.

Liquid phenomena not only move easily, but once they are on the move they are difficult to stop. This is exemplified in many areas such as foreign trade, investment, and global financial transactions (Knorr Cetina 2012; Polillo and Guillen 2005), the globality of transactions and interactions (e.g. on Facebook, Twitter [Birdsall 2012]) on the Internet, and the difficulty in halting the global flow of drugs, pornography, the activities of organized crime, and undocumented immigrants (Ryoko 2012).

Finally, and perhaps most importantly, that which is liquid tends to melt whatever (especially solids) stands in its path. This is clearest in the case of the much discussed death, or at least decline,[10] of the nation-state and its borders in the era of increasing global flows (see Chapter 5). According to Cartier (2001: 269), the "forces of globalization have rendered many political boundaries more porous to flows of people, money, and things."

It is clear that if one wanted to use a single term to think about globalization today, liquidity would be at or near the top of the list. That is not to say that there are no solid structures in the world – after all, we still live in a modern world, even if it is late modernity, and modernity has long been associated with solidity. And it does not mean that there is not a constant interplay between liquidity and solidity with increases in that which is liquid (e.g. terrorist attacks launched against Israel from the West Bank during the Intifada) leading to counter-reactions involving the erection of new solid forms (e.g. that fence between Israel and the West Bank), but at the moment and for the foreseeable future, the momentum lies with increasing and proliferating global liquidity.

> **Liquidity:** Increasing ease of movement of people, things, information, and places in the global age.
>
> **Gaseousness:** Hyper-mobility of people, things, information, and places in the global age.

FLOWS

Flows:
Movement of people, things, information, and places due, in part, to the increasing porosity of global barriers.

Closely related to the idea of liquidity, and integral to it, is another key concept in thinking about globalization, the idea of **flows** (Appadurai 1996); after all liquids flow easily, far more easily than solids. In fact, it is the concept of flows that is widely used in the literature on globalization[11] and it is the concept that will inform a good deal of the body of this book.[12]

Because so much of the world has "melted" or is in the process of "melting" and has become liquefied, globalization is increasingly characterized by great *flows* of increasingly liquid phenomena of all types, including people, objects, information, decisions, places, and so on.[13] For example, foods of all sorts increasingly flow around the world, including sushi globalized from its roots in Japan (Bestor 2005; Edwards 2012), Chilean produce now ubiquitous in the US market (and elsewhere), Indian food in San Francisco (and throughout much of the world), and so on. In many cases, the flows have become raging floods that are increasingly less likely to be impeded by, among others, place-based barriers of any kind, including the oceans, mountains, and especially the borders of nation-states. This was demonstrated once again in 2008 in the spread of the American credit and financial crisis to Europe (and elsewhere), which continues to be felt today: "In a global financial system, national borders are porous" (Landler 2008: C1).

Looking at a very different kind of flow, many people in many parts of the world believe that they are being swamped by migrants, especially poor undocumented migrants (Moses 2006; Wang 2012). Whether or not these are actually floods, they have come to be seen in that way by many people, often aided by media personalities and politicians in many countries who have established their reputations by portraying them as "illegal" immigrants flooding their country. For example, conservative pundit Ann Coulter is known for her inflammatory attacks on immigrants, such as "assimilating immigrants into our culture isn't really working. No, they're assimilating us into their culture" (Blumenfeld 2013). A well-known government official is Arizona's Joe Arpaio, sheriff of Maricopa County, who spoke out against undocumented immigration and illegally targeted Latinos during traffic stops and raids; Arpaio was later found guilty of violating Latinos' constitutional rights (Santos 2013). Undoubtedly because of their immateriality, ideas, images, and information, both legal (blogs) and illegal (e.g. child pornography), flow (virtually) everywhere through interpersonal contact and the media, especially now via the Internet.[14] To take a specific example within the global circulation of ideas, "confidentiality" in the treatment of AIDS patients flowed to India (and elsewhere) because of the efforts of experts and their professional networks. The arrival of this idea in India made it possible to better manage and treat AIDS patients who were more likely to seek out treatment because of assurances of confidentiality. Confidentiality was very important in this context because of the reticence of many Indians to discuss publicly such matters as sexually transmitted diseases and AIDS (Misra 2008: 433–67).

Decisions of all sorts flow around the world, as well as over time: "The effect of the [economic] decisions flowed, and would continue to flow, through every possible conduit. Some decisions would be reflected in products rolling off assembly lines, others in prices of securities, and still others in personal interactions. Each decision would cascade around the world and then forward through time" (Altman 2007: 255). At the moment, much of the world is experiencing slow growth (United Nations 2013a) and continues to be adversely affected by the 2007–2008 financial crisis, including a wide array of bad economic decisions made in the previous decade or more, especially in the United States.

Even places can be said to be flowing around the world as, for example, immigrants re-create the places from which they came in new locales (e.g. Indian and Pakistani enclaves in London). Furthermore, places (e.g. airports, shopping malls) themselves have become increasingly like flows (for more on this and the transition from "spaces of places" to "spaces of flows," see Castells 1996).

Even with all of this increasing fluidity, much of what would have been considered the height of global liquidity only a few decades, or even years, ago now seems increasingly sludge-like. This is especially the case when we focus on the impact of the computer and the Internet on the global flow of all sorts of things. Thus, not long ago we might have been amazed by our ability to order a book from Amazon.com and receive it via an express package delivery system in as little as 30 minutes through the use of drones (*CBS News* 2013). But an even more liquid form of delivery is the ability to download that book in seconds on Amazon's Kindle system (a wireless reading device to which books and other reading matter can be downloaded).

TYPES OF FLOWS

It is worth differentiating among several different types of flows. One is **interconnected flows**. The fact is that global flows do not occur in isolation from one another; many different flows interconnect at various points and times. Take the example of the global sex industry (Farr 2005, 2013). The sex industry requires the intersection of the flow of people who work or are trafficked in the industry (usually women) with the flow of customers (e.g. sex tourists). Other flows that interconnect with the global sex industry involve money and drugs. Then there are the sexually transmitted diseases that are carried by the participants in that industry and from them branch off into many other disease flows throughout the world.

> **Interconnected flows:** Global flows that interconnect at various points and times.

A very different example of interconnected flows is in the global fish industry. That industry is now dominated by the flows of huge industrial ships and the massive amount of frozen fish that they produce and which is distributed throughout the world. In addition, these huge industrial ships are putting many small fishers out of business and some are using their boats for other kinds of flows (e.g. transporting undocumented immigrants from Africa to Europe) (LaFraniere 2008: A1, A10). Over-fishing by industrial ships has emptied the waters of fish and this has served to drive up their price. This has made the industry attractive to criminals and the result is an increase in the global flow of illegal fish (Rosenthal 2008a: A1–A6).

Then there are **multidirectional flows**. Globalization is not a one-way process as concepts like Westernization and Americanization (see Chapter 3) seem to imply (Marling 2006; Singer 2013). While all sorts of things do flow out of the West and the United States to every part of the world, many more flow into the West and the US from everywhere (e.g. Japanese automobiles, Chinese T-shirts, iPhones manufactured in China, Russian sex workers, and so on). Furthermore, all sorts of things flow in every conceivable direction among all other points in the world.

> **Multi-directional flows:** All sorts of things flowing in every conceivable direction among many points in the world.

Still another layer of complexity is added when we recognize that transplanetary processes not only can complement one another (e.g. the meeting of flows of sex tourists and sex workers), but often also conflict with one another (and with much else). In fact, it is

Conflicting flows: Transplanetary processes that conflict with one another (and with much else).

usually these **conflicting flows** that attract the greatest attention. This is most obvious in the case of the ongoing "war" on terror between the United States and Islamist militants and jihadists (e.g. al-Qaeda). On the one hand, al-Qaeda and other Islamist militants are clearly trying to maintain, or to increase, their global influence and, undoubtedly, to find other ways of engaging in a range of terrorist activities. For its part, the US is involved in a wide variety of global processes designed to counter that threat, stymie al-Qaeda's ambitions, and ultimately and ideally to contain, if not destroy, it. This encompassed first the US invasions of Iraq[15] and Afghanistan, and now the ongoing involvement in global flows of military personnel and equipment to other locales (e.g. Pakistan, Syria, and, increasingly, African countries); and counter-terrorism activities (e.g. drone strikes) designed to find and kill its leaders, and ongoing contact with intelligence agencies of other nations in order to share information on Islamist militants, and so on.

Reverse flows: Processes which, while flowing in one direction, act back on their source.

Then there are **reverse flows**. In some cases, processes flowing in one direction act back on their source (and much else). This is what Ulrich Beck (1992) has called the *boomerang effect*. In Beck's work the boomerang effect takes the form of, for example, pollution that is "exported" to other parts of the world but then returns to affect the point of origin. So, for example, countries may insist that their factories be built with extremely high smokestacks so that the pollution reaches greater heights in the atmosphere and is thereby blown by prevailing winds into other countries and perhaps even around the globe (Ritzer 2008b: 342). While this seems to reduce pollution in the home country, the boomerang effect is manifest when prevailing winds change direction and the pollution is blown back to its source. In addition, nations that are the recipients of another nation's air pollution may find ways of returning the favor by building their own smokestacks even higher than their neighbors.

HEAVY, LIGHT, WEIGHTLESS

There is another set of conceptual distinctions, or metaphors, that are useful in thinking about globalization. In addition to the change from solids to liquids (and then gases), we can also think in terms of change that involves movement from that which is *heavy* to that which is *light* (this is another distinction traceable to the work of Zygmunt Bauman) and most recently to that which is lighter than light, that which approaches being *weightless* (the gases mentioned above).

The original Gutenberg Bible (mid-fifteenth-century Germany) was usually published in two volumes, ran to close to 1,400 pages, and was printed on very heavy paper or vellum. It was in every sense of the term a heavy tome (almost like the one you are now reading), difficult, because of its sheer weight and bulk, to transport. Fast forward to 2015 and a much lighter bound copy of the Bible could easily be purchased from Amazon.com and transported in days via express mail virtually anywhere in the world. That Bible had also become weightless since it could be downloaded using the Kindle system or another e-reader.

More generally, it could be argued that both pre-industrial and industrial societies were quite "heavy," that is, characterized by that which is difficult to move. This applies both to those who labored in them (e.g. peasants, farmers, factory workers), where they labored (plots of land, farms, factories), and what they produced (crops, machines, books, automobiles). Because of their heaviness, workers tended to stay put and what they produced (and what was not consumed locally) could be moved, especially great distances, only with great effort and at great expense. Later advances, especially in technology, made goods, people, and places "lighter," easier to move. These included advances in both transportation and technology that made all sorts of industrial products smaller, lighter, and easier to transport (compare the mini-laptop computer of today to the room-size computer of the mid-twentieth century).

Karin Knorr Cetina (2005: 215) has written about what she calls "complex global microstructures," or "structures of connectivity and integration that are global in scope but microsociological in character." She has described financial markets (Knorr Cetina and Bruegger 2002; Knorr Cetina 2012) in these terms and, more recently, global terrorist organizations such as al-Qaeda. We will have more to say about these global microstructures (see Chapter 12), but the key point here is that while Knorr Cetina sees these global microstructures as having several characteristics, of primary importance is their "lightness" in comparison to "heavy" bureaucratic systems. Thus, unlike the armed forces of the United States, Islamist militants (e.g. al-Qaeda) are not heavy bureaucratic structures, but rather light "global microstructures." It is their lightness that gives them many advantages over the extremely cumbersome US military, and the huge bureaucracy of which it is a part.

It could be argued that we moved from the heavy to the light era in the past century or two. However, by about 1980, we can be said to have moved beyond both of those epochs. We are now in an era that is increasingly defined not just by lightness, but by something approaching weightlessness. That which is weightless, or nearly so, clearly moves far more easily (even globally) than that which is either heavy or light. The big changes here involved the arrival and expansion of cable and satellite television, satellite radio, cell phones, personal computers, tablets, and, most importantly, smart phones and the advent of the Internet (and networking sites such as Twitter). It is with the personal computer and the Internet that globalization reaches new heights in terms of the flow of things and of social relationships in large part because they, and everything else, have approached weightlessness.

An excellent example of this can be found in the world of music. Vinyl records were quite heavy and the shift to cassettes and later CDs did not make music much lighter. However, the creation of advanced technologies such as iPods and smart phones allows us to carry around thousands of once very heavy albums in our pockets, or we can play it from the cloud. We can carry that music with us anywhere in the world and we can exchange music over the Internet with people around the globe.

To take another example, in the past, if we needed to consult with a medical specialist in Switzerland, we would have had to fly there and take our x-rays and MRI images with us, or else had them snail-mailed. Now, both can be digitized and sent via the Internet; x-ray and MRI results have become weightless. Our Swiss physician can view them on her computer screen. We do not even need to go to Switzerland at all (in a sense we have become weightless, as well). We (or our local physician) can confer with our Swiss physician by phone, e-mail, or a video hook-up (e.g. Skype) via the Internet. It is information, rather than things, that is increasingly important in the contemporary world. Information, especially when it is translated into digital, computerized codes (that's what happens to our x-rays and MRI images), is weightless and can be sent around the globe instantly.

Of course, there are still many heavy things in our increasingly weightless world. Factories, offices, buildings, large and cumbersome machines (including MRI machines), newspapers, hardback books, and even some people (made "heavy" by, for example, minority status, poverty, a lack of education) continue to exist. All, of course, are nevertheless being globalized to some degree in one way or another, but their weightiness makes that process more cumbersome and difficult for them. For example, the global parcel delivery systems (e.g. FedEx, DHL) have become very efficient, but they still need to transport a physical product over great distances. Clearly, that process is still quite weighty, in comparison to, say, the downloading of weightless movies from Netflix (a website that began by allowing members to receive heavier DVDs via snail-mail) or viewing them on-demand. In fact, of course, it is increasingly the case that that which is weightless (e.g. iTunes and downloadable music in general, downloadable movies, blogs) is destroying that which is comparatively heavy (e.g. the CD, the DVD, newspapers).

The ideas of increasing liquidity and weightlessness being employed here do not require that the world be "flat" or be considered as such (see Chapter 4) (Friedman 2007, 2012). Fluids can seep through all sorts of tall and wide structures and, in the case of a flood, those structures can even be washed away (as was the Berlin Wall, for example, and more metaphorically, the Iron Curtain), at least temporarily. Further, that which is weightless can waft over and between the tallest and widest structures. Thus, the world today is increasingly characterized by liquidity and weightlessness, but it is *not* necessarily any flatter than it ever was.[16] Those tall, wide structures continue to be important, especially in impeding (or attempting to), the movement of that which is solid and heavy. It is less clear how successful these structures will be in impeding that which is liquid, light, or weightless.

The most obvious of such structures are the borders (Crack 2007; Rumford 2007a) between nation-states and the fact that in recent years we have witnessed the strengthening (heightening, lengthening, etc.) of many of those borders. Similarly, the Chinese government has sought to restrict the access of its citizens to at least some aspects of the Internet that the government feels is dangerous to its continued rule. The electronic barrier that the government has constructed is known as the "Great Firewall" (French 2008: A1, A6). (A firewall is a barrier on the Internet; the idea of the "Great Firewall" plays off China's Great Wall.)

The huge "digital divide" in the world today (Ayanso et al. 2014), especially between developed and developing countries (or the North and South), is another example of a barrier. The relative absence in developing countries of computers and the supporting infrastructure (telephone and broadband connections) needed for a computerized world creates an enormous barrier between these groups. In terms of computerization, the world may be increasingly flat (although certainly not totally flat) among and between developed countries in the North, but it has many hills in the developing countries and huge and seemingly insurmountable mountain ranges continue to separate the North from the South.

The history of the social world and social thought and research leads us to the conclusion that people, as well as their representatives in the areas in which they live, have always sought to erect structural barriers to protect and advance themselves, and to adversely affect others, and it seems highly likely that they will continue to do so. Thus, we may live in a more liquefied, more weightless, world, but we do *not* live in a flat world and are not likely to live in one any time soon, if ever. Even a successful capitalist, George Soros, acknowledges this, using yet another metaphor, in his analysis of **economic globalization** when he argues: "The global capitalist system has produced a very *uneven* playing field" (Soros 2000: xix, italics added).

Economic globalization: Growing economic linkages at the global level.

HEAVY STRUCTURES THAT EXPEDITE FLOWS

The liquefaction of the social world, as well as its increasing weightlessness, is only part of the story of globalization. As pointed out already, another major part is the fact that many heavy, material, objective structures continue to exist and to be created in the globalized world.[17] Some are holdovers from the pre-global world, but others are actually produced, intentionally or unintentionally, by global forces. In studying globalization we must look at *both* all of that which flows (or "wafts") with increasing ease, as well as all of the structures[18] that impede or block those flows (see below for more on these), as well as that serve to expedite and channel those flows. To put it another way, we must look at *both* that which is light and weightless as well as that which is solid and heavy and that greatly affects their flow in both a positive and a negative sense. This is in line with the view of Inda and Rosaldo (2008a: 29):

> we will examine the materiality of the global. This refers to the material practices – infrastruc-
> ture, institutions, regulatory mechanisms, governmental strategies, and so forth – that both
> produce and preclude movement. The objective here is to suggest that global flows are patently
> structured and regulated, such that while certain objects and subjects are permitted to travel,
> others are not. Immobility and exclusion are thus as much a part of globalization as
> movement.

For example, there are various "routes" or "paths" that can be seen as structures that serve to both expedite flows along their length (see Figure 1.1 for major global transportation routes), as well as to limit flows that occur outside their confines.

- Intercontinental airlines generally fly a limited number of well-defined routes[19] (say between New Delhi and London) rather than flying whatever route the pilots wish and thereby greatly increasing the possibility of mid-air collisions (see Figure 1.2 for some of the major global airline routes).
- Undocumented immigrants from Mexico have, at least until recently, generally followed a relatively small number of well-worn paths into the US. Indeed, they often need to pay smugglers large sums of money and the smugglers generally follow the routes that have worked for them (and others) in the past.
- Goods of all sorts are generally involved in rather well-defined "global value chains" (see Chapter 7 for a discussion of this concept) as they are exported from some countries and imported into others.
- Illegal products – e.g. counterfeit drugs – follow oft-trod paths en route from their point of manufacture (often China), through loosely controlled free-trade zones (e.g. in Dubai), through several intermediate countries, to their ultimate destination, often the US, where they are frequently obtained over the Internet (Bogdanich 2007: A1, A6).

Then there are an increasing number of formal and informal "bridges" (Anner and Evans 2004) which have been created throughout the globe that expedite the flow of all sorts of things. This idea applies perhaps best to the passage of documented people across borders through the process of migration (Sassen 2007a). It is clear that in the not-too-distant past there were many structural barriers to the flow of people. There are even a few places in the world today where this remains true – e.g. between the US and Cuba. However, with the

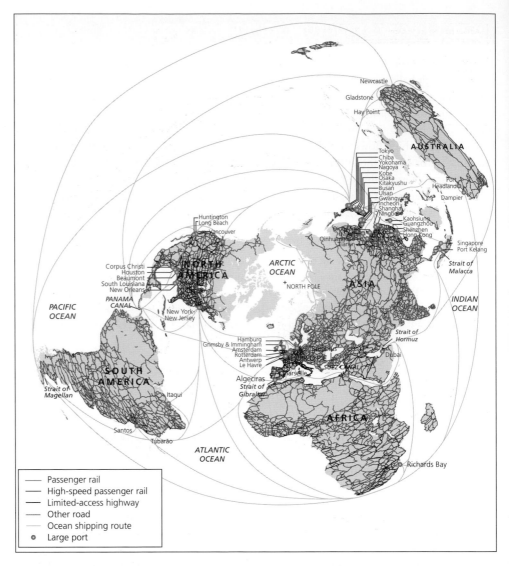

Figure 1.1 Transportation routes. Nearly all of the world's freight headed for international destinations is transported via ships in standardized containers. These sealed metal containers have dramatically altered the face of international freight transport. They are designed to be easily transferred from one mode of transport to another, for instance, from a ship to a train, thereby increasing efficiency and reducing cost. As with passenger airline traffic, maritime freight traffic is concentrated. The largest ten ports, led by Singapore, Rotterdam, Shanghai, Hong Kong, and South Louisiana, handle more than 50% of global freight traffic. Source: de Blij, Harm J., and Roger Downs. 2007. *College Atlas of the World*. Washington, DC: National Geographic Society, p. 59.

Figure 1.2 Airline passenger volume. Air travel, the dominant mode of international passenger transportation, was once limited to the wealthy and those traveling for business. With increased competition, lower fares, and a growing global economy, air travel has boomed over the last 30 years. It is expected to steadily increase over the next five years, particularly in China and other parts of Asia, despite economic instability in the airline industry and concerns over terrorism. Air traffic is concentrated in the Northern Hemisphere between Europe and North America, with increasing volume to East Asia. Nearly 600 million passengers pass through the doors of the world's ten busiest airports, led by Atlanta, Chicago, London, Tokyo, and Los Angeles. Source: de Blij, Harm J., and Roger Downs. 2007. *College Atlas of the World*. Washington, DC: National Geographic Society, p. 58.

end of the Cold War, there are now many bridges for people (and products) to cross openly not only between the countries of the old East and West, but also among and between virtually every country and region of the world. However, undocumented migrants are likely to need to be more covert in their movements. All sorts of illegal products are also less likely to move openly across such "bridges" where they would be highly visible to the authorities.

Thus, there are also more hidden structures that permit movement of undocumented people and illegal products.

It is also the case that an increasing number of people, perhaps nearly everyone, is involved in, and affected by, global relations and flows and personally participate in global networks (Singh Grewal 2008) of one kind or another (networks of communication and information technology, interpersonal networks involving individuals and groups).[20] While global networks span the globe (e.g. cables under the oceans that permit transoceanic communication [Yuan 2006: A1]), or at least much of it, there are other types of networks including transnational (those that pass through the boundaries of nation-states [Portes 2001b]), international (those that involve two or more nation-states), national (those that are bounded by the nation-state), and local (those that exist at the sub-national level) (Mann 2007). Networks can expedite the flow of innumerable things, but they are perhaps best-suited to the flow of information (Connell and Crawford 2005). People involved in networks can communicate all sorts of information to one another in various ways – telephone calls, snail-mail, e-mail, blogs, social networking sites, and so on. These networks have revolutionized and greatly expanded the global flow of information. As with all other structures, such networks can be blocked in various ways (e.g. the "Great Firewall").

All sorts of networks have been made possible by the Internet. The Internet can be seen as being of enormous importance in allowing information of various sorts to flow in innumerable directions. One important example involves the formation of the networks that became and constitute the alter-globalization movement (see Chapter 15). It (as well as its various political actions, most notably the anti-WTO [World Trade Organization] protests in Seattle in 1999 [Smith 2001]), like much else in the world today (e.g. the popular uprisings in Turkey and Egypt in 2013), was made possible by the Internet:

> By significantly enhancing the speed, flexibility, and global reach of information *flows*, allowing for communication at a distance in real time, digital *networks* provide the technological infrastructure for the emergence of contemporary network-based social forms . . . allowing communities to sustain interactions across vast distances. . . . Using the Internet as technological architecture, such movements operate at local, regional, and global levels. . . . (Juris 2008: 353–4)

Finally, it is not only individuals who are increasingly involved in networks. An increasing number of social structures (e.g. states, cities, law) and social institutions (the family, religion, sport) are interconnected[21] on a global basis and these, too, enable and enhance global flows. For example, the international banking system has an infrastructure that facilitates the global movement of funds among a network of banks. Included in that infrastructure are IBANs ([International Bank Account Numbers]), rules, norms, and procedures on how such money transfers are to occur, and a highly sophisticated technical language that allows those in the business to communicate with one another wherever they are in the world. Another example involves global (Sassen 1991, 2013) and world cities (Derudder et al. 2012) (see Chapter 13) that are increasingly interconnected with one another directly rather than through the nation-states in which they happen to exist. The financial markets of the world cities of New York, London, and Tokyo are tightly linked with the result that all sorts of financial products flow among them and at lightning speed. More generally, in this context, we can talk in terms of the "global economy's connectedness" (Altman 2007: 255). To take another example, there are (or were) seven local, interconnected AIDS INGOs (International Non-Governmental Organizations) and they played a key role in, among other things, improving the treatment of the disease in India (Misra 2008). The Indian NGO (Non-Governmental Organization), like others, is, in turn, "operated in a globally and nationally situated web of governmental and extra governmental agencies" (Misra 2008: 441). Once again, however, barriers are erected to limit such interconnections (e.g. the unwillingness of at least some countries to acknowledge AIDS, or at least the full extent of the disease and of its consequences).

HEAVY STRUCTURES AS BARRIERS TO FLOWS

While there is no question that the world is increasingly characterized by greater liquidity, increased flows, as well as various structures that expedite those flows, we also need to recognize that there are limits and barriers to those flows. The world is not just in process, there are also many material structures (trade agreements, regulatory agencies, borders, customs barriers, standards, and so on) in existence. As Inda and Rosaldo (2008a: 31) argue: "Material infrastructures do not only promote mobility. . . . They also hinder and block it." Any thoroughgoing account of globalization needs to look at *both* flows and structures and, in terms of the latter, the ways in which they *both* produce and enhance flows as well as alter and even block them. In other words, there is interplay between flows and structures, especially between flows and the structures that are created in an attempt to inhibit or to stop them.[22] As Shamir (2005: 197) puts it, globalization is an epoch of increased openness *and* "simultaneously an era of growing restrictions on movement." Borders, of course, are major points at which movement is blocked. There are many examples of this including the toughening of border controls in France (and elsewhere in Europe) because of growing hostility to refugees (Fassin 2008: 212–34).

There are challenges to the idea that all there is to globalization is flows and fluidity (Tsing 2000). In examining global flows (some of which have been anticipated above), we also need to consider those agents who "carve" the channels through which things flow, those who alter those channels over time, national and regional units that create and battle over flows, and coalitions of claimants for control over channels.

A focus on the above kinds of agents and structures, rather than flows, promises a more critical orientation to globalization in terms of the structures themselves, as well as in terms of who creates the structures through which things flow as well as who does and does not control and profit from them.

The idea of flows is criticized for other reasons, as well. For example, there is a kind of timelessness to the idea of flows[23] and, as a result, it implies that they are likely to continue well into the future and there is little or nothing that could be done to stop them. This implies that everyone – scientists and businesspeople who profit from flows, as well as those at the margins of those flows and perhaps even those hurt by them – are all swept up in the same processes.[24] The focus on flows tends to communicate a kind of enthusiasm for them and the erroneous idea that virtually everyone benefits from flows of all types.

A similar idea is "frictions," or the "awkward, unequal, unstable . . . interconnection across difference" (Lowenhaupt Tsing 2005: 4). The main idea is that the global flows that create interconnections do *not* move about smoothly; they do not move about without creating friction. Friction gets in the way of the smooth operation of global flows.[25] However, friction not only slows flows down, it can also serve to keep them moving and even speed them up. Highways can have this double-edged quality by both limiting where people and vehicles can go while at the same time making movement "easier and more efficient" (Lowenhaupt Tsing 2005: 6). More generally, "global connections [are] made, and muddied, in friction" (Lowenhaupt Tsing 2005: 272). The key point in this context is that flows themselves produce friction that can slow or even stop global flows: "without even trying friction gets in the way of the smooth operation of global power. Difference can disrupt, causing everyday malfunctions as well as unexpected cataclysms. Friction refuses the lie that global power operates as a well-oiled machine. Furthermore, difference sometimes inspires insurrection. Friction can be the fly in the elephant's nose" (Lowenhaupt Tsing 2005: 6). A prime example of this today is the many frictions being produced in many parts of the world by large numbers of documented and undocumented immigrants, and the backlash against them. In 2011, Spain won approval from the EU to "keep Romanians from seeking work there, arguing that its battered economy could not absorb fresh inflow of workers" (Castle and Dempsey 2011). In 2012, Greece completed a 6.5-mile fence along its border with Turkey, which was considered the most porous entry point for undocumented immigrants entering Europe (Besant 2012).

As has already been mentioned, the most important and most obvious barriers to global flows are those constructed by nation-states. There are borders, gates, guards, passport controls, customs agents, health inspectors, and so on, in most countries in the world. (The great exception is the countries that are part of the European Union [EU] where barriers to movement among and between member countries have been greatly reduced, if not eliminated. The EU is a kind of structure that allows people and products to move much more freely and much more quickly. At the same time, it serves to reduce the need to use hidden channels since there is far less need to conceal what is moving among and between EU countries.) Although many people (undocumented immigrants) and things (contraband goods) do get through those barriers, some of them are successfully blocked or impeded by the barriers. However, it is far more difficult to erect barriers against many newer phenomena, especially the non-material phenomena associated with cell phones and the Internet.

Specific examples of barriers created by the nation-state involve blocking economic transactions that it regards as not in the national interest. For example, in 2006 the US government blocked a deal in which a Dubai company was to purchase an American company involved in the business of running America's ports (*Economist* 2006: March 10). The government felt that such ownership would be a threat to national security since foreign nationals, perhaps enemies, could acquire information that would allow terrorists easy entrée to the ports. In another example, in 2012, the US government blocked a Chinese firm from acquiring wind farm projects in Oregon that are "within or near restricted air space at the Naval Weapons Systems Training Facility" (Paletta et al. 2012). The site is a training facility for attack squadrons and a testing site for military drones. In 2013, the US government discussed blocking the sale of Smithfield Foods, the nation's largest pork producer, to a Chinese firm. The reasons cited included a threat to American economic interests and the potential safety problems of importing Chinese pork (Wyatt 2013).

However, many of the barriers created by nation-states that we assume are, or can be, successful do not in fact deal with the flows they are supposed to stem. It remains to be seen whether the new fence between Mexico and the US can reduce the flow of undocumented immigrants to the US. Similarly, it is not clear that the wall between Israel and the West Bank will stop the flow of terrorists into Israel during more intense periods of conflict in the Middle East.

More generally, in a study of the confluence of legal and illegal global imports, Nordstrom found that the global flow of illegal goods is almost impossible to stop. For one thing, the illegal is often shipped with, or even part of, the legal so that stopping one means stopping the other. For another, the global economy would grind to a halt if there really were serious efforts to, for example, search all cargo entering every country in the world. Even holding "up one line of trucks, one train, one ship" ripples through the global supply chain (Nordstrom 2007: 196). Nordstrom estimates the "most sophisticated ports in the world can inspect a maximum of only 5% of the cargo passing through customs," but even inspecting that much cargo would tax any port and its authorities beyond the limit of its capacities. Global economic gridlock would occur if 5% of cargo was really inspected; a total global economic meltdown would occur if all cargo was inspected.

Nordstrom found that not only do illegal products flow freely across borders, but so do people. She traveled by freighter to and from the US and found that "security does not exist, in fact it cannot exist, in the world today" (Nordstrom 2007: 181). She boarded the freighter and left the US without anyone checking her or stamping her passport and her arrival in Europe was no different: "When I went ashore, I couldn't even find a person to tell me how to get out of port and into town. No customs, no immigration, no one to even ignore me" (Nordstrom 2007: 187). On both sides of the Atlantic she moved freely among the containers, some of them open, stored onshore.

There are many different kinds of organizations that, while they may expedite flows for some, create all sorts of barriers for others. Nation-states are, in fact, one such organization and they (generally) work to the advantage of their own citizens (and their flows as well as the flows of things important to them) in many different ways while creating many roadblocks for those from other countries. For example, nation-states create protectionist (Reuveny and Thompson 2001) tariff systems that help their own farms, corporations, and so on to succeed by making the products of their foreign competitors more expensive. That is, the tariffs help the flow of products from a nation-state's own farms and manufacturers while inhibiting the flow into the country from its foreign competition. Another example is found in the two-tier system of passport control at international airports where natives usually pass through quickly and easily while foreigners often wait in long lines. Part of the reason for this difference is that there are generally fewer officials, at least proportionally, for visitors than natives and visitors are often asked far more questions before they are allowed to enter.

Corporate organizations, say a multinational corporation like Toyota, are devoted to optimizing the flow of their automobiles to all possible markets throughout the world. They also seek to compete with and out-perform other multinational corporations in the automobile business. If they are successful, and Toyota has been extremely successful (it has supplanted General Motors as the world's largest automobile manufacturer), the flow of automobiles from those corporations is greatly reduced, further advantaging Toyota.

Labor unions are also organizations devoted to the flow of some things while working against the flow of others (Bronfenbrenner 2007). Unions often oppose, for example, the flow of undocumented immigrants because they are likely to work for lower pay and fewer (if any) benefits (e.g. health insurance) than unionized citizens. Similarly, they oppose the flow of goods produced in non-union shops in other countries (and their own) since the success of the latter would adversely affect the shops that are unionized and that, in turn, would hurt the union and its members.

While organizations of many types, including nation-states, corporations, and labor unions, serve as structures that can operate against global flows, the fact is that there are signs that many organizations are changing and are themselves becoming more fluid and increasingly open.

One of the roots of this change is open-sourcing and the Internet. The best-known example of open-sourcing is Linux, a free computer-operating system. Anyone in the world with the needed skills can make changes in, and contributions to, it. (The best-known operating systems are produced by Microsoft [now Windows 8]. They cost a great deal and are closed in that only those who work for the company can, at least legally, work on and modify them.) In recent years a traditionally closed organization – IBM – has embraced not only the Linux system, but opened up more and more of its own operations to outside inputs. The Internet has a number of open systems associated with what is known as Web 2.0 (Beer and Burrows 2007; Birdsall 2012). One example is the free online encyclopedia Wikipedia (or wikis more generally[26]) where again (virtually) anyone, anywhere in the world, can contribute to the definition of terms on it. The contrast here is the traditional (and costly) dictionaries (e.g. *Merriam-Webster's Dictionary*) and encyclopedias written by selected experts (*Encyclopedia Britannica*) and closed to contributions from anyone else.

However, in spite of this new openness, most organizations and systems remain closed to various flows. This usually benefits (often economically) those in the system and disadvantages those outside the organization. Even with the new open systems, there are structural realities that help some and hinder others. For example, to contribute to Linux or Wikipedia one must have a computer, computer expertise, and access to the Internet (especially high-speed access). Clearly, those without economic advantages – in the lower classes in developed countries or who live in the less developed countries of the South (i.e. those on the other side of the "digital divide") – do not have any, many, or all, of those things. As a result, they are unable to contribute to them or to gain from them to the same degree as those in more privileged positions or areas.

SUBTLER STRUCTURAL BARRIERS

This brings us to a series of other structural barriers that also serve to contradict the idea of total global fluidity. These structures are less blatant, more subtle, than the kinds of structures discussed above, but in many ways more powerful and more important from a social point of view. Included here are a variety of structures that serve to differentiate and to subordinate on the basis of social class, race, ethnicity, gender (see Chapters 13 and 14), and region of the world (North–South). In fact, these phenomena tend to be interrelated. Thus in the disadvantaged South, one is more likely to find large numbers of poor people in the lower social classes, disadvantaged racial and ethnic minorities, and women who are discriminated against on the basis of gender (Moghadam 2007). As a result, various efforts by the North to subordinate the South serve to further disadvantage people there in all of those categories. Furthermore, these categories overlap – a black female who is a member of the Ibo tribe in Africa is likely to be in a lower social class. (And there is a similar overlap among those who are advantaged – for example, white, upper-class, male Anglo-Saxons in Europe and North America.) Thus, the combination of these disadvantaged statuses ("intersectionality" [Collins 2000, 2012]) has a disastrous effect on those in oppressed groups.

Those who occupy superordinate positions in these hierarchies tend to erect structures that halt or slow various flows. These restrictions are designed to work to their advantage and to the disadvantage of others. Good examples involve the operations of the International Monetary Fund (IMF), World Trade Organization (WTO), and World Bank (see Chapter 6), which, for example, can serve to restrict flows of badly needed funds into Southern nations unless, for example, those nations engage in restructuring and austerity programs that are designed to slow down their economies (at least in the short run). Such austerity and restructuring programs often involve insistence that welfare programs be cut back or eliminated and the result is that the most disadvantaged members of Southern countries – racial and ethnic minorities, women, those in the lower classes – are hurt the most by these programs.

Those in superordinate positions also encourage certain kinds of flows that work to their advantage (and to the disadvantage of subordinates). For example, the so-called "brain drain" (Dube and Rukema 2013; Manashi Ray 2012) (see Chapter 10) is a global phenomenon and it most often takes the form of highly trained people leaving the South and moving to the North. Those in the North actively seek out skilled people in the South and expedite their movement to the North. At the other end of the spectrum, also encouraged, although less these days, is the movement of unskilled workers to the North to occupy poorly paid menial positions such as farm, or household, work.

It is also the case that the prototypical Northern male upper-class white Anglo-Saxon Protestant has, in the contemporary world, acquired a great deal of fluidity and "lightness" in the form of mobility, and thus is able to move about the globe quite readily and easily. In contrast, the Southern female, lower-class, black, Ibo is far less fluid, much "heavier," and therefore has far less capacity to move about the globe.

Zygmunt Bauman (1998: esp. Ch. 4) has illuminated this difference with his conceptual distinction between tourists and vagabonds. The Northern prototype would be **tourists** who move about the world because they *want to* (and because they are "light"), whereas the Southern prototype would be ("heavy") **vagabonds** who, if they are able to move at all, are likely to do so because they are compelled to move (e.g. forced to migrate to escape poverty [and to find work], by war, because of discrimination, and the like). Moving about the world voluntarily as a tourist is a much more pleasant and rewarding experience than being forced to move about as a vagabond. A further complicating matter for vagabonds is the fact that they are often forced to move many different times. For example, undocumented immigrants in the US (estimated at 11.1 million people) are often forced to change jobs and homes frequently, and may also be forced to return to their home countries, perhaps several times (Passel and Cohn 2012). Tourists, on the other hand, are forced to do little if anything – they go just about where they want, when they please, and they stay pretty much as long as their visas (and pocketbooks) permit.

Tourists: People who move about the world because they *want to* because they are "light."

Vagabonds: Those likely to move because they are forced to.

The vagabonds tend to be those who have one or more (and sometimes all) of the disadvantaged statuses mentioned above – they are more likely to be poor, black, a member of a maligned ethnic group, female, and from the South. The tourists, on the other hand, tend to be well-to-do, white, members of a high-status ethnic group, males, and from the North. Of course, there are many exceptions to this – there are tourists from the South and vagabonds from the North – but the general point about the relationship between advantaged/disadvantaged characteristics and tourists/vagabonds holds up quite well.

While the advantages of those in the North over those in the South remain, the South has been increasingly successful, at least in some instances, at gaining advantages by better

Structures:
Encompassing
sets of
processes
that may
either impede
or block
flows or serve
to expedite
and channel
them.

controlling flows into and out of that part of the world. For example, Middle Eastern oil used to be largely controlled by Northern corporations (e.g. Shell) which kept the price low and made sure that the more developed North was adequately supplied with comparatively inexpensive oil. This adversely affected oil-producing countries which did not get the price they deserved and furthermore a large proportion of the profits went to the Northern corporations and *not* the Middle Eastern countries from which the oil came. Now, of course, those countries (through OPEC, see Chapter 6) control the flow of oil and are profiting enormously from it.

In the end, then, globalization involves *flows* – of liquids, gases, and so on – *and* a wide range of **structures** that not only expedite, but also impede, and even halt, those flows.

ON THE INCREASING UBIQUITY OF GLOBAL FLOWS AND STRUCTURES

Globalization (especially global flows and structures) is increasingly ubiquitous (Boli and Petrova 2007). Indeed, our everyday lives have been profoundly affected by this process.

Global flows and structures have become an inescapable part of our *everyday experience*. They are not just flows and structures that are "out there" affecting the world as a whole. It is not just the largest social structures and processes that are affected, but also the most personal and intimate parts of our everyday lives, even our consciousness (Robertson 1992). Furthermore, these flows and structures are not seen by most as being imposed on them against their wills, but rather they are seen as legitimate by most and are even sought out by them. As a result, they are more welcomed than they are seen and treated as unwelcome impositions. Of course, the disadvantaged in the world are the ones who are not likely to welcome global flows and structures. It is the case that one hears increasingly loud voices raised in the North, and especially in the South, against global flows and structures and the problems caused by them. This is true of the poor in the North (and their representatives) and especially of those who live in the global South. Nevertheless, even the protests and opposition in the North and South add to the sense of the ubiquity of global flows and structures and their impact on daily life.

Global flows and structures are increasingly *taken-for-granted* aspects of the social world. That is, they no longer seem to most to be exotic phenomena or even open to question, doubt, or debate. This is quite remarkable since the ideas of global flows and structures, as well as globalization in general, have only been in general usage since about 1990. Global flows and structures no longer affect mainly societal elites; they have descended to the lowest reaches of society. That is not to say that the latter have benefited equally, or even at all, from the global flows and structures; they may even have been adversely affected by them, but they *have* been affected by them.

The above is, in effect, a more micro-perspective on global flows and structures. However, we must not forget the more macro-level aspects of the ubiquity of globalization. There is, for example, the globalization of *social entities*, or social structures, especially cultural and organizational forms including the state and the multinational corporation. Then there is the globalization of civil society (see Chapter 5), and of those social institutions (e.g. Intergovernmental Organizations [IGOs] and International Non-Governmental Organizations [INGOs]) that occupy a position between the state and the market and people in society.

THINKING ABOUT GLOBAL FLOWS AND STRUCTURES

Several concepts are useful for thinking about globalization in general, especially the global flows of focal concern here (Held et al. 1999).

1. How *extensive* are the global flows, relations, networks, interconnections? Obviously, such phenomena have existed for centuries, if not millennia, but what is unique today is how much *more* extensive they have become. They now cover a much greater portion of the globe, involve many more global flows, and will likely grow even more extensive in the future.

2. How *intensive* are the global flows, relations, networks, interconnections, and so on? While these phenomena may, in the past, have lacked much intensity and, as a result, been more epiphenomenal, they are now much more central and important. This is due, at least in part, to the increasingly frenzied activity associated with these flows, as well as to the similarly intense attention to, and concern about, them. For example, many people today are virtually addicted to such things as e-mail to friends throughout the world and to social networking websites that include participants from around the globe.

3. What is the *velocity* of global flows, relations, networks, interconnections, and so on? It is not just their extensity and the intensity that matters, but also the speed at which they move. It is clear that globalization brings with it, and is characterized by, increasingly rapid movement of virtually everything. Velocity is closely related to many of the concepts discussed above (and thereby closely related to globalization) including liquidity, gaseousness, lightness, and weightlessness. Increases in any and all of these characteristics tend to lead to movement around the globe at greater and greater speed.

4. What is the *impact propensity* of global flows, relations, networks, interconnections, and so on? Again, while these flows may have had little likelihood of having a deep and widespread impact in the past, the increasing propensity to have such effects is characteristic of globalization. Think, for example, of the huge global impact of September 11 because of the fact that it was known about, and even viewed, simultaneously throughout much of the world.

This same set of ideas can – and should – also be used to think about the various structures that have emerged to both expedite and impede globalization:

1. How *extensive* are the structures that expedite and impede globalization? It is clear that the structures designed to expedite globalization (for example, export-processing zones, see Chapter 4) are far more extensive than they once were and it is likely that they will grow even more extensive in the future. Structures designed to impede globalization (e.g. tariffs, customs restrictions, border controls, etc.) are undergoing something of a renaissance today, especially in light of the Great Recession.

2. How *intensive* are the efforts to construct or destroy, expand, or contract structures that expedite and impede globalization? At the moment, for example, efforts to further lower tariff barriers globally seem to have lost intensity, whereas efforts to create new barriers (e.g. that fence between the US and Mexico) seem to be at a fever pitch.

3. What is the *velocity* of the efforts to construct structures that expedite and impede globalization? While the construction of the US–Mexico fence, for example, was moving along at a rapid pace beginning in 2006, the Obama administration halted construction of this impediment in 2010 (Hsu 2010).

4.   What is the *impact propensity* of the efforts to construct structures that expedite and impede globalization? Specifically, what is the impact of such structures on global flows, relations, networks, interconnections, and so on? In terms of that fence between the US and Mexico it is clearly hoped, at least by the American government, that undocumented immigration from and through Mexico will be greatly reduced. However, some in the US question its potential impact. The mayor of a border town in Texas said: "You can go over, under and around a fence . . . and it [the fence] can't make an apprehension" (Blumenthal 2000: 12).

CHAPTER SUMMARY

Globalization is a transplanetary process or set of processes involving increasing liquidity and the growing multidirectional flows of people, objects, places, and information, as well as the structures they encounter and create that are barriers to, or expedite, those flows. The sheer magnitude, diversity, and complexity of the process of globalization today lead to the conceptualization of the current era as the "global age." Globalization can be analyzed through conceptual metaphors such as solids, liquids, gases, flows, structures, heavy, light, and weightless.

Prior to the "global age," people, things, information, places, and objects tended to harden over time. Thus their common attribute was "solidity," the characteristic of being limited to one place. Solidity also refers to the persistence of barriers that prevented free movement of people, information, and objects in that era. Although solidity persists, it is "fluidity" that is more characteristic of the "global age."

Over the last few decades, that which once seemed solid has tended to "melt" and become increasingly mobile or "liquid." A range of technological developments in transportation and communication have enabled far greater global movement of what was previously solid. The difficulties posed by the fact that many things and people retain some solidity can now also be dealt with more readily.

As this process of increased mobility continues, liquids tend to turn into gases. This implies additional attributes of being light and a capacity to flow even faster and with greater ease. The flow of information in the global age closely approximates this characteristic of gaseousness. The new liquids and gases that are being created have both constructive as well as destructive effects.

Bauman's ideas on liquidity inform this book's orientation to globalization. Liquid phenomena do not easily, or for long, hold their shape. They are not fixed in either space or time. Most importantly, liquids tend to dissolve obstacles in their path.

A closely related concept is the idea of "flows." Globalization is increasingly characterized by flows of liquid phenomena including people, objects, decisions, information, and places. Many global flows are interconnected – they do not occur in isolation. Others might be multidirectional flows – all sorts of things flow in every conceivable direction among all points in the world. Conflicting flows add another layer of complexity to the analysis of global processes. Finally, reverse flows often have a boomerang effect. That is, they flow back to their source and often have a negative effect on it.

Globalization can also be analyzed through metaphors of heavy, light, and weightless. Historically, there has been movement from that which is heavy to that which is light and most recently to that which approaches weightlessness. Pre-industrial and industrial societies were "heavy," characterized by that which is difficult to move. Advances in transportation and technology made goods, people, and places lighter. We are currently in an era defined not only by lightness but also increasingly by weightlessness.

This does not imply that the world is flat. Some structures continue to be important in impeding the movement of that which is liquid, light, or weightless. Borders between nation-states and the "digital divide" are important examples of such barriers.

Other heavy structures expedite flows. "Routes" or "paths" serve to both expedite flows along their length as well as to limit flows that occur outside their confines. There are also formal or informal bridges that expedite flows. More concealed structures facilitate the illegal movement of people and products. An increasing number of people also participate in global networks, involving networks of communication and information technology, as well as interpersonal networks. Further, an increasing number of social structures (states, cities, law) and social institutions (the family, religion, sport) are interconnected through networks and thus enable global flows.

The idea of flows communicates the sense that virtually everyone benefits from them. Concepts such as awkward connections (points of weak or no connection) and frictions (difficult, unequal, and unstable connections) facilitate a more nuanced analysis showing that some benefit little from global flows.

Nation-states as well as other organizations such as corporations and labor unions may expedite flows for some while creating barriers for others. For instance, protectionist tariff systems aid the flow of products from a nation-state's own farms and manufacturers, while inhibiting similar flows from foreign competitors.

There also exist subtler structural barriers which are in many ways more powerful than the material structures such as national borders. These structures serve to differentiate and subordinate on the basis of social class, race, ethnicity, gender, age, sexual orientation, and region of the world. These phenomena often tend to be interrelated. Those who occupy superordinate positions in these hierarchies tend to erect structures in order to impede flows that are not beneficial to them. They also encourage flows that work to their advantage.

Global flows and structures have now become ubiquitous in everyday experience; they have come to be taken-for-granted. There has also been a generalization of global flows and structures, such that their impact spreads across all levels of society. Four directions of enquiry can be pursued in the analysis of structures and flows – extensiveness, intensiveness, velocity, and impact propensity.

DISCUSSION QUESTIONS

1. Examine the dual role of structures as barriers to, and facilitators of, global flows. Are subtler structural barriers more effective than material barriers?

2. What is the significance of networks in the current age of globalization? Is it possible for networks to act as deterrents or barriers to flows?

3. Do liquids dissolve structures blocking their path, or do they merely circumnavigate them?

4. Discuss the impact of increased liquidity and gaseousness on hierarchical social structures.

ADDITIONAL READINGS ···

Zygmunt Bauman. *Liquid Modernity*. Cambridge: Polity, 2000.

Zygmunt Bauman. *Culture in a Liquid Modern World*. Malden, MA: Cambridge: Polity Press, 2011.

Arjun Appadurai. *Modernity at Large: Cultural Dimensions of Globalization*. Minneapolis: University of Minnesota Press, 1996.

Jonathan Xavier Inda and Renato Rosaldo, "Tracking Global Flows." In Jonathan Xavier Inda and Renato Rosaldo, eds. *The Anthropology of Globalization: A Reader*, 2nd edn. Oxford: Blackwell, 2008.

Manuel Castells. *The Rise of the Network Society*, 2nd edn. Oxford: Wiley-Blackwell, 2009.

George Ritzer, ed. *Blackwell Companion to Globalization*. Oxford: Blackwell, 2007.

George Ritzer, ed. *Wiley-Blackwell Encyclopedia of Globalization*. Oxford: Wiley-Blackwell, 2012.

Ben Derudder, Michael Hoyler, Peter J. Taylor, and Frank Witlox. *International Handbook on Globalization and World Cities*. Northampton, MA: Edward Elgar Publishing, 2012.

NOTES ···

1 The French call this *mondialization*. See, for example, Ortiz (2006). However, as is clear from his book's title, Jean-Luc Nancy (2007) distinguishes between mondialization, defined as the open creation of the world, and globalization which is seen as a more closed and integrated process.

2 Wolf (2005: ix) is slightly more circumscribed in his judgment saying that globalization "is the great event of our time."

3 The term "social" here and elsewhere in his book is used very broadly to encompass social process in various sectors – political, economic, social, etc.

4 It should be noted that while the concept of globalization, if not this particular definition, is now very familiar to all of us, it is actually of very recent vintage. Chanda (2007: 246) reviewed an electronic database that archives 8,000 sources throughout the world (newspapers, magazines, reports). He does not find a reference to globalization until 1979 and then only in an obscure European administrative document. By 1981 there are still only two mentions of the term globalization, but then such references take off reaching over 57,000 in 2001. Interestingly the number drops off after that, but it has begun to rise once again. It seems likely that the number of references to globalization will soon exceed that of the previous peak in 2001.

5 This definition requires several amplifications or clarifications. First, the idea that globalization is transplanetary is derived from Scholte (2005). Second, while globalization is transplanetary, little traverses the entire planet. The latter is the outer limit of globalization, but it is rarely approached. Third, the definition as a whole seems to imply a "grand narrative" of increasing globalization, but it is recognized that globalization occurred on a far more limited scale at earlier points in history (see Chapter 2) and that the changes described here are often uneven and that in some cases (e.g. in the case of immigrants, see below) there was greater liquidity, things flowed more easily, in earlier epochs. Fourth, it should be pointed out that *not* all of the phenomena mentioned in this definition are equally liquid or flow to the same degree. Clearly, communication is the most liquid and flows the most easily; places and people are far less liquid and their flow is much more limited. However, places are much more likely now than in the past to flow around the world as represented by the global presence of many fast food restaurants and other chains. In some senses, people (e.g. as immigrants) moved more easily in the late nineteenth and early twentieth century when nation-states had far fewer restrictions on immigration than they do today (but those restrictions

have increased greatly recently). However, *overall* people today are more liquid and flow more easily globally as, for example, tourists, business travelers, and the like, and even as immigrants, at least in some senses (e.g. the flow is much more multi-directional than it was in that earlier epoch). It is even more the case that social relationships are more liquid, and flow more easily, than they did in the past. Fifth, Tomlinson (2007: 352) offers a definition of globalization that has much of the flavor of the perspective being offered here: "complex, accelerating, integrating *process* of global connectivity . . . rapidly developing and ever-densening *network* of *interconnections* and interdependencies that characterize material, social, economic and cultural life in the modern world"; another definition emphasizing flows, interconnectedness, and also barriers can be found in Yergin and Stanislaw (1998: 383).

6 For other metaphors applied to globalization, see Kornprobst et al. (2008).

7 This reflects the tensions that always exist in globalization since the Greeks resent this theft. This resentment has grown recently with the building of a new Acropolis Museum in Athens (part of it opened In 2008) which makes a point of highlighting the missing portions of the Parthenon.

8 As we will see, capitalism is very much implicated in globalization, but as we will also see throughout this book, there is much, much more to globalization than capitalism or economics more generally.

9 A similar point of view is offered by the popular journalist Thomas Friedman with his notion "fluid networks" which operate in a largely unimpeded manner across what he sees as an increasingly "flat world"; for more on Friedman's thinking, and a critique of the idea of a flat world, see Chapter 4.

10 For a rebuttal to this argument, see Weiss (1998).

11 In addition to "flow" Chanda (2007) uses terms like "flowing," "water," "ripples," and "waves" in discussing globalization. "Tracking Global Flows" is the title of Inda and Rosaldo's (2008a) Introduction to an anthology of work in anthropology on globalization, and flows is the organizing principle of that book. The five substantive sections of that book deal with the flow of capital, people, commodities, the media, and ideologies. Paul Gilroy (1993: 190) often uses images of ships and sea voyages in his discussion of global "flows." See also Ong (2006a).

12 This is in line with one of the two approaches outlined by Martin, Metzger, and Pierre (2006). That is, that which is truly global is not simply similar changes in many countries.

13 John Urry (2009) sees this as part of the fact that everything these days seems to be on the move and, as a result, we need a new "mobilities" theory to deal with that reality.

14 Although, as we will see, especially in Chapter 13, great global inequality, especially in this case the "digital divide," prevents large portions of the world from receiving many of these flows.

15 Although, contrary to US propaganda, al-Qaeda did not have much of a role, if any, in Iraq.

16 George Soros (2000: xix) argues, for example, that global capitalism has "produced a very uneven playing field."

17 For a similar point of view, see Shamir (2005: 197–217).

18 While this discussion will focus on structures, it is clear that structures are created, run, and staffed by human agents who direct their operations. This is in line with the general tendency in social theory to be concerned with the relationship between structure and agency. See Ritzer (2008b: 394–420).

19 In fact, such routes, "trade routes," have existed for centuries (e.g. the Silk Road of the thirteenth century) and continue to exist, although they have been greatly affected and modified by technological advances of all sorts. See Ciolek (2007: 1180–4).

20 Castells (2000); Holton (2007); in fact, the idea of networks is so important to the study of globalization that there is even a journal called *Global Networks: A Journal of Transnational Affairs*.

21 One who emphasizes interconnections is Nayan Chanda in *Bound Together: How Traders, Preachers, Adventurers, and Warriors Shaped Globalization*. New Haven: Yale University Press, 2007.

22 Meyer and Geschiere (2003) also discuss the "dialectics of flow and closure," although their concerns are more microscopic than here in the sense that they are concerned with the closure of identity in the face of flows of people.

23 As the song from *Showboat* says, "Ol' Man River . . . He Keeps on Rollin' Along."

24 For a similar view, see Ho (2005).

25 Lowenhaupt Tsing (2005: 6) addresses power here rather than flows.

26 Tapscott and Williams (2006); for a critique of this see Keen (2007).

GLOBALIZATION II

SOME BASIC ISSUES, DEBATES, AND CONTROVERSIES[1]

Globalization: A Basic Text, Second Edition. George Ritzer and Paul Dean.
© 2015 John Wiley & Sons, Ltd. Published 2015 by John Wiley & Sons, Ltd.

Chapter 1 presented an overarching and integrated perspective on globalization as well as at least some details on a *few* of its (innumerable) elements. However, we have proceeded to a large extent as if globalization in general, as well as the particular perspective on it offered here with its focus on flows and barriers, processes and structures, is not in dispute. Indeed, the entire field of globalization studies is riddled with differences of opinion and great debates (Dean and Ritzer 2012; Guillen 2001; Ritzer and Atalay 2010). In this chapter we present some of these differences. The goal is to offer a more nuanced sense of globalization.

We begin with an issue that, from the tenor of the discussion in the first chapter, would appear to be a non-issue. That is the question of whether or not there is some set of developments that can legitimately be called globalization. While the prior discussion, as well as the reality of this book and its title, indicates that the answer to that question will, in the end, be in the affirmative, it is worth reviewing the debate over the very existence of globalization.

IS THERE SUCH A THING AS GLOBALIZATION?

The "great globalization debate" is between those who are skeptical about the process (the "skeptics") and those who accept it as a reality (the "globalists") (Held and McGrew 2000).

Globalists:
Believe that there is such a thing as globalization and that it encompasses virtually the entire globe.

Skeptics:
Contend that there is no such thing as globalization.

Globalists take the position that there *is such a thing* as globalization and it encompasses virtually the entirety of the globe. The **skeptics** contend that there *is no such thing* as globalization because vast portions of the globe, and a significant portion of the world's population, are wholly, or in significant part, outside of, and even actively excluded, from the processes generally associated with it. It is argued that since the term globalization implies a truly global phenomenon, the exclusion of such a large proportion of the globe serves to deny the existence of globalization. Furthermore, to the skeptics, there are various barriers, especially those created by the nation-state and regional groups of such states, that greatly restrict, if not prevent, global flows.

Globalists respond that just because some parts of the world are relatively uninvolved does not mean that the vast majority of them are not enmeshed, often deeply, in a series of relationships that meet the definition of globalization. The globalists further argue that it is impossible, or at least nearly so, to find any part of the world totally unaffected by globalization.

The globalists tend to see a broad process of globalization, but to the skeptics there is no one process of globalization, but rather many globalizations (Therborn 2000) (there is a scholarly journal entitled *Globalizations*). In fact, there are even several different ways of thinking about globalizations including multiple general processes (e.g. economic, political, etc.), as well as differences between globalization as experienced by the haves and have-nots (de Souza Santos 2006). Thus, to the skeptics the term globalization is an oversimplification and obscures a wide array of processes that are affecting the world in many different ways.

The globalists respond by agreeing that there is much to support the argument of multiple globalization processes and hence the use of the term globalizations has much merit. However, in their view, this is simply a terminological difference and both concepts (globalization and globalizations) acknowledge the importance of globalization. Indeed, the use of the term globalization in this book generally covers both a general process as well as a multitude of sub-processes that are encompassed by it (see below).

The globalists see globalization as not only in existence today, but as growing ever more powerful and pervasive. In this view, globalization involves a set of processes that led, among many other things, to the supplanting of the nation-state as the preeminent actor in the world. In Yergin and Stanislaw's terms, the nation-state lost (primarily to the market) the "commanding heights" it had, until recently, occupied; that loss "marks a great divide between the twentieth and twenty-first centuries" (Yergin and Stanislaw 1998: xiii). Thus, for example, once a structure able to control its borders, the nation-state has been supplanted in importance, at least in this realm, by global flows of all sorts. It is those flows that are of key importance and the nation-state has grown unable (or unwilling) to stop them. While the nation-state has declined in importance in the global age, "this era is not the end of the nation-state, even less the end of government" (Yergin and Stanislaw 1998: 396).

To the skeptics, at one time there may have been a process that could have been called globalization, but it is now coming to an end (Rugman 2012). They argue that in recent years the nation-state has reasserted itself and has regained, or is regaining, its historic role as the key world player. This is reflected, for example, in current US actions involving its Mexican border with increased border patrols, back-up by National Guard units, use of more high-tech surveillance equipment (including drones), and the border fence. The globalists tend to see globalization as a relatively new phenomenon, but to the skeptics globalization is simply a new term for an old, even ancient, process through which various parts of the world relate to one another.

Economically, the globalists emphasize such structures as multinational corporations (MNCs [Bonanno and Antonio 2012]), the transnational economy, and the emergence of a new global division of labor. The skeptics argue that within the economy, there are few genuine MNCs – most continue to be based in their original national locations (e.g. Daimler in Germany and Toyota in Japan). Further, as mentioned above, the skeptics retain a focus on the nation-state and national economies. It is regional blocs of nations as well as specific nations – not MNCs – that engage in new forms of economic imperialism. In addition, the nation-state, especially powerful conglomerations of them (G-8, etc.; see Chapter 6 for a discussion of this organization and others), continue to regulate and exert great control over the global economy.

The response of the globalists is that while it is true that most MNCs retain their associations with the nation-states from which they emanated originally, that association has grown less important over time. For example, while General Motors' vehicles were once produced exclusively in the US, its parts now come from all over the world and are assembled in markets across several continents.

The globalists also argue that the power or the weakness of the nation-state has nothing to do with the reality of globalization. Indeed, the nation-state, powerful or weak, is a key part of globalization. For example, the ability of the nation-state to control global flows of migrants – as well as drugs or human trafficking – ebbs and flows, but that has no bearing on the continued existence and reality of globalization or the fact that the nation-state is a player of note in it. The globalists also contend that while the continuing power of nation-states, singly and collectively, is undeniable, their ability to control economic markets is steadily declining and in some markets (e.g. financial markets) their control is already minimal.

Politically, the globalists emphasize multilateralism whereas the skeptics continue to focus on intergovernmentalism. That is, the globalists see all sorts of relationships possible in a global world, many of which do not involve governments, while the skeptics argue that the world continues to be dominated by relations among and between national governments.

In terms of global order, the skeptics continue to emphasize the role of the international order of nation-states and international governance, while the globalists see a multi-layered global governance involving much more than simply nation-states (e.g. NGOs and INGOs). Further, the globalists see the increasing importance in this domain of the growth of global civil society, a global polity, and a cosmopolitan orientation to the world. All of these, as we will see, serve to reduce the role of nation-states and international governance.

Culturally, the globalists give great importance to the rise of a global popular culture, a culture that is common to large numbers of people and most, if not all, areas of the world. Skeptics reject the idea of a common global popular culture, including and especially one dominated by the US. To them, the whole idea of such a culture has been exaggerated. To whatever extent a common global popular culture existed, it has declined in recent years with the reassertion of national and regional cultural independence, and culture in general has grown increasingly varied and is shaped by many different sources with many different effects. For example, the Internet has been nationalized to a large degree and one could speak of a German or a Japanese Internet.

In a related point, the globalists emphasize the decline of people who rigidly adhere to fixed political identities. Such a decline leaves people much more open to global popular culture. In contrast, the skeptics point, once again, to the more recent resurgence of nationalism and national identities. This is not only important in itself from the point of view of globalization, but strong national identities would serve to restrict the influence of a global popular culture.

We will have occasion to return to many of the issues debated by the globalists and the skeptics in the course of this book. However, it is important to state unequivocally at this point that, in the end, and in spite of the merit of some of the positions and criticisms of the skeptics, we conclude, unsurprisingly, that there *is* a set of processes and structures that can legitimately be labeled globalization. In that sense, this book, as mentioned in Chapter 1, adopts a globalist position on globalization, albeit one that is not insensitive to at least some of the arguments of the skeptics.

IS IT GLOBALIZATION OR TRANSNATIONALIZATION?

Trans-nationalism: Processes that interconnect individuals and social groups across specific geo-political borders.

Trans-nationality: Rise of new communities and formation of new social identities and relations that cannot be defined as nation-states.

In a related debate, some scholars argue that rather than globalization, we have **transnationalism** (Morawska 2007), or "processes that interconnect individuals and social groups across specific geo-political borders" (Giulianotti and Robertson 2007: 62). A related concept is **transnationality**, or "the rise of new communities and formation of new social identities and relations that cannot be defined through the traditional reference point of nation-states" (William Robinson 2007: 1199–201).

Globalization and transnationalism are often used interchangeably, but transnationalism is clearly a more delimited process than globalization. Transnationalism is limited to interconnections that cross geo-political borders, especially those associated with two, or more, nation-states.[2] An example is Mexican immigrants in the US sending remittances home to family members in Mexico. Globalization includes such connections, but is not restricted to them and encompasses a far wider range of transplanetary processes (e.g. direct relationships between people in many places in the world networking via the Internet).[3] Further, geo-political borders are only one of the barriers encountered, and often overcome, by globalization.[4] Some phenomena, labor unions for example, are better thought of as transnational than as global. That is, the relationship between labor unions in, for example, the US and Sweden is more important than are moves toward a global labor movement (see Chapter 15). Transnationalism is most often used in thinking about, and research on, immigrants who move from one country to another, but who continue to be involved in various ways with the country from which they came (Portes 2001b).

The case of baseball is useful in clarifying the distinction between globalization and transnationalism (Kelly 2007: 79–93). Baseball is a transnational sport because many of its fundamentals – techniques, strategies, etc. – and players have circulated across the borders of a small number of nations, especially Japan, Taiwan, Cuba, the Dominican Republic and, of course, the US. However, it is *not* global because it has not flowed on a transplanetary basis to a large portion of the world.

In contrast, football (soccer) would be much more clearly a global sport because it exists in virtually every area of the world. For example, over 200 of the world's nations are members of a global organization, the Fédération Internationale de Football Association (FIFA). Another example of globalization in the realm of sports is the summer (and winter) Olympics sponsored by the International Olympic Committee (IOC) in which about the same number of nations participate (for more on this see Chapter 8).

From the perspective of this book, the reality is that both transnationalism and globalization are present in the world today. Some phenomena can be considered transnational while others are truly global; the nuances are subtle but the distinction helps clarify the ubiquitous nature of globalization.

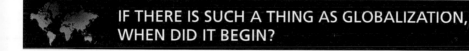

IF THERE IS SUCH A THING AS GLOBALIZATION, WHEN DID IT BEGIN?

We will offer in this section five different ways of thinking about what turns out to be a very complex issue – the origin of globalization.

HARDWIRED

Nayan Chanda (2007: xiv) argues that "globalization stems, among other things, from a basic human urge to seek a better and more fulfilling life". This leads him to trace "the initial globalization of the human species, [to] when in the late Ice Age, a tiny group of our ancestors walked out of Africa in search of better food and security. In fifty thousand years of wandering along ocean coasts and chasing game across Central Asia, they finally settled on all the continents." Chanda's view that globalization is hardwired into humans is not the one accepted here since we argue that we are now living in a distinctive global age.

Chanda focuses on four specific aspects of globalization that relate to a basic "urge"[5] for a better life – trade (or commerce), missionary work (religion), adventures and conquest (politics and warfare). All of these are key aspects of globalization, all can be traced to early human history, and all, as well as much else, will be dealt with in this volume.

CYCLES

The second perspective is that globalization is a long-term cyclical process. It is not only difficult in this view to find a single point of origin, but the effort is largely irrelevant since there long have been cycles of globalization and it is those cycles that are of utmost importance, not any particular phase or point of origin (Scholte 2005). This view, like Chanda's, tends to contradict the idea that we live today in a new "global age." Rather, this suggests that there have been *other* global ages in the past and that what now appears to be a new global age, or the high point of such an age, is destined to contract and disappear in the future. Eventually, it, too, will be replaced by a new cycle in the globalization process.

PHASES

In an example of the third approach to the beginnings of globalization, Nederveen Pieterse (2012) sees eight great epochs, or "phases," of globalization, that have occurred sequentially, each with its own point of origin:

1. Eurasian Phase (starting 3000 BCE). Agricultural and urban revolutions, migrations, increased trade, and ancient empires grew out of Eurasia.
2. Afro-Eurasian Phase (starting 1000 BCE). Commercial revolutions commenced in the Greco-Roman world, West Asia, and East Africa.
3. Oriental Phase I (starting 500 CE). The world economy emerged alongside the caravan trade in the Middle East.
4. Oriental Phase II (starting 1100). Improvements in productivity and technology emerged throughout East and South Asia, with increased urbanization and development of the Silk Routes.
5. Multicentric Phase (starting 1500). Trade expanded across the Atlantic Ocean and into the Americas.
6. Euro-Atlantic Phase (starting 1800). The Euro-Atlantic economy developed through industrialization and the colonial division of labor.
7. 20C Phase (starting 1950). MNCs and global value chains emerged throughout the US, Europe, and Japan, and the Cold War ended.
8. 21C Phase (starting 2000). A new geography of trade encompasses East Asia and emerging economies, with a global rebalancing of power and economic flows.

From this, Nederveen Pieterse concludes that globalization is *not* unique to today's world. However, his historical or phase-based view also rejects the cyclical view of globalization. Past epochs are not returning, at least in their earlier form, at some point in the future. Instead, globalization functions as growing connectivity, which develops and accelerates around various centers across time.

Robertson (1990: 15–30) offers a very different, and far more recent, set of epochs (or phases). He traces the beginnings of globalization to the early fifteenth century, but he does not see it really taking off until the late 1800s:

1. Germinal Phase in Europe (early fifteenth to mid-eighteenth century). Important developments during this period were the sun-centered view of the universe, the beginnings of modern geography, and the spread of the Gregorian calendar.
2. Incipient Phase mainly in Europe (mid-1700s to the 1870s). Among the key developments in this period were the "crystallization of conceptions of formalized international relations," a "more concrete conception of humankind," and "[s]harp increases in

conventions and agencies concerned with international and transnational regulation and communication" (1990: 26).

3. Take-Off Phase (1870s to the mid-1920s). Among the key developments in this period were the "[v]ery sharp increase in number and speed of global forms of communication. Rise of ecumenical movement. Development of global competitions – e.g. Olympics, Nobel Prizes. Implementation of World Time and near-global adoption of Gregorian calendar. First *World* war. League of Nations" (1990: 27).

4. Struggle-for-hegemony phase (1920s to the mid-1960s). This period was characterized by war (WW II) and disputes (Cold War) over the still fragile globalization process. The UN was formed during this period.

5. Uncertainty Phase (1960s to the early 1990s[6]). Many global developments occurred during this period including inclusion of the Third World in the global system, end of the Cold War (and bipolarity), spread of nuclear weapons, world civil society, world citizenship, and global media system consolidation. Robertson saw "crisis tendencies" in the global system in the early 1990s, but, if anything, globalization has accelerated since then (although it may still contain such crisis tendencies).

Were Robertson to address this issue again, he might find that yet another epoch began at the turn of the twenty-first century. These epochal views tend to contrast with the focus here on the current global age since they do not see it as particularly unique.

EVENTS

A fourth view is that instead of cycles or great epochs, one can point to much more specific events that can be seen as the origin of globalization.[7] In fact, there are *many* such possible points of origin of globalization, some of which are:

- the Romans and their far-ranging conquests in the centuries before Christ (Gibbon 1998);
- the rise and spread of Christianity in the centuries after the fall of the Roman Empire;
- the spread of Islam in the seventh century and beyond;
- the travels of the Vikings from Europe to Iceland, Greenland, and briefly to North America in the ninth through the eleventh centuries as examples of, and landmarks, in globalization;
- trade in the Middle Ages throughout the Mediterranean;
- the activities of the banks of the twelfth-century Italian city-states;
- the rampage of the armies of Ghengis Khan into Eastern Europe in the thirteenth century (*Economist* 2006: January 12);
- European traders like Marco Polo and his travels later in the thirteenth century along the Silk Road to China. (Interestingly, there is now discussion of the development of an "iron silk road" involving a linked railroad network through a variety of Asian countries that at least evokes the image of the lure of Marco Polo's Silk Road.[8]);
- the "discovery of America" by Christopher Columbus in 1492. Other important voyages of discovery during this time involved Vasco Da Gama rounding the Cape of Good Hope in 1498 and the circumnavigation of the globe completed in 1522 by one of Ferdinand Magellan's ships (Joel Rosenthal 2007);

- European colonialism, especially in the nineteenth century;
- the early twentieth-century global Spanish flu pandemic;
- the two world wars in the first half of the twentieth century.

It is also possible to get even more specific about the origin of globalization, especially in recent years. A few rather eclectic recent examples include:

- 1956 – the first transatlantic telephone cable;
- 1958 – while it was possible to fly across the Atlantic in the 1930s on seaplanes that made several stops along the way, the big revolution in this area was the arrival of transatlantic passenger jet travel with the first being Pan Am's flight from New York to London (with a stopover for refueling required in Newfoundland);
- 1962 – the launch of the satellite Telstar and soon thereafter the first transatlantic television broadcasts;
- 1966 – the transmission from a satellite of the picture of the earth as single location leading not only to a greater sense of the world as one place (increased global consciousness [Robertson and Inglis 2004]), but also of great importance to the development of the global environmental movement;
- 1970 – the creation of Clearing House Interbank Payment System (CHIPS) making possible global electronic (wire) transfers of funds (now $1.5 trillion a day in 2012) among financial institutions;
- 1977 – the Society for Worldwide Interbank Financial Telecommunications (SWIFT) came into being making possible more global transfers of funds by individuals;
- 1988 – the founding of the modern Internet based on Arpanet (which was created in 1969). While it took the Internet several years to take off, this was a turning point in global interconnection for billions of people;
- 2001 – the terrorist attacks on the Twin Towers in New York and on the Pentagon in Washington, as well as later terrorist attacks on trains in Madrid (March 11, 2004) and London (July 7, 2005), among others. The following is a specific example in support of the idea that 9/11 can be taken as a point of origin for globalization (at least of higher education): "Since the terrorist attacks of September 11, 2001, internationalization has moved high on the agenda at most universities, to prepare students for a globalized world, and to help faculty members stay up-to-date in their disciplines" (Lewin 2008: 8).
- 2009 – due to the highly interconnected global economy, the Great Recession sent shockwaves throughout the world. Some of its many effects included changes to global migration patterns, declines in global remittances, and explosions in unemployment and debt, and it led to many battles over austerity measures – effects that are likely to continue shaping globalization.
- 2014 – mobile-cellular phone subscriptions reach approximately 7 billion, which is almost the human population on Earth (International Telecommunication Union 2014). This suggests that humans are now more interconnected than ever before, even though many parts of the world still have limited access (see Figure 2.1 for the number of mobile-cellular subscriptions in countries around the world).

This focus on specific historical events is less general than the approach taken in this book that focuses on the current global age.

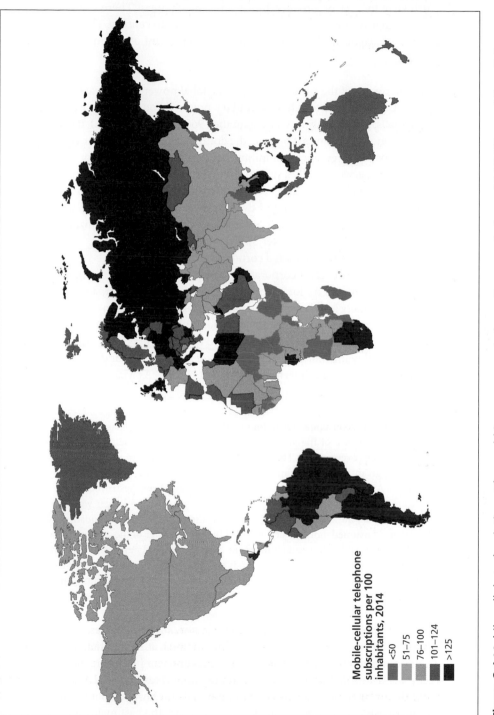

Figure 2.1 Mobile-cellular subscriptions. The world is more connected now than ever before with 7 billion mobile-cellular phone subscriptions. Nonetheless, the number of subscriptions per country is uneven. Source: data from ITU, Mobile-Cellular Subscriptions (http://www.itu.int/en/ITU-D/Statistics/Pages/stat/default.aspx).

Mobile-cellular telephone subscriptions per 100 inhabitants, 2014

<50
51–75
76–100
101–124
>125

BROADER, MORE RECENT CHANGES

The fifth view focuses on broader, but still recent, changes. There is a sense in this view that a sea change occurred in the last half of the twentieth century. Three of these momentous changes have been identified by scholars as the point of origin of globalization as it exists today:

1. The emergence of the United States as *the* global power in the years following WW II.

    The US not only projected its military power throughout the world (Korea in the early 1950s; disastrously in Vietnam in the 1960s and early 1970s), it extended its reach in the economic realm as it became the dominant industrial power when the war decimated most of its competitors militarily (Germany, Japan) and/or economically (the Axis powers as well as Allies such as France and Great Britain). Many other aspects of America's global reach either accompanied these changes or soon followed. Among them was the diplomatic clout of the US government, the reach of the US media, the power of Hollywood, and so on. Such a view closely aligns globalization with the idea of Americanization (see Chapter 3).

2. The emergence of multinational corporations (MNCs).

    While the world's great corporations can be traced back to the eighteenth and early nineteenth centuries in, for example, Germany, Great Britain, and the United States, they were initially largely associated with their nations of origin and did the vast majority of their business within those countries (Bonanno and Antonio 2012). However, over time, those corporations did more and more business internationally. In so doing, they were following Marx's dictum that because of stagnant or declining profits capitalism had to expand into international markets or die. As Marx and Engels (1848/2000: 248–9) put it:

    > The need of a constantly expanding market for its products chases the bourgeoisie over the entire surface of the globe. It must nestle everywhere, settle everywhere, establish connections everywhere. The bourgeoisie has, through its exploitation of the world market, given a cosmopolitan character to production and consumption in every country.... . All old-established national industries have been destroyed or are daily being destroyed. They are dislodged by new industries ... that no longer work up indigenous raw material, but raw materials drawn from the remotest zones; industries whose products are consumed, not only at home, but in every quarter of the globe. In place of the old wants, satisfied by the production of the country, we find new wants, requiring for their satisfaction the products of distant lands and climes. In place of the old local and national seclusion and self-sufficiency, we have intercourse in every direction, universal interdependence of nations.

    For example, the once-great American automobile companies – Ford and General Motors – not only originated in the US, but focused, at least initially, on selling into the American market and most, if not all, of the component parts were produced by them or sub-contractors in the US. Of course, they did import raw materials of various kinds (and they did sell their automobiles overseas, especially in Europe), but in the main, the bulk of their business was done in the US. Furthermore, the vast majority of top executives, employees, and investors were American. However, that began to change over the course of the twentieth century as these corporations exported more of their automobiles to other parts of the world, opened factories in other countries to sell cars under their brand names (or others), targeted their products to the distinctive needs (e.g. for smaller, more fuel-efficient cars) of those countries, and more recently began to move more and more of their automobile production aimed at the US market to other countries, either in factories of their own or in the factories of sub-contractors in those countries.

In these and other ways, Ford and General Motors have become multinational corporations and MNCs are, because of their very nature, inherently part of globalization. Indeed, MNCs are not only involved in globalization but this process is internalized into the organization as all sorts of global flows (parts, people, money) occur *within* the corporation.

The case of the other of the one-time "Big Three" American automobile companies – Chrysler – is even more striking in this regard. Initially, Chrysler followed the same course as Ford and GM and became increasingly multinational. However, Chrysler has long been the most marginal of the Big Three and, famously, had to be bailed out in 1979 by a controversial loan from the US government. However, that was only of short-term help and in 1998 Chrysler was taken over by the German manufacturer of Mercedes Benz automobiles which changed its name to Daimler-Chrysler AG. This clearly represented the formation of a MNC, although Daimler-Benz itself (as well as Chrysler) was a multinational corporation before that since, among other things, it actively sold its automobiles in the US as well as in many other parts of the world. However, this marriage was short-lived and Daimler sold off its interest in Chrysler in 2007. After filing for bankruptcy in 2009, Chrysler was again bailed out (as was GM) by the US government during the Great Recession. Today, Chrysler is owned by Fiat, a MNC headquartered in Italy.

3. The demise of the Soviet Union and the end of the Cold War.

It could be argued that globalization is even more recent and did not truly begin until the fall of the "Iron Curtain" and the Soviet Union in 1991. With those events, the division of the world into mainly "capitalist" and "communist" spheres rapidly eroded as did all sorts of barriers that existed between them. Major parts of the world were opened for the first time since the early twentieth century to all sorts of global flows – immigration, tourism, media, diplomacy, and especially the capitalistic economic transactions of MNCs and other businesses. The global processes that had spread throughout most of the "free" world before 1991 flooded into the now independent states of the old Soviet Union, especially Russia, and most of its allies.

Vestiges of communism exist as of this writing, especially in Cuba, North Korea and, at least nominally, in China (Larry Ray 2012). Cuba remains, in the main, outside of global capitalism, largely because of the US embargo against trading with Cuba, in force since 1962 and expanded and codified several times since then. However, the embargo itself is a manifestation of globalization – the US setting up barriers in order to limit or halt the flow of trade with Cuba and to inhibit or prevent other nations from around the world from trading with Cuba. China, of course, is becoming a, if not soon, *the* major force in global capitalism even though the government remains communist, at least in name (Panitch et al. 2013). In any case, China is actively involved in globalization not only economically, but in many other realms as well (e.g. the Chinese Ministry of Culture participated actively in the prestigious Venice Biennale art exhibition [Platt 2013]).

The perspective adopted in this book on the current global age is most in accord with this focus on broader changes in the last half of the twentieth century. While all of the other perspectives deal with global processes, they were far more limited in geographic scope and far less extensive and intensive than the global processes that took off in the late twentieth century. Thus the perspective adopted here is that globalization is a relatively recent development with its major points of origin occurring after the close of WW II.

GLOBALIZATION OR GLOBALIZATIONS?

While we can discuss globalization in general terms, such a discussion obscures the important fact that there are, as pointed out earlier, various types of globalization – various globalization*s* – that need to be identified and the relationships among and between them teased out (Hoffman 2002). The following are *some* of the major types[9] of globalization that will be dealt with in this book.

ECONOMIC

As we've seen, to many observers, economic globalization is globalization.[10] While economic globalization is certainly of great importance, perhaps of greatest importance, there are other important types of globalization (see below).

POLITICAL

While heavily influenced by economic globalization, political globalization cannot be reduced to economics alone. For example, US wars against Iraq in 1991 and 2003 certainly had an economic motivation (for example, protecting the supply of Middle East oil, perhaps even gaining more control over Iraq's oil), but there were many other factors (misguided fears of "weapons of mass destruction" and of al-Qaeda in Iraq, demonization of Islam in general and of Saddam Hussein in particular, and so on).

> **Political globalization**: Political relations that exist at a global level, including inter-national relations.

Those who study **political globalization** tend to think in terms of inter-national relations. However, the key contribution of globalization studies in this domain is to encompass, but look beyond, inter-national relations to other kinds of political relations that exist at a global level (So 2012). Examples include those involving global organizations, especially the United Nations (UN), relations between regions and cities that bypass the nation-states in which they exist, and more specific phenomena such as terrorist organizations (e.g. al-Qaeda) that are not based in, or associated with, any particular nation-state; they are "state-less." Indeed, statelessness and the increasing problems associated with it (e.g. in the tribal territories of Pakistan, Syria, in several countries in Africa [e.g. Somalia, Congo] which seem to have a government in name only) are of increasing global interest and concern.

CULTURAL

There is a wide variety of cultural flows that exist, at least in part, independently of the other major forms of globalization (Tomlinson 2012). Examples include food (Italian, Chinese, Indian, etc.), television offerings (BBC and al-Hurra), movies (from Hollywood and Bollywood), museum shows, touring rock and classical music performances, and so on. Of course, these forms of **cultural globalization** cannot be divorced totally from the other major forms of globalization. They often have roots in particular nation-states (e.g. India's Bollywood) and their global movement may lead to political outcries in various countries (the hostility to American-style fast food among at least some in France, Italy, and elsewhere). More importantly, all of these forms of cultural globalization are affected by economic considerations (e.g. whether or not they can at least earn back their expenses, if not show a profit, in other geographic locales) and have economic consequences (the continued production of new cultural offerings depends upon previous ones showing a profit, or at least not losing money).

> **Cultural globalization**: Cultural influences that exist at a global level, between and among various nations.

RELIGION

Most of the world's religions (Christianity, Islam, Judaism, etc.) are global in scope and often seek to extend their global influence (Abrutyn 2012). For example, Catholicism, with about a billion adherents, is a global operation run from the Vatican. There are Catholics, Catholic churches, and Catholic priests in most parts of the world and all sorts of information flows to and from them and the Vatican. Many other religions, both large and small, are, or seek to be, global in scope and work toward that through proselytizing throughout the world, sending missionaries, and opening religious centers (churches, mosques, synagogues, and so on). Great attention these days is devoted to the global spread of Islam, especially Islamic fundamentalism, although it has been a globalizing religion since its creation in the seventh century (it spread through the Middle East, northern Africa, and as far as Spain) (Vertigans and Sutton 2002).

SCIENCE

Science today is inherently a global enterprise as its knowledge base is formed by inputs from many parts of the world and that knowledge is disseminated virtually everywhere (Drori 2012a). This has been true for quite some time (e.g. work on atomic and sub-atomic theory in the first half of the twentieth century), but has been made much easier by various technological advances. The advent of the Internet was of particular importance in enhancing the global character and reach of science. Many scientific journals are now online and can be accessed by scientists in most parts of the world. Furthermore, many scientists no longer wait for journals to accept and publish their articles; they now publish their work online. Such work, often in its early stages, can be read by scientists everywhere. It can affect their own work almost instantaneously, or they can offer rapid feedback or corrections to the original author(s) who can quickly revise a work and publish the revised paper online. To take one other example, large if not massive collaborations among scientists around the world are now much more likely because of the Internet and video conferencing.

HEALTH AND MEDICINE

Health and medicine have been increasingly globalized in many different ways (Linn and Wilson 2012). Diseases can and do proliferate globally. There is also the global spread of medical knowledge and expertise as well as technologies useful in diagnosing and treating various diseases. As with scientific knowledge, much medical knowledge is available online and disseminated rapidly around the world.

SPORT

Sport, too, has been globalized in various ways (Andrews and Mower 2012). We have already touched on a few of the major organizations involved in the globalization of sport; other sports that are quite global in reach are professional tennis and golf. The global media, especially television, have played a key role in the globalization of sport and creating global interest in, and an audience for, sport.

EDUCATION

Higher education has spread through increasing areas of the world and the systems of higher education have grown increasingly similar (Mitchell and Nielsen 2012; Ramirez 2012). This is even truer of schools of business administration, especially those that offer MBA programs (Clegg and Carter 2007). Recently, American universities have, in effect, been opening "franchises" in various countries, especially the oil-rich Persian Gulf area (Lewin 2008: 8). Universities are now even graded on the World Reputation Rankings (Gutterplan 2013).

However, primary and secondary schools have not done as well in keeping up with globalization. Three key failures have been associated with today's primary and secondary schools as they relate to globalization:

1. Schools are generally not engaging young people in learning with the result that when asked, most students say that school is "boring." The various facets of globalization – economic, sociocultural, demographic – are everyday realities for young people, but the schools offer little that is relevant to those realities.
2. Schools, especially in the North, are not responding adequately to the needs of the large numbers of immigrant youth from the South. They often "quickly become marginalized as racially, ethnically, religiously, and linguistically marked minority groups... . The results of these general trends are painfully obvious in multiple measurable ways: from the high dropout rates among immigrant, ethnic and racial minorities in many wealthy countries, to stark differences in achievement patterns between native and racialized minorities" (Suarez-Orozco and Smith 2007: 3).
3. Arguably the most alarming problem is associated with the failures of schools in the South and the fact that 61 million children of primary school age and 71 million children of lower secondary school age in the South are not enrolled in schools (UNICEF and the UNESCO Institute for Statistics 2012). As a result, they fall ever-further behind children in the North. In addition, these failures contribute to the enormous problem of illiteracy which is concentrated in the South and growing illiteracy there can only serve to widen the gap between North and South.

Primary and secondary schools need to change in order to adapt to the realities of the new global world.

The above gives at least a sense of the range of globalizations, but, in fact, even this iteration touches only on a small number of the globalizations to be dealt with in this volume.

One important point about the idea that there are multiple globalizations is the fact that it further complicates the whole idea of finding a point of origin for globalization. Clearly, there are different points of origin depending on whether one is focusing on globalization in the economy, or politics, or science, or higher education, and so on. It clearly makes far more sense in the search for origins (assuming one wants to search for them) to specify different origins for each of the many forms of globalization than to seek out a single point of origin for globalization as a whole. Furthermore, even within each of the forms, there are sub-areas each of which is likely to have a different point of origin for the beginning of globalization (for example, malaria has been spreading globally for centuries while Avian flu has yet to [and may never] affect large numbers of humans throughout the world).

WHAT DRIVES GLOBALIZATION?

This is another highly complex question with no easy answers. For example, if we accept the fact that there are multiple globalizations, then it is clear that it would be illusory to think that we could find a single driver, or even a small number of drivers. Yet, to seek out the drivers of each and every form of globalization would be a long and tedious process. At this point, at least, we need to restrict ourselves to a search for the drivers of globalization at the most general level. While we will focus on globalization in general, many of these same factors apply to at least some of the more specific globalizations.

One way to approach this is through one of the classic divisions in the social sciences – the distinction between material and ideal explanations. A *material*, or materialist, explanation would tend to focus on objective factors and forces. While there can be other material forces (e.g. the nation-state in the political realm), this generally comes down, as it did for Karl Marx (who was a materialist), to a focus on economic factors such as "forces" and "relations" of production, technology, and so on. It is this kind of thinking that leads many to the view that it is capitalism in general, or the contemporary MNC, that is the most important driving force in contemporary globalization.

The polar view, as it was for Marx, is that it is not material factors, but rather *ideal* factors, that are the main drivers of globalization. The emphasis on ideal factors was characteristic of the philosopher G. W. F. Hegel and his followers, the "young Hegelians." Marx came of age in this intellectual context, but famously planted Hegel on his feet by focusing on material rather than ideal factors. However, Marx retained a secondary interest in such idea systems as ideology (for more on ideology, at least as it relates to the neoliberal view of globalization, see Chapter 4). Today, the idealist position on globalization is that the main drivers of the process are changes in thinking and ideas, as well as in information and knowledge. We have come increasingly to think in global, rather than in local, or even in national, terms. And, our knowledge base has followed suit so that it, too, is increasingly global in scope. A good example of the latter involves the issue of global climate change. In some ways (because, for example, of movies and books like Al Gore's [2006] *An Inconvenient Truth*) we have come to know a great deal about global climate and climate change, perhaps a lot more than we know about our local climate (Brulle et al. 2012). And this greater knowledge about global climate change is leading at long last to more serious global efforts to deal with its causes and consequences. Thus, in this view, globalization is driven not by material changes, but by changes in ideas and knowledge.

Of course, there is a middle ground on this which sees *both* material and ideal factors as being of great importance. In terms of the history of social theory, Max Weber was the most famous social theorist to adopt such a view. While he set out, in contrast to Marx and the Marxists, to show the importance of ideal factors (e.g. the role of the ethos of Protestantism in the rise of capitalism in the West [Weber 1904–1905/1958]), this was in the context of a larger view that recognized the importance of *both* ideal and material factors (Weber 1927/1981). Actually, in the end, Weber saw material factors as the main drivers, but what is of greatest importance from our point of view is that he accorded importance to *both*. Thus, from this perspective, we can see globalization as being driven by a range of both material *and* ideal drivers. This is clear today in the global green movement which is driven by both ideas (e.g. those of Al Gore) and material realities (high gasoline prices or the drive for greater profit).

DOES GLOBALIZATION HOP RATHER THAN FLOW?

To the degree that globalization exists, does it flow or hop? In spite of occasional conflicts, it can be comforting to conceive of globalization in terms of flows. That is, it seems to suggest a kind of global equality with all parts of the globe being penetrated, at least theoretically, by these flows to more or less the same degree. However, as we all know, the world is characterized by great inequality (see Chapters 13 and 14). Therefore, all flows do not go everywhere in the world and, even when they do, they affect various areas to varying degrees and in very different ways. However, it is also possible that the idea of flows communicates the wrong, or at least a distorted, sense of globalization and that another metaphor might be more appropriate, at least for some parts of the world.

This is exactly what James Ferguson suggests in his work on Africa. He argues, rather, that at least in the case of Africa (and this idea applies elsewhere, as well), globalization "hops" from place to place rather than flowing evenly through the entire continent:

> We have grown accustomed to a language of global "flows" in thinking about "globalization," but flow is a particularly poor metaphor for the point-to-point connectivity and networking of enclaves … as the contemporary African material shows so vividly, the "global" does not "flow," thereby connecting and watering contiguous spaces; *it hops instead*, efficiently connecting the enclaved points in the network while excluding (with equal efficiency) the spaces that lie between the points. (Ferguson 2006: 47, italics added)

The idea that globalization hops, rather than flows, at least in some parts of the world (such as Africa), implies that while some areas are strongly, often positively, affected by it, others are not.

This relates to the "enclaves" discussed by Ferguson. While some areas – enclaves in Africa (and elsewhere) – are deeply implicated in global processes, those processes simply hop over most other areas of that continent. Among those enclaves are the national parks that are such highly desirable destinations for well-heeled tourists from the North. (Note: throughout this book the terms "North" and "South" will be used to refer the two major parts of world – the highly developed North [especially the US and the EU] and the less developed South [especially Africa, South America, and some parts of Southeast Asia][11]). Highly desirable locales have been partitioned off so that Northern tourists can "hop" into them, experience a highly sanitized bit of Africa, and then hop out. In doing so, the areas may be cordoned off (perhaps with barbed wire) and patrolled by the military or private guards who may operate with "shoot-to-kill" orders if any "poachers" are found in the enclaves. The problem is that many of the so-called "poachers" are, in fact, locals who have been excluded from areas that may be, for example, their traditional hunting grounds. The more general point here is that globalization hops into these enclaves (in the form of tourists and their money) but it jumps over most other areas in Africa, including those in which the "poachers" now live. Not only are the latter not helped by global flows, but they are adversely affected by the barriers that exclude them from areas that were once part of their domain.

This all points to a very different image of globalization than the one we are accustomed to:

> The "global" we see … in Africa has sharp, jagged edges; rich and dangerous traffic amid zones of generalized abjection; razor-wired enclaves next to abandoned hinterlands. It features entire countries with estimated life expectancies in the mid-thirties and dropping; warfare seemingly without end; and the steepest economic inequalities seen in human history to date. It is a global where capital flows are at once lightning fast and patchy and incomplete; where the globally networked enclave sits right beside the ungovernable humanitarian disaster zone. It is a global not of planetary communion, but of disconnection, segmentation and segregation – not a seamless world without borders, but a patchwork of discontinuous and hierarchically ranked spaces, whose edges are carefully delimited, guarded, and enforced. (Ferguson 2006: 48–9)

It may well be that we need to think of globalization both in terms of flows *and* in terms of processes that hop from place to place. As a general rule, globalization flows more easily through the developed world (although even there it flows around many areas inhabited by the poor), whereas it bypasses many locales in the less developed world, or even skirts them completely. The metaphors of "flows" and "hops" obviously exist uncomfortably with one another; it is difficult to think of flows as hopping. Rather, to be consistent with the idea of flows, we need to think in terms of some of the "heavy structures," that block those flows, especially in less developed parts of the world. That is, because of those barriers many positive flows are forced to bypass less developed areas.

IF THERE IS SUCH A THING AS GLOBALIZATION, IS IT INEXORABLE?

Assuming there is such a thing as globalization, is its further development and expansion inevitable? The inevitability of globalization is a view that is widespread both in academic work and especially in more popular sources. It is, for example, the view of Thomas Friedman (1999, 2005, 2012) who, in *The World is Flat*,[12] argues that globalization is expanding in various ways and directions. Daniel Altman (2007: x) contends that "the forces often labeled 'globalization' … are here to stay." Nayan Chanda (2007: 320) argues that "[c]alls to shut down globalization are pointless."

Globalization does seem inexorable as it encompasses more and more areas of the social world. However, ideas like inexorability and inevitability are always problematic from the point of view of the social sciences. It is certainly the case that there are quite strong social trends here and a very strong likelihood that they will continue, and even accelerate, in the years to come. Yet, that is not the same as saying that such changes are inevitable. Indeed, the social sciences in general point to the view that there are *never* any inevitabilities and this applies in particular to such a wide-ranging and globe-straddling process as globalization. For example, the current counter-reactions in, especially, the US, Europe, and South Africa to widespread immigration, especially unauthorized immigration from less developed nations (in South Africa's case, Zimbabwe), is leading, or at least could lead, to less rather than more globalization, at least in terms of flows of these types of people. Thus, the counter-reactions (e.g. violence against Zimbabweans in South Africa) against globalization constitute an important check on its seemingly inevitable expansion.

Furthermore, thinking in terms of such inevitabilities serves to reduce people to the status of "judgmental dopes" (Ritzer 2008c: 387) who can do nothing but blindly accept such changes. While it is true that people may often be overwhelmed by such large-scale changes, they *always* retain the ability to act singly and collectively to modify, if not prevent, such changes. While people may at times seem like judgmental dopes, at other times they are much more likely to act as powerful agents (Giddens 1984) and even "dangerous giants."[13]

This relates to the distinction between "globalization from above" and "globalization from below" (Kellner 2002; Langman 2012). We can define **globalization from above** as a process that is created and controlled by centralized and powerful groups, such as the wealthy elites or MNCs (especially those associated with the North), and imposed on less powerful groups. Globalization from above is associated with neoliberalism (see Chapter 4) and popular writers like Thomas Friedman. When looked at in this way, globalization is to a large degree imposed on individual actors in *both* the North and the South, and the greatest benefits go to a minority of powerful states, MNCs, and wealthy individuals.

While much of globalization is certainly from above, social scientists are particularly attuned to globalization from below that serves, at least to some degree, to counteract it and shape its outcomes via more democratic processes. **Globalization from below** can take the form of marginalized groups and social movements, which struggle to make globalization benefit more people and to make global processes more democratic. In addition, globalization from below can also involve whole nations (largely in the less developed world). From the perspective of globalization from below, people are agents, even "dangerous giants." Through grassroots activism, strikes, boycotts, and social movement mobilization, they fight against the inequities produced through globalization from above.

Globalization from below generally relates to the counter-reactions to globalization from above. As a result, it is often called the "anti-globalization" movement, but this would be a misnomer because the movement is generally not against globalization per se, but rather specific forms of that process, especially globalization from above. (Terms like *alter-globalization* or *global justice movement* are also often affixed to it – for more on this, see Chapter 15.) Thus the various groups and organizations associated with that movement (most generally the World Social Forum) oppose impositions by, for example, the US, Wal-Mart, and the IMF. These organizations and groups cannot be seen as being anti-globalization because in many cases they are global themselves and their ambition is to create and sustain global processes and movements that stand in opposition to globalization from above.

Alter-globalization is generally seen to have come of age in protests against the World Trade Organization (WTO) in Seattle in 1999 (although there were precursors such as protests in Madrid in 1994). In Seattle, the protestors forced the postponement of the opening session of the WTO meeting and violent protests occurred for days. The media attention to

Globalization from above: Process that is created and controlled by centralized and powerful actors, such as wealthy elites or MNCs (especially in the North), and imposed on broader society.

Globalization from below: Marginalized groups and social movements that struggle to make globalization benefit more people and for global processes to be more democratic.

these activities gave important visibility and momentum to the alter-globalization movement. This movement took a more collective form with the creation of the World Social Forum (WSF) in Porto Alegre, Brazil in 2001. That organization has met every year since, usually in January because that is the month that the group that represents much of what it is opposed to, the World Economic Forum (WEF) (composed mainly of business and political leaders, although others – journalists, intellectuals – may also be invited), meets annually in Davos, Switzerland. Both the WEF and, more importantly in this context, the WSF (as well as the organizations and groups that are involved in it) are global in nature and therefore WSF cannot be considered as being anti-globalization. Rather, it is an example of globalization from below.

A particularly good example of this is the Italian-based Slow Food Movement. Founded in 1989 and getting its spark from protests against the opening of a McDonald's at the foot of the Spanish Steps in Rome, Slow Food has become a social movement involving over 100,000 members in about 150 countries around the world (Galli and Degliesposti 2012). Thus, Slow Food is global in character and involved in various ways in globalization. It is clearly not anti-globalization, but it is opposed to various types of globalization from above, most obviously the global proliferation of McDonald's and other fast-food chains that offer industrialized fast food. More positively, Slow Food is in favor of the support and even global distribution of local foods that are produced by traditional methods and that have not come to be controlled by agro-industries. Slow Food has expanded in various directions and is involved in various activities, many of which are global in scope and opposed to globalization from above. For example, since 2004 it has sponsored a meeting, Terra Madre, that involves representatives from many countries around the world brought together to discuss such issues as organic foods, small-scale farming and fishing, and above all the sustainable production of food. At the same time, it opposes such forms of globalization from above as the global exportation and proliferation of genetically modified foods.

The most general point here is that globalization is not restricted to the actions of those on "top" (e.g. nation-state and MNC leaders), but also comes from the "bottom" in the actions of people and groups that have a different, often conflicting, vision of globalization. Of course, there are also many other people and groups that are anti-globalization. Such anti-globalization groups struggle against any form of globalization and reinforce separation and isolation. These groups reject, rather than seek to change, global institutions (e.g. United Nations) and connections. Perhaps the most important point in this context is to recognize that globalization, or at least any specific type of globalization, is not inexorable because of the actions of the groups associated with alter-globalization (and in some instances, anti-globalization).

DOES *GLOBAPHILIA* OR *GLOBAPHOBIA* HAVE THE UPPER HAND?

The preceding is related to the chasm that exists between those who are fans of, and favor, globalization (**globaphilia**) and those who fear it and are opposed to it (**globaphobia**). Those who are globaphiliacs see much to celebrate about globalization. They tend to emphasize its positive, and to deemphasize its negative, sides. Those associated with globaphobia tend to see people as "victims" of globalization and its largely negative consequences. Then there are middle-ground positions on this: "neither *globaphobia* nor *globaphilia* seem

Globaphilia: Emphasis on the positive aspects of globalization, especially greater economic success and the spread of democracy.

Globaphobia: Emphasis on the negative aspects of globalization, especially for the less well-off parts of the globe.

entirely justified. Globalization is neither a limitless source of benefit to humanity, as some claim, nor is it guilty of all the ills for which it is held responsible" (de la Dehesa 2006: x).

GLOBAPHILIA

A great deal of attention has been devoted, at least until recently, to the economic success attributed to globalization (Kahn 2012). It is clear to supporters that the North has gained disproportionately from globalization. There is a tendency to ignore the "losers" in the process, including not only most of the South, but also those in the North who have not been beneficiaries of these economic gains. While the losers are ignored, they are expected to take solace in the assumption that while they may not yet have gained much, they will soon, if only they are patient. Adopted here is the view that a "rising sea raises all boats" and eventually most, if not all, will be beneficiaries of globalization's economic advances.

Another positive view associated with globaphilia is that globalization will bring with it increasing democratization. There is an assumption that economic progress leads to democracy and/or democracy leads to economic progress (Friedman 2002). In addition, there is the view that democracy itself is being spread by globalization, despite the fact that globalization has brought both democracy and authoritarian regimes (Moghadam 2013).There are various other positive outlooks associated with globaphilia including the idea that globalization is furthering the spread of "civil society" (Kellogg 2012). Civil society (see Chapter 5) involves those organizations and institutions that are separable from the nation-state and the market and that are able to represent some alternative, if not opposition, to them and their hegemony. The spread of democracy throughout the world is seen as furthering civil society in those countries that move in that direction. After all, the ability of civil society to stand up to the power of the state and the market serves to reduce authoritarianism and to foster democratization. Furthermore, globalization is seen as bringing with it global organizations, especially INGOs like Greenpeace and the World Wildlife Federation, that are themselves part of global civil society. Characteristically, what globaphiliacs ignore is the ways in which globalization can adversely affect civil society through the power of some global INGOs (e.g. World Economic Forum) as well as through global processes such as the market, the emergence and spread of authoritarian regimes, and military incursions. All of these can short circuit, and even destroy, indigenous civil society.

GLOBAPHOBIA

While globaphilia predominates, at least in the United States, there is no shortage of globaphobia there, and more generally in other parts of the world, especially the less developed areas (Watts 2012). Clearly much of the criticism of globalization, especially as it relates to capitalism, comes from scholars, especially those who are more liberal and left-leaning. There is also no shortage of more popular criticisms of globalization from not only the left (e.g. Noam Chomsky [2003, 2013]) but also the right (e.g. Pat Buchanan [2011]). Furthermore, there are the new widespread alter-globalization movements that have their basis in critical perspectives on globalization.

Pat Buchanan is a prominent conservative critic of globalization. He is best known as a US political commentator (and for several unsuccessful runs for president), and has authored several books on globalization, especially attacking American involvement overseas, immigration, and the supposed decline of the American way of life (Buchanan 2011).

Buchanan argues that the US should kick the UN out of its New York headquarters and that it should cease involving itself in any "new world order" that limits the United States' ability to manage its own affairs. He is highly conservative in the sense that he wants to protect Americans, especially American jobs, from competition from both cheap imports and immigrants.

Buchanan is especially critical of immigrants generally and undocumented immigrants in particular, which in his view pose a threat to American culture and the American way of life. For example, his book titles include *The Death of the West: How Dying Populations and Immigrant Invasions Imperil Our Country and Civilization*, and *State of Emergency: The Third World Invasion and Conquest of America*. In his view this, too, poses a threat to American culture and economic strength. He believes we should reduce the number of immigrants permitted to enter the US and that we should not allow entry for those immigrants reluctant to adopt US and Western culture. Once again, Buchanan's position is essentially a conservative one because he wants to conserve the jobs and lifestyles of Americans (his most recent book is titled *Suicide of a Superpower: Will America Survive to 2025?*). Here, as in the case of international trade, Buchanan has little or no interest in the well-being of immigrants to the US (again, especially undocumented immigrants), to say nothing of the Native Americans present before European Americans, or workers in India and in other less developed parts of the world who are the recipients of work outsourced from the US.

When we turn to criticisms from the left, there is no shortage of them either, including from such notable political figures as Venezuela's late president, Hugo Chávez. The latter, in a speech to the United Nations in 2006, lambasted the US as an imperialistic nation endeavoring to create a world empire through globalization. In the process, Chávez called President George W. Bush a "devil." At several points during his speech he held aloft a book authored by the noted American linguist, turned left-wing political analyst, Noam Chomsky (2003, 2013).

Noam Chomsky is not opposed to globalization per se. Rather, his target is neoliberal globalization dominated by the US and its economic interests (2003, 2013). To put it another way, he is opposed to corporate globalization, a process aimed at opening markets in order to maximize profits and the interests and economic well-being of investors. However, he favors globalization as it is represented by, for example, the labor movement and by the World Social Forum. In other words, Chomsky favors globalization from below rather than from above; he favors alter-globalization. Most generally, he argues that no one really opposes globalization as an overall process; it is the specific ways in which it is presently operating that he and other left-wing critics oppose.

Chomsky is critical of neoliberal economic globalization on several grounds. For one thing, such globalization is largely sponsored by the US and is designed to further its interests as well as those of American corporations and the "haves" within the US. More generally, it works to the benefit of the North in general, and the elites there, as well. Related to this is the fact that globalization of this type benefits the few in the world, but does not benefit the masses, the "people." Chomsky obviously favors a globalization that works to the benefit of the vast majority of people in the world, not just a select few.

Chomsky also argues that neoliberal globalization does not enhance, but rather operates to the detriment of, democracy. That is, it enhances the power of the inter-linked corporate and state leaders who exert control over the economy, and much else, without being answerable, accountable to the people. Privatization, which he sees as one element of neoliberalism, "reduces the arena of potential democratic choice" (2003: 138). Furthermore, with truly important matters usurped by those in power, the people are left to decide democratically upon relatively trivial matters: "What remains of democracy is largely the right to choose among commodities" (2003: 139).

As an American, and as a world-famous scholar, Chomsky's stinging attacks on the US are particularly notable. He is critical of not only America in general, and of its economic actions, but also of its political and military undertakings. He was particularly critical of American actions throughout the world during the presidency of George W. Bush. He sees these as part of an American effort to achieve hegemony in the world. It is the vehemence of his critique of the US, and the fact that it is offered by a notable American, that led Chávez to hold Chomsky's book aloft at that UN meeting.

Moving beyond specific arguments such as those offered from the right (Buchanan) and the left (Chomsky), what are the more general criticisms of the globaphobics? As is clear from the above, a major criticism is that globalization has *not* had the positive effects that globaphiliacs like Friedman assume and assert. The critics tend to emphasize globalization's negative effects on the less well-off, especially in the South. The latter are seen as losing more than they gain from globalization. Indeed, what is often emphasized is that instead of catching up as a result of globalization, many of those in the less developed world fall farther behind those in the developed world; the gap grows wider rather than narrower as a result of globalization. Thus, global capitalism, like capitalism in general, serves to benefit the "haves" while disadvantaging the "have nots"; it makes the latter's economic situation worse rather than better, at least relatively. To put this another way, the globaphobic view is that globalization leads to greater global inequality (although this is a hotly debated issue in sociology; see Chapter 13). This is in stark contrast to at least one of the implications of Friedman's "flat world" thesis that globalization is leading to greater global equality.

Needless to say, the globaphiliacs have little use for the globaphobics (and vice versa). For example, Martin Wolf, a prominent neoliberal, often argues that the criticisms of globalization are "wrong," "almost entirely mistaken," "largely, though not entirely, groundless," and so on. Wolf calls one of the most important recent critical works in globalization, Hardt and Negri's *Empire* (see Chapter 4), an "absurdity" (Wolf 2005: 57). His most general judgment of the critics is the following:

> The 1980s and 1990s witnessed the collapse of the Soviet communist tyranny, an unprecedentedly rapid spread of democracy and nigh on universal economic liberalization. East and South Asia, home to 55 per cent of humanity, enjoyed a leap towards prosperity. Yet critics of globalization talk of this period of hope and achievement as if it were a catastrophe. Some do so out of a genuine and understandable dismay over the extent of poverty and misery in a world of plenty, but then reach the *wrong* conclusion on the causes and cures. Others do so because they lament the death of the revolutionary tradition that held sway over the imaginations of so many for two centuries. Most of these critics compare the imperfect world in which we live with a perfect one of their imagining. It is in their way of viewing what has happened in the world, rather than the details of their critique, that those hostile to global economic integration are *most in error*. (Wolf 2005: 308, italics added)

FINDING A MIDDLE GROUND

Some scholars have sought to find some sort of middle ground position between the two extremes discussed above. One example is *In Defense of Globalization* by the well-known economist, Jagdish Bhagwati (2004). However, the title indicates the problems involved in finding such a compromise position since the book is mainly a defense of globalization,[14] especially the economics of it, in the face of a raft of criticisms. Bhagwati uses hard data, subjective impressions, and personal experiences to argue that, in the main, economic globalization has been a good thing. However, he admits that left to itself globalization will produce good results, but not necessarily the best results. Thus, he grudgingly acknowledges that there are not only benefits, but also problems, in globalization today: "Everything does not necessarily improve every time! There are occasional downsides" (2004: 228). His solution to the problems, his suggestion on how to make globalization better, is to manage the process by coming up with more appropriate social policies. Managing globalization is heresy to most economists (especially neoliberals) who believe in a market free of outside interference, but Bhagwati is willing to deviate from established economic dogma. In the process, he offers a comparatively balanced position, but nonetheless his work is most strongly associated with globaphilia.

Another middle-ground position is taken by de la Dehesa who argues that globalization, "although positive overall, entails certain unavoidable, but mainly temporary, negative economic, social, political, and cultural consequences that must be urgently addressed" (2007: 2). De la Dehesa closes his analysis with a long list of the criticisms of globalization and his views on each.

- While "globalization has been accused of increasing the world's poverty level," de la Dehesa concludes that the data and evidence "tend to demonstrate how the world's absolute and relative poverty has been reduced significantly since the 1980s, while globalization has gathered momentum" (2007: 294).
- Globalization "has been accused of significantly increasing the world's inequality," but while measurement is problematic, "there is a considerable amount of empirical evidence demonstrating that inequality among the citizens of the world has been reduced, albeit quite modestly" (2007: 295).
- "[I]t is argued that globalization has enabled multinationals to acquire more power than states and governments and that they have become bigger than most countries." However, "[n]either of these two arguments is substantiated by available empirical evidence" (2007: 295–6).
- He accepts the accusation that "developed countries have been accused of maintaining high levels of protectionism on the goods and services exported by developing countries, such as agricultural and food products, textiles, footwear and clothing," but there is "much evidence that, on average, developing countries protect their production much more than developed countries, even though their protection is much less widespread" (2007: 298).
- He is outraged by the "stinginess" of the developed countries and their reduction of, rather than increase in, aid to developing countries.
- It is "partly true" that international financial organizations (e.g. IMF, World Bank) act in the interests of the developed countries.
- The World Bank does not always work well as far as developing countries are concerned.
- Financial crises have always existed, but it is surprising that the financial markets have not become better than they have in dealing with them.
- He agrees with, and is most concerned about, the fact that "the huge demographic imbalance between wealthy and poor countries could spark a very severe and unsustainable situation in the long run" (2007: 305).

While de la Dehesa presents a reasonably balanced picture, it must be remembered that it is from an economist, reviewing work in economics, who, when all is said and done, finds globalization to be positive.

One final middle-ground position is Kellner's (2002) view that globalization is full of contradictions and includes both winners and losers. He rejects any deterministic view that suggests globalization is all good or all bad, and asserts that it is highly complex and contradictory. Whether globalization is directed from above or from below, Kellner urges us to consider who wins and who loses from globalization in its many different forms in evaluating whether globalization processes are positive or negative.

WHAT, IF ANYTHING, CAN BE DONE ABOUT GLOBALIZATION?

There are clearly large groups of people who are disadvantaged, if not oppressed and exploited, by various aspects of, and by some groups and organizations involved in, globalization. What can they do about the problems as they perceive them?

NOTHING!

In this view, globalization is an inexorable process and there is nothing that can be done to stop it – it is a "runaway world." While there is clearly great economic and political power involved in and behind globalization, the idea that nothing can be done about it only serves to *reify* the process. **Reification** is the idea, derived from Marxian theory, that people come to accord social processes a reality of their own and come to feel that even though they created, and in fact *are* in many ways, those processes, there is nothing they can do about them (Ritzer 2008c: 278–9). As a result, these processes come to have a life of their own and instead of being controlled by people, they come to control people. While reification certainly occurs, it is not inevitable. Those who see globalization as inevitable and beyond their control are guilty of reifying the process and if they persist in doing so, it *will* be beyond their control; there *will* be nothing to be done about it. However, reification, like globalization, is a social process and this means that people are involved in, create, and regularly re-create both reified and globalized structures and processes through their involvement (or lack of involvement) in them (Berger and Luckmann 1967). Thus, just as people create these realities, they can certainly change them by altering the nature of their involvement in them. Of course, this is no easy matter, but in principle no social process, including one as all-encompassing as globalization, is inexorable; all social processes are open to change by those who create them and are involved in them.

> **Reification:** People come to accord social processes a reality of their own and come to feel that there is nothing they can do about them.

EVERYTHING!

The antithetical point of view takes seriously the idea that people construct their social realities, including globalization, and therefore makes it clear that globalization can be affected by their actions. Indeed, it is possible, in this view, not only to slow or alter globalization, but also to stop the process completely. This extreme view seems as unrealistic as its polar opposite. For one thing, globalization has been going on for some time, in some eyes for centuries, if not millennia. For another, there are many different people, groups, organizations, and nation-states involved in globalization and while some may want to dismantle the process, there are many others deeply involved in, and highly committed to, it. And they will fight hard to resist any efforts to alter the process in any significant way. Furthermore, the latter are often the most powerful of the agents involved in globalization (again, MNCs and nation-states, among others, that benefit greatly from it) and they likely constitute powerful opposition to any effort to change the process, let alone dismantle it. It would seem that those who wish to put an end to globalization would need to deal also with far wider political (e.g. democracy) and economic systems (e.g. capitalism), as well as other systems (e.g. cultural) that are key components of globalization and have deep and vested interests in it and its continuation.

NECESSARY ACTIONS ARE ALREADY UNDERWAY

This is the view that whatever problems exist in globalization are already being addressed not only by major players like the UN, IGOs (e.g. the IMF), nation-states, and MNCs, but also by a variety of INGOs that seem to be growing in importance and power in a global world. It is hard to take the actions of the UN, IGOs, nation-states, and MNCs too seriously in this context because they have such vested interests in globalization that they are only likely to undertake and support changes on the margins of the process. In 2013, widespread uprisings in Greece, Turkey, Egypt, and elsewhere sought to shape their countries in reaction to impending global forces and unpopular regimes. There are also social movements and INGOs that are trying to address problematic aspects of globalization (e.g. Greenpeace, the Sierra Club, Slow Food). However, while such INGOs are important, they often pale in comparison to the strength of nation-states and MNCs that oppose them, to say nothing of such IGOs as the World Bank, the IMF, and so on, that are devoted to the continuation, if not expansion, of globalization.

MORE, PERHAPS MUCH MORE, NEEDS TO BE DONE

Many activists, even those involved in INGOs opposed to globalization in its current form, feel that not enough is being done, that much more needs to be done, to deal with at least the most problematic aspects of globalization (e.g. global climate change), if not the process as a whole. Given the great problems associated with globalization already mentioned to this point and to be discussed much more throughout this volume, it is clear that this is the view that is closest to the one taken here. Much can be done and needs to be done to address the ills associated with globalization. In terms of specifics, what needs to be done is defined by the various problems associated with globalization. All of those that can be addressed need to be addressed and they should be addressed in the order of their negative effects on the largest number of people in the largest areas of the globe. Clearly, that means that what needs to be addressed first is the wide range of problems traceable to globalization as they are experienced in, especially, the South, as well as in the impoverished and marginalized areas in the North.

CHAPTER SUMMARY

The study of globalization is home to significant debates and controversies. The major split is between globalists and skeptics. The "great globalization debate" engages with the question of the very existence of globalization. Globalists argue that globalization exists and it encompasses the entire globe. Skeptics contend that there is no such thing as globalization since a significant portion of the world's population is excluded from the processes associated with it. While globalists observe one broad process of globalization, skeptics point to not one, but many globalizations.

Globalists consider globalization an increasingly powerful phenomenon, which, among other things, has led to the decline of the nation-state. Skeptics respond by pointing out that, in recent years, the nation-state has reasserted itself and regained its role as a key world player. Globalists view globalization as a new process while the skeptics argue that it is simply a new term for an old, even ancient, process.

Economically, globalists emphasize structures such as the multinational corporations (MNCs), the transnational economy, and the emergence of a new global division of labor. Skeptics retain a focus on national economies and nation-state-based regional conglomerations, arguing that there are few genuine MNCs today. Globalists maintain that while the continuing power of nation-states is undeniable, their ability to control economic markets is steadily declining.

In terms of the global order, globalists observe the development of various relationships in the global world which do not involve the government. On the other hand, skeptics contend that the world continues to be dominated by relations among and between national governments.

Culturally, globalists tend to accept the idea of a culture common to most areas of the world. Skeptics generally reject the idea of a common global popular culture and argue that culture is becoming increasingly varied.

Some critics argue that we have transnationalism, rather than globalization. Transnationalism is a more limited process which refers largely to interconnections across two, or more, national borders. It may be more accurate to say that transnationalism and globalization both exist today, depending on which phenomena we are analyzing.

The origin of globalization can be analyzed through five perspectives. First, globalization can be seen as being hardwired into humans, in the form of a basic urge for a better life. This instinct results in the spread of globalization through commerce, religion, politics, and warfare. Second, globalization may be perceived as a long-term cyclical process. In this view, there have been other global ages prior to the present one, and each age is destined to contract and disappear, after attaining a peak. Third, globalization can be viewed as a series of historical phases or waves, each with its own point of origin. A fourth perspective argues that the multiple points of origin of globalization are located in seminal historical events. A fifth view focuses on broader, more recent changes in the twentieth century. It argues that the global processes in motion prior to WW II were more limited in geographic scope and less intensive than the global processes of the late twentieth and early twenty-first centuries.

There exist various types of globalizations. Some major categories include economic globalization, political globalization, cultural globalization, globalization of religion, science, health and medicine, globalization of sport, and globalization of higher education. Rather than a single point of origin for globalization as a whole, there are separate points of origin for different globalizations.

The factors that drive globalization are also hotly debated. The materialist approach tends to identify objective factors such as capitalism, technology, and multinational corporations as the driving forces of contemporary globalization. The idealist position stresses the role of idea systems, information, and knowledge as the prime movers in the process. Alternatively, we can see globalization as being driven by both material and ideal factors.

Some scholars have noted that in spite of greater liquidity and ever-more flows of various types, flows do not necessarily go everywhere. Even when they do, they affect different places with varying degrees of intensity. Using another metaphor, it could be argued that globalization "hops" from one locale to another, rather than flowing evenly through all locales. While globalization flows more easily through the developed world, it bypasses many locales in the less developed world.

Disputes exist regarding the future development and expansion of globalization. Some view globalization as an inexorable process. Here, it is important to distinguish between globalization from above and globalization from below. Globalization from above is a process that is created and controlled by centralized and powerful actors, such as wealthy elites or MNCs (especially in the North). Globalization from below, which involves marginalized groups and social movements that struggle to make globalization benefit more people and for global processes to be more democratic, can serve to make the process less inevitable.

A difference of opinion exists between globaphiliacs and globaphobics. Globaphiliacs emphasize the positive aspects of globalization. They argue that globalization leads to great economic growth and a contingent spread of democratization and civil society. Globaphiliacs tend to deemphasize its negative aspects, particularly the people who have not been beneficiaries of the process. The globaphobics' critiques of globalization are diverse, emerging not only from left and liberal quarters, but also from the conservative right. These critics emphasize the negative impact of globalization on the less well-off portions of the world's population. They contend that globalization leads to greater inequality. Some scholars adopt a middle ground in this debate.

Large groups of people feel disadvantaged by various aspects of globalization. Some are of the opinion that globalization is an inexorable process. Others argue that not only can the process be slowed down, it can be stopped completely. Another view is that the problems existing in globalization are being addressed by major players as well as International Non-Governmental Organizations (INGOs). However, many activists feel that much more needs to be done to deal with the most problematic aspects of globalization.

DISCUSSION QUESTIONS

1. Is the current era unique in terms of globalization? What factors contribute to or detract from this uniqueness?

2. Is globalization a homogenizing process? Discuss.

3. Define globalization from below. Is it capable of offering adequate resistance to the pressures created by globalization from above?

4. Discuss the different drivers of globalization. Are materialist factors more influential than idealist factors?

5. Is globalization an inexorable process? Should it be?

6. Does globalization lead to a "flat world"? Discuss.

ADDITIONAL READINGS ....

David Held and Anthony McGrew. "The Great Globalization Debate: An Introduction." In David Held and Anthony McGrew, eds. *The Global Transformations Reader: An Introduction to the Globalization Debate*. Cambridge: Polity, 2000: 1–50.

Stanley Hoffman. "Clash of Globalizations." *Foreign Affairs* 81, 4, 2002: 104/15.

Martin Wolf. *Why Globalization Works*. New Haven: Yale University Press, 2005.

Noam Chomsky. *Hegemony or Survival: America's Quest for Global Dominance*. New York: Metropolitan Books, 2003.

Noam Chomsky. *Power Systems: Conversations on Global Democratic Uprisings and the New Challenges to U.S. Empire*. New York: Metropolitan Books, 2013.

Jagdish Bhagwati. *In Defense of Globalization*. New York: Oxford University Press, 2007.

Guillermo de la Dehesa. *What Do We Know About Globalization? Issues of Poverty and Income Distribution*. Oxford: Blackwell, 2007.

Frank Lechner and John Boli, eds. *The Globalization Reader*. Oxford: Wiley-Blackwell, 2011.

NOTES ....

1   The title of this chapter is derived from an anthology the first author edited many years ago. See Ritzer (1972).

2   Immigrants can be thought of as "transnational" when they are involved in a variety of relationships (e.g. social, economic, political) that cut across the nations of settlement and origin creating a new transnational field (Basch, Schiller, and Blanc-Szanton 1994). While there are certainly many immigrants who fit into this category and their number is likely growing, there has been a tendency to overestimate their number and to conflate transmigrants and immigrants. Thus, Portes (2001a: 183) concludes: "It is more useful to conceptualize transnationalism as *one* form of economic, political and cultural adaptation that co-exists with other, more traditional forms [e.g. assimilation]." He usefully limits the idea of transnational activities to "those initiated and sustained by non-institutional actors, be they organized groups or networks of individuals across national borders. Many of these activities are informal, that is they take place outside the pale of state regulation and control… . they represent goal-oriented initiatives that require coordination across national borders by members of civil society. These activities are undertaken on their own behalf, rather than on behalf of the state or corporate bodies" (Portes 2001a: 186).

3   As globalization accelerates, ever-greater portions of the planet will be encompassed by it.

4   Others include, for example, the oceans in terms of the development of the trans-Pacific cable.

5   By the way, this idea of such a basic "urge" is quite controversial and is critiqued by postmodernists (and others) as being suggestive of "essentialism," or the notion that there is some fundamental characteristic of humans that lies at their essence and explains much of what they do. See Ritzer (1997a).

6   Robertson's analysis ends at this point since his essay was published in 1990.

7   Or as an end to at least a phase of globalization, see James (2001).

8   http://www.bloomberg.com/news/2013-09-22/russia-opens-north-korean-rail-link-for-iron-silk-road-.html.

9   Not surprisingly, this discussion of types overlaps somewhat with the discussion of types of flows in the preceding chapter. This is the case because types of globalization are, to a large degree, types of flows.

10   To take another example, Wolf (2005: 19) says: "Globalization is defined in what follows as integration of economic activities, via markets." See also Rodrik (1997).

11   On the North–South distinction, see, for example, Arrighi, Silver, and Brewer (2007); Persaud (2007).

12   See Chapter 4 for a discussion of Friedman's work in the context of neoliberalism.

13   Goffman (1961: 81). The quotation: "To be awkward or unkempt, to talk or move wrongly, is to be a dangerous giant, a destroyer of worlds. As every psychotic and comic ought to know, any accurately improper move can poke through the thin sleeve of immediate reality."

14   This is also true of de la Dehesa (2006).

GLOBALIZATION AND RELATED PROCESSES

IMPERIALISM, COLONIALISM, DEVELOPMENT, WESTERNIZATION, EASTERNIZATION, AND AMERICANIZATION

Globalization: A Basic Text, Second Edition. George Ritzer and Paul Dean.
© 2015 John Wiley & Sons, Ltd. Published 2015 by John Wiley & Sons, Ltd.

G lobalization has come to be the preeminent term for describing and thinking about processes that affect, and structures common to, large portions of the world today. However, there are many other concepts that either describe earlier historical, or contemporary, realities that deal with at least a portion of that which is encompassed by globalization. In this chapter we deal with several concepts that are related to globalization – imperialism (Berberoglu 2003), colonialism (and postcolonialism), development (and dependency), Westernization, Easternization, and Americanization (and anti-Americanization).

We devote much more attention to Americanization than the other processes even though there is much to indicate, and many scholars argue (and as will be discussed in many places in this book), that the era of American preeminence in the global arena is in decline and can only fall further in the future. For example, Fareed Zakaria (2008, 2011) argues that we are living in a "post-American world." While there is much to recommend such arguments, the fact is that Americanization was of great global importance after WW II and until very recently. While it is greatly weakened, it remains to this day an important global force. Furthermore, even if it were to disappear tomorrow (a highly unlikely possibility), its effects throughout the world would linger and be felt for many years, decades, or even centuries to come. It is important to point out early on that while all of these concepts are discussed separately, many of them overlap, sometimes quite substantially. For example, imperialism is sometimes difficult to distinguish from colonialism; Americanization is a sub-type of Westernization and it has also involved imperialism, colonialism, and a commitment to development (and dependency). Similar overlaps abound among and between all of these concepts. Furthermore, globalization cannot be completely divorced from these other ideas. In some cases their past impact lingers in the global age and they continue to affect globalization. In other cases, they continue to be viable and to affect, and even to be part of, globalization.

Imperialism:
Methods employed by one nation-state to gain power over an area(s) and then to exercise control over it.

Cultural imperialism:
Cultures imposing themselves, more or less consciously, on other cultures.

Media imperialism:
Western (especially US) media and their technologies dominating less developed nations, cultures.

IMPERIALISM

Imperialism is a broad concept that describes various methods employed by one country to gain control (sometimes through territorial conquest) of another country (or geographic area) and then to exercise control, especially political, economic, and military control, over that country (or geographic area), and perhaps many other countries (as, most famously, did the British Empire) (Brewer 2012). It is an idea and reality that came of age in the mid- to late 1800s (although its history, as we will see, is far more ancient), and is therefore rooted, at least since that time, in the idea of the nation-state and the control that it exercises over other nation-states as well as less well-defined geographic areas.

Imperialism can encompass a wide range of domains of control. In the era of the cultural turn in sociology, the latter is of increasing interest and concern and has come to be labeled **cultural imperialism** (more specific manifestations of cultural imperialism are sufficiently important to earn a label of their own with the most important being **media imperialism** [see Chapters 8 and 9 for a discussion of these two forms of imperialism]).[1]

The term imperialism itself comes from the Roman *imperium* (Markoff 2007: 609–14) and was first associated with domination and political control over one or more neighboring nations. The term "empire" is derived from *imperium* and it was used to describe political forms that had characteristics of Roman rule, especially the great power of the leader (the Roman *imperator* or emperor) and the huge chasm between the power of the ruler and the ruled (Gibbon 1998). Over time, the notion of empire, and of the process of imperialism, came to be associated with rulership over vast geographic spaces and the people who lived there. It is this characteristic that leads to the association between imperialism and globalization. In fact, many of the processes discussed in this book under the heading of globalization – trade, migration, communication, and so on – existed between the imperial power and the geographic areas that it controlled.

The term imperialism came into widespread use in the late nineteenth century as a number of nations (Germany, Italy, Belgium, Great Britain, France, United States) competed for control over previously undeveloped geographic areas, especially in Africa. (Before that, Spain, Portugal, and the Netherlands had been other leading imperialist nations.) While used mainly descriptively at first, imperialism came to have a negative connotation beginning, perhaps, with the Boer War (1899–1902). Questions were being raised about the need for political control by the imperial powers. Also being questioned was the longstanding rationale that the "superior" cultures associated with imperial powers were necessary and beneficial to the "inferior" cultures they controlled. While it is true that much culture flowed from the imperial nations to the areas they controlled, culture flowed in the other direction, as well. Imperial nations exercised great, albeit variable, political, economic, and cultural control over vast portions of the world.

In terms of political power, Great Britain exercised great control over a vast empire well into the twentieth century (that included the United States until the end of the Revolutionary War [also called the "War of Independence" from Great Britain] and the Treaty of Paris in 1783; India until its independence in 1947, and so on). The Soviet Union created a great political empire in the early part of the twentieth century by integrating various nations into it (e.g. the Ukraine), as well as exercising great control over other Soviet bloc nations (e.g. Poland, East Germany). The United States has also been an important, perhaps the most important, imperialistic nation, but its political control has generally (but certainly not always) been more subtle and less direct than that exercised by Great Britain and the Soviet Union in their heyday.

Political imperialism declined dramatically after WW II as most imperial nations withdrew, often reluctantly, from the domains they controlled. The imperial power of the Soviet Union continued longer, but it disappeared with the demise of the Soviet Union in 1991. While there is little, if any political imperialism today (i.e. the representatives of an imperial nation ruling a controlled area), other forms of imperialism persist.

In terms of imperialism in an economic sense, the actions of the British were most notable. For example, the British East India Company (the Dutch, French, and Swedish also had East India Companies) exercised great economic (as well as political and military) power on behalf of Great Britain in India. Also important was Britain's Hudson's Bay Company which, from its base in Canada, exercised great control over the fur trade, and later other forms of commerce, in North America. However, it is the United States that dominated the world economy, especially throughout the latter half of the twentieth century, as an imperialistic power, at least in an economic sense.

Vladimir Lenin (1917/1939), the first leader of the Soviet Union, was an important early theorist of imperialism, especially in his book, *Imperialism: The Highest Stage of Capitalism*. Lenin was influenced by J. A. Hobson's (1902/1905/1938) even earlier 1902 book, *Imperialism*. The title of Lenin's work well expresses his view that the economic nature of capitalism[2] leads capitalistic economies, and the nation-states that are dominated by such an economic system, to seek out and control distant geographic areas. This was also Hobson's (1902/1905/1938:

85) view: "Thus we reach the conclusion that Imperialism is the endeavour of the great controllers of industry to broaden the channel for the flow of their surplus wealth by seeking foreign markets and foreign investments to take off the goods and capital they cannot sell or use at home." Control over those areas was needed to provide resources for capitalist industries and also to create new markets for those industries. In other words, a capitalist economic system tended to expand imperialistically throughout the world.

While he recognizes that there are other dimensions to imperialism, Lenin sees "purely economic factors" as the most basic, as the essence of imperialism. His definition of imperialism encompasses five dimensions, all of which highlight economic factors:

1. The concentration of production and capital developed to such a high stage that it created monopolies[3] which play a decisive role in economic life.
2. The merging of bank capital with industrial capital, and the creation, on the basis of this "finance capital,"[4] of a "financial oligarchy["].
3. The export of capital, which has become extremely important, as distinguished from the export of commodities.
4. The formation of international capitalist monopolies which share the world among themselves.
5. The territorial division of the whole world among the greatest capitalist powers is completed (Lenin 1917/1939: 89).

The (mainly European) capitalist nations and firms are seen as having expanded throughout the world and as having carved up that world among themselves. From a revolutionary point of view, Lenin sees imperialism as a parasitic system and one that is part, and reflects the decay, of capitalism. Thus, it is an(other) indication of the rottenness of capitalism and the fact that capitalism is either in danger of collapse or that its decayed carcass will eventually prove easy to discard.

Ironically, although it was not capitalistic, it was Lenin's Soviet Union that became an important imperial power, especially politically, but also through the economic exploitation of the countries in the Soviet bloc. While political imperialism has all but disappeared, economic imperialism remains quite powerful, if for no other reason than the fact that capitalism remains preeminent in the global economic system.

The continuing importance of the idea of imperialism has been challenged in one of the most important books in the study of globalization, Michael Hardt and Antonio Negri's *Empire* (2000). In their view, the often heavy-handed, nation-based forms of imperialism described above have been replaced by a far more subtle and complex network of global political/economic/cultural processes that are exercising a new form of control that is better captured, in their view, by the idea of *empire* rather than imperialism. We will have occasion to examine their work in detail in the next chapter, but the key point is that while the process may have changed, efforts at gaining hegemonic control continue unabated.

Related to Hardt and Negri's argument is the idea that the decline of the importance of the nation-state makes it difficult to continue to talk in terms of imperialism which, at its base, is a view that a given nation (or elements of it, e.g. in the case of media imperialism, the US's *Voice of America*) exercises control over other nations (or geographic areas) around the world. It is this decline that leads to Hardt and Negri's more "decentered" view of globalization. That is, imperialism was a modern process and perspective that was "centered" on the nation-state (Great Britain, the Soviet Union, the US), but the declining importance of the nation-state requires a very different view of control exercised on a global scale. To Hardt and Negri it is the power exercised by a decentered empire that has replaced that exercised by imperialism and practiced by nation-states.

THE NEW IMPERIALISM

David Harvey (2003) has articulated the idea that a "new imperialism" has arisen with the United States as its prime (if not only) representative. He calls this "capitalist imperialism" and sees it as a contradictory fusion of economics and politics. Thus, Harvey offers a more integrated view of imperialism than did Lenin or Hobson. More specifically, it involves a fusion of the *political* – "imperialism as a distinctively political project on the part of actors whose power is based in command of a territory and a capacity to mobilize its human and natural resources towards political, economic, and military ends" and the *economic* – "imperialism as a diffuse political-economic process in space and time in which command over and use of capital takes primacy" (Harvey 2003: 26). There are fundamental differences between the two (political interest in territory and capitalist interest in command, and use, of capital), but the "two logics intertwine in complex and sometimes contradictory ways" (Harvey 2003: 29). For example, to the American government the Vietnam War made sense from a political point of view, but it hardly made sense from an economic perspective and may even have adversely affected the American economy. More generally, Harvey wonders whether we are now seeing an increase in US political imperialism (e.g. Iraq and Afghanistan) while it is declining in importance from the perspective of economic imperialism (e.g. the rise in economic power of China, the EU, India, etc.).

To Harvey, the new imperialism is the uncomfortable mix of these two types under the broad heading of capitalist imperialism. In addition, what is "new" here, at least in reference to the classic imperialism of say the British, is that it is the US that is the paradigm for, and the leader in, the new imperialism. Harvey not only describes US imperialism, but is highly critical of it. He sees it as burdened by a series of internal and external contradictions and problems which make it unsustainable in the long term (and perhaps even in the short term). Whether or not he is correct in that prognostication, he makes a useful contribution to our understanding of imperialism by offering a more balanced sense of its economic and political aspects, as well as their interrelationship.

COLONIALISM

Colonialism is clearly related to imperialism (Williams and Chrisman 1994a), and is sometimes used interchangeably with it,[5] but it has a more specific meaning. At the most extreme, imperialism involves a control *without* the creation of colonies (Harvey 2006: 21). Colonialism generally involves settlers as well as much more formal mechanisms of control than imperialism (Ashcroft 2012a). Thus, colonialism often entails the colonizer creating an administrative apparatus to run its internal affairs, including its settlements, within the colonized country (or geographic area). Edward Said well describes the key differences between imperialism and colonialism, as well as their relationship to one another: "imperialism means the practice, the theory, and the attitudes of a dominating metropolitan centre ruling a distant territory; 'colonialism', which is almost always a consequence of imperialism, is the implanting of settlements on distant territory" (cited in Ashcroft, Griffiths, and

Colonialism: Creation by the colonial power of an administration in the area that has been colonized to run its internal affairs.

Tiffin 1998: 45). While both imperialism and colonialism involve economic and political (as well as cultural) control, imperialism is (following Lenin) more defined by economic control (and exploitation), while colonialism is more about political control.

Although colonialism has an ancient history, it can be said to have had two great and more recent ages. These occurred during and after the Renaissance (fourteenth through seventeenth centuries) and are associated mainly with European societies. The first, beginning in the fifteenth century, was led by European powers, especially Spain and Portugal, and involved creating colonies in Africa, Asia, and the Americas. The second, or modern, phase lasted roughly between 1820 and the end of WW I. It involved other European powers (most importantly Great Britain, France, and Germany), as well as the US and Japan.

Some colonies (e.g. India as a colony of the British) persisted well into the twentieth century. However, during that period the momentum shifted in the direction of *decolonization*, or "the process of revealing and dismantling colonialist power in all its forms. This includes dismantling the hidden aspects of those institutional and cultural forces that had maintained the colonialist power and that remain even after political independence is achieved" (Ashcroft, Griffiths, and Tiffin 1998: 63). Decolonization movements began to succeed with greater frequency as the twentieth century unfolded. They were followed by decolonization and the achievement of political independence (Grimal 1878). Decolonization was particularly important after the close of WW II. That was followed by a period of *neo-colonialism* (Nkrumah 1965), where efforts at control over the former colonies, and other nation-states, grew much more indirect, subtle (e.g. through cultural and educational institutions), and focused on economic control and exploitation. The subtlety of neo-colonialism made it more insidious and harder to detect and therefore more difficult to resist and combat.

POSTCOLONIALISM

> **Post-colonialism:** Developments that take place in a former colony after the colonizing power departs.

Today, few, if any, colonies remain with the result that we can now think in terms of **postcolonialism** (Ashcroft 2012b).[6] Clearly, this implies the era in once-colonized areas *after* the colonizing power has departed (although postcolonial thinking and work could already be well under way before the colonizing power departs). However, in recent years it has come to take on more specific meanings that relate to various developments that take place in a former colony after the colonizing power departs. For example, it relates to a critical issue in globalization studies today, that of national identity, especially the difficulty of gaining identity (as an Indian, for example) after a colonial power (the British in the case of India) has departed. The most notable work[7] on this is Edward Said's *Orientalism* (1979/1994: 93) which deals with this problem in the context of both overt and more subtle negative stereotypes developed in the West about those who live in the East. The issue raised is the difficulty experienced by "Orientals" in developing a positive identity in light of all of the negativity about them in the West which, of course, dominated the East in various ways (imperialism, colonialism, etc., until very recently). This negativity is especially clear in the history of Western literature[8] (and film) about the East (and, as a result, this issue is of special importance in Edward Said's field of literary criticism). In fact, it is argued that "postcolonial theory was a creation of literary study" (Ashcroft, Griffiths, and Tiffin 2006: 5).

Postcolonial theorists focus on literary texts for several reasons. For one thing, literary texts can be used as a way of exercising cultural control over the "natives" (Janmohamed 2006). For example, textbooks written by the colonial power will reflect its perspective including its right to be in power, its superiority, and the inferiority of the "natives." For another, those texts can be subverted by those who oppose the colonial power and can be used to help bring down its regime. Finally, knowledge of the importance of texts can lead to new texts that can be used by newly freed colonies to portray themselves positively and to better understand, critique, and overcome the often continuing legacies of postcolonialism. These postcolonial texts can be an important base for the new society created in the aftermath of colonialism.

However, the focus on texts by postcolonial theorists has been criticized on several grounds. For one thing, it is argued that it is mainly Western intellectuals, especially Europeans, who have produced these texts. Postcolonial thinkers are therefore seen as too closely aligned with those who produced the colonial texts that helped enslave the subalterns. That is, postcolonial scholarship is producing what is "at best only a refined version of the very discourse it seeks to displace" (Ashcroft, Griffiths, and Tiffin 2006: 11). Furthermore, postcolonialists' orientation as European, or at least European-trained, scholars has led to work that is produced for other scholars and therefore largely incomprehensible to the natives without similar academic training. Finally, their work is seen as far removed from the needs and interests of the natives who would be the agents of any movement against colonialism or the legacy of postcolonialism. The work of postcolonialists is seen as quite distant from that of, say, Frantz Fanon (e.g. *The Wretched of the Earth* [1968]) who wrote in more widely accessible terms and was oriented to practical action to bring down both colonialism and the postcolonial legacy.

DEVELOPMENT

Development can be seen as a historical stage (roughly the 1940s to the 1970s) that preceded the global age (Kiely 2012; McMichael 2008: 21). Specifically, development can be viewed as a "project" that pre-dated the project of globalization.[9] As a project, development was primarily concerned with the economic development of specific nations, usually those that were not regarded as sufficiently developed economically. This project was especially relevant after WW II in helping countries devastated by the war, as well as in the Cold War and the efforts by the Western powers, the US in particular, to help various weak nations to develop economically. Much of the latter was motivated by a desire to keep those countries from falling to the communists and becoming part of the Soviet Empire. The focus was on financial aid in order to strengthen these countries' economies, but development also involved technological and military aid.

> **Development:** A "project" primarily concerned with the economic development of specific nation-states not regarded as sufficiently developed.

Development was inherently an elitist project with the nation-states of the North, given, or better taking, the responsibility for the development of the nation-states of the South. (Thus, unlike the later globalization project, development was based on the nation-state as the fundamental unit of concern both as that which was to be aided as well as that which was doing the helping.) The assumption was that not only was the North better off economically (and in many other ways) than the South, but it knew best how the South was to develop. Thus, it tended to help the South on its terms rather than on the South's own terms. Furthermore, there was an assumption that the North was the model, something approaching the ideal model, and the goal was to make the South as much like the North as possible. This often extended beyond simple economics, to making the South resemble the North in many other ways (culturally, morally, politically, etc.). Implied was the fact that the South was "inferior" to the North in various ways and that the only solution was for it to change, or to be changed, so that it came to resemble the North to a greater degree and in many different ways. This tended to be associated with the "Orientalism" that characterized the North (more the West in this case) as well as its academic work, and thinking, on the South (East). Furthermore, it tended to be associated with efforts by the North to exert control over the nation-states of the South. Thus, development was not simply an economic project, but it was also "*a method of rule*" (McMichael 2008: 49).

There is also a whole body of work critical of the development project and development theory known as **dependency theory** (Cardoso and Faletto 1979; Kick 2012). As the name suggests, it emphasizes the fact that the kinds of programs discussed above led not so much to the development of the nation-states of the South, but more to a decline in their independence and to an increase in their dependence on the countries of the North, especially the US. Underdevelopment is not an aberrant condition, or one caused by the less developed nations themselves, but it is built into the development project (as well as into global capitalism). It also involves the idea that instead of bringing economic improvement, development brings with it greater impoverishment. The notion of dependency has wide applicability (e.g. in the food dependency created, at least in part, by food aid).

> **Dependency theory**: Development of the nation-states of the South contributed to a decline in their independence and to an increase in their dependence on the North.

A key work in dependency theory is Andre Gunder Frank's (1969) "The Development of Underdevelopment."[10] One of his arguments is that behind the whole idea of development is the notion that the present of less developed countries resembles the past of the developed countries. Thus, if the less developed countries simply follow the same path taken by developed countries, they too will become developed. However, the developed countries were never in the same position of less developed countries today; the developed countries were *un*developed while the less developed countries were (and are) *under*developed. The result is that the path followed by the former is not necessarily the best one for the latter.

Frank also rejects the idea that the underdevelopment of a country is traceable to sources internal to that country. Rather, he argues that it is a product of the capitalist system and of the relationship between developed and underdeveloped countries within that system. Further, he rejects the idea that the solution to underdevelopment lies in the diffusion of capital, institutions, values, and so on from the developed world. He contends, however, that the less developed countries can only develop if they are independent of most of these capitalist relationships which, after all, are really the cause of their lack of development. It is capitalism that is the cause of development in the developed nations and of underdevelopment in the less developed nations.

Dependency theory has tended to wane,[11] but it has been replaced, and to some degree incorporated, in a broader theory known as **world system theory** (Wallerstein 1974, 2004). This theory envisions a world divided mainly between the *core* and the *periphery* with the nation-states associated with the latter being dependent on, and exploited by, the core nation-states.[12] Nordstrom (2004: 236) critiques this distinction, as well as the North–South differentiation, arguing that the periphery "is not merely 'useful' to cosmopolitan centers; it is critical. It is not the periphery of the economic system; it is central to it."

> **World system theory**: Sees the world divided mainly between the *core* and the *periphery* with the latter dependent on, and exploited by, the core nation-states.

While the development project had some successes, it was basically a failure since the world clearly remained, and remains, characterized by great inequalities, especially economic inequalities, between the North and the South. More pointedly, most nations associated with the South did not develop to any appreciable degree. Indeed, it could be argued that they fell further behind, rather than gaining on, the developed countries. Furthermore, the whole development project came to be seen as offensive since it tended to elevate the North, and everything about it, especially its economic system, while demeaning everything associated with the South. In its place, the globalization project at least sounded more equitable since it was inherently multilateral and multidirectional while development was unilateral and unidirectional with money and other assistance flowing from the North to the South. There is much evidence that the globalization project has not worked out much differently than the development project in terms of differences between the North and South. Furthermore, many of the institutions created during the period of dependency (those associated with Bretton Woods and the UN) continue to function and play a central role in globalization. This raises the question of whether globalization is simply development with another, less offensive, label. This would be the view taken by those who are critics of neoliberalism which undergirds much of contemporary economic globalization (see Chapter 4).

WESTERNIZATION

There are many who not only associate globalization with **Westernization**, but who see the two as more or less coterminous (Bozkurt 2012; Sen 2002). This, of course, is closely related to equating globalization with Americanization (see below), but the latter in this case is subsumed under the broader heading of Westernization, largely by adding its influence to that of Europeanization (Headley 2008, 2012). It is also common, especially today as a result of globalization, to ascribe a negative connotation to Westernization (as it is to Americanization) if one lives in other parts of the world (although critics in the West also view Westernization negatively), especially the South. Specifically, it is tied closely to the notions and earlier periods of Western imperialism and colonialism. Much of the world now blanches at the idea of Western imperialism or colonialism of any kind… and for good reason. However, in rejecting them, what tends to be ignored or excluded is the best of what the West has had to offer, and can still offer, to other parts of the world.

> **Westernization:** Economic, political, and cultural influence of the West on the rest of the world.

Claims of the Westernization of the world are supported in various ways, but it is important to recognize both differences within the West, as well as differences between the West and other parts of the world, even those that *seem* to adopt Western ways (Gray 2000). For example, political democracy is closely associated with the West and the effort to democratize many other parts of the world is linked to Westernization. However, there are great differences between the nature of democracies in the West (e.g. between the US and Great Britain) and, more importantly, between Western democracies broadly conceived and those that have arisen elsewhere. For example, Pakistan is considered a democracy, but it has experienced several periods of autocratic military rule since it was founded in 1947. In late 2007 the country was led by a military leader, martial law had been declared, and the nation was in chaos after the assassination of Benazir Bhutto. All of this calls into question Pakistan's commitment to democracy (although Asif Ali Zardari, Bhutto's widower, was elected president in late 2008 and remained their president until the end of his term in September 2013, becoming the first democratically elected president of Pakistan to complete a tenure) and its ability to sustain it in the face of many destabilizing forces, including the threat posed by Islamist militants (e.g. al-Qaeda and the Taliban) within its borders. In 2013, just two years after toppling Hosni Mubarak's regime, Egypt's military followed popular protest in removing democratically elected President Mohamed Morsi. An interim government was installed, but it is unclear to what degree Egypt's democracy can sustain itself. Democracies that are periodically subject to being overthrown by disaffected generals are very different from the long-lasting democracies in the West. Furthermore, the nitty-gritty of the way democracy works on a day-to-day basis is wildly different from one part of the world to another. There are also non-Western areas of the world – most notably China – that have been able to resist democratization totally and remain totalitarian. Finally, even electoral democracies vary greatly in how well they represent the broader population. For example, while the US is a democracy, there is much empirical evidence that shows it is largely dominated by wealthy elites (Domhoff 2009). Examples like this have led some critics to question to what degree such a form of democracy should be exported throughout the world.

Similarly, the market economies of the West are seemingly triumphant throughout much of the non-Western world, but the ways in which those markets function elsewhere differs greatly from one location to another. In the West in general (although there is great variation within the West, as well) the market is typically quite open and free (hence the term the "free market"), but in other parts of the world such a market is partly or greatly circumscribed. The best example is China in the early twenty-first century which in some cases has an open market, but in others the market is dominated by state-run enterprises and/or controlled by the state. In its early years the post-Soviet economy was quite anarchic, but more recently, buoyed by the booming oil business, it has come to resemble more the Western market, at least in some areas.

Westernization goes beyond politics and economics to include a wide variety of other exports to the rest of the world including its technologies, languages (English as the lingua franca [see Figure 3.1 for map showing significant use of "Global English" in the world today] in much of the world; French is still spoken in many places in the world), law (this is especially important in Hardt and Negri's view of the origin of the Empire's "constitution" in the West, especially the US Constitution), lifestyle (the centrality of consumption), food (the global proliferation of Western-style fast food), and so on. Some of the latter is associated more specifically with the US and therefore with Americanization, but before we deal with the latter we will discuss a process with the same magnitude as Westernization, at least in terms of point of global origin, "Easternization."

However, we close this section with three broad criticisms of Westernization. First, globalization is much more complex than the one-way flow implied by Westernization. Instead, it must be understood "as a process of mutual, if uneven, infiltration: with West permeating the rest and vice versa" (Inda and Rosaldo 2008a: 24). Second, Westernization implies homogenization, that the rest of the world comes to resemble the West, but globalization involves *both* homogenization and heterogenization. Finally, Westernization "neglects those circuits of culture that circumvent the West – those which serve primarily to link the countries of the periphery with one another" (Inda and Rosaldo 2008a: 25). Thus, for example, for Taiwan, the links with China and Japan may be far more important than those with the West. The growth of other power centers (such as the East, especially China) leads to the view that "there is not just one global cultural power center but a plurality of them, even if the West stands out among these" (Inda and Rosaldo 2008a: 29).

EASTERNIZATION

Globalization is often equated to a large extent with Westernization, and more specifically with Americanization. However, this is clearly a very narrow view of globalization that ignores all sorts of processes (e.g. the role of regional powers such as Japan and increasingly China in East Asia). Among the many things that it ignores are many counter-flows and one

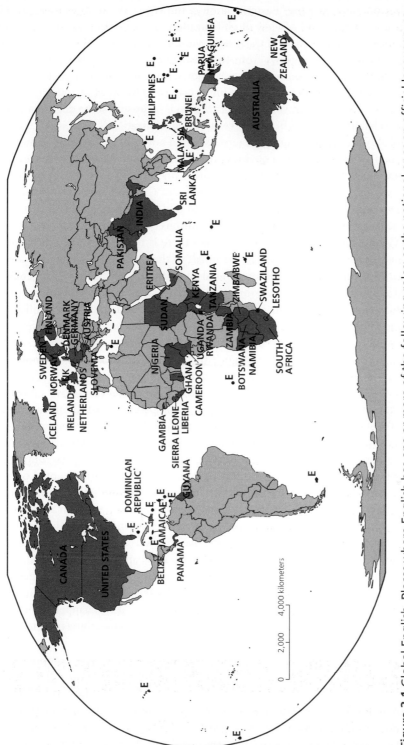

Figure 3.1 Global English. Places where English has one or more of the following roles: as the national or as an official language, as a language in which more than 50% of the general population has fluency, as the lingua franca of government, higher education, and commerce in plural societies, and as an outpost dating from colonial times. Source: de Blij, Harm J. 2008. *Power of Place: Geography, Destiny, and Globalization's Rough Landscape*. Chapter 2: The Imperial Legacy of Language, p. 47. © 2008 Oxford University Press. Used by permission. Data from several sources, including R. G. Gordon, Jr, ed. 2007. *Ethnologue: Languages of the World*. Dallas: SIL International; Encyclopaedia Britannica. 2007. *Encyclopaedia Britannica Book of the Year 2007*. Chicago: Encyclopaedia Britannica; and Graddol, D. 2004.

Easternization: Economic and cultural influences of the East on the West.

that is of particular interest is what Colin Campbell (2007, 2012) has recently called **Easternization**, especially the "Easternization of the West." While this process will be discussed here from the point of view of globalization, it is important to point out that the Easternization of the West has, in Campbell's view, far more to do with factors internal to the West than it does with flows from the East. In that sense, it is very different from Westernization which has more to do with flows from the Western parts of the world. Nonetheless, Campbell does accord some importance to the flow of various influences from the East to the West. In other words, Easternization is, at least to some degree, another process that can be differentiated from, but related to, globalization.

It is probably the case that most Westerners would not think of Easternization as a major influence on their lives. The most obvious influence is undoubtedly the presence and popularity of various ethnic restaurants and cuisine in the West – most importantly Chinese, Thai, Indian, and Japanese food and restaurants. But Campbell points to a wide array of other phenomena that are Eastern in origin and that are increasingly visible in the West. Among them are yoga, a "Zen" outlook on life, various beliefs (e.g. reincarnation), vegetarianism, I Ching, Tarot, Runes, and so on. Then there is the impact of Eastern music and musical instruments on the change in the music of the Beatles in the 1960s as well as the Beatles' growing interest in the East in general and Eastern spirituality in particular.

While Campbell does not discuss this, we could also add the powerful impact of Eastern manufacturers on the American market, especially the market for automobiles (Toyota, Nissan, and Honda from Japan and now Hyundai from Korea – with the likelihood of a growing impact from the newly rising Chinese auto industry) and electronics (Sony and Panasonic, in particular). It could be argued that Eastern manufacturers are not exporting "Eastern" products to the West (there is nothing "Eastern" about automobiles or video recorders; they were Western inventions), but they have made distinctive innovations in production that greatly enhanced their ability to compete successfully in the West.[13] For example, Toyota introduced the Japanese focus on the collectivity into the production process by, for example, developing "quality control groups" (Ritzer 2001: 230–1). These are groups of workers that discuss the production processes and their work routines, weaknesses in them, and ways of improving them. Meritorious ideas are accepted by management and used to improve the production process. The result is not only improved production processes, but also heightened morale as employees see their ideas taken seriously. By "Easternizing" the production of automobiles (and many other things) in this and many other ways (e.g. the *ringi* system of collective decision-making), Toyota (and the other major Japanese manufacturers) was able to catch up with, and vault ahead of, the Western, especially American, manufacturers and capture a major portion of the American (and European) market. They also can be said to have Easternized American manufacturing techniques since when the American companies realized what was happening, they sought to adapt by incorporating many Japanese techniques. For example, some tried to utilize versions of quality circles.

Another Japanese innovation – "just-in-time" delivery of needed components rather than the American "just-in-case" system where large quantities of components were kept in stock at great cost when and if they might be needed – was much more widely adopted by American firms, including many not in automobile manufacturing (Schonberger 1982).

Thus, it is clearly legitimate to discuss Easternization as an important process that is related to globalization. Further, as China continues to explode as a global power, especially economically, we can expect its influence on the West to grow, ushering in a new and expanded form of Easternization. For example, China already has huge reserves in Western currencies, especially American dollars, as a result of its hugely positive balance of trade (far more exports than imports). It possesses the ability, an ability that will grow exponentially in the coming years, to affect greatly the West not only in the way it uses those reserves (e.g. by investing in the West, or not), but also by merely threatening to use those reserves in certain ways. For example, China has so many dollars that should it decide to "dump" them for other currencies (say, the euro), the value of the dollar would go into free fall.

AMERICANIZATION

Americanization is another process that is related to globalization, but is not identical, or reducible, to it (Neil Campbell 2012). We devote the most attention in this chapter to Americanization because it has been such a central part of globalization (at least until very recently), because it continues to be important, and because it has been so widely studied, analyzed, critiqued, and commented upon. We employ Richard Kuisel's (2003: 96) definition: "Americanization is the import by non-Americans of products, images, technologies, practices and behaviour that are closely associated with America/Americans."[14]

While we are dealing with Americanization in terms of its relationship to globalization specifically, it is worth pointing out there is much more to Americanization than that. Reflective of this greater complexity is the fact that there is an entire field known as American Studies, and even an "Americanization theory" (Grainge 2004: 215) of which the study of America's role in globalization is only a small part. This complexity and diversity means, among other things, that it is impossible, as some globalization theorists do,[15] to dismiss an idea that clearly is the subject of so much work and study and means so much more than its role in globalization. While it would be wrong to dismiss the idea in its entirety, or more specifically as it relates to globalization, we need to deconstruct Americanization in order to decide which elements of it, if any, can or should be retained in the larger context of a discussion of its relationship to globalization.

By the way, the term Americanization can mean not only the influence of the US, but also that of Canada and Mexico, as well as Central and South America. After all, they are part of America (North, Central, and South). While we will deal with other complexities below, to handle this one, we will focus on the US[16] when we discuss Americanization.

Long before globalization became a central academic and lay concern, there were many works over a long period of time that dealt with America's global influence, especially on Europe.[17] In addition, there are a number of very recent works that deal with this topic.[18] While the continuation of this work to this day indicates that there has been no diminution of interest in Americanization, there was a particularly heavy concentration on this topic in the 1960s, at or near the summit of America's global power (especially its industrial power given the decades it took Europe [and Japan] to recover economically from the devastation of WW II), and no work epitomizes this better than the Frenchman J.-J. Servan-Schreiber's *The American Challenge* (1968).

Echoing Georges Duhamel's (1931) notion of an American "menace,"[19] Servan-Schreiber saw America as a business, industrial, and economic threat to Europe. His view, and the fear of the day, is reflected in the opening line of his book (which seems laughable in the light of subsequent developments such as the rise of European [e.g. BMW], and the decline of American [e.g. GM], industry): "Fifteen years from now it is quite possible that the world's

Americanization: Imports by non-Americans of that which is closely associated with America/Americans.

third greatest industrial power, just after the US and Russia, will not be Europe, but *American industry in Europe*" (Servan-Schreiber 1968: 3). Whatever the errors in this view in light of today's realities (in addition to those mentioned above, the rise of the EU, Japan, and China), it is reflective of the sense of the day of the power, especially, industrially, of Americanization.

In the ensuing years, fears of Americanization, at least of US industries, declined[20] and were replaced by other ideas and fears, most of which were seen as threatening to the US, as well. One such idea, reflective of the remarkable post-war development of Japanese industry, was "Japanization" (Elger and Smith 1994), and that was later supplemented, and to some degree replaced, by fears of the "Asian Tigers" (e.g. Singapore), the European Union and most recently, and likely more enduringly, China (Huntington 2011).

However, other nations' fears of Americanization and its economic power have certainly not disappeared. Concern about the expansion of American industry was replaced (at least until the Great Recession) to a large degree by a growing fear, reflective of a sea change in the American economy, of American dominance globally in the realm of consumption (Goodman 2007). The fear was no longer of industrial giants, many of which are declining (and disappearing), like US Steel and GM, but rather of the impact of behemoths in the realm of consumption such as Wal-Mart, Coca-Cola, McDonald's, and Visa (Ritzer 1995, 2009). Nothing reflected this change better than the fact that the largest corporation in the world was no longer the production-oriented General Motors, but rather the consumption-oriented retailer, Wal-Mart (Soderquist 2005). With $446.95 billion in revenue and $15.7 billion in profits in 2012, Wal-Mart is the third-largest company in the world and is the world's largest employer (*Fortune* 2013). This fear of the giants in the realm of consumption is reflected in concerns over processes that have been labeled "Coca-Colonization" (Kuisel 1993) (or even "Coca-Globalization" [Foster 2012]), "McDonaldization" (Ritzer 2012), "Disneyization" (Andrews 2012; Bryman 2004), and "Wal-Martization" (Fernie 2012). As new leaders in the field of consumption, almost always US in origin, came to the fore, they led to new labels and new fears. For example, the growth of Starbucks (at least until recently) led to concern over "Starbuckization" (Ritzer 2012). Judging by the proliferation of its coffee shops (over 17,651) in many countries in the world (at least 60 as of this writing) there was clear reason for such concern (Starbucks 2012). Such growth illustrates the exportation of America's consumer products and its "means (or cathedrals) of consumption" (Ritzer 2009) – fast-food restaurants, superstores, shopping malls, and so on – to Europe. (We will deal with all of these, as well as the various processes mentioned above, in Chapter 7.) While the focus may have shifted from production to consumption, scholarly and popular work on, and worry over, Americanization persisted and persists to this day. Now, however, the concern is more over the global economic crisis, with its roots in the US, as a type of Americanization.

Of course, the work on the economy, even that which includes both production and consumption, touches on only a small part of the literature on Americanization. Needless to say, there is also much interest in Americanization in such areas as politics (Harding 2008; Penney 2011), the law (Westbrook 2006), the military, culture, and so on. For example, in the realm of politics, the political campaigns in recent European elections (especially in Great Britain and France) have come to look increasingly like those in America, and prominent American political consultants have played a growing role in them.

Clearly Americanization, from the point of view of this definition, does indeed exist, in that all of these things (products, cathedrals of consumption, the Great Recession, etc.) and much more *are* being exported by the US and being imported in great numbers by other nations. However, this also immediately gets us to another of the complexities mentioned above – which American imports are we talking about? It might be that we can agree that Americanization is an accurate label for the exportation and importation of some of these products (e.g. Coca-Cola and McDonald's), but it does not apply in the case of others (e.g. TVs and video recorders that were largely invented by Americans and pioneered by American corporations, but few, if any, of which are produced there any longer). Thus, in discussing Americanization – as well as its absence – we need to specify the import under consideration. All imports from the US may not involve Americanization, and imports from the US may be declining, but the US remains a major exporter of all sorts of things to other nations, including many that are closely identified with it.

A similar complication occurs when we distinguish among cultural, social, communicative, political, and economic Americanization. Again, in discussing Americanization, which form are we talking about? For example, America has had a powerful influence on China economically, but its political impact in terms of democratization, at least until now, has been comparatively small. There are even differences within each of these domains. For example, within the realm of culture, it has been argued that "musically, the twentieth century was the American century" (Blake 2004: 149), but while that might be true, it almost certainly was *not* the case in painting or sculpture. Similar differences and complexities exist in all of the other realms mentioned above, and many more.

A further complication stems from the fact that there are also many processes closely linked to the US, and being disseminated to the rest of the world, that could be thought of as Americanization. For example, Dezalay argues that the legal field throughout much of the world has been Americanized:

> The Wall Street law firm, invented over a century ago in response to the demands of American finance and industry, has become a model for similar developments everywhere, as the local lawyers, in a struggle for survival, feel they must adopt the model of the *corporate law firm*. (Dezalay 1990: 281)

For another, there is much talk of the Americanization of sport in many places throughout the world with one example being the commercialization, and therefore the Americanization, of sports in New Zealand (Grainger and Jackson 2005). On the global stage, the Olympics have been shaped by Americanization, or its subset, "Californization." Specifically action sports (e.g. beach volleyball and snowboarding) have become very popular at the Olympics and "were incubated in California and are linked to the promotion of American visions of affluence" (Dyreson 2013: 256). One other example is the Disneyization of the European fairy tale (Darcy 2004: 181–96), and one could look more generally, as was mentioned above, at Disneyization, as well as McDonaldization, Wal-Martization, Starbuckization, and the like. However, while all of these are traceable to the US, and have important elements in common, much is lost if they are all simply subsumed under the heading of Americanization. A more nuanced analysis would look at each of these processes to see in what ways they are similar and how they differ, as well as the ways in which each relates to Americanization.

Furthermore, at least some of these processes cannot be restricted to an association with America. For example, McDonaldization has its roots in the bureaucratization and rationalization of German society and Max Weber's analysis of them. And all of them, at least to some degree, have escaped from their roots in the US and are now thriving elsewhere.

There are other ways of slicing and dicing the concept of Americanization, as well. For example, in discussing Americanization, are we focusing on, among many other possibilities, its impact on people's subconscious? On their bodies; the way Americanization is embodied by those in other societies? On the "landscapes" (Campbell 2004) of everyday life? Clearly, we could deal with all of these domains – and many others – and Americanization would mean very different things, and apply in very different ways, in each.

Analyses of Americanization can also be even more fine-grained. One example is the Americanization of the Holocaust (Nelson 2013; Sznaider 2003). Here we have a phenomenon (the Holocaust) that is *not* American in origin and is certainly not usually associated with America and Americanization. Yet, Americans, especially American Jews, have developed a distinctive view of the Holocaust, the importance of having it memorialized, and the ways in which it should be commemorated (e.g. the Holocaust Museum in Washington, DC). And this has been exported elsewhere (even to Berlin, Germany where the Jewish Museum opened in 2001), where we see the emergence of similar structures and ways of memorializing the event.

Then there is the issue of what counts as Americanization? Does something merely need to carry the American label ("made in America") to qualify as Americanization? Or, do those who produce it, and more importantly those who import it, need to *identify* it as American? On the former, many products made in America (e.g. internal components for various machines, tourist trinkets for specific foreign markets) do not bring with them much, if anything, in the way of Americanization. On the latter, one can conceive of very American products that are not so identified by those in other nations. For example, many in Japan think of McDonald's as a Japanese restaurant chain and when they travel are surprised to find it in the US (Watson 1997).

Further complexity results from the diversity that exists among other nations, and even sub-areas (local, regional) within those nations, in terms of their relationship to Americanization. It is clearly the case that some nations, and areas within them, are much more the target of, and more susceptible to, Americanization than others. France is *not* a nation that one thinks of as being receptive to Americanization, but in Kuisel's view it was Americanized, at least to some extent, in the last half of the twentieth century (although it certainly has not lost its distinctive culture and identity), but some areas of France (e.g. small towns and rural areas) were, and are, less Americanized than others. In addition to variation in its impact, Americanization is also more of a public issue in some places than others and there are even locales where it may be a non-issue. That is, Americanization is more likely to spark public outcries and demonstrations in some places than in others. It could even be, and has been, welcomed in many locales.

It could be argued that Americanization has as much, or more, to do with the nation (or area) on its receiving end than it does with America (Hodson 2001). Thus, it might be argued that the focus when examining Americanization should not be on what transpires in the US, but rather on the receiving nations and the dynamics in, and differences among, them.

Then there is the view that a focus on either the US *or* the receiving nation is wrongheaded and that the focus should be on the relationship among and between them. Receiving nations are not passive and may play an active role in shaping Americanization. For its part, what is exported by the US may be shaped by what it (or more accurately elements in it such as big business) thinks other nations will accept and various nations may be receptive to different American exports. Americanization, then, exists in this reciprocal relationship and *not* in either America or the receiving nations alone.

Another way of thinking about the issue of concern here is what has been termed **Americanization without America** (Delanty 2003: 117). That is, for example, a nation can be Americanized by the spread of increasingly universal consumer capitalism without necessarily being affected by America per se. The assumption here is that while consumer capitalism was invented in America, it has now taken on forms that are devoid of, or in the process of losing, their American influence (e.g. McDonald's in Japan). Furthermore, "Americanization" can take place without some American values and/or by reintroducing others (e.g. the "work ethic") that to a large extent have declined or even been lost in the US.

> **Americanization without America:** A nation-state can be Americanized without necessarily being affected by America per se.

There is much diversity in the US and we must specify what aspects of it we are discussing when analyzing Americanization. Thus, for example, we can talk about something like "African Americanization" (White 2004: 164) – for example, in the global dissemination of jazz, hip hop, or rap music – and recognize that some nations are being affected more by it than others. Furthermore, if there is such a thing as African Americanization, there is certainly Native American, Hispanic–American, and Jewish–American Americanization (e.g. as discussed above in the case of the Holocaust), and so on. Furthermore, there is growing diversity in the US increasing the number of possibilities.[21] An example is the growing number of Hispanic Americans and their exports to various countries, especially to Latin America (e.g. of money in the form of remittances; see Chapter 10).

Even if we were to argue, and agree, that Americanization is declining, or even disappearing, it certainly *was* a powerful force in the past and much of globalization, at least until very recently, has been American-led. At the minimum, that (recent) history needs to be recognized for what it was – heavily dominated by Americanization. Furthermore, no matter how far Americanization may have already declined in importance, it will be a long time before most of the nations and areas affected by it in the past will be free of its highly diverse and often powerful effects. The effects of Americanization will continue to be felt in many nations for years to come even if we think of it as slowing or even halting completely (a clearly erroneous view, at least at the present time).

Thus, for example, the modern fast-food restaurant was an American invention (specifically Ray Kroc and the creation of the McDonald's chain beginning in the mid-1950s) that was, and is still being, actively and aggressively exported to the rest of the world. However, many nations have now created their own McDonaldized restaurants (and other forms) that in some cases (e.g. Pollo Campero from Guatemala) are being actively exported back into the US. While this may now be part of the "Latin Americanization" of the US, it has its roots in Americanization (in this case of Latin America) via the export of the fast-food restaurant. While it may be selling food more indigenous to Latin America, even a superficial look at a Pollo Campero restaurant makes it clear that it is a product of Americanization.

However, in many areas Americanization remains as powerful, if not more powerful, than ever. One such area is the criminal justice system in which a recent book argues that there "has been something of an 'Americanization' of criminal justice systems throughout much of the world" (Andreas and Nadelmann 2006: 107). The following reflects some of the specifics of the US's unique role in the globalization of criminal law:

> What makes the US case unique is the extent to which the US government has successfully internationalized its own criminal laws, procedures, and enforcement efforts. No other government has acted so ambitiously in collecting evidence from foreign jurisdictions, apprehending fugitives from abroad, targeting foreign government corruption, and persuading foreign governments to change their criminal justice norms to better accord with its own. No other has

devoted comparable diplomatic and financial resources to pursuing its international law enforcement agenda. And no other has proved so willing to intrude on the prerogatives of foreign sovereigns, challenge foreign political sensibilities, and circumvent and override foreign legal norms. (Andreas and Nadelmann 2006: 106)

This process of Americanization has occurred in many areas, most notably drug enforcement, dealing with undocumented immigration, and the prevention of terrorism and the apprehension of terrorists. The US has not only been increasingly active in all of these areas, but it has also pressed many other governments throughout the world to increase their efforts in these (and other areas).

A BROADER AND DEEPER VIEW OF THE AMERICANIZATION OF CONSUMER CULTURE

Consumerism and consumer culture are at the heart of Americanization. Victoria de Grazia's *Irresistible Empire: America's Advance through 20th-Century Europe* (de Grazia 2005: 3) examines the deeper forces in the Americanization of consumer culture, but with a somewhat different focus on:

> The rise of the great imperium [the United States] with the outlook of a great emporium. This was the United States during the reign of what I call the Market Empire. An empire without frontiers, it arose during the twentieth century, reached its apogee during its second half, and showed symptoms of disintegration toward its close. Its most distant perimeters would be marked by the insatiable ambitions of its leading corporations for global markets, the ever vaster sales territories charted by state agencies and private enterprise, the far-flung influence of its business networks, the coin of recognition of its ubiquitous brands, and the intimate familiarity with the American way of life that all these engendered in peoples around the world. Its impetus and instruments derived from the same revolution in mass consumption that was ever more visibly reshaping the lives of its own citizens.

It was, in her view, the exportation of America's innovations in the realm of mass consumption that helped lead, through mass marketing, to the "fostering of common consumption practices across the most diverse cultures" (de Grazia 2005: 3).

De Grazia does not focus on seemingly superficial exports like Coca-Cola, but rather on much subtler phenomena that settled far more deeply in the fabric of other, especially European, societies and later many other societies. Among the exports dealt with by de Grazia are the service ethic, the chain store, big-brand goods, corporate advertising, and "supermarketing." By the end of the twentieth century Americanization had progressed so far, and these and other changes had taken hold so well in Europe (and elsewhere), that the US had lost its leadership position: "Europe was as much a consumer society as the United States" (de Grazia 2005: 463). As China's economy expands, it stands to become the greatest consumer society in the world and is likely to far surpass the US in its consumption.

However, whatever the decline, America has continued to be highly influential throughout the world. One example is the world of film (Glancy 2013). There is evidence that the film industries in other countries are still seeking to learn from the American way of making movies. For example, American creative and technical advisors are being brought to Russia to teach Russians how to produce movies on time and within budget. Among the other American movie-making techniques employed are the use of focus groups, script doctors, and star-making. As the director of a Russian movie being produced with American help said, "The idea is to absorb the American experience" (quoted in Holson and Myers 2006: 1). Once that experience is absorbed, Russian films, like much else, will be made by locals, but how they do it will have been shaped, at least to some degree, by Americanization.

The arguments made by de Grazia (as well as the case of Russian movies) point in similar directions. First, it is in these deeper, more basic realms, that the most important impact of Americanization is found and felt. Second, if activists really wish to counter Americanization, it is on these levels and against these phenomena that they really must direct their energies. However, it is far more difficult to locate many of these, let alone attack them. (For example, it is easy for Russian activists to oppose American movies, but it will be far harder to deal with Americanization in this realm when American techniques are integrated into Russian movie-making.) Furthermore, many of them have made their way deep into the fabric of societies around the world with the result that an attack on them becomes an assault on one's own society. It is far more difficult to oppose one's own society than it is to oppose an external "enemy" like the US. It is this that makes the task of those opposed to Americanization so daunting, if not impossible.

MINIMIZING THE IMPORTANCE OF AMERICANIZATION

In spite of all of the evidence on the importance of Americanization, the academic literature on globalization tends to minimize or downgrade the significance of the US in global processes.

Some focus on the declining importance of the US (Ferguson 2012; Hardt and Negri 2000; Huntington 2011). Operating from his world-system perspective, Wallerstein offers a nuanced picture of the role of the US in the global world system, but it is dominated by images of decline. Beginning with the near-revolutionary events in the late 1960s (e.g. the student uprisings, the anti-Vietnam War movement), Wallerstein (1992) describes the US as undergoing a long-term decline that it has only been able to stem in part. He argues that "The heyday of US prosperity is over. The scaffolding is being dismantled" (Wallerstein 1992: 16). It could be argued that much of the recent well-being of the US has been built on unusually low-priced imports and that that era is ending (Bradsher 2008a: A1–A6), although Wallerstein wrongly focused on Japan and was unable to see the economic ascendancy of China. While America will retain its military and political power, Wallerstein sees a "terrible" decline psychologically among Americans who will have a difficult time adjusting to their less exalted position in the world system.

Others see the decline of the US linked to the overall decline in the importance of the nation-state (Ohmae 1996; Strange 1996). The declining importance of the nation-state in general, and the US in particular, is also reflected in work that focuses, for example, on the rise in the importance of transnational flows (see Chapter 4) and of global cities (see Chapter 13).[22] Still others argue that the US's massive debt will rapidly speed its decline (Ferguson 2012).

ANTI-AMERICANISM

There is no dearth of anti-Americanism around the world. Various individuals and groups have found many things about the US to dislike, if not despise, including its militarism, its obsession with guns, its continuing use of the death penalty (Singh 2007), its seemingly extraordinary religiosity (especially fundamentalism) (Berggren and Rae 2007), its role in global warming (including its withdrawal from the Kyoto accord), its culture (popular [Hudson 2007] and otherwise), and the imperialism (e.g. television programs, movies, even its [fast] food) associated with it, and especially these days its role in globalization and its association with neoliberalism and the Washington Consensus (Morgan 2007; see Chapter 4), as well as the power of the organizations largely controlled by it (and the developed West), especially the IMF and the World Bank. Indeed, opinions of the US in four selected European countries, while always ambivalent, plunged dramatically after the American-led 2003 invasion of Iraq and throughout Bush's presidency (O'Connor 2007a: xix). More generally, while positive attitudes about the US increased significantly in 2009 after the election of President Barack Obama, they decreased steadily again through 2012 (Pew Research Center, n.d.).

Americanization has long been accompanied by a counter-reaction to it in various places in the world that can be thought of as anti-Americanism. Just as Americanization has proliferated as a process closely linked to globalization, so, too, has anti-Americanism. Not only is it an increasingly global phenomenon, but it is also one that seems to flow far more readily than Americanization to the far reaches of the globe. It also seems more intense than in the past and there is certainly far more attention and publicity devoted to it. But what, exactly, is anti-Americanism?

Although anti-Americanism has become a buzzword in political and academic circles, it (like Americanization) is used by so many, and in so many different ways, that it is today a vague concept lacking in coherence.[23] It is necessary to realize that anti-Americanism is not a homogeneous phenomenon, even if the word itself conveys a sense of a kind of general criticism that is expressed similarly in much of the world. There are distinct forms, causes and expressions of anti-Americanism, in other words there are anti-Americanism*s* (just as we saw in Chapter 2 that there are globalization*s*) rather than an overarching anti-Americanism (Singh 2006). It is such an amorphous concept that both opposition to US cultural, economic, and political policies, as well as more sweeping negative generalizations about the US, are included under the heading of anti-Americanism. It can encompass everything from casual and superficial criticism of the US to a deep-seated and widely shared animosity to it. In O'Connor's (2007b: 1–21) words, "one person's criticism of the United States is another person's anti-Americanism."

We can begin with one well-known definition of anti-Americanism:

> Anti-Americanism is *a predisposition to hostility* toward the United States and American society, a relentless critical impulse toward American social, economic, and political institutions, traditions, and values; it entails an aversion to American culture in particular and its influence abroad, often also contempt for the American national character (or what is presumed to be such a character) and dislike of American people, manners, behavior, dress, and so on; rejection of American foreign policy and a firm belief in the malignity of American influence and presence anywhere in the world. (Hollander 1992: 339, emphasis in the original)

This is a rather breath-taking definition of anti-Americanism encompassing a wide range of specific phenomena. Its attraction is its sweep, but the diversity of phenomena encompassed by that sweep makes it clear that our sense of anti-Americanism needs greater refinement.

There are a number of ways of refining the general idea of anti-Americanism. For example, Naim has analyzed anti-Americanism in terms of several categories (Naim 2002: 103–4).

- *Psychological* and *religious* hostility stemming from, and perpetuated by, long-lasting stereotypes and images of America.

- *Historical* anti-Americanism referring to the resentment toward the US based on its past behavior.
- *Political and economic* anti-Americanism rooted in current political and economic policies of the US.
- Lastly, *cultural* anti-Americanism, or the resentment of America's cultural domination and the displacement of local cultures as a result of America's global cultural imperialism. The cultural aspect of the resentment to the US is focused on the homogenizing effects of US culture, tastes, values, consumer goods, industries, and systems throughout the world.

Perhaps the most important dimension of anti-Americanism focuses on the dangers, the catastrophe, threatened by the rise of American consumerism (Ceaser 2003). Related to this is the idea that what dominates American consumption, and is most threatening about it, are its highly uniform and standardized goods and services. (It may be that we are seeing the rise of a new form of anti-Americanism as others blame American economic excesses for the Great Recession.)

James Ceaser takes the position that the largely European ideas associated with anti-Americanism have served to inhibit dialogue between the US and Europe (as well as between the US and the rest of the world). He argues that Europeans need to free themselves from the grip of anti-Americanism so that a genuine dialogue can take place. Ironically, Ceaser almost certainly wrote just before the single event – the second US invasion of Iraq in 2003 – that has done more than anything else in recent memory,[24] if not in history, to fuel anti-Americanism in Europe and much of the rest of the world as well.

O'Connor (2007b, 2012) recognizes that anti-Americanism takes many forms, but one important form for some people is that it becomes a prejudice. In this case, anti-Americanism can be seen as prejudice when it prejudges America, Americans, and American action, when it offers a one-sided view of things American, and when its view of America is undifferentiated. To overcome such a prejudice, and to develop a far better critique of America, that critique must be "based on details and evidence, rather than broad prejudices and stereotypes; from analysis, not knee-jerk rejection" (O'Connor 2007b: 19). More generally, he argues that this prejudice, like all others, (1) needs to be challenged and confronted; (2) needs to be seen as making clear the need for a more differentiated view of the US; and (3) needs to be viewed as being in opposition to intelligent thought. Thus, "the challenge is how to engage with America without letting anti-American prejudices overwhelm critique" (O'Connor 2007b: 21). Overall, O'Connor argues that to take anti-Americanism seriously, it must be based on intelligent critique well grounded in facts rather than based on prejudice against the US.

COMPARISONS WITH GLOBALIZATION

Globalization continues apace in the early twenty-first century and, if anything, is increasing in scope and importance. Some of the other processes have all but disappeared (colonialism, development) and others seem to have passed their prime and to be in decline (Westernization, Americanization). It could be argued that imperialism, or at least the "new imperialism," has been incorporated into globalization. Given the rise of China as a global power, Easternization, like globalization, is likely to show dramatic growth in the coming years.

Globalization is inherently multidirectional with global flows moving in innumerable directions. It has no single, definable point of geographic origin. All of the others are much more unidirectional, flowing from well-defined points – the imperial powers, the colonial powers, the developed world, the West, the United States, the East.

Globalization is not nation-state based and is likely, as we will see in several places in this book, to pose a threat to the nation-state. All of the other processes tend to be based in one or more nation-states (e.g. Soviet imperialism, British colonialism) and to affect one or more nation-states (e.g. states behind the Iron Curtain, Britain's former colonies).

Another way of saying much the same thing is that globalization is a *decentered* process. All of the others have clear centers from which they emanate and extend their power and influence.

Globalization does not generally involve military and direct (e.g. occupation; imposition of administrators as in colonialism) control by some nations over others. There is power, control, even exploitation, but in the main it tends to be accomplished more subtly than imperialism, colonialism, and even development. The other processes – Westernization, Americanization, Easternization – vary greatly in degree of heavy-handedness and direct- ness. Easternization, at least as it is practiced today,[25] is the subtlest of these practices; Westernization and Americanization have often been quite blunt and direct and, in any case, have been closely tied to imperialism, colonialism, and development.

Because it tends not to be as heavy-handed, globalization (and the processes discussed in this chapter) does not lead to the same intense opposition as did imperialism, colonialism, and to a lesser degree development. In the latter cases, opposition often took the form of armed rebellions and wars designed to end them, although those wars were not always successful.

That is not to say that there are not strong negative reactions against globalization (and development, Westernization, Americanization) as is reflected in the alter-globalization movement and many large and sometimes violent protests mounted against it. Americanization is also prone to eliciting strong (negative and positive) reactions throughout the globe.

To the extent that these other processes continue to exist and to be of significance, it could be argued that globalization is the broadest and most all-encompassing process and can be said to include imperialism, Westernization, Americanization, and Easternization.

Colonialism and dependency are of more historical interest as well as being models of what globalization ought *not* to do and to be like. Unfortunately, globalization often comes to resemble them much too closely.

While this chapter has sought to draw distinctions among various processes and to distin- guish them in one way or another from globalization, the fact is that there are strong over- laps among and between them. If we accept the idea that globalization is the latest and the broadest of these processes, it is possible to conclude that *all* of the others either continue to survive in, or are subsumed under, it. In terms of the former, there are certainly those who see elements of the earlier epochs of imperialism, colonialism, and dependency surviving, if not being alive and well, in the global age and in the process of globalization. This is espe- cially true of those who are critical of the neoliberalism that dominates globalization today (see Chapter 4). They would see globalization as a newer, kinder-sounding label, and a sub- tler method, for more long-standing efforts to exert imperial control over, to colonize, and to create dependency among, many of the weaker nation-states and other areas (e.g. stateless locales) of the world. Beyond that, it is possible to see the other processes – Westernization, Americanization, and Easternization – as sub-processes within globalization that continue to exist to this day and to argue that one or more of them may even increase in importance in the future. Thus, while it makes sense, as we have throughout this chapter, to draw dis- tinctions among and between these processes, they all can also be seen as informing, and as being part of, globalization. In the end, the key point is that in gaining a better understanding of these processes, we gain a more nuanced and sophisticated sense of the fundamental nature of globalization. This is the case whether we carefully distinguish among these processes or see them all as part of a larger process of globalization.

THE ERA OF THE "POSTS"

We have already had occasion to mention post-colonization in the context of a discussion of colonization. However, it is also possible to argue that almost *all* of the processes discussed in this chapter can be described as being in the "era of the posts." That is, they have passed into history, passed their prime, or are showing signs of moving into the past tense. Most, if not all, of them remain important, but what is also important are the signs of their passage into history. Thus, we could talk in terms (and many do) of post-imperialism, post-colonialism, post-development, post-Easternization, and post-Americanization.[26]

One concrete example of this is post-Westernization, specifically the post-Westernization of the sport of cricket (Rumford 2007c: 97–106). As discussed earlier, cricket was at its origin a Western, especially an English, sport. However, in recent years, former British colonies, especially in Asia, have become more equal combatants in global cricket matches and competitions (Fletcher 2011). Indeed, there is an ongoing struggle for control of cricket between the traditional and the nascent powers. This is especially true of India: "In many ways, India is the focal point for both the globalization of cricket – a new focus for generating cricket finance through massive TV audiences and administrative leadership – and for post-Westernization of the game" (Rumford 2007c: 95).

The more general issue, of course, is whether we have moved into a post-Western era in a broader sense. The idea of Easternization, especially in terms of the rise of China, and to a lesser extent India, as global powers, can be taken as an indication of post-Westernization. If the twentieth century marked the peak of Westernization, it may be that the twenty-first century will come to be seen as a post-Western era, as the era of Easternization.

Fareed Zakaria (2008, 2011) has argued that we are living in the post-American age. He is quite clear from the opening sentence of his book that the key issue is *not* the decline of the US, but rather "the rise of everyone else" (2008: 1). Everyone else involves other nation-states (especially China – "the second-most-important country in the world" [2008: 93], but not likely to surpass the US in any domain for decades, at least), as well as various non-state actors (e.g. EU). The US has lost, or is losing, its top position in many realms, large and small, but it maintains and is likely to continue to retain, its politico-military position as the world's dominant, if not only, superpower. However, in virtually every other important domain – "industrial, financial, educational, social, cultural" – the pendulum is swinging away from US dominance (2008: 4). In other words, "we are moving into a *post-American world*, one defined and directed from many places and by many people" (2008: 5). The US is most threatened by these changes, and has the most to lose, but it is likely to remain on top in at least some areas for some time and its effects will be felt long into the future. One of the reasons for the resiliency of the US is the vibrancy of its demographics, at least in contrast to many other parts of the world (especially the EU) where populations are shrinking and immigrants are less welcome. It is this dynamic population that helps to give the US its edge in innovativeness.

While Zakaria focuses on the rest, he is not oblivious to problems in the US that have contributed to its relative decline. He is especially critical of what he considers a dysfunctional government that is able to accomplish little or nothing. Beyond that he recognizes that there are problems in the economy – the US dollar is weak, the savings rate is low, and the costs associated with rapidly growing entitlements (e.g. Medicare) are soaring.

In the end, what this means for Zakaria is that the US will no longer be in a position to dictate to the rest of the world. Instead, the US will need to engage in "consultation, cooperation, and even [shockingly!] compromise" (Zakaria 2008: 233). Nevertheless, the role of the US will remain very important both in terms of setting agendas for the rest of the world and in organizing coalitions in support of its preferred courses of action.

It follows that if we are witnessing a "post-American" world, we might also see a "post anti-American" world. As Meunier (2013: 1) argues, "the financial crisis that erupted in September 2008 seemed to confirm all the worst stereotypes [that Europeans held] about the United States," including their consumerist greed, materialist excess, and blind commitment to free-market ideology. But yet, anti-Americanism did not surge – at least not in Europe, because it was mitigated by the election of Obama, new global trends, and the perception of the relative decline of the US with the simultaneous rise of China. As competing superpowers appear more like the US, and the US loses its ability to dictate the futures of others countries, we will likely see a drop in anti-American sentiment as well.

CHAPTER SUMMARY

This chapter examines several concepts related to globalization – imperialism, colonialism (and postcolonialism), development (and dependency), Westernization, Easternization, and Americanization. While some of these processes had an impact on globalization in the past, others continue to affect and might even be a part of globalization today.

Imperialism describes methods employed by one country to gain territorial control over another, in order to exercise political, economic, and territorial control over it. Such control might be exercised over multiple nation-states as well as less well-defined geographic areas. The idea of imperialism has come to be associated with rule over vast regions. This characteristic leads it to be associated with globalization. Major imperial powers have included Great Britain, the former Soviet Union, and in usually a less direct form, the United States. Today, while political imperialism (direct political control) has declined, other forms persist.

Lenin argued that economic factors are the essence of imperialism. According to this view, factors inherent in capitalism lead nations to undertake imperial ventures. Apart from the economic aspect, cultural imperialism is also an important form of control. This idea emerged primarily in the European context with the belief that "superior" culture should "civilize" the rest of the "less developed" world, through exploratory, missionary, and humanitarian missions. Education and publishing acted as key tools for the dissemination of European ideas. The US has been the most powerful global force from the perspective of cultural imperialism, through the proliferation of American movies, television, and books.

Hardt and Negri argue that heavy-handed state-based imperialism has now been replaced by a decentered empire wherein power operates through a more complex and subtle network of global political, economic, and cultural processes. On the other hand, Harvey makes the case for a new imperialism in the form of *capitalist imperialism* with the US as its prime representative. This form of imperialism consists of a complex and contradictory fusion of political and economic imperialism.

Colonialism involves more formal mechanisms of control over a territory entailing the creation of an administrative apparatus to run a colony's internal affairs. There have been two major, more recent, phases of colonialism – the first began in the fifteenth century and was dominated by Spain and Portugal; the second lasted from the 1820s to the end of WW I and involved Great Britain, France, and Germany, as well as the US and Japan.

The end of WW II saw a strong drive toward decolonization. Colonization was replaced by a more insidious attempt at economic control and exploitation, through *neo-colonialism*. *Postcolonialism* relates to developments in former colonies after the departure of the colonizing power.

Development as a project focused on the economic development of specific nations. It was an inherently elitist project based on the assumption that the North was an "ideal" model of economic growth. In its attempt to move the South as close to this "ideal" as possible, the project extended beyond economics. Efforts were undertaken to replace the "inferior" socio-cultural factors of the South with those in the North, which were presumed to be more conducive to economic growth. This project was motivated by Western apprehensions that weak nations would follow the communist path.

A major critique of the development project emerged in the form of *dependency theory*. Adherents of this theory argued that instead of promoting development, in reality the development project led to the South's greater dependency on the North. Underdevelopment is not traceable to internal sources in a particular nation. Rather, it is a product of the relationship between developed and underdeveloped countries in the capitalist system. Globalization is often criticized as a less offensive version of the development project.

Westernization is a concept that is often perceived as being coterminous with globalization. The term has a strong negative connotation attached to it, due to linkages with earlier periods of Western imperialism and colonialism. However, this view leads to the exclusion of the positive aspects of what the West has to offer to the world. Beyond its politics and economics, Westernization includes other influences such as technology, language, law, lifestyle, and food. As opposed to the unidirectional flow implied by Westernization, globalization involves multidirectional flows. Westernization implies homogenization, while globalization involves both homogenization and heterogenization. In addition, through its focus on the West, Westernization also ignores the linkages among countries in the periphery.

Easternization stresses flows from the East to the West. However, it may have more to do with factors internal to the West than with flows from the East. Among the array of phenomena which are Eastern in origin and are now common in the West are yoga, Zen, vegetarianism, tarot, and the impact of Eastern music. In addition, we can also include here the powerful impact of Eastern (especially Japanese) manufacturers on the American market, through their influence on production and management techniques such as "just-in-time."

Americanization is also a component of the larger process of globalization. It is defined as the export of products, images, technologies, practices, and behavior that is closely associated with America and Americans. Discourse on the issue emerged, at least in part, as a result of concern about, and the study of, America's influence on Europe. While after WW II, the US was seen as the savior (at least by some) of Europe, by the 1960s it was perceived more as a business, industrial, and economic threat to Europe. More recently, the industrial threat posed by the US was replaced by a fear of American dominance in global consumption, through processes such as Coca-Colonization, McDonaldization, and Starbuckization. Apart from the economic realm, the process of Americanization is also evident in Europe, and throughout the world, in such areas as politics, law, military, and culture.

However, this discourse is complicated by other issues, and therefore a more nuanced analysis of Americanization is required. In discussing Americanization, we need to specify the import under consideration. Similarly, the particular form of Americanization – cultural, social, communicative, political, or economic – needs to be specified. While some global processes are traceable to the US, many details of this complicated process would be lost if it was simply subsumed under the heading of Americanization.

The issue becomes more complex when we try to define what counts as Americanization. Does the product or process have to be produced in the US? Or, does it depend on whether it is identified as American by those who import it? It can be argued that the process of Americanization has as much to do with the receiving nation as with the US itself. Receiving nations are not passive entities and they play an active role in shaping the process of Americanization. For instance, many nations have now created their own McDonaldized restaurants, which are then exported back into the US. Anti-Americanism is an intense and non-homogeneous global process, comprising of distinct forms, causes, and expressions.

In contrast to all the other flows, globalization consists of multidirectional flows, with no single point of geographic origin. In addition, while globalization is a decentered process, the others are focused more on nation-states. Globalization generally involves subtler control and hence does not generate the same degree of intense opposition as at least some of the other processes (imperialism, colonialism). Globalization can be said to be the broadest of the processes discussed in this chapter. All of the others either continue to survive in, or are subsumed under, globalization. It could also be argued that, in a sense, most of these processes are past their prime. The current era may then be regarded as an era of the posts – post-imperialism, post-development, post-colonialism, post-Westernization, and post-Americanization.

DISCUSSION QUESTIONS

1. Is globalization simply another name for processes such as imperialism, colonialism, development, Westernization, and Easternization? Examine the similarities and differences among these processes.

2. Are the processes of Westernization and Easternization comparable in terms of scope and magnitude?

3. Trace the shifting definitions of imperialism. Is it relevant as an analytical tool for the current global age?

4. Is Americanization a relevant concept? What particular aspect of it is most relevant today?

5. Has the onset of the Great Recession rendered Americanization an outdated concept? Discuss.

6. What is anti-Americanism and what are its sources? Has it increased or declined over the years?

7. Discuss the concept of the "era of the posts." What are its advantages and disadvantages for thinking about the world today?

ADDITIONAL READINGS

Fareed Zakaria. *The Post-American World: Release 2.0*. New York: W.W. Norton, 2011.

Vladimir Lenin. *Imperialism: The Highest Stage of Capitalism*. New York: International Publishers, 1917/1939.

David Harvey. *The New Imperialism*. Oxford: Oxford University Press, 2003.

Kwame Nkrumah. *Neo-Colonialism: The Last Stage of Imperialism*. Humanities Press International, 1965.

Philip McMichael. *Development and Social Change: A Global Perspective*, 5th edn. Thousand Oaks, CA: Pine Forge Press, 2011.

Immanuel Wallerstein. *The Modern World-System: Capitalist Agriculture and the Origins of the European World-Economy in the 16th Century*. New York: Academic Press, 1974.

Colin Campbell. *The Easternization of the West: A Thematic Account of Cultural Change in the Modern Era*. Boulder, CO: Paradigm Publishers, 2007.

J.-J. Servan-Schreiber. *The American Challenge*. New York: Atheneum, 1968.

Richard F. Kuisel. *Seducing the French: The Dilemma of Americanization*. Berkeley: University of California Press, 1993.

Robert J. Foster. *Coca-Globalization: Following Soft Drinks from New York to New Guinea*. New York: Palgrave Macmillan, 2008.

Victoria de Grazia. *Irresistible Empire: America's Advance through 20th-Century Europe*. Cambridge, MA: The Belknap Press of Harvard University Press, 2005.

Niall Ferguson. *Civilization: The West and the Rest*. New York: Penguin, 2011.

William Marling. *How American is Globalization?* Baltimore: Johns Hopkins University Press, 2006.

Barnett Singer. *The Americanization of France*. New York: Rowman & Littlefield, 2013.

Sean Clark and Sabrina Hoque, eds. *Debating a Post-American World: What Lies Ahead?* New York: Routledge, 2012.

NOTES

1 For a critique of both of these forms of imperialism, see Sparks (2007).

2 Chilcote (2000: 17) is one who associates imperialism with capitalism.

3 As Lenin (1917/1939: 123) puts it later, "the economic quintessence of imperialism is monopoly capital."

4 Lenin (1917/1939: 91) saw finance capital rather than industrial capital as being of central importance: "The characteristic feature of imperialism is *not* industrial capital, *but* finance capital."

5 Lenin (as does Hobson) often uses the terms interchangeably or relates one to the other. For example: "Colonial policy and imperialism existed before this latest stage of capitalism, and even before capitalism" (Lenin 1917/1939: 81–2); see also Williams and Chrisman (1994b: 1).

6 For an excellent collection of essays on this topic, see Ashcroft, Griffiths, and Tiffin (2006); see also

Xie (2007: 986–91) and Krishnaswamy and Hawley (2008).

7 Also of note is the work of Gayatri Spivak and Homi Bhabha.

8 This includes, more broadly, texts and discourse (see Appendix).

9 For a similar view, see Wallerstein (2005: 1263–78).

10 Frank (1969: 17–31); see also Cardoso (1972: 83/95).

11 For one exception, see Edelman and Haugerud (2005).

12 It is this focus on nation-states that leads many who study globalization to argue that world system theory is *not* a theory of globalization because of the decline of the nation-state in the global age.

13 On Japanese innovations in production, see Schonberger (1982).

14 In using the terms "America/Americans" Kuisel clearly has in mind US/US citizens.

15 The work of some of these thinkers will be discussed later in this chapter.

16 The global influences of all other North, Central, and South American countries are too diverse to be encompassed by Americanization as an analytical concept.

17 These include Duhamel (1931); Williams (1962); McCreary (1962); Hebdige (1988); Duignan and Gann (1992); Kuisel (1993); Kroes, Rydell, and Bosscher (1993).

18 Including Campbell (2003); Beck, Sznaider, and Winter (2003); and Campbell, Davies, and McKay (2004).

19 Similarly, Hebdige (1988: 52) wrote of the postwar "spectre of Americanisation."

20 Although, there were other fears in Europe of American global expansion such as concern over the dangers posed by its military, its culture in general and its media in particular, and so on.

21 In fact, it could be argued that the US is undergoing a process of "de-Americanization" and such a view supports the idea of the declining importance of Americanization. Would a de-Americanized America be a force for Americanization around the world? See Robertson (2003: 262–3).

22 Sassen (1991). For a series of studies on would-be global cities, see Marcuse and van Kempen (2000).

23 For at least some meanings of the term, see Ceaser (2003: 3–18).

24 It may now be in the process of being joined, or displaced, by the Great Recession.

25 The Japanese were certainly quite brutal both before and during WW II.

26 Niall Ferguson (2008: April 13: 1) sees Fareed Zakaria's work (2008) as one of the "harbingers of a 'post-American world'."

NEOLIBERALISM

ROOTS, PRINCIPLES, CRITICISMS, AND NEO-MARXIAN ALTERNATIVES

Globalization: A Basic Text, Second Edition. George Ritzer and Paul Dean.
© 2015 John Wiley & Sons, Ltd. Published 2015 by John Wiley & Sons, Ltd.

Neoliberalism:
Liberal
commitment
to individual
liberty, a belief
in the free
market and
opposition
to state
intervention
in it.

While it has come under severe attack in the wake of the global economic crisis, **neoliberalism** has arguably been the most important theory in the field of globalization studies. However, it is more than "just" an important theory, it has profoundly influenced economics (and politics) in the US, as well as in much of the rest of the world. It has both strong adherents and vociferous critics. With much of that economic crisis being linked to the neoliberal belief in the free market and deregulation, critics seemed to be gaining the upper hand (in theory if not in practice). Indeed, it was the deregulation of the banks and financial institutions that led to the high-risk ventures (e.g. financial derivatives) that collapsed in late 2007 leading to the subsequent global crisis. Many of its arguments have not only been heavily attacked, but have demonstrated to be quite disastrous. However, as the economy has regained some growth, many governments appear to be returning to neoliberal "business as usual" (Jessop 2012). Even if governments have backed off from using its rhetoric, neoliberal practices have largely been maintained (Aalbers 2013). Therefore, one cannot understand globalization, and many of its problems, without understanding neoliberalism. It was a key factor (and is not disappearing any time soon) in both the emergence of the global age and the many problems associated with it.

Neoliberalism is a theory that has implications for globalization in general, as well as for many of its elements.[1] It is particularly applicable to economics (especially the market and trade) and politics (the nation-state and the need to limit its involvement in, and control over, the market and trade) (Nederveen Pieterse 2004). It is not only important in itself, but it has also strongly influenced other thinking and theorizing about both of those domains. This is especially the case with various neo-Marxian economic theories (e.g. of David Harvey; see below) that are highly critical of neoliberalism. In the last part of this chapter we will deal with two of the major neo-Marxian alternatives to neoliberalism.

THE PAST, PRESENT, AND FUTURE OF NEOLIBERALISM

Harvey (2005, 2011) deals with neoliberalism as a "grand narrative" involving four basic stages. The first, "classical liberalism," got its impetus from the seventeenth- and eighteenth-century work of thinkers like John Locke and Adam Smith (Macpherson 1962). Many see little or no difference between classical liberalism and neoliberalism. In fact, Martin Wolf (2005) dismisses the concept of neoliberalism arguing that it is simply a derogatory term developed and used by the critics of liberalism (such as Harvey).

The term neoliberalism involves, in Harvey's view, a combination of classical liberalism's commitment to individual liberty with *neo*classical economics devoted to the free market and opposed to state intervention in that market. Liberalism came to be called neoliberalism (Fourcade-Gourinchas and Babb 2002: 533–79) as a result of developments in the 1930s.

The Depression era marked the beginning of Harvey's second stage, or what he calls "embedded liberalism," created, at least in part, in reaction to Keynesian economics and its impact on the larger society. It was "embedded" because the market, entrepreneurs, and corporations, inspired in part by Keynesian theory, came to be ensnared in a "web of social and political constraints and a regulative environment that sometimes restrained but in other instances led the way in economic and industrial strategy" (Harvey 2005: 11). Liberal ideas had to be revitalized and transformed because of the need to counter the interventionism and the collectivism that dominated much thinking (especially Keynesian, as well as Marxian, theories) and many political systems (especially the New Deal in the US and the rise of the Soviet Union) in the early twentieth century (Turner and Gamble 2007: 865–7). Neoliberalism's intellectual leaders were economists, especially members of the Austrian School including Friedrich van Hayek and Ludwig von Mises. An organization devoted to liberal ideas – the Mont Pelerin Society (MPS) – was created in 1947. Its members were alarmed by the expansion of collectivist socialism (especially in, and sponsored by, the Soviet Union) and the aggressive intervention by liberal governments in the market (e.g. Franklin Roosevelt's "New Deal"). Those associated with MPS, especially the famous and highly influential Chicago economist, Milton Friedman, played a key role in the efforts to protect traditional liberal ideas, to develop neoliberal theory, and to sponsor their utilization by countries throughout the world (Goodman 2008a: 3).

Friedman taught economics at the University of Chicago beginning in 1946 and Hayek ("patron saint of the Chicago School" [Klein 2007: 131]) was a colleague there for a time in the 1950s. The Chicago economics department became the center of the neoliberal approach and it produced a number of students who became known as the "Chicago Boys." After they finished their advanced degrees, they either went back to their home countries or served as consultants in various places throughout the world. In either case, they spread the neoliberal doctrine taught at Chicago and by Friedman and played a central role in it becoming policy in a number of nations.

A key development in the history of neoliberalism was the democratic election of Salvador Allende as President of Chile in 1970. Allende was a Marxist and the US, especially through the CIA, sponsored a coup engineered by the Chilean military (with CIA assistance) in September, 1973 (Dallek 2007). Allende was killed in the coup and he was replaced by the general who led it, Augusto Pinochet, who soon became President of Chile.

Many of the Chicago Boys had returned to Chile after their training at the University of Chicago and with Pinochet's ascension to power they were given an opportunity to implement Friedman's neoliberal ideas which, in a highly critical account, Naomi Klein calls the "shock doctrine" (Klein 2007). This involved the view that a total overhaul of an economy required a shock (like the Chilean coup) *and* the economic policies put in place were designed to shock the economy in order to change it dramatically and, at least in theory, to breathe life into it. The basic free-market premises of this economic doctrine were derived from Friedman's teachings and writings (especially *Capitalism and Freedom* [2002]). They involved the privatization of industry, the deregulation of the economy, and reductions in a nation's spending on social welfare programs. In the political arena, laws and regulations were dismantled leaving people to deal with the shock of the resulting lawlessness. Actions associated with each of these profoundly shook the economy, as well as the larger society. The nation's capitalists were the main beneficiaries of this shock therapy, especially privatization, which put them in an ownership position and in control of the newly privatized industries. They also benefited from the deregulation of the economy which left them free to operate – and profit – almost at will. The main victims of this shock therapy were a nation's poor whose economic situation was made worse by the shredding of the social safety net that served to protect them, at least to some degree.

Of far greater global importance was the influence of these ideas, and the shock doctrine, in the 1980s under the conservative political administrations of Margaret Thatcher in Great Britain and Ronald Reagan in the US. Early in their administrations both leaders undertook shock therapy by, for example, taking on, and defeating, powerful labor unions. Such shocks were then used as a basis for radically overhauling their economies by applying the neoliberal ideas of the Chicago School. A decade later, the collapse of the Soviet Union seemingly left few alternatives to neoliberalism. Indeed, shortly after the collapse of communism, Russia and other countries once in its orbit (e.g. Poland) came in for shock therapy and the institution, at least in part, of a free-market economy. Klein offers a number of other examples of the global use of shock therapy[3] including:

- the remaking of Asian economies after the financial meltdown in Asia in 1997;
- the elimination of about a half million of Saddam Hussein's Baathist supporters ("De-Baathification") from government positions in the aftermath of the US invasion of Iraq in 2003 leaving it, and the larger society, unable to function;
- the use of the shock and disorientation of the disaster associated with the tsunami in Asia on December 26, 2004 (Gunewardena and Schuller 2008) to create a "second tsunami" by radically restructuring the economy and society.

Much of the world came to accept, or was coerced into accepting, neoliberalism. Major forces in this were the IMF and the World Bank, both of which were heavily staffed by products of the Chicago economics department ("there was a virtual conveyor belt delivering Chicago Boys to the two institutions" [Klein 2007: 280]), and which practiced a form of shock therapy known as **structural adjustment**. That is, in order to receive aid from these organizations, receiving nations had to restructure their economies and societies in line with neoliberal theory. In addition to liberalizing financial markets and deregulating the economy, this has also meant major cuts to social spending and health care. This neoliberal theory came to be most associated with the US and the Washington-based global organizations it exerted great control over (again the IMF and the World Bank [Plehwe 2007] are prime examples). In fact, neoliberalism (Campbell and Pederson 2001; Harvey 2011) is often referred to as the "Washington Consensus" (Serra and Stiglitz 2008) because of its linkage to the political and economic position of the US and the physical location of such organizations in that nation's capital. The term "Washington Consensus" was coined by, and is associated with the work of, John Williamson (1990a, 1990b, 1993; Cavanagh and Broad 2007). Most generally, in the Washington Consensus "unimpeded private market forces were seen as the driving engines of growth" (Cavanagh and Broad 2007: 1243). Absent was any concern for equity, redistribution, social issues, and the environment.[4]

Structural adjustment: the conditions of economic "restructuring" that are imposed by organizations such as the World Bank and the IMF on borrowing nations. Receiving nations are expected, among other things, to put into place tight monetary and fiscal policies, to liberalize financial markets and trade, to privatize, and to deregulate.

Naomi Klein is highly critical of all of this. The result of the reforms associated with shock therapy is the "dismal reality of inequality, corruption and environmental degradation" (Klein 2007: 280). She touches on Joseph Schumpeter's (1976: 81–6) famous theory of creative destruction (see Chapter 7), which argues that the essence of capitalism is the need to destroy in order to create. However, she argues that in the case of neoliberalism and the shock doctrine, this has "resulted in scarce creation and spiraling destruction" (Klein 2007: 224). She is especially critical of the central role in all of this played by the US, as well as by the global institutions over which it exercises great control.

Structural adjustment in particular has come under attack from many quarters. For example, James Ferguson (2006: 11 ff.) has criticized its impact on Africa. Economically, he argues that it has led to inequality, marginalization, and the lowest economic growth rates ever recorded and, in some cases, even negative growth. Politically, it has led to the decline of the state "whose presence barely extends beyond the boundaries of their capital cities. Vast areas of the continent have been effectively abandoned by their national states" (2006: 13). Corruption is widespread and in many cases once state-based functions have been privatized.

The cause of structural adjustment is not helped by public comments by those in support of it, especially the 1991 memo (later leaked to the press) of the World Bank's then-chief economist Lawrence Summers (who became US Secretary of the Treasury, President of Harvard University,[5] and head of the Barack Obama's White House Economic Council). He argued that the World Bank should encourage the export of pollution and toxic waste to the Third World. His logic was that "the measurement of the costs of health-impairing pollution depends on the foregone earnings from increased morbidity and mortality. . . a given amount of health-impairing pollution should be done in the country with the lowest cost, which will be the country with the lowest wages."[6] For example, the carcinogens that cause prostate cancer would not be as significant a problem in the South because men there are not likely to have a long enough life span to ever get the disease (it is mainly older men who get prostate cancer). More specifically, in the case of Africa, he argued that "the under-populated countries in Africa are vastly *under*-polluted."[7] Such arguments are not likely to win friends in the South for the proponents of structural adjustment and the institutions that they lead.

The Washington Consensus had its heyday in the 1980s and early 1990s (as reflected in the creation of the North American Free Trade Association [NAFTA] in 1994; see Chapter 6), but began to collapse soon after as a result of an avalanche of developments (financial shocks in Mexico in 1994 and 1998; the Asian financial crisis of 1997–1998; the collapse in Argentina of its economy in 2001, the scandals associated with Enron and WorldCom during this period which were linked to excessive application of such neoliberal ideas as deregulation and privatization, and so on). A variety of groups – workers, environmentalists, farmers and peasants, those in poor and less developed nations, and so on – came together in opposition to the Washington Consensus. Then there were the actions of the alter-globalization movements (especially the anti-WTO protests in Seattle), and leftist governments throughout Latin America that have directly challenged this model (Sader 2009; see Chapter 15).

Neoliberalism has recently been called into question in the developed world because of the meltdown in the global economy. The US government was led to intervene in the market in various ways, engineering a 2008 takeover of the investment firm Bear Stearns by J. P. Morgan. Later the US was forced to nationalize, or nearly so, the giant mortgage companies Fannie Mae and Freddie Mac, as well as the huge insurance conglomerate AIG, which were driven to near-insolvency by the same economic crisis. The US government was forced to invest many billions of dollars in the largest American banks (e.g. Citibank) in order to keep them afloat. Huge sums were also invested in the American automobile companies. The US government has since sold off most of its shares in these companies; in some cases these sell-offs have resulted in increased government revenue, and in other cases, in huge taxpayer losses (Krisher 2013; Sparshott and Holm 2012). Such intervention would be anathema to Milton Friedman who long argued for the need to allow the markets to work out such difficulties on their own. The only role he saw for the government was the management of the money supply ("monetarism"), but otherwise the market was to be left to its own devices. From this perspective, Bear Stearns, Fannie Mae and Freddie Mac, AIG, and GM should have all been allowed to fail (as happened in the case of the one-time financial giant, Lehman Brothers).

In Latin America, Friedman's ideas have come under attack for failing to take poverty and inequality into consideration. According to a well-known Peruvian economist: "The problem with Milton Friedman and his fellow libertarians is they never took into consideration the importance of class. . . . They ignored the way elites were able to distort the policies they prescribed for their own benefit" (Goodman 2008a: 3).

Harvey (2005) relates neoliberalism to globalization in various ways. First, the scope of neoliberalism is global in the sense that it has become an economic and political system that characterizes a wide range of societies throughout the world. However, nations have both common paths to neoliberalism as well as basic differences that relate to their different histories and character. Second, neoliberalism is an idea system that has flowed around the world. Third, Harvey sees various international organizations, especially IMF, WTO, and the World Bank, as dominated by neoliberal ideas and as imposing them, in the form of various demands for restructuring, on a number of societies throughout the world. These organizations are, of course, dominated by the US which is indirectly, as well as directly and overtly (e.g. in Iraq, Afghanistan), exporting neoliberalism throughout the globe. At its heart, though, Harvey argues that neoliberalism is the reassertion of global business class power over everyone else. We can add to this fact that opposition to neoliberalism is also global and the reach of that opposition grew during and after the Great Recession.

Harvey saw (and feared) the emergence of a third stage – *neoconservativism* (led by the infamous "neo-cons" [former US Secretary of Defense, Donald Rumsfeld and Paul Wolfowitz, Rumsfeld's aide and later head of the World Bank] associated with the disastrous US policy and war in Iraq) – based on a strong commitment to order and morality *and* the need to impose them on the rest of the world (Kukreja 2012). (It is this third stage, by the way, that moves neoliberalism in a much more overtly political direction.) Given its propensity for authoritarianism, Harvey finds neoconservativism to be dangerous and in need of rejection both in the US and elsewhere in the world where it has gained a significant foothold (e.g. in Singapore and China).

Hope for the future (and a potential fourth stage) lies, unsurprisingly given Harvey's neo-Marxian orientation, in the development of an organic, left alliance involving workers, and racial, ethnic, and gender minorities all of which are to resist neoliberal (and neoconservative) globalization (Watson 2001). He also sees hope in a "stunning" variety of social movements spawned by the abuses associated with neoliberalism. He mentions only a few of them (surprisingly there is no mention of the important move to the left in several Latin American countries), and offers little in the way of positive alternatives to the system being critiqued. Ultimately, Harvey (like Karl Polanyi, see below) favors a system where limited freedoms of the market and profit are replaced by a broader set of freedoms, more open democracy, greater social equality, and greater justice in the economic, political, and cultural realms.

Ideology: Widely shared set of ideas, beliefs, norms, values, and ideals accepted as truth.

While we discuss neoliberalism mainly as a theory in this chapter, another way of looking at it is as being, in whole or in part, an ideology (Steger 2007; Aalbers 2013). An **ideology** may be defined as a system of widely shared ideas, patterned beliefs, guiding norms and values, and ideals accepted as truth by some group. An ideology offers a more or less coherent picture of the world not only as it is, but as it ought to be. While ideology simplifies tremendous complexity, it is often distorted as well. In addition to distortion, ideology also serves to legitimate and to integrate. Indeed, while neoliberal ideas are presented here as theory and science (sophisticated data are often marshalled in support of them), they could also be interpreted as ideology – pro-free-market capitalism and anti-state-controlled socialism; indeed many scholars view neoliberalism as more of a political than a scientific concept (Peck 2010; Jessop 2012).

NEOLIBERALISM: AN EXEMPLARY STATEMENT AND THE BASIC PRINCIPLES

A number of well-known scholars, especially economists, are associated with neoliberalism (e.g. Milton Friedman). Here, we begin by briefly examining some of the ideas of one neoliberal economist[8] – William Easterly – in order to give the reader a better sense of this perspective from the point of view of one of its supporters.

Easterly is opposed to any form of collectivism and state planning[9] because it inhibits, if not destroys, freedom. To Easterly, freedom, especially economic freedom, is highly correlated with economic success. This is the case because economic freedom "permits the decentralized search for success that is the hallmark of free markets" (Easterly 2006a: 35).

Easterly offers several reasons why economic freedom is related to economic success and why central planning has been an economic failure. First, it is extremely difficult to know in advance what will succeed and what will fail. Economic freedom permits a multitude of attempts and the failures are weeded out. Over time, what remains, in the main, are the successes and they serve to facilitate a high standard of living. Central planners can never have nearly as much knowledge as myriad individuals seeking success and learning from their failures and those of others. Second, markets offer continuous feedback on what is succeeding and failing; central planners lack such feedback. Third, economic freedom leads to the ruthless reallocation of resources to that which is succeeding; central planners often have vested interests that prevent such a reallocation. Fourth, economic freedom permits large and rapid increases in scale by financial markets and corporate organizations; central planners lack the flexibility to make large-scale changes rapidly. Finally, because of sophisticated contractual protections, individuals and corporations are willing to take great risks; central planners are risk-averse because of their personal vulnerability if things go wrong.

More generally, neoliberalism as a theory comes in various forms, but all are undergirded by some or all of the following ideas (Antonio 2007). Great faith is placed in the **free market** and its rationality. The market needs to be allowed to operate free of any impediments, especially those imposed by the nation-state and other political entities. The free operation of the market will in the "long run" advantage just about everyone and bring about both improved economic welfare and greater individual freedom (and a democratic political system). George Soros calls this **market fundamentalism**, or the idea that "markets will take care of all our needs."[10] To help bring this about, it is important to champion, support, and expand a wide range of technological, legal, and institutional arrangements that support the market and its freedom. The free market is so important to one neoliberal, Johan Norberg (2003: 16), that he defines capitalism not as "an economic system of capital ownership and investment opportunities" but rather as "the liberal market economy, with free competition based on the right to own one's property and the freedom to negotiate, to conclude agreements, and to start up business activities."

The principles of the free market are not restricted to the economy (and the polity) but can be applied to *every* sphere of society.

> My aim is not for economic transactions to supplant all other human relations. My aim is freedom and voluntary relations in all fields. In the *cultural* arena that means freedom of expression and of the press. In *politics*, it means democracy and the rule of law. In *social* life, it means the right to live according to one's own values and to choose one's own company. And in the *economy*, it means capitalism and free markets. (Norberg 2003: 17, italics added)

Free market: A market free of any impediments.

Market fundamentalism: Markets will take care of all our needs.

Some go even further and argue that transactions in every sphere of life *should* be like those in the economy. The key to all those transactions is the *individual*; neoliberalism is radically individualistic.

Related to the belief in the free market is a parallel belief in *free trade*. Where there are restraints on the free market and free trade, the theory leads to a commitment to **deregulation** to limit or eliminate such restraints. Thus, for example, a so-called "banana war" has raged between the European Union and the US over bananas grown in the Caribbean (Myers 2004). The EU maintained a quota system that discriminated in favor of banana imports from several small Caribbean nations. The US, reflecting the interests of its large corporations involved in the banana business, saw this as a restraint on free trade and it took the lead in bringing complaints to GATT (the General Agreement on Tariffs and Trade) and later the WTO (see Chapter 6). The issue is ongoing, but the fundamental question is whether restraints and limits on free trade are warranted under certain circumstances. While neoliberalism argues that there should be no such restrictions, others argue for them. For example, the Prime Minister of St. Vincent and the Grenadines, small banana-growing Caribbean islands focally involved in the dispute, said:

> The battle is not just about bananas. It is about the readiness of the WTO and the international trading community to meet the special problems of small island states which have vulnerable economies and very limited natural resources. Without special help, their economies will inevitably be destroyed by the juggernaut of free trade. (Gonsalves 2004: x–xi)

There is great belief in the need for the *global capitalist system to continue to expand*. It is presumed that such expansion would bring with it increased prosperity and decreased poverty.

Many of the ideas associated with the neoliberal economy apply to the closely linked concept of the neoliberal state. In *Spaces of Global Capitalism* Harvey (2006: 25) gives us a sense of such a state:

> The fundamental mission of the neo-liberal state is to create a "good business climate" and therefore to optimize conditions for capital accumulation no matter what the consequences for employment or social well-being. This contrasts with the social democratic state that is committed to full employment and the optimization of the well-being of all of its citizens subject to the condition of maintaining adequate and stable rates of capital accumulation.

The clear implication of the above is that in either case, the state is subordinated to the economy, although in the case of the neoliberal state the focus is on those who gain from capital accumulation (the capitalists), while in social democracy the emphasis is on the well-being of all, especially through maintaining something approximating full employment.

Neoliberals argue that free markets and free trade are linked to a *democratic political system*. Thus the political system, especially the freedom of democracy, is associated with economic well-being and with the freedom of individuals to amass great individual wealth. According to Norberg (2003: 61; italics added): "No one can doubt that the world has more than its share of serious problems. The fantastic thing is that the spread of *democracy and capitalism* has reduced them so dramatically. Where liberal policies have been allowed to operate longest, they have made poverty and deprivation the exception instead of the rule."

Deregulation: Commitment by nation-states to limit or eliminate restraints on the free market and free trade.

There is a commitment to *low taxes* and to *tax cuts* (especially for the wealthy) where taxes are deemed too high and too burdensome. Low taxes and tax cuts are believed to stimulate the economy by encouraging people to earn more and ultimately to invest and to spend more.

Tax cuts for business and industry are also encouraged with the idea that they would use the tax savings to invest more in their operations and infrastructure, thereby generating more business, income, and profits. This is seen as benefiting not only them, but society as a whole. Higher profits would "trickle down" and benefit most people in society.[11]

Spending on *welfare should be minimized* and the *safety net* for the poor should be *minimized*. Such spending and such a welfare system are seen as hurting economic growth and even as harming the poor (Norberg 2003: 97). Cuts in welfare are designed to reduce government expenditures and thereby to allow the government to cut taxes and/or to invest in more "productive" undertakings. It also is presumed that without the safety net more poor people would be forced to find work, often at minimum wage or with low pay. More such workers presumably allow companies to increase productivity and profits. Reduction of the safety net also creates a larger "reserve army"[12] that business can draw on in good economic times in order to expand its workforce.

There is a strong and generalized belief in **limited government**. The theory is that no government or government agency can do things as well as the market (the failure of the Soviet Union is seen as proof of that). Among other things, this leaves a government that is, at least theoretically, less able, or unable, to intervene in the market. It also presumably means a less expensive government, one that would need to collect less in taxes. This, in turn, would put more money in the hands of the public, especially the wealthier members of society who, in recent years, have benefited most from tax cuts. Wolf (2005: xvii) argues that the state must not only be limited, but its job is to cooperate with open global markets: "I am arguing for a better understanding by states of their long-run interest in a co-operative global economic order."

> **Limited government**: No government can do things as well as the market and should not intervene in it.

The neoliberal state is very interested in privatizing various sectors (e.g. "transportation, telecommunications, oil and other natural resources, utilities, social housing, education" [Harvey 2006: 25]) in order to open up these areas for business and profit-making. It seeks to be sure that those sectors that cannot be privatized are "cost effective" and "accountable."

It works to allow the free movement of capital among and between economic sectors and geographic regions within the borders of a given nation-state. The neoliberal state also works hard to reduce barriers to the free movement of capital across national borders and to the creation of new global markets.

The neoliberal state extols the virtues of free competition. And it is opposed to, and works against, groups (e.g. unions, social movements) that operate to restrain business interests and their efforts to accumulate capital.

In sum, contrary to many observers, Harvey (2006: 28) argues that "neo-liberalism has not made the state or particular institutions of the state (such as the courts) irrelevant." Rather, the institutions and practices of the state have been transformed to better attune them to the needs and interests of the neoliberal market and economy.

However, the neoliberal state is riddled with internal contradictions. For one thing, its authoritarianism co-exists uncomfortably with its supposed interest in individual freedom and democracy. For another, while it is committed to stability, its operations, especially in support of financial (and other) speculation, leads to increased instability (as is clear from the Great Recession and austerity measures). Then there is its commitment to competition while it actually operates on behalf of monopolization. Most generally, there is the contradiction that its public support for the well-being of everyone is given the lie by its actions in support of the economic elites.

POPULAR NEOLIBERAL "THEORY": THE CASE OF THOMAS FRIEDMAN

Robert Antonio sees Thomas Friedman's work as offering "what may be the most comprehensive, widely read defense of neoliberal globalization" (Antonio 2007: 67–83).

THE LEXUS AND THE OLIVE TREE

In *The Lexus and the Olive Tree* Friedman sought to capture the essence of globalization, especially the tensions associated with it, in his distinction between the modern automobile (the Lexus) and the ancient forces (the olive tree) that continue to dominate much of the world (Friedman 2012). While olive trees "represent everything that roots us, anchors us and locates us in the world," the Lexus represents "the drive for sustenance, improvement, prosperity and modernization – as it is played out in today's globalization system . . . [it] represents all the burgeoning global markets, financial institutions and computer technologies with which we pursue higher living standards today" (Friedman 1999: 27–8). Friedman sees the Lexus as a threat to the olive tree. That is, "all the anonymous, transnational, homogenizing, standardizing market forces and technologies" constitute a threat to local culture and identity (Friedman 1999: 29). While Friedman definitely sees movement toward the Lexus-model in the global world of today, he argues that there is a need for a "healthy balance" between it and the model of the olive tree.

Friedman has a highly positive view of globalization seeing it as involving the democratization of technology, finance, and information. *Above all else, globalization marks the triumph of one of the hallmarks of neoliberalism –* **free-market capitalism**. When a country recognizes the rules of the free market and agrees to abide by them, that is, when it accepts neoliberalism, it dons the "Golden Straitjacket" which involves acceptance of the following ideas, at least some of which were discussed in the preceding section on neoliberalism (note all of the italicized terms that relate in one way or another to a free and open market):

> **Free-market capitalism:** Creation of an open domestic economy.

- the primary engine of economic growth is the private sector;
- maintenance of a low rate of inflation and price stability;
- reduction of the size of the state bureaucracy;
- *lowering or elimination of tariffs* on imported goods;
- *elimination of restrictions* on foreign investment;
- *dropping of quotas;*
- *elimination of domestic monopolies;*
- increase of exports;
- privatization of state-owned industries, utilities;
- *deregulation* of capital markets;
- making currency convertible;
- *opening* of industries and stock and bond markets to direct foreign investment and ownership;

- creation of as much domestic competition as possible by *deregulating* the economy;
- reduction or elimination of government corruption, subsidies, and kickbacks;
- *opening* of banking and telecommunications to private ownership and to competition;
- allowing citizens to *choose* among a range of foreign and domestic pension plans and mutual funds.

Friedman acknowledges that this is a one-size-fits-all model (neoliberalism is often accused of that) and therefore that some are going to be "pinched" and "squeezed" by it. But, as a cheerleader for free-market globalization, Friedman goes no further in his criticisms. As far as he is concerned, nations around the world have no choice, assuming they want to be successful, but to don the Golden Straitjacket and experience the "pinches" with the far more predominant advantages of globalization. Those that do not, or do not do so fully, risk the wrath of the "electronic herd," especially those like electronic stock, bond, and currency traders (the electronic herd also includes large corporations that engage in Foreign Direct Investment), who will flock to countries that adopt market principles fully, but will flee from those that do not.

Friedman recognizes and applauds the fact that with the triumph of the economic market, the political sector and the nation-state shrink in importance (here is the familiar neoliberal linkage between economics and politics). Politicians have some choices but they are limited by economic considerations.

THE WORLD IS FLAT

The World is Flat: A Brief History of the Twenty-first Century (Friedman 2005, 2007) is even better-known and more influential than Friedman's earlier book on globalization.[13] The central point of this book is that the world has grown increasingly flat meaning that the barriers and hurdles to competing successfully in it have declined if not completely disappeared. In other words, the global playing field has been increasingly leveled making it possible for more and more people to play, to compete, and to win. This means that small companies and even individuals anywhere in the world have an unprecedented ability to successfully compete on a global basis.

Friedman lists a number of factors, as well as their convergence, in the emergence of the flat world, as well as in its increasing flatness over time:

1. The end of the Cold War and the destruction of the Berlin Wall.
2. The arrival of IBM personal computers and the Windows operating system.
3. The coming of Netscape in 1995; the "first broadly popular commercial browser to surf the Internet" (Friedman 2005: 56).
4. The standardization of the way things are digitized and transported on the Internet so that people can work on the Internet from anywhere and any computer and communicate to anywhere else and with any other computer.
5. Open-sourcing through self-organizing collaborative communities (e.g. free software, Linux, Wikipedia).
6. Outsourcing and offshoring leading to new forms of collaboration in widely scattered locales throughout the world.
7. Supply-chaining, or "a method of collaborating horizontally – among suppliers, retailers, and customers – to create value" (Friedman 2005: 129).

8. Insourcing allows firms, even small firms, to bring in large ones in order to handle specific functions (e.g. having UPS handle a company's package delivery). The playing field is leveled because small firms can have package delivery – or any other insourced activity – done as well as can huge corporations. At the same time the latter can function better by insourcing many of the same functions.

9. In-forming, or the "ability to build and deploy your own personal supply chain – a supply chain of information, knowledge, and entertainment. Informing is about self-collaboration – becoming your own self-directed and self-empowered researcher, editor. . ." (Friedman 2005: 153).

10. New technologies that amplify and turbocharge the flatteners described above including digital, mobile, personal, and virtual technologies.

That Friedman is not just describing a trend, but praising it as well, is clear when he says that the "world is flattening and rising at the same time" (2005: 231). In other words all are benefiting from the flat world.

The flat world thesis fits within the neoliberal perspective because it implies an elimination of all barriers to free trade (and virtually everything else, for that matter). That is, in a flat world, trade is free to roam everywhere and to get there without impediments. Indeed, the opposite of a flat world is one with lots of barriers in it, some high, some low, that serve to impede free trade. Those barriers are many of the items on the list (see above) of those things militated against by the Golden Straitjacket – tariffs, quotas, restrictions, regulations, etc. These are the kinds of limitations that are anathema to all neoliberals.

It is worth noting the relationship between Friedman's ideas and the perspective laid out in the first chapter of this book. On the one hand, a flat world is conducive to all of the liquefied flows emphasized there. On the other hand, it also takes into consideration the kinds of barriers discussed in Chapter 1. However, where we differ from Friedman is on the desirability of all those flows and on the need to eliminate all barriers to them. While Friedman seems to favor virtually all flows and the elimination of all barriers, we are simply offering tools for the analysis of the global world. If we were forced to make a judgment here, it would be that *not all flows are desirable* (see Chapter 12 for a discussion of some negative flows), and that *at least some barriers are worth retaining* in order to protect some individuals and structures from the ravages of free-floating global flows, especially those spawned by an unbridled neoliberalism. This has been made abundantly clear once again in the aftermath of the Great Recession.

We also differ with Friedman on the existence, or even the possibility, of a flat world. Barriers are built into our definition of globalization. Further, much of sociology is premised on the idea that those with power will erect barriers of all sorts that enhance their interests and that, in the process, adversely affect others and create great inequalities. This book cites a great number of studies that provide evidence for this.

CRITIQUING NEOLIBERALISM

THE EARLY THINKING OF KARL POLANYI

Much of the contemporary critique of neoliberalism, especially as it relates to economics, is traceable to the work of Karl Polanyi,[14] especially his 1944 book, *The Great Transformation: The Political and Economic Origins of Our Time*. He is the great critic of a limited focus on the economy, especially the focus of economic liberalism on the self-regulating, or unregulated, market, as well as on basing all on self-interest. In his view, these are not universal principles, but rather were unprecedented developments associated with the advent of capitalism. Polanyi (1944: 149) shows that the **laissez-faire** system came into existence with the help of the state and it was able to continue to function as a result of state actions. Furthermore, if the laissez-faire system was left to itself, it threatened to destroy society. Indeed, it was such threats, as well as real dangers, that led to counter-reactions by society and the state (e.g. socialism, communism, the New Deal) to protect themselves from the problems of a free market, especially protection of the products of, and those who labored in, it (Munck 2002a). The expansion of the laissez-faire market and the reaction against it is called the **double movement** (Hall 2007). While economic liberalism saw such counter-reactions (including any form of protectionism) as "mistakes" that disrupted the operation of the economic markets, Polanyi saw them as necessary and desirable reactions to the evils of the free market. Presciently, Polanyi (1944: 145) pointed to "the inherent absurdity of the idea of a self-regulating market." He also described as mythical the liberal idea that socialists, communists, New Dealers, and so on were involved in a conspiracy against liberalism and the free market. Rather than being a conspiracy, what took place was a natural, a "spontaneous," collective reaction by society and its various elements that were threatened by the free market. In his time, Polanyi (1944: 251) sees a reversal of the tendency for the economic system to dominate society: "Within the nations we are witnessing a development under which the economic system ceases to lay down the law to society and the primacy of society over that system is secured." This promised to end the evils produced by the dominance of the free-market system, and also to produce *more*, rather than less, freedom. That is, Polanyi believed that collective planning and control would produce more freedom, more freedom for all, than was then available in the liberal economic system.

It is interesting to look back on Polanyi's ideas with the passage of more than 60 years and especially with the rise of a global economy dominated by the kind of free-market system he so feared and despised. Polanyi's hope lay with society and the nation-state, but they have been rendered far less powerful with the rise of globalization, especially the global economy. Very telling here is Margaret Thatcher's (in)famous statement: "there is no such thing as society."[15] Without powerful social and political influences, one wonders where collective planning and social control over the market are to come from. Clearly, such planning and control are more inadequate than ever in the global age. Beyond that, one wonders whether the creation of truly global planning and control is either possible or desirable. Nevertheless, it is likely that were he alive today, the logic of Polanyi's position would lead him to favor global planning and control because of his great fears of a free-market economy, now far more powerful and dangerous because it exists on a global scale.

CONTEMPORARY CRITICISMS OF NEOLIBERALISM

Among the problems with neoliberalism as a theory is the fact that it assumes that everyone in the world wants very narrow and specific types of economic well-being (to be well-off economically, if not rich) and political freedom (democracy). The fact is, there are great cultural differences in the ways in which well-being (to not have to work very hard) and freedom (to be unfettered by the state even if it is not democratically chosen) are defined. Neoliberalism very often comes down to the North, the US, and/or global organizations (e.g. IMF), seeking to impose *their* definitions of well-being and freedom on other parts of

Laissez faire: Policies of non-intervention by the nation-state in market, trade, or the economy more generally.

Double movement: Coexistence of the expansion of the laissez-faire market and the reaction against it.

the world. Furthermore, there is great variation on this among individuals in each of these societies with the result that these definitions are different from at least some of theirs, but are nonetheless imposed on them.

Another problem lies in the fact that the theory conceals or obscures the social and material interests of those who push such an economic system with its associated technological, legal, and institutional systems. These are *not* being pursued because everyone in the world wants them or will benefit from them, but because *some*, especially in the North, are greatly advantaged by them and therefore push them.

Harvey offers a number of other criticisms of neoliberalism including the fact that it produced (and continues to produce) financial crises in various countries throughout the world (e.g. Mexico, Argentina), it helped to commodify virtually *everything*, it contributed to the degradation of the environment, and its economic record was dismal since it redistributed wealth (from poor to rich) rather than generating new wealth. Harvey (2011) calls this process "capital accumulation by dispossession" or the process by which wealth is transferred from the many to the few. While this dispossession takes different forms locally, one example is the neoliberal reforms in Mexico that have promoted widespread privatization of land. This process has forced many peasants off (i.e. dispossessed them of) their land. Thus rather than being a form of subsistence for the farmer, the lands are concentrated into large business interests and have increased their wealth, but have not actually generated any new wealth.

However, neoliberalism is now open to much more severe criticism in the aftermath of the Great Recession. It is clear that neoliberalism played a major role in spawning that recession, especially in its opposition to the regulation of financial transactions and the economy in general. The lack of restraint allowed the economy to expand without limits and then to collapse in disastrous fashion. Even before the collapse, there were indications that it was failing, such as deficit financing in the US, signs of more immediate crisis (e.g. burgeoning budget and balance-of-payment deficits), and the decline of US global hegemony. Despite these findings, however, neoliberalism continues to be applied in practice throughout the world ("the strange non-death of neo-liberalism" [Crouch 2011]).

NEOLIBERALISM AS EXCEPTION

Aiwha Ong makes an important contribution to our thinking about neoliberalism by distinguishing between neoliberalism as exception and exceptions to neoliberalism (Ong 2006b).

One example of *neoliberalism as exception* involves the creation in various parts of the world of special economic zones which are largely separated from the rest of society, free from government control, and within which the market is given more-or-less free reign. These are "exceptions" because the market is not nearly as free elsewhere in society. For example, early in its move away from a communist economic system, China set up "Special Economic Zones" and "Special Administrative Regions" (as well as "Urban Development Zones") characterized by "special spaces of labor markets, investment opportunities, and relative administrative freedom" (Ong 2006b: 19). While the state retained formal control over these zones, de facto power rested with MNCs that set up shop within them. It was those corporations that controlled migration into the zones as well as the ways in which people in the zones lived and worked.

Naomi Klein described the Cavite **Export Processing Zone (EPZ)** in Rosario, a town about 90 miles south of Manila, Philippines, in critical terms (Ong is also a critic) (Klein 2009: 202–29). Cavite is a tax-free zone sealed off from the local town and province. Such zones are independent entities free to police themselves and to prevent those outside them from seeing what is going on inside. They are, in effect, denationalized zones. Inside Cavite's gates are factories devoted to producing goods for some of the leading brands in the world – Nike, Gap, IBM, Old Navy, and so on. However, the brand names are largely invisible, and certainly do not bedeck the buildings in the zone. Furthermore, the buildings are not devoted to the production of any one brand. Rather, various brands are produced side-by-side in the same factory, by the same workers, using the same machinery. The emphasis is on low-cost production and squeezing as much production as possible out of the factories and those who work there.

Klein argues that wherever EPZs exist in the world, they function in much the same way – employees are mostly female, they work for contractors or subcontractors, wages are low (often below subsistence), the jobs are tedious and require little skill. The factories are run in military fashion, often by abusive managers. This is all very attractive to MNCs, as is the fact that the zones are tax-free, at least for the early years that the work is done in them (companies often shut down, or simply change their name, at the end of an initial tax holiday in order to avoid paying taxes). That means that raw materials are shipped in tax-free and finished products leave tax-free. As Klein (2009: 207) puts it, this amounts to "zero-risk globalization."

Conditions in Rosario are atrocious with much pollution, rivers of sewage, scarce running water, crime, exploding population, and so on. The factories are run in an iron-fisted manner with tight restrictions on bathroom breaks (employees are sometimes forced to urinate in plastic bags hidden under their machines), talking, even smiling. Workers not only earn low wages, they may work overtime for a few donuts, but no extra pay. The MNCs that benefit from all this often claim that it is not their business since the work is not being done for them but for sub-contractors.

Neoliberalism by exception can take a variety of forms, many of them less formal and less audacious than those created in China and the Philippines. For example, in Asia several countries have set up special zones for labor, tourism, the growing and harvesting of timber, science parks, and knowledge centers. In a negative sense, these zones are not controlled by national laws on such issues as "taxation, labor rights, or ethnic representation," while in a positive sense these zones are free to "promote opportunities to upgrade skilled workers, to improve social and infrastructural facilities, to experiment with greater political rights, and so on" (Ong 2006b: 78).

Ong calls the political result of constructing these zones **graduated sovereignty**. That is, instead of governing the entire geographic area of the nation-state, the national government retains full control in some areas, but surrenders various degrees of control in others to corporations and other entities. While the creation of these zones may bring a series of economic advantages, it also can create problems for the nation-state that is no longer in full control of its own borders. (This is yet another indication of the decline of the nation-state.) Another example of neoliberalism as exception involves the creation of **growth triangles**, or largely autonomous areas that link contiguous areas of neighboring countries. One example is the Singapore/Jahore-Riau Triangle (Sijori) spanning Indonesia, Malaysia, and Singapore. Such areas allow the exploitation of complementary resources that exist in the border areas between countries.

Export Processing Zone (EPZ): Independent area controlled by corporations and free of national control.

Graduated sovereignty: National government retains full control in some areas, but surrenders some control in others to corporations and other entities.

Growth triangles: Largely autonomous domains linking neighboring countries allowing for the exploitation of resources that exist on the border.

Ong is primarily concerned with neoliberalism as exception, but she also deals with *exceptions to neoliberalism*. These can be double-edged. On the one hand, such exceptions can be used by the state to protect its citizens from the ravages of neoliberalism. For example, subsidized housing can be maintained even if a city's budgetary practices come to be dominated by neoliberal entities and processes. On the other hand, they can be used to worsen the effects of neoliberalism. For example, corporations can exclude certain groups (e.g. migrant workers) from improvements in the standard of living.

NEOLIBERALISM: THE CASE OF ISRAEL

Uri Ram (2008, 2009) has analyzed the globalization of Israel. While he approaches the issue in a variety of ways, one of the dominant themes is the impact of neoliberalism on Israel, especially, but not exclusively, on its economy.

Among the economic changes in Israel in recent years is the trend toward selling off public companies and curbing Israel's traditionally powerful labor unions. This has been pushed by both the rising bourgeoisie and administrative elites who have bought into the Washington Consensus. In addition to those two steps, the neoliberalism of the Washington Consensus led to a variety of other steps including exposing local markets to imports, liberalization of the Israeli currency, deregulation of business practices, reducing taxes, reducing public expenditures, cutting public debt, and drastic reductions in welfare spending (Ram 2008: 20).

As a result of such changes, Israel has improved its global ranking in terms of competitiveness in world markets. Capitalists and upper-level executives have enriched themselves, but the working classes have suffered substantial declines with the result that there are growing disparities in income distribution in Israel. This is related to the growth of a new labor market in Israel that includes the exportation of sites of production, the importation of labor, the subcontracting of employment, and the increase in part-time work.

The power of the capitalist in Israel has been enhanced by two factors:

> First, the development of information, communication, and transportation technologies, which contributed simultaneously to a more concerted and potent management control and to a more fragmented and dislocated labor force; and second, on the basis of the same material infrastructure, the development of transnational networks of material and symbolic transactions, the major components of globalization. (Ram 2008: 96)

Not only do these developments increase the power of the capitalists, they also weaken the public sphere as well as labor unions and labor parties.

The adoption of neoliberal policies has not only led to dramatic changes in the economy, but also in the polity. From its inception, Israel had been dominated by Zionism and Zionist socialism with a corresponding emphasis on a strong state. As a result of the movement toward a neoliberal agenda, there has been movement toward privatization and therefore toward the "destatization of Israeli society" (Ram 2008: 28). Associated with this is the fact that the traditionally dominant political elites have been increasingly replaced by economic elites. Capital has become increasingly hegemonic in Israel.

Similarly, the famous kibbutz[16] system is undergoing radical change. Traditionally, the kibbutz was owned cooperatively and overseen by a general assembly. However, in recent years the economic aspects of the kibbutz have been separated out and come to be run by economic experts. As a result, the kibbutz is increasingly coming to resemble a suburb with associated high-tech industries oriented to the export business.

THE END OF HISTORY

A well-known and wide-ranging argument implies that the neoliberalism discussed throughout this chapter is the culmination of history and that no major changes are to be expected in it. Neoliberalism is not only seen as a good thing, but it is with us for the foreseeable future, if not forever.

This argument is to be found in Francis Fukuyama's (1989, 1992) "The End of History?"; one of the most controversial essays (and books) in recent intellectual history. It achieved great notoriety and was the subject of much discussion, both pro and con. Because of its broad philosophical approach, it was, and is, relevant to a variety of disciplines and topics, not the least of which is globalization. Fukuyama suggests a model of economic and political liberalism that he sees becoming increasingly dominant throughout the globe. To put it more specifically, liberal ideas and liberal structures, especially political and economic, have become increasingly predominant throughout the world.

Fukuyama's starting point is the philosophy of G. W. F. Hegel and his focus on the evolution of ideas. It was Napoleon's victory over the Prussian monarchy at the Battle of Jena in 1806 that marked, in Hegel's eyes, the "end of history" (at least to that point in time) in the sense that it indicated the triumph of the ideas of the French Revolution – liberty and equality – and of the state that incorporated those ideas. That state was liberal in that its system of law protected people's universal right to freedom. It was democratic in that the state's existence required the consent of the governed. Such a liberal state was the end of history in the sense that it, as well as the ideas on which it was based, could not be improved upon.

Fukuyama clarifies what he (and Hegel) means by the "end of history": "This did not mean that the natural cycle of birth, life and death would end, that important events would no longer happen, or that newspapers reporting them would cease to be published. It meant rather, that there would be no further progress in the development of underlying principles and institutions, because all of the really big questions had been settled" (Fukuyama 1992: xii). Thus, the end of history is the end of big ideas and big systems built on the basis of those ideas. Many things continue to happen and to change after the end of history, but those transformations are never again monumental.

The end of history is clear in Fukuyama's discussion of several big idea systems including fascism, communism, and liberalism (both political and economic). His basic argument is that fascism as an alternative idea system was destroyed as a result of the defeat of the fascist powers (Nazi Germany, Japan, Italy) in WW II. This left communism as a competing idea system to liberalism, but it has virtually disappeared with the demise of the Soviet Union and the movement of China toward a liberal (i.e. capitalistic) economic system. It is true that China retains a "communist" state, but that appears to be the case in name only as that state increasingly functions as an adjunct to the capitalistic economy. With the demise of communism (and fascism), we are at the end of history in that there is no longer any ideological alternative to liberalism and now neoliberalism.

One problem with this view is that a similar proclamation by Hegel in the early nineteenth century proved premature. We later witnessed the rise of various alternative ideologies including fascism and communism. This leads one to wonder whether Fukuyama, too, is being premature in his end of history proclamation and whether other big idea systems will arise in the future to compete with (neo)liberalism.

In terms of globalization, the Fukuyama thesis means, in effect, the eventual global hegemony of liberal ideology, as well as the liberal state and a liberal economy. Thus, this perspective is clearly aligned with neoliberalism. In terms of the liberal economy, Fukuyama accords great importance to consumption, consumer goods and a "universal consumer culture" (Fukuyama 1989: 119). Any ideology, state, and/or economy that is unable to deliver the (consumer) goods is doomed to failure in the contemporary world. Since it is only the liberal varieties of each that produce the abundance needed for a consumer society, it is clear that there are no alternatives to them. The implication is ever-increasing homogenization across the globe in terms of the (liberal) ideology, state, and economy.

While Fukuyama is clearly pleased with this development, he worries at the end of his essay about how "boring" the triumph of liberalism, and the absence of alternatives, will be. The earlier ideological struggles led to "daring, courage, imagination and idealism," but that is now being replaced by "economic calculation, the endless solving of technical problems, environmental concerns, and the satisfaction of sophisticated consumer demands."[17] This leads Fukuyama to hope that the realization that we are doomed to centuries of boredom will lead to efforts to get history started again, presumably by the creation of newer and even better sets of big ideas.

There are innumerable weaknesses and problems with Fukuyama's end of history argument. From the point of view of globalization, it subscribes to neoliberal economics with the usual result of ignoring the condition of the global have-nots as well the possibility that their economic situation is made worse, not better, by globalization. Furthermore, it announces rather bizarrely that the issue of class has been resolved successfully in the West and that the Marxian dream of a classless society has been essentially achieved in the United States. This will offer little solace to the tens of millions of Americans who live below the poverty line. It also accords economic centrality to consumption and consumerism and ignores those who are largely left out of consumer society, to say nothing of the disastrous environmental effects of such a society. It also accepts consumerism unquestioningly without addressing the many criticisms of a society that is overly devoted to consumption (Barber 2007). In addition, it reaffirms the centrality of the (liberal) nation-state when many globalization scholars see the nation-state as being of declining importance in the global age. Finally, Fukuyama does not see much of a threat to the global hegemony of liberalism emanating from either religion, including religious fundamentalism, or nationalism. However, at the moment, that hegemony is under attack from both directions – the religious fundamentalism of Islam and the growing nationalism in places like Russia and Venezuela.

More generally, it reaffirms a grand narrative of the historical movement toward the neoliberal society in an era in which the postmodern critique should have led Fukuyama to be more wary of such an approach and more reflexive about it. It also celebrates in a totalistic fashion the global triumph of the West in general and the United States in particular. Fukuyama has an unquestioned belief in material wealth and abundance, as well as in the fact that they will lead to liberal democracy.

It might be for these reasons that Fukuyama's more recent writings seem to back off from his "end of history" argument. For example, in 2011, Fukuyama acknowledged the ascendancy and stability of China, which, contrary to his original thesis, has occurred without the principles and institutions of liberal ideology. At the same time, among other problems, "the American system shows little appetite for dealing with long-term fiscal challenges" (Fukuyama 2011). Fukuyama no longer seems to be claiming that this ideological system cannot be improved upon. Instead, he argues that "US democracy has little to teach China," which boasts state-owned enterprises, a wealth of consumerist goods, and is capable of making "large, complex decisions quickly, and to make them relatively well, at least in economic policy." While their model has many issues of its own (e.g. rising inequality and widespread environmental degradation), it shows no signs of slowing down soon and offers an ideological competitor to the dominant neoliberal ideology. This has led some other commentators to declare "the end of the end of history" (*Economist* 2011).

THE DEATH OF NEOLIBERALISM?

In the wake of the Great Recession, many people called for, and predicted, the beginning of the end of neoliberalism. For example, in a speech in 2008 former French president Nicolas Sarkozy said: "The idea of the absolute power of the markets that should not be constrained by any rule, by any political intervention, was a mad idea. The idea that markets are always right was a mad idea." Referring implicitly to the global economic system dominated to that point by neoliberalism, Sarkozy argued that "we need to rebuild the whole world financial and monetary system from scratch." In other words, we need to scuttle the remnants of the global neoliberal economic system, just as the Keynesian system was scuttled as neoliberalism gained ascendancy, and replace it with some as yet undefined alternative. Accordingly, scholars have begun to theorize what a post-neoliberal society might look like (Macdonald and Ruckert 2009; Peck et al. 2009).

But despite the mounting resistance to neoliberalism in the wake of the Great Recession, many governments have continued their neoliberal policies. For example, the Obama administration continued to staff its cabinet with neoliberal economists (Leonhardt 2011), several European countries have maintained extreme austerity measures that prioritized deregulation over social welfare (Jolly 2012), and "most of the 'solutions' to the crisis are in the spirit of neoliberalism, rather than enraptured by neoliberal spirit" (Aalbers 2013: 1083). If nothing else, the ongoing economic crises and the social movements that have fought back against neoliberalism have reminded us of the importance of neo-Marxian thinking which, at its base, is critical of neoliberalism and the capitalist system that is, to a large extent, erected on a (neo)liberal foundation.

NEO-MARXIAN THEORETICAL ALTERNATIVES TO NEOLIBERALISM

We have already presented critiques of neoliberalism from a neo-Marxian perspective (e.g. those of David Harvey), but neo-Marxists have done more than critique neoliberalism; they have developed their own perspectives on, and theories of, capitalism. While neoliberalism is supportive of capitalism, the neo-Marxists are, needless to say, critical of it. In this section we offer two examples of a neo-Marxian approach that are explicitly and implicitly critical of the neoliberal theory outlined in this chapter.

TRANSNATIONAL CAPITALISM

Leslie Sklair distinguishes between two systems of globalization (Sklair 2002). The first – the neoliberal capitalist system of globalization – is the one that, as we have seen, is now predominant. The other is the socialist system that is not yet in existence, but is foreshadowed by current alter-globalization movements, especially those oriented toward greater human rights throughout the world (see Chapter 15). The alter-globalization movements, and the possibility of socialism, are made possible by the problems in the current system of neoliberal globalization, especially class polarization and the increasing ecologically unsustainable capitalist globalization.

While the nation-state remains important in his view, it is the case that Sklair focuses on transnational practices that are able to cut across boundaries – including those created by nation-states – with the implication that territorial boundaries are of declining importance in capitalist globalization. As a Marxist, Sklair accords priority to economic transnational practices and it is in this context that one of the central aspects of his analysis – *transnational corporations* – predominates. Underlying this is the idea that capitalism has moved away from being an inter-national system to a globalizing system that is decoupled from any specific geographic territory or nation-state.

The second transnational practice of great importance is political and here the *transnational capitalist class* predominates (Sklair 2009, 2012). However, it is not made up of capitalists in the traditional Marxian sense of the term. That is, they do not necessarily own the means of production. Sklair differentiates among four "fractions" of the transnational capitalist class. The first is the *corporate fraction* made up of executives of transnational corporations and their local affiliates. Second, there is a *state fraction* composed of globalizing state and inter-state bureaucrats and politicians. The third, *technical fraction* is made up of globalizing professionals. Finally, there is the *consumerist fraction* encompassing merchants and media executives. These four fractions are obviously very different from the capitalists conceptualized by Marx.

The transnational capitalist class may not be capitalist in a traditional sense, but it is transnational in various ways (see Figure 4.1 for a look at the richest of the transnational capitalist class and their official countries of residence). First, its "members" tend to share global (as well as local) interests. Second, they seek to exert various types of control across nations. That is, they exert economic control in the workplace, political control in both domestic and international politics, and culture-ideological control in everyday life across international borders. Third, they tend to share a global rather than a local perspective on a wide range of issues. Fourth, they come from many different countries, but increasingly they see themselves as citizens of the world and not just of their place of birth. Finally, wherever they may be at any given time, they share similar lifestyles, especially in terms of the goods and services they consume.

The third transnational practice is culture-ideology and here Sklair accords great importance to the *culture-ideology of consumerism* in capitalist globalization. While the focus is on culture and ideology, this ultimately involves the economy by adding an interest in consumption to the traditional concern with production (and the transnational corporations) in economic approaches in general, and Marxian theories in particular. It is in this realm that the ability to exert ideological control over people scattered widely throughout the globe increased dramatically primarily through the greater reach and sophistication of advertising, the media, and the bewildering array of consumer goods that are marketed by

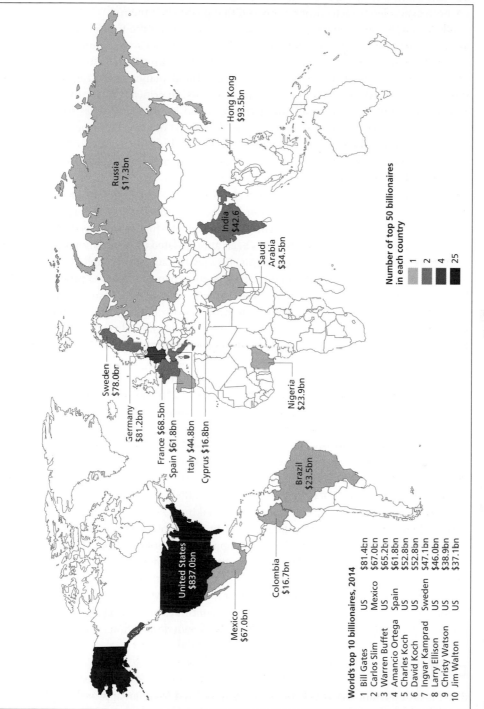

Figure 4.1 The top 50 billionaires. This figure shows the world's top 50 billionaires, which is just a small fraction of the transnational capitalist class. While the wealthiest individuals are spread around the globe, they are disproportionately concentrated in the USA. Source: data from Bloomberg Billionaires: Today's ranking of the world's richest people (http://www.bloomberg.com/billionaires/2014-06-04/adq).

Map labels:

Hong Kong $93.5bn

Russia $17.3bn

India $42.6

Saudi Arabia $34.5bn

Sweden $78.0br

Germany $81.2bn

France $68.5bn

Spain $61.8bn

Italy $44.8bn

Cyprus $16.8bn

Nigeria $23.9bn

Brazil $23.5bn

United States $837.0bn

Colombia $16.7bn

Mexico $67.0bn

Number of top 50 billionaires in each country
1
2
4
25

World's top 10 billionaires, 2014

1	Bill Gates	US	$81.4bn
2	Carlos Slim	Mexico	$67.0bn
3	Warren Buffet	US	$65.2bn
4	Amancio Ortega	Spain	$61.8bn
5	Charles Koch	US	$52.8bn
6	David Koch	US	$52.8bn
7	Ingvar Kamprad	Sweden	$47.1bn
8	Larry Ellison	US	$46.0bn
9	Christy Watson	US	$38.9bn
10	Jim Walton	US	$37.1bn

and through them. Ultimately, they all served to create a global desire to consume what benefits transnational corporations, as well as the advertising and media corporations that are both examples of such corporations and that profit from them.

Ultimately, Sklair is interested in the relationship among the transnational social practices and the institutions that dominate each by arguing that transnational corporations utilize the transnational capitalist class to develop and solidify the consumerist culture and ideology that grew increasingly necessary to feed the demands of the capitalist system of production. As a Marxist, Sklair is not only interested in critically analyzing capitalist globalization, but in articulating an alternative to it and its abuses. He sees some promising signs in the protectionism (anathema to neoliberalism) of some countries that see themselves as exploited by transnational corporations. Also hopeful are new social movements such as the green movement seeking a more sustainable environment and the various alter-globalization groups that have sprung up in recent years. He is particularly interested in various human rights movements in which, he believes, can be found the seeds of the alternative to neoliberal capitalist globalization, i.e. socialist globalization. He predicts that these and other movements will gain momentum in the twenty-first century as they increasingly resist the ways in which globalization has been appropriated by transnational corporations. In fact, in good Marxian dialectical terms, he sees the success of capitalist globalization sowing the seeds of its own destruction. That is, its expansion tends to provide the opponents with resources (derived from the economic success of transnational capitalism), organizational forms (copied from the successful organizations in global capitalism), and most obviously a clarity of purpose. That is, as the transnational corporations grow more successful, so do their abuses and the need to supplant them as the central players in the global system.

Precariat:
the growing number of part-time workers, temporary workers, and others living precariously without stable jobs, occupational identities, or social protections.

Another group that has emerged as a result of neoliberal policies, and is likely to fight against neoliberalism, is the **precariat**. In his book, *The Precariat: The Dangerous New Class*, Guy Standing (2011a) describes the growing number of part-time workers, temporary workers, and others living precariously without stable jobs or social protections. As neoliberalism has promoted "flexible" labor policies and dismantled welfare states and other social protections, people around the world increasingly find themselves in these precarious jobs, without a particular occupational identity or a sense of what their next job will be. While Standing does not believe that they constitute a new social class yet, they do share common experiences and are a "class-in-the-making." As they begin to recognize their common vulnerabilities, such as their insecurity in the job market and inability to build a career, they will attain a class consciousness opposed to neoliberalism. Standing points out that these shared experiences have already motivated many marches against austerity programs in Greece, the widespread rejection of mainstream political parties in Spain, and protests by educated but unemployed youth in the Middle East (Standing 2011b). Accordingly, as the transnational capitalist class continues promoting neoliberalism and the precariat grows, it might be sowing the seeds of its own destruction.

EMPIRE

The most important and widely discussed and debated Marxian approach to globalization is Michael Hardt and Antonio Negri's *Empire* (2000) (as well as the closely associated *Multitude* [2004]). Although they have reservations about postmodern social theory, they analyze the postmodernization of the global economy. They associate modernity with *imperialism* (see Chapter 3), the defining characteristic of which is a nation(s) at the center that controls and exploits, especially economically, a number of areas throughout the world. In a postmodern move, they *decenter* this process thereby defining Empire as a postmodern reality in which such dominance exists, but *without* any single nation (or any other entity) at its center. To put this argument another way, modern sovereignty can be traced to a *place*, but in its postmodern form as **Empire** sovereignty exists in a non-place.[18] Sovereignty exists in a non-place because there is no center, it is deterritorialized, it is virtual in the form of communication (especially through the media) and, as a result, the spectacle and the reality of Empire is everywhere; it is omnipresent.

Empire: Decentered global dominance.

Empire does not yet exist fully; it is in formation at the moment, but we can already get a sense of its parameters. Empire governs the world with a single logic of rule, but there is no single power at the heart of empire. Instead of a single source of command, power is dispersed throughout society and the globe. Even the US, in spite of its seeming hegemony in the world today, is not an empire in these terms nor does it lie at the heart of Hardt and Negri's sense of an empire. However, the sovereignty of the US does constitute an important precursor to Empire and the US continues to occupy a privileged position in the world today. Nonetheless, it is in the process of being supplanted by Empire.

Empire is lacking in (or will lack) geographic or territorial boundaries. It can also be seen as lacking temporal boundaries in the sense that it seeks (albeit unsuccessfully) to suspend history (shades of Fukuyama!) and to exist for all eternity. It also can be seen as lacking a lower boundary in that it seeks to expand downward into the depths of the social world. This means that it seeks control of the basics of the social world (thought, action, interaction, groups), and goes even further in an effort to use biopower to control human nature and population; *both* peoples' brains and their bodies.[19] In a way, Empire is far more ambitious than imperialism in that it seeks to control the entirety of life down to its most basic levels.

The key to the global power of *Empire* lies in the fact that it is (or seeks to be) a new juridical power. That is, it is based on the constitution of order, norms, ethical truths, a common notion of what is right, and so on. This juridical formation is the source of the power of Empire. Thus, it can, in the name of what is "right," intervene anywhere in the world in order to deal with what it considers humanitarian problems, to guarantee accords, and to impose peace on those who may not want it or even see it as peace. More specifically, it can engage in "just wars" in the name of this juridical formation; the latter legitimates the former. Such wars become a kind of sacred undertaking. The enemy is anyone or anything that the juridical formation sees as a threat to the ethical order, as it defines such an order, in the world. Thus the right to engage in just war is seen as boundless encompassing the entire space of civilization. The right to engage in it is also seen as boundless in time; it is permanent, eternal. In a just war, ethically grounded military action is legitimate and its goal is to achieve the desired order and peace. Thus Empire is not based on force per se, but on the ability to project force in the service of that which is right (precursors of this can be seen in the two US wars against Iraq, as well as the incursion into Afghanistan).

Empire is based on a triple imperative. First, it seeks to incorporate all that it can. It appears to be magnanimous and it operates with a (neo)liberal facade. However, in the process of inclusion, it creates a "smooth" world in which differences, resistance, and conflict are eliminated. Second, Empire differentiates and affirms differences. While those who are different are celebrated culturally, they are set apart and aside juridically. Third, once the differences are in place, Empire seeks to hierarchize and to manage the hierarchy and the differences embedded in it. It is hierarchization and management that are the sources of the real power of Empire.

Empire is, then, a postmodern Marxian perspective on globalization and the exertion of power around the world. However, instead of capitalists, or capitalist nations, exerting that power, it is the much more nebulous Empire that is in control. If there are no more capitalists in Empire, what about the proletariat? To Hardt and Negri, the time of the proletariat is over. But if the proletariat no longer exists to oppose Empire, where is the opposition to it to come from? After all, operating from a Marxian perspective, Hardt and Negri must come up with an oppositional force. In fact, they do not disappoint on this score and label that oppositional group the "multitude." This is an interesting choice of a term for many reasons. First, it is much more general and abstract than the proletariat and also moves us away from a limited focus on the economy. Second, it is clear that there are lots of at least potential opponents of Empire; indeed, those in control in Empire constitute only a small minority vis-à-vis the multitude.

The *multitude* is that collection of people throughout the world that sustains Empire in various ways, including, but *not* restricted to, its labor (it is the real productive force in empire). It includes a vast number of groups that are marginalized in, and exploited by, Empire; at each point of domination, there will be resistance. The multitude encompasses marginalized "cultures, races, ethnicities, genders, and sexual orientations; different forms of labor; different ways of living; different views of the world," which are all unified by their opposition to capital (Hardt and Negri 2004: xiii). Among other ways, the multitude also sustains Empire by buying into the culture-ideology of consumerism and, more importantly, in actually consuming a variety of its offerings. Like capitalism and its relationship to the proletariat, Empire is a parasite on the multitude and its creativity and productivity. Like Marx's proletariat (which all but disappears in this theory), the multitude is a force for creativity in Empire. Also like the proletariat, the multitude is capable of overthrowing Empire through the autonomous creation of a counter-Empire. The counter-Empire, like Empire, is, or would be, a global phenomenon created out of, and becoming, global flows and exchanges. Globalization leads to **deterritorialization** (and the multitude itself is a force in deterritorialization and is deterritorialized) and the latter is a prerequisite to the global liberation of the multitude. That is, with deterritorialization social revolution can, as Marx predicted, occur, perhaps for the first time, on a global level.

Deterritorialization: Declining significance of the geographic location in which culture exists.

Thus, while Hardt and Negri are certainly critics of globalization, whether it be modern neoliberal capitalist imperialism or postmodern empire, they also see a utopian potential in globalization. Thus, globalization per se is *not* the problem, but rather the neoliberal form that it has taken, or takes, in imperialism and Empire. That utopian potential has always been there, but in the past it has been smothered by modern sovereign powers through ideological control or military force. Empire now occupies, or soon will, that controlling position, but its need to suppress that potential is counterbalanced by the need of the multitude to manifest and express that utopian potential. Ultimately, it is in globalization that there exists the potential for universal freedom and equality. Further, globalization prevents us from falling back into the particularism and isolationism that has characterized much of human history. Those processes, of course, would serve to impede the global change sought by the multitude. More positively, as globalization progresses, it serves to push us more and more in the direction of the creation of counter-Empire. This focus on the global serves to distinguish Hardt and Negri from other postmodernists and post-Marxists who tend to focus on the local/national and the problems and potential that exist there.[20] In contrast, in their view, a focus on the local serves to obscure the fact that the sources of both our major problems and our liberation exist at the global level, in Empire.

While Hardt and Negri foresee counter-Empire, they, like Marx in the case of communism, offer no blueprint for how to get there or for what it might look like. Like communism to Marx, counter-Empire will arise out of actual practice (*praxis*), especially that of the multitude. Counter-Empire must be global, it must be everywhere, and it must be opposed to Empire. Counter-Empire is made increasingly likely because Empire is losing its ability to control the multitude. Thus, Empire must re-double its efforts (e.g. through police power) and this serves to mobilize the multitude and make counter-Empire more likely. As postmodernists, Hardt and Negri reject a focus on the agent of the type found in Marxian theory, specifically the centrality accorded to the proletarian revolutionary agent who is increasingly conscious of exploitation by capitalism. Instead, they focus on such non-agential, collective actions by the multitude as desertion, migration, and nomadism. In accord with their postmodern orientation and its focus on the body, Hardt and Negri urge a new "barbarism" involving new bodily forms of the kind that are now appearing in the realm of gender, sexuality, and esthetic mutations (such as tattooing and body piercing). Such bodies are less likely to submit to external control and more likely to create a new life; the basis of counter-Empire. Thus, the revolutionary force is not conscious agents, but new bodily, corporeal forms.

While Hardt and Negri retain a Marxian interest in production, they do recognize a new world of production and work in which immaterial, intellectual, and communicative labor are increasingly central. Thus, control over those engaged in such work – a key element and increasing proportion of multitude – is of increasing importance. However, while they are controlled through global communication and ideology (especially via the media), it is also through communication and ideology that the revolutionary potential of the multitude will be expressed. The key to communication is that it flows easily and effectively across the globe. This makes it easier for Empire to exert control, to organize production globally, and to make its justification of itself and its actions immanent within that communication. Conversely, of course, it is also the mechanism by which the multitude can ultimately create counter-Empire.

CHAPTER SUMMARY

This chapter examines the impact of neoliberal theory on globalization. Neoliberal theory, as well as the discourse that emerged as a reaction to it, has significantly influenced economics and politics. It can also be seen as being, in whole or in part, an ideology.

Neoliberal theory emerged in the 1930s as a combination of the liberal commitment to individual liberty and neo-classical economics. The free operation of the market and minimal intervention by the state were the cornerstones of the theory. The end of the Depression era marked the second stage of development of the theory; it entered a phase of embedded liberalism. Under the influence of welfare-state-based Keynesian economics, the market, corporations, and individuals came to be embedded in a regulative environment. The Austrian School, under the leadership of Hayek and von Mises, launched a staunch effort to counter such interventionism. The movement grew stronger, as the University of Chicago became an important center of neoliberal thinking and a training ground for neoliberals under the tutelage of Milton Friedman.

A key mechanism in neoliberal economics was the administering of a "shock doctrine," designed to invigorate the economy through shock tactics such as privatization of industry, deregulation, and reduction of public spending on social welfare programs. While the initial experiment in Chile proved unsuccessful, modified versions were applied by the Thatcher and Reagan governments in the UK and the US respectively.

Later, much of the world was coerced into accepting neoliberalism, at least in part through the efforts of the IMF and the World Bank, which practiced a particular form of shock therapy known as "structural adjustment." In order to qualify for financial loans from these institutions, receiving countries had to restructure their economies in line with neoliberal policy. The theory was referred to as the Washington Consensus, due to its close association with the US. The structural adjustment approach has been severely criticized for leading to a growth in inequality. It has also faced opposition from alter-globalization movements.

The third stage entails a transition of neoliberalism to neoconservatism, which has a strong commitment to order and the need to impose it on the rest of the world. A potential fourth stage lies in the development of an organic, left alliance involving workers, and racial, ethnic, and gender minorities all of which are to resist neoliberal (and neoconservative) globalization.

Under neoliberalism, the operation of free markets is considered to be crucial. It emphasizes a commitment to deregulation of the markets. Free markets are also portrayed as being intrinsically linked to a democratic political system that facilitates individual economic well-being. Tax cuts are advocated as a mechanism to stimulate investment in the economy, which consequently demands a reduction of government expenditure, especially in terms of welfare expenditure.

Although the theory advocates "limited government," it favors state intervention to facilitate the business interests and the reduction of barriers to the free movement of capital across national borders. Rather than rendering the state irrelevant, neoliberalism has modified the functioning of the state in order to facilitate the functioning of the market. Friedman contends that this removal of barriers has leveled the global playing field. This enables everyone to benefit from a supposedly *flat world*.

Polanyi's critique of neoliberalism highlights the fact that the laissez-faire system came into existence through the assistance of the state. Left to itself, that system threatens to destroy society. Free markets induce a natural collective reaction by society.

Neoliberalism has been criticized for its narrow definition of well-being, which is equated with economic well-being. The theory also conceals the vested interests of those who push for such an economic system. Adoption of neoliberal theory has produced severe financial crisis in various countries, and has led to increasing commodification as well as environmental degradation.

Ong emphasizes that *neoliberalism as an exception* can be distinguished from *exceptions to neoliberalism*. An instance of the former would be special economic zones, wherein markets have the maximum freedom. While formal control of these areas is in the hands of the nation-state, de facto power rests with the MNCs that operate within these zones. Exceptions to neoliberalism are double-edged. While the state can use exceptions to protect citizens from volatility under neoliberalism, they might also be used to worsen the effects of neoliberalism.

Fukuyama locates the end of history in neoliberalism. Neoliberalism is not only seen as a positive development, but also as an inextricable part of the foreseeable future. While this has been a popular argument for many years, inherent weaknesses of the argument, and recent developments, have made Fukuyama's thesis less convincing.

Neoliberal theory has evoked implicit as well as explicit criticism from neo-Marxian thinkers. Sklair places emphasis on transnational practices that are able to cut across boundaries – through transnational corporations, the transnational capitalist class, and the culture-ideology of capitalism. Transnational corporations utilize the capitalist class to develop and solidify the consumerist ideology that is necessary to meet the demands of the capitalist system. Hardt and Negri critique the neoliberal form of globalization in terms of imperialism and empire. They locate a postmodern turn in imperialism, leading to a decentering of the imperialist empire and the creation of Empire. However, they accord positive potential to the process of globalization, foreseeing a counter-Empire characterized by non-agential collective action.

DISCUSSION QUESTIONS

1. Are globalization and neoliberalism two sides of the same coin? Discuss.

2. What are the positive developments that emerged from the neoliberal perspective? Discuss the reasons for the popularity of this perspective in various academic, policy, and business spheres.

3. Discuss Fukuyama's perspective on the "end of history." In light of current events can it be said that we might witness the end of neoliberalism?

4. Examine Polanyi's critique of neoliberalism. How does it differ from later neo-Marxist critiques implied in the work of Sklair or Hardt and Negri?

5. Is neoliberalism to "blame" for the Great Recession?

ADDITIONAL READINGS

Milton Friedman. *Capitalism and Freedom*. Chicago: University of Chicago Press, 1950.

David Harvey. *A Brief History of Neoliberalism*. Oxford: Oxford University Press, 2005.

Johan Norberg. *In Defense of Global Capitalism*. Washington, DC: Cato Institute, 2003.

Naomi Klein. *The Shock Doctrine: The Rise of Disaster Capitalism*. New York: Metropolitan Books, 2007.

Narcís Serra and Joseph E. Stiglitz, eds. *The Washington Consensus Reconsidered: Towards a New Global Governance*. New York: Oxford University Press, 2008.

Colin Crouch. *The Strange Non-Death of Neo-Liberalism*. Malden, MA: Polity, 2011.

Thomas Friedman. *The Lexus and the Olive Tree: Understanding Globalization*. New York: Picador, 2012.

Karl Polanyi, *The Great Transformation: The Political and Economic Origins of Our Time*. Boston: Beacon Press, 1944.

Aiwha Ong. *Neoliberalism as Exception: Mutations in Citizenship and Sovereignty*. Durham, NC: Duke University Press, 2006.

Leslie Sklair. *Globalization: Capitalism and Its Alternatives*. Oxford: Oxford University Press, 2002.

Michael Hardt and Antonio Negri. *Empire*. Cambridge, MA: Harvard University Press, 2000.

Jamie Peck. *Constructions of Neoliberal Reason*. New York: Oxford University Press, 2010.

NOTES ···

1   In fact, it could be seen as more a *metatheory*, as a theory that overarches many specific theories, than a theory. However, we will mainly treat it as a theory in this chapter; see Ritzer (1991).

2   On the role of neoliberalism in another Latin American country, see Babb (2001).

3   She also argues that it has been used within the US, as well, such as the example of the natural shock of Hurricane Katrina, and its aftermath, in New Orleans.

4   Many feel that the Washington Consensus has eroded and has long since passed its peak; see Held (2005: 95–113); Broad (2004: 129–54).

5   Where he made news by making comments about women that were almost as reprehensible as those that follow about less developed nations.

6   Cited in Ferguson (2006: 70).

7   Cited in Ferguson (2006: 70).

8   Others are Dollar and Fischer; Dollar and Kraay (2002: 195–225); also see Fischer (2003: 1–30).

9   http://www.freetheworld.com/release_2006.html; Easterly (2006a: 29–41). More generally, see Easterly (2006b).

10 While a capitalist, Soros (2000) is critical of this idea, especially that a free market will take care of common interests and a democratic society.

11 Another argument is that increases in government expenditures trickle down to those in the lower social classes.

12 This is Karl Marx's concept; see Ritzer (2008c: 61).

13 For one of many critiques see Steingart (2008).

14 Many have applied Polanyi's ideas to the contemporary world. See, for example, Munck (2006: 175–86; Da Costa and McMichael 2007).

15 www.margaretthatcher.org/speeches.

16 The kibbutz was a collective, usually based in agriculture, that operated on socialist principles.

17 Fukuyama (1989). Reprinted in Tuathail, Dalby, and Routledge (1998: 114–24).

18 Hardt and Negri are using this term differently from others we will discuss such as Auge and Ritzer (see Chapter 8). Their meaning is closer to Castells' "spaces of flows" (as opposed to spaces of places).

19 Here Hardt and Negri are drawing on the work of Foucault.

20 See, for example, Seidman (1991; Antonio 1991).

GLOBAL POLITICAL STRUCTURES AND PROCESSES

Globalization: A Basic Text, Second Edition. George Ritzer and Paul Dean.
© 2015 John Wiley & Sons, Ltd. Published 2015 by John Wiley & Sons, Ltd.

The focal concern in this chapter is the political structures[1] involved in globalization. However, these structures, like all structures, are often better seen as processes (and flows) or as encompassing sets of processes. For example, a nation-state or a bureaucracy is often thought of as a structure, but in the main it is the sum of the processes (communication, decision-making, etc.) that take place within it. To put this another way, structures can be seen as "congealed flows." In that sense, the bulk of this chapter also deals with political processes (and flows). A primary focus of this chapter is to show how the nation-state, and its associated flows and structures, have been transformed within the era of globalization. As global and regional political organizations have emerged, and political processes spill across national borders, the nation-state continues to change in fascinating and unexpected ways. However, before we get to our focus on political structures, we need to be more explicit about the political flows themselves.

ON POLITICAL PROCESSES AND FLOWS

While the focus in this chapter will be on the development and nature of a wide range of political structures relevant to globalization, there certainly are a number of separable political processes and flows of various sorts that are relevant to an understanding of contemporary globalization. In fact, it could be argued that virtually all of the flows discussed throughout this book are political and of great relevance to political structures of all sorts. Some, of course, are of more direct political relevance than others.

- The global flow of people (Chapter 10), especially refugees and undocumented immigrants, poses a direct threat to the nation-state and its ability to control its borders.
- The looming crises associated with dwindling oil and water supplies (Chapter 7) threaten to lead to riots and perhaps insurrections that could lead to the downfall of existing governments.
- The inability of the nation-state to control economic flows dominated by MNCs, as well as the current economic and financial crisis that is sweeping the world (Chapter 7), is also posing profound threats to the nation-state (e.g. in Eastern Europe).
- Environmental problems of all sorts (Chapter 11), especially those related to global warming, are very likely to be destabilizing politically.
- Borderless diseases (Chapter 12), especially malaria, TB, and AIDs in Africa, pose a danger to political structures.
- War (Chapter 12) is the most obvious global flow threatening the nation-states involved, especially those on the losing side.
- Global inequalities (Chapters 13 and 14), especially the profound North–South split, threaten to pit poor nations against rich nations.
- Terrorism (Chapter 12) is clearly regarded as a threat by those nations against which it is waged.

Thus, a significant portion of this book deals with political processes, or with many processes that are directly or indirectly related to politics. In addition, there is a discussion (especially in Chapter 15) of various efforts to deal with global problems, many of which (e.g. trade protection and liberalization; efforts to increase political transparency and accountability) are political in nature. Finally, political structures (e.g. nation-states, UN) initiate a wide range of global flows (e.g. the violence sponsored by Robert Mugabe's government in Zimbabwe has led to the mass migration of millions of people from the country).

THE NATION-STATE

A series of treaties, known as the Peace of Westphalia (1648), ended the Thirty (and Eighty) Years' War(s) in Europe and instituted an international system which recognized sovereign states as its core. Thus, it is not sovereign states that were new (absolutist states, for example, had long existed), but rather the recognition accorded them at Westphalia. The treaties were widely interpreted as giving states the right to political self-determination, to be considered equal from a legal point of view, and as prohibiting them from intervening in the affairs of other sovereign states. Critics of the traditional interpretation of Westphalia contend that none of these things were inherent in the original treaties, but were read into it later by those who wanted to buttress the state system. Furthermore, it is argued that this interpretation set in motion an anarchic and conflictive relationship between states and perhaps set the stage for inter-state wars, especially WW I and WW II. Nevertheless, nation-states[2,3] remained preeminent until the current era of globalization when global processes began, at least in the eyes of many observers (including ours[4]), to undermine the nation-state (Hayman and Williams 2006).

The nation-state, of course, has two basic components – "nation" and "state." **Nation** "refers to a social group that is linked th[r]ough common descent, culture, language, or territorial contiguity" (Cerny 2007: 854). Also important in this context is **national identity**, the "fluid and dynamic form of collective identity, founded upon a community's subjective belief that the members of the community share a set of characteristics that make them different from other groups" (Guibernau 2007: 849–53; Chua and Ser Tan 2012). While the notion of a nation was highly circumscribed (e.g. regionally) in the Middle Ages, from the seventeenth century on the idea of nation was broadened and enlarged by a number of forces (political leaders, bureaucrats, the bourgeoisie, the proletariat, intellectuals, etc.) that pushed for **nationalism**, a doctrine and/or political movement that seeks to make the nation the basis of a political structure, especially a state (Hobsbawm 2012). The **state** emerged as a new institutional form in the wake of the demise of the feudal system. The state offered a more centralized form of control (in comparison to, say, city-states) and evolved an organizational structure with "relatively autonomous office-holders outside other socioeconomic hierarchies, with its own rules and resources increasingly coming from taxes rather than from feudal, personal or religious obligations" (Cerny 2007: 855). Also coming to define the state was its claim to sovereignty. This involved the ability to engage in collective action both internally (e.g. collect taxes) and externally (e.g. to deal with other states, to engage in warfare, etc.). The **nation-state** can therefore be seen as an integration of the sub-groups that defined themselves as a nation with the organizational structure that constituted the state.

THREATS TO THE NATION-STATE

As a result of the heritage of Westphalia, we came to think of the nation-state as an autonomous, rather self-contained,[5] entity, but in fact many of the global processes that slice through it (see below, as well as throughout this book), indicate that the nation-state is not,

---

Nation: Social group linked through common descent, culture, language, or territorial contiguity.

National identity: A fluid and dynamic form of collective identity; members of the community believe that they are different from other groups.

Nationalism: Doctrine and (or) political movement that seek to make the nation the basis of a political structure.

State: Organizational structure outside other socioeconomic hierarchies with relatively autonomous office-holders.

Nation-state: Integrates sub-groups that define themselves as a nation with the organizational structure of the state.

and undoubtedly has never been, such a "container." As a result, one observer concludes (and the authors would agree) that the "state is today highly contingent and in flux" (Cerny 2007: 854).

Global flows and processes

The nation-state is especially threatened by the global economy and global economic flows. An extreme argument is made by Ohmae who contends that "The uncomfortable truth is that, in terms of the global economy, nation-states have become little more than bit actors" (1996: 12). He talks in terms of a borderless global economy that nation-states are unable to control.

A similar argument is made by Strange who contends that the decline of the nation-state is linked to technological and financial changes, as well as to "the accelerated integration of national economies into one single global market economy" (Strange 1996: 13–14). While nation-states once controlled markets, it is now the markets that often control the nation-states. (We will have much more to say about these economic factors in the next two chapters.) In this context, Strange takes on the Westphalia system and dubs it a "Westfailure." She does so because the state has failed to control the financial system (she cites the Asian financial crisis, but the Great Recession is an even better example), to protect the environment, and to deal with social inequality (Strange 1999: 345–54).

There are a variety of other factors threatening the autonomy of the nation-state including flows of information, undocumented immigrants, new social movements, war, terrorists, criminals, drugs, money (including laundered money, and other financial instruments), sex-trafficking, and much else. Many of these flows have been made possible by the development and continual refinement of technologies of all sorts. The nation-state has also been weakened by the growing power of global and transnational organizations (e.g. the EU) that operate largely free of the control of nation-states. Another factor is the growth of global problems (AIDS, TB, global warming; see Chapters 11 and 12) that cannot be handled, or handled very well, by a nation-state operating on its own. A more specific historical factor is the end of the Cold War which had been a powerful force in unifying, or at least holding together, some nation-states. One example is Yugoslavia and its dissolution with the end of the Cold War, but the main one, of course, is the dissolution of the Soviet Union into a number of independent nation-states (Russia, Ukraine, Georgia, etc.). Then there are "failed states" (Boas and Jennings 2007) (e.g. Somalia) where there is, in effect, no functioning national government, as well as states that are in the process of breaking down (Li 2002; Foreign Policy and Fund for Peace 2013). Clearly, failed states, and states that are disintegrating, are in no position to maintain their borders adequately.

One way of summarizing much of this is to say that the nation-state has become increasingly *porous*. While this seems to be supported by a great deal of evidence, the fact is that no nation-state has *ever* been able to control its borders completely (Bauman 1992: 57). Thus, it is not the porosity of the nation-state that is new, but rather what is new is a dramatic *increase* in that porosity and of the kinds of flows that are capable of passing through national borders.

International human rights

Another threat to the autonomy of the nation-state is the growing interest in international human rights (Blau 2012; Chatterjee 2008; Donnelly 2013). Indeed, the issue of human rights, defined as the "entitlement of individuals to life, security, and well-being" (Turner

1993, 2007a: 591) has emerged as a major global political issue. It is argued that because these rights are universal, the nation-state cannot abrogate them.[6] As a result, global human rights groups have claimed the right to be able to have a say about what is done to people within (for example, torture of terror suspects) and between (for example, illegal trafficking in humans [Farr 2005]) sovereign states. Thus, in such a view, human rights are a global matter and not exclusively a concern of the state (Brysk 2013; Levy and Sznaider 2006). Furthermore, the implication is that the international community can and should intervene when a state violates human rights or when a violation occurs within a state border and the state does not take adequate action to deal with the violation.

A concern for human rights on a global scale emerged in reaction to the Holocaust (Bauman 1989) and other twentieth-century atrocities. On December 10, 1948, the UN General assembly approved a Universal Declaration of Human Rights. Below are a few of the Articles of this Declaration most relevant to its relationship to the nation-state.

Article 1

All human beings are born free and equal in dignity and rights. They are endowed with reason and conscience and should act towards one another in a spirit of brotherhood.

Article 2

Everyone is entitled to all the rights and freedoms set forth in this Declaration, without distinction of any kind, such as race, colour, sex, language, religion, political or other opinion, national or social origin, property, birth or other status.

Furthermore, no distinction shall be made on the basis of the political, jurisdictional or international status of the country or territory to which a person belongs, whether it be independent, trust, non-self governing or under any other limitation of sovereignty.

Article 13

(1) Everyone has the right to freedom of movement and residence within the borders of each State.
(2) Everyone has the right to leave any country, including his own, and to return to his country.

Article 15

(1) Everyone has the right to a nationality.
(2) No one shall be arbitrarily deprived of his nationality nor denied the right to change his nationality.

Article 19

Everyone has the right to freedom of opinion and expression; this right includes freedom to hold opinions without interference and to seek, receive and impart information and ideas through any media and regardless of frontiers.

Article 22

Everyone, as a member of society, has the right to social security and is entitled to realization, through national effort and international co-operation and in accordance with the organization and resources of each State, of the economic, social and cultural rights indispensable for his dignity and the free development of his personality.

Article 30

Nothing in this Declaration may be interpreted as implying for any State, group or person any right to engage in any activity or to perform any act aimed at the destruction of any of the rights and freedoms set forth herein.

What this Declaration and its Articles suggest is that human rights take precedence over the nation-state and that the UN is seeking to exert control over the state, at least on these issues.

As a result, at least in part, of growing interest in human rights in recent years, more people throughout the world have come to define themselves as global citizens and agitated against human rights abuses throughout the world. The creation of the International Criminal Court (ICC) in 2002 created a venue in which those accused of human rights abuses could be tried and found guilty (Schabas and McDermott 2012). However, such an international system is seen by some as a threat to the sovereignty of the nation-state (Sorensen 2007). As a result, the US, for one, has refused to recognize the ICC.

"Shadows of war"

Carolyn Nordstrom sees a different kind of threat to nation-states in what she calls the "shadows of war." Shadows of war are defined as "the complex sets of cross-state economic and political linkages that move outside *formally* recognized state-based channels" (Nordstrom 2004: 106, 2010). These "shadows of war" are *not* restricted by or to the nation-state; it is these "extra-state" processes (those that exist outside formal state channels; e.g. flows of black market goods) that are of central importance, especially in less developed countries. The myriad flows (e.g. of pharmaceuticals) that occur in this way help in the development of those countries and link them to transnational and cosmopolitan consumption sites. She concludes:

> The sheer power carried in extra-state systems – the power to shape global economic and political realities – demonstrates the partial nature of state authority. And this demonstrates that the state's power is not preeminent, but a carefully crafted illusion that exists only because a population chooses to grant it believability.
>
> No single system of power reigns supreme, no ultimate hegemony prevails in the world. (2004: 235)

Nordstrom accords great importance to the "extra-state." On the one hand, when a nation-state collapses, in order to survive the people who live in such locales rely on extra-state networks that link people and countries globally. These are very flexible systems that are capable of adapting to the most extreme circumstances. On the other hand, it is often the case that extra-states (such as al-Qaeda) pose a greater threat to nation-states, including those that achieve superpower status, than do other nation-states. "Looking at the history of extra-state groups defeating the colonial world, people have learned that the extra-state is the most powerful way of challenging the state and combating a superpower" (Nordstrom 2004: 249).

As part of these shadows of war, there has been a significant growth in the informal economy and complex trade networks that take place outside of legally regulated spheres (i.e. they are extra-state). Nordstrom (2010: 161) refers to these as "vanishing points – places where formal analyses and policy effectively cease." For example, after a tsunami pummeled war-torn Sri Lanka in 2005, the informal economy accounted for approximately 70% of all economic activity. This included various activities, from agricultural work, women selling their vegetables at the market, or providing domestic work in wealthy homes, to the trade in arms. Despite this activity, the national government and international agencies (e.g. World Bank, UN) do not measure or analyze it, and there are few government or civil society programs that target it. These extra-legal vanishing points are inherently violent, especially to women, who provide much of the labor. These women are subject to exploitative working conditions, and sexual violence, as a result.

Transnational discourse communities

A very different kind of threat to the nation-state is posed by the development of transnational discourse communities (TDCs) (Bislev et al. 2002; Plehwe 2010). TDCs involve, at the level of discourse, "increased interconnectedness between the local and the global" (Bislev et al. 2002: 199). They serve to demonstrate in yet another domain the decline of nation-states both as a source of such discourse for local governments within them, as well as in their inability to block the flow of this discourse. Thus, for example, cities as far apart as Phoenix in the US and Bremen, Germany share directly ideas on managing their cities derived from a TDC, the Bertelsmann Network. The point is that it is this network and the managerial ideas it disseminates that are influencing these two cities rather than, or at least independent from, the nation-states (US, Germany) in which they exist.

The Bertelsmann Network is a comparatively small TDC. Of far greater importance are organizations like the World Bank and the IMF and their discourses. There is also a diverse group of professional and expert organizations that are TDCs. For example, the International Social and Environmental Accreditation and Labeling (ISEAL) Alliance brings together researchers and practitioners to develop and improve sustainability standards throughout the world. The ISEAL Alliance works with governments, consultants, private businesses, NGOs, and other stakeholders to promote more socially responsible and environmentally sustainable business practices. These communities of discourse are affecting directly the nature of local government in various locales throughout the world.

IN DEFENSE OF THE NATION-STATE

There are at least some who contest the position taken above. A variety of arguments are made including that the nation-state continues to be *the* major player on the global stage (Gilpin 2001), that it retains at least some power in the face of globalization (Conley 2002), that nation-states vary greatly in their efficacy in the face of globalization, and that the rumors of the demise of the nation-state are greatly exaggerated.[7]

Daniel Beland argues that "the role of the state is enduring – and even increasing – in advanced industrial societies" (Beland 2008: 48). He sees greater demands being placed on the state because of four major sources of collective insecurity: terrorism (see Chapter 12), economic globalization leading to problems such as outsourcing and pressures toward downsizing, as well as the current economic crisis (see Chapter 7), threats to national identity due to immigration (see Chapter 10), and the spread of global diseases such as AIDs (see Chapter 12). Further, the state does not merely respond to these threats, it may actually find it in its interest to exaggerate or even create dangers and thereby make its citizens more insecure (Glassner 2000). A good example is the US and British governments' arguments prior to the 2003 war with Iraq that Saddam Hussein had Weapons of Mass Destruction (WMDs) that posed a direct threat to them. The US even claimed that Iraq could kill millions by using offshore ships to lob canisters containing lethal chemical or biological material into American cities (Isikoff and Corn 2006). The collective insecurity created by such outrageous claims helped foster public opinion in favor of invading Iraq and overthrowing Saddam Hussein.

The other side of this argument in support of the nation-state is that global processes of various kinds are just not as powerful as many believe. For example, global business pales in comparison to business *within* many countries, including the US. For another, some question the porosity of the nation-state by pointing, for example, to the fact that migration to the US and other countries has *declined* substantially since its heights in the late nineteenth and early twentieth centuries (Gilpin 2001). More recently, migration into the US fell from 2007 to 2011 (Passel and Cohn 2012). Furthermore, we could also look to China for an example of a nation-state that remains incredibly powerful in the face of globalization; indeed it has harnessed globalization (through its extensive importation of raw materials and exports of manufactured goods) while maintaining tight control of its own territory (although at great cost to the environment and many of its own people).

A related point is that it would be a mistake simply to see globalization as a threat to, a constraint on, the nation-state; it can also be an *opportunity* for the nation-state (Conley 2002). For example, the demands of globalization were used as a basis to make needed changes (at least from a neoliberal point of view) in Australian society, specifically allowing it to move away from protectionism and in the direction of (neo)liberalization, to transform state enterprises into private enterprises, and to streamline social welfare. In this, the rhetoric of globalization, especially an exaggeration of it and its effects, was useful to those politicians who were desirous of such changes. In other words, Australian politicians used globalization as an ideology in order to reform Australian society.

"IMAGINED COMMUNITY"

Imagined community: A nation exists primarily as a set of ideas in people's minds.

Whether or not it is being superseded by globalization, the nation-state remains important. In thinking about the nation-state, especially in the era of globalization, we need to understand that it is not a "natural" phenomenon, but is rather a social and political construction. This means that the nation-state had to be literally created as, for example, the early leaders of the United States did in fusing the original independent states into a unified nation-state. It also means that the nation-state has to be defined by those within it, as well as those without, as such an entity. This can occur in various ways, but one of the key ideas in thinking about the unification of the nation-state is Benedict Anderson's (2006) notion of **imagined communities**.

Anderson (2006: 6) *defines* the nation as "an imagined political community." Clearly, this means that for Anderson a nation exists primarily within the realm of ideas, subjectively within people's minds as an image. Anderson attributes four characteristics to an imagined nation. First, it is *imagined* because it is impossible in all but the smallest communities to have face-to-face contact with more than a few of one's peers. Because there are at least some, and likely many, not available for personal contact, one must imagine who they are, what they believe, what holds them together, and so on. Second, it is imagined to be *limited* "because even the largest of them, encompassing perhaps a billion living human beings, has finite, if elastic, boundaries, beyond which lie other nations. No nation imagines itself as coterminous with mankind" (Anderson 2006: 7). Third, the nation-state is imagined to be *sovereign*, that is as being free. Finally, it is imagined to be a *community* "because, regardless of the actual inequality and exploitation that may prevail in each, the nation is always conceived as a deep, horizontal comradeship" (Anderson 2006: 7).

Anderson sees the eighteenth century as the beginning of the dawn of the nation (in the sense that he defines it) and nationalism, and he links it to two key developments – the modern novel and the modern newspaper – that he includes under the heading of "print capitalism." Key to the modern novel was the idea of an actor moving calendrically through "homogenous, empty time." He sees this as "a precise analogue of the idea of the nation, which also is conceived as a solid community moving steadily down (or up) history" (Anderson 2006: 26). The novels tended to have a national imagination as well as an imagination of the characters moving through the sociological landscape presented in them.

In the case of the newspaper, the reader also operates with a sense that what appears in its pages operates calendrically. This is the case when one reads about a community – say the refugees in and from Syria – for several days in a row. However, it is also the case when the story disappears from the newspaper for a time. The reader assumes that the Syrian community continues to move along and thus has little trouble picking up the "story" (note the similarity to a novel and its story line) when articles once again are published on Syria. In addition, large numbers of people buy and read the newspaper on a given day and a given reader imagines that she is part of the larger community that is reading the same stories.

It was the mass sale and distribution of novels and newspapers that was critical to the rise of the imagined nation. It was also important that they were produced not in the language of the elites (e.g. Latin), or in many different vernaculars, but in a limited number of print languages. It was through this that people who previously could not understand one another

> gradually became aware of hundreds of thousands, even millions, of people in their particular language-field, and at the same time that *only those* hundreds of thousands, or millions, so belonged. These fellow-readers, to whom they were connected through print, formed, in their secular, particular, visible invisibility, the embryo of the nationally imagined community. (Anderson 2006: 44)

Print capitalism also gave a new fixity to language that helped give solidity and long-term continuity to the notion of the nation. However, while a national print language was important historically, that does not mean that today nations (as well as nation-states) and print languages are coterminous. Clearly, various languages exist within a given nation-state (India encompasses many different languages) and languages stretch far beyond the borders of given nation-states (people in many countries speak French).

The imagined community is clearly a much greater reality than ever before because of developments far beyond print capitalism and not dealt with by Anderson. We are thinking here of the new digital media – especially social media networks, cell phones, e-mail, the Internet, blogs, Twitter (Gruzd et al. 2011), etc. – that allow widely dispersed populations to maintain, create, and disseminate a continuing sense of an imagined community. Globalization has meant not only the dispersal of many people but it has also provided them with newer technologies that allow them to be part of truly (global) imagined communities. Thus, although the nation-state itself may be of declining importance, it may be as important, and in fact more important, today in the age of globalization as an imagined reality.

One of the many examples of the application of the concept of imagined communities to globalization studies is Frank Lechner's (2007, 2012) work on the Dutch, especially in the way they conceive of themselves through soccer. One of the things the Dutch have done is to use soccer as a way of re-imagining their nation. In 1974 the Dutch national soccer team reached the World Cup finals and, although they lost to the German team, the accomplishment was seen as a demonstration of the fact that a small country like the Netherlands could compete on the global stage, not only in soccer but in many other things. In other words, success in world soccer allowed the Dutch to imagine their nation-state as being powerful, perhaps far more powerful than it was in actuality. Further, the source of the success of the team, as well as the nation-state, was seen as resulting from an integration of the collective, or the system, with the creative individual, either as player or citizen. The team was seen as being able, through its play, to "stretch" the soccer playing field and this mirrored the ability of the Dutch to literally stretch the physical dimensions of the country itself by, for example, reclaiming land from the sea. In this, the Dutch are not unique. Many nations imagine themselves in terms of the World Cup and global soccer more generally and, in fact, many think of themselves as superior, unique, and whole because of their successes in that realm.

However, the whole notion of a distinctive Dutch style in soccer is contested. Further, much the same could be said about soccer in many other nations, as well. And, there are mythical aspects of the Dutch sense of not only their soccer but of their nation as a whole. Indeed, the whole idea of a distinctive Dutch nation-state, or of any nation-state, for that matter, involves selective memory and application. Furthermore, those imaginings are not carved in stone, but are affected by, and are changing as a result of, globalization. The Dutch, as well as those in many nations, are re-imagining themselves in the wake of globalization, especially immigration. The key point, however, is not the specific nature of the "imagined communities," but the fact that they seem to be both broadly needed in, and created in a wide range of, national settings.

CHANGES IN GLOBAL NATION-STATE RELATIONS

Beyond the nation-state there has been a wide range of formal and informal political relations among and between nation-states that have served to structure international, and more recently, global relations. Thus, during WW II the major divide was between those nation-states associated with the Allies (mainly US, Great Britain, France, Russia) and those linked to the Axis (primarily Germany, Japan, Italy). During the Cold War, the major split was between Soviet bloc countries and those allied with the West. In the nearly two decades since the collapse of the Soviet Union the global political situation has been more fluid and various efforts have been made to offer a picture of the new global political world.

Parag Khanna (2008a, 2008b: 34 ff.) offers one interesting perspective on this emerging new world.[8] He bases his analysis on a distinction between globalization and geopolitics[9] (Steinmetz 2012). Basically, globalization involves free flows, especially of an economic nature. In contrast, geopolitics involves largely political and military efforts aimed at gaining control over, but frequently disrupting, those flows (and much else). While the US was hegemonic in the era of geopolitics, it is greatly weakened as globalization competes with, and gains ascendancy over, geopolitics. However, based on the fact that the widely acknowledged prior epoch of globalization (see Chapter 6) was brought to an end by the geopolitics associated with the onset of WW I, Khanna (2008a: 341) worries that geopolitics may once again undermine globalization.

Khanna argues that with the demise of the Soviet Union in 1991, US geopolitical hegemony was expected to last well into the future, but it failed to get past the end of the century. Instead, he sees the emergence in the twenty-first century of a new Big Three in the world – the EU, China, and the US. As Khanna (2008b: 64) puts it, the "web of globalization now has three spiders." However, in his view, the US is the one of the Big Three that is declining while the other two are likely to continue their recent ascent. (However, he does not foresee the US being replaced by the other two; they will co-exist and compete actively and aggressively with one another.) He dismisses the other possibilities for world power status – Russia (Blum 2008) is being depopulated and is reduced to being run by "Gazprom.gov";[10] Islam is sharply divided (especially, Sunnis vs. Shias) and wars rage within it; India is far behind China and does not seem to have the same kind of global ambitions and appetite.

There is a lengthy set of points to be made about the strength of the EU, but there is mixed evidence about its future role in the world. On the one hand, the EU has a great number of strengths to suggest it will continue to grow in importance.

- EU membership is growing, at least for the moment, and there is a fairly lengthy list of nation-states eager to enter.
- New pipelines bring the flow of oil to EU countries from Libya, Algeria, and Azerbaijan.
- The EU is already the largest market in the world having surpassed the US.
- Europe is a leader in technological developments.
- London is replacing New York as the global financial capital.
- Europe (and the EU) is more of a political model for those in Africa or the Middle East than the US.

On the other hand, the EU has experienced several challenges in recent years.

- Following the Great Recession in the US, there has been a "euro crisis" in which member countries suffered ballooning deficits and a real-estate bubble (Riera-Crichton 2012).
- As a response to increasing deficits, several EU countries (e.g. Greece, Portugal, Italy, Spain) implemented severe austerity measures that limited public spending and provoked massive public protest.
- Support within Europe for the EU has fallen, with the residents of several countries (France, Spain, Greece, and Britain) indicating greater opposition than support for the Euro Zone (Kanter 2013).

The relative position of the EU is even more difficult to assess when we consider that while the relative value of the euro has been consistently stronger than the US dollar since 2002, the size of the gap has varied in recent years. In addition, when China was considering where to locate its first foreign office to manage its sovereign wealth fund, it snubbed both New York and London and instead located it in Canada's financial capital, Toronto (Hoffman and Perkins 2011). To what degree the EU ascends as a global hegemon may be determined by its ability to maintain the strength of the euro and the unity of its member states.

China, however, is clearly expanding as a global power in a variety of ways.

- As of 2012, China surpassed the US as the world's largest trading nation.
- It is making all sorts of deals with, and sending a wide range of personnel (engineers, military personnel, etc.) to, a number of locales in the world – Africa, Latin America, etc.
- Its trade with the world is massive and has been growing and it continues to buy major companies in the US and Europe.
- China continues to secure access to natural resources (such as oil and gas) from all over the world, including the building of over 200 dams around the globe.
- In 2013, China announced plans to move 250 million rural peasants to its cities to provide a steady stream of labor, especially for its export sectors.
- Of course, China's greatest power is in East Asia where it is aided by the fact that about 35 million ethnic Chinese live throughout the other countries of East Asia and are well-positioned within their economies.
- China is drawing more and more nations in the region into its political orbit and there is a possibility that it could eventually stand at the center of an Eastern version of NATO.

When the US is also taken into account, what is being produced, then, is "three hemispheric pan-regions, longitudinal zones dominated by America, Europe and China... because a vertically organized region contains all climatic zones year-round, each pan-region can be self-sufficient and build a power base from which to intrude in others' terrain" (Khanna 2008b: 37). This ability to intrude into each other's world is exacerbated by globalization and made easier in a "shrinking world."

The main battleground among the Big Three will be what Khanna calls the "second world" that is distinct from the core first-world countries and the peripheral third-world countries (Wallerstein 1974). These are the "swing states" over which the Big Three will compete and the outcome of that battle will determine who will win out in the geopolitics of the future. The most important of these swing states are in "Eastern Europe, Central Asia, South America, the Middle East and Southeast Asia" (Khanna 2008b: 39).

OTHER GLOBAL POLITICAL DEVELOPMENTS AND STRUCTURES

LEAGUE OF NATIONS

The idea for the League of Nations emerged as a result of, and during, WW I. The League was formulated during the Paris Peace Conference of 1919, and began operations in January 1920. Its significance was that it was a global political organization and it was a forerunner to the much more important United Nations. It was not the first such organization (there was the largely nineteenth-century Concert of Europe and its periodic meetings), but it was the broadest and most inclusive – that is, the most global – to that date. Although the US played a key role in the formation of the League, it did not become a member when the Senate refused to ratify the agreement because it did not want to cede war-making powers to such an organization. Without the US, the League came to be dominated by Europe and lost its global reach and the legitimacy that could have been derived from such a sweep. The League was formally "buried" in April, 1946, but its demise was foreordained by the absence of the US and by the fact that it was never a truly global organization (Northedge 1989; Ostrower 2012).

The League was also done in by a series of failures including its inability to stop Japan from conquering Manchuria (1931) and to prevent Italy from taking over Abyssinia (now Ethiopia) in 1935. Of course, its greatest failure, and the most important cause of its demise, was WW II.

The League did make some contributions to international cooperation and global governance (especially the Permanent Court of International Justice at the Hague). The UN in general, as well as other global organizations such as the IMF, continue to reflect innovations made by the League in the global arena. The ultimate significance of the League was as an early form of political globalization and as a forerunner to the far more important United Nations.

UNITED NATIONS

Clearly, the United Nations (UN), in spite of its myriad problems, is the premier global organization in the realm of politics. It succeeded the failed League of Nations, although the UN incorporated many of its principles and some of its functions and characteristics. It, like the world wars that preceded and precipitated it, was an indicator of globalization, at least in the political realm.

The UN began operations on October 24, 1945. It is organized on the basis of the nation-states (there were 193 member states in 2014) that are its members. As a "state-centric" organization (Weiss, Forsythe, and Coate 2004; Weiss and Zach 2007), the UN stands in opposition, at least in general, to those who argue that globalization has brought, or is bringing about, the demise of the (nation-)state. The UN is a global setting in which nation-states meet and deliberate. However, the UN is not merely a setting in which nation-states meet, but it is also an independent actor.

As an arena for nation-state decision-making

The two best-known state-based organs in the UN are the Security Council and the General Assembly. The latter is the UN's main deliberative body, while the former is responsible for the maintenance of international peace and security (Charron and Boulden 2012). The day-to-day operations of the UN are handled by the Secretariat, employing about 6,400 people in New York and approximately another 36,600 people throughout the world (United Nations 2012). The ability of the UN to function adequately is greatly and chronically hampered by severe budget limitations.

The UN can be seen as concerned primarily with four broad areas. The first involves *military* issues. The UN was envisioned as a major force in managing peace and security, especially in inter-state relations. However, it was marginalized during the Cold War[11] largely because in the Security Council both the US and the Soviet Union could veto proposed interventions. A turning point in the military role of the UN was the 1991 authorization by the Security Council of the use of force to deal with Iraq's invasion of Kuwait. Throughout the 1990s the UN engaged in a wide variety of actions that were not anticipated by its founders and which had been regarded previously as the province of states. These included interventions in civil wars in less developed countries, "election and human rights monitoring, disarmament, and even the assumption of state functions (in Cambodia and East Timor, for example)" (Weiss and Zach 2007: 1219). However, the expansionism of the UN in these areas was tempered by failures in the 1990s in Somalia and Yugoslavia. In the military realm it is also important to mention the fact that the UN has been actively involved in arms control and disarmament. The second area involves *economic* issues. In this realm, the main focus of the UN has been to promote actions that would lead to reductions in global inequality. Third are *environmental* issues (e.g. pollution, hazardous wastes) which are dealt with primarily through the United Nations Environment Programme.[12] Finally, there are matters of *human protection*. A variety of UN-sponsored human rights treaties and agreements have protected human rights (see above) around the world.

The UN is both a creation and creature of the United States. Its name was suggested by President Franklin Delano Roosevelt, the UN charter was adopted in San Francisco and it has been housed in New York City since the 1950s. The US has also been the largest single contributor to the UN. However, the UN is minuscule in comparison to the US – its budget is about 0.07% of the budget of the US government. It is for this reason that the UN continues to be relatively weak and that the US has felt free to go it alone whenever it has serious disagreements with it (Ferguson 2004).

United Nations Conference on Trade and Development (UNCTAD)[13]

UNCTAD was created in 1964 by the UN General Assembly primarily to improve the economic situation of less developed nations, as well as to improve the nature of their relationship to the developed nations. It sought markets for the manufactured goods of less developed countries and stable prices for their commodities. It was opposed by the developed nations because it opposed the (neo)liberalism that predominated at the time of its formation. However, in 1992 it changed course, accepted the predominant neoliberal economic system, ceased to seek systemic change, and sought instead the integration of less developed countries into the global economy (Williams 2007). UNCTAD continues to focus on trade and development, but its goal is to improve the position of less developed nations in these areas by finding ways of allowing them to benefit more from, and function better in, the global economy.

United Nations Educational, Scientific and Cultural Organization (UNESCO)

With headquarters in Paris, UNESCO has been in existence since 1946. Its primary focus is in the areas of education, the natural and social sciences, and culture (Singh 2010). It had a number of successes in its first four decades of existence, but it was hampered by the Cold War and more recently by the neoliberalism of economic globalization. It has sought the free movement of knowledge and information, but neoliberals favor turning these into goods which can be bought and sold on the market. The triumph of neoliberalism has meant that both the budget and the activities of UNESCO have been in decline.

INTERNATIONAL ATOMIC ENERGY AGENCY (IAEA)

IAEA became well known in early 2003 when its current leader, Mohammed ElBaradei, led a team to look into the status of nuclear weapons in Iran. (It had earlier shown that contrary to US assertions, Saddam Hussein's Iraq had no nuclear weapons.) Its subsequent report indicated that Iran failed to meet safeguard obligations relative to nuclear development and weaponry. As of 2014, Iran had made significant progress on developing its nuclear program (Sanger and Broad 2013) and while the IAEA continues to advocate dissolving this program, newly elected President Hassan Rouhani shows no signs of stopping Iran's nuclear development.

The IAEA is an autonomous organization established on July 29, 1957. It is not controlled by the UN, but it does report to both the General Assembly and the Security Council. The vast majority of the nations involved in the IAEA are members of the UN. The Iran case illustrates one of the IAEA's best-known roles as the world's "watchdog" on nuclear issues. As such, it inspects nuclear facilities to ensure that they are for peaceful use, disseminates information and standards designed to help make sure that nuclear facilities do not become dangerous, and serves as a center for scientific information on the peaceful use of nuclear technology.

GROUP OF EIGHT

The Group of Eight (G8) began as the Group of Six (France, Germany, Italy, Japan, United Kingdom, the US) in 1975; Canada was added in 1976 and Russia officially became a member in 1998. At the heart of the G8 is a two- to three-day annual meeting of the leaders of the countries involved. In addition, there are an increasing number of more specialized meetings involving representatives of Group of Eight nations and more and more official bodies have been created to deal with specialized issues (Kirton et al. 2001). The main significance of the G8 lies in the fact that its summit meeting "remains the only place where the leaders of all of the world's major states regularly meet to provide wide-ranging global governance, based on democratic principles" (Kirton 2007: 552). The G8 has addressed a series of specific political (arms control, regional security, human rights, etc.) and economic (e.g. exchange rates, international trade, relations with developing nations) issues.

At the 2013 meeting in Northern Ireland, economic issues and the Syrian conflict were at the top of the meeting agenda. At the time, the war in Syria was responsible for approximately 93,000 deaths, but little progress was made given divisions within the G8; Russia was allied with Syria's President Bashar al-Assad while the remaining members opposed his ruling party (Calmes and Castle 2013). Key economic issues discussed included illegal tax evasion and legal loopholes used by MNCs to avoid taxes, although measures taken against these problems were left to individual member states.

The G8 has also been heavily criticized in recent decades (Higo 2012). On the one hand, the member countries no longer represent the world's most important economic powers. For example, China, India, and Brazil have surpassed many G8 countries, and their notable absence in discussing global economic policy has upset many countries. On the other hand, annual G8 meetings are always intense sites of protest, sometimes attracting hundreds of thousands of activists. Protestors argue that the G8 pushes a neoliberal agenda of market liberalization that disproportionately benefits wealthier nations and elites. They further contend that while the G8 claims to fight poverty its policies actually reinforce and exacerbate poverty both in its own countries and in the developing world.

REGIONAL POLITICAL ORGANIZATIONS

Below we deal with some of the more important regional political organizations (Cooper, Hughes, and de Lombaerde 2008). We will not cover all of them; the focus will be on more formal than more informal regional organizations.

ORGANIZATION OF AMERICAN STATES (OAS)

The OAS was created on April 30, 1948, and initially it included all of the states in Central and Latin America, as well as Cuba and the US (Horwitz 2011; Phillips 2007). Over the years, Canada and the other Caribbean states joined the OAS, but Cuba, while technically remaining a member, was suspended in 1962 in light of the ascendancy of a communist government in Cuba headed by Fidel Castro. The OAS has not been a notably successful regional organization largely because of profound differences between the US and other members. While the OAS is devoted to multilateralism, the US continues to favor a unilateral approach to Latin America. This is reflected not only in its staunch, and continuing (in spite of the replacement of Fidel Castro by his brother Raul as president of the country in 2008), opposition, indeed hostility, to Cuba, but also in many other areas such as dealing with the flow of narcotics from Latin America and the flow of undocumented immigrants from and through Mexico. The relationship between the US and Latin American countries has grown more strained with the rise to power of Hugo Chávez in Venezuela and the movement to the left in other Latin American regimes (e.g. Ecuador, Bolivia). This has also created strains among Latin American countries between those that have moved left and those that have not.

ASSOCIATION OF SOUTHEAST ASIAN NATIONS (ASEAN)

ASEAN was founded in 1967, with Indonesia, Malaysia, the Philippines, Singapore, and Thailand as the original members, to foster regional cooperation in Southeast Asia among its smaller, developing nations. It has now grown to ten members with the addition of Brunei, Vietnam, Laos, Myanmar, and Cambodia.[14] ASEAN operates on the basis of the following principles which clearly reflect its political character and its base in the nation-states that compose the organization:

- mutual respect for the independence, sovereignty, equality, territorial integrity, and national identity of all nations;
- the right of every State to lead its national existence free from external interference, subversion, or coercion;
- non-interference in the internal affairs of one another;
- settlement of differences or disputes by peaceful manner;
- renunciation of the threat or use of force; and
- effective cooperation among member nations.[15]

In addition, it takes as its other goals the acceleration of "economic growth, social progress and cultural development in the region."[16]

Although ASEAN was founded as a largely political organization (Leifer 1989), it has come to be dominated by economic issues (Nesadurai 2003), especially dealing with the impact of neoliberal economic policies on the region and its member nations. For one thing, it sought to adapt to neoliberalism by creating the ASEAN Free Trade Area (AFTA) to reduce both tariff and non-tariff barriers to free trade. For another, it sought, beginning in 1998, to nurture new domestic firms by giving domestic investors priority over foreign investors. This was both to prevent the firms from coming to be controlled by outsiders and to help them grow so that they could compete with the MNCs. However, in 2001 the focus shifted to attracting foreign investment. Finally, it responded to the 1997–1998 Asian financial crisis by seeking to develop regional financial systems that could help to prevent future financial crises.

The relatively small size of their economies led ASEAN to form ASEAN Plus Three (APT) and to include three powerful Northeast Asian countries – Japan, China, and South Korea. In May, 2000, they agreed on the Chiang Mai Initiative to provide funds to member nations in case of a financial crisis. The actions of ASEAN show "how a group of small developing countries have pragmatically employed regional cooperation to help them mediate a range of pressures from globalization. It also explains the seemingly paradoxical phenomenon of a worldwide resurgence of regional integration projects since the 1980s in tandem with globalization" (Nesadurai 2007).

AFRICAN UNION (AU)[17]

The Organization of African Unity (OAU) began in 1963, but it was succeeded by the African Union in 2002 (Murray 2004; Süderbaum 2012). The change represented a switch from a focus mainly on pan-Africanism and collective self-reliance to more of one on benefiting from globalization as well as avoiding its adverse effects. Given the great problems within Africa, it remains unclear how successful the AU will be in either taking advantage of globalization or avoiding being victimized by it.

GLOBAL GOVERNANCE

The decline of the nation-state, along with at least some of its governance function, and the fact that the Intergovernmental Organizations and treaties have not been sufficient in solving transnational issues, have given rise to proliferating forms of global governance. Governance refers to the "processes and institutions, formal and informal, whereby rules are created, compliance is elicited, and goods are provided in pursuit of collective goals" (Hale and Held 2011: 12). Global governance goes beyond the traditional forms of cooperation between sovereign nation-states (e.g. interstate diplomacy, treaties, and international law) to include a broader variety of networked organizations and individuals that had not previously participated directly in creating and enforcing rules (Cox and Schilthuis 2012). Governance has shaped global politics in important ways, and is a rapidly growing area of both activity and research.

There are at least three new forms of global or transnational governance. First, there is *governance through multi-stakeholder initiatives*. This form of governance brings together various public and private actors into public policy networks and partnerships. It usually involves at least one state actor (but not always) and various international institutions as well as INGOS and private sector organizations of various sorts. Multi-stakeholder initiatives provide governance in the form of service provision (e.g. the Global Fund to Fight AIDS, Tuberculosis, and Malaria) and standard-setting (e.g. the World Commission on Dams).

The second, and common, form of global governance involves the creation of voluntary regulations. In voluntary regulation systems, MNCs (or other actors) agree to a set of social and/or environmental practices that go beyond the stated or enforced set of laws in the area in which they operate. Sometimes these standards are created by the companies themselves in a given sector (e.g. a code of conduct) and are little more than public relations tools. But in other cases, the standards are developed, monitored, and enforced through an extensive network of international organizations (e.g. NGOs, social movement organizations, states, Intergovernmental Organizations, etc.). One example of this voluntary form of regulation is the Forest Stewardship Council (FSC), which seeks to promote sustainable forestry. The FSC brings together environmental and social NGOs, forestry corporations, and scientific institutions in the development of forestry standards that are monitored and enforced through independent third-party certification. Many of these private regulatory schemes (which also include fair trade; see Chapter 15) rely on mobilizing consumers to purchase certified products and punish those companies who do not submit to this voluntary regulation.

Not all systems of voluntary regulation feature a specific set of standards that are monitored and enforced. For example, the "Global Compact" created by former UN Secretary-General, Kofi Annan encompasses ten basic principles by which businesses around the world should voluntarily conduct their affairs (Soederberg 2007: 500–13). It facilitates learning and capacity building in the development and implementation of these social and environmental principles (e.g. businesses should support human rights, eliminate compulsory labor, and promote greater environmental responsibility), but is not enforced or monitored.

Third, there are transnational arbitration bodies where global governance has been accorded to courts and lawyers, but whose authority is not based in international law (Hale and Held 2011). For example, the North American Free Trade Agreement (NAFTA) has an environmental side-agreement that strives to make sure that member countries follow their own environmental laws (Hale 2011). Through the North American Commission for Environmental Cooperation (CEC), citizens may submit evidence exposing their country's failure to enforce their environmental law. Through independent investigation, the commission's process can establish a factual record of violations that can put pressure on states to adhere to their own national laws. The World Bank has similar procedures as well. The authority of these arbitration bodies, or "info courts," is "based on information and persuasion, not law," or at least not any law that they have the power to enforce (Hale and Held 2011: 115). These processes have led to some improvements but they are limited in scope.

One important area of governance is the world economy (Hirst and Thompson 1999). All the forms of governance identified above are involved in overseeing the world economy. There are at least five interdependent levels at which that governance can operate:

1. The major political entities, especially the G3 (Europe, Japan, and North America), can govern through various agreements "to stabilize exchange rates, to coordinate fiscal and monetary policies, and to cooperate in limiting speculative short-term financial transactions" (Hirst and Thompson 1999: 191).

2. States can create various international regulatory agencies to deal with a specific economic issue (e.g. the WTO).

3. Trade and investment blocs such as EU, NAFTA, and AFTA (ASEAN Free Trade Area) can govern large economic areas.

4. Nations can develop policies to enhance themselves and the ability of their corporations to compete in the global marketplace.

5. Regions within nations can integrate economic activities that take place within their borders in order to increase their ability to compete globally and to protect themselves from large shocks that might adversely affect them.

There is some evidence of, and some increasing pressure toward, the emergence of various forms of global governance. James Rosenau (2002; Rosenau and Czempiel 1992) links this to the increasing "fragmegration" (see below) of the global order. This reflects increasing global diversity as well as the array of contradictory forces that have been unleashed as a result. Among those contradictory forces are globalization and localization, centralization and decentralization, and integration and fragmentation (fragmegration).

There are a series of more specific factors behind the growth in demand for more global governance. At the top of the list must be the declining power of nation-states. If states themselves are less able to handle various responsibilities, this leaves open the possibility of the emergence of some form of global governance to fill the void. A second factor is the vast flows of all sorts of things that run into and often right through the borders of nation-states. On the one hand, this could involve the flow of digital information of all sorts through the Internet. It is difficult, if not impossible, for a nation-state to stop such flows and in any case it is likely that such action would be politically unpopular and bring much negative reaction to the nation-state involved in such an effort. For example, the flow of criminal elements and their products (drugs, laundered money, people bought and sold in sex trafficking, etc.), is a strong factor in the call for global governance. In these cases and others, there is a need for such things as some degree of order, some sort of effective authority, and at least some potential for the improvement of human life. These are but a few of the things that can be delivered by some form of global governance.

Another set of issues that has led to calls for global governance involve horrendous events within nation-states that the states themselves either foment and carry out, or are unable to control. For example, in Darfur, Sudan, hundreds of thousands have been killed and millions of people displaced and the lives of many more disrupted in a conflict that dates back to early 2003. The government of Sudan and its military have been implicated in the conflict between ethnic and tribal groups and the Sudanese government has been resistant to outside interference in its internal affairs. Of course, this is far from the only event of its kind. Other prominent examples in recent history include death and disruption in Rwanda (in 1994 militant Hutus killed hundreds of thousands of Tutsis and more moderate Hutus), and Kosovo (a semi-independent province in Serbia and the site of conflict in the 1990s between ethnic Albanians and Serbs and the mass murder of Albanians). One could even go back to WW II and argue that the Holocaust could have been prevented, or at least mitigated, had there been a viable form of global governance to put pressure on Nazi Germany and ultimately to intervene in a more material way, perhaps militarily (see Figure 5.1 for a global map of areas of recurrent conflict).

Then there are global problems that single nation-states cannot hope to tackle on their own. One, of course, is the global financial crises and panics (including the current ones)

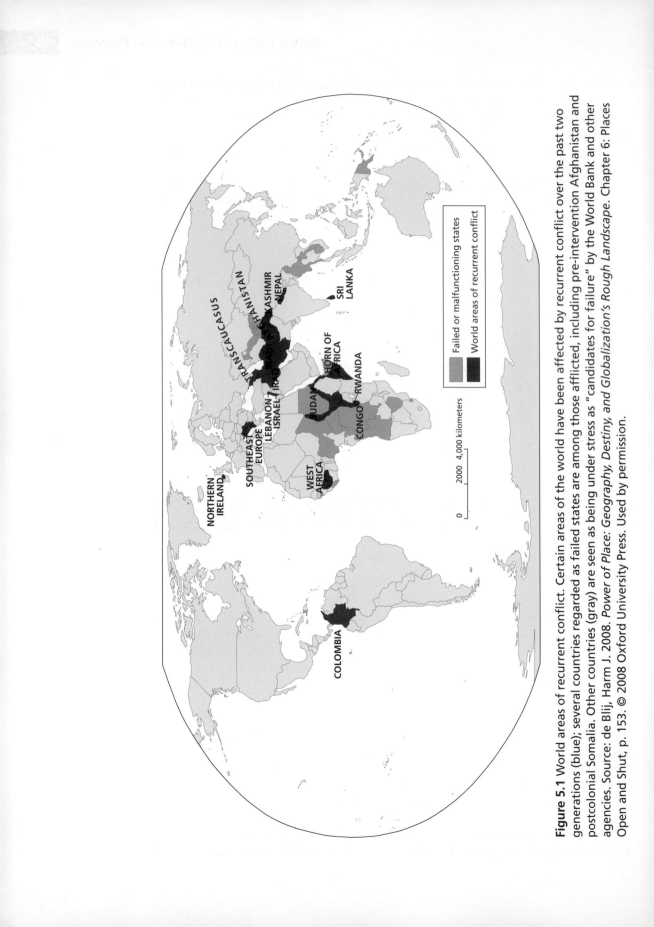

Figure 5.1 World areas of recurrent conflict. Certain areas of the world have been affected by recurrent conflict over the past two generations (blue); several countries regarded as failed states are among those afflicted, including pre-intervention Afghanistan and postcolonial Somalia. Other countries (gray) are seen as being under stress as "candidates for failure" by the World Bank and other agencies. Source: de Blij, Harm J. 2008. *Power of Place: Geography, Destiny, and Globalization's Rough Landscape.* Chapter 6: Places Open and Shut, p. 153. © 2008 Oxford University Press. Used by permission.

that sweep the world periodically and with which nations are often unable to deal on their own. Indeed, some nations (e.g. the ASEAN nations discussed above) have often been, and are being, victimized by such crises. Unable to help themselves, such nations are in need of assistance from some type of global governance.

It is important to remember, however, that governance structures are not all created to meet general functional needs but can also be developed to pursue narrow interests. For example, MNCs have sought participation in many of these governance structures both to have more direct involvement in rule-setting processes (although they often participate directly in domestic and international legislative processes as well) and to avoid state-enforced regulations that could have more powerful enforcement mechanisms. It is often in corporations' interests to voluntarily agree to weak social and environmental standards that have no legal enforcement. So while some governance structures are shaped from below, many social movements heavily criticize corporate or industry-led governance structures as exacerbating, rather than solving, global problems.

Nation-states have long struggled to deal with problems like these through various inter-state systems (e.g. alliances such as NATO), but the more recent trends documented above are toward (1) the development of more truly global structures and methods of dealing with various sorts of issues and problems; and (2) the involvement of a more diverse array of actors in the rule-setting process. This greater inclusiveness can mean that rule-setting and enforcement is more democratic (e.g. the management of sustainable forests through the Forest Stewardship Council), but that is not necessarily the case. As noted above, many new governance procedures continue to be driven by state and non-state elites which exclude broader members of society and help their members to pursue their narrow interests collectively.

CIVIL SOCIETY

While civility and civil society have ancient roots and examples (e.g. in Aristotle), John Keane (2003) traces what we now consider civil society to the appearance of the West on the global stage beginning around 1500 (see also Eberly 2008). Until the nineteenth century (Lipschutz 2007), civil society was not distinguished from a state dominated by laws. The philosopher G. W. F. Hegel played a key role in re-defining civil society as that which exists between the family and the state; a realm that is not only separated from them, but one where an individual can participate directly in various social institutions. To Hegel, like Marx and Engels (and Keane), the economy was considered part of civil society.

The major figure in social theory[18] associated with the idea of civil society is Alexis de Tocqueville. Tocqueville lauded the early American propensity to form a wide range of associations (e.g. religious, moral) that were not political in nature and orientation. Such civil associations allowed people to interact with one another and to develop, renew, and enlarge feelings, ideas, emotions, and understandings. Such civil associations also allowed people to band together and to act. Without such associations they would be isolated and weak in large-scale contemporary societies (Tocqueville 1825–1840/1969: 513, 515).

The distinction between the market (and state, family) and civil society is a twentieth-century innovation usually associated with the Italian Marxist thinker, Antonio Gramsci

(1992). In his view, to challenge the hegemony of the state (controlled by the market which, in turn, dominated the family), the opposition had to gain positions in civil society (e.g. universities, the media) in order to generate their own ideas to counter the hegemonic ideas emanating from the capitalist economic system.

While the West often conquered the world through uncivilized, even violent means, it "gave birth as well to modern struggles for liberty of the press, written constitutions, religious toleration, new codes of 'civil manners' (often connected with sport), non-violent power-sharing, and talk of democracy and human rights, whose combined 'ethos' gradually spawned the growth of civil society institutions" (Keane 2003: 44). A robust civil society was already in existence by the nineteenth and early twentieth centuries (e.g. peace societies, cooperatives, workers movements), but it was soon set back dramatically by the two world wars. It is largely in the aftermath of WW II that the modern civil society movement took shape and expanded dramatically.

Mary Kaldor (2003, 2007: 153–7) accords central importance to the 1970s and 1980s, especially in Latin America and Eastern Europe. In both regions, there was opposition to military dictatorship and efforts to find an autonomous and self-organizing base outside of the state in order to oppose the military. It was also during this period that civil society became increasingly global as improved travel and communication made linkages among various civil society groups throughout the world increasingly possible. These groups mounted appeals to international authorities and were able to create a global political space for themselves where they argued for, and helped bring about, international agreements on such issues as human rights. Of great importance in the 1990s "was the emergence of transnational networks of activists who came together on particular issues, including landmines, human rights, climate change, dams, HIV/AIDS, or corporate responsibility" (Kaldor 2007: 155). Much of the contemporary "alter-globalization" movement (see Chapter 15) is now an integral part of global civil society.

Civil society: Process through which individuals negotiate, argue, struggle against, or agree with each other and with those in authority.

Following Kaldor (2007: 154; Kaldor et al. 2012), **civil society** is defined (we will soon offer a definition of global civil society) as: "the process through which individuals negotiate, argue, struggle against, or agree with each other and with the centers of political and economic authority." It is a realm in which people can engage each other more or less directly and in which they can, among other things, analyze and criticize their political and economic institutions. People can do this, and thereby act publicly, by acting through "voluntary associations, movements, parties, and unions" (Kaldor 2007: 154). Thus, civil society involves *both* settings and actions that take place within those settings. It also represents an ideal toward which many people and groups aspire – an active, vital, and powerful civil society that can influence, and act as a counterbalance to, potent forces in the realm of the polity and the economy (Seckinelgin 2002). It is particularly the case that civil society stands as a counterbalance and an alternative to *both* the nation-state and the economic market, especially the capitalist market.

While historically civil society was nation-state-centered, that is, linked to groups and actions within states,[19] in more recent years it has been associated with more global actions and therefore with a somewhat different set of organizations including "social movements, nongovernmental organizations (NGOs), transnational networks, religious organizations, and community groups" (Kaldor 2007: 153). In other words, we have moved increasingly toward the notion of a global civil society (Alexander 2006a; Kellogg 2012), although civil society remains a force within states and societies, as well (Smith and West 2005).

John Keane (2003: 8, italics in original) offers a definition of **global civil society** as:

> *a dynamic non-governmental system of interconnected socio-economic institutions that straddle the whole earth, and that have complex effects that are felt in its four corners. Global civil society is neither a static object nor a fait accompli. It is an unfinished project that consists of sometimes thick, sometimes thinly stretched networks, pyramids and hub-and-spoke clusters of socio-economic institutions and actors who organize themselves across borders, with the deliberate aim of drawing the world together in new ways. These non-governmental institutions and actors tend to pluralise power and to problematise violence; consequently, their peaceful or 'civil' effects are felt everywhere, here and there, far and wide, to and from local areas, through wide regions, to the planetary level itself.*

> **Global civil society**: Global, non-governmental, pluralistic form of society composed of interlinked social processes oriented to civility.

This definition emphasizes five tightly linked characteristics of global civil society; it is *non-governmental, a form of society composed of interlinked social processes, oriented to civility (non-violence), pluralistic (including the strong potential to reduce conflict)*, and *global*.

Keane gives us a good feel for *global* civil society, as well as both its unfinished and varied character. However, one of the things that sets Keane's view on civil society apart is his argument that the economic market is deeply implicated in civil society. While many see civil society as distinct from *both* the nation-state and the market, Keane (2003: 76) puts forth the "no market, no civil society" rule. Civil society could not survive without the market, money, and the money economy. Indeed, there is no clear dividing line between civil society and the market; the market is embedded in civil society and vice versa. For example, those who work in the market draw upon the civil society's norms of sociability such as "punctuality, trust, honesty, reliability, group commitment and non-violence" (Keane 2003: 77).

Keane (2003: 78) draws three basic conclusions from this relationship: "markets are an intrinsic *empirical* feature, a functionally intertwined prerequisite, of the social relations of actually existing global civil society"; "global civil society as we know and now experience it could not survive for more than a few days without the market forces unleashed by turbo-capitalism"; and "the market forces of turbocapitalism could themselves not survive for a day without *other* civil society institutions, like households, charities, community associations and linguistically shared social norms like friendship, trust and cooperation."

To buttress his point, Keane argues that labor is not restricted to the market economy, but is a kind of social activity also found in non-market settings like households and charities, arts and entertainment, recreation, intimate relationships, communications media, and sacred settings and institutions. Further, markets and capitalist firms even have a civilizing effect on civil societies through, for example, their forms of face-to-face negotiations and by nurturing social codes such as those associated with charity (e.g. the Bill and Melinda Gates Foundation).

However, Keane also recognizes that the capitalist market can disturb, even disrupt, global civil society through, for example, the great social inequality it produces or by choosing where to invest and, especially, where not to invest and from where it chooses to withdraw investments. Of perhaps greatest importance from a negative point of view is the tendency for the capitalist market to strengthen "the hand of market domination over the nonprofit institutions of society, which tend to be pushed and pulled, twisted and torn into bodies that obey the rules of accumulation and profit maximization" (Keane 2003: 90). Indeed, it is for this reason that many argue for the need to distinguish between market-based organizations and civil society.

In contrast to Keane, Jeffrey Alexander differentiates civil society (or what he often calls "the civil sphere") from the market and the economy. However, he goes much further to also separate civil society from the state, religion, family, and community (Alexander 2006b: 7, 2010). Thus, civil society is to Alexander independent of these and other structures and institutions. It is a sphere that possesses its own ethics and institutions. Yet, it is not merely an idea or an ideal, it also exists in the "real world." That is, it has a local existence in both time and space. However, there is a set of ideals associated with it including community, solidarity, justice, and democracy. As such, civil society is not a reality that is ever, or could ever be, completed. Rather it is an ongoing and ever-present project.

This is especially the case in the era of globalization where civil societies that were created in nation-states now must be extended to the global level. In fact, Alexander argues that without a global civil society the promises of national civil society may die. The challenges and the dangers of today's world have become global with the result that civil society must itself become global if it is to have any chance of countering them and, more generally, of creating a true civil society.

In practice, civil society has been dominated for decades by critical agents and agencies, but more recently neoliberalism and neoliberal organizations (e.g. the World Bank) have picked up on the idea to create organizations (NGOs), often funded by government and international agencies, oriented to reforming the market and government. Some see these NGOs as compromising the very notion of civil society and argue that they should not be thought of as part of it. However, as both Keane and Kaldor point out, civil society is a broad and internally contradictory category that includes a wide range of groups.

How do we account for the recent rise of civil society in general, and NGOs in particular? A number of factors are involved. Perhaps the most important are the various flows that we have already mentioned many times, including flows of both resources (money, information, popular culture, etc.) and threats (e.g. pollution, drugs, sex trafficking, etc.) (Mathews 1997). As the power of the nation-state to deal with these flows, and in the case of negative flows (see Chapters 11 and 12) to mitigate or prevent them, the role of civil society in general, and of myriad NGOS in particular, has grown.

A variety of movements and organizations have come together since the 1990s to become significant components of the global civil society. One type involves various groups of transnational activists participating in efforts to deal with global warming, AIDs, landmines, and so forth. Then there is the global alter-globalization movement as well as the anti-war movement, especially its most recent iteration spurred by the invasion of Iraq. Of growing significance in the realm of global civil society is the wide range of organizations dealing primarily with issues that relate to the environment, human rights, and economic development. Among the most notable of these are INGOS (see below) such as CARE, Worldwide Fund for Nature, Greenpeace, Amnesty International, Friends of the Earth, Médecins Sans Frontières, Oxfam, and so on. Perhaps of greatest importance today in thinking about civil society are groups that represent the poor, especially those in less developed countries, and their efforts to improve the position of the poor within the global economy.

INTERNATIONAL NON-GOVERNMENTAL ORGANIZATIONS (INGOs)

INGOs are international not-for-profit organizations that perform public functions but are not established or run by nation-states (examples in addition to those mentioned above include Transparency International, Global Witness, Center for Public Integrity, Clean

International Non-Governmental Organizations (INGOs): International not-for-profit organizations performing public functions but not established or run by nation-states.

Clothes Campaign, International Organization for Standardization [ISO], International Electrotechnical Commission [IEC], and various professional associations). They are private, voluntary, and nonprofit and most are oriented to bringing about some sort of social and/or political change. INGOs are advocates for any number of things, but they also "routinely influence the domestic policies of states, participate in multilateral forums and institutions, promote interstate cooperation, and facilitate political participation on the part of governments and the public" (Warkentin 2007).

The first modern INGOs are traceable to the nineteenth century (the International Red Cross was founded in Switzerland in 1865), but they have boomed in recent years. As their number, influence, and power have grown, they have become highly controversial. Some see them as the harbingers of a future democratic civil society. Others are highly critical of them (see below).

While many INGOs have grown highly influential, their power does not involve rational-legal authority (Weber 1921/1968) (such as having their leadership being duly elected), but rather comes from rational-moral authority (Thomas 2007). This stems from the fact that they claim (often successfully) that they represent and express universal human interests, are democratic both as organizations and in terms of their goals, and are committed to global progress and the creation of a more rational world. Their great moral power also comes from their neutrality; their disinterestedness. At the most general level, they serve to frame global policy issues in areas such as women's rights, population, education, and the environment.

As moral powers, they are less actors on the world stage than they exist to advise states, firms, and individuals on how they ought to act on various issues and under an array of circumstances.

INGOs have several characteristics that make them invaluable in the global arena. First, they are often grassroots organizations and therefore are much more in touch with the needs and interests of their membership than larger, more formal, and more bureaucratized organizations associated with nation-states or the international community. Second, they are often more effective in achieving their goals than other types of organizations (for example, they are often able to get relief faster to people in poor countries or to victims of disasters). Third, they are very good at garnering media attention in efforts to force more formal organizations (e.g. states) into action.

A turning point in the history of INGOs occurred in 1992 when a treaty to control the emission of greenhouse gases was signed as a result of the actions of a variety of groups that not only exerted external pressure, but were actually involved in the decision-making process. A number of other successes followed:

1. Review by the World Bank of its funding strategies.
2. Creation by the UN of a high commissioner for human rights.
3. Prevention of the approval of the Multilateral Agreement on Investment (which would have liberalized foreign investment and limited the role of nation-states in such actions).
4. Protests at World Trade Organization meetings, especially the Seattle action of 1999.
5. Formal representation at the World Economic Forum in Davos, Switzerland.

One of the most notable successes of INGOs was an international treaty spearheaded by the International Campaign to Ban Landmines (ICBL). The treaty was signed in 1997 by

122 nations which agreed to stop selling and using landmines. On the surface the fact that so many nation-states were involved in signing the treaty would seem to indicate that this was an accomplishment linked to the old state-centered system. In fact, however, much of the credit went to the approximately one thousand NGOs that had been involved in lobbying in about 60 countries for such a treaty (Bond 2000).

However, there are negative sides to the growth of INGOS (and civil society).

- Fundamentally INGOs are special interest groups and therefore they may not take into consideration wider sets of concerns and issues.
- In addition, they are not democratic, often keep their agendas secret, and are not accountable to anyone other than their members.
- They are elitist (many involve better-off and well-educated people from the North), that is undemocratic, organizations that seek to impose inappropriate universal plans on local organizations and settings.
- Thus, they have the potential to be "loose cannons" on the global stage.
- They are seen as annoying busybodies that are forever putting their noses in the business of others (Thomas 2007).
- And, they often pander to public opinion and posture for the media both to attract attention to their issues and to maintain or expand their power and membership.
- As a result, they may distort the magnitude of certain problems (e.g. overestimating the effects, and misjudging the causes, of an oil spill) in order to advance their cause and interests.
- Their focus on one issue may adversely affect the interest in, and ability to deal with, many other important issues.
- The nature of the focus, and indeed the very creation, of an INGO may be a function of its ability to attract attention and to raise funds. As a result, other worthy, if not more worthy, issues (e.g. soil erosion, especially in Africa), may fail to attract much, if any, attention and interest.
- In some cases, well-meaning INGOs conflict with one another, such as those wishing to end certain practices (e.g. logging) versus those that see those practices as solutions (e.g. logging producing wood as a sustainable resource that is preferable to fossil fuels).
- Then there are those critics who point to the fashionableness of certain issues and the fact that INGOs may be driven by what is considered in vogue and not what really needs attention.
- Control of the North over INGOs has actually increased leading to questions about their relevance to the concerns of the South.
- However, perhaps the strongest criticism of INGOs is that they "seem to have helped accelerate further state withdrawal from social provision" (Harvey 2006: 52). In that sense they can be seen as neoliberalism's "Trojan horses" furthering its agenda while seeming to operate against some of its worst abuses.

Thus, global civil society is extremely broad and includes organizations and parties that may well be in conflict with one another (e.g. the Western neoliberals who dominate the major INGOs and the often non-Western critics of neoliberalism, including radical religious fundamentalists, who dominate less well-organized groups). What they all have in common is that they exist more or less outside the confines of the nation-state and offer at least the possibility that people can be a part of ongoing debates in the world and perhaps even involved in movements toward greater democracy and emancipation (Munck 2002a; Teune 2002).

Beyond their moral power, some INGOs (see below) have become formally involved in **Intergovernmental Organizations** (IGOs) that are international in scope (e.g. UN) (Martens 2001). INGOs stand to gain from such formal associations in various ways. There are *symbolic* gains such as greater legitimacy associated with being involved with such an internationally visible organization. There are also the more *material* gains since such an organization might provide badly needed funding to various INGOs; work may even be sub-contracted to INGOs and they can earn income for performing the required tasks.

Of course, there are dangers to INGOs involved in this course of action. They can easily become co-opted by the IGO involved. Less extremely, INGOs may need to become more rationalized, bureaucratized, and professionalized[20] in order to deal with the needs and demands of the IGO. This, in turn, can lead to a more subtle change of orientation, and a decline in radicalism, in an INGO. Other possible changes in INGOs include a loss of flexibility (as they must satisfy the demands of the IGO which, after all, may well be the source of badly needed funds), a decline in capacity to act quickly, and, perhaps most troubling, a loss of autonomy and perhaps even identity.

For their part, IGOs are affected by the involvement of INGOs. They, too, can gain symbolically and increase their legitimacy through the involvement of high-minded INGOs. Further, they can gain in a material sense because of the fact that less bureaucratized INGOs can perform tasks that would be much more costly, and done much more slowly and inefficiently, were they performed by IGOs.

The mutual involvement of INGOs and IGOs is perhaps clearest in the case of UNESCO since INGOS were involved in it from its inception in 1945. In fact, in order to handle its large and diverse responsibilities, UNESCO created a variety of INGOs such as the International Council of Museums (ICOM). In other cases, UNESCO funded existing INGOs (e.g. the International Council of Scientific Unions [ICSU] in existence since 1931) in order to handle tasks (in the case of ICSU the promotion of scientific research and its application to the betterment of humankind) that it otherwise might be required to handle. Finally, UNESCO helped INGOs by either not getting involved in domains already well-handled by INGOs or by withdrawing from areas when a viable INGO emerged. Thus, with the emergence of the World Wildlife Fund (WWF) in 1961, UNESCO effectively ceded to it environmental issues with which it had, up to that time, been concerned.

> **Intergovernmental Organizations (IGOs):** Organizations such as the UN that are international in scope.

INGOs AND GLOBALIZATION

On the one hand, it could be argued that INGOs have arisen as part of globalization. But a more critical view might be that as neoliberalism has spread around the world as an integral part of economic and political globalization, functions once handled by the nation-state have been scaled back or eliminated. Many INGOs can be seen as coming into existence to fill various voids left by the withdrawal of the nation-state. More extreme is the role played by neoliberalism and its agencies (e.g. the World Bank) in the less developed world. For example, the restructuring demanded by these agencies in the third world has often meant that national governments retreat from handling various functions. Without INGOs in these areas, many of these functions might not be handled at all.

CHAPTER SUMMARY

This chapter examines the development and functioning of global political structures. Starting with more traditional structures such as the nation-state, the discussion moves on to the development of regional and global political structures and processes.

The origin of the modern nation-state is traced to the Peace of Westphalia, and its treaties which led to the notion that nation-states are autonomous. Later developments led to the fusion of the cultural concept of a nation and the structure of the state, to the idea of the nation-state. With globalization, the nation-state faces innumerable challenges, leading to a significant loss of control over economic flows and transnational organizations. A debate has emerged over whether the "nation-state is dead." Although the role of the nation-state has declined, it is still an important political structure. However, in the global age, the "porosity" of the nation-state, the increasing global flows flow through it, should be a focal concern.

Benedict Anderson's "imagined community" is an important idea in thinking about the nation-state. As a result of the development of "print capitalism," it came to be conceived of as being actively constructed, socially and politically, by people who identify with the community that is represented by the nation-state. This concept is extended further by examining how the nation-state transcends its geographic boundaries in the face of rapidly developing technology and increasing immigration flows. Emphasis is placed on the "re-imagining" of the nation-state in the light of such global flows.

In terms of the changing geo-political scenario, the world can be seen as evolving through three stages – bipolar (during the Cold War), unipolar (ascendancy of the US), and finally to a tri-polar future with the US, EU, and China as the three centers of power.

Also examined is the emergence of larger global political structures such as the League of Nations, the United Nations, as well as more specific organizations such as UNCTAD, UNESCO, G8, and IAEA.

The concept of global governance is an increasingly important concern today. This has emerged as an alternative, or at least a supplement, to the inter-state system in addressing various global problems. Global governance has developed in response to the decline of the nation-state, as well as to global crises that nation-states cannot control.

Also of great political importance is civil society. Although it has ancient origins, the modern concept of civil society was fleshed out by thinkers such as Hegel and Gramsci. Civil society came to be conceived of as clearly separated from the state on the one hand and the market and family on the other. However, there are contemporary debates over whether civil society is truly separate from the market, in light of the disruptive influence that the latter might have on the former. This can be traced, in part, to the tension that is internal to civil society which is comprised of a number of highly disparate organizations. Local civil society now co-exists with "global civil society." Non-Governmental Organizations (NGOs) co-exist with International Non-Governmental Organizations (INGOs).

There is a perception that global civil society could be a "replacement" for the nation-state. In many areas it is seen as already filling the vacuum created by the decline of the nation-state. While civil society has its strengths (greater efficiency, closer to the people), it also faces challenges in terms of a narrowness of focus, and charges of elitism and control by the North. INGOs may also share a symbiotic relationship with Intergovernmental Organizations (IGOs), which, while being beneficial in symbolic and material terms, creates challenges for the INGOs in terms of loss of radicalism and autonomy.

DISCUSSION QUESTIONS

1. Examine the interaction between the nation-state and civil society, differentiating between local and global civil society.

2. Make the case *for* the "death of the nation-state" focusing especially on the role played by global flows in the "demise" of the nation-state.

3. Make the case *against* the "death of the nation-state" focusing especially on the role played by barriers (especially those erected by the nation-state) to global flows.

4. Analyze the concept of global governance and discuss the adequacy of such a government as a political tool in the "real world."

5. Discuss the advantages of, and challenges to, the nation-state, in the context of "imagined communities."

6. Examine the relevance of global political structures such as the UN in light of global flows and processes.

ADDITIONAL READINGS

Robert J. Holton. *Globalization and the Nation-State*. New York: St. Martin's Press, 1998.

E. Ohmae. *The End of the Nation-State: The Rise of Regional Economies*. New York: Free Press, 1996.

Susan Strange. *The Retreat of the State: The Diffusion of Power in the World Economy*. Cambridge: Cambridge University Press, 1996.

Carolyn Nordstrom. *Shadows of War: Violence, Power, and International Profiteering in the Twenty-First Century*. Berkeley: University of California Press, 2004.

Eric Hobsbawm. *Nations and Nationalism Since 1780: Programme, Myth, Reality*, 2nd edn. New York: Cambridge University Press, 2012.

Benedict Anderson. *Imagined Communities*. Revised edition. London: Verso, 2006.

Parag Khanna. *The Second World: Empires and Influence in the New Global Order*. New York: Random House, 2008.

Paul Diehl and Brian Frederking, eds. *The Politics of Global Governance: International Organizations in an Interdependent World*. Lynne Rienner Publishers, 2010.

Thomas Hale and David Held, eds. *Handbook of Transnational Governance*. Malden, MA: Polity Press, 2011.

John Keane. *Global Civil Society*. Cambridge: Cambridge University Press, 2003.

Alison Brysk. *Human Rights and Private Wrongs*. New York: Routledge, 2013.

NOTES

1 Although some of the economic structures – e.g. the EU – have at least some political aspects and implications – indeed everything discussed in this book has political relevance.

2 For studies of the relationship between one nation-state and globalization, see Kim (2000); Mohammadi (2003).

3   While we now tend to think of the nation-state as virtually synonymous with a political structure, the fact is that there have been, and still are, other important political structures including "village societies, city-states, multilayered and feudal and warlord-dominated societies, tribal societies, federations and confederations of various kinds, and empires"; Hayman and Williams (2006).

4   However, the bailout of its economy by the US, Great Britain, Germany, and others could only have been accomplished by the nation-state; no international or global body had the funds to do it.

5   The nation-state's borders were seen as the perimeter of the "container" protecting it from unwanted outside influences and allowing it to retain most, if not all, of what it needed to function on its own.

6   Although, as we will see in Chapter 10, the nation-state remains central in various ways including the definition of a refugee as one who crosses a national border.

7   See, for example, Wolf (2005); Conley (2002).

8   Khanna has written a popular work, but he draws on many noted scholars of geopolitics including Richard N. Rosecrance, Samuel Huntington, Robert Gilpin, and John Agnew.

9   Unfortunately, he is not as clear as he might be on these two terms; see footnote on p. xxi in Khanna (2008a).

10   Gazprom is a huge Russian conglomerate, but its main business is in natural gas. It is thought to exercise undue influence on the Russian government.

11   The Cold War is a term used to define the conflicting relationship between the Soviet Union and its allies and the West, especially the United States, between the end of WW II and the fall of the Soviet Union in 1991. It was a "cold" war because it never became a "hot," a shooting, war involving the protagonists, at least directly.

12   www.unep.org.

13   www.unctad.org; Taylor (2003).

14   www.aseansec.org; Nesadurai (2007).

15   www.aseansec.org.

16   www.aseansec.org.

17   http://www.au.int/.

18   For a major contemporary example of social theory in this area, influenced at least in part by Tocqueville's work, see Alexander (2006b). For a recent overview of Tocqueville's work, see Ritzer (2008a: 81–105).

19   For an argument that this is still the case, at least to some degree, see Vogel (2006).

20   On the interrelationship of these processes, at least from the point of view of Weberian theory, see Ritzer (1975: 627–34).

STRUCTURING THE GLOBAL ECONOMY

Globalization: A Basic Text, Second Edition. George Ritzer and Paul Dean.
© 2015 John Wiley & Sons, Ltd. Published 2015 by John Wiley & Sons, Ltd.

Because of the importance of the economy in globalization, we devote two chapters to it. In this chapter the focus is on economic structures, while in the next the focus shifts to economic processes and flows. However, it is useful to reiterate the point that this is a largely artificial distinction since structures are composed of processes and processes can be structured.

We will show how the economic structure known as the Bretton Woods System emerged and shaped global economic flows for decades. In response to newer global developments, this system has been superseded by several new global institutions, which are the focal point of many conflicts that will be explored in subsequent chapters. But, first, in order to understand the major economic structures involved in globalization today one must have a sense of their place in economic history (Frieden 2006; Tonkiss 2012).

BEFORE BRETTON WOODS

A PRIOR EPOCH OF GLOBALIZATION

One important view is that a global economic system, specifically a global capitalist system, emerged in about 1896 and reached something of a peak throughout the world in 1914.[1,2] There are some interesting analogies between the growth of the global capitalist economy during that period and today.[3]

- During the earlier epoch global progress was spurred by such developments in transportation as the railroad and the steam ship, whereas in more recent years it is the airplane that played a central role in that development.
- The telegraph greatly enhanced global communications in the early twentieth century, while it is the Internet that plays that role nearly a century later.
- Global economic development, both then and now, depended on large-scale flows of capital.
- In addition, such development in both periods entailed large-scale immigration and even the growing importance of remittances to those who remained in the homeland (for a discussion of remittances today see Chapter 10).
- More generally, global economic specialization (Smith 1776/1977) among the nations of the world became the norm, then and now.
- Furthermore, this specialization operated on the basis of the "law" of *comparative advantage* (Ricardo 1817/1971); that is, that nations should concentrate on what they do best. This comparison is internal – that is, a nation should concentrate on what it does best in comparison to the other things *it* does (or could do) and *not* in comparison to what other nations do.
- This is related to another similarity between today and a century ago and that is an emphasis on free trade and the elimination of trade barriers (e.g. tariffs).[4]

Not only are there structural similarities between global economic development in the two periods, but the problems created in the two epochs are also similar. First, poor nations and the peoples who inhabit them were and are subjugated by the operations of the global economy. Second, not all parts of the world (e.g. traditional economies) gain(ed) (or gain[ed] equally) from the growth of the global economy. There were/are even sub-areas within those parts of the world that did advance that did/do not share equally in the gain. Third, not only were/are there losers in this economic competition among geographic areas, but also certain industries and social classes lose out, at least in comparison to the winners. Fourth, within nations the poor tend(ed) to suffer most when those nations are forced to repay their debts to other, more developed, nations. In sum, the global economy of a century ago (and much the same could be said today) "was not equally good for everyone and was bad for many" (Frieden 2006: 26).

While a strong case can be made for a prior epoch of economic globalization, what is not recognized in this argument – and what is central to this book – is that there is far more to globalization than that which relates to the economy. For example, Jeffry Frieden mentions the global spread of the English language and of soccer/football, but he fails to accord such cultural phenomena the importance they deserve. Further, while Frieden devotes more attention to political issues, they are usually part of, or subordinated to, economics and economic globalization. Thus, he (and many others) fails to give political and cultural globalization their proper role in his overall perspective on globalization. The cultural and the political are just two of the aspects of globalization given short shrift, or ignored, by Frieden. Thus, even if we accept his argument (shared by others) that economic globalization is not new, this argument tells us little or nothing about these other aspects of globalization. Nonetheless, the argument about a prior epoch of economic globalization is very useful in terms of the discussion to follow on the emergence of more recent global economic structures.

ECONOMIC DEVELOPMENT DURING AND AFTER WW II

Frieden sees the development of economic globalization after WW II in the context of this prior epoch of economic globalization, as well as its collapse as a result of WW I, the Depression, and WW II. All of these events had negative effects on almost all major economies (the US economy was a major exception, at least in terms of the effect of the two world wars). Of particular importance in the 1930s was the movement of many countries – notably fascist Italy and Germany – in the direction of **autarky**, or the turn inward of a nation in order to create as much economic self-sufficiency as possible. Such a turn inward is, of course, anathema to globalization which requires that various entities – including nation-states – be outward-looking, rather than inward-looking, not only in the way they view the world but in their actual dealings with other parts of the world. For its part, the US in the 1930s had a strong tendency toward *isolationism*,[5] although such an orientation was not quite as antithetical to economic globalization as autarky, largely because it was more political than economic.

Autarky: Turn inward of a nation-state in order to become as economically self-sufficient as possible.

However, even in the midst of WW II, the Western world, especially the US and Great Britain, began planning for a more open international economy. A great fear was the recurrence of the Depression after the end of WW II, especially because of the difficulties those societies would have in absorbing the massive manpower created by the demobilization of the military when the war ended. There was also fear of a resurrection of barriers to trade and the free flow of money that had become commonplace prior to WW II. The focus of the planners was on reducing trade barriers and on creating conditions necessary for the free flow of money and investment. Another concern was the creation of conditions needed for financial stability around the globe. This was the background for a meeting in July 1944 at the Mount Washington Hotel in Bretton Woods, New Hampshire, which led to the beginning of the "Bretton Woods System" by the end of the three-week meeting.

BRETTON WOODS AND THE BRETTON WOODS SYSTEM

A key factor in the Depression was thought to be a lack of cooperation among nation-states. That lack of cooperation was associated with high tariffs and other import restrictions and protectionist practices, as well as the propensity of governments to devalue their currencies in order to gain an edge in global trade over other countries. The latter also made exchange rate wars among the nations involved more likely.

Those concerns were the backdrop for the creation of the Bretton Woods system and its five key elements (Bordo and Eichengreen 1993; Boughton 2007). First, each participating state would establish a "'par value' for its currency expressed in terms of gold or (equivalently) in terms of the gold value of the US dollar as of July 1944" (Boughton 2007: 106). For example, the US pegged its currency at $35 per ounce of gold, while, to take one example, Nicaragua was 175 cordobas per ounce. This meant that the exchange rate between the two currencies was five cordobas for one dollar.

"Second, the official monetary authority in each country (a central bank or its equivalent) would agree to exchange its own currency for those of other countries at the established exchange rates, plus or minus a one-percent margin" (Boughton 2007: 106–7). This made international trade possible at or near the exchange rate for the currencies of the countries involved without the need for any outside intervention.

Third, the International Monetary Fund (IMF) was created (Babb 2007) (as was the forerunner of the World Bank – see below) to establish, stabilize, and oversee exchange rates. Forty states became IMF members in 1946 and were required to deposit some of their gold reserves with it. The IMF was empowered to approve the par values of currencies and member states could not change that value by more than 10%. If a currency was destabilized, the IMF was prepared to lend member states the money needed to stabilize their currency.

Fourth, the member states agreed to eliminate, at least eventually, "all restrictions on the use of its currency for international trade" (Boughton 2007: 107).

Finally, the entire system was based on the US dollar (at the end of WW II the US had about three-fourths of the world's gold supply and accounted for over one-fifth of world exports). The US agreed to make the dollar convertible into other currencies or gold at the fixed par value. The dollar became, in effect, a global currency. Of course, as the Bretton Woods system came into existence and had a chance to develop, it changed dramatically over time.

Bretton Woods had its most powerful effects on global trade, the global monetary order, and global investment (Peet 2003). On *global trade* a key point was the idea of the "unconditional most-favored-nation" which "required governments to offer the same trade concessions [reductions in trade barriers, non-discrimination against a nation's products] to all" (Frieden 2006: 288). Restrictions on international trade were reduced over the years through various meetings ("rounds") under the auspices of GATT (General Agreement on Tariffs and Trade) and later the WTO (see below).

In terms of the *monetary order*, it was the IMF that took center stage. The goal was to provide security, as well as flexibility, to the monetary order. What emerged between 1958 and 1971 was a system in which the US could not change the value of its dollar, while all other countries could, but as infrequently as possible. This made exchange rates stable enough to encourage international trade and investment which otherwise would have been discouraged by dramatic fluctuations in those rates.

In terms of *global investment*, a key role was envisioned for the World Bank, but massive US aid through the Marshall Plan, and rapid European post-war recovery, made its work in that period of much less significance than had been anticipated. A key development in terms of investment involved MNCs, especially American-based firms in fields like automobiles and computers, constructing their own plants and/or investing in indigenous companies in other countries. This kind of investment took center stage because the industries involved required very large, often global, organizations in order to function effectively. In addition, this kind of investment made it possible to get around trade barriers by opening plants within the countries with such barriers.

The global openness encouraged by Bretton Woods also contributed to the emergence or expansion of social welfare programs, indeed the welfare state, in many countries. Welfare states sought to deal with various problems – recession, layoffs, reductions in wages, and bankruptcies of uncompetitive firms. The creation of a social safety net within a given country served to protect it and its citizens from these problems, at least to some degree. In the process, it gave a nation and its entrepreneurs the cover they needed to be actively involved in the global marketplace.

The combination of all of these aspects and dimensions of Bretton Woods satisfied many different nations and constituencies (e.g. capital and labor) and in the process "oversaw the most rapid rates of economic growth and most enduring economic stability in modern history" (Frieden 2006: 300).

Given this brief background on Bretton Woods, let us now look in more detail at some of the economic organizations spawned by it either directly or indirectly.

INTERNATIONAL TRADE ORGANIZATION

We can begin with the International Trade Organization (ITO) because, while it was a creation of Bretton Woods, it never really got started. It was killed largely by US opposition based most broadly on perceived threats of the ITO to its national sovereignty. Further, some (protectionists in the US) found it too oriented toward free trade, while other Americans (free traders) thought it too protectionist. Given the contradictory nature of this assault, it was clear that the ITO had little chance of winning political support in the US. In fact, opposition to the ITO was so strong that President Harry Truman never submitted it to Congress because it was sure to be killed there. The ITO was dead before it started, but the idea of free(r) trade was not. This is clear in the discussion to follow of GATT, as well as of the World Bank.

GENERAL AGREEMENT ON TARIFFS AND TRADE (GATT)

GATT was a system for the liberalization of trade that grew out of Bretton Woods and came into existence in 1947 (Hudec 1975). It operated until 1995 when it was superseded by the World Trade Organization (WTO) (see below). While GATT focused on trade in goods, the WTO also took on responsibility for the increasingly important trade in services. While GATT was simply a forum for the meeting of representatives of countries, the WTO is an independent organization.

GATT was deemed more acceptable than the ITO by the US (and others) and in 1947 a number of initial trade agreements were negotiated by 23 nations. Since then, multinational trade agreements have been negotiated under GATT's (and later the WTO's) institutional umbrella. Over the years a number of "rounds" of negotiation were completed (e.g. the Kennedy Round ending in 1967; the Tokyo Round which concluded in 1979). It was out of the Uruguay Round (1986–1993) that an agreement was reached to create the WTO. While GATT has been superseded by the WTO, many of its elements were incorporated into the WTO, although they continue to change and evolve as a result of changing global economic realities. Negotiations on trade have continued under the auspices of the WTO and as of this writing the highly disputatious Doha Round has just ended in failure. Over the years, WTO negotiations have dealt with such issues as reducing tariffs on the trading of goods, dealing with non-tariff barriers (e.g. quotas, national subsidies to industry and agriculture), and liberalizing international trade in agriculture. More recently, attention has shifted to such issues as "international trade in services, trade-related international property rights (TRIPS), and trade-related investment measures (TRIMS)" (House 2007).

Trade-Related Intellectual Property Rights (TRIPS)

Intellectual property rights (IPRs) are an increasingly important issue in the world today and as it relates to globalization (Bedirhanoglu 2012). These involve intangible ideas, knowledge, and expressions that require their use be approved by their owner. Involved here is a wide range of intellectual property such as movies, books, music recordings, and computer software that exist, or whose value lies, largely in the realm of ideas. There are other, more material, products such as pharmaceuticals and advanced technologies, that are also viewed as having a significant intellectual component. Historically involving phenomena such as "patents, copyrights, trademarks, and trade secrets" (Rangnekar 2007), IPRs have now expanded to include the kinds of things discussed above. There were national IPRs agreements long before the current era of globalization, but profound differences among such agreements led to the need for the development of a global agreement rather than a series of national agreements. That global agreement – **Trade-Related Aspects of Intellectual Property Rights** (TRIPS) (Correa 2000) – was negotiated through the WTO, as a result of the 1986–1994 Uruguay Round of negotiations. This agreement serves to protect the interests of those individuals, organizations, and states that create ideas. However, there is global inequality in the generation of these ideas with the result that the most developed nations, as well as organizations and individuals in them, benefit from TRIPS, while less developed nations and their constituents often feel that this serves to continue to advantage the developed nations and to disadvantage them. (This is one of the many global realities that contradict Thomas Friedman's "flat world" thesis [Friedman 2005]). More generally, there are those who protest the whole idea of commodifying intellectual and cultural products (May 2002). Then there are more specific complaints such as those against the pharmaceutical industry for biopiracy which can involve both the effort to control genetic resources and therefore not to share them equitably and equally. Biopiracy can also involve gaining control over (stealing) indigenous medical knowledge, as well as of the ingredients discovered by indigenous peoples that they may well continue to use (e.g. plants), to treat various illnesses (Kamau and Winter 2013). For example, indigenous communities in South Africa have long used pelargonium sidoides, a variety of geranium, to treat various respiratory diseases, as well as bronchitis (Hall 2013). In 2000, a German company, Schwabe, developed a pharmaceutical based on the plant and the medical knowledge of the indigenous communities. Not only did the company refuse to compensate the community, but it sought to obtain exclusive copyright for the medical usage of the plant

Trade-Related Aspects of International Property Rights (TRIPS): WTO agreement to protect the interests of those that create ideas.

(the patents were cancelled in 2010). This is thought of as piracy because there is little or no effort to reward indigenous peoples for their discoveries. This is a rapidly growing issue, with many similar examples, as corporations seek to profit from the hundreds of years of medical knowledge in these communities that have no concept of intellectual property.

All of this has led to disputes over the legitimacy of intellectual property as a whole and there have been many more specific disputes over who has rights to specific forms of intellectual property. The WTO has a dispute settlement system to deal with these issues.

Trade-Related Investment Measures (TRIMs)

Trade-Related Investment Measures (TRIMs) "are a range of operating or performance measures that host-country governments impose on foreign firms to keep them from having a distorting effect on trade in goods and services" (Grimwade 2007: 1178; Chiang 2012a). There are a number of specific restrictions and constraints on foreign firms that can be included under this heading, including:

> **Trade-Related Investment Measures (TRIMs):** WTO agreement on trade measures governments can impose on foreign firms.

1. Requirements for local content or sourcing. Minimum amounts of local content or local sourcing are specified for inputs into final products.
2. Export Performance Criteria. This spells out how much of a foreign producer's output must be exported.
3. Trade Balancing Requirements. Limits the value of goods imported by a foreign firm to the amount it exports.
4. Foreign Exchange Restrictions. Limits the inflow of foreign exchange to foreign firms.
5. Export Controls. Limits on the amount a foreign firm can export (Grimwade 2007: 1178–80).

There are many other restrictions that can be placed on foreign firms, but nation-states also use various inducements (e.g. subsidies and tax allowances) to get foreign firms to invest in their country, or to increase their investments.

TRIMs are another subject of dispute between the North and the South (disputes that can be hashed out within the WTO). The less developed countries in the South tend to favor TRIMs because they allow them to better control foreign investment. The more developed countries in the North tend to be critical of TRIMS largely because they limit the ability of corporations that stem primarily from the North to do business and earn profits in less developed nations. More generally and from a straight neoliberal position, they are critical of TRIMS for being barriers to the free flow of money and products.

WORLD TRADE ORGANIZATION (WTO)

The WTO is a multilateral organization headquartered in Geneva, Switzerland, with, as of mid-2014, 160 member nations (Krueger 2000, 2012; World Trade Organization 2013). Its focus on trade places it at the heart of economic globalization and has made it a magnet for those opposed either to the broader process of trade liberalization and promotion or to some specific aspect of WTO operations. The WTO encompasses much of what was GATT's mandate, but has moved onto other issues and areas such as services (General Agreement on Trade in Services [GATS] [Batista 2012], intellectual property [TRIPS], and so on).

Each member state in the WTO has an equal vote. To a large extent, the WTO is the organization of these member states and not (with some exceptions) a supranational organization. Agenda items to be voted on generally flow from a number of more informal groups.

There are stresses and strains between developed and developing nations in the WTO that are manifest in and between these groups, as well as in the WTO as a whole. One bone of contention has been meetings of the larger trading powers in the so-called "Green Room" and the exclusion of smaller powers from these meetings. Protests over such matters have led to more transparency in the internal operations of the WTO (and elsewhere). There is also no mechanism for involvement of INGOs in WTO decision-making and this has led INGOs to stage regular protests and demonstrations against the WTO.

While GATT focused on tariff reduction, the WTO has come to focus more on non-tariff-related barriers to trade. One example is differences between nations on regulations on such things as manufactured goods or food. A given nation can be taken to task for such regulations if they are deemed to be unfair restraints on the trade in such items. However, the WTO has been criticized for not going far enough in countering the trade barriers retained by developed countries in such domains as agricultural products and some services.

Of course, the WTO continues to be concerned with tariff barriers, as well as restrictions on trade in services. The WTO also deals with other types of protectionism. Overall, WTO operations are premised on the neoliberal idea that all nations benefit from free and open trade and it is dedicated to reducing, and ultimately eliminating, barriers to such trade. While there are winners under such a system, there are also losers.

"Rounds"

The most recent of the "rounds," the Doha Round, began in Doha, Qatar in 2001 and continues today (as of mid-2014). The talks had been highly contentious from the beginning and stalled at several different points. The ostensible goal of this round of trade talks was to help the less developed countries in the world, but a major issue was a dispute between the US and the EU over farm subsidies. The US offered to limit farm subsidies to $22.5 billion per year. While this is less than half of what current agreements permit, it was about $3 million *more* than US farm subsidies in 2005. European negotiators saw this as an effort to increase, not reduce, US subsidies. For its part, the US wanted Europe to cut its farm subsidies by 50%. Both sides were hampered in making concessions by their powerful farm blocs. For an agreement to have been reached, less developed countries would also have needed to reduce their tariffs on farm goods. Comparatively poor countries resisted such cuts, arguing that they should not have to make sacrifices in order for rich countries to open their markets. As of this writing, agriculture remains at the top of the Doha Agenda.

The negotiations, and even the future of such talks, were in doubt from the beginning of the re-opening of the Doha Round in mid-2008, and their conclusion remains unclear. This was the case because so many member nations had become involved (160) that negotiations had grown complicated and cumbersome (Krueger 2012). Earlier rounds were easier not only because of the smaller number of nations involved, but also because an agreement among a few nations, especially the EU and the US, would ordinarily be the basis of a general decision. However, that was no longer the case with so many more nations involved and with the general shift in economic power toward the East in general, especially China and India (Castle 2008: B2). The collapse of the Doha talks has several implications including a demonstration of the rising power of India and China (as well as of the less developed nations), and the declining power in such deliberations of the US and the EU. Talks on trade will continue, but they are likely to be in more limited bilateral negotiations than in the global negotiations that have characterized WTO talks (Saggi and Yildiz 2011).

OTHER ORGANIZATIONS

The *Group of Thirty* (G30) is neither a governmental nor a state-based organization (Chiang 2012b). It was founded as a nonprofit organization in 1978 with a grant from the Rockefeller Foundation. Its goal was the examination of "economic and financial issues in a way that is relevant to policy makers and practitioners in an era of globalization" (Tsingou 2007: 556). It is composed of people drawn from high-level positions in international institutions (e.g. Bank of International Settlements), national supervisory agencies (e.g. Governor of the Bank of Mexico), major financial institutions (e.g. senior managers from Citigroup), and academia (especially economists). It has produced a number of influential studies on topics such as clearance and settlement in national securities markets and the use of over-the-counter derivatives.

The *Group of 77* involves developing nations and is part of the UN. Created in 1964, the Group of 77 is a misnomer since it now numbers 133 nations. It was formed because of a concern that Bretton Woods and GATT did not serve the interests of developing nations (Collins 2012). Its increasing size and diversity has created various divisions (e.g. large versus small; rich and poor nations) within it that, among other things, led to the creation of the Group of 21.

The *Group of 21* developing nations came into existence at the 2003 meetings of the WTO under the leadership of Brazil, South Africa, and India. Its major focus, at least initially, was on agricultural issues.

INTERNATIONAL MONETARY FUND (IMF)

The goal of the IMF is macroeconomic stability for both member nations and, more generally, the global economy (Lee 2012a). More specifically, the IMF deals with exchange rates, balances of payments, international capital flows, and the monitoring of member states and their macroeconomic policies. The IMF is a lightning rod for critics who see it as supporting developed countries and their efforts to impose their policies, including neoliberalism, on less developed countries. Its supporters see it as key to the emergence and further development of the global economy.

As a result of changes in the global economy, the nature and functions of the IMF have changed since its creation in 1944. In the beginning it managed the exchange rate system created at Bretton Woods. The IMF closely watched a nation's balance-of-payments in order to be sure it could sustain the agreed-upon exchange rate for its currency. If there were problems in the latter, the IMF concerned itself with two matters. The first were policy errors by a nation which, presumably, could be corrected. The second were more fundamental economic problems (relating, for example, to productivity). Above all, the IMF wanted to be sure that a nation did not use such problems as an excuse to lower its exchange rate and therefore improve its competitive position vis-à-vis other nations. If a fundamental disequilibrium occurred, the IMF had the power to authorize a change in the exchange rate of a nation's currency.

When the fixed, albeit adjustable, exchange-rate system collapsed in the early 1970s, the first of the IMF's functions changed so that it was in charge of the much more amorphous goal of seeking stable exchange rates in order to prevent exchange rate wars among its member nations. By the end of the 1970s developed nations had fully recovered from WW II and ceased seeking adjustment loans; such loans were now given to developing countries with balance-of-payments problems. With a new clientele, the conditions for such loans changed and became more stringent, including the demand for **structural adjustments** in such nations.[6] Among such adjustments were demands for a tight monetary policy and fiscal austerity. More specifically, the IMF might demand "currency devaluation, measures to reduce government spending or (more rarely) increased taxation, deregulation of interest rates and of foreign exchange transactions, slower expansion of domestic credit creation, and measures to manage and reduce external indebtedness" (Killick 2007: 1095). In particular, reduced government spending often meant less spending on health care and aid to the poor. These policies were traceable to a growing belief that balance-of-payments imbalances were caused by inflationary policies and processes (i.e. "loose" monetary policy, expansionist fiscal policies) in a given nation. Structural adjustments were designed to rein in such tendencies toward inflation and became conditions ("conditionalities") of help from the IMF. A nation receiving help agreed to alter its policies in order achieve a balance of payments in a short period of time (usually a year).

> **Structural adjustment**: Conditions of economic "restructuring" imposed by organizations such as the World Bank and the IMF on borrowing nation-states.

As the IMF became the lender of last resort for developing countries in the late 1970s and 1980s, it underwent further changes. Such countries were unlikely to be able to achieve a balance of payments in a short period of time. Thus, longer-term structural adjustment programs were required. The IMF adopted general models of the requirements for the operation of a market economy and these tended to be imposed on developing economies without regard for differences among and between their economies. These structural adjustments not only took the IMF into uncharted waters and new directions, but they also became highly controversial and ultimately a target of groups opposed to globalization, at least as the kind of globalization that was conceived and practiced by the IMF.

Such protests were also related to the IMF governance structure which is dominated by the US (with about 17% of the total IMF vote and veto power over any strategic decision); developed nations control more than 50% of the votes. (Votes are a function of a fixed number for each nation *plus* additional voting power based on each nation's quota of contributions to the Fund.) The managing director of the IMF usually comes from Western Europe; the deputy managing director from the US. In order to cope with criticisms of this structure, the IMF has been moving in the direction of greater transparency in its dealings with member nations, dealing more with NGOs, and being more concerned with social issues (e.g. poverty) in its dealings with developing nations.

The changing nature of global economic crises in the late twentieth century led to further changes in the IMF. It shifted from an interest in balance-of-payments issues that were related to current (trade and income) accounts to capital account movements of financial assets. This led to the creation of a Capital Markets Department to monitor financial markets and to suggest ways of stabilizing them.

In the 1990s the IMF was actively involved in helping to resolve the economic crises in Latin America, Asia, and Russia. However, critics contend that IMF policies were largely responsible for creating many of these crises, especially Argentina's 2001 financial collapse. Nonetheless, the Fund continued loaning large amounts of money, but as the countries involved repaid their loans (including Argentina), income to the IMF declined and by 2007, with interest income declining, it found itself running a deficit (about $400 million a year). The IMF increasingly seemed marginal or irrelevant. Accordingly, it began to focus on other issues such as working to "prevent crises, monitoring the global economy and providing technical assistance" (Weisman 2007b: C1). Others thought it should focus on data gathering and the dissemination of financial information in order to forestall economic surprises. The IMF faced other problems such as protests from the rest of the world over the continuing dominance of it by the Western powers. Further, the countries bailed out in the 1990s had become powerful economically and increasingly resented being dictated to by the Fund. There were also lingering resentments over IMF interventions that demanded austere budgets and other fiscal tightening in exchange for loans. As the Russian IMF representative described it, the resentment was over the traditional approach of the IMF – "you need our money, we tell you what to do" (Weisman 2007b: C5).

However, the Great Recession brought about a dramatic change in the fortunes of the IMF. The flows of international capital dried up and a number of economies were on the brink of disaster (Iceland, for example), or close to it (Hungary, Ukraine). The IMF called on developed economies to increase their contributions and the IMF's loan portfolio increased from $15.6 billion in 2008 to $52.6 billion in 2010, and now has hundreds of billions of dollars. Some countries that had avoided IMF loans previously, because of their strict conditionalities (e.g. Iceland), ultimately accepted funds from the IMF. Even healthy economies (Brazil, South Korea) were receiving economic help from the IMF (Landler 2008: B4). The long decline of the IMF was at an end, and more recently, significant IMF loan packages have gone to Pakistan and Cyprus. The most controversial recipient, however, is Greece, which has received hundreds of billions of dollars (including multiple IMF loans and loans from other agencies), which have been poorly managed and failed to set Greece on a financially sustainable path (Lowrey 2013). Among its many conditionalities, Greece was forced to slash public spending, which increased unemployment and sparked massive public protests throughout the country.

WORLD BANK

The World Bank (officially The International Bank for Reconstruction and Development [IBRD]), a specialized agency of the UN, is the most important element of the World Bank Group (WBG) (Gilbert and Vines 2000; Lee 2012b). IBRD (or the Bank) was established in 1944 at Bretton Woods and began operations in 1946. Membership is open to all member states of the IMF and as of this writing it includes 188 nations. It provides funds to government-sponsored or -guaranteed programs in so-called Part II countries (member states that are middle-income or creditworthy poorer nations). It also provides advice and analytical services to such states. Among the missions of the Bank are:

- encouraging "development of productive facilities and resources in less developed countries";
- funding for "productive purposes" when private capital cannot be obtained on reasonable terms;
- encouraging international investment in order to promote international trade and development and equilibrium in balance of payments;
- helping member countries improve their productivity, standard of living, and labor conditions (Bradlow 2007: 1264).

Over the years the Bank has expanded far beyond its original focus on projects involving physical infrastructure (e.g. transportation, telecommunication, water projects, etc.) capable of generating income. It now deals with a broad range of issues related to economic development including "population, education, health, social security, environment, culture... aspects of macroeconomic policy and structural reform... [and] poverty alleviation" (Bradlow 2007: 1265). In addition, it now makes loans to deal with a variety of governance matters such as "public-sector management, corruption, legal and judicial reform, and some aspects of human rights and broader policy reforms" (Bradlow 2007: 1265). Support is also given to help women deal with gender inequality and discrimination. The Bank continues to expand its range of concerns and activities (e.g. most recently, child labor, reconstruction after a conflict, etc.). NGOs and affected peoples have grown increasingly involved in projects financed by the Bank.

Decisions are supposed to be made on purely economic, not political, grounds and the Bank is not supposed to intervene in the political affairs of member states. However, exactly what is deemed political is not defined and it is often difficult to ascertain whether, and to what degree, political considerations have been involved in Bank decisions (e.g. neoliberal economic policies can be seen as politically contentious).

All of the member states have a say in the WBG, but a state's number of votes varies depending on its size and its importance in the world economy. Each member state appoints a governor to the Board of Governors which meets once a year. There is also a 24-member Board of Executive Directors empowered to handle the most important functions (e.g. financing operations, budget) of the larger and more unwieldy Board of Governors. The president of the Bank is chief of the Bank's operating staff. The president is officially appointed to a five-year renewable term by the Board, but by tradition the president is appointed by the President of the United States. This was much in the news in 2007 when the then-president of the Bank, Paul Wolfowitz (and prominent neoconservative; neoliberal; see Chapter 4), a close advisor to President George W. Bush who had nominated him to the post, was forced by the Board to resign.[7]

The resources of the Bank include both a relatively small sum paid in by member countries and a much larger amount that can be called in by the Bank if it finds it needs the money. The Bank uses its potential access to the latter to issue highly rated bonds and in this way raises about $25 billion per year. It is this money that provides the bulk of the funds that it uses to finance loans of various sorts. Countries that receive the loans benefit from the fact that the Bank offers low interest rates. Since its money is borrowed, the Bank depends on the ability of nations to which it has loaned money to pay back those loans. Its lending decisions are based on a given country's ability to repay loans.

Over the years, especially since the 1980s, the operations of the Bank have become increasingly controversial. First, the Bank is seen as dominated by rich developed nations and less developed countries and non-states (e.g. NGOs) have little say in it. Second, there are concerns that the Bank serves certain interests (e.g. the nation-state, international capital, wealthy nations, and economic elites in developing nations) and thereby adversely affects those of others (especially the poor and less developed nations). Critics point out that developing countries often pay more in interest to developed countries than they receive in aid. Third, as a result of its expanded mandate described above, the Bank is seen as having lost focus and of encroaching on the activities of other agencies (thereby weakening them).

In late 2007, a controversy arose over the Bank's annual World Development Report, this one devoted to agriculture. Given its mandate to use funds from rich nations to reduce poverty in poor ones, the report was a shocker since it showed that the Bank had long neglected agriculture in sub-Saharan Africa. This neglect occurred in spite of the fact that sub-Saharan Africa is one of the poorest regions in the world and one that is almost totally dependent on agriculture. In fact, in the 1980s and 1990s the Bank had helped push the public sector in sub-Saharan Africa, which was seen as inefficient and dominated by poor management practices, out of agriculture on the neoliberal assumption that agriculture would improve if privatization and market-forces (e.g. through the de-control of prices) were allowed to operate. However, the private sector has not filled the void and this has had disastrous consequences for agriculture in the region (e.g. farmers find it difficult to get credit). As one economist put it, "markets can't step in and won't step in when people have nothing. And if you take help away, you leave them to die" (quoted in Dugger 2007: A3). Said another economist: "Here's your most important client, Africa, with its most important sector, agriculture, relevant to the most important goal – people feeding their families – and the bank has been caught with two decades of neglect" (quoted in Dugger 2007: A3). While some observers felt that the Bank was not given enough credit for its positive contributions, and much of the blame lies with African governments, the Bank itself acknowledged its mistakes in this domain.

With the 2007 Report, the Bank announced its intention to return to a focus on agriculture in developing nations, especially in Africa. It is late in doing so since both the Bill and Melinda Gates and the Rockefeller foundations have already been focusing on this issue in Africa. While many of the details are to be worked out and negotiated with African governments, the Bank has decided to shift back to an earlier focus on agriculture from later concerns with such issues as health (e.g. AIDs) and primary education (Dugger 2007: A6). Of course, the Bank, like the IMF, has become deeply immersed in the economic issues produced by the Great Recession and that might sidetrack it, at least for a time. (Even before the recession, the Bank was following, and being concerned about, debt levels, especially of developing countries.)

In spite of a wide range of difficulties, the Bank is an important force globally. First, it is a forum for a vast number of nations to discuss development and development financing. Second, it remains a significant source of funds for developing countries. Third, it is an important source of information on development and provides valuable advice and support to the nations that are its members. Fourth, it not only promotes development but a specific form of *neoliberal* development.

THE END OF BRETTON WOODS

While many of the economic organizations discussed above remain in place and of great importance in the global economy, and many of those to be discussed below were at least inspired by Bretton Woods, it can be argued that Bretton Woods itself died on August 15, 1971. President Richard Nixon took the US off the gold standard resulting in a devaluation of the dollar and the end of the standard by which the currencies of other nations operated.

The demise of the Bretton Woods system is traceable to several factors (Frieden 2006: 339–60). For one thing, it had been based on the preeminence of the US and the dollar, but other nations and currencies grew in importance (e.g. Japan and the yen, the European Union's euro, and more recently China and the yuan). Second, international finance was restored to major importance after years of being subordinated to a focus within national economies.

The agreements and understandings that undergirded international trade and investment also came under attack. There was an agreement among GATT members not to raise tariffs on nonagricultural products. However, countries began to find other ways to protect themselves from foreign competition. For one thing, they accused other countries of "dumping" their products, that is, selling products at less than the cost of production in order to dominate a given market. For another, countries sought to convince other nations to "voluntarily" restrict (through Voluntary Export Restraints – VERs) their exports to them. This indicated a move back toward protectionism and away from the openness that was the hallmark of GATT.

CHANGES IN, AND CRITIQUES OF, BRETTON-WOODS-ERA ORGANIZATIONS

In the twenty-first century, the organizations that were spawned by Bretton Woods – the World Bank, the International Monetary Fund, and the World Trade Organization – are undergoing dramatic changes (Weisman 2007a: C1, C8). Said a former US Secretary of Treasury: "The Bretton Woods system has become outmoded.... It has served us very well for a long time, but these institutions haven't changed with the times. They need to be rethought and restructured" (Weisman 2007a: C8).

Recent changes in the organizations are traceable to several major forces including globalization (a concept and a process not even dreamt of in 1944), major trade disputes, and the increasing power and ambition of growing economic powers, especially in Asia. In terms of the latter, the World Bank has been loaning large sums of money to countries whose economies sometimes did not need such loans. Furthermore, the Bank's loans to "middle-income" and "high-income" economies (e.g. Greece) have far exceeded the loans given to "low-income" economies (in recent years, more than half of the IMF's lending has gone to European countries that had rarely received IMF loans before [Ewing 2013]). Even in terms of the funds that do go to poor countries, the World Bank is an increasingly small player in comparison to various international and private aid organizations. As a result, one professor said: "... it's hard to see what good it [the World Bank] has done anywhere" (quoted in Weisman 2007a: C8). The Bank argues it is helping large numbers of the poverty-stricken in less developed countries, while its critics say it is the opening of markets there, and not bank loans, that have helped in poverty reduction. And even worse, its critics contend that World Bank policies actually exacerbate poverty in these countries through its structural adjustment programs and aid that largely benefit the wealthy.

Then there is the issue of the leadership of these organizations, especially the preeminent position occupied in them by the US. This has become increasingly controversial for various reasons including the fact that the US is not contributing as much money as it used to, at least in comparison to other nations.

The IMF is saddled with such problems as relentless criticism of past austerity programs imposed on poor countries in exchange for bailouts, the bailouts themselves for legitimating and supporting bad policies by countries receiving them, by a shift in global power away from the US and Europe and toward countries like China, and the fact that the IMF has been rendered increasingly less relevant by a growing global economy. Thus, former US Secretary of State George Schulz says, "If it [IMF] disappeared tomorrow, I don't think people would miss it very much" (quoted in Weisman 2007a: C8). On the other hand, there are those who argue that while things are relatively calm for the moment, the IMF will be needed during the next global financial crisis.

The biggest problem facing the WTO is the possibility that the failure of the Doha Round could lead to a reversal of the long trend toward more open trading systems. The fear is a new era of protectionism which, in turn, would lead to a slowdown in the global economy. This fear was exacerbated in the Great Recession as one began to hear outcries in the US to "buy American." Similar calls were being heard elsewhere in the world.

One of the most effective critics of Bretton-Woods-era organizations is the noted economist Joseph E. Stiglitz. His critique is especially powerful because he had great practical experience as a member of President Bill Clinton's Council of Economic Advisors and as Chief Economist at the World Bank. Thus, he was able to view the operations of the global economic system not only from the inside, but also from prominent positions within powerful institutions within that system. It is that this is a critique from within, rather than from those who are on the periphery of the system and who feel they are being exploited by it, that gives Stiglitz's argument so much power.

To Stiglitz (2002: ix), globalization is defined as "the removal of barriers to free trade and the closer integration of national economies."[8] It should be clear, therefore, that he is falling into the familiar trap, especially common among, but not restricted to, economists, of defining globalization as economic globalization. As has been pointed out on several occasions, and as this book makes abundantly clear, there is much more to globalization than its economic aspects. It should also be clear that to Stiglitz, economic globalization *is* neoliberal economic globalization (especially "closer integration" and the "removal of barriers"), but he takes this position at the same time that he is a critic of it.

Stiglitz argues that economic globalization *can* be a positive force and *can* enrich everyone in the world, including the poor. However, this has not been the case because of the way globalization, especially international trade agreements, have been managed, including their imposition on less developed nations. As a result, Stiglitz sees an increase in global poverty as well as a growing gap between the global rich and the global poor. In this way globalization has *not* fulfilled its promise. Furthermore, globalization has not provided the global economic stability that many thought it promised (Stiglitz refers to not only the Asian financial crisis, but to the others in Russia and Latin America).

Stiglitz accepts various criticisms of the West. For example, he agrees with the argument that the West has been hypocritical in seeking the elimination of trade barriers in other parts of the world, while maintaining its own barriers to trade. He also accepts the idea that the West has been the driving force in an economic agenda that has furthered its interests while disadvantaging less developed parts of the world.

In terms of the IMF, Stiglitz sees several major changes since its creation at Bretton Woods in 1944. The IMF was created on the basis of the belief that markets often worked badly, but now has become a strong champion of market supremacy. It was founded on the idea of the need to pressure developing countries to expand economically (e.g. increase expenditures, reduce taxes, lower interest rates – all designed to stimulate the economy), but now will provide funds to developing countries only if they "engage in policies like cutting deficits, raising taxes, or raising interest rates that lead to a *contraction* of the economy" (Stiglitz 2002: 12–13, italics added). Stiglitz attributes this about-face in the IMF to the 1980s and the Reagan–Thatcher years. The IMF and the World Bank became missionary institutions pushing neoliberal, "Washington Consensus" ideas (such as market liberalization [the removal of barriers], fiscal austerity, and privatization) on developing countries that were inclined to go along because they badly needed funds from them.

Originally, the IMF was to maintain global stability by dealing with *macroeconomic* issues such as a "government's budget deficit, its monetary policy, its inflation, its trade deficit, its borrowing from abroad" (Stiglitz 2002: 14). In short, the task of the IMF was to be sure a nation was living within its means. The World Bank was supposed to eradicate poverty by dealing with *structural issues* such as "what the country's government spent money on, the country's financial institutions, its labor markets, its trade policies" (Stiglitz 2002: 14).

However, the IMF grew increasingly imperialistic, seeing almost all structural issues as having macroeconomic implications. As a result, it saw virtually everything falling within its domain. It not only felt that it had the answers to dealing with these issues, but it tended to apply one set of answers to every country; in Stiglitz's words, "it tends to take a 'one-size-fits-all' approach" (Stiglitz 2002: 34). It also tended to ignore the inputs from the countries it was ostensibly helping. And the countries that were ignored had little recourse because they needed the funds that the IMF was offering in exchange for structural changes and reforms. In spite of its great ambitions, or perhaps because of them, Stiglitz sees the IMF as a failure in terms of its missions of providing funds (to create jobs, etc.) to countries to weather economic downturns and more generally to create greater global economic stability. (It certainly failed in terms of the latter and it remains to be seen whether its efforts in the Great Recession to provide funds to countries in need will work.) Among the more specific failures of the IMF was the fact that its structural adjustment programs did not bring sustained growth, its imposition of economic austerity often stifled economic growth, and the opening of markets too quickly to competition led to job losses and increased poverty. In Stiglitz's view, the IMF has not only failed, but its failure (and that of the World Bank) has been magnified by the fact that it came to play a much greater global role than was originally envisioned.

Once distinct, the World Bank and the IMF became increasingly intertwined. Early on, the World Bank focused on making loans for specific projects (e.g. roads, dams), but later moved to broader "structural adjustment loans." However, such loans required the approval of the IMF and, along with its approval, the IMF also often imposed various conditions on the receiving nations. As a result, the IMF moved from its original role in dealing with crises to becoming a perpetual part of life for developing countries.

Another set of critiques focuses on who is in charge of the IMF and the World Bank. As we saw above, the top positions at the IMF and the World Bank are held by Europeans and Americans. More generally, the nations and the largest corporations and financial institutions of the developed countries dominate these organizations. This, of course, leaves the rest of the world out of leadership positions and is the source of considerable dissatisfaction. There is no overarching global system to be sure this system functions better and more equitably. As a result, we have what Stiglitz calls "*global governance without global government*" (Stiglitz 2002: 21). The system is run by the few with the few as the main beneficiaries. Most of the people in the world have no say in these systems and are either not helped or are adversely affected by them.

Still another criticism of the IMF is the lack of transparency in its decision-making and in its operations. Those countries served by it do not know how it operates or the bases for its decisions. Further, the IMF is not accountable to those nation-states.

Stiglitz offers a long list of more specific IMF errors and blunders:

1. The privatization of state-run systems (e.g. steel mills) was often done too quickly and the new privatized businesses were often ineffective, in part because they weren't ready to operate on their own. As a result, consumers suffered, as did workers as privatization brought with it job loss. Privatization often also went hand-in-hand with corruption (see below).
2. The push to liberalize financial and capital markets, and to reduce barriers to trade, often hurt small emerging countries (e.g. through higher unemployment) and contributed to the financial crises of the 1990s. Furthermore, resentment was generated in those countries because the pressure to liberalize them came with restrictions on finance, capital, and trade.
3. The emphasis on foreign investment often adversely affected indigenous businesses in less developed countries.
4. The IMF failed in the sequencing and pacing of the changes: "forcing liberalization before safety nets were put in place, before there was adequate regulatory framework, before the countries could withstand the adverse consequences of the sudden changes in market sentiment that are part and parcel of modern capitalism; forcing policies that led to job destruction before the essentials of job creation were in place; forcing privatization before there were adequate competition and regulatory frameworks." (Stiglitz 2002: 73)
5. The IMF failed to deal with a variety of issues such as job creation, land reform, improved education and health services, and helping workers adversely affected by its policies.

More recently, Stiglitz chaired the "Commission of Experts of the President of the UN General Assembly on Reforms of the International Monetary and Financial System." The Commission was given the task to evaluate what reforms in the global financial system are necessary to avoid another Global Recession. In the subsequent report, Stiglitz (2010: 59) argued that "while 'blame' should rest on the financial sector, government failed to protect the market from itself and to protect society from the kinds of excesses that have repeatedly imposed high costs on taxpayers, workers, home owners, and retirees." Much of this government policy, Stiglitz noted, is driven by an ideological belief in free markets and a distrust of government. He is clear in arguing that the International Financial Institutions (IFIs, i.e. the World Bank, IMF, and WTO) were inadequate in preventing the crisis, and need to be reformed. First, the IFIs must improve their credibility in the eyes of developing nations by giving them more voice in the institutions. Second, there must be greater coordination among the international institutions, which could be accomplished through a new agency that he calls the "Global Economic Coordination Council." The Council should consist of an international panel of experts that identity global systemic risks, and are interdisciplinary in nature to be able to identify social and environmental challenges as they relate to systemic economic problems (the Council should also represent different geographic regions and levels of development). Third, the IFIs should abandon their particular free-market ideology (which contributed to the crisis) in favor of a "diversity of ideas [that] may contribute both to global stability and to a strengthening of democracy" (Stiglitz 2010: 14).

ORGANIZATION FOR ECONOMIC COOPERATION AND DEVELOPMENT (OECD)[9]

This is a broad group of, at the moment, 34 developed nations. The OECD is the broadest group of the world's wealthiest nations (Abbott 2012). While the OECD has little formal power, it is highly influential.

The OECD is the successor to the Organization for European Economic Cooperation (OEEC), created in 1948 to foster economic cooperation among European nations. The OEEC focused on the reconstruction of Europe after WW II and the distribution of US economic assistance aimed at achieving that goal. Thus, it was closely associated with the US and its goals of open, multilateral, and cooperative international relations.

In the 1950s other schemes and organizations oriented to European economic integration emerged, including the European Economic Community (or the Common Market). The US was not included in the latter and wanted to create a successor to the OEEC that focused on transatlantic cooperation. As a result, the OECD was reconstituted as the successor to the OEEC in December 1960. In the beginning, the OECD included the US and 17 western European countries, Turkey, and Canada. Over the years, 14 nations have been added, including a number of nations in Europe and other parts of the world (e.g. Japan, Australia). In addition, the OECD has relationships with more than 70 other nations throughout the world to which it supplies policy advice and analytical support in order to better integrate them into the global economy.

The OECD is an IGO centered in Paris. Each member state is represented on the Council and decisions are made by consensus. Ambassadors from the nations meet on a regular basis and ministers meet annually. Key to the OECD are about two dozen committees that deal with such issues as development assistance and maritime transport, as well as many other expert and working groups. Overall, there are approximately 250 committees and working groups and about 40,000 officials come from various nations to do the work involved in them. There is also a Secretariat with over 2,500 civil servants. They focus on such specific areas and issues as economic affairs, the environment, and education.

Overall, the OECD:

1. Gathers statistics on economic globalization.
2. Watches over the economic performance of nations.
3. Promotes the liberalization of flows of capital and the globalization of finance, and banking, as well as FDI and transnational organizations.
4. Seeks to deal with the difficult issue of taxation, and the problems of double taxation and tax evasion, in a global economy.
5. Is involved in regulations dealing with global environmental issues.

The OECD is closely associated with neoliberalism. It played a key role in the development of the idea of reforming economies through a combination of tight monetary and fiscal policies combined with structural reform. In restoring weak economies, the OECD hoped reformed societies would become more active participants in the global free market.

The OECD has much influence but little actual power. It "continues to further economic globalization by promoting free cross-border movements of goods and capital and by promoting more or less coordinated development of national policy responses to the challenges created by economic and technological developments in the context of globalization" (Ougaard 2007: 917).

EUROPEAN UNION (COMMON MARKET)

The European Union was a product of the post-WW II era, as well as the Bretton Woods era. A key figure in its development was Jean Monnet who believed that the fragmentation of Europe put it at a disadvantage vis-à-vis the US in the era of industrial capitalism, mass production, and mass consumption. To compete, Europe had to become more unified in order to create a large and integrated market and large corporations and financial institutions, like those in the United States.

A key development in the ultimate emergence of the EU was the formation, under a plan formulated by Monnet, to create a more integrated coal and steel community in Europe. Conflict over these materials and markets had long bedeviled the relationship between France and Germany. In 1950 the European Steel and Coal Community (ECSC), with Monnet as its first president, emerged out of this context (it began operations in 1952). It included not only France and Germany, but also Italy, Belgium, the Netherlands, and Luxemburg. Monnet left his post in a few years to form a private Action Committee for the United States of Europe. This, in turn, led to the creation of an organization devoted to the development of cooperative relations on atomic energy – European Atomic Energy Community (Euratom) – and the more ambitious European Economic Community (EEC). Both of these organizations began operations in 1958. (The EEC, along with ECSC and Euratom, became the European Community [EC] in 1992 [Rumford 2002, 2007b]).

By the 1960s the six member-nations of the EEC were moving toward a unified market. In 1971 that effort was buttressed dramatically when the original six were supplemented by the addition of the United Kingdom (the French had long resisted the inclusion of the British), Ireland, and Denmark. With this, the EEC became larger economically than the United States and it had a significantly larger population. It has undergone further growth since then and now, as the EU, has 28 member-states (the most recent additions include Romania, Bulgaria, and Croatia). It is now the largest domestic market in the developed world (soon to be surpassed by China) with over 510 million citizens. While the US is not involved in the EU, it was an important driver in its creation and the US continues to be closely associated with the EU.

The Maastricht Treaty (named after the Dutch city in which the agreement was signed) was finalized on February 7, 1992. From an economic point of view, the key outcome of this meeting was the creation of a monetary union, the European Central Bank, and the common EU currency – the euro (see below):

> The European Union now had all the economic hallmarks of a country: a single market, a single currency and central bank, a common trade policy, and common economic regulations on such matters as antitrust and the environment. For all economic intents, Western Europe was one economic unit – indeed, by most measures, the largest economic unit in the world, bigger than the United States and twice the size of Japan. (Frieden 2006: 384)

Maastricht also had a series of political consequences such as greater political cooperation among EU members (e.g. on foreign policy) and a strengthening of the European Parliament (the legislature for the EU with elected members). The 2009 Lisbon Treaty later sought to strengthen the EU's democracy by further empowering the European Parliament and creating a single, elected president, among other changes. This was meant to grant citizens more voting power in what the European Commission does.

However, the EU has faced a legitimacy crisis more recently. Support for the EU has declined in most member countries, with the greatest dissatisfaction coming from Britain, "where pressure is mounting to quit the EU" (Dixon 2013). In France, air traffic controllers expressed dissatisfaction with the centralized government when they went on strike after the European Commission proposed to speed up the integration of air traffic management throughout the Continent (Clark 2013). Increasingly, critics have called to decentralize more power back to individual nations.

The concerns were expressed significantly by voters in May 2014. It was the first election since voting was expanded in the Lisbon Treaty – and the most important vote in ten years – giving Europeans more influence over key positions. After four days of balloting in 28 countries, citizens voted a large cohort of populist leaders, mostly from the far right, into the European Parliament (Higgins 2014). For example, a neo-fascist group in Germany, and a neo-Nazi party (Golden Dawn) in Greece each won a seat in Parliament. In Hungary, the anti-Semitic Jobbik party obtained the second-largest number of votes. The UK Independence Party, which proposes withdrawing Great Britain from the EU, won more votes than any other party in the UK. Far-right parties also did well in Austria, Denmark, and Sweden. These groups achieved success by appealing to voters with anti-immigrant rhetoric and claims that the EU threatened their national identities.

Not all countries saw a surge in far-right sentiment. Mainstream parties in many countries (e.g. the Netherlands and Italy) still fared well. In Greece, where austerity measures have ignited resistance throughout the country, a leftist coalition (Syriza) obtained more votes than the governing center-right New Democracy party. Overall, the voting was not significant enough to develop a populist majority in Parliament and centrist parties will maintain control. But commentators argued that the vote shook "the political establishment and call[ed] into question the very institutions and assumptions at the heart of Europe's post-World War II order" (Higgins 2014). It was hoped that increasing the voting power of European citizens would improve the EU's legitimacy, but the voting backlash suggests a more complicated position and its future remains uncertain.

EURO ZONE

The Euro Zone encompasses those nations in Europe (18 in total) that have adopted the euro as their basic currency. Most, but not all, nations using the euro are members of the EU. For example, the Principality of Monaco and the Republic of San Marino both have adopted the euro but are not EU members. The reverse is also true; Slovenia joined the EU in 2004 but did not become a member of the Euro Zone until January 1, 2007. However, while the euro was seemingly readily accepted by most European nations when it was officially launched in January, 2002, and it has become a very strong currency (especially vis-à-vis the dollar), it has encountered opposition. Some western European nations (e.g. Great Britain, Sweden, and Denmark) have never accepted the euro, and retain their traditional currencies. There is also growing opposition to the euro in some of the nations that have accepted it (Italy, France, the Netherlands) on a variety of grounds (e.g. it is believed to have led to an increase in prices and to have depressed economic growth rates because of the policies of the European Central Bank which sets policies for Euro Zone nations). While some countries (e.g. Lithuania) have failed to meet the requirements (e.g. for inflation levels) needed to qualify for the Euro Zone, others (Poland and Hungary) have, on their own accord, postponed attempts to join it.

The criticisms of the euro seem to be mounting. As mentioned above, one of the main criticisms is that the arrival of the euro has not brought about anticipated economic growth. In fact, the economy of Great Britain, which has eschewed the euro and remains committed to the pound, has generally outperformed Euro Zone countries. Another criticism relates to the European Central Bank's policies, which are not seen as flexible enough to take into account the different needs of the 15 European nations that currently use the euro. As of 2013, the Euro Zone has faced a significant crisis, plagued by high unemployment, growing deficits, and economic stagnation. With this crisis, and the many loans provided to European nations (e.g. Portugal, Ireland, and Greece), the IMF's power has increased in the Euro Zone and their economic advice has often been given priority over that of national leaders (Ewing 2013).

Of course, the euro has its defenders and advocates. Among the arguments for the euro is that it has reduced the cost of financial transactions, has made cross-border business easier, and has had the psychological effect of binding together various European countries. It is also seen as leading the nations involved in the direction of more disciplined economic policies (e.g. lower rates of inflation, smaller budget deficits).

NORTH AMERICAN FREE TRADE AGREEMENT (NAFTA)

Turning to North America, the developments in Europe spurred the US and Canada to sign a bilateral trade agreement in 1988. This was uncontroversial because it involved two developed, albeit unequally developed, nations. What was controversial, especially in the US, was the addition of Mexico to the agreement. The inclusion of a much less developed country like Mexico distinguished what eventually became NAFTA from the EU which included, especially early on, only highly developed countries and thus far has never included one as little developed as Mexico.

Negotiations to create NAFTA began in 1990 and were completed in 1992. A series of side agreements on such issues as the environment and labor were required, but NAFTA finally came into effect on January 1, 1994. It is based on the idea that the three nations involved were to eliminate most barriers to trade and investment over the ensuing 15 years (Kay 2012). The US, especially under former President George W. Bush, sought to expand the idea to include all 34 countries in the Western hemisphere (except Cuba) in the Free Trade Area of the Americas (FTAA). This idea has not only not caught on, but encountered increasing opposition from Latin American nations such as Venezuela.

NAFTA has both strong supporters and opponents. Its supporters emphasize that trade among the countries involved has increased dramatically and, at least initially, there was significant job growth in Mexico. However, there is a long list of criticisms of NAFTA including the facts that:

- wages declined rather than increasing in Mexico;
- the initial gain in Mexican jobs has given way to a loss of jobs, especially to China;

- Mexican farmers have been disadvantaged in comparison to American farmers who receive substantial subsidies from the government;
- US workers have also lost jobs (Kletzer 2007: 6) because their firms have moved to Mexico (or Canada) and the ability of those firms to fight for jobs and better working conditions has been weakened;
- wages have declined in the US.

NAFTA also suffered significant opposition based on related social and environmental issues, both during its development and after its implementation (Kay 2012). In fact, NAFTA inspired an unprecedented coalition of labor unions, peasants and farmers, human rights groups, consumer organizations, and environmental NGOs. The response did prompt the first Bush administration to address some labor and environmental protections, and was the first multilateral trade agreement to include some enforcement of labor and environmental laws – but its mechanisms were limited to domestic law and were very weak. Critics contended the provisions did not go nearly far enough and that NAFTA ultimately worsened environmental degradation and labor issues (especially increasing income inequality). Furthermore, Canada cut social programs in order to compete better within NAFTA.

MEXICAN CORN

Corn is a staple in the Mexican diet, particularly because it is a key ingredient in the tortilla, an essential part of Mexican food. Because of globalization, and NAFTA in particular, Mexico now grows less of its own corn and therefore imports more from other nations, especially the United States. Critics argue that this makes nations like Mexico more vulnerable to the vagaries of the global market and ultimately to higher prices. This appears to be precisely what has happened to the price of corn and therefore tortillas; hardest hit by the price rises on these staples are the poorest members of Mexican society.

This issue came to a head in early 2007 when the former Mexican president, Felipe Calderón, was forced by protests over rising corn and tortilla prices to coerce producers (and some retailers such as Wal-Mart, a huge player in the Mexican retail market) into signing an agreement that fixed the price of corn products. This was particularly interesting and important because Calderón is an advocate of free trade. His action was caused by a significant rise in corn prices on the global market leading to a one-third rise in the price of tortillas (McKinley, Jr 2007a: A11). This price rise hit half of the Mexican population (107 million) particularly hard since they live on four dollars a day, or less, and may spend as much as one quarter of that meager income on tortillas.

One cause of the price rise is the US where corn prices had risen because of increased demand as a result of the growing interest in using corn to produce ethanol (as an alternative to gasoline) (see Chapter 11). But the public uproar in Mexico was fueled more by the belief that the big tortilla producers and corn flour distributors were creating the problem through the hoarding of corn supplies in the hope that they could drive prices still higher.

On January 31, 2007, thousands of workers and farmers marched through Mexico City and went on to the central square to protest the rise in corn prices and more generally neoliberal globalization. Said a spokesperson for the marchers: "While other countries are looking for alternatives to neoliberal policies, in Mexico, the government has lagged behind and insisted in applying a model that, after a quarter century, has shown its inefficiency and inequality" (Malkin 2007: A6). Among the goals of the protestors were greater protection of

Mexican farmers through renegotiation of aspects of NAFTA that relate to agriculture, reduction or elimination of Mexican dependence on imports of corn from the US (Mexico gets about 25% of its corn from the US), and movement toward the broader objective of "food sovereignty." Exactly one year later, on January 31, 2008, Mexican farmers again took to the streets (McKinley, Jr 2008). This time, under NAFTA, Mexico's corn import taxes were set to expire. Farmers claimed the policy would drive them out of business, especially since American farmers receive subsidies that keep the price of their corn artificially low. The broader issue here is that there has been a long-term trend away from Mexican self-sufficiency in corn production (and food more generally), which has led to a decrease in sovereignty over its labor as well (Otero 2011).

THE REACTION TO NAFTA IN THE US

The reaction to NAFTA in the US has, at best, been mixed. In the 1992 presidential election, Ross Perot, an independent candidate for president, gained notoriety for contending that if NAFTA was passed (as it was the next year), a "giant sucking sound" would be associated with jobs being lost to Mexico. As noted above, the event sparked a widespread coalition of farmers, unions, environmentalists, and consumers to protest the treaty. The issue resurfaced in the 2008 presidential primary campaign as the two leading candidates for the nomination of the Democratic Party agreed that NAFTA was costing the US jobs and, were they to be elected, they would seek to have the treaty renegotiated (although Obama never did renegotiate the treaty [Harwood 2010]). However, while job losses in industrial states such as Ohio have occurred, it is very difficult to link them to NAFTA. It is far more likely that many of those jobs have been lost not to Mexico, but to Asian economies. NAFTA makes for an easy political target, but it is not clear that it has been a major cause of job loss to Mexico and what is ignored are the gains in the US, especially those that make the Mexicans angry about NAFTA. In fact, political and business leaders in all three countries involved seem to favor NAFTA and appear to want more rather than less economic integration (*Economist* 2008: March 6 ["An Unreliable Ally"]).

MERCOSUR

MERCOSUR (Roett 1999, 2012) is sometimes called the Southern Common Market. It was created by the Treaty of Asuncion in 1991 with the goal of a common market in South America by 1995. The original members, with full voting rights, were Argentina, Brazil, Paraguay, and Uruguay, with Bolivia, Chile, Colombia, Ecuador, and Peru as associate members. There were predecessors to MERCOSUR going back to as early as 1960, but they were more motivated by the idea of import substituting industrialization (McMichael 2008), while MERCOSUR was inspired by globalization and strongly influenced by neoliberal thinking. Between 1991 and 1995 the vast majority of tariff and non-tariff barriers among the countries involved were eliminated. Bolivia and Chile were added to MERCOSUR in 1996. Venezuela was admitted hurriedly in 2006, and achieved full membership in 2010. However, its former president's (Hugo Chávez) philosophy and policy of "twenty-first century socialism" was at odds with the neoliberalism of MERCOSUR. Rather than playing down these differences, Chávez announced on his arrival for a January 2007 meeting that his goal was "decontaminating the contamination of neoliberalism"

(Rohter 2007b: A11). One of Chávez's ideas was to create a development bank, the Bank of the South (for more on this see Chapter 15), in MERCOSUR to serve as an alternative to the World Bank. Among other things, this set up a conflict between Chávez and Luiz Inácio Lula da Silva, then President of Brazil and supporter of MERCOSUR's neoliberal orientation. Ultimately, the different visions of MERCOSUR and disagreements of member nations have largely stalled its development, and its future remains uncertain. Many believe that its greatest value for its members is as a "political counterweight to the United States" (Roett 2012).

OPEC

While it is a narrower and more specialized organization than the others discussed in this chapter, mention must also be made in this context of the Organization of Petroleum Exporting Countries (OPEC) which was formed in 1960 and included the major oil exporters of the day – Iran, Iraq, Kuwait, Saudi Arabia, and Venezuela (Mason 2012). There are currently 12 members: Algeria, Angola, Ecuador, Libya, Nigeria, Qatar, and the United Arab Emirates have been added. It was motivated by the comparatively low price being paid for oil at the time and the fact that oil prices had long failed to keep up with inflation. However, in its early years OPEC had little impact as the oil business continued to be dominated by the large Western oil companies. In 1973, as a result, at least in part, of the Israeli–Arab War, OPEC increased the price of oil to $3.60 a barrel by the end of 1973 and then to $10.40 a barrel by the end of 1974 (Pirages 2007). It also created a quota system in order to sustain such prices. However, larger events prevented OPEC from exercising control over oil prices, let alone steadily increasing them. Thus, after reaching nearly $40 a barrel in 1981 (in part, at least, a result of the fall of the Shah of Iran and the coming to power of Ayatollah Khomeini in 1979), prices dropped dramatically throughout the 1980s, partly as a result of a global economic slowdown traceable to such high (for the time) oil prices. After bottoming out at about $11 a gallon in 1999, oil prices increased dramatically (peaking, at close to $150 a barrel in mid-2008). However, as the Great Recession gained momentum and demand for oil declined, oil prices declined to nearly $30 a barrel in early 2009 and increased to around $120 a barrel in 2012.

THE MULTINATIONAL CORPORATION (MNC)

Multinational corporation (MNC): Corporation that operates in more than two countries.

By most accounts the other major player – strong actor – in economic globalization (beyond the nation-state and the organizations discussed above) is the **multinational corporation (MNC)** (Bonanno and Antonio 2012). Also of importance are transnational corporations (TNCs).[10] While TNCs involve operations in more than one country, MNCs operate in more than two countries. We will generally use the term MNC in this book to encompass both MNCs and TNCs. There are many who believe that the MNC has grown more powerful, perhaps much more powerful, than the nation-state[11] *and* any of the organizations described above that are based on nation-states. For example, de la Dehesa (2006: 85) argues: "We have to get used to the fact that, thanks to the globalization process, companies rather than states will be the leading actors in the world economy."

There is no question that MNCs are increasingly important on the global scene. Adapting Dicken's (2007: 106) definition of a TNC, an MNC is "a firm that has the power to *coordinate* and *control* operations" in more than two countries "even if it does not own them." This means that they operate in an array of economic, political, social, and cultural environments. While MNCs have proliferated and grown in recent years, companies that operate, have interests, and have activities outside a home country (if one can be identified) are not new and this was exemplified by, among others, the East India Trading Company (fifteenth century to late nineteenth century) and Hudson's Bay Company (late seventeenth century, with vestiges to this day).

Such a sense of an MNC is hard to quantify, but if we rely on ownership data (a more restrictive criteria than those posed in the definition above), there are about 61,000 MNCs in the world today carrying out production through over 900,000 affiliates. They account for about a tenth of the world's Gross National Product (GNP) and about a third of total world exports. While there are many MNCs, the fact is that a relatively small number of "global corporations" (Toyota, IBM) predominate. And the vast majority – 96 of the top 100 – are in the developed world (Dicken 2007). However, as we will see, it is the case that MNCs from developing countries are increasing in number and importance.

MNC activity is usually measured by **Foreign Direct Investment (FDI)**. This involves investments by one firm in another firm that exists abroad in a different nation-state with the intention of gaining control over the latter's operations (Moran 2012). It can also involve setting up a branch (subsidiary) operation in another country. FDI has grown substantially in recent years and this is a major indication of the growth of MNCs. More than two-thirds of the world's FDI is directed toward the developed *not* the less developed countries.

Another form of MNC activity is **portfolio investment**. This involves the purchase of equity in companies in other countries, but the motivation is financial gain and not to obtain control over those companies.

Why do companies become multi- (or trans-) national? One set of reasons relates to market-oriented investments made necessary by the geographic unevenness of markets. A company may reach a saturation point in its domestic market; identify new markets that require its direct presence; find that unless it becomes trans- or multi- national it will have its markets restricted because of political regulations (e.g. import tariffs); find that a foreign market is so idiosyncratic that it can deal with it only by being physically present in it; and discover that there are strong cultural and political reasons for it to be present in other countries.

There are also reasons relating to market-oriented investment necessitated by the geographic unevenness of assets. A company in these circumstances may invest in another country in order to access natural and human resources. The latter can involve accessing either human resources with high skill and knowledge and/or low-paid personnel with little in the way of skill or knowledge whose attraction is their low cost.

Dicken outlines various ways in which corporations become trans- or multi- national. One is **greenfield investment** which involves the building of totally new facilities in another country. This is obviously favored by host countries, but is highly risky from the point of view of the MNC. A second is merger and acquisition (e.g. the acquisition of America's Chrysler Corporation by the German Daimler-Benz – now dissolved). A third is strategic collaborations which, while they have existed for quite some time, have grown in number, increased in scale, and become increasingly central to a firm's transnational strategy. Strategic collaborations among companies in different countries have various objectives

Foreign Direct Investment (FDI): Investment by a firm in one nation-state in a firm in another nation-state with the intention of controlling it.

Portfolio investment: Purchase of equities in companies in other countries for financial gain, not control.

Greenfield investment: Building of totally new corporate facilities in another country.

such as gaining access to specific markets and technologies, sharing the risks associated with market entry, sharing other costs and uncertainties, and achieving economies associated with synergy. There are, of course, risks involved in this such as losing control over key technologies and the great complexity involved in running strategic collaborations.

However they are created, MNCs lead to the development of far more complex networks. For starters, the firm's internal network now needs to be tied into networks in other countries. These larger, more complex networks are inherently more difficult to control. There are difficulties involved in finding a balance between centralized control and local sensitivity; economies of scale in production and responsiveness to local market conditions; core and peripheral knowledge; and global integration and local responsiveness. Then there are more specific issues such as the location of corporate headquarters (usually the home country); core research and development centers (also usually the home country); sales and marketing (usually dispersed globally); and production activities (also usually dispersed).

In terms of the latter, there are various possibilities:

- globally concentrated production in a single location. This produces economies of scale, but it maximizes transportation costs and doesn't make use of local expertise;
- production specifically for a local or national market – this limits economies of scale;
- production of a specialized product for a regional market (e.g. the EU);
- segment production and locate different parts in different geographic locations producing a form of transnational vertical integration.

There is great variation in MNCs, but interestingly Dicken argues that few of them are actually truly global. They are more likely to be regional (e.g. in Europe, North America, or East Asia). However, they do vary in terms of size and shape.

There are also always tensions involving MNCs including those with nation-states, local communities, labor, consumers, and civil society organizations. MNCs have also helped lead to the creation of counter-forces such as multi-scalar regulatory systems (e.g. WTO), international institutes of technical standards (e.g. ISO – International Organization for Standardization), and the resurgence of the nation-state.

While most observers emphasize the power of MNCs and their increasing ascendancy over the nation-state, Dicken demurs. He sees the nation-state as of continuing importance and as having various advantages over the MNC (e.g. its control over continuous territories versus the discontinuous territories under the MNC's control). To Dicken, MNCs are not the "unstoppable juggernauts" they are to other observers and critics, especially vis-à-vis the nation-state.

Dicken's perspective also runs counter to the dominant view that the global world is increasingly placeless or defined by non-places (Auge 1995; Ritzer 2007). Dicken contends that as far as MNCs are concerned, place and geography still matter. He contends that MNCs continue to evidence various characteristics traceable to their home base, their place of origin, including their cognitive, cultural, social, political, and economic traits. As he puts it, no matter how transnational they become, MNCs continue to evince the "aroma of native land." Thus, he sees little evidence that these organizations are "converging towards a single model" (Dicken 2007: 135). He also rejects the view of various perspectives (see Chapter 9) that argue that MNCs throughout the world are becoming standardized, homogenized.

THE DEVELOPING WORLD'S MULTINATIONALS

While we have had multinational corporations for some time, one of the things that is new about them in recent years is that more of them are coming from bases in the South rather than the North. Not only that, they are expanding and growing by acquiring corporations, sometimes well-known corporations, based in the North. For example, an Indian company, Tata Motors (part of Tata Group, India's largest industrial conglomerate), purchased two of the world's best-known (but struggling) automobile brands – Jaguar and Rover – in 2008, and boosted sales (Bajaj 2012a). The Tata Group also has a partnership with British Petroleum (BP) to make solar panels (Bajaj and Werdigier 2011) and a joint venture with AirAsia to increase air travel between India and Malaysia (Paul 2013). Overall, the Tata Group has over 450,000 global employees spread across 80 countries, and is seeking to expand in many areas, especially the US (Vora 2013). Another Indian MNC, Mittal, bought Arcelor, to become the largest steelmaker in the world, named ArcelorMittal after the merger (and now headquartered in Luxembourg). Brazil's Petrobras is a leader in deep-sea oil drilling, operates in 24 countries, and is among the world's largest 25 MNCs (based on revenues). More generally, Foreign Direct Investment (FDI) still flows disproportionately from developed to developing economies. In 2012, the FDI flows into developed countries totaled $560,718 billion while the FDI flows into developing countries totaled $702,826 (a difference of $142 billion). FDI outflows from developing countries are increasing, and accounted for about 30% of total FDI outflows in 2012.

WORLD ECONOMIC FORUM

With origins in 1971, the World Economic Forum (WEF)[12] meets annually in January in Davos, Switzerland.[13] It includes an elite group of elected officials, leaders of important institutions, and corporate leaders from throughout the world. It was founded as an independent, not-for-profit organization that is global in scope. As the name suggests, its focus is on the economy and its motto is "entrepreneurship in the global interest" (Lim 2012). Among its members are thousands of leading corporations in the world; to qualify for membership, corporations (and banks) must have at least $1 billion in annual turnover or have an equal amount of capital. There are a series of invited speakers, panels, informal meetings, and closed-door one-on-one discussions at the annual meetings. Themes at these meetings have included globalization, technology, health, cooperation, and so on. The WEF has influenced a variety of global economic and political events and developments.

Such involvements have been among the things that have mobilized opposition to, and protests against, the WEF, especially since 1999. Critics see such elite influence on political and economic matters as inappropriate. More generally, critics see it as an economic, especially a capitalistic, organization, devoted, in spite of its claim to humanitarianism, to the continued expansion, and increased profitability, of the capitalist system. They note that meeting participation is dominated by top corporate executives and government officials, but there is almost no involvement from NGOs, religious organizations, or labor unions (Lim 2012). Similarly, the WEF is critiqued for its commitment to, and furtherance of, neoliberalism. Among other things, such criticisms and protests led to the creation of the socially (rather than economically) oriented World Social Forum (WSF; see Chapter 15) in Porto Alegre, Brazil in 2001 as an alternative to the WEF. The WEF has responded to such developments by becoming more open to NGOs and by having more open meetings and discussions.

The theme of the January, 2012, meeting was "The Great Transformation: Shaping New Models." Ironically, it bore the same name as Karl Polanyi's book, *The Great Transformation*, in which he critiqued free markets as being disastrous for society (see Chapter 4; it is ironic because the meeting participants generally promote these free-market policies). Those attending included nearly 40 heads of state and a record 2,600 leaders in business, government, and civil society. Meeting organizers (World Economic Forum 2012) boasted "the great transformation is generating tremendous opportunities for humankind to live in a more prosperous, more peaceful world that is greener and socially more inclusive" and that "inclusion is critical." However, the meeting continued to be highly exclusive in terms of who was allowed to participate.

The theme of the 2013 meeting was "resilient dynamism," which the WEF described as "tackling immediate problems and long-term challenges at the same time." The meeting came amidst massive public unrest over austerity measures, and was meant to signal WEF efforts to deal with these issues while promoting long-term economic competitiveness.

THE MYTH OF ECONOMIC GLOBALIZATION?

All of the above (as well as what is to come in the next chapter) points to the growing importance of economic globalization. While that is the predominant view, as well as the one adopted here, there are those who do not accept it. For example, Paul Hirst, Grahame Thompson, and Simon Bromley (2009) famously argue that globalization, especially economic globalization, is a myth. They argue that such a highly internationalized economy, although it may not have been labeled "global," is not unprecedented. In fact, the current world economy may well be less open than the world economy during the period 1870 to 1914 (see the beginning of this chapter). Most companies continue to be based in nations in terms of assets, production facilities, and sales (this is also Dicken's view). Their multinational business stems from such a national base. And there does not appear to be much in the way of movement toward the development of multinational businesses. There is no massive shift of investment and employment from advanced to developing countries. Foreign Direct Investment (FDI) continues to be mainly in the advanced industrial economies and not in less developed countries. Trade continues to involve mainly Europe, Japan, North America, China, and India; it is not truly global. It is those nations that possess the ability to govern the global economy (Hirst et al. 2009).

While these are solid arguments, they really come down to the point that contemporary economic globalization may not be as new or as great as many contend. However, they do not contradict the idea that today's economy is globalized. The view adopted here is that the economy is more global than Hirst et al. argue and that it continues to grow even more globalized, at least at this moment.

CHAPTER SUMMARY

This chapter examines the major global economic structures. Similarities between the current global capitalist system and a prior system which functioned during 1896–1914 are analyzed. Turmoil beginning with WW I ended the earlier global capitalist system and set the stage for the emergence of the current global capitalist system.

Fears of another Depression after WW II led to the Bretton Woods system in 1944. This was an attempt to create institutional structures which would foster international economic cooperation and encourage the free flow of capital around the world. The US dollar was adopted as the standard, almost a "global currency," in order to establish stable international exchange rates.

The Bretton Woods system led to the creation, either directly or indirectly, of various global economic structures. While the International Trade Organization (ITO) was unsuccessful because of a lack of US support, the General Agreement on Trade and Tariffs (GATT) sought to facilitate the liberalization of trade by the reduction of tariff barriers. GATT was eventually replaced by the World Trade Organization (WTO), which added a concern for the reduction of non-tariff barriers. The includes the General Agreement on Trade in Services (GATS), protection of intellectual property through TRIPS, and TRIMS measures that allow a nation-state to control the distorting effects of foreign investment. The WTO is a forum for international negotiations on trade, with member countries participating in successive "rounds" of discussions.

Bretton Woods also led to the creation of the International Monetary Fund in order to create a stable global monetary system and to act as a "lender of the last resort." Another key institution was the World Bank, which started out (and continues) with a specific focus on developing physical infrastructure in middle-income nations. The IMF and the World Bank have come under criticism for furthering the neoliberal agenda. The IMF (and later the World Bank in consultation with it) imposed structural adjustment programs on developing countries, extending loans only if certain "conditionalities" (reduction of government expenditure and integration with the world market) were met by the borrowers.

Joseph Stiglitz criticizes these institutions for their policy of imposing liberalization on developing countries, especially their use of a one-size-fits-all, ideological approach. Stiglitz believes that premature opening of markets under the structural adjustment programs increased the vulnerability of some countries to economic crises, and that the Great Recession was largely a matter of bad policy. The lack of transparency and the dominance of the US and Europe in the governing structure of these organizations has also been severely criticized.

Regional coalitions also play a key role in the global economic system. While the European Union, with its common market and the establishment of the euro as a common currency, is perhaps the best known, others include NAFTA, MERCOSUR, and OPEC. While these organizations face various internal challenges, they also engage with (and provide important mechanisms for nation-states to engage with) economic globalization.

Also analyzed is another significant economic player – the multinational corporation (MNC). Many believe the MNC has grown more powerful than the nation-state. MNC activity is measured in terms of Foreign Direct Investment and portfolio investment. MNCs employ various mechanisms such as greenfield investments, mergers and acquisitions, and strategic collaborations. Although the vast majority of MNCs are based in the North, there is significant growth of successful MNCs from the South. There is growing tension between MNCs, nation-states, and civil society.

There are those who argue that economic globalization is a "myth." For example, they contend that the world economy is actually less open than in earlier epochs. The position taken here is that the world economy is much more global than is argued by such critics.

DISCUSSION QUESTIONS

1. Discuss the relevance of Bretton Woods' institutions such as the IMF and World Bank in the current global context.

2. Analyze the "global" nature of multinational corporations.

3. Make a case that economic globalization is a "myth."

4. Examine the "paradoxical" role of regional coalitions in the global economic system.

5. Examine the role of the nation-state with respect to the changes in the world economic system.

ADDITIONAL READINGS

Jeffry A. Frieden, *Global Capitalism: Its Fall and Rise in the Twentieth Century*. New York: W.W. Norton & Co., 2006.

Joseph E. Stiglitz. *Globalization and Its Discontents*. New York: W.W. Norton and Co., 2002.

Joseph E. Stiglitz. *The Stiglitz Report: Reforming the International Monetary and Financial Systems in the Wake of the Global Crisis*. New York: New Press, 2010.

Chris Rumford. *The European Union: A Political Sociology*. Oxford: Blackwell, 2002.

Peter Dicken. *Global Shift: Mapping the Changing Contours of the World Economy*. 6th edn. New York: Guilford Press, 2011.

Guillermo de la Dehesa. *Winners and Losers in Globalization*. Oxford: Blackwell, 2006.

Paul Hirst, Grahame Thompson, and Simon Bromley. *Globalization in Question*. 3rd edn. Malden, MA: Polity, 2009.

NOTES

1 Typical of economic historians and economists more generally, as well as many journalists and laypeople, Frieden seems often to equate global capitalism with globalization. For example, "The opening years of the twentieth century were the closest thing the world had ever seen to a free world market for goods, capital, and labor. It would be a hundred years before the world returned to that level of *globalization*." (Frieden 2006: 16; italics added).

2 However, it is important to bear in mind that such a view of globalization relates *only* to the economy and tells us little about globalization in general, as well as about the globalization of other realms such as political and cultural globalization.

3 However, there are certainly factors that are specific to each period. One example is the triumph of the gold standard in the earlier epoch as a result of the rejection by the American electorate of its passionate supporter – William Jennings Bryant – in the presidential election of 1896.

4 However, it would be a mistake to assume that trade was totally free and that tariffs were eliminated. Many barriers remained, again then as now, because, for example, nation-states wanted to protect their farmers as well as their most vulnerable, often their newest, industries.

5 There was great concern in the Great Recession about a return to isolationism.

6 While there are no hard-and-fast dividing lines, the World Bank also engaged in structural adjustment

programs which tended to focus on such issues as "the civil service, privatizations, reforms of international trade policies, reforms at the sectoral level (such as agriculture, education, utilities), the improvement of property rights and other measures to promote the growth of the private sector, anti-corruption measures, and so on" (Killick 2007: 1095; see also Babb 2005).

7   He was forced to resign because of improprieties involving an intimate relationship with a prominent woman associated with the Bank.

8   Stiglitz (2002: 9) also offers a more detailed definition: "the closer integration of the countries and peoples of the world which has been brought about by the enormous reductions in cost of transportation and communication, and the breaking down of artificial barriers to the flows of goods, services, capital, knowledge, and (to lesser extent) people across borders."

9   www.oecd.org.

10   Dicken (2007; Pearce 2007); see also the UN journal, *Transnational Corporations*.

11   One exception is Wolf (2005: 247).

12   www.weforum.org.

13   There are, as well, a range of more specific meetings during the year.

GLOBAL ECONOMIC FLOWS

PRODUCTION AND CONSUMPTION

Globalization: A Basic Text, Second Edition. George Ritzer and Paul Dean.
© 2015 John Wiley & Sons, Ltd. Published 2015 by John Wiley & Sons, Ltd.

In 2012, Julie Keith, a mother of two in the United States, opened a box of Halloween decorations she bought at Kmart, a major US discount chain. Inside the box, she found a note from a man who said he was imprisoned in a Chinese labor camp, where he was forced to work 15 hours per day, seven days a week (Jacobs 2013). The note requested, "Sir: If you occasionally buy this product, please kindly resend this letter to the World Human Right Organization." The note, which travelled 5,000 miles before reaching its recipient, reveals one of the many interesting and hidden dimensions of global economic flows. Having examined various economic structures in the previous chapter, we now turn to an examination of these flows, especially as they relate to production and consumption.

We begin by showing how the world economy operates through global trade, production networks, and commodity flows. We document how countries are positioned differently within these flows and processes. By extending our analysis to financial globalization, the role of corporations, and consumption, we explain how basic capitalist dynamics drive the processes of globalization forward through all these different sorts of flows.

TRADE

A good place to get a quick snapshot of global trade (Mann and Pluck 2007) (see Figure 7.1 for a map showing the value of trade between major regions of the world), as well as net economic flows in and out of a nation-state, is a nation's trade surpluses and deficits.

TRADE SURPLUSES AND DEFICITS

Of special interest and importance as far as trade surpluses and deficits are concerned are the positions of the two global economic giants in terms of their trade balances – the US and China.[1] On the one side is the US which had a trade *deficit* of $471.5 billion in 2013. This figure was down from a record high $752.4 billion deficit in 2006 (US Census Bureau 2013). For its part, China announced that it had a trade *surplus* of $231.1 billion in 2012 (*UPI* 2013: January 9). China's surplus was 48% greater than it had been in the previous year (2011). China is now the world's largest exporting country, and the second-largest importer. The US deficit with China alone was $315.1 billion in 2012, meaning that the US has a larger deficit with China than with all other countries combined. Despite these large numbers, only 8.1% of total US consumer spending on goods is on products imported from China (Hale and Hobjin 2011), but this number continues to grow. Therefore, while the trade deficit with China has certainly hurt American industry, it is increasingly helping the American consumer who has access to a wide range of low-priced imports from China (and elsewhere).

GLOBAL TRADE: ECONOMIC CHAINS AND NETWORKS

Trade in goods and services is clearly central to the global economy. Much of that trade takes place in interconnected circuits of one kind or another. These interconnections are clear, as are the basic flow- and process-oriented themes of this book (see Chapter 1), in the various chains and networks that exist in the global economy, specifically in global trade.

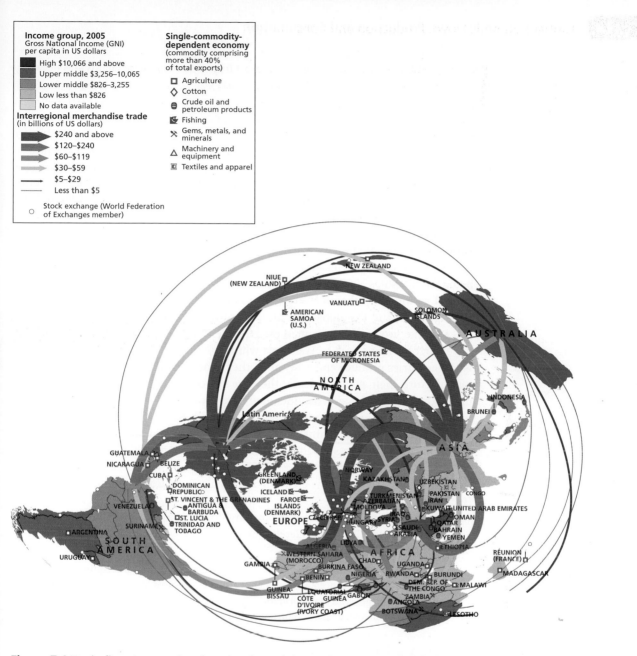

Figure 7.1 Trade flow. International trade of goods is a major avenue of globalization. The arrows show the value of trade between major regions of the world. More than half of world trade occurs between high-income areas such as Japan, the United States, and Western Europe (as well as China). Trade is increasing, however, between these high-income countries and developing countries in Asia, South America, and Africa. Lowered trade barriers offer opportunities for low-income countries, although still limited. Labor-intensive merchandise, such as textiles, can be produced and exported at a low cost from developing nations. Trade in agricultural commodities is a key issue between developing and high-income countries. Two billion families in the world make a living from farming. About 60 countries are dependent on commodities for more than 40% of their export income – in some African countries the figure is 80%. Stormy meetings of the World Trade Organization (WTO) focus on making the European Union (EU) and the United States end subsidies to their farmers to increase trade opportunities for developing nations. Source: de Blij, Harm J., and Roger Downs. 2007. *College Atlas of the World*. Washington, DC: National Geographic Society, pp. 56–7.

Gary Gereffi[2] has outlined several of the most important economic chains and networks involved in global trade (Gereffi 2005: 160–83, 2012).

Supply chains: Value-adding activities in the production process beginning with raw materials and ending with a finished product.

- **Supply Chains** is a general label for value-adding activities in the production process. A supply chain begins with raw materials and follows the value-adding process through a variety of inputs and outputs and ultimately to a finished product. For example, the process might begin with some comparatively inexpensive raw material (say cotton) and at various steps along the way workers and technologies add value to the cotton (e.g. transforming it into thread, producing a T-shirt) so that in the end the finished product – the T-shirt in this case – has greater value than the cotton with which the process began (Rivoli 2009).

International production networks: Networks of producers involved in producing a finished product.

- **International production networks** involve the networks of producers involved in the process of producing a finished product. MNCs are seen as playing a central role, as being the "flagships," in these networks.

Global commodity chains: Value-adding chains, global industries, *and* the sellers of global products.

- **Global commodity chains** (Gereffi and Korzeniewicz 1994) bring together value-adding chains and the global organization of industries. They also accord a central place to the growing importance of the sellers of global products. This includes buyer-driven chains such as Wal-Mart which play an increasing role in determining what industries produce and how much they produce. Since such companies do not manufacture their own products, they are buyers of products that are then sold under their brand names. Also included here are "brand companies," or "manufacturers without factories" (the best known of these is Nike [Rothenberg-Aalami 2004: 335–54]). Buyer-driven chains are distinguished from producer-driven chains (e.g. Toyota). There is a focus on the governance structure of global commodity chains (e.g. are they governed by producers or buyers?). Also of concern is the role of lead firms (Wal-Mart, Nike) in the creation of "global production and sourcing networks" (Gereffi 2005: 168).

Global value chains: Various phases of production, delivery to final consumers, final disposal.

- **Global value chain** is emerging as the overarching label for all work in this area and for all such chains. Here is the way Gereffi describes global value chains:

> These highlight the relative value of those economic activities that are required to bring a good or service from conception, through the different phases of production (involving a combination of physical transformation and the input of various producer services), delivery to final consumers, and final disposal after use. (Gereffi 2012)

This conceptualization has several advantages. First, it "focuses on value creation and value capture across the full range of possible chain activities and end products (goods and services)" (Gereffi 2005: 168). Second, "it avoids the limiting connotations of the word *commodity*, which to some implies the production of undifferentiated goods with low barriers to entry" (Gereffi 2005: 168). Third, while it accepts a number of ideas from earlier approaches – the nature and consequences of organizational and geographic fragmentation; the role of power in the chain; and "industry (re-)organization, coordination, governance" (Gereffi 2005: 168), the ways in which firms are linked in the global economy – it goes beyond them to include the broader institutional contexts (e.g. trade policy, trade regulations, trade standards) of these chains. However, the most important advantage of the idea of global value chains is that it encompasses both production and consumption (and even post-consumption).

GLOBAL VALUE CHAINS: CHINA AND THE US

To give specificity to the idea of global value chains we look at several specific examples of such chains, all of which involve trade between China (Brandt and Rawski 2008) and the US (although many other countries in the world are involved in these or similar chains.)

Scrap metal

An important example of a global value chain involves scrap metal (Seabrook 2008). This seems like a rather prosaic commodity, but it is more important than many think and its fate tells us a great deal about globalization. For one thing, about two-thirds of the steel made in the US comes from recycled steel rather than from iron ore and coke ("virgin steel"). For another, this is big business, especially since prices for scrap metals (e.g. steel, copper) increased dramatically as a result of skyrocketing global demand for such commodities. In addition, it is not surprising that, given its high level of consumption (of cars, lawnmowers, and the like), *the* major global source of scrap metal is the US, but increasingly the work involved in extracting usable metal from scrap is done elsewhere in the world, especially China.

Scrap metal is interesting in this regard because, by definition, its origins go back to other chains involved in the use of raw materials (say, iron ore) and the production of finished products (say, automobiles). Furthermore, it also includes consumption of those products as well as their ultimate disposal as scrap or junk. For example, we would need to go back to the extraction of raw materials for an automobile (perhaps in part made from scrap), the production of the automobile, its sale to a consumer, its use by the consumer and perhaps others (in the case of used cars), and ultimately to the end of the useful life of the car. It is at this point that the junked car is transformed into various types of scrap, especially scrap metals.

Unsorted aluminum and copper scrap is shipped from scrap metal companies in the US to recycling companies in China. Why ship it all the way to China? The reason, of course, is primarily the willingness of people there to do work that most Americans would refuse *and* to do it for very low wages; those who do the recycling work in China are paid about $140 a month. Here is a description of the work:

> Inside the open-walled shed, four hundred women, working in groups of twenty, surrounded fifteen-foot piles of metal. The women wore gloves and masks and white uniforms. They picked through the pieces by hand, sorting the aluminum into different grades... and each grade had its own bucket. They also separated out small pieces of copper wire and whatever else they might find... American coins, left in gummy car ashtrays, were not uncommon. (Seabrook 2008: 57)

The men did the smelting work turning the scrap into liquid metal which is later cooled in molds.

A few examples, among many, of the uses to which the scrap metal can be put include the use of aluminum to make "engine casings of new cars... as well as irons, coffee pots, grills and frying pans" (Seabrook 2008: 55). As we might expect, some of the scrap metal that is sent to China is turned into various products that are shipped back to the US to be sold as new products and then, once again, eventually scrapped. More interesting is the fact that much of that which is made from the scrap is now increasingly likely to be used in China itself to create the infrastructure for that country's meteoric growth and expansion: "Most of the scrap metal that goes to China is turned into materials for the Chinese construction industry – rebar, beams and floor decking. That steel flows into the skyscrapers sprouting all around Chinese cities and into new factory towns, the copper is used to wire the millions of houses being built for China's new middle class." The great irony of this is that "China's industrial might is being constructed out of the ruins of [the US]" (Seabrook 2008: 55).

The future seems clear since the world's largest scrap yard has recently been built not far from Shanghai. A large steel mill is nearby to process the scrap metal. While American scrap yards depend on huge mechanical mega-shredders, the Chinese scrap yard relies on "hundreds of men working at tables with alligator shears, cutting every piece of scrap by hand. The result looked like metal pasta. The mega-shredder, for all its grunt, couldn't do that" (Seabrook 2008: 59). While China continues to import many recycled metals (in 2012, about 65% of China's scrap copper was imported [Bloomberg News 2013]), it seems likely that in the future the Chinese will no longer need American scrap metal; they will not need to engage in trade with the US for such scrap since they will be producing more than enough of their own.

Waste paper

One of the richest women in the world is Zhang Yin (estimated worth $3.05 billion and her family is worth billions more). The source of her wealth? Her business, Nine Dragons Paper (72% of which is controlled by the Zhang family) and Los Angeles-based America Chung Nam (the largest exporter to China), takes mountains of waste paper from the US, ships it to China, recycles it into corrugated boxes, the boxes are used to ship goods to various places around the world – including the US – and, once the boxes have arrived at their destination and been unpacked, they are turned into scrap and the process begins all over again.

Nine Dragons Paper is already one of the world's largest producers of paper and it could possibly soon be number one in the world surpassing such well-known giants as Weyerhauser. It is difficult to compete with Nine Dragons Paper because the company works with less expensive paper, its factory burns comparatively inexpensive coal, and it uses the latest technologies (while competitors like Weyerhauser are saddled with less efficient technology that is three or four decades old) (Barboza 2007a: C1, C8).

T-shirts

The neoliberalism that undergirds the global market is based on the belief that markets should be free, open, and have no barriers to free and open trade. While there have been many efforts to lower or remove such barriers, the fact is that such barriers remain in many areas. One particularly interesting and instructive example is found in Pietra Rivoli's work on the global value chain for T-shirts (Rivoli 2009). The global value chain here involves, among other things, cotton grown in and shipped from the US; T-shirts manufactured in China or Bangladesh; the shipping to, and sale of, those new T-shirts in the US; the eventual disposal (often very quickly) of them; and finally the shipping and sale of those used T-shirts in Africa. Below we look at this global value chain, but this time instead of focusing on the various steps involved, we will deal primarily with the nature of the various markets involved.

We can begin with cotton production in Texas. With its high labor costs, how is it the US can lead the world (at least most of the time) in cotton production and export? While part of the answer lies in the fact that the industry is embedded in a set of other highly advanced institutions (e.g. American universities that do cutting-edge scientific research on cotton production), the fact is that a large part of the answer lies in the fact that US government subsidies ($4 billion in 2000) distort the global market and give American producers a tremendous advantage. For example, as a result of the 2002 Farm Bill, American farmers got a minimum of over 72 cents per pound, while the average market price was 38 cents. This amounts to a government subsidy of about 34 cents per pound so that US cotton can compete on the global market. In fact, the WTO (heavily controlled by the US) ruled that in this the US violated global trade rules giving it a great advantage. The irony, of course, is that the US champions free trade and often chastises other nations for doing precisely what it does in the market for cotton.

The American cotton industry is aided – unfairly – in other ways. For example, American textile manufacturers are prevented from using foreign cotton even when they can get it at a lower price. The US government pays American textile manufacturers to use American cotton. And the US government helps in other ways as well, such as its Crop Disaster Program and its Farm Loan Program. Few, if any, of America's global competitors in the cotton market have support of this type and certainly not of this magnitude.

These subsidies and other programs put producers in other countries at a disadvantage. Another major cotton exporter, Brazil, fought back. It filed a claim with the WTO (see Chapter 6), alleging that the US was not following the agreed-upon rules of global trade. In 2004, the WTO ruled in favor of Brazil, but the US ignored the ruling and kept the subsidies in place (Joffe-Walt 2010). The US appealed, and lost the appeal, but still refused to change its subsidies until Brazil threatened a variety of economic sanctions against the US (this action was approved by the WTO). Then the two sides met to negotiate, and while the US argued it was impossible to eliminate subsidies immediately, it agreed to pay Brazilian cotton farmers $147 million per year until the subsidies were addressed in the next Farm Bill in 2012. However, after a delay on the Farm Bill vote in 2012, the Bill was rejected by Congress in June, 2013 (Chakraborty 2013). Americans continue to pay Brazil the annual payment, but having failed on their obligations to address the subsidies, the United States has exacerbated tensions and left the door open for Brazil to impose heavier economic sanctions on the US.

Similarly, the global trade in T-shirts, especially those produced in China, has not been free and open, especially with respect to the sale of Chinese-made T-shirts in the US. The Multi-Fibre Agreement (1975–2005) put quotas on the number of T-shirts that could be imported into the US from various producing countries. The main purpose of the law was to prevent China from garnering all, or close to all, of that market. In fact, were this to be a free and open market, China *would* have dominated most of the market because according to many observers it produces the best quality T-shirts at the lowest price. The Multi-Fibre Agreement was a state-imposed mechanism to limit the ability of the Chinese to sell T-shirts in the American market. After it expired at the end of 2005, imports of Chinese T-shirts to the US (and the EU) were capped for three more years (Chanda 2007: 82).

So where do all those T-shirts go when Americans (and consumers from other countries) don't want them anymore? Many of them end up in the bins of second-hand stores, such as the Salvation Army or the Goodwill. A very rare T-shirt, like a Rolling Stones 1972 tour shirt, might find its way to a hip vintage store where it can sell for up to $300. But most

T-shirts have a less profitable fate. And because the supply of second-hand T-shirts far exceeds the demand for them in the US, it has driven a successful export industry. As Rivoli (2009: 216) observes, "between 1995 and 2007, the United States exported nearly 9 billion pounds of used clothing and other worn textile products to the rest of the world." Some of these items are dumped into African countries, with the unintended consequence that they have the potential to destroy local apparel manufacturing. For example, a recent study found that "used-clothing imports are found to have a negative impact on apparel production in Africa, explaining roughly 40% of the decline in production and 50% of the decline in employment over the period 1981–2000" (Frazer 2008: 1764). Many other unwanted T-shirts end up being sold to a rag cutter, where they are cut and then sold to wiping-rag manufacturers. The most unwanted T-shirts go through a shredder and these recycled materials might be used in carpet pads, mattresses, cushions, caskets, and more recently, as insulation in eco-friendly construction (Rivoli 2009: 226).

iPhones

The global value chain for the Apple iPhone is fascinating and very complex. The phone's conceptual design is created in the US, and the processor is produced in Texas. Beyond that, "advanced semiconductors have come from Germany and Taiwan, memory from Korea and Japan, display panels and circuitry from Korea and Taiwan, chipsets from Europe and rare metals from Africa and Asia" (Duhigg and Bradsher 2012). Then the phone is assembled in China, often using the infamous contractor, Foxconn (they are well known for widespread labor abuses). The lack of adequate labor regulations in China (and throughout Asia) provides Apple with a cheap and flexible labor force. For example, Apple had last-minute design changes (the use of a new glass screen) to its new model and this required fully reconfiguring the assembly line. However, the new screens would be arriving at the same night that the necessary overhaul was to take place. One report described how the Chinese factory handled the situation: "A foreman immediately roused 8,000 workers inside the company's dormitories, according to the [Apple] executive. Each employee was given a biscuit and a cup of tea, guided to a workstation and within half an hour started a 12-hour shift fitting glass screens into beveled frames" (Duhigg and Bradsher 2012). After only four days, the factory was turning out more than 10,000 iPhones each day for consumers around the world. Of course, the flipside of this efficiency is that those 8,000 workers are living in poor conditions (at least by American standards) in company dormitories. They work long hours for little pay, and working conditions are often very bad. For example, there is evidence of forced labor, child labor, forced unpaid overtime, industrial accidents from unenforced workplace regulations, and workers committing suicide at Foxconn, which alone employs 1.2 million Chinese workers (Barboza and Duhigg 2012).

Once the phones are produced, they are distributed to markets around the world, and the value chain for iPhones gets even more interesting. While many of the phones are shipped to the US and Europe,[3] some of them are then smuggled by tourists, airline personnel, small businesspeople, and full-time smugglers to other nations, mainly China, where consumers also love high-tech gadgets like the iPhone. For example, in Hong Kong, the iPhone 4S sold for $125 less than it did in mainland China. For a poor Chinese worker, smuggling iPhones can appear more desirable than assembling them. It is no wonder then, that in the first two months of 2012, over 3,000 smart phones were confiscated at Shenzhen Bao-an International Airport near Hong Kong (Matthews 2012).

"Used" factories

While China is manufacturing and shipping all sorts of products throughout the world, another of the things that China has imported from other parts of the world is entire factories that had come to be considered obsolete in their country of origin. For example, Germany had a number of steel plants that had become outmoded by the 1980s. For one thing, they were not as efficient as the newer plants constructed elsewhere in the world (e.g. Japan). For another thing, their antiquated technology was not only highly inefficient, but it tended to pollute the environment to a degree that was no longer acceptable in the West. Finally, the era of profitable heavy industries in the West was ending and steel was just one of many industries that were moving to other parts of the world.

All of this occurred at a time when China was beginning to develop in a variety of different areas, including its heavy industries such as steel. The Chinese quickly concluded that it was far cheaper to buy dated factories in places like Germany than to build new ones from scratch. In one case they purchased a seven-story blast furnace and sent their own workers to Germany to dismantle it. The workers painstakingly labeled every part of the furnace, dismantled it, and packed the parts in thousands of wooden crates for shipment back to China. Of the Chinese workers, a German company official said: "They worked day and night.... They could never have done it that fast if they were governed by German labor laws" (Kahn and Landler 2007: A12). The Chinese used such equipment and factories to great advantage in helping them to become a production and exporting colossus. However, the factories have done to the Chinese environment what they did at one time to the environment in Germany and elsewhere in the world – it has become severely polluted with sulfur dioxide, carbon dioxide, etc. In fact, while the air has become clean in the Ruhr area where many of these factories once existed, it has become highly polluted in the parallel areas in China. Of course, China has the jobs and the growing income, while Germany has lost work and income. On the other hand, the Germans now live in a relatively clean environment and they can still afford to buy all the relatively inexpensive imports from China. The Ruhr area is now characterized by educational and high-tech centers, and it attracts more tourism than was previously the case.

Automobiles

However, China has also moved beyond the era of importing unwanted German factories; it is building more of its own and they are increasingly sophisticated. For example, Geely is an automobile manufacturer and its first crudely built automobiles (less than 5,000 of them) rolled off the assembly line in 2000; by 2006 it was producing 180,000 far more sophisticated autos that sold not only in China, but Latin America, the Middle East, and Europe (Fairclough 2006: A1, A14). In 2010, Geely sold over 415,000 vehicles, bought Volvo (a Swedish car company), and positioned itself as part of a rapidly growing Chinese automobile industry. In fact, China quickly became the world's largest automobile manufacturer and in 2012, they produced almost one out of every four cars sold in the world (15.5 million in total) (International Organization of Motor Vehicle Manufacturers, n.d.). It is now far easier for China (and countries like it) to enter, and become a major player in, the automobile industry (and others) for a number of reasons including widespread knowledge of needed technologies, the expertise derived from previous joint ventures with Western and Japanese manufacturers, the hiring of experts (especially engineers) from established firms in those areas, the ability to purchase components from the same manufacturers through-out China and the world used by long-established automobile companies, and the ability to outsource many aspects of the production process.

Joint ventures with established auto companies are underway and venture capitalists are investing in the Chinese auto industry. Said Geely's chairman: "Globalization is changing the world distribution of industries. Industry here is developing from the simple to the sophisti-cated" (quoted in Fairclough 2006: A14). In the meantime, American and Japanese auto com-panies are opening more joint venture factories in China (e.g. GM entered a joint partnership with SAIC Motor in China, to produce electric cars [Bradsher 2011]). Chinese companies are also starting to invest heavily in Detroit and other US locations (Vlasic 2013).

INCREASING COMPETITION FOR COMMODITIES

A wide range of commodities constitute the starting point for many of the global value chains discussed above. However, one of the most striking developments in recent years has been the increasing global competition for various commodities. The best-known and most obvious example is oil (see below), but much the same thing has happened in the markets for natural gas, copper, nickel, silver, gold, as well as even more mundane commodities such as rice, wheat, corn, and soybeans (Krauss 2008: C1, C8). The increasing demand for these commodities, and many others, is no longer fueled mainly by the needs of the countries we traditionally think of as highly developed (e.g. the US, the members of the EU, Japan), but now by massive development in other parts of the world, especially India (Dossani 2008) and China. The latter, especially China, are industrializing at a rapid pace. Between 2008 and 2011, China's economic growth was between 9.2 and 10.4% each year, although it dipped slightly to 7.8% in 2012 (by contrast, the US economy shrank in 2008 and 2009, and grew at 2.2% in 2012). Those relatively new industries place large and increasing demands on all sorts of commodities, especially the oil needed to power them (China accounted for 40% of the increased global demand for oil in 2012 [Lelyveld 2013]). While China is now the second-largest consumer of oil in the world, and is the most significant consumer of many base metals, it is important to remember that the North, especially the US, remains the major consumer of most of the world's commodities.

However, demand for commodities goes well beyond that of specific industries needing specific commodities for their production processes. This industrial development is linked to the emergence of a similarly expanding consumer society with consumers in countries like China and India demanding the same sorts of products that consumers in the US and the EU possess. The result involves the need for everything from more airplanes to transport people who now want to see the world, to gas-guzzling and polluting trucks to deliver the things they want to consume, to the automobiles they now want to have both as consumables and as technologies that allow them to consume much else (e.g. tourism within China and Asia). All of these planes, trucks, and cars require gasoline, need to be produced in factories that consume huge amounts of energy, and in order to be produced all of them require a wide range of commodities. A global commodities specialist sums this up well: "It is absolutely a fundamental change in the global economic structure.... Global commodities ranging from oil to base metals to grains are moving higher as billions of people in China and around the world get wealthier and are consuming more as they produce products for us, and increasingly for themselves" (quoted in Krauss 2008: C1). As an economist put it,

"The world is coming alive and the lights are coming on across Asia.... What we are dealing with is a tremendous demand for resources" (quoted in Krauss 2008: C8).

The developing countries, especially China, are devouring huge quantities of many commodities (of course the developed countries long have, and continue to, devour much larger quantities of these commodities). For example, while China has approximately one fifth of the world's population, it consumes almost half of global cotton production, 45% of coal production, and almost 40% of its aluminum production (Roache 2012).

The result of all of this is massive increases in the price of all sorts of commodities (e.g. the price of copper tripled and that of zinc doubled in a five-year period in the early twenty-first century; the cost of both wheat and soybeans increased by 70% in 2007). The prices of many commodities reached record highs in 2008, before dropping off quite dramatically as the Great Recession gained momentum.[4] More recently, China has been investing in commodities of all sorts to fuel its growth.

THE ECONOMIC IMPACT OF THE FLOW OF OIL

The economic impact of oil over the last century cannot be underestimated. It has been the driving force of both industrialization and mechanized warfare. As nations and economies have developed, they have pursued more and more oil (Labban 2012). Not only does this greater demand lead to higher prices, but it becomes harder and harder to find additional resources (e.g. new oil fields) and increasingly difficult to obtain them. Thus, oil wells far out in the ocean are more expensive to build than those on land, and the oil itself is harder to get and, as a result, more expensive. Getting oil from sand pits is more difficult and costly than from underground oil wells. All of these increasing difficulties translate into higher costs and higher prices. And these changes have ripple effects throughout the economy. For example, the high price of oil and gasoline has led to increased efforts to create and use various biofuels, especially ethanol (see Chapter 14) from corn (among other sources including sugar cane). The result is a huge increase in demand for, and the price of, corn (see discussion of Mexican corn in Chapter 6). This has motivated the increased use of hydraulic fracturing (i.e. fracking) to obtain oil. This method can be less costly in the short-term but it carries significant environmental risks (e.g. groundwater contamination and air pollution), including many unknown risks because extraction companies do not disclose the chemicals used in fracking.

OIL WEALTH

There was a huge influx of petrodollars into oil-producing countries after 2002 and especially in 2007 and 2008, as a result of the great run-up in oil prices through mid-2008. In 2000 oil exports earned OPEC about $243 billion; by 2007 it was estimated to rise to $688 billion (Weisman 2007c: A1, A16). While these figures dropped significantly during the Great Recession, they quickly rose again and in 2012, OPEC earned a record $982 billion from oil revenues (Makan 2013). Saudi Arabia alone earned an estimated $312 billion in 2012. Since they cannot possibly spend it all, they need to invest their revenues somewhere. Said the chairman of an energy company, "The oil-producing countries simply cannot absorb the amount of wealth they are generating.... We are seeing a transfer of wealth of historic dimensions" (quoted in Weisman 2007c: A16). This huge and growing income has enormous implications, but at the minimum those nations, their leaders, and their corporations (private and state-run) have huge sums of money to invest. The decisions on where they should invest their money give them great power and influence. One of the things the beneficiaries of this boom are doing – or not doing – is investing in Northern (especially American) companies. The North is likely to benefit greatly if the money flows back in the form of new investments, but it is likely to suffer if the oil-producing nations turn inward, or elsewhere (especially China), in order to get a higher return on their investment.

On the one hand, the Abu Dhabi Investment Authority invested $7.5 billion in the American-based Citicorp and with that investment became one of the company's largest shareholders. Citicorp had found itself in economic difficulty and in need of an influx of cash because of bad investments related to the 2007 financial crisis (see below). In 2010, they also acquired Harrods department store in London for $2.3 billion. On the other hand, in the aftermath of the Arab Spring, the sovereign wealth funds from these oil-producing nations have shifted more of their investment dollars back to the region. In particular, they have been putting more money into education, health care, and infrastructure (including Qatar, which is preparing for the World Cup in 2022) (Hamdan 2012).

Many other American-based companies have been the recipients of huge investments of petrodollars including Advanced Micro Devices, Carlyle Group, and Walt Disney. While such investments are a good thing from the point of view of the economic condition of these corporations, some worry about oil-producing nations "buying up America" (and other countries) and gaining control over its key corporations.

However, investments in the US are not as attractive as they once were. In part, this is because of the rise in, and increasing attractiveness of, other economies (notably China). And in part it is because the decline in the US dollar in recent years can lead to an erosion in the value of foreign investments in the US. On the other hand, the declining dollar makes investments in the US cheaper and therefore more desirable to other countries.

The increase in the price of oil, and the increasing difficulty in obtaining enough of it, is both roiling and restructuring the globe and the position of many nations, corporations, and individuals in it (Labban 2012). At the national level we have become accustomed to thinking of OPEC nations such as Saudi Arabia and Abu Dhabi as profiting handsomely from the oil business,[5] but in recent years other nations have also become wealthy and more important global players as a result of the oil boom. Russia, nearly bankrupt in the late 1990s, is awash with oil money and it is using it in various ways, including reasserting itself on the global stage (e.g. the invasion of Georgia in late 2008) in ways reminiscent of the old Soviet Union. Venezuela, taking the lead from former President Hugo Chávez (see, especially, Chapter 15), is using oil profits to fuel a move toward socialism and to acquire a more powerful position in Latin America. It has also used them to fund massive public spending and to create subsidies designed to offer Venezuelans free health care and education and less expensive food. Angola ended a decades-long civil war in 2002; oil revenues have helped their country grow steadily since then. The government was investing in roads, airports, and railroad tracks.

At the individual level great wealth and affluence is being produced at the very top. Individual Russians are traveling the world, buying expensive art, and bidding up the price of the most desirable real estate in, for example, London (Russia's controversial rock band, "Pussy Riot," produced a video in 2013 accusing President Putin and his allies of stealing the country's oil profits [Mackey and Roth 2013]). In Angola most of the wealthiest people are current and former government officials. They drive the luxury cars seen throughout the capital city, where luxury apartments now are visible above the skyline and some night clubs demand a $100 cover charge. While such people are clearly skimming a large proportion of oil income off the top, the great majority of Angolans are profiting little, if at all, from the oil boom. So starting in 2011, inspired by the Arab Spring, people began protesting the concentration of oil wealth. After a year of intense protests, the government responded by starting their own sovereign wealth fund to diversify the economy and begin to distribute its wealth, but it is not yet clear if much of this money will reach the poor (Polgreen 2012). While Angola is an extreme case, there is little evidence in many other parts of the world that the poor are benefiting greatly from the oil boom.

The International Energy Agency has urged advanced nations to work with India and China to reduce the burgeoning use of oil. It is the increased demand, especially from China and India, which is playing a huge role in pushing up the price of oil on the world market. Increased use there, and elsewhere, is also tied, of course, to higher carbon dioxide emissions (projected to increase by 57% over the next quarter century) and accompanying disastrous effects on the globe's climate. It is estimated that global energy demand will increase 56% by 2040, driven by India and China, whose energy consumption alone will more than double (Zhou 2013). Energy demand in the US (the world's second-largest consumer after China) is expected to increase by 9%. For their part, representatives of China and India argue that they are being unduly singled out in this issue. After all, the developed countries have already developed and China and India should be given an opportunity to catch up before there is any discussion of limiting their expansion. The problem is that waiting for them to address their energy and emissions issues would make it too late to reduce much of the earth's warming, given what we now know about climate science (see Chapter 11).

OIL IMPORTS TO OIL-RICH NATIONS

Global concern about oil usually focuses on its consumption by oil-importing nations. However, we are on the cusp of a change where some nations that are currently oil producers will need to import oil in order to meet increasing demand due to economic development and the requirements of increasing numbers of automobiles, homes, and businesses (as the world's third-largest oil producer, the US has faced this situation for quite some time). In fact, Indonesia has already made this transition and in the near future Mexico and Iran are expected to shift from being net exporters to net importers of oil (Iran has been further affected by US sanctions on oil, implemented in late 2011). In other cases (Russia and some OPEC nations), increasing internal demand will lead to reductions in oil exports. The net result is clear: since 2006, net global exports of oil have decreased slightly each year (from 45.6 million barrels per day in 2006 to 43.7 million barrels per day in 2011). This does not seem to be much, but it needs to be seen in light of inflexible demand, limited new production facilities, and the growth of developing countries. For example, it is projected that by 2030, China and India alone could use all of the world's oil exports. In the absence of available alternatives, this will lead to the use of unusual sources and the opening up of areas currently closed to oil production (Krauss 2007: 1, 22). This has already happened in Canada's tar sands, where oil extraction is already taking a heavy environmental toll. Another possibility is the relaxation on restrictions of drilling for oil in Alaska and off the US coast, which continues to provoke controversy in the US.

The oil-producing states still lag behind the greatest oil users in the world in overall use of oil, especially the US (and soon China), but it is surprising that per-person oil consumption in some of the producer states – e.g. Bahrain, Kuwait, Qatar, United Arab Emirates – exceeds that in the US. Some oil-producing nations subsidize oil leading to artificially low prices for gasoline and this leads to more cars, drivers, and gasoline consumption. In early 2013, gas prices were 80 cents in Kuwait, 45 cents in Saudi Arabia, and only 4 cents per gallon – practically free – in Venezuela (compared to a high of $9.98 per gallon in Turkey) (Randall 2013). Many in those countries are newly rich and their relatively youthful populations are eager to acquire all sorts of things, including automobiles. Farmers are replacing horse carts with gas-guzzling trucks, tractors, and the like.

INCREASING FOOD PRICES

In a number of quite obvious ways, increased fuel prices lead, in turn, to higher prices for many other things. For example, higher fuel prices mean higher transportation costs for all sorts of products and that eventually is reflected in higher prices for those products. The cost of transportation itself rises with the result that the cost of driving increases as does the price for airline tickets. For another, many products are made from oil (e.g. plastic) and higher oil prices mean higher prices for all of those products.

RACE TO THE BOTTOM AND UPGRADING

Race to the bottom: Countries involved in a downward spiral of competitiveness.

A dominant idea in thinking about less developed economies from a global perspective is the so-called **race to the bottom**. The basic argument is that for less developed countries to compete and succeed in the global economy, they must undercut the competition in various ways such as offering lower wages, poorer working conditions, longer hours, ever-escalating pressure and demands, and so on. It is often the case that one nation is willing to go further than the others in order to attract the interest of MNCs. An ever-spiraling decline in wages, etc., occurs in the "winning" less developed nation, at least until it is undercut by other countries eager for work and willing to offer even lower pay, poorer working conditions, and so on. In other words, the countries that get the work are those that win the race to the bottom. These, of course, are almost always pyrrhic victories since the work is earned on the basis of creating poorly paid and horrid circumstances for the workers within the "victorious" nation.

UPGRADING IN THE LESS DEVELOPED WORLD?

The current global economic system is based, at least in part, on a race to the bottom by less developed countries and the exploitation of them and their industries by the more developed countries. However, we must not ignore the fact that there is evidence of a process of upgrading in less developed countries and their industries (Bair and Gereffi 2003; Gereffi 2012). That is, at least some of them enter the global economic market at or near the bottom, but over time begin to move up. This, for example, is clear in China today, where the early success of Chinese industry was based on their victory in the race to the bottom, but the Chinese are now moving away from that and to the production of higher-value products with higher pay and better working conditions for at least some Chinese workers.

Another example is to be found in Mexico, especially its *maquiladoras* (Gereffi 2005: 163). The early, first-generation *maquiladoras* were labor-intensive, employed limited technologies, and assembled finished products for export (e.g. apparel) using components imported from the US. Second-generation *maquiladoras* "are less oriented toward assembly and more toward manufacturing processes that use automated and semi-automated machines and robots in the automobile, television, and electrical appliance sectors" (Gereffi 2005: 163). In their third generation, *maquiladoras* "are oriented to research, design, and development, and rely on highly skilled labor such as specialized engineers and technicians," and they "have matured from assembly sites based on cheap labor to manufacturing centers whose competitiveness derives from a combination of high productivity, good quality, and wages far below those prevailing north of the border" (Gereffi 2005: 163). Of course, this indicates that while the *maquiladoras* may have advanced, the lot of the workers may not have kept pace with this development.

This point can be made more generally under the heading of **industrial upgrading** through which economic actors – nations, firms, and even workers – "move from low-value to relatively high-value activities in global production networks" (Gereffi 2005: 171). This can occur in four sequential stages – assembly, original equipment manufacture (OEM), original brand name manufacturing (OBM), and original design manufacturing (ODM). Depending on the nation and industry in question (e.g. apparel, electronics, fresh vegetables), one sees varying degrees of movement up this hierarchy.

> **Industrial upgrading**: Nation-states, firms, and even workers move from low-value to relatively high-value production.

A similar point is made, albeit in far more general terms, by Rivoli in her study of the global market for T-shirts (Rivoli 2009). If one takes the long historical view, the nations, especially specific areas and the industries located there, that won the race to the bottom are now among the most successful global economies in the world. In textiles, the race to the bottom was won first by England (especially Manchester), then the US (New Hampshire and later Charlotte, North Carolina), then Japan (Osaka), and Hong Kong. Most recently it was the Chinese and their textile industry and it is clear that, having won the race to the bottom in that industry, they are moving up industrially and economically.

Rivoli generalizes from this to argue that nations and areas within them must win the race to the bottom in order ultimately to succeed. Victory in this race is, in her view, the "ignition switch" that turns the economy on and gets it rolling. Thus, she concludes that those who criticize globalization from below are misguided in their efforts to end this race. However, she does recognize that activists have, through their actions over the years, altered the nature of the race by raising the bottom. More generally she concludes that the "bottom is rising" (Rivoli 2009).

However, Rivoli's view on this is hotly debated and much disputed because not all countries are eventually able to upgrade their economies (Klein 2009). In addition, this view has a clear association with neoliberalism. As a result, it seems to endorse the race to the bottom for all countries interested in development. This not only leads them into poverty for at least a time, but it greatly advantages the wealthy North which is guaranteed a continuing source of low-priced goods and services as one country replaces another at the bottom. Winning the race to the bottom is no guarantee of adaptive upgrading, but it is a guarantee of low wages and poverty for an unknown amount of time.

OUTSOURCING

Outsourcing is the transfer of activities once performed by an entity to a business (or businesses) in exchange for money. It is a complex phenomenon that is not restricted to the economy, not only a macro-level phenomenon, and not simply global in character.

> **Outsourcing**: Transfer of activities once performed by an entity to a business (or businesses) in exchange for money.

Dealing with the first issue, while outsourcing in the economic realm is of greatest importance and the issue of concern here, it also occurs in many other institutions such as health care and the military. In terms of the former, one example involves the fact that the work of the radiologist is increasingly being outsourced. This is made possible because the material with which radiologists deal (x-rays, results of MRIs) is now usually digitized and therefore sent easily and quickly via the Internet to radiologists anywhere in the world. Thus, a digitized x-ray taken in London can be read quickly and easily by a lower-paid radiologist in Asia. Similarly, the military has outsourced many of its functions. For example, NATO forces from various countries serving in Afghanistan may be flown there on leased Ukrainian airplanes or by the commercial airlines of NATO nations rather than on planes from their own air forces. While both of the preceding examples exist outside the economy, they *are* examples of outsourcing and *are* manifestations of globalization.

Second, we need to go beyond the macro-level of outsourcing (e.g. a British corporation outsourcing work to one in India) to deal with it at the meso- and micro-levels. Thus, we can include under the heading of outsourcing at the meso-level restaurants that outsource the cooking of their food to outside organizations (e.g. Sysco produces meals that restaurants then simply reheat) and at the micro-level parents who outsource the care of their young children (Pyle 2006) or aged parents to institutions, specifically day-care and assisted-living centers.

Inclusion of these levels makes for a more satisfying and more complete sense of outsourcing, although much of it may not relate directly to globalization. Nonetheless, globalization is often involved even at these levels as exemplified by the fact that the micro-level of care for children or aged parents in developed countries is often outsourced to immigrants, documented or undocumented, from less developed countries. These migrants can be seen as part of a global care-chain[6] and those who care for children, as well as the children themselves, as part of the globalization of parenthood. It is even the case that motherhood is being outsourced with, for example, Indian women serving as surrogate mothers for couples from Israel (Gentleman 2008: A9).

The form of outsourcing most closely and importantly associated with globalization is **offshore outsourcing** which involves sending work to companies in other countries. For example, a variety of Indian firms have become very important settings for the outsourcing of various kinds of work – the best known of which is that performed by call centers (Aneesh 2012) – from, especially, the US and Great Britain (although offshore outsourcing is a two-way street and such work is also finding its way into these developed countries). Indian companies are even making progress in performing outsourced call-center work for Japanese firms necessitating, of course, the employment of those fluent in Japanese (*Economist* 2007: October 11). While blue-collar manufacturing work has long been outsourced offshore, and the offshore outsourcing of low-level service work is of more recent vintage, what is eye-catching is the increasing offshore outsourcing of high-level white collar and service work such as IT (information technology), accounting, law, architecture, journalism, and medicine. There are many advantages of offshore outsourcing to both outsourcers (e.g. 24/7 availability of workers) and outsourcees (e.g. job and wealth creation) and that is why it has grown so dramatically and is likely to continue to grow. However, there are many costs, especially in the country doing the outsourcing and most notably in job loss and destruction. It is the array of costs that has made offshore outsourcing a hot-button issue in the US and other developed nations and has led to calls for the government to act to restrict it.

Offshore outsourcing: Transfer of activities to entities in other countries.

However, as we saw above in the case of health care and the military, offshore outsourcing is not restricted to the economy and is therefore globalizing in a far broader sense than is usually understood. For example, the offshore outsourcing of war has a long history (including British outsourcing of fighting much of the Revolutionary War to paid mercenaries, especially the Hessians), but it boomed, at least in the case of the US, following the end of the Cold War. A variety of for-profit private organizations have emerged to which various war functions are outsourced. So many aspects of the war in Iraq are outsourced that one journalist joked that President George Bush's "coalition of the willing" might thus be more aptly described as the "coalition of the billing."[7]

In-sourcing involves the fact that offshore outsourcing necessarily involves tasks being taken in by other firms in other countries. In the case of the US (and other developed countries), the work that is outsourced to, say, India is simultaneously in-sourced by that country. It is also the case that while they are offshore outsourcing a great deal of work, the US and Great Britain, among others, are also in-sourcing some work that had been performed in other countries.

CREATIVE DESTRUCTION AND OUTSOURCING

The theory that is most often employed, especially by neoliberals, to think about outsourcing is Joseph Schumpeter's *creative destruction* (Schumpeter 1976: 81–7). While it is acknowledged that much outsourcing is destructive (although in-sourcing, in particular, shows its constructive side), the overall view is that it is, at least in the long run, constructive, good for the economy and ultimately the capitalist system. However, this is far too rosy a picture. There are largely or purely destructive aspects of offshore outsourcing. For example, in the case of the US, offshore outsourcing can be seen as being responsible for job loss, the hollowing out or complete destruction of businesses and industries, the evisceration of the military and health-care system, and the emptying of many lives that were once filled with tasks (care for children, aged parents) that they once found highly meaningful.

The theory of creative destruction has its origins prior to the current era of globalization, and of offshore outsourcing. It is well suited to deal with, for example, jobs lost in one part of the US (destruction) but gained (created) in another part of the country. It is ill equipped to deal with a situation in which the jobs lost in one country (perhaps *only* involving destruction there) are created in another. Neoliberals also emphasize that, within a country, jobs lost in one industry are created in another industry, but the reality is that the new jobs created (at least in the US) tend to be jobs that pay a much lower wage. Schumpeter and his disciples always combine creativity and destruction because of their focus on a single country. However, in the global age (if not always) they clearly can be, and are, separated with the likelihood that creativity occurs in one country while destruction occurs in another. Disentangling creativity and destruction in this way would make the concept of creative destruction more applicable to the global age.

FINANCIAL GLOBALIZATION

The world's economies have become more tightly interconnected as a result of globalization. One reflection of that is the well-known phrase, "When the American economy sneezes, the rest of the world catches a cold." However, dramatic economic events in other parts of the world also have an impact on most, if not all of, the world's economies. This is clear, for example, in the global impact of the financial crises that struck Asia and Russia in the 1990s. However, it remains the case that the more powerful the economy, the greater the effect of its crises on the rest of the world. The corollary is that problems in weaker economies have less of an effect across the globe. Thus, Argentina had a serious financial crisis in the late 1990s and early 2000s, but its impact on the global economy was comparatively small.

THE GREAT RECESSION

Thus, when the US suffers a financial crisis it does have a profound effect on the rest of the world's economies. This was demonstrated most recently in the 2007–2008 financial crisis and the Great Recession, which was the worst global economic crisis since the Great Depression (Orr 2012). There are several factors that contributed to this financial crisis, the effects of which continue to be felt today. First, growing inequality in the US was brought about by the loss of unionized manufacturing jobs, offshoring various types of labor, and the decades-long slashing of government spending which has led to a decrease in purchasing power for many American workers. From 1975 to the last years of the first decade of the twenty-first century, the ratio of American household debt to income doubled.

Second, the dot-com bubble that burst in 2000 drove many investors into real estate, a more tangible investment that was perceived as less risky. Money poured into the housing industry as new homes were built and as house prices began to skyrocket. Banks of all sizes were providing loans that did not follow banking regulations and to people who should not have qualified for them. As Orr (2012) describes it, the rising home prices and "the ensuing housing bubble enabled many workers to borrow against their rising home equity to finance home improvements, send their children to college, pay medical bills or simply maintain their standard of living in the midst of stagnant wages." But when the bubble burst, and home prices began to fall in 2005, workers could no longer borrow against their over-inflated equity. Not only did this mean that consumption slowed significantly, but foreclosure rates increased dramatically and many people lost their homes.

Home foreclosures were compounded by the sub-prime mortgages crisis. These were mortgages that offered low interest rates (rates below the prime interest rate) for a short period of time after which the interest rate was to increase dramatically. The interest rate jump served to raise significantly homeowners' monthly payments, and many borrowers did not have the income to afford the monthly payments. Sub-prime mortgages were often given by predatory lenders who either did not disclose how the loan worked or simply lied about the loans. Therefore, many of those who bought homes at the sub-prime rate did not realize that such an increase would occur or how much more they would need to pay each month. Others believed that they would be able to refinance their homes at an attractive fixed interest rate when the initial low-interest rate ended, but they found that the emerging crisis had left banks unable or unwilling to offer them new credit at low rates.

The crisis began in earnest when large numbers of homeowners were unable to make their monthly payments and the banks foreclosed on their homes. Banks would ordinarily sell foreclosed homes, but the booming housing market of the early 2000s had collapsed and many banks were left with far too many valueless properties and this translated into large write-offs and huge losses. More importantly, many low-income homeowners were ruined as a result of losing their homes and their investments in them. The losses experienced by American banks contributed to a global banking crisis and other financial and economic institutions were adversely affected, as well. This was a big factor in the huge bailout of the financial system by the US government in late 2008. The government, fearing a complete economic meltdown, funneled billions dollars (including a $700 billion financial rescue plan in October 2008) into the country's largest banks and financial companies to keep them operating and to continue to make credit available.

Another underlying cause of the global crisis was deregulation throughout the financial industry. Most importantly, the Glass-Steagall Act was repealed in 1999.This repeal allowed commercial banks to merge with investments banks. It enabled American banks not to hold many of the mortgages that they wrote, but rather to "securitize" (bundle) them with other mortgages and sell the bundles as "mortgage-backed securities" to other banks and financial institutions, often throughout the world (Gotham 2006). By selling the mortgages in these packages, the banks which made the risky loans were not the ones who would suffer the losses if the loans failed. Those who bought these bundles of debt rarely fully understood, or even cared about, the details of the securities that were in the bundles. The assumption was that mortgages were generally safe and if there were some risky investments in the bundle, they were more than compensated for by the safe ones. When the sub-prime crisis developed, financial institutions in the US and throughout the world came to realize that a large portion of the bundles of debt that they had purchased was valueless. Because the US Securities and Exchange Commission allowed investment banks to increase their levels of debt and essentially regulate themselves, the extent of the crisis was greatly exacerbated. This all led financial institutions to mark down billions of dollars in assets and some nearly went bankrupt. These instances of deregulation were championed by neoliberals, but they are further examples of how neoliberal theory often deviates from practice. Specifically, while neoliberal theory suggests that market deregulation makes economies more efficient, in practice it often leads to corruption, malpractice, and financial crisis (which is consistent with Polanyi's theory of the double-movement – see Chapter 4).

Not surprisingly major banks (e.g. Citicorp, Washington Mutual) and other financial institutions (e.g. Fannie Mae, Freddie Mac, AIG – all eventually nationalized in whole or in part by the US) in the US experienced severe difficulties either because they had issued sub-prime mortgages or had invested in bundles of securitized mortgages. However, the crisis was not restricted to the US. For example, the Northern Rock bank in Great Britain was saved from bankruptcy in late 2007 by an infusion of money from the Bank of England (*Economist* 2008: January 24). In early 2008 the British government reluctantly took control of (nationalized) Northern Rock, at least temporarily (Werdigier 2008a: C1, C4). The crisis continued to expand in 2008 and 2009 involving the global economy to an ever-increasing degree.

Throughout late 2007 there was much discussion of whether and how much the sub-prime crisis, and the related implosion of the housing market, was going to affect the overall American economy. By early 2008 it became clear that the impact was going to be profound with indications increasing that the US economy was facing a recession later in 2008. The US Stock Market dropped dramatically to more than 15% below its peak in late 2007, and after a slight recovery dropped again in late 2008 (Grynbaum 2008: C1, C7). This occurred in the context of a view that because of the great strength and growth of other economies around the world (e.g. the EU, Japan, China, India), they were much less likely to catch a "cold" just because the US "sneezed" (Goodman 2008b: C1, C4). Another way of putting this is that a number of the more powerful economies in the world had "decoupled" from the US economy. That is, they had become strong enough, had enough internal demand, and could do business with so many other countries, that their economies were no longer closely linked ("coupled") with that of the US (Gross 2008: 39–42). This seemed to be especially true of emerging economies which trade a great deal with each other, as well as with countries such as China (*Economist* 2008: March 6 ["The Decoupling Debate"]).

However, this quickly proved fallacious. Since the US is the major consumer of much of the world's products, a recession or financial crisis there was likely to have a profoundly negative effect on many global economies dominated by the production of goods exported to the US. Indeed, there were significant drops in industrial production throughout much of the world as economies contracted (i.e. entered into recession). Unemployment rose rapidly in all countries: in 2009, unemployment in the Euro Zone was around 9.5%, with the highest unemployment rate in Spain at 18.7% (The Associated Press 2009) and youth experiencing higher rates throughout Europe. The negative effect on other economies could, in turn, adversely affect their ability to buy American goods and services, or to invest in the US and its businesses, further worsening the crisis there. Countries around the globe saw drops in travel and consumer spending. Thus, the effects of the crisis flowed easily and rapidly back and forth throughout the world.

Even the booming Chinese economy began to feel the pinch. Sales of T-shirts and knitwear declined significantly and some Chinese factories were in danger of being forced out of business (Bradsher 2008b: C1, C4). The Chinese economy clearly remains closely tied to the American economy. This may be even truer of less robust economies than that of China (and India). For example, the Japanese economy seemed to feel the effects of the American decline more than these other economies. Said a Japanese economist: "Now we see 're-coupling'…. The economy of Japan is proving disappointingly fragile to external shocks" (quoted in Bradsher 2008b: C4).

In another reflection of globalization, Citicorp sought to solve its financial problems caused by the sub-prime crisis by soliciting massive investments from other parts of the world, especially the oil-producing states of the Middle East. The Abu Dhabi Investment Authority invested $7.5 billion in Citigroup in 2007. This served to make Citicorp itself a more global company (even though the investment lost big when the bank nearly collapsed, and the Abu Dhabi Investment Authority would ultimately spend years arguing they were defrauded on their investment [Stempel and Raymond 2013]). On the other hand, such foreign investments in US corporations led to increasing fears in the US of other nations buying into, and coming to control, large American corporations (Goodman and Story 2008: 1, 29).

The biggest concern about foreign control involved financial investments in the US by **sovereign wealth funds**. These funds are owned by nation-states (not corporations or individual investors) and when they invest in other countries, it is in fact those nation-states that are doing the investing. Among the largest sovereign wealth funds are the Abu Dhabi Investment Authority (ADIA), the Government of Singapore Investment Corporation, and the China Investment Corporation. In a sense, the activities of these funds involve a new form of state capitalism. It is estimated that sovereign wealth funds will be valued at over $5.6 trillion globally by the end of 2013 (Rao 2013). The largest are Norway's Government Pension Fund (begun in 1990) valued at $737.2 billion, and the Abu Dhabi Investment Authority (begun in 1976) valued at $627 billion (Sovereign Wealth Fund Institute 2013).

Sovereign wealth funds: Funds controlled by nation-states that often invest in other countries.

In one sense the flow of money from sovereign wealth funds to beleaguered companies in the US and elsewhere is just business as usual in a global world; it is just another global flow of one of the things that flows most readily around the globe – money. At the same time, it has led to cries for the creation of barriers to those flows. In the US the worry is that through sovereign wealth funds, other nations were gaining control over its institutions (e.g. its banks and financial institutions) and its resources. Said one US Senator: "In the short run, that they are investing here is good.... But in the long run it is unsustainable. Our power and authority is eroding because of the amounts we are sending abroad for energy and consumer goods" (quoted in Thomas, Jr 2008: C4). As a result, many American politicians were in favor of greater control over, and restrictions on, the flow of money from sovereign wealth funds to the US. Similar reactions have occurred in other countries (e.g. France, Germany).

Finally, while the Great Recession is technically over, its effects continue to be felt today. Unemployment in many countries, including the US and Europe, remains relatively high. Also, some countries have suffered political turmoil from their economic problems. As noted in previous chapters, Greece faced a severe economic downturn from the Great Recession and defaulted on its loans. A variety of European banks and the IMF stepped in to prevent further financial collapse. As part of the IMF's required structural adjustments, Greece was then forced to cut back on its social services, thus exacerbating economic problems for many of the poor and working class throughout the country. Massive protests and political unrest have continued throughout Greece.

CORPORATIONS, PEOPLE, AND IDEAS

We turn now to a different set of global economic flows involving new corporate organizational forms, MBA students, corporate leaders, and management ideas.

CHANGING CORPORATE STRUCTURE

For much of the twentieth century business organizations (Clegg and Carter 2007) were dominated by Taylorist/Fordist organizational forms (characterized by bureaucratization, industrialization, and the strict subjugation and control of employees). It was the power of this type of organization that helped make possible much of the conquest of the globe by capitalism. However, this type of organization is being undermined today as globalization accelerates and grows more pervasive. There is a new global world and business, in particular, is in the process of creating new organizational forms across vast expanses of geographic space. In fact, it could be argued that this space is the last frontier of business.[8]

New organizational forms are being made necessary by the new realities of the global economy and of doing business globally. One way of putting this (although it is, as we have seen, highly flawed) is that business organizations are becoming increasingly "flat" rather than hierarchical (Friedman 2007). Another, is that they are growing more like networks; what is being created is the "network organization" (Castells 2000). Yet another possibility is that organizations are growing increasingly virtual and in so doing are involving their clients and customers to a greater degree in the work of the organization. In this, they are part of the movement toward systems that involve "peer production" or "user-generated content." That is, they are growing more like a range of phenomena that can be included under the heading of Web 2.0 including Facebook, Twitter, Tumblr, and blogging (Beer and Burrows 2007; Birdsall 2012; Ritzer et al. 2012). What distinguishes Web 2.0 is that the content is increasingly produced by the users. The essential point from the perspective of this chapter is that new organizational forms are proliferating throughout the world.

MBA STUDENTS

MBA students are on the move. For example, American-trained MBA students, many of whom are now from many nations in the world, are increasingly likely to spend part of their years in school overseas learning about business in other societies. Some American business schools (e.g. Anderson School of Management at UCLA) are offering joint programs and degrees with Asian universities (e.g. Jiao Tong University in Shanghai). In such joint programs, students take courses at participating universities in the US and Asia and perhaps elsewhere in the world, as well. In other cases, several universities throughout the world offer collaborative programs (e.g. one involves Paul Merage School of Business at the University of California, Irvine, Indian Institute of Technology, Peking University, and City University of Hong Kong). That is, business training, like business itself, is increasingly global. The Provost at the University of Southern California said that its goal was to create a university where "students and faculty can cross academic and geographic boundaries to innovate, an institution with a public service mission that spans continents" (quoted in Flanigan 2008: C5).

The students who graduate from such programs will find it increasingly easy to move among and between corporations in many different parts of the world. This will make them *and* those corporations more global.

MANAGEMENT IDEAS

While new organizational forms and personnel flow around the world, ideas about, and that relate to, them flow around the world even more easily. The global dissemination of these ideas is much more important because once the ideas are known in many different locales, organizational forms based, at least in part, on them can be erected in virtually all of them.

What we have seen in recent years is the growth of a new global management ideas industry that is creating blueprints for organizational forms that are flowing to, and being used throughout, the world (Clegg and Carter 2007; Clegg 2012). This view is consistent with the more general view articulated by John Meyer and his associates about the global spread of models and the development of institutional isomorphism (see Chapter 8) (Meyer 1980).

There are several major forces involved in the global spread of these new management ideas. One is *large IT firms* which played a key role in both globalization (through their global technologies) and in the development of new management ideas. They infiltrated organizations throughout the world, bringing with them not only their technology and systems, but, most importantly for our purposes, ideas on how to manage organizations.

Second is *management consultants*, especially those associated with the large accounting firms. They helped to produce, and were a significant part of, the rise of an "audit culture" in many places in the world. Such a culture emphasized such things as calculability and verification. This allowed accounting firms to proliferate globally and to spread their influence widely. In addition, they used this point of entry to create and to sell all sorts of other management services and ideas to firms throughout the world. Most generally, such consultancies expanded because they were able to create anxiety among their client organizations and then to sell those organizations services designed to reduce that anxiety.

Third is *MBA programs*. Not only those with MBAs, but the graduate programs that create them, are increasingly common throughout the world. Like much else associated with globalization, especially as it relates to the economy, these programs had their origins in the US and represent the domination of an American educational model on a global scale. In fact, such programs have become *the* global model of management education. In the process, they have served in various ways to rationalize or "McDonaldize" management globally (see Chapter 8). Examples include MBA-speak, the *de rigueur* use of PowerPoint presentations, and the creation of a homogenized body of management knowledge, all of which has been exacerbated by the growth of international credential bodies for MBA programs. While MBAs and their programs have been criticized for these and other reasons (the role of MBAs in recent accounting scandals and corporate collapses), globalization is seen as favoring the survival and further expansion of MBA programs. This expansion is not only occurring, but MBA programs, including those in the US, are themselves becoming increasingly global in character. The dean at the Marshall School of Business at the University of Southern California argued that the reason American universities and programs, especially the new global MBA programs, are prized throughout the world is that "we have a different kind of pedagogy.... We are much more inclusive of students, allowing their participation on many levels, in contrast to the classic Oxford lecture model. The students learn from one another, particularly in the global classes where individuals from different cultures work together" (quoted in Flanigan 2008: C5).

Fourth is management *gurus*. This is another American creation and it remains an area dominated by Americans like Tom Peters (co-author of *In Search of Excellence* [Peters and Waterman 1988]). These people created simplified (McDonaldized) management ideas and published best-selling books devoted to them. The books have come to be widely sold and translated throughout the world. The gurus themselves are in great demand as highly paid speakers around the globe. In these and other ways gurus have produced and disseminated globally accepted ideas on basic management practices.

Fifth is *management fashions*. Gurus are major producers of ideas and imaginaries that have become fashionable in MBA programs and with managers throughout the world. Like the gurus and others who create them, management fashions are often American in origin. These fashions may be attractive because of their aesthetic (e.g. narratives on how effective they have been) and technical (tools and techniques) dimensions. Thus, what are currently considered best practices are copied, regulations compel organizations to adopt them, and some fashions become normative among business organizations throughout the world.

This global conjunction of organizations, students, managers, and management ideas raises several questions, especially: Where are innovations to come from if all major business organizations around the world are increasingly following much the same model? Will these organizations be able to respond adequately and creatively to threats posed by their role in various environmental problems (e.g. global warming)?

CONSUMPTION

While aspects of globalization that relate to consumption have been mentioned above, especially in the discussion of global value chains, in this section we focus more directly on consumption itself in a global context (Brändle and Ryan 2012; Sassatelli 2008).

Consumption is highly complex, involving mainly consumer objects, consumers, the consumption process, and consumption sites (Ritzer, Weidenhoft, and Goodman 2001). Before we get to those topics, it is important to note that there has been a tendency to closely associate consumption, as well as the globalization of consumption, with America and Americanization. This is largely traceable to the affluence of the US after the close of WW II and the economic difficulties encountered by most other societies in the world during this period. Thus, the US developed an unprecedented and unmatched consumer society for several decades after the end of the war and at the same time began exporting it – and its various elements – to much of the rest of the world. While much of American consumer society came to be adopted elsewhere, it was also modified in various ways, even in the immediate aftermath of WW II in the European nations ravaged by the war and being aided through America's Marshall Plan (Kroen 2006).

The latter point brings us to the issue of globalization and how it is implicated in all of this beyond the mere fact that consumption sites, goods, and the like have become both ubiquitous and increasingly similar throughout the world. In a world increasingly dominated by neoliberalism, the emphasis in the economy is to greatly increase global flows of everything related to consumption and to greatly decrease any barriers to those flows. Of particular interest here is the expediting of global flows of consumer goods and services of all types *and* of the financial processes and instruments that expedite those flows. Thus, for example, the relatively small number of credit card brands with origins in the US (especially Visa and MasterCard) are increasingly accepted and used (including by locals) throughout more and more parts of the world. This not only serves to expedite global consumption, but also the flow of global consumers (including tourists).

Hyperconsumption: Buying more than one can afford.

More importantly, this serves to expedite the global flow of **hyperconsumption** (buying more than one can afford) and **hyperdebt** (owing more than one will be able to pay back). The global flow of many of the same goods and services, and the increasing global use of credit cards and other credit instruments, leads more and more societies throughout the world in the direction of American-style hyperconsumption and hyperdebt. Many countries that at one time were very conservative, as far as consumption and debt are concerned, plunged headlong in these directions. China and India, with their enormous populations enjoying an unprecedented economic boom, also appear to be headed in much the same direction. Thus, globalization means that hyperconsumption and hyperdebt, as well as the problems associated with them, are increasingly likely to become global phenomena and problems (as they have in the Great Recession).

Hyperdebt: Owing more than one will be able to repay.

The case of Great Britain is highly instructive. Until recent decades, it was not easy to go into debt and the British tended to regard any debt beyond a mortgage as shameful. However, it was then that American banks such as Citigroup and Capital One made great headway in the British market with new products, low- and no-interest loans, and much advertising. While regulators in Germany and France restricted growth in credit card debt, British officials remained on the sidelines. "As a result, the British market became the largest and most sophisticated in Europe," with huge amounts of debt (Werdigier 2008b: B7). And one now hears the same kinds of things from British consumers that one has been long accustomed to hearing from American consumers. For example, a Glaswegian media relations executive, $63,000 in debt, said: "It was so easy to get the loans and the credit that you almost think the goods are a gift from the shop.... You don't fully realize that it's real money you are spending until you actually sit down and consolidate your bills and then it's a shock" (quoted in Werdigier 2008b: B1).

Nonetheless, Great Britain is an extreme case of the globalization of American-style debt. Other European societies, most notably Germany, have not followed this path. Said one British professor: "Culturally, maybe also because of the defeat in the war, Germans remain reluctant to borrow and banks are often state-owned, pushing less for profits from lending" (quoted in Werdigier 2008b: B7).

While there was, and continues to be, an important American component to the globalization of consumption, it is important to recognize that the heyday of the US in this area (and many others) is long past and in any case there has always been much more to the globalization of consumption (and everything else) than Americanization (Brewer and Trentmann 2006). That is, local areas have certainly not always, or perhaps ever, been overwhelmed by American imports, but have integrated them into the local cultural and economic realities, that is they have "glocalized them" (see Chapter 8).[9] Furthermore, other nations and regions have been significant exporters of important aspects of consumer society (e.g. Mercedes-Benz and BMW automobiles from Germany). Finally, much of consumption remains largely, if not totally, local in character (e.g. "binge" consumption in Belize [Wilk 2006]). The growing consumption of khat, or *qat*, [a mild stimulant] in Kenya (Anderson and Carrier 2006) is not only locally defined, but there is active resistance to external definitions of it (the US defines it as a dangerous drug).

CONSUMER OBJECTS AND SERVICES

Much of consumption revolves around shopping for and purchasing objects of all kinds (Quarter Pounders, snowboards, automobiles, etc.), but in recent years an increasing amount of consumption relates to various services (legal, accounting, educational, etc.). While many objects and services remain highly local (e.g. the khat mentioned above; the services of street-based letter writers for illiterate Indians; see Chapter 8), an increasing number have globalized. On the one hand, there are, for example, the global objects such as automobiles from the US, Germany, and Japan. On the other hand, there are global services such as those offered by accounting firms (e.g. KPMG International), as well as package delivery services (e.g. DHL).

Of particular importance in terms of objects and services is the issue of brands and branding (Holt 2004; Arviddson 2012). Brands are of great importance both within nations as well as globally. Indeed, much money and effort is invested in creating brand names that are recognized and trusted throughout the world. In fact, all of the corporate names mentioned in the previous paragraph have achieved global brand recognition. In her best-selling book *No Logo: Taking Aim at the Brand Bullies*, Naomi Klein details the importance of the brand (e.g. Nike, McDonald's) in the contemporary world and the degree to which they are both globalized (logos are virtually an international language) and having a global impact (Klein 2009).

CONSUMERS

Increasing numbers of people throughout the world are spending more and more time as consumers. Not long ago it was very different as most people spent most of their time as producers. Not only do more people spend more time consuming, but they increasingly are more likely to define themselves by what they consume (Bimmers, Patek Philippe watches, and so on) than by their roles as producers and workers. Therefore, there has emerged a global consumer culture – where people all around the world are defining their identity through the objects and meanings associated with consumption. Furthermore, consumers are on the move throughout the world, often as tourists. Not only is tourism a form of consumption, but much tourism is undertaken in order to consume the goods and services on offer at other locales throughout the world.

CONSUMPTION PROCESSES

Increasing numbers of people know what is expected of them as consumers; they generally know what to do in the consumption process wherever they happen to be in the world. This includes knowing how to work their way through a shopping mall, use a credit card, or make a purchase online. Others have not yet encountered, let alone learned how to handle, these processes, but many of them certainly will in the not-too-distant future. Where these processes are known, there is a remarkable similarity throughout the world in the process of consuming in a supermarket, a shopping mall, or a fast-food restaurant.

CONSUMPTION SITES

American and Western-style consumption sites – shopping malls, fast-food restaurants, clothing chains, discounters such as Wal-Mart, Disney-like theme parks, Las Vegas-style casino hotels, Internet sites such as Amazon.com and ebay – have spread throughout much of the world. Discussed below are some highly diverse examples of this.

Wal-Mart stores in India

Until its recent boom, India had not attracted much attention from large global retailers and in any case the government has not typically allowed direct foreign ownership of such businesses. Modern stores make up a tiny fraction of retail operations in the country. However, with India's $500 billion market (as of 2013) that is expected to grow 20% per year, it is the "next great frontier for global retailers" (Bose 2013). It is no surprise then that the retail giant, Wal-Mart, known for its low-priced products, is aggressively pursuing expansion into India. Until recently, foreign retailers could not operate in India. It is only since the passing of a 2012 law that "Indian policy makers said foreign companies like Wal-Mart could directly enter the retail business with a local partner as long as they did not own more than 51 percent of the business" (Bajaj 2012b). As a result, the company has partnered with Bharti Enterprises and is transforming many dimensions of the retail business, all the way from how crops are grown and sold to retailers to setting fixed prices in large warehouse-like stores.

But now Wal-Mart is running into the same resistance that it has faced throughout the world: the local mom-and-pop shops that it threatens to drive out of business are protesting the company's expansion. In the process of modernizing India's inefficient retail sector, retailers like Wal-Mart have the potential to radically transform the consumption patterns of Indians by replacing networks of small producers, middlemen, and small retailers with big-box stores. For example, Ravi Mahajan's family has owned a wholesale general store in a northern Indian city for 40 years. He says he has already lost 50% of his family's business to Wal-Mart and that the business will be "destroyed" if foreign companies are permitted to open as many retail stores as they like. While staging a protest, "he and dozens of other traders burned an effigy with a bloated belly and a crudely drawn face, meant to represent multinational marauders" (Bajaj 2011).

The key point, however, is not only that global retails like Wal-Mart are expanding in India, but that they reflect a particular type of consumption that is both American in character and McDonaldized. Thus, this is a clear example of grobalization rather than glocalization (see Chapter 8 for a definition of all these terms) and of the successful expansion globally of American consumption sites and ways of consuming.

Big Boy in Bangkok

On the other hand, there are examples of American consumption sites that have changed dramatically in adapting to local realities, in other words, that have glocalized. A few years ago the first author was in Bangkok, Thailand, and walked past a vaguely recognizable restaurant. Most of what was visible reflected local Thai culture, as did most of the food for sale. As he moved further into the restaurant he saw hidden away in a corner the statue of the Big Boy that was the symbol – and name – of a once successful chain of American restaurants. He had recognized the restaurant because it clearly had started out as part of the chain, but over the years it had glocalized to such a great degree that it was barely recognizable as a Big Boy restaurant; he was sure locals had no idea it was or even what the Big Boy statue (if they even saw it) represented.

The Big Boy restaurant in Bangkok represents, then, the polar opposite of Wal-Mart in India. The former has glocalized to an extraordinary degree, while the latter remains a good example of grobalization and shows little in the way of adaptation to the local environment.

Global theme parks

Another example of globalization in the realm of consumption sites is the emergence of the global theme park industry. Salvatore Anton Clavé details both the global expansion of the theme park, as well as the expansion of what he calls a "global model" of the kind championed by Disney (Clavé 2007: 78; Andrews 2012). That is, not only have idiosyncratic (glocalized) theme parks proliferated throughout much of the world (the classic is Tivoli Gardens in Copenhagen, Denmark), but so have those based on a standard (grobalized) model. This can be seen as part of what Alan Bryman calls the process of Disneyization (see below) and the first author has called the McDisneyization in the realm of tourism (of which theme parks are a part) because the model combines elements of both McDonaldization and Disneyization (Ritzer and Liska 1997).

Not only have theme parks proliferated globally, but the fact that they have become "destinations" for many means that they have affected both national and international travel. Thus, for example, Disney World in Orlando, Florida, is not only a destination for Americans, but also for many in the general region (e.g. Latin America) as well as those from other parts of the globe such as Europe and Asia. Thus, they have become global destinations and as such had a profound effect on global travel and the global travel business.

Like McDonaldization, Disneyization clearly involves globalization (Andrews 2012; Bryman 2004). As is true of McDonald's restaurants, Disney theme parks adapt in various ways to local realities. Note the following adaptations made by Tokyo Disneyland:

- the Hall of Presidents was dropped because it was so specific to the US and its presidents;
- Main Street USA was replaced by World Bazaar;
- there is a Japanese-style ghost house;

- there are Japanese restaurants catering to Japanese tastes in food;
- picnics are permitted;
- ride operators' commentaries are modified to include "Japan-specific puns, jokes, and creative explanations" (Bryman 2004: 164).

While one finds these and other adaptations, Bryman concludes that as with the case of McDonaldization, Disney's basic operating principles tend to remain the same in Japan as they are in the US. To put this another way, Disneyization involves much more grobalization than glocalization.

GLOBAL RESISTANCE

The global spread of chain stores, theme parks, and so on, has led to many concerns and to resistance in many parts of the world (one now even sees resistance, or at least increasing concern, in the US). While we discuss resistance to consumption sites here, there is far broader global opposition to all aspects of consumption, especially hyperconsumption (e.g. Slow Food, the Voluntary Simplicity Movement, etc.).

For example, in Paris there is much concern about the Champs-Elysées, "the most beautiful avenue on earth," and the increasing dominance on it of large outlets, often megastores, associated with global chains such as McDonald's, Adidas, Gap, Benetton, Disney, Nike, Zara, Virgin, Cartier, Louis Vuitton, and Sephora, as well as huge auto showrooms for Toyota, Renault, and Peugeot (Sciolino 2007a: A1, A8). A major reason: burgeoning rental costs on the Champs-Elysées increasingly mean that it is only the large chains that can afford them. As a result, local institutions such as clubs and movie theaters are disappearing from the Champs-Elysées. A movement has emerged to stop the "banalization" of at least the most famous avenue in Paris, if not the world; to stop what has already occurred in other major areas such as Times Square in New York and Oxford Street in London. A first step was the banning of the opening of an H&M megastore (a Swedish chain with about 1,500 shops in nearly 30 countries) on the Champs-Elysées. A study commissioned by the city of Paris concluded that "the avenue progressively is losing its exceptional and symbolic character, thus its attractiveness" (quoted in Sciolino 2007a: A8). An alternative view, however, is that these changes represent a democratization of the Champs-Elysées. They offer an escape for the less affluent, especially multi-ethnic young people, some of whom have been expressing their general dissatisfaction with French life. Furthermore, there is evidence that resistance to such stores on the Champs-Elysées is waning. When Abercrombie & Fitch opened there in 2011, the store opening was not greeted by protest but by eager consumers (Clifford and Alderman 2011).

It is not surprising to see such concerns expressed in Paris, but what is more surprising is the expression of similar concerns in the home of many of the global chains – the United States, in particular New York City. The occasion for the reaction was the increasing spread of chain stores from an already saturated Manhattan to the other four boroughs of the city. In 2012 there were, for example, over 200 Starbucks coffee shops in the city, and they were making their way to outlying parts of it. On recent visits to New York (the first author grew up there), he had great difficulty finding traditional New York "hole in the wall" breakfast joints; most of them seem to have been replaced by Starbucks and other chains. Wal-Mart, noted above for sparking protests in India, has long faced resistance opening stores in cities throughout the US, most notably New York City and

Washington, DC (Greenhouse and Clifford 2013). The resistance in New York was so strong that Wal-Mart recently announced that they would be scaling back their efforts to expand there. Similar proliferation led San Francisco to pass a proposition that any proposal for a new chain store or restaurant must be reviewed by the city's planning commission. Said the city supervisor: "Our position is: We're San Francisco; you can do what you want in other cities, but here we are going to protect local neighborhood character" (quoted in McGeehan 2007: 24). The main concern in New York (and San Francisco), as well as in Paris (and many other world cities), is that the proliferation of chain stores will drive out distinctive local businesses, destroy the unique character of many neighborhoods, and generally produce a boring sameness in the city so that it will not only be difficult to differentiate one area from another, but one city from any other. Of course, many consumers want the chains, and many neighborhoods welcome them, as well, because of the increase in business for all that they bring with them. The real issue is the mix of local and chain stores and the general tendency for the latter to drive the former out of business yielding landscapes that are dominated by the chain stores and, in the worst-case scenario, nothing but chain stores.

It must be noted in closing that a very large proportion of the world's population is excluded from many of the kinds of consumption and consumption sites discussed in the last several pages. That is clearly the much greater global problem in this domain, a problem we will return to in Chapters 13 and 14.

CHAPTER SUMMARY

This chapter focuses on global economic flows. Global trade operates through various economic networks such as supply chains, international production networks, global commodity chains and, most importantly, global value chains. Global value chains follow the creation of value through different stages, from the creation of a product, to its disposal after use.

Commodities are often the first link in this chain. The demand for commodities sky rocketed, fueled primarily by enormous demand in the developed countries and increased consumption in developing countries (especially China). Oil is a case in point. Not only did prices escalate because of increased demand, but it is also becoming increasingly difficult to procure oil. These problems will be exacerbated in the future by a decrease in the global supply of oil, as well as by the fact that some of the current oil-exporting countries will start to import (rather than to export) oil to meet their domestic needs.

Some countries stimulate trade and investment through low prices and low wages. This often leads to a "race to the bottom" among countries vying for increased investment and export business. However, some theorize that after a point, there is a move toward industrial "upgrading." Countries that entered the world market at the bottom, such as China and Mexico, move on to produce higher-value products at higher wages. However, as some countries upgrade, some countries remain at the bottom, and still others enter at the bottom guaranteeing a supply of low-priced, low-wage products to the North.

Outsourcing is also an important global flow. Offshore outsourcing involves contracting work to companies located in other countries. Apart from the economic domain, this process is also prevalent in the health care and military domains. Not only does the process operate at a macro-level but, increasingly, it can also be observed at micro- and meso-levels.

National economies across the globe are highly interconnected through financial markets; cyclical fluctuations in one country will have an impact on many others. However, the more powerful the economy, the greater the likelihood that the crisis will spread around the world. One very recent example is the US financial crisis, which led to the Great Recession.

Global economic flows also include the movement of corporations, people, and ideas, across both geographic and virtual boundaries. The flow of consumer goods and services is also being expedited. Hyperconsumption (buying more than one can afford to) and hyperdebt (owing more money than one can afford to re-pay) are important concepts in this analysis. Not only do people spend more time in consumption, they are also increasingly defining themselves through their consumption practices.

Consumption sites are increasingly becoming global. However, there is much more to the process than Americanization. Global consumption sites can reflect grobalization (Wal-Mart stores in India) as well as glocalization (Big Boy restaurant in Bangkok). Global theme parks such as Disney World contribute significantly to this process. Resistance to these sites of consumption, as well as hyperconsumption and hyperdebt, is also global.

DISCUSSION QUESTIONS

1. Locate the major barriers to global economic flows. Are they effective? Are they necessary?

2. Examine the linkages between the process of "race to the bottom" and "upgrading."

3. Examine the linkages between the process of outsourcing and the "race to the bottom."

4. Examine globalization in the sphere of consumption as well as production.

5. Does the ongoing global economic crisis signal the end of hyperconsumption and hyperdebt?

ADDITIONAL READINGS ···

Giovanni Arrighi. *Adam Smith in Beijing: Lineages of the Twenty-First Century*. London: Verso, 2007.

Pietra Rivoli. *Travels of a T-Shirt in a Global Economy: An Economist Examines the Markets, Power, and Politics of World Trade*, 2nd edn. Chichester: John Wiley & Sons, Ltd, 2009.

Gary Gereffi and Miguel Korzeniewicz, eds. *Commodity Chains and Global Capitalism*. Westport, CT: Praeger, 1994.

Joseph Schumpeter. *Capitalism, Socialism and Democracy*. London: Routledge, 2006.

Barry Smart. *Consumer Society: Critical Issues and Environmental Consequences*. Thousand Oaks, CA: Sage, 2010.

Douglas Holt. *How Brands Become Icons: Principles of Cultural Branding*. Cambridge, MA: Harvard Business School, 2004.

Adam Arvidsson. *Brands: Meaning and Value in Media Culture*. London: Routledge, 2006.

Naomi Klein. *No Logo: 10th Anniversary Edition*. Toronto: Vintage, Canada, 2009.

Alan Bryman. *The Disneyization of Society*. London: Sage, 2004.

NOTES ···

1 Because of China's economic successes, and the political failures of the US in Vietnam and more recently in Iraq, it may well be that China will not only replace the US as the global leader economically, but politically as well. See Arrighi (2007).

2 For a critical examination of his perspective, see Hassler (2003: 513–32).

3 Many more are bought in the US, but not registered. They are used in the US for various applications; they only need to be registered to be used as phones.

4 Many believe that the price rise for many commodities was produced by speculators and that the speculative "bubble" burst in mid-2008. Nevertheless, increasing demand is likely to drive prices higher again in the future.

5 Dubai has used its oil wealth to diversify its economy by expanding tourism, construction, real estate, and trade. As a result, oil now accounts for only 5% of Dubai's GDP.

6 http://prospect.org/article/nanny-chain.

7 http://dir.salon.com/story/news/feature/2003/03/12/foreign_aid/.

8 While a dramatic image, one wonders why this would be the last frontier. For example, one could envision, adopting a Foucauldian perspective, business organizations seeking ever-greater bio-physical control over human beings as yet another frontier to be conquered in the future.

9 However, in thinking about glocalization in this context, we must always keep in mind that what has been glocalized are grobalized phenomena like McDonald's restaurants, Disney theme parks, and Visa credit cards.

GLOBAL CULTURE AND CULTURAL FLOWS

Globalization: A Basic Text, Second Edition. George Ritzer and Paul Dean.
© 2015 John Wiley & Sons, Ltd. Published 2015 by John Wiley & Sons, Ltd.

B ecause much of it exists in the form of ideas, words, images, musical sounds, and so on, culture tends to flow comparatively easily throughout the world. In fact, that flow is increasingly easy because culture exists increasingly in digitized forms. Thus, the Internet permits global downloading and sharing of digitized cultural forms such as movies, videos, music, books, newspapers, photos, and so on. Further, those who see themselves as part of the same culture can maintain contact with one another through e-mail or via virtual face-to-face contact on Skype. They can also remain immersed within the culture in which they exist and/or from which they come by, for example, reading online newspapers from home. While the global flow of digital culture is increasingly easy, the fact is that there are still barriers to its flow, especially the lack of access by many (the "global digital divide"), mostly in the South, to the Internet.

While culture does flow comparatively easily across the globe, not all cultures and forms of culture flow as easily or at the same rate. For one thing, the cultures of the world's most powerful societies (most notably the US) flow around the world much more readily than the cultures of relatively weak and marginal societies. Similarly, some types of culture (pop music, for example) move quickly and easily around the globe, while others (innovative theories in the social sciences) move in slow motion and may never make it to many parts of the world.

This chapter on culture permits the introduction of additional theories of globalization beyond the neoliberal and neo-Marxian theories discussed in Chapter 4. These are theories of cultural differentialism, hybridization and convergence (Nederveen Pieterse 2009). While these theories are treated here under the heading of culture, they have much broader applicability to many issues covered in this book such as the previously discussed topics of economics and politics. In politics, for example, it could be argued that nation-states throughout the world remain stubbornly different ("differentialism"), are growing increasingly alike ("convergence"), or involve more and more combinations of various political forms drawn from many different parts of the world ("hybridization"). In spite of this broader applicability, the focus here will be on these three types of theories as they relate to global culture.

What makes these three theories particularly attractive from the perspective of this book is that they are all about our focal concern with flows and barriers and take very different positions on them and their relationship to one another. In *differentialism*, the focus is much more on barriers that prevent flows that would serve to make cultures (and much else) more alike. In this view, cultures tend to remain stubbornly different from one another. In the *convergence* perspective, the barriers are much weaker and the global flows stronger, with the result that cultures are subject to many of the same flows and tend to grow more alike. In its extreme form, convergence suggests the possibility that local cultures can be overwhelmed by other, more powerful cultures, or even a globally homogeneous culture. Finally, in the *hybridization* perspective, external flows interact with internal flows in order to produce a unique cultural hybrid that combines elements of the two. Barriers to external cultural flows exist in the hybridization perspective, and while they are strong enough to prevent those flows from overwhelming local culture, they are not strong enough to block all external cultural flows entirely. That which does succeed in gaining entry combines with local culture to produce unique cultural hybrids.

CULTURAL DIFFERENTIALISM

The concept of **cultural differentialism** emphasizes lasting differences among and between cultures largely unaffected by globalization or any other bi-, inter-, multi-, and trans-cultural processes and flows. This is not to say that culture is unaffected by any of these processes, especially globalization, but it is to say that *at their core* they are *largely unaffected* by them; they remain much as they always have been. In this perspective, globalization occurs mainly, if not only, on the surface with the deep structure[1] of cultures largely, if not totally, unaffected by it. Cultures are seen as basically closed not only to global processes, but also to the influences of other cultures. In one image, the world is envisioned as a mosaic of largely separate cultures. More menacing is an image of a billiard ball table, with billiard balls (representing cultures) seen as bouncing off others (representing other cultures). This is more threatening because it indicates the possibility of dangerous, potentially catastrophic, collisions among and between at least some of the world's cultures.

> **Cultural differentialism:** Cultures tend to remain stubbornly different from one another.

This theory has a long history, but it has attracted increasing attention and adherents (as well as critics) in recent years because of two sets of events. One is the terrorist attacks on September 11 (and after in London, Madrid, etc.) and the subsequent wars in Afghanistan and Iraq. To many, these events are seen as the product of a clash between Western and Islamic culture and the eternal differences between them. The other is the increasing multiculturalism of both the US (largely the growth of the Hispanic population) and of Western European countries (largely the growing Muslim populations) and the vast differences, and enmity, between majority and minority populations.

CIVILIZATIONS

The most famous, and controversial, example[2] of this theory is Samuel Huntington's *Clash of Civilizations and the Remaking of the World Order*.[3] Huntington (2011) traces the beginnings of the current world situation to the end of the Cold War and the reconfiguring of the world from one differentiated on a political-economic basis (democratic/capitalist vs. totalitarian/communist) to one based on cultural differences. Such cultural differences are nothing new, but they were largely submerged (as in the old Yugoslavia and in the differences between, among others, Serbs and Croats) by the overwhelming political-economic differences of the Cold War era. In the last two decades ancient identities, adversaries, and enemies have resurfaced. Huntington uses the term *civilization* to describe the broadest level of culture and cultural identities (indeed, to him civilization *is* culture "writ large"). What he sees is the emergence of fault lines among and between these civilizations. Given the historic enmities among at least some of the civilizations involved, these fault lines have created a highly dangerous situation.

Huntington differentiates among seven or eight world civilizations: Sinic (Chinese), Japan (sometimes combined with the Sinic as Far Eastern), Hindu, Islamic, Orthodox (centered in Russia), Western Europe, North America (along with the closely aligned Australia, New Zealand), Latin America, and (possibly) Africa.

He sees these civilizations as differing greatly on basic philosophical assumptions, underlying values, social relations, customs, and overall outlooks on life. To Huntington, human history is, in effect, the history of civilizations, especially these civilizations. Every civilization shares a number of characteristics including the fact that there is great agreement on what they are (although they lack clear beginnings and there are no clear-cut boundaries between civilizations which, nonetheless, are quite real). Civilizations are among the most enduring of human associations (although they do change over time), are the broadest level of cultural identity (short of humanity in its entirety), are the broadest source of subjective self-identification, usually span more than one nation-state (although they do not perform state functions);[4] are a totality, and are closely aligned with both religion (see below) and race.

Huntington offers a modern grand narrative of the relationships among civilizations. For more than 3,000 years (approximately 1500 BC to 1500 AD) civilizations tended to be widely separated in both time and space. As a result, contacts among them were apt to be almost non-existent. The contacts that did occur tended to be limited or intermittent, but when they occurred they were likely to be quite intense.

The next phase, roughly from 1500 to the close of WW II, was characterized by the sustained, overpowering, and unidirectional impact of Western civilization on all other civilizations. Huntington attributes this to various structural characteristics of the West including the rise there of cities, commerce, state bureaucracy, and an emerging sense of national consciousness. However, the most immediate cause was technological, especially in ocean navigation and the military (including a superior military organization, discipline and training, and, of course, weaponry). In the end, the West excelled in organized violence and while those in the West sometimes forget this, those in other parts of the world have not. Thus, by 1910, just before the beginning of WW I, the world came closer, in Huntington's view, than at any time in history to being one world, one civilization – Western civilization.

The third phase – the multi-civilizational system – is traceable to the end of the expansion of the West and the beginning of the revolt against it. The period after WW II and until about 1990 was characterized by a clash of ideas, especially capitalist and communist ideologies, but with the fall of communism, the major clashes in the world came to revolve around religion, culture, and ultimately civilizations. While the West continues to be dominant, Huntington foresees its decline. It will be a slow decline, it will not occur in a straight line, and it will involve a decline (at least relatively) in the West's resources – population, economic products, and military capability (traceable to such things as the decline of US armed forces and the globalization of the defense industries making generally available weapons once obtainable only, or largely, in the West). Other civilizations will increasingly reject the West, but they will embrace and utilize the advances of modernization which can and should be distinguished from Westernization.

While the West declines, the resurgence of two other civilizations is of greatest importance. The first is the economic growth of Asian societies, especially Sinic civilization. Huntington foresees continuing growth of Asian economies which will soon surpass those of the West. Important in itself, this will translate into increasing power for the East and a corresponding decline in the ability of the West to impose itself on the East. He sees the economic ascendancy of the East as largely traceable to the superior aspects of its culture(s), especially its collectivism in contrast to the individuality dominant in the West. Also helpful to the economic rise of the East are other commonalities among the nations of the region (e.g. religion, especially Confucianism). The successes of Asian economies are not only important in themselves, but also for the role they play as models for other non-Western societies.

This first of Huntington's arguments is not that surprising or original. After all, we witnessed the dramatic growth of the post-WW II Japanese economy and we are now witnessing the amazing economic transformation of China and India. Few would disagree with the view that projecting present economic trends, the Chinese economy will become the largest in the world in the not-too-distant future and that India will experience great economic growth, as well.

More controversial is Huntington's second major contention involving the resurgence of Islam. While the Sinic emergence is rooted in the economy, Islamic expansion is rooted in dramatic population growth and the mobilization of the population.[5] This has touched virtually every Muslim society, usually first culturally and then socio-politically. It can be seen as part of the global revival of religion. It also can be seen as both a product of, and an effort to come to grips with, modernization.

Huntington goes beyond pointing to these developments to paint a dire portrait of the future of the relations between the West and these other two civilizations, especially Islam. Conflict will occur at the fault lines among and between civilizations, especially the Western, Sinic, and Islamic civilizations. Thus, he foresees dangerous clashes in the future between the West (and what he calls its "arrogance"), Islam (and its "intolerance"), and Sinic "assertiveness." Much of the conflict revolves around the West's view of itself as possessing "universal culture," its desire to export that culture to the rest of the world, and its declining ability to do so. Furthermore, what the West sees as universalism, the rest of the world, especially Islamic civilization, sees as imperialism. More specifically, the West wants to limit weapons proliferation, while other civilizations want weapons, especially the now-infamous "weapons of mass destruction." The most notable instance of this at the moment is the great heat associated with the possibility that Iran is in the process of constructing nuclear weapons. (Another is use of poison gas against rebel forces in Syria in 2013 ostensibly by the government of Bashar al-Assad.) While Iran elected a comparatively moderate president, Hassan Rouhani, in June 2013, it continues the development of its nuclear program and is believed to be close to building its first nuclear weapon. The West also seeks to export democracy to, even impose it on, other societies and civilizations (Iraq and Afghanistan are notable examples in the Islamic world), which often resist it as part of the West's idea of universal culture. And, the West seeks to control and to limit immigration (especially from Islamic civilizations), but many from those civilizations have found their way into the West, or want to be there. As this increases, Huntington sees cleft societies developing *within* both Europe and the United States (in the latter, fault lines will develop not only between Westerners and Muslims, but also between Anglos and Hispanics [Huntington 2004: 30–45]). Huntington's predictions seem to have been borne out, at least in part, in recent years as much tension and conflict has arisen between Muslims and "natives" in Europe (notable instances have occurred in France [Erlanger 2013], the Netherlands [Erlanger 2011], and Denmark [Higgins 2013]), and between Hispanics and "native" Americans over undocumented immigrants from Latin America.

Huntington has earned numerous criticisms and great enmity for his controversial statements about Islamic civilization and Muslims (Huntington 2011). For example, he argues that wherever Muslims and non-Muslims live in close proximity to one another, violent conflict and intense antagonism are pervasive. And Huntington puts much of the blame for this on Muslims and what is, in his view, their propensity toward violent conflict. He argues that from the beginning, Islam has been a religion of the sword; it glorified military values and there is a history of Islamic conquest. The relationship between Islam and other civilizations has historically been one of mutual indigestibility. (Of course, Western imperialism and military adventurism – often with Islam as a target – has played a key role in this.) Islam also lacks a strong core state to exert control over the various elements that constitute its civilization. But of greatest importance to Huntington are the pressures created by the demographic explosion within Islam. The high birth rate in Islam will force many to move out of the heart of Islamic society in search of income and work. This will serve to bring Muslims and their culture into more and more contact – and conflict – with those in other civilizations.

Huntington is concerned about the decline of the West, especially of the US. He sees the US, indeed all societies, as threatened by their increasing multi-civilizational or multicultural character. For him, the demise of the US effectively means the demise of Western civilization. Without a powerful, uni-civilizational US, the West is, in his view, minuscule.

Huntington argues that for the West to survive and prosper the US must do two things. First, it must reaffirm its identity as a Western (rather than multi-civilizational) nation. Second, it must reaffirm and reassert its role as the leader of Western civilization around the globe. The reassertion and acceptance of Western civilization (which would also involve a renunciation of universalism), indeed all civilizations, is the surest way to prevent warfare between civilizations. The real danger, for Huntington, is multiculturalism within the West and all other civilizations. Thus, Huntington ultimately comes down on the side of cultural continuity and something approaching cultural purity within civilizations. Thus, for him, at least in some ideal sense, globalization becomes a process by which civilizations will continue to exist and move in roughly parallel and largely independent fashion in the coming years. This constitutes a reaffirmation of the importance of civilization, that is, culture, in the epoch of globalization.

Beyond Huntington's specific and highly controversial arguments is a more general theory of culture, especially of the global flow of culture, as well as of the barriers to that flow. At a general level, cultural differentialism emphasizes the barriers to cultural flows and the ways in which those barriers lead cultures to remain largely distinct from, and potentially in conflict with, one another.

It should also be noted that much of the controversy behind Huntington's thesis is that it promotes cultural racism and Islamophobia (Marranchi 2004; Saeed 2007). First, his attempt to characterize any civilization as a monolithic entity may be overly simplistic. He ignores important differences within the West, or within Sinic, or Islamic cultures. For example, consider the differences in US and French attitudes on the recent wars against Iraq and Afghanistan or the different adherents of Islam, many of which do not promote the violence that Huntington assumes from them. Second, his explicit concerns about the fall of Western civilization and its vulnerability to multiculturalism reflect a belief in the inherent superiority of the West and inferiority of Islam and other "civilizations." It is on this basis that he legitimates the West's need to assert itself and is concerned about its waning ability to impose itself on other civilizations. Given that there are significant racial overlaps with each civilizations (e.g. white Westerners and Asian Sinic culture), this theoretical framework reduces each group to a simplified set of cultural criteria and assigns superiority to some groups over others. Most importantly, it promotes a fear toward Islam.

RELIGION

Given the centrality of religion to Huntington's civilizations, as well as the strongly cultural character of religion, this is a good place for a discussion of that topic and its relationship to globalization (Beyer 1994). The relationship between the two is very much in the news these days (e.g. reactions in various parts of the world to Muslim migrants, their modes of dress [especially head scarves and veils[6] worn by women], and their increasingly ubiquitous mosques). However, it is clear that this relationship is quite ancient since religion globalized before virtually anything else. In fact, if one focused only on religion, it could be argued that globalization is at least 2,000 years old, and undoubtedly much older than that. While the global spread of various religions is nothing new (see Figure 8.1 for a map of the dominant religions, and more generally belief systems, in the world), it has taken on a new magnitude and importance in the contemporary era of globalization. The focus here is on institutional religion, especially Christianity, Islam, Hinduism, Buddhism, and Judaism (Abrutyn 2012), and at least a few of the ways in which they relate to globalization.

Islam

The founder of Islam is Muhammed who lived in the seventh century. Islam was born on the Arabian peninsula and within a century of Muhammad's death it had spread as far as Spain and China (Arjomand 2007; Lapidus 1988). The lands encompassed by Islam were seen as the center of the world, with all else subordinated to it. Important to its spread was its universalistic world-view; Muslims were not a chosen people and humanity had a common destiny. Its universalistic ideas (e.g. God-given standards that led everyone to search for goodness) led to the belief that they had to be diffused throughout the world. On the one hand, such a world-view led to a global mission to rid the world of competing idea systems such as idolatry and superstition. On the other hand, Islam saw itself as building on, going beyond, but not destroying Judaism and Christianity. Thus, "Islam was the first of world's great religious civilizations to understand itself as one religion among others" (Keane 2003: 42).

Believers in Islam, as well as their armies, spread westward (into Spain and France) and eastward into Byzantium, Persia, and eventually India and China. They traveled with the belief that they were the messengers of Islam and that the rest of the world was eagerly waiting for, if not being actively denied, their message. Thus, the belief emerged that "Islam would prevail among the world's peoples, either by willing acceptance, or by spiritual fervour, or (in the face of violent resistances) by conquest" (Keane 2003: 42). Because there was only one God, and therefore only one law, such a view – and mission – took no notice of nation-states and their borders.

In the end, of course, the grand ambitions of Islam were thwarted. One factor was the efforts of alternate religions, especially Christianity. Another was that "the principle of *jihad*, the duty to struggle for God against His doubters and enemies, was rarely put unconditionally" (Keane 2003: 43; Peters 1979). Thus, Islam was willing to compromise with its opponents and this had a negative effect on its ambitions. Furthermore, because Muslims believed that ultimate victory was assured, contact, trade, and traffic with non-believers was considered acceptable, even encouraged. "The point was to change the world by using all means, including the stretching of one's perceptual horizons, so that all human beings, young and old, rich and poor, black and white, male and female, Christian and Jew, would come to regard Islam as *the* universal religion" (Keane 2003: 43). While these efforts were ultimately only a limited success (because of the Crusades as well as because of military defeats that forced Muslims out of Italy, Spain, and Portugal), the history of such efforts remains strong among many of the 1.6 billion devotees of Islam and helps to inform the contemporary thinking of jihadists.

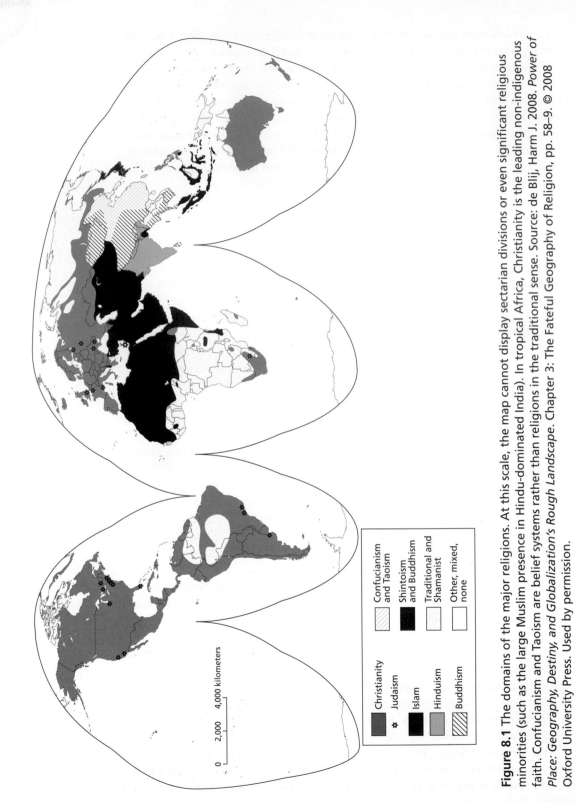

Figure 8.1 The domains of the major religions. At this scale, the map cannot display sectarian divisions or even significant religious minorities (such as the large Muslim presence in Hindu-dominated India). In tropical Africa, Christianity is the leading non-indigenous faith. Confucianism and Taoism are belief systems rather than religions in the traditional sense. Source: de Blij, Harm J. 2008. *Power of Place: Geography, Destiny, and Globalization's Rough Landscape*. Chapter 3: The Fateful Geography of Religion, pp. 58–9. © 2008 Oxford University Press. Used by permission.

Christianity

✿ Judaism

Islam

Hinduism

Buddhism

Confucianism and Taoism

Shintoism and Buddhism

Traditional and Shamanist

Other, mixed, none

0   2,000   4,000 kilometers

Today, a wide swath of countries running across northern Africa, the Middle East, and as far west as Pakistan are predominantly Muslim. Islam has also spread rapidly throughout the West largely as a result of people migrating in search of work. Well known are large Islamic populations in various countries in Europe, most notably Great Britain, but Islam has spread far more broadly, even to the US (Detroit is a center of Islamic life there) and Australia. In the post 9/11 era, this has led to tensions in many parts of the world, with some of the most notable examples occurring in the Netherlands, including the trial of Geert Wilders, the right-wing Dutch politician who was charged (and later acquitted) of using anti-Islam hate speech when he made "provocative statements including comparing the Koran with Hitler's 'Mein Kampf' and calling for an end to Muslim immigration" (Jolly 2011). Also of note are the transnational Islamic communications, especially via the Internet, as well as the international organizations that serve to hold these widespread populations together.

Hinduism

There are over 1.03 billion Hindus in the world today, but the vast majority (about 975 million) live in India (Pew Forum 2012). Hinduism is generally thought of as religion even though it lacks many of the characteristics of a religion such as "a founder, an essential set of fundamentals of belief and practice, or a church" (Madan 2007: 571). Nonetheless, Hinduism has spread across six continents. It is spread by both migrants and itinerate religious teachers. While it is heavily concentrated geographically, Hinduism has been important as part of the "Easternization of the World" (see Chapter 3) in, for example, the spread of yoga, Transcendental Meditation, etc. (Campbell 2007).

Buddhism

Buddhism arose in the Indic Ganges Basin in about the sixth century BC and began to have a transnational influence about three centuries later (Taylor 2007). There are approximately 488 million Buddhists in the world today, although the vast majority are in Asia (China has the largest number of Buddhists followed by Thailand). However, Buddhism has spread throughout the globe (Abrutyn 2012). In fact, Buddhism has spread in various ways (there is even a "cyber-Buddhism") producing a number of different variants; many Buddhisms. There are so many varieties that Taylor argues that "we are unlikely to see a 'McBuddhization' of the world" (Taylor 2007: 111). (McDonaldization is a concern, however, for other religions as reflected, for example, in John Drane's [2012] *The McDonaldization of the Church*.)

However, another possibility for Buddhism is decline, even disappearance, especially in Japan. The Japanese have tended to rely on Buddhism for funerals (in Japan it is often called "funeral Buddhism" [Onishi 2008: A6]), while drawing on other religions (e.g. Shintoism, Christianity) for other purposes (e.g. weddings). However, there is a declining interest in using Buddhism for funerals. Instead of having them in Buddhist temples (or at home), many Japanese are using funeral homes (which may supply a Buddhist priest). Some are eschewing funerals altogether by being cremated. In either case, the temples are in decline, although other factors are involved in that, as well (e.g. an aging population). Said one head priest: "If Japanese Buddhism doesn't act now, it will die out" (quoted in Onishi 2008: A6).

Christianity

Christianity (about 2.2 billion adherents) is one of the two fastest-growing religions in the world today (the other is Islam) (Garrett 2007; Pew Forum 2012). Christianity spread throughout the Middle East following the death of Christ. It grew and spread within the Roman Empire and was an important contributor (along with internal problems within Rome such as corruption and incompetence and external assaults by the "barbarians") to the latter's famous "decline and fall" (Gibbon 1998). Emperor Constantine moved Rome in the direction of greater religious tolerance and he, himself, became a Christian. Both by giving Christianity a greater opening in the Roman Empire, and through his founding of the city of Constantinople, Constantine helped set in motion the development of a schism (a formal rupture took place in 1054 and continues to this day) between the Latin-speaking Roman Catholic Church (Casanova 1997) in the West (Pelikan 1971) and the Greek-speaking Eastern Orthodox Church in the East (Pelikan 1974) (at the time, more Christians lived in the East than in the West). By the time of the schism, Christianity had already long become a religion oriented to the "Christianization" of the world. The Crusades were a major event in the history of that Christianization, and of globalization more generally. They began in 1095, shortly after the formal schism had taken place. The Crusades were designed to liberate the Holy Land from Muslims (and others) who had gained control of Jerusalem in 638 CE. This is still a hot-button issue for Muslims as reflected in the firestorm that erupted when former US President George W. Bush used the word "crusades" in a speech shortly after the 9/11 terrorist attacks.

Overall, Christianity today is still growing and expanding globally. A decline in Europe is more than compensated for by strong growth in the South – Asia, Africa, and Latin America (Coleman 2007). Those areas will become the center of Christianity in the not-too-distant future; the global South will dominate Christianity (Jenkins 2002).

Growth is so strong in Latin America that it is predicted that 80% of the world's Christians will be Hispanic by 2050. Southern Christianity is different from Christianity as it has been generally understood and practiced in the North. On the one hand, it is "more Pentecostal, morally conservative, and evangelical" (Garrett 2007: 143). On the other hand, it is also the main source, and remains the center, of *liberation theology* which is more liberal, if not radical, in nature and is oriented toward helping the economically deprived and the oppressed. Liberation theology arose in the 1950s and 1960s, and spread through large portions of the world from the 1960s to the 1980s. Since that time, its growth has slowed at least in part because of opposition from the Vatican (Alves 1969; Segato 2007).

However, it is important to remember that there were not just outflows of Christianity from Europe, but reverse-, as well as cross-, flows producing new variants of Christianity. Multidirectionality is especially important in the case of Christian Pentecostalism which began in the US in the early twentieth century, specifically in a poor black and white revival held in Los Angeles in 1906. Pentecostalism grew rapidly worldwide (Martin 2002) producing many variations and localized forms that are linked to one another through publications, conferences, electronic media, and travel. It is now the second-largest, and fastest-growing, Christian identification in the world with somewhere between 150 and 400 million adherents. It has come to exceed in size all forms of Christianity but Catholicism. Its growth has been especially great in Asia, Africa, and Latin America (Lechner and Boli 2005). Indeed, its center is in those geographic areas. Missionaries from there now often travel back to the US and Europe.

It is also important to keep in mind that the spread of institutionalized religion was not unrelated to other institutions and aspects of globalization. For example, the spread of Christianity in the sixteenth to eighteenth centuries was closely related to the spread of European political power and influence.

Judaism

Judaism is one of the smallest of the world's religions; only about 14 million people in the world define themselves as Jews, representing about 0.2% of the world's population (Ben-Sasson 1976; Goldberg 2007; Pew Forum 2012). However, for a variety of reasons, the importance of Judaism, both historically and contemporaneously, has been far greater than one would expect looking simply at the numbers involved. By the late nineteenth century there were 12 million Jews in the world who, as a result of the diaspora (see Chapter 10), had migrated from the Middle East and had come to be spread in small enclaves throughout much of the world. There was, and continued to be, a large concentration of Jews in Europe, but migrations to North America, as well as to Israel (then under Ottoman control) began during this period. By WW II the number of Jews in the world had grown to 16 million, but the Holocaust led to a reduction of the Jewish population to about 10 million. The founding of Israel in 1948 marked an important turning point for Jews and the mostly Jewish population of Israel is now in excess of 5 million people. Another large concentration of Jews lives in the US; over 80% of all of the 14 million Jews alive today live in either the US or Israel with only about 2.5 million living elsewhere (especially in Europe). The spread of Jews throughout the world, Zionism (which helped lead to the founding of Israel), the Holocaust, anti-Semitism, and the current and seemingly never-ending conflict between Israel and its Muslim neighbors over Palestine are just a few of the factors that make Judaism of great global significance.

CULTURAL HYBRIDIZATION

Cultural hybridization emphasizes the mixing of cultures as a result of globalization and the production, out of the integration of the global and the local (Cvetkovich and Kellner 1997; Stockhammer 2012), of new and unique hybrid cultures that are not reducible to either local or global culture. From this perspective, the focus is on the integration of global processes with various local realities to produce new and distinctive hybrid forms that indicate continued global heterogenization rather than homogenization. Hybridization is a very positive, even romantic, view of globalization as a profoundly creative process out of which emerges new cultural realities, and continuing, if not increasing, heterogeneity, in many different locales.

> **Cultural hybridization:** Mixing of cultures leading to unique combinations.

Glocalization is the concept that gets to the heart of cultural hybridization[7] as well as to what many contemporary theorists interested in globalization think about the essential nature of global processes (Giulianotti and Robertson 2012). **Glocalization** can be defined as the interpenetration of the global and the local resulting in unique outcomes in different geographic areas.

Based on the work of Roland Robertson (Friedman 1994; Robertson 2001), the essential elements of the perspective on globalization adopted by those who emphasize glocalization are that the world is growing more pluralistic (glocalization theory is exceptionally

> **Glocalization:** Interpenetration of the global and the local resulting in unique outcomes in different geographic areas.

alert to differences within and between areas of the world); individuals and local groups have great power to adapt, innovate, and maneuver within a glocalized world (glocalization theory sees individuals and local groups as important and creative agents); social processes are relational and contingent (globalization provokes a variety of reactions – ranging from nationalist entrenchment to cosmopolitan embrace – that produce glocalization); and commodities and the media are *not* seen as (totally) coercive, but rather as providing material to be used in individual and group creation throughout the glocalized areas of the world.

A discussion of some closely related terms (and related examples) will be of considerable help in getting a better sense of glocalization, as well as the broader issue of cultural hybridization (Canclini 1995; Nederveen Pieterse 2009). Of course, **hybridization** itself is one such term emphasizing increasing diversity associated with the unique mixtures of the global and the local as opposed to the tendency toward *uniformity* often associated with globalization. A cultural hybrid involves the combination of two, or more, elements from different cultures and/or parts of the world. Among the examples of hybridization (and heterogenization, glocalization) are Ugandan tourists visiting Amsterdam to watch Moroccan women engage in Thai boxing, Argentineans watching Asian rap performed by a South American band at a London club owned by a Saudi Arabian, and the more mundane experiences of Americans eating such concoctions as Irish bagels, Chinese tacos, Kosher pizza, and so on. Obviously, the list of such hybrids is long and growing rapidly with increasing hybridization. The contrast, of course, would be such uniform experiences as eating hamburgers in the United States, quiche in France, or sushi in Japan.

Yet another concept that is closely related to glocalization is **creolization** (Hannerz 1987). The term "creole" generally refers to people of mixed race, but it has been extended to the idea of the creolization of language and culture involving a combination of languages and cultures that were previously unintelligible to one another (Cohen 2007; Knörr 2012).

While all of the above – glocalization, hybridization, creolization – should give the reader a good feel for what is being discussed here under the heading of cultural hybridization, the following examples should also help.

> **Hybridization:** External flows interact with internal flows producing a unique cultural hybrid that combines their elements.

> **Creolization:** Combination of languages and cultures previously unintelligible to one another.

MUSLIM GIRL SCOUTS

An interesting example of hybridization in the US involves Muslim girls (Sarroub 2005) who participate in one of the quintessentially American institutions, the Girl Scouts (Muslim involvement in the Boy Scouts is thus far less significant, although they are making attempts to be more inclusive [Seelye 2010]) (MacFarquhar 2007: A1, A22). Muslim girls are now wearing a Girl Scout sash (with American flag, troop number, and merit badges) along with the flowing headscarf that is traditional Muslim garb. For some Muslim girls, the Girl Scout garb tends to reduce tension when they interact with non-Muslims. At a cookout, hot dogs and s'mores are served, but such food meets the dietary restrictions of Islamic law (the hot dogs are made of beef not pork). One Girl Scout broke the fast of Ramadan with a hot dog and s'mores exclaiming, "It's delicious! . . . It's a good way to break my fast" (quoted in MacFarquhar 2007: A22). Another won a ribbon, a Bismallah (in the name of God) ribbon, from her group for writing some of God's names in Arabic calligraphy and for memorizing a verse in the Koran that involves protection from gossips and goblins. (Such religious badges are not issued by Girl Scouts, USA, but it does endorse having them issued by specific groups.) However, her favorite badge was awarded for learning "how to make body glitter and to see which colors look good on us and how to clean our nails" (quoted in MacFarquhar 2007: A22).

The Girls Scouts have adapted to Muslims, as well, especially if a given troop is predominantly or wholly Muslim. In one mostly Muslim troop, the Girl Scout Promise is: "On my honor I will try to serve Allah and my country, to help people and live by the Girl Scout law" (quoted in MacFarquhar 2007: A22).

A similar process of hybridization is also happening with the Girl Scouts' global sister organization, Girl Guides. This organization, founded in Britain in 1910, has 10 million members around the world (Mark McDonald 2012). Given its linkage to Britain, the Girl Guides' oath had a reference to the Queen in which girls swore to "do my duty to God, to serve the Queen and my country." However, in 2012, the Girl Guides of Australia removed the reference to both God and the Queen (and a promise that the girls would be obedient). As the organization has become more culturally diverse (including more Jewish and Muslim members), the Girl Guides of Australia has sought to promote more inclusiveness and to create more space for cultural expression. This modified cultural form continues to exist alongside both the Girl Scouts (in the US) and other instances of Girl Guides (around the world).

SALSA

Salsa, a Latin American export, has become a global dance craze. As the salsa has been exported throughout the world, it has *not* come to be practiced in the same way in different geographic locales. In fact, there are important differences even among Latin American countries in the way salsa is danced – in Cuba, it is "vigorous and athletic, with much clockwise circling," in Puerto Rico the "New York style" is preferred with "straighter movements" and "dancers moving to and fro as if on tracks"; in Columbia and Venezuela there is an "elegantly restrained style, with much back-stepping, smaller hand-movements and little use of the elaborate arm-tangling moves beloved by Cuban dancers" (*Economist* 2008: March 27). Thus, salsa has been glocalized even within Latin America let alone throughout the world.

APPADURAI'S "LANDSCAPES"

Arjun Appadurai's *Modernity at Large: Cultural Dimensions of Globalization* (1996) emphasizes the concept – global flows – that, as we saw in Chapter 1, is central to this book, as well as the disjunctures among them. These flows and disjunctures serve to produce unique cultural realities around the world; they tend to produce cultural hybrids.

Appadurai discusses five global flows – *ethnoscapes, mediascapes, technoscapes, financescapes*, and *ideoscapes*. The use of the suffix -*scape* allows Appadurai to communicate the idea that these processes have fluid, irregular, and variable shapes and are therefore consistent with the idea of heterogenization and not homogenization. The fact that there are a number of these scapes and that they operate independently of one another to some degree, and are perhaps even in conflict with one another, makes this perspective also in tune with those that emphasize cultural diversity and heterogeneity. Furthermore, these scapes are interpreted differently by different agents ranging all the way from individuals, to face-to-face groups, sub-national groups, multinational corporations, and even nation-states. And, these scapes are ultimately navigated by individuals and groups on the basis of their own subjective interpretations of them. In other words, these are imagined worlds and those doing the imagining can range from those who control them to those who live in and traverse them. While power obviously lies with those in control and their imaginings, this perspective gives to those who merely live in these scapes, or pass through them, the power to redefine and ultimately subvert them.

At the center of Appadurai's thinking are the five landscapes mentioned above. **Ethnoscapes** involve those who are mobile, groups and individuals on the move (tourists, refugees, guest workers) that play such an important role in the more rapidly changing world in which we live (Chun 2012). This involves actual movement as well as fantasies about moving. Furthermore, in an ever-changing world, people cannot afford to allow their imaginations to rest too long and thus must keep such fantasies of movement alive.

Technoscapes are the ever-fluid, global configurations of high and low, mechanical and informational technology (see, especially, Chapter 9) and the wide range of material (downloading videos, e-mail) that now moves so freely and quickly around the globe and across borders that were at one time impervious to such movement (or at least thought to be) (Mele 2012).

Financescapes involve the processes by which huge sums of money move through nations and around the world at great speed through commodity speculations, currency markets, national stock exchanges, and the like (Powell 2012a). The great importance of this scape was highlighted, if it was ever downplayed, by the global recession that spread rapidly throughout the world following its onset in late 2007.

Mediascapes involve both the electronic capability to produce and transmit information around the world as well as the images of the world that these media create and disseminate (Kuipers 2012). Involved here are those who write blogs online, citizen journalists who provide news to outlets such as CNN, Al Jazeera, global filmmakers and distributors, television stations (SkyNews is a notable example), and newspapers and magazines.

Ideoscapes, like mediascapes, are sets of images (Martínez 2012). However, they are largely restricted to political images either produced by states and in line with their ideology, or the images and counter-ideologies produced by movements that seek to supplant those in power, or at least to gain a piece of that power. For example, Nancy Netting (2010) has described marital ideoscapes, which are communicated among Indian youth, and promote the freedom to choose a partner based on romantic love, instead of abiding by traditional norms for arranged marriage.

Three things are especially worth noting about Appadurai's landscapes. First, they can be seen as global processes that are partly or wholly independent of any given nation-state. Second, global flows not only occur through the landscapes, but also increasingly in and through the *disjunctures* among them. Thus, to give one example of such a disjuncture, the Japanese tend to be open to ideas (ideoscapes, mediascapes), but notoriously closed to immigration (at least one of the ethnoscapes). More generally, the free movement of some landscapes may be at variance with blockages of others. Studies in this area must be attuned to such disjunctures and to their implications for globalization. Third, territories are going to be affected differently by the five landscapes and their disjunctures lead to important differences among and between cultures. The focus on landscapes and their disjunctures points globalization studies in a set of unique directions. However, the key point here is that such a focus is in line with the idea of hybridization.

Ethnoscapes: Actual movement, as well as fantasies about moving, of mobile groups and individuals.

Technoscapes: Fluid, global configurations of technology and the wide range of material that moves freely and quickly around the globe.

Financescapes: Processes by which huge sums of money move through nation-states and around the world at great speed.

Mediascapes: Electronic capability to produce and transmit information and images globally.

Ideoscapes: Flows of images primarily political in nature.

CULTURAL CONVERGENCE

While differentialism is rooted in the idea of lasting differences among and between cultures, and hybridization emphasizes differences resulting from the interaction of the global and the local, **cultural convergence** is based on the idea that globalization tends to lead to increasing sameness throughout the world. Those who support this perspective see cultures changing, sometimes radically, as a result of globalization, specifically flows of global culture and the relative weakness of barriers to those flows. The cultures of the world are seen as growing increasingly similar, at least to some degree and in some ways. There is a tendency to see global assimilation in the direction of dominant groups and societies in the world.

> **Cultural convergence**: Cultures are subject to many of the same global flows and tend to grow more alike.

While the different perspectives to be discussed in this section do focus on cultural convergence, they certainly do *not* argue that that is all that is happening in globalization or that local cultures (Wherry 2008) are disappearing completely, or even necessarily being altered in some fundamental way. While globalization often overwhelms local realities, or at least changes them dramatically, those realities frequently survive in some form or other.

One example is the delivery of home-cooked meals to workers throughout Mumbai (with an estimated metropolitan population of over 20 million people in 2012) by what are called *dabbawallas* (*dabba* is the food box and *wallas* are the people who deliver them) (Kai 2007: C1, C7). Here is the way the system works:

> A network of wallas picks up the boxes from customers' homes or from people who cook lunch to order, then deliver the meals to a local railway station. The boxes are hand sorted for delivery to different stations in central Mumbai, and then re-sorted and carried to their destinations. After lunch the service reverses, and the empty boxes are delivered back home. (Kai 2007: C7)

Color codes on the boxes are crucial because they tell the *wallas* where the food comes from, which train stations it must pass through, and where it is ultimately to go. Once they arrive at the right station, the boxes are unloaded, sorted, carried by wooden cart, and ultimately personally delivered to each recipient. As the wife who cooks lunch for one of those recipients said, "The old fashioned, inexpensive dabbawalla system is a rare survivor in this fast-paced world" (quoted in Kai 2007: C7).

CULTURAL IMPERIALISM

The idea of *cultural imperialism* indicates that one or more cultures are imposing themselves, more or less consciously, on other cultures thereby destroying local culture, in whole, or more likely in part. There are many examples of cultural imperialism in the world today with local cultural practices being threatened, or even being destroyed, by the flow of culture from other parts of the world, especially from the North to the South.

Indian sari weavers

One of the traditional crafts being threatened with destruction as a result of globalization is hand-woven silk sari-making in India (Wax 2007: A1, A17). These silk saris can take as much as two months to make by hand. They involve elaborate designs (such as leaves, elephants, and birds) made with strands of gold thread and green silk. There are about a million sari makers in India today and they are threatened by machine-made saris (such technologies have their roots in Western culture). While some of these are made in India – employing far fewer and less skilled workers – others are being made in, where else, China. Said the head of a local committee in India: "This is the ugly, painful side of globalization" (quoted in Wax 2007: A17). As a result, a local cultural product (the silk sari), practice (making such saris by hand), and practitioners (skilled sari makers) are being threatened by mass manufactured saris (often polyester) made by machine and less skilled workers in China.

India's professional letter-writers

Another example of cultural imperialism involves the destruction of India's professional letter-writers. Traditionally, men would place themselves in prominent locations (e.g. near the post office) and write letters for poor, often illiterate migrants. They would be paid a pittance for each letter, but many letter-writers were able to survive on their earnings. However, the spread of cell phones (another product of Western culture) into India, including the possibility of text messaging, is making the professional letter-writer obsolete. However, "creative destruction" (Schumpeter 1976: 81–7; see Chapter 7) is taking place, in at least some cases, as the children of these letter-writers obtain jobs in telecommunications (and other high-tech industries), often at much higher pay than the parent ever earned. Disappearing in much the same way are bank tellers (replaced by ATMs), phone-booth operators (by cell phones), and rural moneylenders (supermarket chains now do business directly with farmers eliminating the need for such middlemen). On the other hand, all sorts of new occupations are being created such as shopping mall attendants (such malls only appeared recently in India), cashiers in fast-food restaurants, auto sales executives, and software engineers. Much of the above involves cultural imperialism with the exportation to India of such creations and expressions of Western culture as ATMs, supermarkets, shopping malls, and fast-food restaurants. However, what is being destroyed are cultural practices indigenous to India (letter-writing, rural money-lending), as well as the occupations that engage in those practices. Replacing them are cultural practices (e.g. selling and consuming fast food) and occupations (software engineers) that are more global in character and less tied to the specific nature of Indian culture. That is, Indian fast food and software engineering have more in common with global culture than they do with Indian culture.

Examples such as these have led to the argument that what we are seeing throughout the world is increasing convergence as a result of cultural imperialism. In fact, UNESCO was sufficiently concerned about the issue of cultural imperialism and its deleterious effect on cultural diversity that on November 2, 2001, it adopted a Universal Declaration on Cultural Diversity.[8]

In spite of many examples of, and much hand-wringing about, cultural imperialism (including UNESCO's great concern about threats to cultural diversity), many observers have argued that the danger of cultural imperialism is greatly exaggerated. Mike Featherstone (1995: 13–14) was an early critic of the idea of a global culture, as well as associated ideas such as cultural imperialism and increasing global homogeneity: "The process of globalization, then, does not seem to be producing cultural uniformity; rather it makes us aware of new levels of diversity. If there is a global culture, it would be better to conceive of it not as a common culture, but as field in which differences, power struggles and cultural prestige contests are played out."

John Tomlinson (2007) sees many obvious examples of increasing similarity around the globe in the operations of the global capitalist system and its effects, but there are also many global differences and countervailing trends. Globalization is uneven and neglects and even excludes some areas. Thus, globalization, to Tomlinson, is not quite global. However, he is critical of the view that a global culture is being formed, most generally by cultural imperialism emanating from the West, especially the United States. Involved in this view is the simultaneous loss of distinct, non-Western cultural traditions. He sees this perspective as focusing on the superficial[9] issue of the global distribution of cultural goods (e.g. Coke, Big Macs, iPods, and the like).

Deterritorialization

Central to Tomlinson's work is the issue of *deterritorialization*, or the declining significance of the geographic location in which culture exists; culture is no longer as tied as it once was to the constraints of local geography. This means that in Tomlinson's terms "global connectivity" is reaching into local culture and the localities of everyday life. This transformation is both perplexing/disruptive and exhilarating/empowering (here Tomlinson is following the theorizing of Anthony Giddens[10]). Involved is the penetration of everyday life by distant forces and the dislodging of everyday meanings from the anchors of the local environment. In the long run, it may be that this weakening of traditional bonds between cultural experience and geographic territory will be the most far-reaching effect of cultural globalization. However, Tomlinson is careful to point out that this does not simply involve loss, but localities also thrive on globalization. Yet, he admits that the culture produced by locality (if such a narrow source of production was ever the case[11]) is no longer the single most important factor in our lived reality. It has been attenuated by deterritorialization with the integration of distant events, processes, and relationships into everyday lives. Tomlinson singles out the role of the media and communication technology for their role in deterritorialization (Kellner and Pierce 2007). He is very even handed, arguing that while there might be negatives associated with all of this and their effects on emotions, social relations, and cultural identity, there are also many positive potentialities including a new sensibility of cultural openness, human mutuality, and global ethical responsibility.[12]

WORLD CULTURE[13]

A distinctive theoretical approach to convergence in general, and cultural convergence in particular, is known as **world culture** theory (Meyer et al. 1997). They argue that there has developed, especially in recent years, a series of global models in a variety of different domains – politics, business, education, family, religion, and so on – and that their spread has led to a surprising amount of uniformity throughout the world. This is, in part, a result of the fact that such global models have become more codified and publicized than at any time in history. In addition, there are more organizations involved in, and they are more active in, educating and advising various populations about the models. As a result, there is a striking amount of structural **isomorphism** throughout the world as a result of the spread of these models (DiMaggio and Powell 1983). These models have been spread by a wide variety of cultural and associational processes. An assumption behind this approach is the decline of the nation-state as a significant player in the global world. Indeed, the authors often describe the world society in terms of "statelessness." As a result, the models of

> **World culture:** Spread of global models leading to global convergence.

> **Isomorphism:** A series of global models has led to a great uniformity throughout the world.

concern in this theory are able to flow relatively freely throughout world and are not impeded to any great extent by the nation-state.

While a variety of forms of isomorphism are discussed by world culture theorists, culture is accorded pride of place. In fact, world culture scholars describe the world in terms of an enactment of culture. More specifically, culture is associated with a "cultural order" and "institutions," both of which are seen as "rationalized" (e.g. carried and legitimated by professional and scientific organizations). Culture is seen as shaping (and being shaped by) the macro- (states and the state system), meso- (organizations like schools and firms, associations including voluntary associations), and micro- (individual citizenship and identity) levels throughout the world.

John Boli and Velina Petrova (2007) demonstrate the general tendency in this approach to emphasize homogenization. While they acknowledge the existence of global resistance, their emphasis is on the spread of world culture, standardized cultural models, and the tendency toward organizational isomorphism around the globe. All of this is part of a "soft" model of increasing global homogeneity. These things tend not to be imposed on people, institutions, or societies, but rather are more likely to be welcomed by them. Thus, globalization, in their view, tends to be seen as something legitimate rather than as something that is imposed on people illegitimately. People tend to feel increasingly part of, included in, a global culture. While global culture can be constraining, the emphasis in this approach is on how that culture is enabling; how it permits people to self-actualize.

There has been a globalization of models that place great value on the individual. They are manifest in the educational system (the emphasis on the education and well-being of the individual student), the economy (it is individuals who are to be paid, to have property rights, etc.), an increasingly pervasive ideology of human rights, and so on. Then there are global models for the state that expect it to be responsible to its citizens for schooling, medical care, development, gender empowerment, control over state corruption, etc. Not only have we seen the spread of global models for the state, but also of methods for assessing the performance of the state. There is also the spread of methods for deciding whether the state is, in fact, handling its responsibilities, including the possibility that the state can fail to fulfill its responsibilities to such a degree that it can be considered a "failed state." A failed state is characterized by high levels of poverty, violence, and social disorder. In the realm of economic organizations, the corporation has become the globally favored model. A global model of corporate morality has emerged, as well. Fairly standard organizational forms have also developed globally for universities, sports clubs, hobby groups, and professional associations.

The power of globalization from this perspective is that it is *both* internal and external to actors. Culture is manifest cognitively in the individual, but it also exists outside the actor in the form of the larger culture and increasingly isomorphic organizations that reflect that culture. The school is crucial here since it is a prime agent for teaching world culture and it is an organizational form that is both increasingly similar throughout the world and is a structural reflection of world culture.

While the thrust of this is to emphasize increasing global homogeneity, there is also diversity, glocalization, and resistance. The emphasis is not on globalized homogeneity inducing resistance, but rather globalization is seen as producing legitimate differences and diversity.

One way of getting at world culture is to examine the INGO as an organizational form that is shaped by it. There is a common set of principles among most INGOs throughout the world (Boli and Thomas 1997). They include universalism, individualism (e.g. the one-person, one-vote rule), rational voluntaristic authority (rational individuals organizing themselves on a global basis to undertake purposive action and employing rational procedures; the collectivities in which they exist create and come to employ rules that are efficient, just, and equitable), rational progress (economic development, collective security, justice, and the self-actualization of individuals), and world citizenship (everyone is seen as having various rights and obligations, including the taking of actions to deal with global problems; everyone is seen as a citizen of the global polity).

McDONALDIZATION

The McDonaldization thesis (Ritzer 1997b, 2012) is based on Max Weber's classic, turn-of-the-twentieth-century, theory of the rationalization of the West. In fact, Weber's theory of rationalization was, at least in part, an early theory of globalization since he tended to see not only the Occident (i.e. the West) increasingly dominated by rationalization, but much of the rest of the world was destined to rationalize, as well. Weber's model for the rationalization process was the bureaucracy, while the end-of-the-twentieth-century McDonaldization thesis takes the fast-food restaurant as its model. The McDonaldization thesis also brings the theory into the twenty-first century, and views rationalization extending its reach into more sectors of society and areas of the world than Weber ever imagined. Of greatest concern here is the fact that McDonaldization is a force in global cultural homogenization.

McDonaldization is defined as the process by which the principles of the fast-food restaurant are coming to dominate more and more sectors of American society, as well as the rest of the world. It is the latter aspect of the definition that makes it clear that McDonaldization is a globalizing force.

The nature of the McDonaldization process may be delineated by outlining its five basic dimensions: efficiency, calculability, predictability, control through the substitution of technology for people, and, paradoxically, the irrationality of rationality.[14] The key point for our purposes is that these five principles, as well as the McDonaldization process of which they are part, are becoming increasingly global.

First, a McDonaldizing society emphasizes *efficiency*, or the effort to discover the best possible means to whatever end is desired. Workers in fast-food restaurants clearly must work efficiently; for example, burgers are assembled, and sometimes even cooked, in an assembly-line fashion. Customers want, and are expected, to acquire and consume their meals efficiently. The drive-through window is a highly efficient means for customers to obtain, and employees to dole out, meals. Overall, a variety of norms, rules, regulations, procedures, and structures have been put in place in the fast-food restaurant in order to ensure that *both* employees and customers act in an efficient manner. Furthermore, the efficiency of one party helps to ensure that the other will behave in a similar manner.

Second, great importance is given to *calculability*, to an emphasis on quantity, often to the detriment of quality. Various aspects of the work of employees at fast-food restaurants are timed; this emphasis on speed often serves to affect adversely the quality of the work, from the point of view of the employee, resulting in dissatisfaction, alienation, and high turnover rates. Similarly, customers are expected to spend as little time as possible in the fast-food restaurant. In fact, the drive-through window reduces this time to zero, but if the customers desire to eat in the restaurant, the chairs may be designed to feel increasingly uncomfortable

McDonaldization: Process by which the principles of the fast-food restaurant are coming to dominate more of the world.

in order to impel them to leave after about 20 minutes. This emphasis on speed clearly has a negative effect on the quality of the dining experience at a fast-food restaurant. Furthermore, the emphasis on how fast the work is to be done means that customers cannot be served high-quality food that, almost by definition, requires a good deal of time to prepare.

McDonaldization also involves an emphasis on *predictability* meaning that things (products, settings, employee and customer behavior, and so on) are pretty much the same from one geographic setting to another (globalization!) and from one time to another. Employees are expected to perform their work in a predictable manner and, for their part, customers are expected to respond with similarly predictable behavior. Thus, when customers enter, employees ask, following scripts, what they wish to order. For their part, customers are expected to know what they want, or where to look to find what they want, and they are expected to order, pay, and leave quickly. Employees (following another script) are expected to thank them when they do leave. A highly predictable ritual is played out in the fast-food restaurant – one that involves highly predictable foods that vary little from one time or place to another.

In addition, great *control* exists in McDonaldized systems and a good deal of that control comes from technologies. Although these technologies currently dominate employees, increasingly they will be replacing them. Employees are clearly controlled by such technologies as french-fry machines that ring when the fries are done and even automatically lift the fries out of the hot oil. For their part, customers are controlled both by the employees who are constrained by such technologies as well as more directly by the technologies themselves. Thus, the automatic fry machine makes it impossible for a customer to request well-done, well-browned fries.

Finally, both employees and customers suffer from the *irrationality of rationality* that seems inevitably to accompany McDonaldization. That is, paradoxically, rationality seems often to lead to its exact opposite – irrationality. For example, the efficiency of the fast-food restaurant is often replaced by the inefficiencies associated with long lines of people at the counters or long lines of cars at the drive-through window. Another of the irrationalities of rationality is dehumanization. Employees are forced to work in dehumanizing jobs and customers are forced to eat in dehumanizing settings (e.g. in their cars) and circumstances (e.g. on the move). The fast-food restaurant can be a source of degradation for employees and customers alike.

The most important irrationality of rationality, at least from the point of view of globalization, is that McDonaldization is a force for increasing global homogeneity.[15] This is because fast-food restaurants and many other businesses and organizations throughout the world are based on the same fundamental principles – efficiency, predictability, calculability, and control. This serves to give them a high degree of structural similarity even though they may sell (or do) very different things, even things (e.g. foods) that are quite local in nature. They are also similar in the sense that they all tend to spawn various irrationalities of rationality. Thus, the McDonaldization thesis describes a process of increasing global homogenization, but it is critical of that process for helping to reduce global differences and to produce a rather depressing sameness throughout the world.

McDonaldization, expansionism, and globalization

The fast-food restaurant in general, and McDonald's in particular, has been a resounding success in the international arena. More than half of McDonald's restaurants are outside the US (in the mid-1980s only 25% of McDonald's were outside the US). The vast majority of new restaurants opened each year are overseas – in 2012, McDonald's opened 1,000 new restaurants outside the US (although overall sales flat-lined in 2013). As of 2013, it had over 34,000 locations in 118 countries. Two-thirds of McDonald's revenue comes from its overseas operations. The highly McDonaldized Starbucks has also become an increasingly global force. Despite a setback in growth in 2008, Starbucks continues to grow and as of 2013, it has 19,000 stores in 59 countries besides the US, with a strong presence in Latin America, Europe (it is particularly visible in London), the Middle East, and the Pacific Rim.

Many highly McDonaldized firms outside of the fast-food industry have also had success globally. Perhaps the most famous (or notorious) example is Wal-Mart. Although Wal-Mart opened its first international store (in Mexico) in 1991, it now operates over 6,238 international units in 26 countries (in 2012, 40% of Wal-Mart's net sales were outside the US).

Another indicator of globalization is the fact that other nations have developed their own variants of McDonaldized fast-food restaurants. Canada has a chain of coffee shops, Tim Hortons (merged with Wendy's in 1995), with 4,264 outlets (804 in the United States). Paris, a city whose love for fine cuisine might lead one to think it would prove immune to fast food, has a large number of fast-food croissanteries; the revered French bread has also been McDonaldized. India has a chain of fast-food restaurants, Nirula's, which sells mutton burgers (about 80% of Indians are Hindus, who eat no beef) as well as local Indian cuisine. Mos Burger is a Japanese chain with over 1,740 restaurants that, in addition to the usual fare, sells Teriyaki chicken burgers, rice burgers, and Oshiruko with brown rice cake. Russkoye Bistro, a Russian chain, sells traditional Russian fare like pirogi (meat and vegetable pies), blini (thin pancakes), Cossack apricot curd tart, and, of course, vodka. Perhaps the most unlikely spot for an indigenous fast-food restaurant, war-ravaged Beirut of 1984, witnessed the opening of Juicy Burger, with a rainbow instead of golden arches and J. B. the Clown standing in for Ronald McDonald. Its owners hoped that it would become the McDonald's of the Arab world. After the 2003 war with Iraq, a number of clones of McDonald's ("Madonal," "Matbax") quickly opened there. In spite of the great hostility between the governments of Iran and the US, many Iranians are very positive toward Americans and America and this is reflected in their fast-food restaurants. While there were almost no American chains there as of 2013 (KFC opened a branch there in 2012), there are local shops that are modeled after them such as an ice cream shop that emulates Baskin-Robbins down to its 31 flavors, a T. G. I. Friday's clone featuring burgers, Cobb Salad, and waiters with familiar Friday's garb, as well as "Starcups and Kabooky Fried Chicken" (Blackman 2008: A11).

Now McDonaldization is coming full circle. Other countries with their own McDonaldized institutions are beginning to export them to the US. The Body Shop, a British cosmetics chain, had over 2,500 shops in 60 nations in 2013. Three hundred of them were in the US. Furthermore, American firms are now opening copies of this British chain, such as Bath and Body Works. Pollo Campero, a Guatemalan chain specializing in fried chicken, is currently in 12 countries and is spreading rapidly throughout the US.

As the model of the process, McDonald's has come to occupy a central position throughout the world. At the opening of McDonald's in Moscow, it was described as the ultimate American icon. When Pizza Hut opened in Moscow in 1990, customers saw it as a small piece of America. Reflecting on the growth of fast-food restaurants in Brazil, an executive associated with Pizza Hut of Brazil said that his nation is passionate about things American.

Beyond fast food

While the fast-food restaurant is the model for the process of McDonaldization, the process extends far beyond it. A wide range of studies have analyzed the McDonaldization of higher education (Hayes and Wynyard 2002), the church (Drane 2012, 2008; White and Yeats 2011), social work (Dominelli 2010; Dustin 2007), and much else.[16] The point is that not only have many sectors of society been McDonaldized, but those sectors, like McDonald's itself, are increasingly global in character.

Let us close this section with an unusual example of McDonaldization, this time as it relates to the globally distributed drug, Viagra. Viagra is designed to help deal with erectile dysfunction (ED), but it could be argued that it also serves in many ways to McDonaldize sex (e.g. by making more predictable the ability of males to perform sexually). Viagra, and its use, have become global phenomena. Wide-scale use of Viagra has become a subject of concern (and some humor), not only in the US, but elsewhere in the world. In Spain, Viagra has been stolen from pharmacies; it has become a recreational drug demanded even by young people; and this has led to enormous sales even at high retail prices (the wholesale price in 2013 was $22 per pill), and illegal sales (at discos, for example) of a single pill for as much as $80. Why this great demand for Viagra in a society noted for its macho culture? According to a spokesperson for the company that makes Viagra, it is linked to McDonaldization: "We used to have a siesta, to sleep all afternoon. . . . But now we have become a *fast-food nation* where everyone is stressed out, and this is not good for male sexual performance" (quoted in Bilefsky 2007: 14, italics added).

McDonaldization, as a theory of globalization, certainly emphasizes convergence, but it does *not* argue that everything throughout the world is growing increasingly homogeneous. Overall, we do see the global proliferation of systems that operate on the basis of the basic principles of McDonaldization. However, while that represents some degree of convergence, there is considerable variation around the world in terms of the degree, and the way in which, McDonaldized systems operate efficiently, predictably, and so on. Further, McDonaldized systems often provoke resistance and this helps to lead to continued, or even greater, differences in many parts of the world.

Interestingly, most of the debate over McDonaldization and globalization has focused on the wrong issue. In the main, it has focused on the end-products arguing against convergence because the products differ, at least to some degree, from one geographic locale to another. However, McDonaldization is *not* about end-products (e.g. Big Macs), but rather about the system and its principles. That system has been globalized, and in many different domains, but it operates at least slightly differently from sector to sector and in different parts of the world. There is convergence, but it does not result in uniformity and homogeneity.

THE GLOBALIZATION OF NOTHING

The globalization of nothing (Ritzer 2007), like McDonaldization, implies growing convergence as more and more nations around the world are increasingly characterized by various forms of nothing (see below for the definition of this concept). The argument is that there is an *elective affinity*, using a term borrowed from Weber (1921/1968), between globalization and nothing. That is, one does not cause the other, but they do tend to vary together. Note: the argument is *not* that globalization is nothing; indeed it is clear that, if for no other reason than this lengthy book, the process is of enormous significance.

Central to this argument is the idea of **grobalization** (a companion to the notion of glocalization) which is defined as the imperialistic ambitions of nation-states, corporations, organizations, and the like and their desire, indeed need, to impose themselves on various geographic areas throughout the world (Ryan 2007: 2022–3). Their main interest is in seeing their power, influence, and in some cases profits *grow* (hence the term *grobalization*, a combination of grow and globalization) throughout the world. Grobalization involves a variety of sub-processes, three of which – capitalism, Americanization, as well as McDonaldization – are not only central driving forces in grobalization, but also of great significance in the worldwide spread of nothingness.

Nothing involves (largely) empty forms; forms largely devoid of distinctive content.[17] (Conversely, **something** is defined as [largely] full forms; forms rich in distinctive content.) It is easier to export empty forms (nothing) throughout the globe than it is forms that are loaded with distinctive content (something). The latter are more likely to be rejected by at least some cultures and societies because the content conflicts, is at variance, with local content. In contrast, since they are largely devoid of distinctive content, empty forms are less likely to come into conflict with the local. In addition, empty forms have other advantages from the point of view of globalization including the fact that since they are so minimalist, they are easy to replicate over and over and they have a cost advantage since they are relatively inexpensive to reproduce.

A good example of nothing in these terms is the shopping mall (especially chains of malls) which is an empty structure (largely) that is easily replicated around the world. These malls could be filled with an endless array of specific content (e.g. local shops, local foods, etc. – something!) that could vary enormously from one locale in the world to another. However, increasingly they are filled with chain stores, themselves meeting the definition of nothing, carrying a wide range of various types of . . . nothing! That is, chain stores throughout the world sell goods that are more or less the same everywhere they are sold. Since more and more countries in the world have these malls, chain stores, and chain-store products, this is an example of the grobalization of nothing and of increasing global convergence.

There are four sub-types of nothing and all of them are largely empty of distinctive content and are being grobalized. The four types are **non-places**, or settings that are largely empty of content (e.g. the malls and chain stores discussed above); **non-things** such as chain-store products and credit cards (there is little to distinguish one credit card from the billions of others, all of which work in exactly the same way for all who use them anywhere in the world); **non-people**, or the kind of employees associated with non-places, for example, telemarketers (who may be virtually anywhere in the world) who interact with all customers in much the same way relying heavily on scripts; and **non-services** such as those provided by ATMs (the services provided are identical; the customer does all the work involved in obtaining the services) as opposed to human bank tellers. The grobal proliferation of non-places, non-things, non-people, and non-services is another indication of increasing convergence.

SPORT: GLOBAL, GLOCAL, GROBAL

Sport (Andrews and Mower 2012) is a particularly appropriate topic to examine at this point. It is a very important cultural phenomenon, it is globalizing to a great degree, and it is an excellent domain in which to examine the relationship between the last two theories[18] – hybridization (especially glocalization) and convergence (especially grobalization).

Grobalization: Imperialistic ambitions of nation-states, corporations, and organizations, and their imposition throughout the world.

Nothing: Social forms largely devoid of distinctive content.

Something: Largely full social forms, those rich in distinctive content.

Non-places: Settings largely devoid of distinctive content.

Non-things: Objects largely devoid of distinctive content.

Non-people: Those who occupy positions that lead them to be devoid of distinctive content at least in those positions.

Non-services: Services largely devoid of distinctive content.

Sport has become increasingly global throughout the twentieth and early twenty-first centuries "with the growth of international sporting bodies, competitions, tournaments, migratory flows of competitors and associated globally extensive forms of media representation, especially in the form of terrestrial (later satellite) television and the internet" (Smart 2007: 7). In fact, it has become increasingly possible to think in terms of a global sporting, or athletic, system.

The beginnings of this development can be traced to the late 1800s and early 1900s. Tennis was arguably the first global sport. The forerunner of the Davis Cup took place in the US in 1878 and involved players from the US, Canada, and England. The first international team-tennis competition of what later became known as the Davis Cup occurred in 1900. The number of teams involved was limited at first, but by the 1960s, 50 or more nations were competing for the Cup.

Also of importance in the history of global sports is the first "modern" Olympics that occurred in Athens in 1896 (Guttman 2002, 2007). What became known as the Summer Games has taken place every four years since then (except during WW I and II). While 13 nations participated in the first games, over 200 nations now compete in the Summer Olympics. It was joined by the Winter Olympics in 1924. Today, the Summer and Winter Olympics occur at alternate two-year intervals. Both are global events in many senses of the term, although the summer games are far more popular, and involve many more participants, than the winter games. Both are global because so many nations participate and so many people come from so many parts of the world not only to compete, but also to be in the audience. Perhaps of greater importance is the fact that they have become great global media events with, for example, 1 billion people around the world watching the opening ceremony of the 2012 Olympic Games in London. This has been fostered by the fact that global corporations and brands have found that sponsoring a portion of the television coverage of the games is good for the global increase and spread of the sales of their products.

However, the most global of sports is certainly soccer (called football in most places outside the US). Football is run globally by the Fédération Internationale de Football Association (FIFA), founded in 1904. FIFA has 209 member nations and is therefore larger than the UN (the UN has 193 member nations). The World Cup is watched by billions of people around the world. What occurs in those matches is global news (e.g. the head-butting incident involving Zidane in the 2006 World Cup final was front-page news throughout the world). There are super-clubs like Manchester United (in England) and Juventus (in Italy) that are far more important globally than, say, the New York Yankees in baseball or the Los Angeles Lakers in basketball. Soccer's media-darlings such as Argentina's Lionel Messi and Portugal's Cristiano Ronaldo are bigger global celebrities than even the American basketball player, Michael Jordan, in his prime. There is a huge global market for paraphernalia (e.g. team jerseys) associated with major soccer teams.

Also of great importance are the global sports companies that attach themselves to these sports and their stars and sell their paraphernalia globally. Among the most famous of these are Adidas, Reebok, and Nike. Not only are their names known around the world, and their products used worldwide, but their logos (e.g. the Nike "swoosh" [Goldman and Papson 1998]). Adidas's stripes are also recognized almost everywhere in the world (Klein 2009). Global sports have generated global sports stars (e.g. Messi, Tiger Woods) and these stars have been used by the sports companies to sell their wares throughout the world (Smart 2007). Of course, the sports stars have earned many millions of dollars for being "used" in this way. In fact there is a symbiotic relationship between the athletes and the sports companies with each involved in not only selling each other, but themselves.

Isolated role of US

There is a tendency to see the US as the hegemonic power in the world of sports, but there is much that contradicts that idea. In fact, in many realms of the sports world, the US is second-rate or a relatively insignificant factor (e.g. global soccer). Its greatest success is in sports – especially baseball and American football – that enjoy their greatest popularity and have their greatest appeal within the borders of the US. As Eriksen (2007: 48) puts it, "the United States, often seen as the main source of global culture, despised by middle classes everywhere else, is almost an island unto itself when it comes to team sports." The relatively isolated status of the US in the realm of sports is well illustrated by the case of baseball. Baseball did begin to spread beyond the confines of the US well before the spread of the English sports of soccer and rugby (although after the spread of cricket). It had moved to Cuba by 1860, China in 1863, and Japan and Korea by the early 1870s (Kelly 2007). However, despite its early start, the spread of baseball slowed. In fact, it was Japan that later did more to disseminate baseball by promoting it in its empire in countries like Korea, Taiwan, Southeast Asia, and Oceania in the Pacific.

There are several factors that limited the global spread of baseball. First, it became a big business in the US monopolized by a small number of owners. They helped to stabilize and systematize the sport "into regular seasons, stadium fixtures, continuing player contracts and monopolistic associations of owner-operators" (Kelly 2007: 84). This tended to solidify baseball in an American context and left little room for, or interest in, global expansion. Second, baseball was "promoted in highly nationalistic terms as embodying American values and inculcating an American character" (Kelly 2007: 84). Finally, unlike soccer or cricket, baseball was not disseminated through colonialism, but more informally and less coercively by missionaries, teachers, and so on.

While the most successful example of the spread of baseball is to be found in Japan, baseball there is quite different from the game played in the US. It has been aggressively appropriated by the Japanese. As one former American baseball star put it after playing a year in Japan: "This isn't baseball – it only looks like it" (quoted in Kelly 2007: 88). The following is a good comparison of the differences between baseball in the two countries: "Free-spirited, hard-hitting, fun-loving, independent-minded American baseball players are pitted symbolically against team-spirited, cautious, self-sacrificing, deeply deferential, intensely loyal [Japanese] samurai with bats" (Kelly 2007: 86). Nonetheless, Bud Selig (the Major League Baseball Commissioner in the US) continues to promote a "real World Series" where the top US and Japanese teams would play in a championship match (Rogers 2013). As of this writing, Major League Baseball was exploring this possibility, which could help further the globalization of baseball.

Basketball was invented in the US by James Naismith (born in Canada) in 1871 and it was exported throughout the world through the efforts of the YMCA (founded in England). It was dominated by the US, especially with the emergence of the professional National Basketball Association (NBA; founded in 1946) and the amateur National Collegiate Athletic Association (NCAA) and its national basketball championships (begun in 1939). The US continued to dominate global basketball through much of the last half of the twentieth century.

However, in recent years basketball has become a much more global phenomenon and the US has lost its hegemonic position in the sport (Veseth 2005). This is reflected in the increasing difficulty US teams, even those dominated by star professional players, have had in recent years in winning international tournaments, including Olympic championships (although the US men and women did win the respective 2012 championships in London). It is also reflected in not only the increasing presence of foreign players in the NBA, but also by the fact that they have become some of the dominant players in the league (e.g. Marc Gasol of Spain). However, this flow is not one way; lesser US basketball players (and those in other sports such as American baseball players going to Japan) often play in leagues in Europe.

Professional athletes ("sports workers" [Sayers and Edwards 2004: 243–8], albeit often very highly paid ones) have increasing global mobility; more and more of them can be seen as "border crossers" (Maguire and Stead 1998). There are several types of border crossers in the sports world, including "pioneers" (those who move to a new country with a zeal to bring and promote their sport), "settlers" (those who move to a new country and remain there), "mercenaries" (those solely motivated by money and who are likely to move from locale to locale depending on where the rewards are greatest), and "nomads" who move about "simply because they enjoy migration and being strangers in a new culture and society" (Grainger 2008: 303). It should be noted that there are also totally nomadic global sports like professional golf and tennis where athletes are constantly moving from tournament to tournament throughout the world (Grainger 2008: 288). Whatever the reason, an increasing number of athletes have been, and are, flowing throughout the world.

Again contrary to the Americanization thesis, much of this flow is into rather than out of the US (as well as other countries in the North; this has prompted concern in the South about a "brawn drain" (Bale 1994) paralleling worry about the "brain drain" – see Chapter 10). In addition to the influx of foreign players into the NBA, there is the signing of an increasing number of Japanese players by Major League Baseball. In 2012 the Texas Rangers signed star Japanese pitcher Yu Darvish (an icon of Japanese baseball) for a long-term salary of over $60 million and, more striking, they paid his team, the Hokkaido Nippon Ham Fighters, $51.7 million just for the right to negotiate with him. In 2007 one of America's Major League soccer teams, the Los Angeles Galaxy, signed the British superstar David Beckham to a contract that earned him $255 million (including $50 million in salary and the rest in lucrative endorsements) over five years (Badenhausen 2012).

While in various ways global sport appears to contradict the Americanization thesis, Barry Smart points out that in many broader senses global sport has been "Americanized." Included under the heading of the Americanization of global sport are "the extensive commercialization of sport that first became evident in America, exemplified by the cultivation of sport as an entertainment spectacle, developments in television sports broadcasting, and the extension of a culture of celebrity to include sports stars" (Smart 2007: 23).

There is movement of professional athletes in various sports from less to more developed countries. For example, no country sends more baseball players to the US than the Dominican Republic (Marcano and Fidler 2012). These border crossers often view baseball as a vehicle for social mobility, but because of the unequal power relations between the Dominican Republic and the US, such exchanges involve many abuses (as depicted in the documentary *Ballplayer: Pelotero* [dirs. Ross Finkel, Trevor Martin, and Jon Paley]). To note one example, over 100,000 boys train full time in the Dominican Republic in hopes of eventually playing in the US. However, only a very few of them succeed. Furthermore, this system involves the buying and selling of these boys as commodities. One less widely known example is the movement of rugby players from Samoa to New Zealand where they can earn much more money and acquire much greater, even world, fame (Grainger 2008). This can be seen as neo-colonial exploitation with the imperial nation (New Zealand in this case) exploiting a natural resource (talented athletes) of a former colony. The very best Samoan rugby players now compete in, and for, New Zealand and this has served to diminish the quality of the game in Samoa.

Local, glocal, grobal

A central issue in the study of the globalization of sport is the degree to which it has been glocalized (its global aspects have been integrated with more local aspects) (Giulianotti and Robertson 2004). There is a wide-scale belief among those who study the topic that sport has been glocalized to a large degree and that glocalization is the best concept for thinking about the globalization of sport. While it is certainly the case that there *is* a great deal of glocalization in sport, this is far from the entire picture as far as the globalization of sport (or anything else) is concerned.

Roland Robertson and Richard Giulianotti have directly addressed this issue as it relates to sport, especially football (soccer) (Giulianotti and Robertson 2007). They go beyond the idea of glocalization involving the interpenetration of the global and the local to argue that glocalization involves the "societal *co-presence* of sameness and difference" (Giulianotti and Robertson 2007: 60) of "homogenizing and heterogenizing trends in globalization *tout court*" (Giulianotti and Robertson 2007: 61). They see the concept of glocalization as encompassing *both* homogenization and heterogenization.

However, this combination of homogenization and heterogenization under the heading of glocalization obscures the often conflicting pressures toward one or the other. What is needed is the distinctions, discussed above, between grobalization and glocalization, as well as something and nothing. Based on those distinctions, it is the grobalization of nothing that tends to produce homogeneity in whatever locale it asserts itself and gains hegemony. In contrast, the glocalization of something inherently involves heterogeneity since what is "something" (indigenously conceived, controlled, and rich in the distinctive content of that locale) in one setting will be different from something in another setting (conceived and controlled in a different locale with inevitably different distinctive content).

Much of what is often interpreted as the glocal in sport is, in fact, better thought of as grobal. For example, while much attention is paid to the way cricket has been glocalized (in India, for example; see below), the fact is that cricket was grobalized by the British. Also important in the grobalization of sport in the late nineteenth and early twentieth centuries were international sporting organizations and competitions, national governing bodies and leagues (Andrews and Ritzer 2007: 32), multinational corporations (and their global brands), and the media. All of these served to grobalize sport and produce increasing homogeneity in sport throughout the world. That is not to say that there are not also pressures toward heterogenization and that those are best captured by the concept of glocalization. While it is true that there are forces for homogenization (and heterogenization) in the glocal, overall it is the combination of glocalization and grobalization that produces that which is unique in a given locale and that tends toward the heterogeneous rather than the homogeneous. Thus, it is best to use the concept of grobalization, especially the grobalization of nothing, when we focus on homogeneity and the concept of glocalization (of something) for the production of heterogeneity.[19]

In his analysis of sport, especially the highly local Gaelic football and hurling, Eriksen (2007: 56) argues that they are not examples of glocalization of something, but rather

> represent something that cannot, and will not, be globalized because they symbolize a cultural identity that is by default associated with a particular place . . . Ritzer's sociology of globalization needs a third term to grasp this kind of phenomenon which is exclusively global . . . Ritzer's approach . . . is limited because it rules out the possibility of anything being merely local . . . the self-contained, local system continues to exist, by carving out a niche where there is sufficient nourishment and no external competition.

In effect, Eriksen wants to add the "local" to the "grobal" and the "glocal" as key concepts for analyzing globalization, especially of sport. The problem is that it is difficult to think of *any* phenomenon in the world of sports, or any other realm, that is totally self-contained, devoid of any impact from the global. This is especially the case with the examples used by Eriksen – hurling and Gaelic football – since their roots are in Ireland, the country which is almost always rated, and considered, the *most* globalized country in the world.

Cricket: local, glocal, or grobal?

The sport of cricket has attracted a lot of attention from those interested in globalization in general and of sport in particular (Kaufman and Patterson 2005; Rumford and Wagg 2010), with perhaps the best-known work on it done by Appadurai (1996). His argument is that cricket has become decolonized, indigenized in India so that it is "no longer English-mediated" (Appadurai 1996: 104). That is, it has been glocalized, if not localized. He recognizes that cricket was brought to India by England; it was one aspect of colonization. England needed to create teams that it could play against. India and the other colonies were perfect for this role. However, the Indians have transformed cricket (just as the Japanese transformed baseball) and made it their own.

Of particular importance has been the role played by the media and language in the transformation of cricket in India. Mass Indian publications – books, magazines, and pamphlets – liberated cricket from its "Englishness" and dealt with cricket matches in native terms; they "vernacularized" cricket. The game came to be played widely in the streets, playgrounds, and villages of India so that it became inculcated in the bodily practice of many Indians. Indians also read about their favorite teams and stars and heard about them on the radio and saw them on TV. This served to make cricket an important part of the fantasy lives of many Indians.

In India, and elsewhere in former English colonies, cricket has come to be dominated by the locals and not by England; they have "hijacked" the game from the English (Mustafa 2013). In the process, they have transformed cricket, making it a much more aggressive game, one that is less "sportsmanlike," and perhaps most importantly, much more spectacular (just as the Japanese game of baseball is more spectacular than the American version). To Appadurai (1996: 107), cricket "now belongs to a different moral and aesthetic world." It has become an "instrument for mobilizing national sentiment in the service of transnational spectacles and commoditization" (Appadurai 1996: 109). Thus, to take one example, it is at the heart of matches between rivals India and Pakistan that resemble a war. As a result, in such matches, as well as in many other international cricket matches, "England . . . is no longer part of the equation" (Appadurai 1996: 109).

While there is much merit in Appadurai's analysis, it is important to remember that cricket was grobalized by the English. It is out of the interaction between the cricket grobalized by the English that was centrally conceived, controlled, and lacking in distinctive content ("nothing") and the indigenously conceived, controlled, rich in distinctive content cricket ("something") produced by glocalization in India, that the distinctive form of Indian cricket emerged. As with all other cultural forms, cricket cannot be reduced to glocalization or grobalization, or something or nothing. In today's world, all cultural forms involve elements of all of these.

CHAPTER SUMMARY

This chapter examines the global flows of culture, which tend to move more easily around the globe than ever before, especially through non-material digital forms. Three perspectives on global cultural flows are examined – differentialism, hybridization, and convergence.

Cultural differentialism emphasizes the fact that cultures are essentially different and are only superficially affected by global flows. The interaction of cultures is deemed to contain the potential for "catastrophic collision." Samuel Huntington's theory of a clash of the civilizations best exemplifies this approach. According to him, after the Cold War, political-economic differences were overshadowed by new fault lines which were primarily cultural in nature. Increasing interaction among different "civilizations" (such as the Sinic, Islamic, Orthodox, Western) would lead to intense clashes, especially economic conflict between the West and Sinic civilization and bloody political conflict between the Western and the Islamic civilizations. This theory has been critiqued for a number of reasons, especially its portrayal of Muslims as being "prone to violence."

The process of globalization, considered as involving the spread of religion (closely related to civilizations), could be said to be more than 2,000 years old. The growth of major world religions such as Islam, Hinduism, Buddhism, Christianity, and Judaism, is examined, as is also the fact they involve global flows as well as the processes through which they adapt to other flows.

The cultural hybridization approach emphasizes the integration of local and global cultures. Therefore, globalization is considered to be a creative process which gives rise to hybrid entities that are not reducible to either the global or the local. A key concept is "glocalization," or the interpenetration of the global and local resulting in unique outcomes in different geographic areas. Another key concept is Arjun Appadurai's "scapes" (global flows involving people, technology, finance, political images, and media) and the disjunctures between them, which lead to the creation of cultural hybrids.

The cultural convergence approach stresses homogeneity introduced by globalization. Cultures are deemed to be radically altered by strong flows. Cultural imperialism, wherein one culture imposes itself and tends to destroy at least parts of another culture, is also analyzed under the heading of this approach. One important critique of cultural imperialism is based on the idea of "deterritorialization" of culture. This means that it is much more difficult to tie culture to a specific geographic point of its origin.

McDonaldization involves the global spread of rational systems, based on the principles of fast-food restaurants, such as efficiency, calculability, predictability, and control. This process is extended to other businesses, sectors, and geographical areas. Grobalization (in contrast to glocalization) is a process wherein nations, corporations, etc. impose themselves on geographic areas in order to gain profits, power, and so on.

Globalization can also be seen as a flow of "nothing" (as opposed to "something"), involving the spread of non-places, non-things, non-people, and non-services. The interplay between these processes (grobalization and glocalization; nothing and something) can be clearly seen in the globalization of sports, a phenomenon that is an important part of culture.

DISCUSSION QUESTIONS

1. Analyze the three main perspectives discussed in this chapter with respect to the deterritorialization of culture.

2. Analyze "clash of the civilizations" as a perspective on globalization. What are the advantages and disadvantages of utilizing a "civilizational" approach?

3. Critique "differentialism" and "convergence," using the concept of "scapes."

4. Make a case for cultural hybridization in the study of religion.

5. Contrast glocalization with grobalization. Examine the relative significance of each to the study of globalization.

ADDITIONAL READINGS

Jan Nederveen Pieterse, *Globalization and Culture: Global Melange*, 2nd edn. Lanham, MD: Rowman and Littlefield, 2009.

Stockhammer, Philipp, ed. *Conceptualizing Cultural Hybridization: A Transdisciplinary Approach*. New York: Springer, 2012.

Frederick F. Wherry. *Global Markets and Local Crafts: Thailand and Costa Rica Compared*. Baltimore: Johns Hopkins University Press, 2008.

Benjamin Barber. *Jihad vs. McWorld*. New York: Times Books, 1995.

Samuel P. Huntington. *The Clash of Civilizations and the Remaking of the World Order*. New York: Simon and Schuster, 2011.

Peter Beyer. *Religions in Global Society*. London: Routledge, 2006.

Peter Beyer. *Religion and Globalization*. London: Sage, 1994.

John Drane. *The McDonaldization of the Church: Consumer Culture and the Church's Future*. Macon, GA: Smyth & Helwys Publishing, 2012.

George Ritzer. *The McDonaldization of Society: 20th Anniversary Edition*. Thousand Oaks, CA: Pine Forge Press, 2013.

George Ritzer. *The Globalization of Nothing*, 2nd edn. Thousand Oaks, CA: Pine Forge Press, 2007.

Chris Rumford and Stephen Wagg, eds. *Cricket and Globalization*. Newcastle upon Tyne, UK: Cambridge Scholars Publishing, 2010.

NOTES

1 Social theorists known as "structuralists" tend to take the view that there are "deep" structures that are largely unaffected by surface changes. Further, they see those deep structures as being of great importance, far more important than that which exists on the surface. Famous examples include Karl Marx, Sigmund Freud, and Claude Lévi-Strauss.

2 See also Barber (1995).

3 Huntington (2011). For at least a partial test of Huntington's (and Fukuyama's) thesis, see Diez-Nicolas (2002).

4 For example, due to a long history of out-migration, the Chinese nation extends not only to "greater China" – the nation-states of China and Taiwan, as well as to Hong Kong – but far beyond it with large numbers of Chinese people found, often in enclaves, in almost all parts of the world. The Chinese state does not govern these people. See Harding (1993).

5 Increased oil wealth in a number of Muslim countries is also important.

6 For a series of articles on this, see *Sociology of Religion* 68, 3 (2007); Gokariksel and Mitchell (2005: 147–65).

7 Although it serves to obscure many things about the global–local relationship including the fact that some processes are simply incompatible; they cannot be combined. More generally, glocalization ignores global–local conflicts.

8 http://unesdoc.unesco.org/images/0012/001271/127160m.pdf.

9 For my part, I am not so sure that they are superficial, but in any case my concern, and that of others, is the global spread of systems, like those of McDonald's and Disney, and *not* their products.

10 See, for example, Giddens (1990).

11 For a critique of this view, see Caldwell and Lozada, Jr (2007).

12 This stands in contrast to a view of ethics in a postmodern age which rejects such a totalizing ethic, see Bauman (1993).

13 This approach is emphasized in Boli and Lechner (2009).

14 In fact, these were also the basic characteristics of Weber's rationalization process.

15 For some evidence against this argument, at least as far as values are concerned, see Esmer (2006).

16 A variety of these other applications are to be found in essays in Ritzer (2006).

17 For another critique of globalization that relies heavily on the concept of nothing, albeit defined much differently, see Nancy (2007).

18 It is hard to make a strong argument for differentialism within the world of sports.

19 The issue is more complex than this because the grobalization of something would lead to greater heterogeneity and the glocalization of nothing would tend toward homogeneity. Thus all four combinations of the grobalization–glocalization and nothing–something conceptualization must be employed in order to understand globalization more fully

HIGH-TECH GLOBAL FLOWS AND STRUCTURES

TECHNOLOGY, MASS MEDIA, AND THE INTERNET

Globalization: A Basic Text, Second Edition. George Ritzer and Paul Dean.
© 2015 John Wiley & Sons, Ltd. Published 2015 by John Wiley & Sons, Ltd.

This chapter deals with three of the most cutting-edge aspects of the social world in general, and globalization in particular. Grouped under the heading of high-tech global flows and structures are technology, the media, and the Internet. While for discussion purposes many technologies (e.g. containerized shipping, universal product codes [UPCs]) are treated separately in this chapter, the media and the Internet are themselves technologies. Further, the Internet encompasses many crucially important new technologies, and the media are being transformed by a variety of new technologies (including the Internet – for example blogs are increasingly supplanting newspapers) that facilitate and direct global flows, and in doing so compress time and space. However, some flows can be threatening to governments and transnational corporations that have constructed a variety of barriers to stop, slow, and monitor certain types of flows. This chapter will further analyze responses to these barriers on the part of civil society, and the technologically mediated struggles involved in shaping the processes of globalization.

TECHNOLOGY, TIME-SPACE COMPRESSION, AND DISTANCIATION

As mentioned in Chapter 2, technological changes of all sorts (many of which have been touched on in previous chapters) have played a huge role in globalization. Such changes have affected global processes for a century, or more, depending on how one conceives of the history of globalization, but they have accelerated in recent years (especially in the global age) creating, or at least expediting, global processes. In particular, global flows have been hastened by **time-space compression** (Harvey 1989). A variety of new transportation and communication technologies, driven mainly by capitalist corporations seeking to expand around the world, have effectively shrunk the power of space and reduced the time required by a wide range of processes (Kivisto 2012).

Time-space compression: the shrinking of space, and the reduction of the time required by a wide range of processes, brought about by changes in transportation and communication technologies advanced mainly by capitalist corporations.

The creation of the world's first container ship in 1956 is one example of a technological development in the realm of commerce that resulted in significant time-space compression. Instead of loading and unloading goods of various sorts individually or in small batches, containers already filled with products are loaded on, and unloaded from, ships. A new era of shipping was born that allowed much more rapid loading and unloading of ships, and the seamless transfer of containers between ships and from ships to trucks or trains. Because of the greater speed, space was compressed in the sense that it took less time to complete a ship's journey and the unloading of its cargo. That new technology cut the cost of transportation of goods dramatically. Of course, container technology has improved further over the years, with the result that time, space, and the costs of shipping have been reduced much further. For example, we now have so-called "monster ships" that can carry 18,000 containers, which is equal to the carrying capacity of more than 20 miles of trucks. As a result of modern containerization: "It often costs more to send a container by road one hundred miles from port to its final destination than it does to ship the container by sea from Shanghai to Rotterdam" (Chanda 2007: 57).

Of course, the development and expansion of air freight greatly speeded up the transportation of goods, reduced distances even more, and in some cases even reduced costs (although it is still cheaper to transport many things – automobiles, for example – by ship). A key technological development here was the introduction in 1970 of the Boeing 747 (now being phased out for newer, smaller and more fuel-efficient planes), with its wide body, and the arrival soon afterward of a cargo version of the plane.

Another important advance also occurred in 1970 with the founding of Federal Express (FedEx). While FedEx was, and is, an innovative organization, the key technological advance associated with it involved the use of computer technology to track deliveries of packages by jet planes and other conveyances. The rest is history as FedEx has become a household name and a visible presence throughout the world. While it delivered a mere 186 packages on its first day (Chanda 2007), the company now delivers more than 3.4 million packages daily. The delivery of packages has been sped up dramatically and as a result great distances are covered more quickly.

Then there is the seemingly modest creation of the Universal Product Code (UPC) which began in grocery stores in the US in June, 1974. "Today, more than five million bar-coded products are scanned and sold all over the world. Sensors housed in store shelves can now read the bar codes on boxes of shoes, shirts, or shampoo, and automatically alert suppliers when stocks run low, allowing replenishments to arrive quickly without the need for costly inventories" (Chanda 2007: 65). This has greatly expedited the movement of products from all over the world to warehouses and ultimately retail outlets across the globe.

From the point of view of globalization, in fact perhaps from any point of view, all of these developments pale in comparison to the creation of the first personal computers in the mid-1970s and then the Internet in the 1990s. (Of course, personal computers and the Internet are now deeply implicated in, and essential to all, of the technological developments mentioned above, as well as most others.) These developments paved the way for global Internet transactions and the coordination of global commodity chains (see Chapter 7). For example, computer networks have enabled global corporations, with headquarters in Germany, to coordinate their production facilities in India and China, in order to fill orders from customers in the United States. Economic flows, therefore, are dramatically faster and distance is much less important than it once was.

In addition to altering time and space in global business, transportation and communication technologies have also compressed the time-space involved in interpersonal relationships in various ways. For example, telecommunications devices (e.g. cell phones, Skype) and social media (e.g. Facebook, Orkut, Habbo, Qzone, and Twitter) have connected people around the world in ways and with a rapidity that were not possible previously. Giddens (1994) sees these connections as brought about by **time-space distanciation**, or the stretching of social relations across time and space. These technologies have decoupled time from space, enabling relationships that do not depend on the co-presence of their participants.

While the concept of time-space distanciation is very similar to Harvey's notion of time-space compression, there are important differences between them. For example, time-space compression does not necessarily mean that we can relate to others who are not co-present. More importantly, Harvey and Giddens see different driving forces behind these new social relations. As a Marxist, Harvey theorizes the implosion of time and space, and the social relations that result from that implosion, as being driven by global capitalism and its corporations (e.g. Facebook, Google). In contrast, Giddens theorizes time-space distanciation as driven by technological change that is independent of capitalist pursuit of profit. In other words, Giddens decouples technological change from capitalism and does not see capitalism as a determining force in that change.

The preceding are just a few of the technological advances that have contributed greatly to the globalization of commerce and of interpersonal relations. Not only are there innumerable other technological advances in these areas that could be mentioned here, but the

> **Time-space distanciation:** the stretching of social relations across space and time brought about by technological change.

globalization of every other realm covered in this volume has been affected, and greatly expedited, by technological change.

However, we should be careful not to exaggerate the technological impacts on global flows. They have not eliminated the role of time and space in how we experience life, but instead, we should view technology as *mediating* time and space (Dyb and Halford 2009; Tsatsou 2009). For example, in the world of global capitalism, global cities like New York and London have become critical hubs for the flows of global finance (see Chapter 13). It is true that the distance between them has been compressed, but many important functions remain anchored in these physical places. In interpersonal relationships, the Internet and social media (e.g. Facebook) may connect people in distant areas of the globe but those people remain situated in their local environments; furthermore, much of social media (e.g. Foursquare) also serves to facilitate and strengthen face-to-face interactions (e.g. through meetups, flash mobs, or even hookups) in nearby locations. In each of these examples, social relations are assisted by high-tech flows that connect various locations without eliminating their importance.

MEDICAL TECHNOLOGIES

New health-care technologies (e.g. MRIs, CAT scans, PET scans, DaVinci robotics) have not only been created at a rapid rate, but because of global improvements in transport, they flow around the world much more rapidly than ever before. These are extraordinarily expensive technologies largely created in the North. The developed countries are able to afford these technologies and they spread throughout the North. This is especially the case for the world leaders, Japan and the United States, which possess an extraordinary number of these technologies relative to the size of their populations. The machines are not only more likely to exist in developed countries, but they are more likely to be used intensively because patients, either on their own or because of health insurance, are able to afford the very expensive scans, tests, and surgeries (e.g. of the prostate with the DaVinci robotic system) associated with them. Furthermore, the wide-scale existence of such expensive machines leads to pressure to use them; it is costly to purchase such machines and they cannot be allowed to remain idle for long periods of time. Also concentrated in developed countries are the highly trained personnel needed to run and maintain the machines, administer the tests, and interpret the results of, say, an MRI. In contrast, few of these technologies flow to less developed, Southern countries, they are used there less intensively, and there are relatively few trained people there capable of conducting the tests and interpreting the results.

These flows have also facilitated the processes of time-space compression and distanciation in the growing field of telemedicine (Frederick 2013). Through the use of new advanced technologies, telemedicine enables health services to be administered across borders and to remote regions within countries. Practitioners can now use medical devices to "measure glucose, blood pressure, international normalized ratio (INR) and numerous other laboratory parameters integrated with question-based algorithms. These devices are able to stream video from the patient's home to a health care provider via the Internet" (Waruingi et al. 2013: 7). For example, in Akwa Ibom State in Nigeria, health services have not kept up with the rapidly expanding population. Patients in Akwa Ibom (at least the patients who have health insurance or can afford to pay the fees) can access medical services remotely by having their CT scans, MRIs, or blood work sent to India for testing and evaluation.

The technologies compress time and space, enabling medical consultation and services to be delivered across great physical distances. In the United States, more than 50% of hospitals now use at least one telemedicine service (Frederick 2013).

The rapid global flows of pharmaceuticals of all types have also expanded medical delivery to various parts of the world. Clearly, the superstars of the pharmaceutical industry – Lipitor and Crestor (high cholesterol), Plavix (heart disease), Nexium (gastrointestinal reflux), Prevacid (heartburn), Advair and Singulair (asthma), Humira (inflammatory diseases), Remicade (arthritis), Abilify and Seroquel (schizophrenia), Cymbalta (depression), Viagra (male impotence) – are global phenomena. In fact, while the US accounts for about one-third of the $956 billion in pharmaceutical sales worldwide, sales in emerging markets are growing more rapidly than US sales.[1] The key point is that as these drugs are approved and come to be seen as efficacious, they are likely to flow around the world, especially to developed countries and to the elites in less developed countries.

Unfortunately, the drugs that are most likely to be produced and distributed globally are those that are considered likely to be most profitable. Those are the drugs that address the health problems and concerns (e.g. hypertension, high cholesterol, arthritis, mental health problems, impotence, hair loss, and so on) of the wealthier members of global society. It is the relatively well-to-do who are most able to afford diets likely to lead to high cholesterol and they are therefore the likely consumers of Lipitor. Similarly, overeating is apt to be associated with wealth and excessive food consumption is associated with acid reflux and heartburn and the use of drugs such as Nexium.

Drugs that might save many lives, but that are not likely to yield great profits because those who need them are mainly the poor in less developed countries, are either never likely to be produced or, if they are, their flow to those parts of the globe is likely to be minimal. Thus, for example, Africa is the home to many diseases (e.g. malaria), some of them killing millions of people each year, but because these are largely poor people in poor countries, the major drug companies (based primarily in the wealthy developed countries) have little interest in doing the research and paying for the start-up and production costs necessary to produce drugs that are not likely to be profitable and may even lose money.

Then there is the case of the cocktail of drugs needed to keep those who suffer from AIDS alive, sometimes indefinitely. A number of these drugs are needed by an AIDS patient and they are very expensive. As a result, wealthy (or, at least well-insured) victims in developed countries have virtually unlimited access to these drugs. However, few of these drugs flow to the less developed parts of the world where AIDS is now spreading most rapidly.[2] Large and rapidly increasing numbers of people in less developed countries are contracting the disease and dying horrible deaths from it, but the high cost of the necessary drugs puts them out of reach for most of those who suffer from AIDS in those countries.

The examples above further illustrate the way that place – and especially wealth – mediate both telemedicine (Dyb and Halford 2009) and the flows of pharmaceuticals brought about by new medical technologies. The pharmaceutical drugs themselves are so "light" that they resemble a weightless gas. Yet the potential profit of these drugs – especially blockbuster drugs like Humira (with worldwide sales exceeding $10 billion in 2013) – leads their manufacturers to closely monitor and limit their flows. Impoverished areas might be skipped over entirely as drugs are transported around and flown over these spaces. The role of wealth remains important for understanding how such technologies move through time and space, and the degree to which social relations are stretched across these spaces (i.e. the extent of time-space distanciation).

SPACE-BASED TECHNOLOGIES

The space that surrounds the globe is, by its very nature, global and already involves, and will increasingly involve, globalization. Although the US has dominated this domain, especially through the launching of satellites, other nations are involved and, more generally affected by, activities in space. In the military realm, space continues to be largely an American realm. For example, it uses its satellites (and commercial satellites) for surveillance of enemies and potential enemies throughout the world (Risen 2012). However, that dominance is being, and will be, contested by others, especially China, and the ultimate fear here on many levels, including from the perspective of globalization, is a war in and over space that could truly devastate every part of the globe.

However, space-based technology is not restricted to military uses. Satellites are used to transmit TV and other images around the world. Of growing importance are the global positioning systems (GPS) that rely on satellites to allow those flying civilian airplanes, as well as millions of automobile drivers, to use global navigational systems (GNS) in order to locate where they are and how they should get to where they intend to go (Bovet 2007). There are now many varieties of inexpensive and portable GNS devices embedded in smart phones or installed in automobiles that can be used for other purposes such as providing guidance for those who wish to go off trekking or mountain-climbing. Smaller and cheaper "microsatellites" are also poised to bring new commercial applications, such as insurance companies taking before and after pictures of natural disasters or commodity traders monitoring crop yields (Eisenberg 2013).

There are several other non-military examples of developments that seek to compress time and space between people and outer-space. For example, the Virgin Galactic is scheduled to be the first ever space tourism venture (Chang 2013). The project has recruited more than 500 wealthy travelers to travel to space at the price of $250,000 per ticket. Finally, Google has sponsored the Google Lunar X Prize, which will be awarded to the first private team that can launch a robotic spacecraft to the moon and travel its surface to send back images. Teams from around the world are competing to improve our access to the moon. As Harvey argued in his theory of time-space compression, these efforts are largely driven by capitalist firms.

LEAPFROGGING

The popular image of technological change, as it relates to globalization, is that such advances flow around the world gradually and systematically; they compress time and space slowly and systematically. While this does occur in many cases and in many places (especially in the North), it is also the case that global technological changes can occur erratically and irregularly; the flows can be sporadic. And, of course, one of the reasons for that is the fact that barriers to such flows exist in many parts of the world, especially in the South. For example, the lack of electricity in many parts of the world serves to exclude many new technologies.

Instead of flowing smoothly around the world, technological advances (e.g. the medical technologies discussed above) often "hop" over some areas while "landing" in others. Similarly, some geographic areas are able to skip over some technological advances and go straight to later developments.

Leapfrogging mainly involves developing nations bypassing earlier technologies enabling them to adopt more advanced technologies. For example, some developing countries have gone straight to solar energy or energy from biomass rather than building huge,

Leapfrogging: Developing nations bypassing earlier technologies and adopting more advanced technologies.

centralized systems (e.g. enormous and very expensive power plants operating on the basis of coal, oil, or nuclear energy) for the transmission of power.

An example of leapfrogging can be found in Al-'Arakeeb, a Bedouin village in southern Israel (Schejter and Tirosh 2012). The Israeli–Bedouin people have a unique ethno-regional identity, but they have long been treated as second-class citizens (Marx 2008). Many of the Bedouin live in makeshift villages in a "restricted area," where their villages are considered "unrecognized" by the Israeli government. While the Bedouin are citizens of Israel, their villages are not connected to the national networks of water, electricity, or telecommunications. Not only has this lack of basic infrastructure resulted in poor living conditions, it has made them vulnerable to the unilateral demands of the Israeli government.

In 1951, three years after Israeli independence, the Bedouin living in Al-'Arakeeb were relocated from their ancestral lands. According to residents, the military promised residents that they could return to their lands after six months, but the villagers were never officially resettled there. After several decades, the villagers began returning to Al-'Arakeeb in the 1990s without authorization from the Israeli government. The village grew to 300 residents, and became a target of the Israeli government. In July 2010, the Israeli army and police brought in bulldozers and leveled the entire village in almost one day.

As a marginalized people disconnected from electricity and telecommunications networks, the Bedouin had few traditional means to fight the demolition. But unlike many other Bedouin communities engaged in land conflicts in the Negev, the people of Al-'Arakeeb were able to gain limited exposure in the Israeli and international media through leapfrogging. Using generators to power laptops or mobile phones, tech-savvy residents began organizing themselves through social media and reaching out to journalists. One high school student started a page called "We are all Al-'Arakeeb," where he posted pictures and videos of what was taking place in the village. They sent pictures via mobile phones to journalists, and began using Twitter to connect with foreign journalists, diplomats, and supporting foundations. As a result, their situation has been featured in stories on CNN and the BBC, and in the *New York Times* and the *Guardian*, among others. Through leapfrogging, mobile communication technologies "have helped marginalized communities [like the Bedouin] acquire a voice" (Schejter and Tirosh 2012: 304). Leapfrogging has integrated them into civil society:

> As this case study demonstrates, mobile and wireless technologies have enabled the rewriting of the rules to a certain extent. They have allowed 'Arakeebians to overcome the concerted effort to marginalize them and take part – limited as it may be – in civic society. Batteries and generators brought electricity … cellular technology, satellite television, and mobile Internet made "unrecognized" Al-'Arakeeb a member of the international community. (Schejter and Tirosh 2012: 312)

Bypassing twentieth century fixed-line phone systems and going directly to twenty-first century mobile phone technology is one of the most common examples of leapfrogging in the developing world. For example, in Bangladesh there are barely more than one million land-line phone connections in a nation of 155 million people. However, there are already 100 million cell-phone users (Telecompaper 2013).

Globally, there are over 7 billion people and 6 billion mobile phone subscriptions, but about 1 billion people – mostly in Africa and Asia – do not yet have access to cell phones. Bringing more cell phones (and many other technologies) to these areas would have an enormous impact on people's lives. It would also have a significant global impact, especially on the world economy and global social relationships. And many of those without cell phones understand this since as soon as they have a modest increase in income, they invest in telecommunications technologies, especially the cell phone. This technology can increase their well-being (e.g. by enabling them to get help in case of emergency) and their productivity.

However, as promising as leapfrogging may be to developing countries, most technologies that spread in this way do *not* spread very widely throughout developing countries or do not have comparable capabilities (Napoli and Obar 2013). This is the case because of a lack of basic twentieth-century infrastructure in these countries such as roads, railroads, schools, electrical grids, water pipelines, and sewerage systems (*Economist* 2008: February 7 ["Of Internet Cafes and Power Cuts"]). While many developing countries have leapfrogged over PC-based Internet access to mobile-based cellular Internet access, they often lack 3G networks, which limits their ability to harness mobile Internet access; in other words, technological infrastructures are not functionally equivalent and partially reproduce the global digital divide. While leapfrogging may be useful to some in developing countries, more fundamental changes in infrastructure are needed in order to make most new technologies truly available to the bulk of the population.

In addition to a lack of infrastructure, other barriers to the spread of advanced technology in less developed countries are widespread illiteracy, a lack of research and development capacity, a lack of strong systems to finance development, insufficient training in informational literacy, and the absence of strong and stable governments. In terms of the latter, twenty-first-century rioting and warfare in Kenya, Chad, Somalia, and elsewhere created all sorts of problems, including not only serving as barriers to technological development, but perhaps setting such development back years, if not decades. Not only do they prevent new developments, but they also serve to adversely affect such existing infrastructure as roads, railroads and railroad tracks, shipping facilities, and airports. All of these tend to deteriorate as a direct result of hostilities or more indirectly because of neglect. Money and attention are devoted to conflict rather than to the care and maintenance, let alone advancement, of infrastructure. This all shows that global flows of technology, or the time-space compression and distanciation that result from them, do not occur evenly.

MASS MEDIA

The term "mass media" refers to media intended to reach large audiences, and includes traditional media such as newspaper, radio, television, and film. These forms of media (as well as the newer social media discussed later in the chapter) facilitate time-space compression and distanciation. Beginning with the printing revolution in early modern Europe, books and other printed materials stretched social relations across time and space in fundamentally new ways (Warf 2008). Advances in printing technology made this media much cheaper and easier to produce. For the first time, ordinary citizens had access to stories and descriptions of faraway places and historical knowledge. Newspapers began appearing in the late 1700s, and by 1850, daily papers were available throughout much of Europe. Through the dissemination of knowledge, people began developing a heightened consciousness of other parts of the world that facilitated communication across vast distances.

With the advent of radio, time and space became further compressed through instantaneous communication on radio waves. Media messages were no longer reliant on having to be put into a physical form, and thus not constrained by paper, ink, or other objects on which the message is encoded. Like Franklin D. Roosevelt's famous "fireside chats" in the 1930s and 1940s, politicians could now enter the homes of millions of voters. Corporate advertisers made direct appeals to consumers. In short, radio stretched these political and economic relationships beyond the corridors of government buildings or store shelves. Like printed media, radio continued to remove the need for a person to be physically present to experience social life.

Television and film went a step further by using video to "stimulate co-presence between television performers and their absent audiences" (Moores 1995: 329). Through a television set, social relations were dis-embedded from their physical context and re-embedded immediately across vast stretches of space. This form of mass communication is still largely one-way (rather than the multidirectional interactions enabled by social media), but television continued to simulate a fuller social experience without constraints of time and space.

In returning to the metaphors used in this book, mass media messages strongly resemble liquids and – even more so – gases. Early daily newspapers flowed like liquid throughout much of Europe and later to all reaches of the globe. With radio, television, and films, they more closely resembled gases. Communicated via invisible radio waves, satellite transmissions, or more recently digital cable, media messages move seamlessly around the world. Of course, this does not mean that such flows are even or have been experienced in the same ways. The following sections will illustrate some of the ways in which these relationships are stretched and compressed to benefit particular powerful groups, and have sparked their own forms of resistance. We will further see how at least some of these media flows are motivated by capitalist pursuits, which Harvey (1989) theorized as the primary force to compress time and space.

MEDIA IMPERIALISM

Media imperialism is a sub-category under the broader heading of cultural imperialism (see Chapter 8). The conventional view for quite some time was that it was the Western (especially US) media, and the technologies associated with it, that was imperialistic and that dominated less developed nations and their cultures (Rhomberg 2012a). Thus, it was television programs created in the US, movies from Hollywood (Cowen 2002), books by American authors and published originally in the US, US media conglomerates such as Fox and Time Warner, and so on, that were seen as imposing themselves on less developed nations and playing a key role not only in their media, but in shaping their culture. For example, the idea that American movies have dominated not only less developed nations, but much of the world as a whole, is supported in *Global Hollywood 2*: "Los Angeles–New York culture and commerce dominate screen entertainment around the globe, either directly or as an implied other, and the dramatic success of US film since the First World War has been a model for its export of music, television, advertising, the Internet and sport" (Miller et al. 2005: 9).

While still a powerful view, other views have emerged on this issue that indicate that Western, especially the American, media are not as powerful as they once were or had been thought (Sparks 2007). First, alternative global media giants have arisen to compete with those emanating from the West (Morley and Robins 2013). One example is the Arabic Al Jazeera which began operations in 1996 and is based in Qatar. It is a global source of news (Bielsa 2008), designed to compete with CNN and the BBC. Al Jazeera has even focused its attention on the US and expanded its operation there in 2013 (Stelter 2013). Other examples are Bollywood, India's answer to Hollywood and the source of large numbers of movies that are distributed throughout much of the world (Rizvi 2012), and more recently Nollywood, which is the budding film industry of Nigeria (Krings and Okome 2013).

Then there are the local and regional media which have always been important and, in many ways, their power has grown in recent years. Another factor is the expansion of the Internet as a source of highly diverse media of all sorts. Finally, the global distribution of, say, an American movie or television program does not mean that it is going to be viewed and understood everywhere in the same way that its creators intend or interpreted in the same way as it is by an American audience. The idea that media products are interpreted differently by different audiences throughout the world is in line with the widely accepted contemporary view, most associated with postmodern social theorists, that media products are simply "texts" and what is of greatest importance is not what authors "intend," but rather the interpretations of the "readers" and "viewers." People are not passive recipients of the media, but actively construct their products. Thus, the emphasis on the power of the person/ reader/viewer serves to undermine the whole idea of media imperialism.

Much has been written about this in the past in terms, for example, of the way in which non-American viewers interpreted popular TV programs such as *Dallas* (Ang 1985). However, we need to think about this more in terms of contemporary TV offerings such as the wildly popular *24* (which returned to network TV in mid-2014 after a hiatus of several years). To most viewers in the US this was seen as an inspiring vision of how the nation can respond, often quite ruthlessly, to new global threats that emerged after 9/11. Some American viewers were concerned about the negative images offered of their supposed adversaries, especially Muslims, but such a reaction was likely much more extreme among Muslim viewers in the US, as well as in other parts of the world. Less extremely, many viewers in Europe were likely to read this program as a celebration of American individualism, aggressiveness, and its over-willingness to take dangerous and reckless actions that further endanger, rather than improve, the chances of world peace. The meaning of *24*, like that of every other cultural product, is in the eyes of the beholder and the culture in which the beholder exists profoundly shapes that interpretation.

For another example, consider AMC's *Breaking Bad*. American audiences saw the main character, a high school chemistry teacher, Walter White, diagnosed with lung cancer, in a largely positive light. He struggled to secure adequate medical care, and in fearing death, he sought to leave his family financially secure. White ultimately turned to cooking and selling methamphetamine to help out his family, but struggled to keep the family together. Many critics contended that somehow American viewers found his character so compelling because they could all relate to him in some way (for example, a father and husband trying to provide for his family) (St. John 2013). While *Breaking Bad* became one of the most popular shows in the US (with nearly 3 million viewers for the series finale in late 2013), with some claiming it as "the best show ever,"[3] the show failed to catch on in many countries around the world. For example, in the UK, seasons one and two had so few viewers that no broadcaster aired another season. One commentator noted that for people "who have relied for decades on the National Health Service – where money never changes hands for medical care – the thought of someone turning to crime in order to pay for cancer treatment is more far-fetched than a body-switching time lord" (Thomas 2012). In other words, they may have rejected the premise of the show and found it much more difficult to relate to the charismatic protagonist. Just like the series *24* and other cultural products, how audiences interpret *Breaking Bad* varies across culture.

"MEDIA WERE AMERICAN"

In 1977 Jeremy Tunstall authored a book entitled *The Media Are American.* Over two decades later he published *The Media Were American: US Mass Media in Decline* (2008). The timing of the publications, and the nature of their titles, tell us much of what we need to know about the role of American mass media in an increasingly globalized world. Tunstall's basic point in the most recent book is that the global influence of the American media peaked in the mid-twentieth century and has been in decline ever since. It is not American media, nor media from any other country, that dominates the world. Rather, national media have not only survived, but are increasingly important (they are dominant in countries which include the overwhelming majority of the world's population). The largest countries in the world are now either media self-sufficient, or have a rough balance of imports and indigenous media. That leaves a large number of countries (about 150), with a relatively small total population, that are largely dependent on media imports. Overall, outside the US about 10% of world media time is devoted to US media, about 10% to other media imports (largely from the immediate region, continent, subcontinent or language area), and about 80% to domestic and national media.

A variety of other findings point to the fact that no media dominate the world. While Euro-American media are the world leaders, people in fact spend more time with their national media than with any such imports. CNN is indeed global but it is largely watched by Americans abroad; few locals anywhere in the world watch CNN, at least on a regular basis. In Brazil (and elsewhere) it is telenovelas that are predominant and they are produced by a large Brazilian company, Globo. There are regional media pecking orders with, for example, Mexico the leader in Latin America. China is a growing media power in East Asia in general, especially in Taiwan, Hong Kong, Singapore, and Malaysia (Yang 1996).

NEW GLOBAL MEDIA

In spite of the arguments against media imperialism, the fact is that we have witnessed the rise of the "new" global media (e.g. Apple's iTunes, Facebook, Twitter, Google, Microsoft, YouTube, Tumblr) with great power to impose their systems on large portions of the world (Alexander and Aouragh 2014; McChesney 1999). While the major players change over time, especially through mergers of various types, the global media (this applies to traditional media such as newspapers, TV, movies, as well as to the newly emerging media on, or related to, the Internet) are increasingly dominated by a relatively small number of huge corporations. In virtually all sectors the goal is to produce a relatively noncompetitive global environment in order to maximize profits. This process is fairly well advanced in the "old media" and it is ongoing in the case of the "new media." There, competition continues, but largely because the process is so new and the dust has yet to settle. Thus, for example, while Facebook succeeded in overwhelming a number of early competitors (e.g. Friendster and MySpace) for the position of the dominant social networking site, it continues to compete with the possibility of new competitors arising in this relatively new arena. Furthermore, giants in the industry such as Newscorp, Microsoft, Google, and Yahoo are either seeking to create their own versions of successful new media (including Google+ which was designed to compete with Facebook), especially on the Internet. They are also seeking to either buy into, or gain control over, already successful websites (for example, Google bought YouTube in 2006, and attempted to purchase Yahoo in 2011; Yahoo bought Tumblr in 2013), as well as those that show signs of being successful. While control over the new Internet media is far from clear or resolved, it seems clear that in the long-run they, too, will succumb to becoming an increasingly less competitive world.

INDYMEDIA

The movement in the direction of global media giants is countered, at least to some degree, by the rise of independent media ("Indymedia") as another source of media diversity that serves to counter media imperialism (Pickard 2012). Indymedia have come to be associated with globalization, especially the alter-globalization movement (see Chapter 15). The first independent media center associated with the alter-globalization movement was created at the first big protest against globalization at the Seattle meetings of the WTO in late 1999: "Indymedia journalists reported directly from the streets, while activists uploaded their own text, audio, video, and image files" (Juris 2005). Such centers soon sprang up throughout the US and later throughout the world. Indymedia have always been committed to participatory decision-making, horizontal organizing, global justice, inclusiveness, openness, and transparency. They play a particularly important role during protests, actions, and gatherings through e-mails, formal updates, and the virtually immediate upload and dissemination of videos and images, including live video and audio streaming. Expertise on such matters is now widespread and Indymedia are not dependent on professionals in the media. They often cover stories ignored by the mainstream media. Indymedia are also involved in disseminating information and technologies so that activists throughout the world can become involved.

Also worth mentioning here as a threat to the aspirations of the global media are "hacktivists" – those who hack into computer programs in order to further various causes, in this case the alter-globalization movement.

However, the future of Indymedia remains unclear. As noted by Pickard (2012), "as a kind of community news blog, much of what marked Indymedia as innovative no longer seems revolutionary given the proliferation of blogs, social media, and user-generated content." Many Indymedia centers have shut down or significantly lost membership to more recent social media outlets, including the giants discussed above. Nonetheless, Indymedia served as one of the early, large-scale efforts at Internet activism, built on democratic organizing principles, and functioning as an open-publishing global network.

THINKING ABOUT THE GLOBAL MEDIA

Much of current thinking on the media in general, and especially on the relationship between globalization and the media, has its roots in Marshall McLuhan's prescient ideas on the "global village" (McLuhan and Fiore 2005). McLuhan focused on the medium itself (although Herbert Marcuse [2006] argued that the problem was not technologies such as the media, but rather the way they were employed in capitalism). In the new media age, McLuhan famously argued, the "medium is the message." That is, it is the medium (e.g. television) that is most important, not necessarily the content (e.g. a particular television program) presented on and via the medium. This led to a new sense of the power of the media to shape individual subjectivity and culture, not only locally but globally. As important as his insights were, McLuhan failed to link the global proliferation of the media to their origins in large-scale social structures and social institutions.

Guy DeBord (1967/1994) is a French social theorist known for his work on spectacle, media spectacle, the globalization of such a spectacle, and the ability of spectacle to produce and reproduce capitalism and consumer culture on a global scale. Over the years, media spectacles have grown ever-grander and they can be flashed around the world with blinding speed. The increasing sophistication and ubiquity of media spectacles makes it increasingly difficult to distinguish the concrete referent from the spectacle. Of course, as the media have grown more powerful, their role in the globalization of spectacle has increased dramatically.

This is perhaps best exemplified by the emergence of TV news as entertainment. The focus is on the spectacular visual rather than on what are the most important news events of the day. If an event has no significant visual associated with it, it is likely to get little or no TV time. On the other hand, news with little or no importance to most people (e.g. a crane collapse in New York City) gets lots of TV attention because effective, even powerful, visuals are associated with it. Of course, the most important spectacles are those associated with events that are *both* very important and that offer powerful visuals. Perhaps the ultimate example of this is the terrorist attacks of 9/11 and the sight, shown endlessly on television, of the collapse of the twin towers. Similar visuals and spectacle were associated with the bombing of the London underground (7/7/05), the subway in Madrid (3/11/04), and the Boston Marathon (4/13/13) – as well as violent clashes between Turkey's government and protestors in 2013.

This focus on media spectacles tends to emphasize the global power of the media, but other perspectives (Rojek 2003) have focused on the importance of marginal voices and counter-hegemonic narratives rather than the global media. From a global point of view, this means that it is not just the hegemonic messages from the media giants that circulate throughout the world, but so do counter-hegemonic messages from the margins. For example, through the use of cell phones and social media (e.g. Twitter) in the less developed world, such messages can be transmitted rapidly to large numbers of people. From this perspective, a world of differences can now circulate globally and serve as a counterweight to the global power of the media. Since the mass media tend to produce and/or to disseminate hegemonic discourses, it is those on the margin who are the major source of counter-hegemonic discourse throughout the world, such as the dissent in the Arab Spring that began in December 2010.

While this is an optimistic perspective, a more pessimistic view is presented in various circles, including in a variety of neo-Marxian theories, especially those associated with what is known as the Frankfurt School (Wiggershaus 1994). The theorists associated with that school of thought tended to shift the traditional focus of Marxian analysis away from the economy, and to the culture, of which the media are a significant component. To the Frankfurt theorists, the media were of economic significance as a new source of capital realization, but of far greater importance was their role in the social control of people and their unprecedented ability to influence and shape the larger culture. Instead of leading to counterhegemonic discourses, the Frankfurt thinkers tended to see the media, and other components of what they called the "culture industry," as foreclosing the possibility of emancipatory discourse and action.[4]

The view of the Frankfurt School has tended to win out over the more optimistic view. As a result, the emphasis tends to be on the effect of the global media rather than the counter-reactions of people to it and its messages. Global media culture is seen as overwhelmingly linked to both MNCs and to globalization from above rather than globalization from below (Kellner and Pierce 2007). Not only are the global media heavily influenced by MNCs, but they often are MNCs themselves. As a form of globalization from above, that which emanates from the global media is largely controlled by the MNCs. These global media giants are, in the main, largely unregulated and they tend to produce largely homogeneous products (e.g. newscasts, entertainment programming). Since they are global in nature, they are usually beyond the control of any single nation-state. In fact, the nation-state is often reduced to the role of distributing cultural forms and commodities for the media conglomerates. While there are globally known examples of powerful media conglomerates (CNN, Fox) based in the US, there are many others including Brazil's Globo and Mexico's Televisa. They are all examples of globalization from above in that they extend media and consumer culture into diverse communities, serve to blur national boundaries, and they have at least the potential not only to supplement, but replace, local culture.

Despite the global reach and power of media conglomerates, one finds the global-local (or better grobal-glocal; see Chapter 8) struggle in this realm as indigenous viewers work to counter, or at least redefine, global messages. There is even the (remote) possibility that the indigenous – especially when a number of indigenous movements, perhaps across the globe, band together – can triumph over the global (globalization from below). In the more traditional media there is EZLN's Radio Insurgente associated with the Zapatista Movement. In fact, new media, especially those associated with the Internet (e.g. blogs), make such opposition more likely and powerful. The role of the Internet and social media in facilitating these forms of resistance, including the so-called "Twitter Revolution," will be discussed more below.

However, some of these media activities from below are themselves spectacles (e.g. the Live 8 concerts involving U2's Bono) and this raises the point that they may well serve more to further than to counter the development of the society of the spectacle discussed by DeBord. Clearly, a far more radical step would be a restructuring of the media and using it in other less – or even non- – spectacular ways.

Mentioned above are media spectacles associated with various terrorist attacks, but others include those associated with the invasion of Iraq in 2003, the subsequent toppling of the statue of Saddam Hussein in Baghdad, and George W. Bush's appearance on an aircraft carrier announcing (prematurely) the end of hostilities in Iraq ("mission accomplished"). However, these spectacles can cut both ways. They can serve not only to control people (e.g. leading them to believe that the war in Iraq was over), but also to energize them (e.g. Al-Jazeera's use of many of the same spectacles to help create opposition to the Iraq war and to the US more generally), and to make the contradictions that exist within them abundantly clear (as was the case when the televising of accelerating hostilities in Iraq made it clear that Bush's pronouncements about the end of the war were simply untrue). Similarly, the contradiction between the American claim to the moral high ground and reality was made clear when photos taken by American soldiers of the abuses at the Abu Ghraib prison escaped the filters of the mainstream media and made their way via the Internet directly into people's homes throughout the world. Overall, some see the development of such alternate media sources as a positive development. Indeed, they argue that these represent signs that a shift away from the control of the media conglomerates, a democratization of the global media, is underway (Kellner and Pierce 2007: 383–95).

THE INTERNET AND SOCIAL MEDIA

The Internet is one of several digital technologies that have all had a profound effect on many things, including globalization. Digital technologies store and transmit data based on the binary (or dichotomous) coding of data. (This is in contrast to analog which involves the continuous coding of data). Other digital technologies include the computer, chips, semiconductor processors, DVDs, wireless routers, digital projectors, tablets, 3-D printers, and various wearable technologies (e.g. Google Glass).

Since its birth in the 1990s, the Internet has profoundly affected almost every aspect of life, especially in the developed world. In the case of globalization, the Internet has expedited the globalization of many different things and is itself a profound form and aspect of globalization. The Internet is global in several senses, but the most important is that while its users are not equally divided between the North and South, rich and poor, etc., they do exist virtually everywhere in the world (Drori 2006). Like the mass media described above, it stretches relations across space and time in various social, economic, and political domains. People can engage in all kinds of activities and interactions in real time and across tremendous physical distances. But unlike the mass media, the Internet better facilitates interactivity – especially through social media.

The Internet is also global in the sense that it was produced and is maintained by a number of global and transnational corporations and organizations including multinational corporations (e.g. Intel, Cisco), and IGOs and INGOs (e.g. World Intellectual Property Organization [WIPO] which regulates intellectual property rights, Internet Corporation for Assigned Names and Numbers [ICANN] which coordinates domain names, and United Nations Education, Science, and Culture Organization [UNESCO] which promotes computer and Internet use in schools) throughout the world. Thus, the compression of time and space through the Internet has been driven, at least in part, by capitalist corporations.

ONLINE SOCIAL NETWORKING

Involved here are social networking sites (SNSs) such as Facebook (with over 1.25 billion registered users as of this writing) and Google+ that involve communication, networking, and the creation of friendship networks among those involved (Boyd and Ellison 2007; Zhang and Leung forthcoming). They are part of social media which also includes Wikipedia, the blogosphere, podcasts, and many others. What defines social media is the fact that the material on it is generated by the users (consumers) rather than the producers of the system. Thus, those who operate on social media can be called **prosumers** because they engage in the interrelated process of production and consumption such as is the case with interaction on Facebook and the entries on Wikipedia (Ritzer 2014; Ritzer and Jurgenson 2010; Ritzer, Dean, and Jurgenson 2012).

Prosumers: Those who engage in the interrelated process of production and consumption.

Given the character of the Internet, all of these sites are global in nature. That is, assuming one is on the "right side" of the "digital divide" (see Chapter 13), wherever one is in the world, one will be able to "prosume" on these sites. Further, while Facebook, Twitter, Tumblr, LinkedIn, Pinterest, and Google+ are some of the most popular SNSs in the US, Canada, and Australia, there are many other such sites throughout the world. Some popular sites include Weibo, a microblogging site in China (600 million users); Orkut, which was popular in India and Brazil although its users are rapidly declining; hi5, which is popular in Nepal, Mongolia, Thailand, Romania, and several countries around the world; Odnoklassniki, especially popular in Russia; and Skyrock, popular in France.

It is the global nature of many SNSs, and the ability of people throughout (much of) the world to participate in these sites, that make them a truly global phenomenon. Because of the speed by which social networking sites have grown and permeated so many aspects of our lives, it is easy to take their consequences for granted. Above all, this form of media best reflects two of the orienting concepts for this chapter. For example, social networking sites illustrate the process of time-space compression in which users from literally anywhere with an Internet connection can chat and participate in groups in real time. Most of the platforms themselves are also driven by global corporations that are seeking to enlist as many free users as possible in the hope that they can later translate these massive networks into profit. Similarly, we observe time-space distanciation in the stretching of social community and relationships across enormous areas and through which people relate to one another in meaningful ways. Through the exchange of videos and pictures (including the emergence of the "selfie") and commenting on profiles and uploaded content, prosumers can develop intimate bonds online. They bridge both online and offline networks, often reinforcing local networks with deeper connections. These forms of social media far exceed earlier technologies, such as e-mail, forums, and chat rooms, in their ability to coordinate online events and relationships.

Social networking sites have also shaped how individuals manage their identity in a global world (Cunningham 2012). Through online profiles and status updates, individuals seek to manage how they represent themselves to the world and influence the impressions that others have of them. The motivations of these online personas range from performing for friends or intimate partners (e.g. on Facebook or Instagram), and sharing interests with one's followers (e.g. on Weibo or Twitter), to crafting one's professional persona (e.g. on LinkedIn). Users can experiment with new identities, including new forms of gender, sexuality, or politics, in constructing how they are portrayed to both local and distant relations (Leung 2011). Of course, as prosumers post so much personal information about themselves online, this raises concerns over privacy, especially given the levels of corporate and government surveillance documented in the sections below. Finally, social networking sites are likely to become increasingly important in the future, if for no other reason than the fact that it is young people who are the ones who are most involved in them. Relatively speaking, social networking sites and social media more generally are in their early stages and promise even greater advances as the Internet reaches more parts of the world and social media continues to be integrated with more and more other technologies.

SPAM AND COMPUTER VIRUSES

The Internet has given rise to many types of flows, some of which can be harmful to society, or at the very least, annoying. Among these negative flows are spam and computer viruses. Spam is unsolicited bulk e-mail, often of a commercial nature (e.g. offers of products to enhance sexual performance), and while it is a bane to the World Wide Web, it stems from virtually everywhere on the globe (especially Eastern Europe, Russia, China, and Nigeria), goes everywhere, and until very recently, has been difficult to contain. It is one of the *flows* that are a defining feature of globalization. Virtually as soon as methods are devised to stop the influx of spam, spammers find ways to get around those defenses. Programs are widely for sale on the Internet that allow anyone from anywhere to get into the spam "business."

And, one needs virtually no computer expertise in order to become a contributor to the increasing avalanche of spam around the world. As of 2012, spam comprised approximately 72% of all e-mails, suggesting the entire system is being shaken because of the mass of useless and sometimes offensive messages that one must wade through in order to get to legitimate messages. However, spam decreased steadily throughout 2012 and hit a five-year low. Because of better spam protection in e-mail systems and the improvement in software security engineering, spam may be a "dying business" (Rapoza 2013).

The idea of a computer virus made its first appearance in science fiction in the late 1960s and early 1970s. Over a decade later a graduate student wrote the first program that was able to replicate and propagate itself. His professor, seeing its similarity to a biological phenomenon, suggested it be called a "computer virus." The first global computer virus was likely created in Pakistan in 1986. Since then, of course, many different viruses (and worms), some benign, some malicious ("malware"), have been created, circled the globe, and in some cases caused great damage to computers and computer systems. Some of these viruses (e.g. CodeRed, MyDoom, Stuxnet, Conficker, Heartbleed; for a global mapping of the spread of the CodeRed virus, see Figure 9.1), unbeknown to computer owners and/or users, "infect" computers and can be used illegally to access personal information. For example,

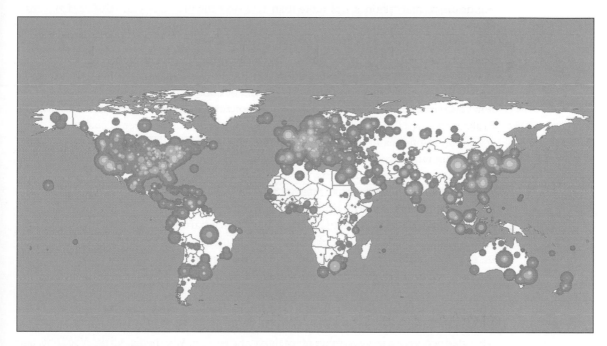

Figure 9.1 Spread of computer virus. This map shows the spread of the CodeRed worm on July 19, 2001, which disproportionately affected small businesses and home users. Some 360,000 computers were infected, spreading in early (light gray), middle (mid-gray), and late (dark gray) zones. Clearly, not all software programs are benign. Programs designed to intentionally disrupt, damage, or interfere with computer functions, files, and data are commonly referred to as computer viruses. Much like human-spread viruses, they range in complexity, severity, and speed of transmission. One particularly fast-spreading type of virus is called worms. They spread themselves automatically by controlling other software programs such as e-mail. Source: de Blij, Harm J., and Roger Downs. 2007. *College Atlas of the World*. Washington, DC: National Geographic Society, p. 61.

they can be used to gain access to credit card numbers and then those numbers can be used to charge all sorts of goods and services illegally. A new sort of virus, known as "ransomware" emerged in 2013. The rapidly spreading CryptoLocker virus worked by encrypting files on a user's hard drive, then demanding a $300 ransom to obtain the decryption key. It effectively made it impossible to access files on one's computer, making the computer useless without the decryption key. It is estimated that its creators received as much as $30 million from paid ransoms in its first 100 days (Matthews 2013).

At the same time, global organizations, including law enforcement agencies (e.g. Department of Homeland Security), have emerged to try to warn people about new viruses and to develop counter-measures to protect against them (Subramanian 2012). To the degree that these organizations are successful, they are barriers to the largely free flow of computer viruses around the globe. But these agencies can also be the creators of computer viruses. See Chapter 12 for a description of how the NSA and Israeli military created the Stuxnet worm and used it to attack Iran's nuclear program in an act of cyberwarfare.

THE INTERNET IN CHINA

As of early 2014 there were 618 million Internet users in China, an increase – aided by the explosion in smart phones – of more than 10% over the previous year (BBC 2013). China already has more than twice the number of Internet users than the second-highest country (the US). Since only 45% of China's population currently uses the Internet, China will become the world leader in Internet use by an increasingly wide margin.

What is most interesting about the Internet in China today from the perspective of this book is how well it illustrates the basic argument about the relationship between global flows and structural barriers to those flows. Among the major flows through the Internet in China are pirated films, music, and TV shows that can be watched free of charge; the delivery to smart phones of mobile-Internet content (e.g. music); online multiplayer games; online communities with social networking and instant messaging; gossip, photos, videos of American and European sports, etc.

On the surface it seems that Internet flows in China are not much different from the flows elsewhere in the world. However, what *is* different are the active efforts by the Chinese government[5] to erect barriers to that flow. In fact, that barrier – known to foreigners as the "Great Firewall" – exists, although many Chinese Internet users are completely oblivious to its existence. (Iran, North Korea, Myanmar, and Saudi Arabia also block at least some Internet traffic, although cyberactivists there are increasingly rebelling against such restrictions and finding ways around them [Powell 2012b].) This is part of a larger effort by the Chinese government to block various flows including the censoring of news, control over television, and limits on bookshops and movie theaters. Barriers on the Internet include restricted access to a large number of foreign websites (e.g. Wikipedia, Flickr, YouTube, and Facebook). There are filters on China's main search engine, Baidu, designed to keep out material regarded by the government as politically sensitive (Google has faced a list of challenges in trying to operate in China). For example, Chinese Internet users are not permitted to access content about the Tiananmen Square protests of 1989, freedom of speech, human rights organizations, Tibet's struggle for independence, or any news that the government considers a threat to social stability or the ruling party.

The Chinese government deploys a number of strategies to police this content. For example, Sina Weibo (or simply "Weibo," similar to a hybrid of Facebook and Twitter) is China's main micro-blogging platform and one of the country's most popular sites. Chinese officials work swiftly to censor content posted on Weibo. A study of censored posts on Weibo found that "nearly 30% of the total [controversial posts that are deleted] occur within 5–30 minutes. Nearly 90% of the deletions happen within the first 24 hours" (Zhu et al. 2013). China has also increased penalties for posting controversial content online. For example, "people who post defamatory rumors online could face three years in jail if those comments are popular enough to attract more than 5,000 readers or more than 500 re-posters. Online commenters will also be in danger if the allegedly defamed person commits suicide, hurts him or herself, or suffers from mental disorders" (Einhorn 2013). Considering all of China's Internet censorship, experts estimate approximately 100,000 people are employed by the state and private companies to police the Internet (*Economist* 2013: April 21).

Overall, there are many flows into and through China on the Internet, but much else is limited or blocked altogether. The result, at least at the moment, is a fairly unique Internet world in China (for example it has its own online communities). However, the long-run question here, and in much else that relates to China in an increasingly global world, is how long these differences will remain? That is, how long can China buck the tide of global flows and erect barriers that few if any other countries in the world erect?

In fact, there are already early signs of rebellion against the Great Firewall, although of course the history of China, especially in the crushing of the Tiananmen Square revolt, shows that the government could destroy that rebellion in its infancy. The resistance is currently taking many forms, from lawsuits by Internet users against government-owned service providers claiming that blocking sites is illegal, to a growing network of software writers who develop code aimed at overcoming government restrictions. An Internet-based word-of-mouth campaign has taken shape, in which bloggers and webpage owners post articles to spread awareness of the Great Firewall, or share links to programs that will help Internet users evade it (French 2008: A6). They also use nicknames and code words to spread information on Weibo and other sites to stay ahead of the censors. Working transnationally, many human rights organizations (e.g. Chinese Human Rights Defenders) also work with dissidents to promote human rights and greater Internet freedoms in China.

INTERNET SURVEILLANCE

Readers might not be surprised by the level of government control of the Internet in a country with an authoritarian regime like China, but what about the rest of the world? While the American government has publicly promoted a free and open Internet and opposed broader Internet censorship, it has aggressively, albeit secretly, engaged in surveillance of both domestic and international Internet communications. In a recent information leak (from former US intelligence contractor Edward Snowden) that caught the world's attention in 2013, classified documents showed how the US National Security Agency (NSA) and their British counterpart, the Government Communications Headquarters (GCHQ), spy on their citizens. The documents show that while these governments have not sought to stop or censor the flow of communications, they secretly observe, record, and act on this information.

In general, the NSA and GCHQ have "broadly compromised the guarantees that internet companies have given consumers to reassure them that their communications, online banking and medical records would be indecipherable to criminals or governments" (Ball, Borger, and Greenwald 2013). The techniques include covert measures enabling NSA's control over international encryption standards, the use of supercomputers to break codes, and working with private companies to access their products and services. Both the NSA and GCHQ have worked closely with Internet service providers and software developers to build weaknesses into their programs. Documents show that GCHQ has worked with the largest service providers in Britain, including Google, Facebook, Yahoo, and Hotmail. Marissa Mayer, the CEO of Yahoo, reported that they would be imprisoned for revealing secrets about working with the US government (Rushe 2013). These relationships have granted the NSA and GCHQ covert "backdoors" into their customers' information and networks. This has allowed the spy agencies to secretly collect data and the communications of both domestic and international targets.

The American and British governments claim this is necessary to fight terrorism and is vital for collecting information that keeps people safe. Security analysts, however, have pointed out that such vulnerabilities can be exploited by anyone. Furthermore, a federal judge on a secret US court even rebuked the NSA in 2011 for "repeatedly misleading the court that oversees its surveillance on domestic soil," including the systematic searches of Americans' Internet communications (Savage and Shane 2013). Nonetheless, leaders of other countries, such as France's former President Sarkozy, have publicly supported similar systems. Sarkozy suggested that the Internet is uncivilized and not accountable to democratically elected governments, and therefore such systems are needed (Wood 2012). The justifications for these surveillance mechanisms, however, are very similar to Russia's case for greater Internet governance or China's "Great Firewall."

Also worth mentioning is the role that global corporations play in promoting Internet surveillance. In addition to serving as agents of various governments, they also have their own interests in monitoring, tracking, and observing users' behaviors online. The information that Facebook or Orkut users post about themselves, or that Google collects about users' searches, serve as huge data sources for corporate surveillance. Corporations mine this data to then produce targeted ads that subtly seek to shape consumer behavior and promote consumer culture that benefit those companies and their clients.

GLOBAL INTERNET GOVERNANCE

Given the issues of censorship, privacy, and surveillance raised above, global Internet governance is a particularly important issue today. The current form of global Internet governance emerged in the 1990s through a complex process of negotiation between a variety of stakeholders, including the Internet "technical community, intellectual property owners, hi-tech corporations, internet service providers, civil society organizations, intergovernmental organizations, and national governments" (Gelernter and Regev 2010: 73). In response to these various coalitions and negotiations, the US government created the Internet Corporation for Assigned Names and Numbers (ICANN), a nonprofit group that assigns IP addresses and domain names, and is the formal center of global Internet governance. On the one hand, "the computers storing the database lie in the hands of the US government, despite international demands," but on the other hand, its development and functioning does represent a broad multi-stakeholder coalition (Gelernter and Regev 2010: 73).

More recently, however, attempts to assert state control over the Internet have been globalized. In December 2012, 152 countries sent delegations to the World Conference on International Telecommunications in Dubai to discuss the International Telecommunication

Regulations (ITRs). According to conference organizers, the regulations "serve as the binding global treaty designed to facilitate international interconnection and interoperability of information and communication services, as well as ensuring their efficiency and wide-spread public usefulness and availability." At the end of the conference, delegates debated a proposal that could dramatically shift authority for Internet governance. Countries pushing for greater Internet governance sought to (1) move the oversight powers (e.g. assigning domain names) from ICANN, which continues to operate through a US government contract, to an international body (i.e. the International Telecommunications Union); and (2) strengthen the authority of individual countries to monitor the Internet in their own countries (Pfanner 2012).

Russia and other proponents of the proposal argued that providing individual countries with greater authority was necessary for national security, while critics contended that it would be utilized for censorship. Critics further argued that, as in the case of China, such powers would be used to monitor and disrupt mass movements that might oppose the government (Gjelten 2012). Many countries opposed the resolution, including the US, which stated it would sign no treaty that addressed Internet governance. No solution was reached in Dubai, but the struggle reflects the increased efforts to assert greater control over the Internet, and to limit its existence as an open, free, and autonomous space.

It was not until March 2014, in the aftermath of Edward Snowden and his leak of information about US surveillance, that the US announced it would finally step back from its unique role in governing the Internet. As noted above, it came to light that partially because of their close relationship to ICANN (among many other public and private agencies), US spy agencies were intercepting Internet traffic from around the world in a massive global surveillance effort. It lent new urgency to the need for a global non-governmental body to oversee Internet governance. Fadi Chehadé, the president and chief executive of ICANN, ironically stated: "We are inviting governments, the private sector, civil society and other Internet organizations from the whole world to join us in developing this transition process. All stakeholders deserve a voice in the management and governance of this global resource as equal partners" (Wyatt 2014). As of this writing, global meetings are being held to determine how the new organization would be structured and administered, with the transition scheduled for 2015.

WIKILEAKS

Attempts to control flows of information have not gone unchallenged, and it is not only governments and corporations that have utilized the Internet to empower themselves. Wikileaks, a website launched in 2006, posts confidential documents with the goal of improving transparency around the world. Through its electronic drop-box and encryption software, its platform enables individuals to upload documents securely and anonymously. It then makes these documents available on the Internet. Their website states:

> Publishing improves transparency, and this transparency creates a better society for all people. Better scrutiny leads to reduced corruption and stronger democracies in all society's institutions, including government, corporations and other organisations. A healthy, vibrant and inquisitive journalistic media plays a vital role in achieving these goals. We are part of that media.

Since its founding, Julian Assange has been the controversial figure at the head of Wikileaks. Assange is an Australian Internet activist and journalist, with a background in computer programming.

Each release of Wikileaks documents has provoked its own unique controversy (Yagatich 2012). For example, among the leaked documents was the Standard Operating Procedure for Camp Delta, which was the acting protocol for military personnel stationed at Guantánamo Bay, and military incident reports from Iraq and Afghanistan (among other things, these documented violations of the Geneva conventions on war). In 2012, Wikileaks began publishing more than 2.4 million hacked emails from the Syrian government and corporations, which were "embarrassing to Syria, but … also embarrassing to Syria's opponents" (Taylor 2012).

One of the most infamous and well-known leaks came in November 2010, when Wikileaks began publishing hundreds of its 250,000 classified US diplomatic cables. The leaks were coordinated with traditional news outlets in the US (*New York Times*), the UK (*The Guardian*), Germany (*Der Spiegel*), France (*Le Monde*), and Spain (*El País*), which reported the leaks and their contents. Some of the cables revealed that American diplomats were ordered to collect information such as "office and organizational titles; names, position titles and other information on business cards; numbers of telephones, cellphones, pagers and faxes," thus blurring the boundary between diplomacy and spying (Mazzetti 2010). Other cables showed major strategic differences between US and Pakistan over how to deal with the Taliban and al-Qaeda (Perlez et al. 2010). Still another set showed that American diplomats were highly active in pushing sales of jetliners overseas, turning diplomats into corporate salespeople (Lipton et al. 2011). The documents revealed, in striking detail, how government actually functions. A US soldier, Private Bradley Manning, later admitted to leaking the "information to help enlighten the public about 'what happens and why it happens' and to 'spark a debate about foreign policy.'" He was ultimately sentenced to 35 years in prison (Savage 2013). The US government sought actions against Assange, who took refuge at the Ecuadorian embassy London in June 2012, when Ecuador granted him political asylum. He remained there in late 2014 when this book was going to press.

Although Assange and his supporters insist that Wikileaks is an attempt to improve transparency (Sifry 2011), the actual effects of Wikileaks are unclear. The leaks have clearly provided insight into secret government and corporate dealings with an unprecedented level of detail. They provide information about secret trade negotiations, military decision-making, and the blurred boundaries between government and private interests. But states and corporations have largely responded by taking steps to make the information more secure, rather than more freely available (Shane 2010). Furthermore, some critics have accused Wikileaks of unnecessarily endangering the lives of people identified in the leaks.

The key point from the perspective of globalization is that technology has made it possible for information to be shared anonymously and to flow instantaneously around the world. But the story of Wikileaks ultimately reveals that in this era of high technology, powerful interests will go to great lengths to keep this information secure. While the information itself resembles the gases increasingly associated with globalization, barriers are constantly erected to contain the gas and prevent it from flowing around the world. The struggle to direct, contain, or free these flows will continue far into the future.

SOCIAL MEDIA AND SOCIAL MOVEMENTS

While governments and corporations have either sought to control, or at least monitor, global Internet flows, thereby shaping globalization from "above," organizations (e.g. Wikileaks) and social movements have also harnessed these technologies to shape globalization from "below." Indeed, the Internet, social media, and cell phones have become centrally important tools for activists and social movements around the world (Moghadam 2013).

One of the most important uses of the Internet and social media for social movements is for linking various movements and networks together to coordinate activities and help activists develop a collective identity. For example, Avaaz.org launched in 2007 "with a simple democratic mission: organize citizens of all nations to close the gap between the world we have and the world most people everywhere want." Avaaz (which means "voice" in several Middle Eastern, European, and Asian languages) addresses many global, regional, and national issues, from genocide and war to climate change and poverty. The site is truly global in that it is translated into 15 languages and draws on thousands of volunteers to create and promote campaigns around the world. While some campaigns are focused online (e.g. Internet petitions), many actions are also aimed at organizing protests offline, but all campaigns harness the quick and efficient use of the Internet to spread information and mobilize action.

Perhaps the most famous example of the use of social media and cell phones in social movements is the so-called "Twitter Revolution" (Jurgenson 2012). The term originated amidst mass protest in Moldova in 2009 (Mungiu-Pippidi 2009), and was popularized through the subsequent wave of popular uprisings in North Africa and the Middle East. It refers not only to the use of Twitter on computers and mobile devices, but also to the broader use of social media in social movements. For example, in Iran, protestors turned to Twitter after the controversial 2009 re-election of President Mahmoud Ahmadinejad. The government had shut down traditional media outlets, so the use of Twitter, especially via mobile phones, was an especially effective way to spread information and organize actions. It was through Twitter and other social media that activists and bystanders learned about the death of Nedā Āghā-Soltān. Āghā-Soltān, a philosophy student, was shot by government forces and her last moments were recorded on video and then went "viral" throughout social media. The event was described as "probably the most widely witnessed death in human history" (Mahr 2009), and the video went on to win the prestigious George Polk Award for video journalism. It was the first time that the award was given to an anonymous producer. Āghā-Soltān, and the video, became rallying cries for the opposition.

The role of social media and the Internet can be further seen as these popular protests spread to other countries, such as Egypt in 2010–2011. Protests were sparked in part by the brutal death of Khaled Mohamed Said, a 28-year-old Egyptian man, who was severely beaten and died while in police custody. Photographs of Said's disfigured face went viral online and helped mobilize a discontented populace against then-President Hosni Mubarak. Protestors used social media, and especially a Facebook group titled "We Are All Khaled Said," to organize mass protests (the page was started by Wael Ghonim, at the time a Google marketing executive). Protests continued to grow larger so the government shut down the Internet to squash the uprising, but the movement was already highly organized and was ultimately successful at overthrowing the Egyptian ruler of 30 years. Social media continued to play a part in social movements in Tunisia, Bahrain, Yemen, and other countries throughout the region and the globe.

The examples above demonstrate how the Internet, social media, and cell phones can be utilized to quickly spread information useful for activism and to organize protest events in real time. As Harvey argued at the beginning of this chapter, they compress time and space so that networks of activists can be linked across long distances. Relative to mass media, they also enable broader participation through "citizen journalism" and provide access to news and news-making in ways that did not exist previously. In other words, these technologies facilitate global flows and can be used to leverage the weaknesses of national regimes. However, these technologies are no guarantee of effective social movements and conceptualizing the technologies themselves as "revolutionary" has its critics.

The term "Twitter Revolution," or analogous terms such as "Facebook Revolution," are controversial for several reasons. First, many critics disagree with the use of a corporate name applied to revolutions that are organized and executed by mass popular protest. Second, others note that Twitter (and Facebook) is only one of many tools – and not even the most essential element – of movement organizing that helped activists accomplish their goals. Critics such as Malcom Gladwell (2010) argue that such tools are no replacement for effective organizing and campaigning; revolutions happened before social media and they will continue to unfold without social media.

HIGH-TECH FLOWS AND BARRIERS

As we've seen, perhaps no change has done more to further the process of globalization than the Internet. It occupies pride of place in many analyses of globalization. As discussed in Chapter 4, perhaps the most famous is Friedman's analysis of globalization as involving a "flat world"; the major example of such a world is the Internet (Friedman 2005). The Internet is flat in the sense that virtually anyone anywhere can become involved in it. As noted above, we also see that the Internet, and social media in particular, can help social movements in promoting change and providing new ways for everyday citizens to exercise power. However, as was pointed out in Chapter 4, we have deep disagreements with the argument that the world is naturally becoming flatter because of the Internet. That is, the whole of social history indicates that there are *always* strong pressures to erect barriers that serve to impede movement of all types. Both the flat world thesis and the weaknesses in the argument are nicely illustrated in the case of the Internet in China today and the continuing efforts by various states to erect barriers to the Internet or to monitor it. In addition to some countries promoting greater control over the Internet, other countries (e.g. the US and UK) are using the Internet to monitor both its citizens and non-citizens to maintain its power, at both national and global levels. Therefore, it is important to view the role of technology within globalization as one that facilitates both flows and new types of barriers. In Kellner's terms, it can help to facilitate globalization from above *and* globalization from below, but there is nothing inherently flattening about the technology itself.

CHAPTER SUMMARY

High-tech flows and structures such as technology, media, and the Internet are closely interconnected. Technology plays an important role in expediting global processes. Significant cornerstones have been the development of containerized ships, air freight, the personal computer, and the Internet. These technologies can usefully be conceptualized as bringing about time-space compression and distanciation. Time-space compression refers to the shrinking of space, and the reduction of the time required by a wide range of processes, brought about by changes in transportation and communication technologies advanced mainly by capitalist corporations. The concept of time-space distanciation is very similar, in that it conceives of the stretching of social relations across space and time. However, distanciation is argued to be brought about by technological change, independent of the capitalist pursuit of profit, and to specifically involve the ability to relate to others who are not co-present.

The global flow of technology does not go to all parts of the world, and it might "skip" areas due to the presence of barriers such as lack of electricity. There are instances of countries "leapfrogging" in the process of technological advancement; they skip certain technologies and move on directly to more advanced developments. Barriers to technology include lack of basic infrastructure (such as electricity), illiteracy, lack of strong systems of finance, and unstable political conditions.

The global flow of mass media is often characterized as media imperialism. TV, music, books, and movies are perceived as being imposed on developing countries by the West. Media imperialism undermines the existence of alternative global media originating from developing countries themselves such as Al Jazeera and Bollywood, as well as the influence of the local and regional media. The Internet can be seen as an arena for alternative media. Cultural imperialism denies the agency of viewers, but people around the world often interpret the same medium (e.g. a movie) in significantly different ways.

Global media are dominated by a small number of large corporations. This is being extended from old media to new social media. As a result, in the long run, the Internet could end up being less diverse and competitive. Global media have been seen as tending toward homogenization, both through McLuhan's concept of the "global village" as well as the more pessimistic approach of the Frankfurt School, which theorizes the creation of a "culture industry" under capitalism. However, the sector is witnessing a grobal-glocal struggle and the potential for democratization of global media is largely dependent on the further development of alternative media sources.

The Internet is a truly global phenomenon since it is used in all parts of the world. It is produced and maintained by global corporations, IGOs, and INGOs, thus reducing the influence of the nation-state. Social networking sites (e.g. Facebook, Weibo), like other social media (e.g. Wikipedia), involve the creation of content by the users themselves; they are prosumers who both produce and consume content.

The Internet has prompted a flat world thesis; anyone can be involved in it, at least theoretically. However, there are efforts to create barriers to impede, or at least monitor, such movements. For instance, the "Great Firewall" erected by the Chinese government is an effort to control Internet access and use, while the American government has been involved in wide-scale surveillance of people all over the world. The latter case has raised additional concerns about the American involvement in global Internet governance, which is now scheduled to transition into a more international structure. Other organizations, such as Wikileaks, and social movements have also utilized the Internet to promote globalization from below. Using social media, as in the so-called "Twitter Revolution," they have sought to promote more government transparency, democracy, and equality.

DISCUSSION QUESTIONS

1. How have high-tech flows changed the nature of time and space? What are the most important forces in shaping these changes?

2. What is media imperialism? How do global flows of technology affect media imperialism?

3. Discuss the idea that "the world is flat" in the context of global flows of technology.

4. Discuss the potential of the Internet to be a global "democratic" space.

5. Discuss the impact of global technological flows on the nation-state.

6. How is social networking changing the ways people relate both online and offline?

ADDITIONAL READINGS

Marshall McLuhan and Quentin Fiore. *The Medium is the Massage*. Berkeley: Gingko Press, 2005.

Colin Sparks. *Globalization, Development and the Mass Media*. London: Sage, 2007.

Ien Ang. *Watching Dallas: Soap Opera and the Melodramatic Imagination*. London: Routledge, 1985.

Jeremy Tunstall. *The Media Were American: US Mass Media in Decline*. Oxford: Oxford University Press, 2008.

Toby Miller, et al. *Global Hollywood 2*. London: British Film Institute, 2005.

Gili S. Drori. *Global E-Litism: Digital Technology, Social Inequality, and Transnationality*. New York: Worth, 2006.

Micah Sifry. *Wikileaks and the Age of Transparency*. New York: OR Books, 2011.

Barney Warf. *Time-Space Compression: Historical Geographies*. New York: Routledge, 2008.

David Morley and Kevin Robins. *Spaces of Identity: Global Media, Electronic Landscapes and Cultural Boundaries*. New York: Routledge, 2013.

Matthias Krings and Onookome Okome, eds. *Global Nollywood: The Transnational Dimensions of an African Video Film Industry*. Bloomington, IN: Indiana University Press, 2013.

Dwayne Winseck and Dal Yong Jin, eds. *The Political Economies of Media: The Transformation of the Global Media Industries*. New York: Bloomsbury, 2011.

NOTES

1 http://www.ifpma.org/fileadmin/content/Publication/2013/IFPMA_-_Facts_And_Figures_2012_LowRes SinglePage.pdf.

2 As we will discuss in Chapter 12, AIDs, like many other diseases, flows very rapidly through these less developed nations and through entire continents, especially Africa.

3 The authors believe *The Wire* is the best TV show ever, at least from a sociological perspective.

4 However, one member of the Frankfurt School, Herbert Marcuse, offered a more dialectical and less one-sided view on the impact of the media on culture.

5 Google allowed this and participated in it in order to retain access to the huge Chinese market. It argued that some censure was better than no market penetration at all in China.

GLOBAL FLOWS OF PEOPLE

MIGRATION, HUMAN TRAFFICKING, AND TOURISM

Globalization: A Basic Text, Second Edition. George Ritzer and Paul Dean.
© 2015 John Wiley & Sons, Ltd. Published 2015 by John Wiley & Sons, Ltd.

This chapter examines three types of global flows of people: migration, human trafficking, and tourism. The vast majority of the chapter will be devoted to the first type – migrants[1] – because of their increasing importance in globalization studies (Gold and Nawyn 2013) and the growing number of problems associated with, and encountered by, them.

These different types of global flows[2] can also be related to our key interest in this chapter, and the book, on global flows and barriers. In particular, many migrants, especially if they have low skills or are undocumented, have great, and increasing, difficulty moving about the world because they are "heavy" (e.g. if they lack education and training, are prostitutes, etc.) and because they encounter many structural barriers that impede their movement (Cohen 1995). Other migrants are much "lighter," given their valuable skills that may be in high demand, and are often encouraged through favorable migration policies to move freely through their borders. Similarly, while human traffickers (i.e. pimps) face some barriers to moving their "heavy" victims within and between nations, they continue to find porous borders and contribute to the explosion in trafficking flows that has occurred over the last several decades.

MIGRANTS

There has undoubtedly been a great deal of population movement associated with globalization. Much of this movement comes from migration, and while migration can occur within a single country (also known as "relocation"), this chapter focuses on international migration. The United Nations defines an **international migrant** as "any person who lives temporarily or permanently in a country where he or she was not born, and has acquired some significant social ties to this country." As of 2013, the UN estimates there are 232 million international migrants, or about 3.2% of the world's population (United Nations 2013b). To some observers, this represents a large and growing number and, in fact, it constitutes an increase of 36% since 1990. However, to other observers, the sense that we live in a global era of unprecedented international migration is exaggerated (Guhathakurta et al. 2007). While international migration has ebbed and flowed over time, the current rate is unspectacular in comparison to at least some of the recent past. Further, rates of migration in order to find work, while high and the subject of much media interest, lag behind the mobility rates for goods, services, and technologies.

> **International migrants**: People who live in a country where they were not born and have important social ties to that country.

While the contemporary numbers may not be impressive in comparison to the past, migrants do make up a significant percentage of the population of many regions and countries. For example, Europe (72 million) and Asia (71 million) are the regions attracting the largest numbers of international migrants (United Nations 2013b). However, the US remains the country with the largest migrant population; in 2010, 40.4 million people were foreign-born (12.9% of the total population). The US–Mexico corridor is also the world's largest route for international migrants. Other countries with large numbers of international migrants include Germany and France, owing to work migration and their geographic proximity to Africa, oil-producing nations such as the United Arab Emirates, and rapidly developing countries, including Malaysia, Singapore, and Thailand.

A combination of push and pull factors is usually used to explain migration. Among the *push* factors are the motivations of the migrants, contextual issues in the home country (e.g. unemployment, low pay) making it difficult or impossible for them to achieve their goals, and major disruptions such as war, famine, political persecution, environmental catastrophe, or an economic depression. Then there are such *pull* factors as a favorable immigration policy in the host country, higher pay and lower unemployment, family reunification, formal and informal networks in such countries that cater to migrants, labor shortages, and a similarity in language and culture between home and host country.

The precise push and pull factors are usually the way that observers differentiate between types of migration (Faist 2012). The first form are **temporary labor migrants**, which include guest workers and overseas contract workers. These migrants move to a country to work for a limited amount of time with the intention of sending much of their income back to family in their home country. Similarly, **irregular migrants** (i.e. undocumented migrants) are people who move across borders without proper documentation, or overstay their approved permits, and often do so for economic reasons.

Third, **highly skilled migrants** are people who move with special work qualifications. For example, managers, executives, professionals, technicians, and similarly trained workers respond to favorable labor markets or the needs of TNCs and international organizations. When coming from less developed countries in the global South, the exit of highly skilled migrants can contribute to a significant brain drain (see below).

Fourth, **forced migrants** include **refugees** and **asylum seekers** and are compelled to leave their home countries. While refugees are forced to flee for their safety and often move in mass numbers (e.g. because of war, or environmental catastrophe sometimes brought about by climate change), asylum seekers[3] want to remain in their countries but are unable (e.g. for political reasons). In 2013, the UN estimated there were 15.4 million internationally displaced refugees and 937,000 asylum seekers[4] (Euronews 2013).

Fifth, **family reunification migrants** are individuals who have family ties across borders. This type of migrant often seeks to reunite with migrants that have moved for economic reasons, and fit into one of the categories above. They both draw upon existing networks and reconfigure those networks through migration. Finally, **return migrants** are those who, after spending time in their destination country, go back to their home country.

MIGRATION

International migration has four components – "the in-migration of persons to a country other than that of their place of birth or citizenship; the return migration of nationals to their home country after residing abroad; the out-migration of nationals from their home country, and the out-migration of foreigners from a foreign country to which they had previously immigrated" (Kritz 2008). Our primary concern in this section will be with the out-migration of nationals and their in-migration to other countries. These migrants increasingly come from developing countries and move to developed or rapidly developing countries.

Our ability to discuss migration (as well as human trafficking) is hampered by the fact that there are great difficulties in tracking population flows. First, many countries do not collect such data. Second, those countries that do collect such data may not report them to international agencies. Third, population flows are defined differently in different countries; there are also differences in defining the permanency of a move and the residency period required for migrant status. Fourth, few countries keep track of their expatriates. Finally, there are overwhelming difficulties in keeping tabs on undocumented migrants (and survivors of human trafficking). One must keep these limitations on data clearly in mind in discussing migration.

Temporary labor migrants: guest workers and overseas contract workers that move to a country for a limited amount of time.

Irregular migrants: migrants that enter, or stay in, a country without proper documentation.

Highly skilled migrants: workers with special qualifications (e.g. managers, executives, professionals, technicians) who migrate for better economic opportunities.

Forced migrants: refugees and asylum seekers who are forced to leave their home country.

Refugees: Those forced to leave their homeland, or who leave involuntarily, because they fear for their safety.

Asylum seekers: Refugees who seek to remain in the country to which they flee.

Family reunification migrants: individuals whose family ties motivate them to migrate internationally.

Return migrants: people who, after spending time in their destination country, go back to their home country.

Unlike much else in the modern world (trade, finance, investment), restrictions on the migration of people, especially labor migration, have *not* been liberalized (Tan 2007). The major exception is in the European Union, but elsewhere in the world restrictions on migration remain in place. How do we explain this anomaly?

For one thing, in order to prosper economically, nations must try to keep the labor they need, both highly paid skilled workers and professionals of various types, and masses of low-paid semi-skilled and unskilled workers. If nations routinely lost large numbers of such workers, their ability to compete in the global marketplace would suffer.

For another, the influx of large numbers of migrants into another country often leads to conflict of various types usually between the newcomers and those who have been in place for quite some time, although there also may be conflict between different groups of newcomers. Thus, many nations prefer to maintain significant barriers to migration.

Finally, the concern over terrorism in many parts of the world, especially in the United States and in many European nations, has served to reinforce, if not increase, the restrictions on migration. This is especially clear in the immense difficulties involved in migrating to the United States today. This difficulty has even been extended to people traveling on business and to students wishing to study in the US. Even those who are tourists (i.e. vacationers) now often find the process of clearing border control in the US burdensome and even offensive. There is concern that these barriers and difficulties will cause people to take their business elsewhere and the best students to study in other countries, as well as lead to a significant decline in tourism and the income to be earned from it.

Shamir (2005) discusses the emergence of a "mobility regime" which seeks to contain the movement of migrants not only between, but even within, national borders. For example, by late 2008 Great Britain began issuing identity cards to foreigners from outside the EU to be better able to track their movement within the country, and therefore to be better able to contain their movement, should the need arise (*New York Times* 2008: March 7, A7). This desire for surveillance and containment is traceable to fear, real or imagined, of the dangers of terrorism (and crime) associated with immigrants.

While much attention has been devoted in recent years to barriers to the movement of migrants (see Figure 10.1 for a global map showing the major locales where there are significant efforts to stem the flow of undocumented immigrants), it is important to note that at the same time barriers have been reduced in terms of movement between, for example, the EU nations (this was pre-dated by the 1985 Schengen agreements – now part of EU law – which eased border controls among the European signatories). In the case of NAFTA, some restrictions on movement have been eased between the US, Canada, and Mexico (e.g. for business executives and highly skilled workers), while other barriers remain in effect and, in fact, have been strengthened and increased.

Since many of these barriers are created by nation-states, it is clear that they are a product of the Westphalian era (see Chapter 5) of the preeminence of the nation-state. Prior to that era, people moved about geographic space rather freely, but with the rise of the nation-state much more notice was taken of such movement and many more barriers were erected to limit and control it. However, as late as the end of the nineteenth century, there was still much freedom of movement, most notably in the great Atlantic migration to the US from Europe. It is estimated that about 50 million people left Europe for the US between 1820 and the end of the nineteenth century (Moses 2006: 47). Prior to 1880, entry into the US was largely unregulated, anyone who wanted in, could get in! In 1889 an International Emigration Conference declared: "We affirm the right of the individual to the fundamental

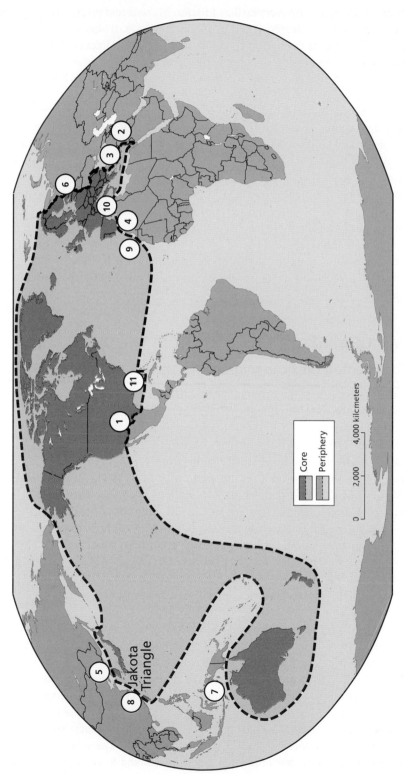

Figure 10.1 The world divided: core and periphery in the early twenty-first century. The numbers refer to places where governments try to stem the tide of undocumented migrants moving from periphery to core. Source: de Blij, Harm J. 2008. *Power of Place: Geography, Destiny, and Globalization's Rough Landscape.* Chapter 1: Globals, Locals, and Mobals, pp. 14–5. © 2008 Oxford University Press. Used by permission.

liberty accorded to him by every civilized nation to come and go and dispose of his person and his destinies as he pleases" (cited in Moses 2006: 47). It was WW I that changed attitudes and the situation dramatically; nation-states began to impose drastic restrictions on the global movement of people. Today, while there is variation among nation-states, "there is not a single state that allows free access to all immigrants" (Moses 2006: 54).

However, while authorized migration is restricted in various ways (although there are exceptions in some locales for highly skilled migrants), there seems to have been an increase in irregular (i.e. undocumented) immigration, even in the smuggling of people into (and out of [Shane and Gordon 2008: 1, 17]) various nations. In some cases, nations have laws requiring them to accept refugees (see below) escaping war, political persecution, and so on. For those who make it with or without authorization into another country, the burgeoning business of global remittances (see below), as well as technological developments that have made such transfers of funds quicker and easier, has tended to encourage and support migration. Furthermore, there has been a selective reduction in barriers to migration in many countries (especially the rise of "guest worker" programs that promote temporary labor migrants to increase the supply of cheap labor). This is driven by various factors in host countries, including labor shortages, the needs of MNCs for workers, and aging populations.

FLOWS OF MIGRANTS TO AND FROM THE US

Undocumented Mexican migrants to the US

More than one-tenth of the US population (40.4 million of a total of about 312 million) were born outside the US and many of them arrived after a(nother) great boom in immigration that began in the early 1990s. Many entered the US as irregular migrants without authorization. They come from various countries (Philippines, China, El Salvador), but the largest number (at least one-half) come from Mexico (as of 2012 about 6 million Mexicans are in the US without documentation [Valdes 2013]). (It is estimated that more than 10% of Mexico's total population [116 million] live in the United States.) In fact, the majority of Mexican immigrants are in the US without authorization (they may have crossed the border without documentation [about 85% of those who cross the border do so without documentation], or have remained after their visas expired). They come (and often stay) because while they may be paid poverty wages by US standards (approximately $300 per week), that may be as much as four times what they could earn in Mexico (Preston 2006: A24). Furthermore, there are more jobs and better future job opportunities in the US than in Mexico.

Life is not easy for undocumented Mexican immigrants in the United States. While they may be better off economically than they were in Mexico, and than those who remained in or returned to Mexico, their life is problematic in various ways. First, while they have improved their lives from an economic point of view, they remain largely marginal economically in the US context. Second, their family life is often in shreds with many family members (and friends) still in Mexico (Navarro 2006a: A1, A20, A21). They are separated from them by a border that has recently become increasingly difficult to breach from the Mexican side for those who are not entering the US with authorization. These new restrictions seem to have deterred few, but it "has resulted in a greater demand for smugglers, higher prices for smuggling and more deaths from crossing the border. It has also discouraged people from going back home" (Alvarez 2006a: A20). Those who do go back home face increasingly dangerous conditions trying to re-enter the US (Cave 2011), and an increasing number of them are dying during the journey (Santos and Zemansky 2013). The economic situation of immigrants is complicated by the fact that they are asked for, and often feel obligated to give, financial aid (remittances) to relatives (and friends) who remain in Mexico (roughly $20 billion in 2012 [Mallén 2013]) and who are worse off than they are. Third, those who are in the US without documentation are haunted by the possibility of being apprehended by the immigration authorities, "*la migra*" (Alvarez 2006b: A1, A20, A21).

The life of undocumented Mexican immigrants in the US often shrinks to just the few square blocks of their immediate neighborhood where they feel safe from *la migra*. This is also an area where they are not asked for what they do not have – the crucial indicators of legitimacy – insurance cards, credit cards, Social Security cards, and "Green" cards (which offer legal permanent residence in the US and enable immigrants to get a job legally; people often pay large sums for fraudulent Green cards). Local information networks warn them of the presence of government authorities. Some places (e.g. the nearby Wal-Mart) become no-go zones when there is word that it is being watched by *la migra*. It is even deemed a good idea to be wary of neighbors who just might inform on them. Undocumented Mexican immigrants rely heavily on the underground economy. When they need to cash a check, they often rely on check-cashing enterprises that charge exorbitant fees. Yet, with all these problems (and more), many prefer life in the US to their old life in Mexico. Said one: "Living here without papers is still better than living there" (quoted in Alvarez 2006b: A20).

One woman who had lived (without authorization) in the US for six years, returned to Mexico (i.e. as a return migrant) distressed about what was happening to her family there. Three years later, however, she was forced to exclaim: "Look how I live … I was used to something else" (quoted in Navarro 2006a: A1). She now lives in a cinderblock house in Mexico that had been carved into four tiny apartments. The family shares two toilets and two showers outside the house. Her bedroom lacks a window. The kitchen has no refrigerator or sink. To do the dishes she needs to fill buckets with water from a faucet also found outside the house.

Many, including the woman described above, leave the US because they regret the inability to interact with family members who remained in Mexico and the loss of their support network. However, upon their return to Mexico, many of these people must deal with the separation from family and friends who remain behind in the US. And, they are now separated by the newly reinforced border as well as the difficulty in obtaining the funds necessary to finance an unauthorized trip across it to visit those still in the US. Adding to the dissatisfaction of many who return to Mexico are the relatively poor wages and occupational prospects there. Furthermore, they now have the experience of life in the US to compare to what it is like in Mexico. For many, the life they left in the US seems far better than the way they now live in Mexico. This led the woman described above to exclaim: "If I had the money, I'd leave today" (quoted in Navarro 2006a: A21).

Migrants through Mexico and to the US

In addition to the large number of undocumented immigrants from Mexico, many others make their way from various Central American nations to the US. As of 2011, there were over 2 million of these unauthorized immigrants in the US, up from 1.8 million in 2000, but down from 3 million in 2007 (Hoefer et al. 2012; Thompson 2008: A17). Most of these immigrants came from El Salvador (660,000), Guatemala (520,000), and Honduras (380,000). To get to the US, the vast majority must travel through much of Mexico and across the Mexico–US border. One route is through Mexico's southern neighbor, Guatemala, wading across the Suchiate River (an "open border"), on to the city of Tapachula, and from there undertake an arduous 1,500-mile trip to the US border. The latter involves a 250-mile walk along the Chiapas coast to Arriaga where they swarm aboard moving trains (an average of 300–500 people per day find their way on to such trains) and hang precariously from them en route to the US. Many are injured or die falling from the moving trains. One Honduran migrant, Donar Antonio Ramirez Espinas, had both of his legs sheared off above the knees when, riding between cars, he dozed off and fell from the train. "I fell face down, and at first I didn't think anything had happened…. When I turned over, I saw, I realized, that my feet didn't really exist" (quoted in McKinley, Jr 2007b: 12). Before getting to the train, migrants must run a gauntlet of crooked federal police and robbers (and rapists) who are likely to steal most of their already meager amount of money and other possessions.

In early 2007, Misael Mejia (27 years old) made this trek from Comayagua, Honduras. It took him 11 days to walk from the Suchiate River to Arriaga to await the train. While there, he and several others were ambushed by three men, one with a machine gun. "'They told us to lay down and take off our clothes…. I lost my watch, about 500 Honduran lempiras, and 40 Mexican pesos,' about \$31" (quoted in McKinley, Jr 2007b: 12). Yet, Mejia was undeterred, driven by hope of higher pay (he earned \$200 a month as a driver in Honduras, but his brother in Arizona earns \$700 a week as a carpenter). Said Mejia, "I felt hopeless in Honduras…. Because I could never afford a house, not even a car. There is nothing I could have" (quoted in McKinley, Jr 2007b: 12).

Increased law enforcement

In the past, most migration, especially from Mexico, was for temporary labor and was a round-trip journey. However, it is increasingly becoming one-way as migrants settle, often without authorization, into life in the US (and elsewhere in the world). There are several reasons for this. First, they are more likely to be able to get jobs outside of the agricultural sector. Such work is less seasonal and more likely to be regular and stable. Second, many are moving beyond the southwestern border states and deeper into the US thereby making a return to Mexico more difficult and more expensive. Third, with the tightening of border controls since the 1980s, and especially after 9/11, it is simply more difficult and more expensive to find a way to return to Mexico. According to one sociologist, "Having run the gauntlet of enforcement resources at the border, migrants grew reluctant to repeat the experience and hunkered down to stay, causing rates of return migration to fall sharply" (quoted in Navarro 2006b: A20). About 47% of undocumented immigrants returned to Mexico between 1979 and 1984, but the percentage of returns had declined to 27% between 1997 and 2003. But because the number of overall migrants leveled off during the Great Recession (they have climbed again slightly since the Recession), return migrants have become an increasingly larger proportion of people attempting to re-enter the US without documentation. As migrants return to Mexico to visit family, it is becoming more common for them to get caught attempting to cross the border back to the US again. In total, "56 percent of apprehensions at the Mexican border in 2010 involved people who had been caught previously, up from 44 percent in 2005" (Cave 2011). Nonetheless, the longer immigrants stay in the US, the lower the probability that they will return. Thus, one of the ironies of increased US border controls is that *more* undocumented immigrants from Mexico remain in the US rather than returning (as many would have in an earlier era of easier border-crossing). Furthermore, these migrants in the US might be more likely to be followed by family reunification migrants, seeking to reunite with their parents, siblings, and other family members there.

And the controls on the 2,000-mile Mexican border have continued to increase with thousands of new border patrol agents and national guardsmen. This control includes 650 miles of border fence, with proposals to extend fencing along the entire span (Preston 2011). The focus on extending the border fence, however, has shifted toward increased use of guards and surveillance as costs for constructing the fence have ballooned. In 2009, the Department of Homeland Security spent approximately $21 million per mile to build the fence near San Diego, California. To build the entire fence would cost tens of billions of dollars. The US is not alone in constructing such a fence – for example, India has built fencing along much of its border with Bangladesh; Israel has its wall between it and the West Bank.

The fence between the US and Mexico, as well as increased border patrols, was said to have produced a 22% drop in apprehensions of undocumented immigrants at the border, but others claim that the drop may be, at least in part, the result of other factors (e.g. weaker "pull" factors as a result of the economic recession). As noted above, while undocumented immigration decreased during the Great Recession, it has increased again since the recovery (Valdes 2013). There are also real questions as to whether such a fence is really useful given the terrain. Limited experience with a far less lengthy fence near San Diego is not hopeful for supporters of such a fence. That fence merely led many undocumented immigrants to use other, more dangerous, routes into the US.

In addition, while some proponents of immigration reform seek to ease the path to citizenship, there are proposals to make it tougher for undocumented immigrants to become US citizens by making the English and history exams more difficult, and by delving more deeply into applicants' past lives. While such changes may never occur, they reflect the current mood in the US, at least among more conservative politicians and citizens. It is the case, however, that the cost of applying for citizenship has drastically increased, from $225 in 1999 to $680 in 2013, thereby pricing some individuals out of applying for citizenship (Emanuel and Gutierrez 2013).

In addition to the fence, the US employs many other tools to police its borders with Mexico. For example, "unmanned Predator Bee drones float at 12,000 feet, helping to guide officers in bulletproof helicopters, in jeeps, on horseback, on mountain bikes and all-terrain buggies towards any would-be migrants. Seismic sensors catch footfalls, magnetic ones notice cars, infra-red beams are useful for tunnels" (*Economist* 2008: January 3 ["Keep Out"]). In addition, 21,000 border patrol agents stand guard there, with some anti-immigration advocates calling for 40,000 agents at the border (Blow 2013). Others have called for enforcement and stricter penalties levied on employers who hire undocumented immigrants.

The impact of increased enforcement of immigration laws is being felt throughout the US even as far north as upper New York State where natives engaged in already marginal farming are increasingly threatened by the loss of their low-paid undocumented immigrant workers from Mexico (Bernstein 2006: 20). Not only are the workers more likely to be picked up by immigration authorities, but the farm owners themselves now worry about criminal prosecution. There is a pervasive climate of fear as undocumented workers are suspicious of everyone and farmers fear that jealous neighbors might inform on them for employing such people. The result of increased law enforcement is that deportation rates are up dramatically.

Some of those who support the more stringent law enforcement do so out of a concern for the immigrant workers, their low wages, and their otherwise highly exploited status as farm workers. However, others do so because they feel undocumented immigrants drag down wages for everyone and they resent the costs associated with public services accorded to them. In contrast, native farmers (among others) tend to support the immigrant workers because they contend that they are unable to find anyone else to do the work. Migrants are also supported by those who are concerned that the human rights of undocumented immigrants are being abused (e.g. fathers being arrested and leaving behind wives and American-born children to fend for themselves) in the current crack-down.

Returning undocumented immigrants

The tightening of restrictions on undocumented immigrants in the US (and elsewhere) has had all sorts of implications and repercussions. One is that at least some are choosing to return home (if they can) rather than put up with the increasing difficulties of remaining in the country to which they emigrated (Salaff 2013). One such group is several hundred thousand Brazilians who came to the US in the 1990s and early 2000s on tourist visas and then remained as irregular, or undocumented, immigrants. A large number of them married and had children who were born in the US. Many are now returning home because of increasing fear of deportation, declining economic possibilities in the US especially associated with the Great Recession, loss of homes due to the sub-prime mortgage crisis, the impossibility of renewing expiring driver's licenses because of tighter rules in recent years, the absence of good public transportation, the decline in the value of the dollar relative to the Brazilian currency (the real), and the improving economy and job prospects (at least at the time) in Brazil (Bernstein and Dwoskin 2007: A32). More generally, many are distressed by the fact that for most of them no route exists to legal status in the US. This dooms them to a life of fear of being caught by immigration authorities and of being deported. Said one man who decided to return with his family to Brazil (they would be banned by law from returning to the US, even as visitors, for ten years): "If we had papers, we'd stay forever... . We love this community" (quoted in Bernstein and Dwoskin 2007: A32). Their American-born children are often reluctant to leave the US with them (and they don't need to) and this is an additional burden for their families who return to Brazil. Even if their American-born children do return to Brazil, their families worry that the children will resent being forced to leave the place where they were born.

FLOW OF MIGRANTS ELSEWHERE IN THE WORLD

It is not only in the US that control over borders is a major issue.

Migrants in Europe

Since the ratification of the Maastricht Treaty, a number of nations have been added to the EU including less developed Eastern European nations such as Bulgaria and Romania in 2007 and Croatia in 2013. One of the key points of the Maastricht Treaty was to move toward Europe as an increasingly borderless society, at least as far as the member nations and their citizens are concerned. However, the influx of immigrants from the less developed east to the more developed west has led to major issues in a number of countries in Western

Europe and calls by many for a reassertion of border controls. As in the US, there is growing concern about unauthorized immigration in Europe and there are increasing efforts to reduce or eliminate the flow of undocumented immigrants.

Great Britain

In Great Britain, there is great public debate over various aspects of the EU, but especially the impact of the free movement of workers from Eastern Europe. After the admission of new members (including Poland) to the EU, Great Britain (and a few other EU nations) opened their doors to immigrants from those nations and the result was an influx of over a half million people. Predictably, these immigrants took many low-paying jobs and were perceived as a threat because the jobs they obtained might have gone to British workers and because of their overall impact in driving down wages for all, especially at the lower end of the occupational hierarchy. These fears resurfaced with the admission of Bulgaria, Romania, and Croatia to the EU; perhaps the ultimate fear for many is the proposed admission of Turkey to the EU.

Many larger issues are involved in this debate. There are those who argue that the influx of low-wage immigrants aids a country like Great Britain by making its products less expensive and therefore more competitive in the global marketplace. They also often take jobs that natives are reluctant to take because of the low wages or the intrinsic nature of the work. Their low wages are also seen as tending to dampen the tendency toward inflation. And, the taxes paid by immigrant workers help pay for public services. In spite of such advantages, in 2013 Britain tried to make immigration rules stricter. Conservative Prime Minister David Cameron sought to make it easier to deport foreigners who commit crimes, increase penalties for employers hiring unauthorized immigrants, and force private landlords to check tenants' citizenship status; others called for curbing immigration even further (Castle 2013).

Sweden

For many decades, Sweden has been considered a very tolerant and welcoming place for immigrants. Sweden has been particularly welcoming to refugees from war-torn countries, including many Muslims, who have both contributed significantly to Sweden's workforce and also benefited from its generous welfare state. Even into the 2000s, Sweden seemed "immune" from the anti-immigrant sentiment that had been increasing in Europe.

However, this welcoming atmosphere has begun to change. In Sweden about 17% of the population of 9.5 million is now foreign-born (Demsteader 2010); approximately one in four Swedes is either foreign-born or has a parent born outside the country (Daley 2011). While they are, on average, better off economically than immigrants in many other countries, unemployment rates among immigrants are very high (16% in immigrant neighborhoods and twice that for people under 25 [Higgins 2013]). Backlash against immigrants has swelled and social conflicts have increased. For example, in 2010, Sweden's far-right party ran on an anti-immigration platform, and the party garnered 6% of the vote, shocking many Swedes. There was even a "racist sniper" who targeted foreign-born Swedes before being arrested in 2012 (*The Local* 2013). Sweden has experienced immigrant riots in 2013, similar to those in France in 2005 and Great Britain in 2011 (Higgins 2013).

Greece

EU countries are involved in a system, Frontex, designed to police their borders. Frontex has patrol boats, spotter airplanes, radar on land, and other high-tech devices (*Economist* 2008: January 3 ["Keep Out"]). A traditional route for undocumented immigrants to

EU countries was to travel, perhaps hundreds of miles, by flimsy boat, to places like the island of Lampedusa off of Italy, or Spain's Canary Islands. A newer, and much shorter, route is from Turkey to three Greek Islands – Lesbos, Chios, and especially Samos – that lie very close to Turkey and therefore the gateway to the Middle East and Asia. Although it is a short dinghy ride from Turkey to Chios, the waters there are treacherous and the trip is quite dangerous. In spite of the danger (and the cost of using intermediaries like smugglers and lawyers), many have used this route including migrants from "Iraq, Afghanistan, Somalia, Libya, Lebanon, Eritrea, the Palestinian territories and Iran" (Brothers 2008: A3). Others travel across land from Turkey to Greece. Overall, Frontex estimates that 55,000 people crossed the border in 2011 (a 17% increase over the previous year) (Kennedy 2012). Officials now estimate that 1 in 20 people in Greece are undocumented immigrants. As a result, Greece "has become the back door to the European Union, making member countries ever more resentful as a tide of immigrants from the Middle East, South Asia and Africa continues to grow" (Kennedy 2012).

Among those that suffer in this are forced migrants who have a legitimate reason to seek asylum in Greece. In fact, Greece has been criticized by the EU for not dealing adequately with the issue of asylum seekers. EU rules stated that the first country reached by an immigrant is the one that is supposed to deal with asylum issues. But because Greece had such a backlog of refugees and living conditions there were so poor, the European Court of Human Rights had to change the law in 2011. They no longer required that migrants' request for asylum had to be filed in the country through which they entered the EU.

One of the ironies in this case is that it was not too long ago that it was large numbers of Greeks who were emigrating from their homeland. Further, during WW II the three islands in question were often sites for the debarkation of Greeks seeking to escape the German army by taking small boats to Turkey.

As the flow of undocumented immigrants to Greece has increased, so has Greek resistance to it. Those undocumented immigrants who are caught are put in detention for three months and then forced to leave Greece within 30 days. Like the US, Greece is also building a wall, or $7.3 million fence, on its border with Turkey (although few people believe it will have an impact). Support for conservative, anti-immigrant Greek politicians has also grown. According to the chief of police for the three Greek islands: "Greece was not ready to accept such vast numbers of immigrants" (quoted in Brothers 2008: A3). The example of an Ethiopian law student is illustrative of the problems of even highly desirable undocumented immigrants:

> He bribed Ethiopian border officials, hid in a truck carrying coffee to Sudan, endured seven days in the Sahara, spent months in a grim camp in Libya, suffered a terrifying voyage across the Mediterranean, hitched a lift in a frozen-meat lorry in Turkey, scavenged in a forest for days and feared he would drown in a fishing boat that carried him into the EU. He paid several thousand dollars for the journey and ended up locked in a cramped and stinking warehouse on the island of Samos, crammed with asylum-seekers. Dejected, he says he wants to go home. (*Economist* 2008: January 3 ["Keep Out"])

Yet, large numbers of undocumented migrants still make it to Europe, as well as to the US. In the end, these barriers will not keep out those who are desperate to get to these destinations (and they likely keep in those who might want to leave). There is some evidence of a decline of undocumented immigration in Europe, especially those coming from Africa. However, the issue is whether the decline will continue in the long term, or whether it is nothing more than a blip on the otherwise upward trend in migration from Africa. The latter appears more likely given the problems seemingly endemic to Africa – warfare, poverty, and ethnic and religious conflict. Said one migrant from Darfur: "We were already dead when we were in Sudan and Libya. If we died on the boat, it's all the same" (quoted in Fisher 2007: 10).

Undocumented immigrants in Asia

The problem of undocumented immigrants is not restricted to the EU and the US. It is an issue elsewhere, including Asia. For example, 16% of the workforce in Malaysia are foreign-born. Out of a country of 29 million people, it is estimated that over 1 million of them are undocumented immigrants (Gangopadhyay and Ng 2013). Most are from Indonesia, but others come from the Philippines, Bangladesh, Nepal, and Myanmar. They are there to work in various manual occupations, as well to labor in the service industry. However, many, especially those who are there without authorization, live in fear of harassment, arrest, whippings, imprisonment, and deportation.

In 2005 a group, created in the 1960s to combat communism, was deputized and transformed into a strike force ("Rela" – Peoples' Volunteer Corps) to search out undocumented immigrants throughout Malaysia. They are permitted to stop a "suspect" on the streets or to enter the homes of suspects. Rela's leaders are armed. Rela has grown to about a half million uniformed volunteers and is larger than Malaysia's police and armed forces; about 135,000 of these volunteers were expected to be used in raids in late 2013 that sought to eventually capture and deport 400,000 undocumented immigrants in the following months (*Business Standard* 2013). Human rights groups accuse it of various abuses such as "violence, extortion, theft, and illegal detention." A 2007 Human Rights Watch report said: "They break into migrant lodgings in the middle of the night without warrants, brutalize inhabitants, extort money and confiscate cell phones, clothing, jewelry, and household goods before handcuffing migrants and transporting them to detention camps for illegal immigrants" (quoted in Mydans 2007: A4). Rela's director-general responded: "… if you talk about human rights, you cannot talk about security" (quoted in Mydans 2007: A4). Those who are caught and detained are tried and, if convicted, can get up to five years in prison, or a whipping followed by deportation. Said one undocumented immigrant serving as lookout for an apartment he shares with several other undocumented immigrants: "We always fear, especially at night… . Maybe there will be a raid. Where will we run? I worry for my wife and children. I've been thinking of moving to the jungle [many have done just that]" (quoted in Mydans 2007: A4). Rela's director-general responds by saying that undocumented immigrants are Malaysia's enemy number two. The first? Drugs.

The issue of immigration, often unauthorized, is also of concern in central Asia where large numbers of people are moving north from impoverished and declining countries such as Uzbekistan and Tajikistan to comparatively oil-rich Kazakhstan and Russia. According to Russian estimates, approximately 10 million documented immigrants and another 3 million undocumented immigrants, including Uzbeks, Tajiks, and Kyrgyz nationals, are currently working, some of them seasonally, in Russia (Guillory 2013). Similar to the US, Great Britain, Sweden, and Greece, anti-immigrant sentiment has risen in Russia and politicians have responded with further crackdowns.

Problems arise because receiving nations do not seem to know how to categorize such immigrants and they are often treated very badly, sometimes even turned into slaves or semi-slaves. One Uzbek immigrant contended that immigrants were being sold in an open public market (see section below on human trafficking). In spite of such treatment, the immigrants keep coming because economic conditions are so poor back home. They take jobs in construction (buildings, roads), in factories, or in market stalls of various types. While the immigrants already encounter personal problems, there has been a rise in Russia in anti-immigration sentiments and demonstrations, and there is the potential there, and elsewhere in the region, for even greater problems (e.g. a rise in ethnic tensions and violence). However, there are also gains for immigrants such as improved conditions at home as a result of remittances (see below) from immigrant workers. While the borders in the region remain open, there has been an increase in the smuggling of undocumented immigrants because the borders are more difficult to cross.

THE CASE AGAINST THE BACKLASH TO UNDOCUMENTED IMMIGRATION

A number of arguments have been made against the various roadblocks currently being erected in the path of immigrants. From the point of view of the South, immigrants from there to the North have benefited enormously and many have sent money back home. Those who return eventually bring with them money saved while working in the North, new skills and technical expertise, and innovative new ideas.

Of course, it could be argued that it is the North that benefits more from immigration, documented or undocumented. It is this that makes the growing opposition in the North even more incomprehensible. Among other things, the North usually gains youthful, vigorous, and ambitious new workers of all types. The latter is especially important to the graying, and perhaps shrinking, workforces in the EU and the US. In some cases, there are few alternatives to hiring immigrants. For example, a hotel owner in Ireland recently advertised for a hotel receptionist. Two hundred people applied, but *none* were Irish.[5] Immigrants often do work (e.g. farm labor, care for the elderly) that natives eschew. Migrant workers are generally more flexible than natives, willing to go almost anywhere and do anything. Additional flexibility is made possible by the fact that migrants may free up natives to take other jobs (e.g. working in day care), or to move on to higher-status, better-paying jobs. Migrant workers also better protect the economy from inflation because of the mixed blessing of their low wages. The North may even see an influx of the best-trained, elite workers from the South. Then there is the fact that migrants are consumers and the more they are paid, the more they spend. As consumers, they contribute to the growth (although there is a debate about just how much they contribute and their contribution is difficult to measure precisely) of the local economy in another way. Related to this is the fact that as they open their own shops and restaurants, they contribute to the diversity of the host country. Overall, the economies of the North have grown historically, and are likely to continue to grow, as a result of immigration, documented and undocumented (Kenny 2012).

Why, then, the fears in the North? Politicians gain much notoriety and support by focusing national attention on unauthorized (or "illegal") immigration and immigrants. After all, the latter are safe to attack, especially the undocumented who cannot vote. Further, they represent a convenient scapegoat for both politicians and much of the public. Few members of the public support undocumented immigrants, or at least want to be seen as supporting them, and many fear them for various reasons. Thus, they are receptive to the arguments of ambitious politicians.

There are also a number of more practical reasons why there is such fear of undocumented immigrants in the North. Some may simply find it disturbing to see a significant influx of people from other cultures, especially dramatic increases in the number of such people that they come in contact with on a daily basis. It is difficult for such immigrants to integrate into the larger culture and some may not want to. For their part, Northerners may not want, or allow them, to integrate. The least skilled workers in the North are the ones who may see their jobs threatened or a decrease in pay as a result of competition from undocumented immigrants and this fear has been heightened by increasing unemployment rates. However, there is evidence that the decline in pay traceable to immigration is relatively small and that over time the wages recover. Furthermore, there is at least some job creation that occurs as a result of immigration – employers move in to take advantage of their low wages, distinctive skills, etc. There is also a fear, especially in the US and the EU, that undocumented immigrants will become reliant on state welfare systems and strain school systems, public housing, and hospitals. However, most immigrants, both documented and undocumented, are prime working age and, in addition to work, contribute to the economy through various taxes (e.g. excise and sales taxes). Of course, fears in the North of all types of immigration were exacerbated by terrorist attacks on or after 9/11.

The most complete case against restrictions on international migration is made by Jonathon W. Moses in *International Migration* (2006). He divides his argument into economic, political, and moral dimensions.

Economically, he argues that immigration has had a positive, *not* a negative, effect on the economy of the US (and other developed nations). In one comprehensive review of existing research, the Brookings Institution concluded "on average, immigrants raise the overall standard of living of American workers by boosting wages and lowering prices" (Greenstone and Looney 2010). Contrary to what many believe, it is not clear that immigrants compete with natives for jobs. It is also not clear that immigrants have less skill than natives; for example, in the US, foreign nationals living the US account for a quarter of new patent applications and foreign-educated nurses are making up an increasing percentage of those taking the US licensure exam (Kenny 2012). In any case, there is great variation in this from nation to nation and from immigrant group to immigrant group. While the wages of native, less-skilled workers may be negatively affected, overall wages are not affected, or may even increase. Immigrants are not a drain on public finances and may even pay more in taxes than they cost in services (one reason for this is that immigrants are usually young and in their prime as far as work is concerned). A very strong economic argument in support of more open immigration in developed countries is the fact that they are dominated by aging workforces and they need an influx of young, vibrant, and "hungry" workers. Yet another economic argument relates to the high (and increasing) cost of restricting immigration through border controls – money that would be saved and could be put to other uses if border controls were eased. For example, as of 2013, the US was processing 400,000 deportations per year (Preston 2013), at a cost of $12,500 per deportation (Cave 2011). As noted above, its US–Mexico border fence has cost as much as $21 million per mile to build.

The above relate to economic benefits to receiving countries, but sending countries benefit economically, as well. Those workers who remain behind are in an improved bargaining position and can better their economic situation and their lives more generally.

Remittances can provide capital that can be used by the countries receiving the money for investments in economic development.

In the political realm, freer immigration can contribute in various ways to greater democratization, less authoritarianism. In terms of sending countries, the fact that people (especially the most highly educated and skilled) can and do leave because of a lack of democracy puts pressure on the political system to reform itself. More generally, it strengthens the ability of individuals to influence political regimes and to push them in the direction of increased democratization. In short, with free(r) migration, nation-states need to be more responsive to their citizens. In a world of freer movement, nation-states would also compete with one another in order to be better able both to keep their best people and to attract those from elsewhere. This could improve nation-states the world over and enhance international exchanges.

There are two basic moral arguments in support of freer migration. First, as an end in itself, free mobility is "a universal and basic human right" (Moses 2006: 58). Second, instrumentally, "free migration is seen as a means to achieve greater moral ends (in particular, economic and political justice)" (Moses 2006: 59). In terms of the latter, greater freedom of movement would lead to a reduction in global economic inequality and would mitigate global tyranny. Overall, Moses emphasizes the moral aspect of freer migration: "Today's migration regime is terribly unjust: it distributes opportunity by fate, and has the effect of condemning people to life sentences in their country of birth. As such, the current regime tends to prioritize the rights of an imagined community (the nation), at the expense of sometimes desperate individuals" (Moses 2006: 9). To the degree that societies value a diverse population with vibrant cultures, this could be a further rationale for promoting immigration.

Of course, all of this challenges much conventional wisdom today about migration and open borders. However, Moses shows that most of that conventional wisdom is erroneous or, at best, only partially correct. There is much fear these days over the crime and terrorism that might be associated with free, or even just freer, global migration. However, Moses argues that freer migration would bring with it greater global cooperation, and global systems, that would allow for greatly improved tracking of flows of people and a much-improved ability to identify and apprehend those intent on criminal or terroristic activities.

REMITTANCES

Remittances:
Transactions by which migrants send money back to their country of origin.

The issue of **remittances** is increasingly important as more and more immigrants, documented and undocumented, make their way into developed countries in order to find work (Ratha and Mohapatra 2012). Those who are successful often end up sending money back to their country of origin for the care and support of various family members. While they are often poorly paid by the standards of developed countries, they are better off than many in their country of origin. Further, they are aware that their absence makes it harder for family members left behind to survive. Thus, remittances have become an increasing reality, and of increasing importance, to developing countries. The World Bank estimated that in 2013 remittances amounted to $410 billion (and were three times the size of global aid budgets) (World Bank 2013). It further projected that this number would grow by 9% each year, totaling $540 billion in 2016. If we included high-income countries in these estimates, global remittances would total $550 billion in 2013 and $707 billion by 2016.

Thriving businesses[6] have arisen in the North to handle the large numbers of transfers of relatively small amounts of funds that banks generally are unwilling to bother with. In addition, banks lack the infrastructure to handle such transfers. The small businesses that handle most of these transfers (as we will see large businesses are also involved) generally use the Internet for the transfers and can function with small offices in cities in the North (London has a large number of them) and in the South to which they send money (*Economist* 2008: January 3 ["Send me a Number"]).

Remittances constitute *the largest source of money* flowing into developing countries from the rest of the world. In some countries in the South remittances constitute a substantial, even stunning, proportion of GNP (48% in Tajikstan, 31% in the Kyrgyz Republic, 25% in Lesotho and Nepal, and 24% in Moldova [World Bank 2013]). Remittances are most likely to go to India (receiving $71 billion), China ($60 billion), the Philippines ($26 billion), and Mexico ($22 billion).

This is usually seen as a boon to those who receive remittances, as well as to the economies of the societies in which they live. Recipients are better able to survive, to buy the basics they need, and even to afford a few luxuries (a TV set, a cell phone). More generally, remittances can:

- reduce poverty rates;
- go directly to those in need and give them experience with banks and in saving;
- help deal with emergencies because flows of money can be increased easily and quickly and because virtually all of the money goes to satisfy important needs for "food, clothes, housing, education and health" (*Economist* 2008: January 3 ["Send me a Number"]);
- be used to raise educational levels;
- be a source of pride and confidence in the receiving community over the success of those able to send remittances;
- be countercyclical, that is remittances can be increased as a result of an economic slump at home (or a natural disaster) (in contrast to money from investors that declines during a slump);
- be preferable to foreign aid because they are more predictable, better aimed at those in need and they are less susceptible to corruption (since they go directly to recipients, officials cannot skim money from them);
- increase a nation's foreign reserves and thereby reduce its borrowing costs;
- be monitored better by intimates than by officials.

Overall, as the Minister of Émigrés in Morocco, put it: "The impact [of remittances] is decisive, enormous, we have a construction boom across the country. This is an important safeguard against poverty and helps to modernize our rural society" (quoted in the *Economist* 2008: January 3 ["Send me a Number"]).

There are negatives associated with remittances as well as the immigration they help to encourage that are difficult to rebut. First, the most skilled and educated in less developed countries would be the ones most likely to leave, and to remain in developed countries, because of the greater earnings and the resulting ability to remit money to loved ones in their home countries. This creates a drain on the economy of the home countries; those most likely to succeed are precisely those most likely to emigrate.

Second, the money that is infused into the local economy does not necessarily translate into economic growth and development. The increases in personal consumption made possible by remittances do not lead to greater investment in the economic infrastructure that could fuel economic development. As one scholar said: "If I ask can you name a single country that has developed through remittances, the answer is no – there's none" (quoted in DeParle 2008: A9). However, some Southern countries (e.g. Brazil, Egypt, El Salvador, Kazakhstan, Guatemala, and Mexico) are making greater efforts to see to it that more of this money is being invested in infrastructure and industry. Banks in these countries are using future remittance flows to acquire cheaper and longer-term financing that can finance infrastructure projects (Ratha and Mohapatra 2012). In any case, greater consumption among the poor can be seen as a good thing.

Third, those who receive remittances can become targets of local gangs interested in stealing either the cash received or the products purchased with that cash.

Fourth, the money sometimes goes to countries that have regimes that are highly dubious such as Zimbabwe and North Korea. That is, while those who send the money are supporting, perhaps only indirectly, regimes of choice, it may be that from a broader global perspective those regimes should not be supported.

Fifth, it is surprisingly costly (although that cost has been declining) to send remittances and those who process such payments also manipulate exchange rates to further enhance their profits and thereby to reduce the actual amount of money being remitted to developing countries.

Sixth, while they may help, remittances are no cure for poverty. On their own, they are unable to lift a country out of poverty. And there is a fear that those who receive remittances will become dependent and reduce their efforts to find ways to make it on their own.

Seventh, there are the problems of those left behind by those who migrate in search of work such as broken families, delinquent children, and the like. Said a UNICEF official: "Behind every remittance, there's a separated family" (quoted in DeParle 2008: A9). Remittances can also be a source of divisiveness within families (Schmalzbauer 2008). Those who go abroad in search of work may be also abused, forced into sex work, beaten, or even killed.

Eighth, the poorest nations are not the greatest recipients of remittances. In fact, it is middle-income countries that are the largest recipients. Similarly, within the poorest countries, the poorest people are *not* the most likely to receive remittances.

Finally, in the end, we are still talking about relatively small sums of money and it tends to obscure the problem of the exploitation of migrants. It also "tends to justify the way the world is being restructured for the benefit of a small elite" (quoted in DeParle 2008: A9).

Overall, then, remittances have been an increasing reality, but perhaps not an unmitigated boon to the economies of developing countries and to the people who remain behind. Yet, there are many whose lives are materially better as a result of remittances. As a pioneer in the area of remittances put it, "Let's not forget, a billion dollars in the hands of poor people is a lot of money" (quoted in DeParle 2008: A9).

Increasing barriers to immigration into the US, especially from Mexico, have affected remittances from the US to Mexico. From 2000 to 2008 such remittances grew from $6.6 billion to $27 billion, at times reaching increases of 20% per year. However, remittances declined after 2008 and were at $22.4 billion in 2012 (Villagran 2013). In addition to increased border restrictions (and the resulting higher cost of an illegal crossing), other reasons for this decline include lower rates of economic growth and a dramatic drop in American housing construction where many undocumented immigrants could get work more easily, the return by many to Mexico, and the fact that those who remain are sending smaller amounts of money back home. Many communities in Mexico are being hurt economically as a result of the decline in remittances.

Western Union and the business of global remittances

The giant in the remittance business is Western Union (DeParle 2007a: A1, A6). The company began in 1851, became famous and important in the telegram business, but declined dramatically with the rise of airmail, faxes, the Internet, e-mail, and the like. It began to rise again with a focus on money transfer. The company is praised for providing immigrants with a safe way for transmitting money, and criticized, as is the rest of the remittance industry, for its high fees (up to 20%) and predatory pricing (it continues to have the highest prices in the industry), as well as its deceptive advertising (it settled a lawsuit in which it was accused of concealing its high fees [Silver-Greenberg 2012]). Its business is seen as enabling immigration and even encouraging unauthorized immigration in the sense that undocumented immigrants come with the knowledge that Western Union will allow them to send money home. For example, the Attorney General of Arizona said that Western Union is "protecting an illegal enterprise in human smuggling…. It's outrageous" (quoted in DeParle 2007a: A6).

As of June 2013, Western Union (and its Vigo and Orlandi Valuta branded services) had 520,000 locations worldwide (in comparison, this is 15 times more locations than McDonald's). They are in small shops, in large supermarket chains, and even part of the Chinese postal system. They are truly global in scope and they advertise their global operations by appealing to the use of remittances: "With more and more people leaving their homelands to make a living in other countries, the value of our services increases immensely and we have committed more resources toward various regions" (Western Union 2013).

While Western Union remains the industry leader, their share of the market has fallen dramatically. In the late 1990s, they controlled a staggering 75% of the market in global remittances (Kitroeff 2013). But with greater competition from other large (e.g. MoneyGram) and small competitors, their market share and fees have fallen. Western Union's market share has now fallen to 15%, while MoneyGram's market share has gone from 22% to 5% in the same time period.

With greater competition to facilitate the global flows of remittances, the costs of sending money worldwide have fallen significantly. In the late 1990s, the average cost to send $300 was 15%, but those costs have fallen to 10% today (Kitroeff 2013). This does vary further by country. For example, the cost of sending $300 to Mexico has fallen from 9.5% to just over 2%. Estefana Bautista, a Mexican migrant who came to Texas in 2005 and left two children behind in Mexico, said her fees have fallen by $5 over the last several years. "I send those five dollars to Mexico," Bautista noted. "My kids know that they're getting a little more money every two weeks." The downside to this growing market, and its diversity of players, is that it has also made it susceptible to counterfeit services, where immigrants have been defrauded out of their paychecks that they send back to their families.

Furthermore, there are potentials for decreasing the cost of remittances through innovative technologies and mobile money transfers (Ratha and Mohapatra 2012). In domestic transfers, mobile phones have already been used in several countries (e.g. Kenya), and they have successfully enabled individuals to send smaller sums of money and to send them more frequently, thus increasing the total amount sent for less cost. While there have been some pilot programs to integrate these mobile technologies into international transfers, their application has been very limited because of regulations that combat money laundering and financing of terror operations across borders.

DIASPORA

Diaspora:
The large-scale dispersal of a population.

The term **diaspora** has a long and rather specific history, but it has come to be adopted by various groups to describe their situation (and that of others); it has also come to be used widely in the popular media to describe a range of population movements (Braziel 2008; Fiddian-Qasmiyeh 2012; McAuliffe 2007; Sheffer 2013). The term is, of course, most associated with the dispersion of Jews to many places in the world in both the years before and after the birth of Christ. In 586 BC, the Babylonians dispersed the Jews from Judea and in 136 AD it was the Romans who chased the Jews out of Jerusalem (Armstrong 1996). In recent years, however, the use of the term has broadened to include the dispersion, dislocation, and deterritorialization of *any* population (Bauman 2000: 314). Most frequently, a diaspora involves the large-scale dispersal of a religious, ethnic, racial, or national group. In addition to the Jews, other groups that have experienced diasporas include the Lebanese, Palestinians, Armenians, and the Irish. In fact, the term has come to be used so widely and loosely that many complain that diaspora discourse has lost a consensus on the meaning of the term (Lie 1995), its meaning has in fact become *less* clear,[7] and it is in danger of becoming little more than a "buzzword" (Cohen 1999: 3). It seems clear that it is best to differentiate among the various diasporas rather than to combine them all under one all-encompassing heading.

Nevertheless, there have been a number of efforts to develop an ideal-typical diaspora by enumerating its various characteristics. Safran, for example, discusses "expatriate minority communities" that are dispersed from some original central location to two or more peripheral locations; have a collective memory or mythology of their homeland that is maintained by the community and that binds them together; involve people who are alienated from the country from which they emanated and are not – and may never be – fully accepted there; involve people who nevertheless idealize a return to their ancestral homeland and maintain a commitment to restore their homeland to its former glories (e.g. independence, prosperity);[8] maintain a relationship to the homeland not only through a commitment to its restoration, but also through group solidarity and consciousness resulting from this commitment. Of course, since this is an ideal type, no single diaspora conforms to all of these dimensions,[9] nor could any of them (Clifford 1994).

In another approach, a diaspora can be seen as involving one, several, or all of the following (Vertovec 1999: 447–62). First, it is a social form. That form is defined by the fact that relationships are maintained even though the population has been dispersed. The population spans transnational borders; they constitute transnational communities. They involve a group of people who collectively define themselves as such even though they may be widely dispersed, perhaps even globally. While they reside in a different locale, they relate to the homeland from which they and/or their forebears came. Second, a diaspora involves a type of consciousness. Those involved have great sensitivity to various interconnections, especially those that span borders, and to attachments that are decentered. They are aware of being different from those around them and of the fact that those they identify with exist in multiple locales, as well as in the homeland. Third, diaspora is a mode of cultural production. The diaspora's cultural objects, meanings, and images are produced in, and involve, global flows. Thus, they are highly fluid and subject to many mutual influences, negotiations, transformations, and contestations. Fourth, a diaspora is political. Individuals and/or collectivities involved in diasporas often become important political players in both their host country as well as internationally (prominent examples include Palestinians and Tibetans) (Bruneau 1995).

However, the preceding are rather static approaches to diaspora that are inconsistent with the more fluid orientation to globalization adopted in this book. A better approach, at least for our purposes, is to be found in Paul Gilroy's (1993: 190) *The Black Atlantic* which, most generally, is concerned with "flows, exchanges and in-between elements." Implied here is a sense of diaspora as process, specifically a transnational process. It is not tied to any specific locale (especially nation-state) but involves a constant dialogue with both real and imagined locales. Thus, the Black Atlantic (Black cultures in the Atlantic basin) cannot be understood as West Indian, British, or American, but as an ongoing relationship involving the Black Atlantic in its entirety. The Black Atlantic (and diasporas in general) is therefore an imagined (and contested) community rather than a specific geographic space(s). Thus, Gilroy (1993: 18) concludes that the Black Atlantic should be seen as "a deterritorialised, multiplex and anti-national basis for the affinity or 'identity of passions' between diverse black populations."

The use of the term diaspora has expanded with the process of globalization. There are not only more diasporas, but more people describe themselves and their relationships with others in these terms. This relates, in Dufoix's (2007) view, to the expansion of "trans-state collective experiences linked to an organized referent (e.g. a state, a land, a nation, a people, a language, a culture)." In fact, the use of the term has become so common that Dufoix (2007: 314) describes the "diasporization" of the world. It shares with globalization "processes such as the shrinking of the world, a disembeddedness of time and space, glocalization, instantaneous communication, the reshaping of geography, and the spatialization of the social." While diasporas were relatively unusual in a world dominated by powerful nation-states and territories, they have proliferated with the decline of the nation-state and deterritorialization. Furthermore, the trans state community networks that characterize diasporas today are made possible by a wide range of technologies (e.g. inexpensive air travel, cheap international phone calls and phone cards [Vertovec 2004: 219–24], cell phones, the Internet, Skype) that make communication among far-flung people possible. Thus, diasporization and globalization are closely linked today, and since the latter will continue to develop and expand, we can expect more and more dispersals that are, or at least are called, diasporas.

New technologies are playing such an increasing role in diasporas that it could be argued that we have seen the emergence of "virtual diasporas" (Laguerre 2002; Oiarzabal and Reips 2012). These virtual worlds have been created through a variety of information and communication technologies, including mobile phones, e-mails, video chats, and social media. These technologies have provided new ways for people to maintain links with one another and for communities to maintain themselves and even to create new communities. Of course, a virtual diaspora requires the prior existence of a real diaspora, the real dispersal of a given population.

One very contemporary example of a diaspora, part of one of the longest-term and truest diasporas, involves the Lebanese (*Economist* 2013: March 16). In the past century, several waves of Lebanese have left the country for Africa and the Americans, and more recently, because of the 2008 street-fighting involving Hezbollah. Continuing instability in the country (political assassinations; the lack of a stable government; clashes between Shias and Sunnis, etc.) and region (e.g. civil war in neighboring Syria) make it hard to run a business or to travel to and from the Lebanon. As a result, there is a "brain drain" (see below) as the most educated and trained Lebanese are those best able to emigrate, increasingly these days to oil-rich Gulf states. For example, the Lebanese-Mexican telecommunications tycoon, Carlos Slim, is the wealthiest person in the world; Nick Hayek, a Swiss-Lebanese man, is CEO of Swatch, the largest producer of Swiss watches. In many cases, Lebanese have gone elsewhere (most commonly, Brazil, the US, and West Africa), secured good, high-paying jobs, and are sending much needed money back to Lebanon. The Lebanese diaspora has a strong sense of their ethnic identity abroad and form close-knit communities in their new countries. They are also highly devoted to their home country and they go to great lengths in order to get back home, especially Christian Lebanese during the Christmas season.

IMMIGRANT ENTREPRENEURS IN THE US

The life of migrants in the US today is not all doom and gloom. For example, the large number of new immigrant groups to the US is creating new, and ever-changing, entrepreneurial opportunities, especially for immigrants who have the understanding, expertise, and skill needed to provide various ethnic groups with what they need in terms of food, clothing, travel, and so on. A 2012 report showed that "10.5 percent of the immigrant workforce owns a business compared with 9.3 percent of the non-immigrant (i.e. U.S.-born) workforce" (Fairlie 2012). What is even more striking is that immigrants are twice as likely to start a new business, compared with the native-born population. About one in four American engineering and technology companies that started between 2006 and 2012 had at least one founder who was born outside the US (Rampell 2013). This is serving both to inject a new source of entrepreneurialism, as well as increasing ethnic diversity, into American culture. While these developments have historically been centered in the largest cities, they are now spreading to the suburbs and to smaller cities. A notable example of this spread is Golden Krust Caribbean Bakery, begun in 1989 by an immigrant from Jamaica. It now has over 100 franchise restaurants throughout the United States. It is much more difficult for undocumented immigrants to create such businesses, but they are often served by them. Those who succeed can begin to engage in tourism and can be better thought of as tourists rather than migrants.

BRAIN DRAIN

The global flow of people has many dimensions and carries with it many implications. People flow around the world for a wide range of reasons and they bring with them a wide variety of things. One of those things that is of overwhelming importance is intellectual capacity and ability. People with great intellect and advanced training and education, with much intellectual capital, are highly prized elsewhere in the world and the loss of such people by a given locale involves what is often called the **brain drain** (Manashi Ray 2012). Clearly, the systematic loss of those highly skilled migrants and their intellectual capital is a source of great concern and would, over the long term, have a negative effect on the locale that is a net loser of its best-educated people.

Brain drain: Systematic loss by a nation-state of people highly prized elsewhere in the world.

The issue of the brain drain has a long history and it has affected, and continues to affect, nation-states in various ways at different points in time (Docquier and Rapoport 2012). Furthermore, the directionality of the flows of those with great intellectual capital often varies from one place and time to another. In some places and times, the flows are primarily outward, while at others they are primarily inward. Whatever the primary direction, in almost all places and times it is bi-directional.

Israel

Concern has grown in Israel, especially at the beginning of the twenty-first century, about a brain drain (Ram 2008: 46). Consider the 2013 Nobel Prize winners in chemistry; three Americans won the prize, and two of those Americans were immigrants from Israel. There is a greater likelihood that those with advanced education will now move from Israel to other countries. Academics, for example, are driven to leave by the general atmosphere of instability and the dangers associated with terrorism and warfare. They are also led to leave because of more mundane problems such as low wages, high taxes, and an inflexible labor market. As a result, since 2008, one in five faculty members have left Israeli universities to work in American universities; one in four Israeli scientists have emigrated to other countries (Fisher 2013).

Japan

In the case of Japan, skilled workers – especially engineers – with high levels of education and training are increasingly active in searching out job opportunities in other Asian countries, especially Taiwan, South Korea, and now China (Reuters 2012). Since its peak in the 1980s and 1990s, the Japanese economy has not only declined, but employees are less likely to have lifetime job security. The result is that it is harder to find jobs in Japan and those that exist are less desirable than in the past. Furthermore, neighboring economies have boomed opening up more job opportunities there for skilled Japanese workers. Higher pay is not the only lure to Japanese engineers. In Taiwan, they are being offered the opportunity to start up whole new businesses (Fackler 2007a: C1, C5). Furthermore they are offered amenities such as Japanese-style schools, restaurants, karaoke bars, and even "massage parlors." In China, the manufacturing boom is attracting highly skilled Japanese workers that could no longer find comparable jobs in their home country. Employers benefit from a newly innovative workforce, which many critics contend is lacking because their educational system favors rote learning. On the losing end of this migration, a Japanese government official argued, "From Japan's perspective, emerging countries are getting a free ride of the benefits we nurtured. So yes, it is a problem" (Reuters 2012). There is concern not only about the loss of talent and technological expertise, but also that Taiwan and China can produce high quality goods at a much cheaper cost, thereby adversely affecting Japan's economy.

The South

While the brain drain is a great concern in the North, it is of even greater concern in the South where there is evidence that some countries' best and brightest are leaving, making it difficult for various tasks to be handled at home. South Africa has large numbers of college graduates each year, but many of them leave for places like Great Britain and Australia. In Morocco those with, for example, computer skills often leave for other nations, especially France. The result is that while Morocco is in great need of upgrading its Internet systems, many of its best-trained people in this area are elsewhere, perhaps members of a Moroccan IT association in Paris. More than half the college graduates in places like Jamaica, Trinidad, and Senegal have moved abroad. In African countries, from where one in five doctors is working overseas, hospitals struggle to care for patients because skilled medical personnel are emigrating to the Gulf States, the EU, and so on. On one medical doctor's recent trip to Africa, he was introduced to a woman with a tumor on her face. She had been waiting for three months for specialized equipment so that the surgery could be performed (Boahene 2013). While waiting, the tumor spread and began affecting her vision in one eye. The visiting doctor reviewed her case and, using available equipment, fully removed her tumor with a two-hour surgery but only after it had permanently compromised her vision. As for many patients, the lack of proper medical expertise cost her dearly. These educated workers are all pulled by higher wages and better living conditions, but they are also pushed by low wages, poor living and working conditions, a crumbling infrastructure, and so on (*Economist* 2008: January 3 ["Open Up"]).

Questioning the brain drain

Brain gain: Nation-states, especially those that are developed, acquire more people with a strong knowledge base than they lose.

Yet, as with much else in globalization, there is another side to this issue. For one thing, there is what has been called the **brain gain** (DeParle 2007b; Manashi Ray 2012). That is, it is also possible that nations will be net gainers in this domain acquiring more people with an increased knowledge base than they lose. Unfortunately, historically and to some extent to this day, it is the rich and powerful countries of the North that are the net gainers in this process. For example, efforts are underway to deal with the problem of a nurse shortage in the US by luring nurses from various other nations, often Southern nations such as the Philippines and India. To the degree that this effort is successful, the US will gain high-quality nurses whereas other nations, often in the South, will lose them. And it is likely to be successful if for no other reason than the pay gap. A 2008 study found that Ugandan nurses start at $115 per month (compared to $3,000–4,000 per month in the US); it is no wonder that 70% of nursing students surveyed wanted to work outside Uganda, with most preferring work in the US or UK (Nguyen et al. 2008).

It is also possible that in some cases nations may regain well-trained personnel who return with even more knowledge and training than they had when they left. This can be thought of as "brain circulation" (Saxenian 2006: 18). Taiwan is a notable example of a nation that has lured back better trained and more experienced personnel to its research and development centers, many of whom had left previously for better opportunities elsewhere.

There are a number of other reasons to question the idea that the brain drain has only negative consequences for the locale that is losing its best-trained and most skilled people. It is not the case that most of the world's migrants are doctors, engineers, and physicists who emigrate in search of money (Moses 2006: 174); more of the émigrés are less- and un-skilled people whose loss to the sending locale is not as great and may even be beneficial (e.g. reducing the economic burden they may place on the state). Émigrés can perform various functions for the sending countries such as providing important networks (involving people and technology) and sending remittances home. The ability of highly trained natives to emigrate can lead others in the sending countries to acquire advanced education and can strengthen the educational system at home. There is also a moral argument here. That is, it is immoral to try to prevent those with skills, indeed anyone, from migrating. Thus, there are those who say that whatever the costs back home, it would be immoral to prevent those who want to leave from leaving.

HUMAN TRAFFICKING

While some migrants move voluntarily and some migrants move because they have to (e.g. owing to lack of economic opportunities, war, environmental disaster), it is the case that all victims of human trafficking are moved by force and coercion. According to the

2000 United Nations Protocol to Prevent, Suppress, and Punish Trafficking in Persons, especially Women and Children, **human trafficking** is:

> The recruitment, transportation, transfer, harboring or receipt of persons, by means of the threat or use of force or other forms of coercion, of abduction, of fraud, of deception, of the abuse of power or of a position of vulnerability or of the giving or receiving of payments or benefits to achieve the consent of a person having control over another person, for the purpose of exploitation.

Human trafficking: The recruitment and movement of people through force or coercion, for purposes of sexual exploitation or forced labor.

While this definition of human trafficking involves the movement of people both within and across borders, we focus here on international trafficking. These flows of trafficked individuals for purposes of sexual exploitation and forced labor have expanded exponentially since the early 2000s (Farr 2005, 2013).

As for any illicit behavior, measuring human trafficking is very difficult and estimates therefore vary significantly. The most commonly cited estimates show that between 700,000 and 2 million people are trafficked internationally each year, but estimates can range up to 4 million people. While we are most concerned with international flows of people here, domestic trafficking is even more widespread, with an additional 2 to 4 million people trafficked annually within countries. It is frequently assumed that trafficking victims only flow from developing to developed countries, but trafficking *within* both developed countries [e.g. the US] and developing countries [e.g. India] is also very common. The vast majority of trafficking victims are women and girls (75%) but many are boys and men, with 27% of them children (United Nations Office on Drugs and Crime [UNODC] 2012). Common global trafficking routes are similar to those for unauthorized immigration. For example, routes into the US are often through Mexico and sometimes through Canada or by air, and typical routes into Europe include going through northern Africa, Northeastern Europe, or Central Eastern European countries (Jakobi 2012).

The human trafficking industry is organized through complex global networks, and with high demand, high profits, and relatively low risk for traffickers, business is booming (Shelley 2010). In 2005 – the most recent year for which global revenues in human trafficking were calculated – the International Labor Organization (ILO) estimated that human trafficking netted $31.6 billion in profits (UNODC 2012). The network is largely driven by transnational criminal organizations that connect with other criminal organizations and ethnically based organizations. It also relies on a variety of "corrupt guardians" (Farr 2005), including immigration officers, embassy officials, border patrol agents, and police officers that either facilitate or ignore the illicit flows of trafficked victims.

We will look separately at sex trafficking and labor trafficking. While most estimates indicate that sex trafficking is more typical, with the United Nations Office on Drugs and Crime (2012) stating it constitutes approximately 79% of human trafficking, some critics contend that labor trafficking is grossly underestimated and the ILO (2012) argues that it is the more common form of trafficking accounting for 68% of all trafficking victims.

SEX TRAFFICKING

People who are victims of sex trafficking are used as sexual slaves or forced into prostitution, where the entire income usually goes to a pimp. For example, Marinela Badea was kidnapped from her home in Romania when she was 17 years old (Townsend 2011).

She was doing her homework when two men appeared at the door. They forced her from her home, and within three hours, they raped Marinela. They held her prisoner then gave her a fake passport and smuggled her into the UK. In a new country where she did not know the language, Marinela was raped an average of 50 times each week at a massage parlor in Manchester. On her first day of forced work, Marinela earned £300, which was more than her family earned in six weeks in Romania, but her pimps kept all of it. She was forced to work 12-hour shifts, seven days per week. Any time Marinela refused to do as she was told, she was severely beaten – often having her head banged on a wall or table – or her trafficker threatened to kill her.

Occasionally, trafficked individuals like Marinela are abducted and brought into the sex trade, but usually they are enticed into it through a deceitful job offer. Traffickers often target areas with high unemployment, and make promises of a job in another country or at the trafficker's own business (e.g. offering work in a restaurant, office, or domestic labor), then later force the person into becoming a sex slave or worker. Some are sold by their parents or relatives (Lee 2012c). However, not all victims are poor women seeking jobs; traffickers also target vulnerable children with family problems (e.g. who might have run away from home) and then serve as their caring (older) boyfriend only to bring them into the sex trade.

Once at their destination, women have their passport confiscated and are told that they must work off a considerable "debt." For example, women taken from Southeast Asia and trafficked into the US, Canada, or Japan for sex work have average debts of $25,000 to $30,000 (Farr 2013). Women trafficked within a smaller region often have smaller debts, but sex services totaling those "debts" are not a guarantee of a woman's freedom. Instead, traffickers often charge fees for room and board, medical fees, and behavioral violations – or they might simply sell them to another trafficker. In addition to controlling women through debts or withholding their identification documents, traffickers commonly beat and rape their women, have guards watch over them, and threaten to use violence against their family back home. Their living conditions are terrible, their work expectations are extreme (providing sexual services for up to 25–30 men per day), and they are exposed to very high rates of sexually transmitted infections.

LABOR TRAFFICKING

Labor trafficking also involves high degrees of exploitation, where workers toil under conditions of slavery, often receiving no wage, no time off, physical abuse, and poor living conditions. Some types of migrants described earlier (especially low-skilled, temporary, and irregular migrants) are especially vulnerable to forced labor conditions.

The number of people in forced labor around the world is very high (the ILO's [2012] estimate of 20.9 million forced laborers globally means that three out of every 1,000 people are trapped in forced labor at any particular time), but most of these people are not trafficked across borders. Unlike sex trafficking, most forced labor occurs in or near one's home or area of residence. It is much less common in labor trafficking to move victims across international borders, but the majority of those trafficked into forced labor are brought from the global South to the global North.

One common form of international labor trafficking is for domestic labor in more affluent countries. Women are often trafficked from countries like China, Mexico, and Vietnam

(Bales et al. 2004), and end up in Europe, North America, the Middle East, Japan, Malaysia, Singapore, South Korea, and Hong Kong. Like many victims of sex trafficking, they are enticed with fraudulent job offers and pay high fees to get them, and once they arrive at their destination, these enslaved domestic workers are unable to leave their employer's home without permission.

Domestic workers are also trafficked into countries using authorized routes by foreign diplomats (Farr 2013). For example, foreign diplomats to the US are permitted to transport domestic workers on special (A-3 and G-5) visas. A Kuwaiti diplomat and his wife brought in Mani Kumari Sabbithi, an Indian national, on one such visa (Frederickson and Leveille 2007). After confiscating her passport once they had brought her into the US, the couple forced her to work 16–19 hours per day, every single day. They also beat her, would not allow her to leave the house, and would not allow her medical care. Sabbithi attempted to sue her "employers" for trafficking and forced labor, but the suit was dismissed in 2009 because the diplomats "were entitled to diplomatic immunity and could not be sued in the United States" and the US Trafficking Victims Protection Act "does not override diplomatic immunity."

TOURISM

In this final section we turn to the kind of flows of people with which we are most familiar – vacationers – those who engage in tourism. However, it is important to remember that tourism (McCannell 1989; Urry 2002; Weaver 2012) is not necessarily global in scope. There have long been global tourists and far more people today are tourists on a global scale than has ever been the case in the past. A key factor, of course, is the rise of the passenger jet airplane and, more recently, the arrival of budget airlines (e.g. Ryanair in Europe) that have made global travel far more affordable for far more people. In spite of this, we must remember how few people travel for pleasure, let alone travel globally. Tourism, especially global tourism, is largely restricted to the world's elites, especially from the North.

Globalization is closely associated with the movement of all sorts of people, including tourists. Because of globalization, far more people are interested in global travel, are knowledgeable about places throughout the world, and have available a wide array of modern, high-speed conveyances able to transport them from one location to another, even the world's most remote places such as the Galápagos Islands off the coast of Ecuador. This, of course, is the site of Charles Darwin's famous research and life today on the islands is much as it was in Darwin's time. One can get to those islands via an international flight to Guayaquil and an internal flight to Baltra, and then travel between the islands by boat. There are a number of companies offering tours of, say, a week's duration that travel between several of the islands. To keep damage to the ecology to a minimum, these usually involve fairly small ships – a maximum of about 100 people. Those on these tours sleep and eat on the boats. Some of these tours are extremely expensive, while others are more budget-conscious, although certainly not inexpensive.

It is the availability of relatively low-priced transportation and organized tours that has played a huge role in the increase in global tourism. As a result, what were once thought to be among the world's most remote and/or unlikeliest of locations have become part of global tourism (see below).

SPECIALIZED FORMS OF TOURISM

**Ecotourism:
Tourists
experience
natural
environments
while doing
little or no
harm to
them.**

Ecotourism involves efforts to allow tourists to experience natural environments while doing little or no harm to them. It is animated, of course, by the fact that so much tourism is destructive to the environment. Many nations seek to encourage ecotourism, but the contradiction is that the more it succeeds, the more tourists will be drawn to these natural environments. No matter how much care is taken, large numbers of tourists are likely to do at least some harm to the environment. The Galápagos are one natural resource for which efforts have been made to practice ecotourism on most of the islands in the chain. There are limits to the number of people who can visit (as well as the number of people who can live there – most of the inhabitants are restricted to one island) and to where they can go and what they can do on the islands (in most cases they cannot stay overnight on the islands, but must sleep on the ships that bring them). As pointed out above, there are also limits to the size of the ships that ply the waters between the islands. Nonetheless, the Galápagos are being stressed by the large numbers attracted to them even though those numbers would qualify as ecotoursists.

**Ethnotourism:
Tourists
experiencing
the way other
people live,
often people
very different
from
themselves.**

Ethnotourism involves efforts to experience the way other peoples live, often people very different from the tourists. Touring the Galápagos is more about seeing natural sights, while a tour of, say, Malaysia might be more about seeing how Malaysians live. *Adventure tourism* involves trips to remote, often difficult, natural environments. The point is the adventure and not necessarily to see natural sights or people. Then there are a variety of other forms of "niche tourism" such as those that focus on sex (Cliff and Carter 1998; Robinson 2007), food, wine, the interests of gays, war, heritage, and so forth.

ADVERSE EFFECTS OF TOURISM

It is certainly true that global tourism is big business and an important source of revenue to many locales (Apostolopoulos et al. 2013). Furthermore, many people are employed in various positions throughout the tourism industry. Tourism is a source of a great deal of fun for many people and to many it is also a highly educational experience. However, tourism is not without its negative sides.

While tourism in some popular destinations such as the Galápagos is carefully managed with the result that damage to the environment is minimal, that is not necessarily true in many other places in the world experiencing huge increases in tourism (e.g. the Acropolis in Athens, Greece; the Forbidden City and Great Wall in China; and the Hagia Sophia area in Istanbul, Turkey).

The temples of Angkor Wat, traceable to the ninth and tenth centuries, in Cambodia were impossible to reach for most tourists for many years because of warfare there and an oppressive political regime. However, in recent years the tourists have returned, and are arriving in droves. Over 2 million tourists visited Angkor Wat in 2013, 12 times the number that came in 2000, and that number is likely to increase dramatically in the coming years. Angkor Wat is Cambodia's largest tourist attraction, and by a wide margin. Its appeal brings in badly needed income, but at the cost of preservation, restoration, and study of the sites. The mass of tourists are also beginning to damage the temples, including damage to the stone path leading to them and to statues and carvings in the temples. Graffiti is spray painted on walls adjacent to sandstone carvings. The Cambodian government would like to do a better job of protecting the temples, but it lacks the money to do so. Contradictorily, the government has embarked on a campaign to bring yet more tourists to Angkor Wat. Sound and light shows have been added and Japanese tourist groups have been granted the right to hold huge moonlit banquets on the grounds. Predictably, a local tourist and preservation official said, "Angkor has become a sort of cultural Disneyland" (quoted in Faiola 2007: A10).

CHAPTER SUMMARY

This chapter analyzes the global flow of people as migrants, victims of human trafficking, and tourists.

Migrants are differentiated by "push" factors (for instance lack of employment opportunities in home countries), as well as "pull" factors (available work elsewhere) motivating the migration. This includes temporary migrants, irregular migrants (who lack proper documentation), and highly skilled migrants. Forced migrants include refugees forced to flee their home countries due to safety concerns, and asylum seekers who wish to remain in the country to which they flee. Family reunification migrants move internationally to reunite with family. Return migrants ultimately move back to their originating country after spending time in their destination country.

Unlike other global flows, labor migration still faces many restrictions. Many of these barriers are related to the Westphalian conception of the nation-state and are intimately associated with it. The state may seek to control migration because it involves the loss of part of the workforce. An influx of migrants can lead to conflicts with local residents. Concerns about terrorism also affect the desire of the state to restrict population flows.

Many countries face issues of undocumented migration. The US faces a major influx of unauthorized immigrants from Mexico and other Central American states. The political backlash has prompted the construction of a giant fence along the US–Mexico border to control this flow of people. However, questions about its efficacy (it is thought that it will only lead undocumented immigrants to adopt more dangerous methods to gain entry) and its extraordinary cost have halted construction. In addition, tighter borders have also had the effect of "locking in" people who might otherwise have left the country. Other countries with similar concerns about undocumented immigration include Great Britain, Switzerland, Sweden, and Greece as well as countries in Asia.

A strong case can be made against the backlash against undocumented immigrants. In the North, such immigrants constitute a younger workforce which does work that locals may not perform, and they are consumers who contribute to growth. They also send remittances back to family members in the country of origin, which improves the lives of the recipients, reduces poverty rates, and increases the level of education as well as the foreign reserves of the home country. Banks are often unwilling or unable to handle the type (small amounts of money) and volume of remittances. As a result, specialized organizations such as Western Union play a major role in the transmission of remittances.

Labor flows also raise concerns regarding a brain drain – it is often people with greater intellect and more advanced education and training who migrate willingly to other countries. However, these arguments are countered by a theory of brain gain, which emphasizes the eventual return to their home country of migrants who are better trained and have access to better networks.

The term diaspora is increasingly being used to describe migrant communities. Of particular interest is Paul Gilroy's conceptualization of the diaspora as a transnational process, which involves dialogue with both imagined and real locales. Diasporization and globalization are closely interconnected and the expansion of the latter will lead to an increase in the former. Today there exist virtual diasporas which utilize technology such as the Internet to maintain the community network.

While migration is motivated by a combination of voluntary and/or involuntary factors, human trafficking is the recruitment and movement of people through force or coercion for purposes of sexual exploitation or forced labor. As an industry, human trafficking has grown significantly since the early 2000s, and there are now between 700,000 and 2 million people trafficked internationally each year (domestic human trafficking is a big problem as well). The majority of trafficking victims are females, many are children, and the profits from trafficking bring huge revenues to the criminal networks that coordinate its global flows.

People who are victims of sex trafficking are used as sexual slaves or forced into prostitution, where the entire income usually goes to a pimp. The most common way in which individuals are sex trafficked is through a deceitful job offer. Traffickers often target areas with high unemployment, and make promises of a job in another country or at the trafficker's own business, then later force the person into becoming a sex slave or worker. Labor trafficking also involves high degrees of exploitation, where workers toil under conditions of slavery, often receiving no wage, no time off, physical abuse, and poor living conditions.

The growth of tourism has been facilitated by access to relatively low-priced transport. However, it is still mostly restricted to elites, especially from the North. Specialized forms of tourism like ecotourism, ethnotourism, adventure tourism, and niche tourism have developed – but they pose many adverse effects on the environment and populations visited.

DISCUSSION QUESTIONS

1. Is the heightened flow of people a unique feature of the current global era?

2. Analyze the concept of an "undocumented migrant." Why might someone use the term "illegal immigrant" rather than calling them an undocumented immigrant? Trace the repercussions of such labeling.

3. Has globalization facilitated or obstructed greater labor migration?

4. Examine the concept of "diaspora as a transnational process," in the context of global technological flows.

5. Compare the "brain drain" and "brain gain." Are these comparable processes? Do they affect different parts of the world differently?

6. How is human trafficking different from migration? What are the most common means through which people become involved in human trafficking?

ADDITIONAL READINGS ···

Jonathon W. Moses. *International Migration: Globalization's Last Frontier*. London: Zed Books, 2006.

Steven Gold and Stephanie Nawyn, eds. *The Routledge International Handbook of Migration Studies*. New York: Routledge, 2013.

Jana Evans Braziel. *Diaspora: An Introduction*. Oxford: Blackwell, 2008.

Ajaya Kumar Sahoo and Johannes G. De Kruijf, eds. *Indian Transnationalism Online: New Perspectives on Diaspora*. Ashgate, 2014.

Paul Gilroy. *The Black Atlantic: Modernity and Double-Consciousness*. Cambridge: Harvard University Press, 1993.

Uri Ram. *The Globalization of Israel*. New York: Routledge, 2008.

Annalee Saxenian. *The New Argonauts: Regional Advantage in a Global Economy*. Cambridge, MA: Harvard University Press, 2006.

Kathryn Farr. *Sex Trafficking: The Global Market in Women and Children*. New York: Worth, 2005.

Louise Shelley. *Human Trafficking: A Global Perspective*. New York: Cambridge University Press, 2010.

Yiorgos Apostolopoulos, Stella Leivadi, and Andrew Yiannakis, eds. *The Sociology of Tourism: Theoretical and Empirical Investigations*. New York: Routledge, 2013.

NOTES ···

1 A good online source of information on migration is *Migration Information Source*; http://www.migrationpolicy.org/programs/migration-information-source.

2 It is important to note that there are other types of global flows of people (e.g. pilgrimages, the best known of which is to Mecca), but they will not be dealt with here, see Boisvert (2007).

3 These terms are usually used interchangeably to describe those seeking protection in another country from various dangers and threats at home. On asylum seekers, see Richmond (2007).

4 Refugees (and asylum seekers) can be differentiated from *displaced persons* ("internally displaced people") who may experience problems similar to those faced by refugees, but when they move, they remain within the nation-state in which they were born or in which they live, see Wilkinson (2006: 4–19).

5 *Economist* (2008: January 3 ["Of Bedsheets and Bison Grass Vodka"]); in an astonishing case of dependence on migrants, 85% of the population of the United Arab Emirates are foreigners.

6 Remittances also occur much more informally, see Pieke, Van Hear, and Lindley (2007: 348–66).

7 Butler (2001). Also see Fludernik (2003: xii).

8 Safran (1991); for other iterations see Cohen (1999).

9 Safran (1991); for other iterations see Cohen (1999).

GLOBAL ENVIRONMENTAL FLOWS

Globalization: A Basic Text, Second Edition. George Ritzer and Paul Dean.
© 2015 John Wiley & Sons, Ltd. Published 2015 by John Wiley & Sons, Ltd.

I n this chapter and the next we deal with what can be termed "negative global flows." As we saw in Chapter 1, the idea of flows owes a large debt to Zygmunt Bauman and his thinking on the liquid society (as well as to the work of others including Arjun Appadurai [Chapter 7]). This analysis now owes a further debt to Bauman (2006: 96) for his discussion of "negative globalization." We will discuss this idea at the beginning of the next chapter where it has greater and more specific relevance to the issues discussed there. While Bauman does not discuss environmental issues under the heading of negative globalization, it is clear that adverse environmental flows are among the most, if not the most, negative aspects of globalization.[1]

One of the most enduring and important issues in the study of globalization involves its relationship to the environment (Christoff and Eckersley 2013; Grainger 2012). The environment is inherently, and has always been, global. That is, we all share the atmosphere, are warmed by the sun, and are connected by the oceans (Yearley 2007). Further, much that relates to the environment has an impact on, and flows around (e.g. weather patterns), the world, or at least large portions of it.

In spite of this, the earliest thinking on globalization tended to ignore the environment, or at least to underplay its significance. There was some early concern for the environmental impact of fallout from nuclear testing and acid rain (Munton and Wilkening 2007). However in the 1980s and 1990s the environmental movement (Rootes 1999) made great progress and a number of notable problems, especially the depletion of the ozone layer (Liftin 2007) and global climate change (Beer 2012), brought the environment to the fore as a global issue and problem.

In the case of these two issues, and many others, it is clear that many throughout the world play a major role in the creation of these problems and that virtually everyone in the world will suffer their adverse consequences. In that sense they are clearly global in nature.

However, while the idea that environmental problems are global problems seems indisputable, it can be challenged in various ways.

- Not everyone or every part of the world is equally responsible for the most pressing global environmental problems. It is clear that those from the most developed countries are disproportionately responsible for them.
- Such problems do *not*, and will not, affect everyone and all areas of the world in the *same way*. For example, the rise of the level of the seas as a result of global climate change will most affect those who live in coastal areas or on islands, and globally this will be poorer people and people of color (see below). Such areas will also be most affected by the expected increase in the number and severity of hurricanes. Tornados are also expected to increase, although they are likely to affect different geographic areas[2] (e.g. the American Midwest more than its coasts[3]). To take another example, those in the North will be better able to find ways of avoiding or dealing with all but the most catastrophic of the problems caused by global warming. On the other hand, those in the South will be far more defenseless and have fewer options (e.g. selling their homes and moving to a less threatened locale). Therefore, they will suffer more from environmental problems of various kinds.
- The main sources of environmental problems change as, for example, the center of manufacturing (with its associated pollutants) is moving from, for example, the US to China.
- There is much dispute over how nations of the world should respond to environmental problems, especially climate change. Given that nations have contributed unequally to

climate change (with the affluent global North contributing more) and that its effects are felt unevenly (with the global South suffering higher burdens), it raises important questions for what constitutes environmental justice (Walker 2012) and climate justice (Foran and Widick 2013).

MODERNIZATION AND ENVIRONMENTAL FLOWS

In Chapter 3 we discussed processes that are related to, and pre-date, globalization, including colonialism, imperialism, and development. These processes were all part of a long process of modernization (defined below) that would have slow, but accelerating, effects on the natural environment. The beginnings of this transition unfolded in this way:

> The indigenous practices and forms of knowledge that preceded colonization were on the whole, if not always sustainable, often ecologically restrained and had successfully managed productive landscapes, sometimes for millennia. These peoples, cultures, and landscapes were disrupted and most often destroyed by new, harsh exploitative colonial resource regimes that were usually insensitive to the environments on which they were imposed. (Christoff and Eckersley 2013: 42)

With colonialism and imperialism came new, intensified forms of resource extraction, which fueled early wealth accumulation and the new industrial powers of Europe, and later, the United States. New ports and cities were built for trade within Europe's newly industrialized centers. People moved from rural areas to the cities, and populations grew, which fueled demand for, and kept resources flowing from, the colonies.

Colonialism and imperialism, as economic systems, also coincided with the Enlightenment and new ways of thinking about the world (Christoff and Eckersley 2013). The first Enlightenment ideal was a notion of human progress that saw history as evolutionary and linear, with human progress likened to evolution in the natural world. Second, given their ships, guns, new medicines, and industrial machinery, those humans who had them (mainly Europeans) came to afford importance to their scientific and technological superiority. Third, Europeans believed in their own moral and racial superiority, asserting that their culture did and should dominate the "inferior" (non-white) people of the world. Fourth, progress was also tied to an anthropocentric worldview. Humans were seen as the center of the natural order of the world and they would inevitably come to dominate and subjugate the non-human world.

This constellation of practices and ideas came to be known as **modernization**, or the supposedly evolutionary process that moved humankind from agricultural and pre-modern societies into the modern era, brought about by wide-scale rational planning (Schmidt 2012). Driven by this notion of modernization, industrialized nations applied their scientific and technical knowledge to economic expansion, cultural domination, and intensifying exploitation of the earth. During this time, there was no conception that humans were negatively impacting the environment or that the environment could not absorb the myriad human demands placed on it – if anything, the natural environment existed explicitly for the betterment of humans.

The long, slow, early phases of modernization would ultimately give way to contemporary globalization that would rapidly accelerate and intensify modernization and its

Modernization: the belief of an evolutionary process that moved humankind from agricultural and pre-modern societies into the modern era, brought about by the reality of wide-scale rational planning.

environmental impacts. This process intensified most quickly after WW II as international trade increased and more countries were integrated into the global capitalist economy. Mass production became increasingly efficient, facilitating mass consumerism in the US, Western Europe, and increasingly in more of the world. Goods that had always been built to be durable and long-lasting were becoming part of a disposable consumer society. Through further technological developments, humans began making all sorts of new chemicals and applying them widely to agriculture (e.g. DDT), war (e.g. agent orange), and consumer goods.

There was little consideration of how these processes affected the environment until the publication of Rachel Carson's book, *Silent Spring*, in 1962. Carson's book focused especially on the unintended effects of the chemical revolution that had taken place since the 1940s and criticized humans' attempt to exploit the earth for their own gain with little regard for the earth's complex ecological systems. While *Silent Spring* was published in the US, it was translated into 22 languages and became a truly international phenomenon. Although it emerged at the same time as new scientific studies with an ecological (rather than anthropocentric) framework, and others (e.g. Aurielo Peccei, Vice President of Fiat and Olivetti) began noting the limits of economic growth, Carson's book is widely considered the source of an emerging global consciousness about the environment and of the modern environmental movement.

The environmental movement therefore brought attention to the implications of resource extraction, energy consumption, industrial production, population growth, and mass consumerism. Several problems associated with these human activities – such as global climate change, loss of biodiversity, and overpopulation – will be explored below. Given that these problems were largely a result of globalizing industrial activity, environmentalists began to demand curbs on economic globalization. They view economic globalization as leading to more manufacturing which, among other things, increases pollution. As a result, they generally demand limits on trade, curbs on the human-made chemicals that have become so commonplace in industrial production, and movement away from the use of nonrenewable resources (e.g. oil). Environmentalists are also critical of the mass consumerism that drives demand for cheaper and cheaper goods.

However, the environmental movement sparked its own opposition, especially among neoliberals. In Chapter 4 we discussed neoliberalism in great detail, as well as the way in which it applies to various aspects of the economy such as trade. The neoliberal perspective views free trade as central to economic globalization. It leads to the view that the efforts favored by environmentalists to limit industrial pollution are impediments to free trade and need to be opposed. If efforts to reduce pollution are implemented, they need to be watered down and, if possible, eventually eliminated. In effect, environmentalists offer an alternative model of globalization to that of the neoliberals (Gareau 2013; Harvey 2005). To environmentalists, environmental issues are not only global in nature, but they also should be accorded priority over economic considerations. The priorities are clearly reversed by neoliberals, especially many economists and virtually all capitalists.

While the environmental and neoliberal economic paradigms are clearly opposed to one another, there are efforts to create models that integrate the two. One example is **ecological economics** (Daly and Farley 2011), which argues that productive economic activity must consider the ecological carrying capacity of the earth. Neoliberal economists view environmental resources as commodities to be bought and sold, and prioritize economic production above any environmental concerns, thereby disregarding environmental limits in

Ecological economics: economic theory that considers the ecological carrying capacity of the earth thus integrating economic theory with environmental knowledge.

emphasizing efficient production. On the other hand, ecological economists argue that without a sustainable environment, markets will eventually be unable to produce anything efficiently. Indeed, if the environment is pushed to its limits, the markets themselves will be threatened. Therefore, ecological economists consider ecological limits and costs when analyzing the efficient use of resources to promote development. In other words, globalization need not be a "race to the bottom" (see Chapter 7) ecologically (and in many other senses), but can be a process that protects and enhances the environment as well as much else that is of importance to all of us and that all of us value greatly (or at least should).

DIFFERENCES AMONG NATION-STATES

Many of the nations of the world, 132 of them, were ranked in 2012 on their environmental performance on a number of dimensions such as air pollution, greenhouse gas emissions, sanitation, agricultural policies, and many others. The highest-ranking nations in terms of sustainability were Switzerland, Latvia, Norway, Luxembourg, Costa Rica, France, Austria, Italy, United Kingdom, and Sweden. The US ranked forty-ninth and was considered a "modest performer." The rising industrial powers China and India had overall rankings of 116th and 125th respectively.

The report notes that some indicators have shown improvement over time. But one important area where the world's nations have not improved is climate change. Here, too, Switzerland was at the top because of its system of hydroelectric power and because its extensive train system tends to reduce the use of cars and trucks. The US performs poorly on greenhouse gas (e.g. carbon dioxide) emissions that contribute to global warming. Because the US alone contributes 25% of all of the world's emissions, it is no surprise that on the climate change measure of the index it ranks 121st out of 132 nations (Barringer 2012).

GLOBAL CLIMATE CHANGE

Global climate change is the defining environmental challenge of today, and has become a rallying point for many in the environmental movement. There is little or no doubt, at least among scientists, that global warming is a real phenomenon brought about by human activity, most notably the huge increase in greenhouse gases. The Intergovernmental Panel on Climate Change (IPCC) is an agency under the auspices of the UN. Established in 1988, it "reviews and assesses the most recent scientific, technical and socio-economic information produced worldwide relevant to the understanding of climate change." It is comprised of thousands of scientists from around the world and is the most authoritative scientific source on the subject. In its 2013–2014 report, the IPCC stated: "warming of the climate system is unequivocal, and since the 1950s, many of the observed changes are unprecedented over decades to millennia . . . carbon dioxide, methane, and nitrous oxide have increased to levels unprecedented in at least the last 800,000 years" (IPCC 2013). Their scientific evidence shows that our current period of warming is unprecedented in observable history and is indeed caused by humans. Furthermore, the predominant view is that global warming is already well advanced and is moving ahead more rapidly than predicted. In 2014, Rajendra K. Pachauri, chairman of the panel, told reporters at a news conference that "nobody on this planet is going to be untouched by the impacts of climate change" (IPCC 2013).

However, there are still some dissenters in the lay public and business community who adhere to the view that the global warming and resulting climate changes that are now occurring are not the result of human actions but simply part of a natural cycle. This view is likely not surprising in certain industrial sectors (e.g. coal and oil), given the material interests these companies have in continuing their profitable business practices even though they may contribute to climate change. However, this skepticism is also reproduced by the media, which often seek to be controversial. For example, one early study found that, between 1988 and 2002, the most prestigious US newspapers vastly overrepresented climate change deniers in their articles (Boykoff and Boykoff 2004). Results showed that 53% of articles gave equal attention to climate scientists and deniers, and 6% of articles emphasized doubts about climate change. In contrast, a study of academic articles published during a similar period (1993–2003) found "robust consensus" among scientists on climate change with no articles voicing significant dissent (Oreskes 2004). A more recent analysis of newspaper editorials written by the conservative columnists most often read in 2007–2010 shows an important trend. Overall, the editorials gave "a highly dismissive view of climate change and critical stance toward climate science among these influential conservative pundits" (Elasser and Dunlap 2013: 754). Thus, popular media coverage serves to confuse the lay public about, and promote misinformation on, global warming.

Anthropocene: a potential new geological era characterized by several accelerating human-made ecological changes, including mass extinctions, global warming, and oceanic changes, that are far-reaching and in many cases permanent.

Given the dramatic reality of global climate change, many earth scientists have argued that we are actually entering a new geological era. They argue that the earth is undergoing a change from the relatively stable Holocene to the **Anthropocene**, which comes from *anthropo* meaning "man," and *cene* meaning "new." The word was popularized by atmospheric chemist and Nobel laureate Paul Crutzen. The Anthropocene is characterized by several human-made and permanent ecological changes, including mass extinctions, global warming, oceanic changes, and more. Regardless of whether or not we have entered a new geological period, the effects on human populations are mounting and increasingly being felt by people around the world.

Rising sea levels

Climate refugees: people displaced by environmental changes brought about by climate change, such as rising sea levels, drought, and increased exposure to hurricanes and floods.

As temperatures rise on earth, glaciers around the world melt, and sea levels rise. And temperatures are currently rising at a faster rate than even the most extreme estimates predicted. We will likely see the global average rise by at least 3 degrees Celsius (5.4 degrees Fahrenheit) by 2047 (Wagner and Weitzman 2013). Scientists further argue that, in that time, the earth's coldest years may have higher temperatures than the hottest years between 1860 and 2005 (Gillis 2013a). With temperatures already rising at a rapid pace, this has increased the rise in sea levels since the mid-nineteenth century to a rate faster than any time during the previous two millennia (IPCC 2013). To put this in perspective, the US state of Louisiana loses 65 square kilometers – or 25 square miles – to rising sea levels every year.

One of the many effects on humans of rising sea levels is the loss of land in coastal areas and the displacement of people living on those lands. **Climate refugees** are people displaced by environmental changes brought about by climate change, such as rising sea levels, drought, and increases in hurricanes, floods, and other environmental disasters (see Chapter 11 for a more complete discussion on global flows of people, including refugees). There are already tens of millions of climate refugees around the world, and by 2050, this number could increase to 150–200 million (Brown 2008; Myers 2005). One particularly vulnerable area is Maldives, a nation of 1,200 islands (200 islands are inhabited) in the

Indian Ocean (Christoff and Eckersley 2013). Maldives' highest point of elevation is a mere 2.3 meters (7.5 feet) above sea level. Much of its population of 395,000 people live only a few feet from the ocean waves. Kivalina, Alaska, is the first American town that will likely be lost to climate change. This is predicted to happen by 2025. The town sits on a small peninsula and is home to 400 indigenous peoples. For generations, they have depended on the sea for their survival, but will soon lose their homes to that sea. As more people become climate change refugees, we can expect to see increasing border conflicts as those people flee to new areas, and greater international conflicts over where these mass migrations will go, raising more pressing security issues.

There is particular concern about how global warming will affect the rapidity with which the huge ice sheets that cover Greenland, the Arctic, and Antarctica will melt (Struck 2007a) (see Figure 11.1 for a map of coastlines endangered by a 10-meter rise in the sea levels). If all of the ice on Greenland *alone* were to melt, global sea levels would rise 23 feet; another 17-foot rise would be associated with similar disintegration in Antarctica. Such a rise would be a global catastrophe leading to the end of life on many islands and in coastal civilization throughout the world. With the sea level likely to rise much more rapidly than was previously believed, vulnerable areas around the world near, at, or below sea level are likely to be swamped much sooner than was previously forecast (Collins Rudolph 2007: D1, D4).

Loss of biodiversity

Through global warming, sea levels rise and salt water spills into freshwater areas. As a result, some areas experience desertification. In conjunction with other human activity (e.g. deforestation, activities that encourage invasive species), these forces of global climate change are already altering natural ecosystems (e.g. wetlands) with profound effects on biodiversity, animal and human food systems, and the overall functioning of local environments (Christoff and Eckersley 2013; Hooper et al. 2012). According to the International Union for Conservation of Nature, nearly 20,000 species of plants and animals are considered at "high risk" of extinction (Pearson 2012). Ecologists have shown that ecosystems rely on the interactions of multiple species within a specific local environment. Pearson (2012) notes:

> These systems provide food, fresh water and the raw materials for construction and fuel; they regulate climate and air quality; buffer against natural hazards like floods and storms; maintain soil fertility; and pollinate crops. The genetic diversity of the planet's myriad different life-forms provides the raw ingredients for new medicines and new commercial crops and livestock, including those that are better suited to conditions under a changed climate.

These are systems that humans still know little about. In fact, out of the 1.7 million known species, fewer than 4% have been evaluated by scientists. Furthermore, for each known species, there are likely two more species that are not yet discovered. The direst possibility for these species is extinction, and according to one estimate, at least 20% of the earth's plants and animals will be at increased risk of disappearing. Even if they do not become extinct, plants and animals are going to change as their environment changes. The problem is that as a result of evolution, plants and animals can adapt to gradual changes, but the changes underway are more rapid than they are accustomed to and these changes are likely to accelerate in the future.

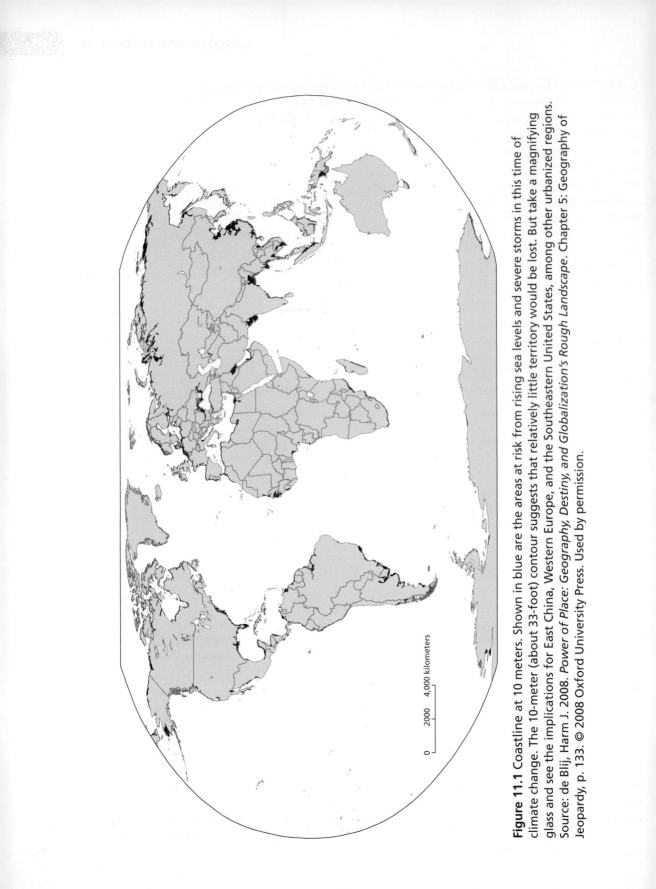

Figure 11.1 Coastline at 10 meters. Shown in blue are the areas at risk from rising sea levels and severe storms in this time of climate change. The 10-meter (about 33-foot) contour suggests that relatively little territory would be lost. But take a magnifying glass and see the implications for East China, Western Europe, and the Southeastern United States, among other urbanized regions. Source: de Blij, Harm J. 2008. *Power of Place: Geography, Destiny, and Globalization's Rough Landscape*. Chapter 5: Geography of Jeopardy, p. 133. © 2008 Oxford University Press. Used by permission.

Polar bears that live on Arctic ice are one animal that is already experiencing the effects of climate change and they are likely to be profoundly affected in the relatively near future. The shrinking and melting of the ice on which they live is making life more difficult, even impossible, for many of them. Polar bears in the Arctic (as well as penguins in the Antarctic) are already reacting and are on the move in an effort to compensate for the changes. Nevertheless, a recent report from the US Geological Survey estimated that two-thirds of the world's polar bears could disappear in the next half-century.

Animals are affected in different ways by global climate change. In terms of adverse effects, migrating birds (e.g. robins) may migrate earlier only to find little food or the ground ice-covered. Rodents (e.g. the American pika) that cannot live in warm temperatures may need to move higher and higher on mountains in order find temperatures that allow them to survive. Frogs may disappear as the climate changes. A few frog species already seem to have disappeared in the Monteverde Cloud Forest of Costa Rica because a reduction in cloudiness has reduced the damp, foggy, and misty weather that they need in order to survive.

Threats to food security

While some climate changes will affect people in various parts of the world (and other living creatures) differently, one change that will affect virtually everyone, everywhere, is changes (e.g. higher temperatures, salt seepage into groundwater, increase in floods and droughts) wrought in farming and therefore in the food supply. This could have disastrous consequences for food security, where climate change might increase water shortages and crop failures (Christoff and Eckersley 2013). In such events, food prices could rapidly increase (Gillis 2013b). The effects will be greatest in the South, in the lower latitudes of the world – India, Africa, Latin America – where a majority of the poor people in the world live. And this does not even take into account other adverse changes such as new pests and diseases that are likely to plague agriculture. As different locales compete for increasingly limited resources, this could further lead to more local and regional conflicts. Finally, in one of its 2014 reports, the IPCC warned that in terms of food security, the worst is yet to come (Gillis 2014).

Global warming and health

Global warming is expected to adversely affect health in a number of different ways (Walsh 2012). Global warming will bring with it more, and more intense, heat waves, and excessive heat can be deadly. A heat wave in Europe in 2003, the worst in almost 500 years, caused about 30,000 deaths from heat-related illnesses. The aging of the population throughout much of the developed world makes more people vulnerable to being made ill and dying due to excessive heat. Increasing urbanization also increases the likelihood of death since cities become "heat islands." Other factors making death from excessive heat more likely are being very young, ill, or poor, or lacking the ability to move away from super-heated areas. However, there are things that can be done to mitigate the dangers of heat stress such as more use of air conditioning (although many people in the world have no access to it or cannot afford it; furthermore it causes other problems such as a great demand on limited energy sources), greater awareness of the dangers associated with excessive heat, and better medical treatment of those afflicted with heat stress. Of course, those in the North are much more likely to be able to avail themselves of these mechanisms.

More severe storms will lead to more deaths, especially from increased flooding due to the storms. Residents are more likely to become stranded and cut off from access to health care in such emergencies. This was one exacerbating factor that affected the US when Hurricane Sandy devastated areas along the Atlantic Coast in 2012 (Lipton and Moss 2012).

Increased heat will speed up chemical reactions and make worse pollution from ozone and soot. Deaths from ozone pollution (mostly among those with lung or heart problems) could rise by 5% by 2050. Increased pollen production could increasingly affect those with asthma and other allergies. Waterborne diseases (e.g. cholera) will increase with higher temperatures and more torrential rains. Food-borne infections (e.g. salmonella) will also increase with hotter weather.

Diseases caused by animals and insects may increase, although there is less certainty on this than on the other health issues discussed above. For example, it is expected that there will be an increase in malaria and dengue borne by mosquitoes. Exposure to malaria is expected to increase by 25% in Africa by 2100. However, here, as elsewhere, actions can be taken to mitigate the problem such as controlling the mosquito population with pesticides (although they pose many other hazards [Carson 1962]), greater use of bed nets (especially by pregnant women and children), and better medical care. Other diseases of this genre that are likely to become more prevalent are schistosomiasis (carried by snails), leishmaniasis (sand flies), Lyme disease (ticks), and yellow fever and the chikungunya virus (both carried by mosquitoes).

OTHER ENVIRONMENTAL PROBLEMS

Most, if not all, environmental problems are global in the sense that many of them flow readily around the world and there are few barriers to those flows. While there is not enough space to address adequately all major environmental problems, this section will deal with some of the other environmental problems facing the world today.

DESTRUCTION OF NATURAL HABITATS

Destruction of natural habitats includes their conversion into human habitats, and clearing or damaging of natural habitats such as the "forests, wetlands, coral reefs, and the ocean bottom" (Diamond 2006: 487). In fact, deforestation was a, or perhaps the, major factor in the collapse of past societies. Today, the most notable deforestation in the world is taking place in Indonesia and the Amazon rain forest (mostly in Brazil) (Meyfroidt 2012), but other parts of the world are also destroying/losing their forests. The Amazon forest is being decimated to allow the area to be "developed" (to create farms and areas for livestock to graze) and for the creation of more human settlements. What is different about Brazil today is that its forest is so huge and it plays such a large role in the global ecology that its destruction will have negative effects on the world as a whole. For example, the burning of all of those felled trees releases large amounts of carbon dioxide that flow around the globe contributing to global climate change. The destruction of the forest leads to other problems for humans including the loss of timber and other raw materials. It is also of great concern, especially in the areas undergoing deforestation, because forests "provide us with so-called ecosystem services such as protecting our watersheds, protecting soil against erosion, constituting essential steps in the water cycle that generates much of our rainfall, and providing habitat for most terrestrial plant and animal species" (Diamond 2006: 487). The loss or decline of the other natural habitats (wetlands, coral reefs, the ocean bottom) will also have a variety of negative consequences for life on earth. For example, the decline of coral reefs (due, for example, to runoffs from agriculture) adversely affects the sea life that exists in and around them.

DECLINE OF FISH AND WHALES

A large fraction of the protein consumed by humans comes from fish and, to a lesser extent, shellfish. However, many fishing areas (e.g. the Mediterranean) are in decline or have collapsed. Without seafood,[4] more people would need to rely on meat for protein and livestock can only be grown at great cost, and with great damage to the environment. In fact, eating meat is associated with a significant rise in global warming because of methane gases released from factory farms and the clearing of forests for lands to raise livestock. Aquaculture, or the farming of aquatic organisms, is not an adequate replacement for the loss of natural fishing areas because it causes a series of ecological and other problems (Goldburg 2008; Rosenthal 2011).

Ocean fishing

Marine life in the world's oceans has been greatly diminished by over-fishing. According to biannual reports from the United Nations Food and Agricultural Organization (FAO), the number of fisheries that are "fully exploited" or "overexploited" has continued to increase steadily. As of 2012, 87% (up from 77% in 2006) of the world's most important fisheries can be considered either "fully exploited" or "overexploited," (FAO 2012). An early twenty-first-century study concluded that industrial fishing had led to a 90% decline in such large predatory fish as swordfish, tuna, and marlin.

A major culprit in the decimation of marine life is industrial fishing. As the amount of sea life declines, the techniques involved compensate by becoming that much more industrialized and intensive. Drift nets were in use until 1992 when they were banned on the high seas by the UN. They were "free-floating veils of monofilament webbing that can be as long as twenty-five miles . . . at the peak of their use in the eighties, there was enough drift netting in the ocean on any given day to encircle the planet, if measured end to end" (Khatchadourian 2007: 68). Clearly, such a technology was capable of ensnaring innumerable forms of marine life, some wanted, others unwanted – with the latter unceremoniously discarded into the sea. Bottom trawling continues and it "involves raking the ocean floor for food on a large scale." Not only does this contribute to over-fishing, but it destroys complex ecosystems in the process (Watling and Boeuf 2013). Longlines are what they sound like and can employ thousands of hooks at a time. They, too, catch lots of unwanted fish that are discarded. In fact, over 20% of the fish hauled out of American waters – over a million tons – is discarded as bycatch. One of the worst examples of bycatch occurs as a result of the use of bottom trawling in the harvesting of shrimp in the Gulf of Mexico. That method leads to over 80% bycatch. Furthermore, innumerable plants and corals are uprooted, caught in the trawling and destroyed in the process. Because several fish species are nearing extinction largely as a result of industrial fishing, a director at the Pew Environmental Group argues that "the responsible thing to do is to stop the fishing until effective management measures are in place that will ensure a reversal of the population decline" (Jolly 2013a).

Whaling

The whale, one of the world's natural wonders has, like many others, been threatened, ultimately with extinction, by many things, especially human actions taken on a global basis. In response, the International Whaling Commission (IWC) was formed in 1946 to manage the global whale population and its habitats. However, the Commission was not very effective and by the 1970s several species of whales were nearly extinct. In the early 1980s, the IWC instituted at least a partial ban on commercial whaling, but several important whaling countries (e.g. Norway, and especially Japan) refused to accept it and continue to hunt whales. Using industrial fishing technology and techniques, the Japanese kill hundreds of whales during the hunting season each year. Japanese whaling is undertaken purportedly for research purposes (up to 1,000 whales are killed each year) and is conducted under the auspices of a government-subsidized agency, the Institute for Cetacean Research. However, little research of any note has emanated from this organization and a good deal of meat derived from these whales ends up in the markets and on the dinner plates of Japanese consumers. As a result, in 2013, Australia sued Japan in an international court for its supposed illegal hunting of whales (as of this writing, a decision had not yet been announced). Another organization fighting illegal whaling is Sea Shepard, a US-based conservation group that dispatches fast ships to harass and interrupt Japan's commercial whaling practices.

DECLINE IN USABLE FARMLAND

Farmland soil is being carried away by the erosion caused by water and wind. Other problems associated with the soil include increasing salinity, decline in soil fertility, and soil acidification/alkanization. As noted above, global warming has also led to desertification of several areas. Usable farmland has declined at the same time that the global population and its need for agricultural products have increased. Furthermore, when people who depend on their environment for survival are unable to farm the land or catch fish in overfished waters, they are forced to turn to other means of feeding themselves. For example, many Somalian pirates were found to be farmers from Yemen who were driven from their lands by desertification (*New York Times* 2010).

INCREASINGLY INACCESSIBLE SUPPLIES OF FOSSIL FUELS

Supplies of relatively easily obtained fossil fuels (oil, coal) are being used up rapidly. Getting at more will require access to reserves that are "deeper underground, dirtier, increasingly expensive to extract or process, or will involve higher environmental costs" (Diamond 2006: 490). One very controversial method used commonly in the US is hydraulic fracturing (i.e. fracking). Fracking is a relatively new technique that applies high-pressure streams of water and chemicals to dislodge pockets of natural gas that could be miles below the earth's surface. The practice has revolutionized the oil and gas industry in the US, but there are a number of concerns about its environmental and health effects. For example, fracking could lead to local earthquakes, the "flowback" of water and chemicals could be cancerous to humans, and large volumes of newly released methane could contribute further to global warming. However, the method has been quickly adopted with little scientific study and the actual effects of these practices are not clear (Hurdle 2013). Given these concerns, Europe has experienced widespread protest against fracking, making them much slower to adopt these techniques, with France and Bulgaria banning the practice altogether (Jolly 2013b). Furthermore, the flow of fossil fuels will grow increasingly problematic and more and more barriers (e.g. oil-producing nations needing to keep an ever-larger proportion of the oil they produce for themselves) will emerge to further reduce the flow.

DECLINE IN FRESH WATER

Water is becoming an increasingly important global issue, or rather raising a number of different issues (Conca 2006; Hoekstra 2012). Among the concerns are water pollution (with one result being water-borne diseases), flooding (especially as a result of global warming), the increasing scarcity of water, the need to choose between water (to drink) and the crops (food) that can be produced with it, and the possibility that the flow of water could slow or stop completely, at least in some locales. The latter involves "desertification" (Glantz 1977) or the decline in the water supply as a result of the degradation and deterioration of soil and vegetation. Indeed, because of the latter, water, once considered a public good, is increasingly becoming a valuable and privatized commodity as many places run low on, and in some cases begin to run out of, drinkable water. (Much water – perhaps two-thirds of all water used for irrigation, as much as half of city water supplies – is simply wasted due, among other things, to leaky pipes.) There is likely to be an increase in the number, and an escalation of the actions, of social movements involved in efforts to deal with various issues that relate to water (see Figure 11.2 for a map of global water risk).

While we usually think of water as abundant and readily accessible, the fact is that about 783 million people, or 11% of the global population, lack basic access to drinking water. Even more people – 2.5 billion – do not have basic sanitation, which poses problems for local water sources and an array of health concerns. The poorest areas of the globe (largely in the South), and the poorest people within those areas, especially women and children (over a billion children lack basic sanitation), experience a disproportionate share of water-related problems. The situation is apt to grow worse in coming years with the possibility that as many as half the world's population will be faced with water security problems by the 2030s.

Fresh water ecosystems (rivers, lakes, wetlands, etc.) are under increasing stress (from dams, pollution, etc.) as are the invaluable services they provide "including controlling floods, filtering water supplies, diluting pollutants, cycling sediments and critical nutrients, and providing rich storehouses of biodiversity" (Conca 2007: 1246). As water is diverted from these ecosystems to human uses, it puts strains on the ability of the environment to accomplish these functions, which can exacerbate problems discussed earlier, including desertification, loss of biodiversity, and food insecurity.

A less visible water problem involves international trade, especially in agricultural and industrial products. For example, when Japan buys crops (which are water-intensive) produced in the US, pressure is put on American water supplies. In other words, Japanese consumers (to use just one example) contribute to the "mining of aquifers and emptying of rivers in North America" (Hoekstra and Chapagain 2008: 1). Without realizing it, people throughout the world are using water from elsewhere in the world ("virtual water"), especially Australia and North America. If they do not realize they are using (or abusing) it, how can they do anything about it?

Astounding quantities of water can be used to produce commodities consumed as much as halfway around the world. For example, according to one estimate, it takes about 140 liters

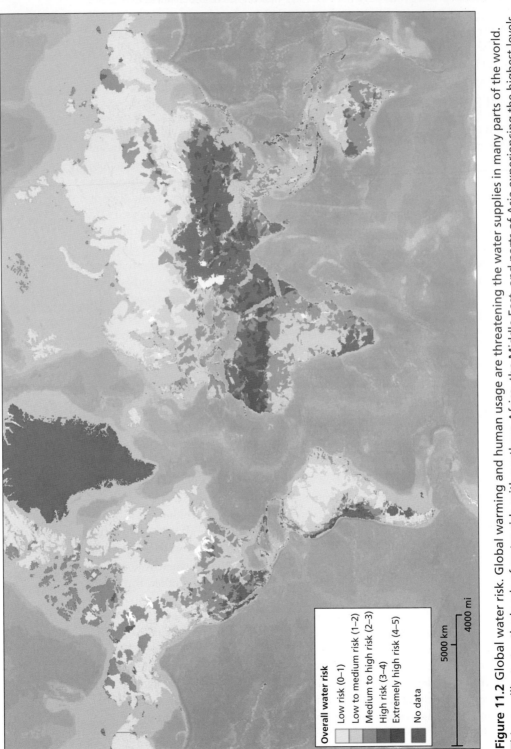

Figure 11.2 Global water risk. Global warming and human usage are threatening the water supplies in many parts of the world. This map illustrates the levels of water risk, with northern Africa, the Middle East, and parts of Asia experiencing the highest levels of risk. As these risks become realized, conflicts over water are likely to increase. Source: Gassert, F., M. Luck, M. Landis, P. Reig, and T. Shiao. 2013. "Aqueduct Global Maps 2.0." Working Paper. Washington, DC: World Resources Institute (http://www.wri.org/ publication/aqueduct-global-maps-20. Attribution 3.0 Unported (CC BY 3.0)).

Overall water risk

- Low risk (0–1)
- Low to medium risk (1–2)
- Medium to high risk (2–3)
- High risk (3–4)
- Extremely high risk (4–5)
- No data

5000 km

4000 mi

of rainwater to produce enough coffee beans to make one cup of coffee! We begin to get a sense of the magnitude of the water problem produced by the consumption of "virtual water" when we multiply that level of water consumption by the many cups of coffee, to say nothing of all the other commodities, that people consume on a daily basis throughout the world (Hoekstra and Chapagain 2008: 7).

Global climate change will make some parts of the world wetter, but other parts will grow drier (as a general rule, already wet areas will grow wetter, already dry areas drier; both floods and droughts will intensify), and it is in the latter that we are likely to see increasingly desperate and expensive efforts to find water (e.g. by drilling ever-deeper in the earth for underground water supplies) (Struck 2007b: A8). Among the areas likely to grow drier are southern Europe, the Middle East, South Australia, Patagonia, and the southwestern US. There are predictions of a dust-bowl-like situation in the American southwest and the resulting possibility of mass migrations. A similar situation, with potentially even more dire implications, is forecast for Mexico where similar conditions will lead to mass migrations to Mexican cities *and* to still more, likely unauthorized, migration to the US. Such an increase threatens to create even far greater problems and animosities than already exist in the US as a result of documented, and especially undocumented, immigration from Mexico. In more general terms, we will see more and more climate refugees.

Another water-related problem is the melting, due to global warming, of mountain-top glaciers that are an important source of the flow of drinking water to many people in the world. As those glaciers melt and fail to re-form fully, they will produce less and less water for those below them who need the water to survive. The affected populations, too, are likely to become climate refugees and they are likely to come into conflict with residents of the still water-rich areas to which they are likely to move. Furthermore, various areas and countries around the world are already trading threats over common or disputed water supplies (as are various areas within countries; in the US – Georgia vs. Florida, and the states in the southwestern US, to take two examples). We will likely see more barriers erected by territories interested in retaining their water supplies and preventing their flow to neighboring territories. Tensions will increase in the future leading, perhaps, to open national and global warfare over water!

The paradox of bottled water

Water is becoming an increasingly important global commodity as many places run low on, and in some cases begin to run out of, drinkable water. At the same time, there has been an enormous growth in the global distribution and sale of bottled water; bottled water has become a global commodity commanding relatively high prices. However, it is too expensive for the poorest people in the world who may be most in need as a result of the decline in available water supplies. Sales of bottled water are most likely to thrive in the relatively well-off areas of the world where there is still plenty of drinkable water freely available. But instead of using this inexpensive and accessible water, increasing numbers of people, especially in the North, are buying bottled water which is sometimes shipped in, at great cost and with profoundly negative effects on the environment, from distant locales (consumers in the US buy half a billion bottles of water each week). All sorts of environmental problems are related to, for example, the great use of fuel by airplanes and ships that transport the bottled water. Also, 80% of empty water bottles end up in landfills (most of them are not able to be recycled) and take approximately 1,000 years to decompose.

One of the most outrageous examples of this is Fiji Water, with $150 million in sales per year. The water is literally produced and bottled in Fiji in the South Pacific and transported thousands of miles to places like New York and London. Aware of the danger it poses to the environment, Fiji Water has announced plans to use renewable energy (build a windmill to power its bottling plant), preserve forests, and cut its carbon footprint by, for example, shipping its bottles of water by sea to the East Coast of the US rather than by truck from Los Angeles (after it gets there by ship). Of course, this says nothing about the environmental cost of shipping to Los Angeles or to the East Coast. In spite of actions like these, the executive director of the Rainforest Action Network said: "Bottled water is a business that is fundamentally, inherently and inalterably unconscionable. . . . No side deals to protect forests or combat global warming can offset that reality" (Deutsch 2007: C3).

TOXIC CHEMICALS

Various industries, especially the chemical industry, "manufacture or release into the air, soil, oceans, lakes, and rivers many toxic chemicals" (Diamond 2006: 491). Among the culprits are "insecticides, pesticides, and herbicides . . . mercury and other metals, fire-retardant chemicals, refrigerator coolants, detergents, and components of plastics" (Diamond 2006: 491). All of these have a variety of immediate, and more usually long-term, negative effects on humans and other forms of life.

There is, for example, the issue of persistent organic pollutants (POPs) which are highly toxic, human-made chemicals. Among these are polychlorinated biphenyls (PCBS) once used as coolants and various pesticides (especially DDT, dichlorodiphenyltrichloroethane) (Dinham 1993, 2007). POPs have four characteristics in common – they are highly toxic, they are persistent, remaining in the environment for years before breaking down and becoming less harmful, they can travel great distances (thus, what is locally produced and may create local problems can easily become a global problem as, for example, the role of PCBs in the decline of the ozone layer and the relationship of that to global health problems resulting from increased exposure to ultraviolet radiation), the "impact of POPs can be magnified through processes of bioaccumulation and biomagnification, in which their concentrations build up along food chains."[5]

Toxic chemicals are especially widespread in industrial agriculture. For example, 5.1 billion pounds of pesticides are used in the US every year, and the rise of genetically modified seeds (which enable the plant to withstand greater amounts of pesticides), have helped increase the amount of pesticides used. These pesticides have a variety of negative effects on the environment and human health. For example, they seep into the ground and can contaminate drinking water (Schwarzenbach et al. 2010), or spill into rivers and streams, ultimately damaging ecosystems. Farm laborers who are exposed to these chemicals experience higher rates of illness. The American Academy of Pediatrics (2012) noted children are particularly susceptible to the effects of pesticides, including lymphocytic leukemia, pediatric cancers, decreased cognitive functioning, impaired neurological development, and behavioral problems.

POPULATION GROWTH

As of mid-2014, the global population is more than 7.17 billion and the UN predicts it will reach 8 billion by 2025. Significant population growth, especially in the South (population will remain stable or decline in much of the North), will exacerbate the kinds of ecological problems discussed above and produce new ones.

In terms of the latter, it is not sheer numbers themselves that matter, or matter most, but rather what the population consumes, and there are huge variations around the world in consumption (see Chapter 7) (Diamond 2008: A19). The roughly 1 billion people who live in the developed countries, especially the 320 million or so in the United States, have a per capita consumption rate of 32, while it is much less in the less developed world, with many countries located there (e.g. Kenya) approaching a rate of 1, or *32 times less* than that in the US. Thus, from an ecological point of view, the greatest problems are produced by those nations (especially the US) with both the largest populations *and* the highest consumption rates.

The latter also points to the looming increase in ecological problems traceable to the booming populations and economies of India and especially China (its 1.35 billion people give it a larger population than the developed world). Their consumption rates still rank far below those in the developed world, but clearly they are increasing rapidly. Enormous strain would be placed on the resources and the ecology of the planet, should (as seems likely) China's consumption rate (and that of India) approach that of the developed countries. Of course, this could be compensated for by a decline in the consumption rate in the developed world (perhaps inevitable with the ongoing global redistribution of wealth), as well as by various conservation efforts. The latter would not be too painful in those countries since it would mainly focus on the many wasteful aspects of consumption (e.g. reduction in at least the excessive rate of growth of oil, forest, and fish consumption).

The present trends and future ecological problems are clear in India in a comparison between a suburb of New Delhi – Gurgaon – and a small village – Chakai Haat – within commuting distance of it. Gurgaon is booming with heavy traffic, shopping malls, and large air-conditioned office buildings. This is the future of India which has 1.2 billion people and where energy consumption is likely to increase more rapidly than any other country with a similar economy, leading to huge increases in carbon emissions. At the moment, however, India, with 17% of the world's population, produces only 5.8% of the world's greenhouse gases. Its total energy (toe) per capita is 0.6 tons of oil equivalent, significantly lower than Brazil (1.4), China (1.8), the world average (1.9), South Africa (2.7), Russia (5.1), and the US (7.1) (Denyer and Lakshmi 2012).

How far India has to go in this area is reflected in life today in Chakai Haat where there is "no access to the electricity grid, cooking stoves are fueled by animal waste and bicycles are the main mode of transportation on rutted country roads. Three diesel-powered generators hum a few hours each night so the village bazaar can be lighted and cellphones recharged" (Sengupta 2008: 4). Many who live in this town, and others like it, work in New Delhi, or suburbs like Gurgaon, with the result that they are very cognizant of the huge difference between these locales and their ways of life. Said one man who works in a garment factory in Gurgaon and lives in Chakai Haat: "There we live in light. . . . Here we live in darkness" (quoted in Sengupta 2008: 4). It is these differences and these people who are going to spearhead the effort to bring light and many other amenities of modern life that require huge amounts of energy to innumerable places like Chakai Haat. As they do, the carbon footprint of nation-states such as India is going to enlarge. And such nation-states are not likely to be very responsive to demands to cut back or slow down their growth not only because growth brings with it so many advances, but also because the West requires so much more energy than they do and its requirements are likely to continue to rise as well.

GLOBAL FLOWS OF WASTE

All parts of the world produce garbage that is dangerous, or at least potentially so. Examples of concern here include "e-waste" such as discarded television sets, computers, printers, cell phones, and so on. However, it is the highly developed Northern countries that produce a disproportionate amount of such waste. Once products have outlived their usefulness (or even long before that) and are reduced to garbage, the developed nations want no more to do with them. They seek to send much of the waste to less developed countries which, for their part, are anxious to receive the garbage since it can be transformed into work, jobs, and profits. Very often the waste that is unloaded on these countries has components and elements (gold, silver, copper) that are of value. However, they are difficult and time-consuming to extract. From the perspective of global corporations and governments, the poorly paid workers of less developed countries are ideal for this unskilled work. Few in the developed world want to do this work, especially for the pay those in the less developed world receive.

Furthermore, many of the things that are found in e-waste are dangerous. For example, a cell phone has about 200 chemical compounds and it is not clear which are hazardous and which are not. When workers in developing countries dismantle, burn, or pour acids on cell phones, it is unclear what toxic chemicals are released and how they are affected by the processes that release them. What is clear is that there are many toxic elements involved and it is the workers in less developed countries who are being exposed to them. Furthermore, the population as a whole in those areas is being endangered since what remains after the valuable e-waste is removed is often carelessly discarded to poison the land, crops, and so on.

One of the roots of this problem is the fact that those in developed countries are discarding electronics of all sorts long before the equipment has exhausted its useful life. Thus, for example, people buy new cell phones – and discard old ones (often, at least initially, by just dumping them in a drawer at home) – not because the old ones have ceased functioning, but because they like the color, design, or additional functions of new ones. Thus, much e-waste is unnecessary. Furthermore, many of the older phones could be recycled, but few people have any interest in doing what is necessary to recycle old phones (Mooallem 2008: 38–43).

But not all of this waste finds its way to landfills in developed or developing countries. Instead, much of it is dumped into oceans and other waterways. Some of the material ends up in the stomachs of birds or marine animals (who are unable to digest many of the human-made substances) and some of it ultimately ends up in the Great Pacific Garbage Patch (also known as the Pacific Trash Vortex). Located in the northern Pacific Ocean, it is a mass of non-biodegradable floating plastics, chemical sludge, and other marine pollution (varying from larger objects like fishing nets and water bottles to micro-sized particles from household cleaners). The Garbage Patch covers an area twice the size of Texas. It is one of several large oceanic waste areas, with each of them forming where the ocean currents intersect in a way that suspends the plastic and other waste in particular locations.

GLOBAL RESPONSES

Many global environmental problems, especially global climate change, are traceable to modernization and economic development. In particular, as economies grow larger and more successful they are likely to do increasing damage to the environment in, for example, the ways in which they produce things (factories that pollute) and what they produce (automobiles that pollute still further). As concerned as nation-states are becoming about damage to the environment, they are not about to either give up the fruits of development or cease seeking to become more developed. This leads to the important concept of sustainable development (Christen and Schmidt 2012; Elliott 2012; Park, Conca, and Finger 2008; Redclift and Woodgate 2013).

SUSTAINABLE DEVELOPMENT

The origin of this concept is a 1987 report to the UN by the World Commission on Environment and Development entitled "Our Common Future." In the view of the authors of the report, **sustainable development** (which should apply to all countries[6]) involves economic and environmental changes that meet the needs of the present, especially of the world's poor, without jeopardizing the needs of the future. While the focus of sustainable development is on physical sustainability, there must also be a concern for equity within the current generation and for future generations.

> **Sustainable development:** Economic and environmental changes that meet the needs of the present without jeopardizing the future.

A key event in the history of global environmentalism, indeed of globalization, was the 1992 meeting in Rio de Janeiro, Brazil labeled the Earth Summit, but formally the United Nations Conference on Environment and Development (Najam 2007). It is known for legitimizing and advancing the concept of sustainable development.

While "sustainable development" was focused on the environment (although not exclusively, given the concern for economic development), the term has come to be used much more broadly, even indiscriminately, to include "using renewable energy and farming organically to increasing local self-sufficiency and undertaking radical political decentralization" (LeLe 2007: 1103).

Globalization can be seen as either a threat or a boon to sustainability. As a threat, globalization can be seen as leading to unsustainable development by "undermining of the regulatory capacities of nation-states and local communities, and the depletion of biological and social diversity in favor of an overconsuming and culturally homogenized lifestyle" (LeLe 2007: 1103). Globalization can aid sustainable development through the "enhanced penetration of markets, diffusion of modern technologies, and globalization of standards" which, in turn, lead to "enhanced efficiency of resource use and demand for cleaner environments" (LeLe 2007: 1103).

While virtually everyone today would be in favor of sustainable development, there are at least three key issues involved in such a notion. The first is the difficulty involved in developing reliable projections about what is likely to happen to an ecosystem in the future. Second, should we simply seek to maintain the current ecosystem (e.g. the rainforests), or can we rely on advances in knowledge and production to compensate, perhaps more than compensate, for what is lost as a result of declines in the ecosystem? The third, and biggest, debate is over the causes of the current unsustainability of our ecosystem. The main difference is between those who argue that the main cause is population growth and those who contend that it is high levels of production and consumption (Dauvergne 2008) in developed countries (as well as China and India). Overall, there is a strong relationship in the debate over sustainability between the environment and economic development. The issue, of course, is whether economic development is possible without causing substantial, if not overwhelming, damage to the environment. Some view sustainable development as not truly being "sustainable" and thus development must be limited.

There are a number of dimensions to the relationship between globalization and sustainability. First, there is the *economic* dimension and the issue of whether economic development irretrievably destroys the environment or whether economic development enables the desire and the ability to better control the factors that are adversely affecting the environment. Second, *technology* can be seen as both producing environmental degradation and creating the possibility (e.g. through dissemination of information about environmental problems and their causes via the mass media or the global spread of green technologies) of limiting the damage. Third, there is the dimension of *awareness*. On the one hand, a nation's integration within the world polity, through the presence of civil and political international organizations, tends to lead to more individual environmental concern (Givens and Jorgenson 2013). On the other hand, it is unclear whether the global media have led to greater awareness of environmental problems and their causes, or whether consumerism also pushed by the global media increased people's blindness to these issues. Finally, there is the *politics* of environmentalism with some global organizations (e.g. the WTO) pushing for more economic growth, while many others (environmental INGOS such as Greenpeace) are seeking to reduce it or to limit its negative impact on the environment. Overall, then, "[w]hile many elements of globalization are clearly detrimental to already fragile efforts at environmental protection, there are those who believe that the economic benefits resulting from globalization will increase societal capacity to deal with environmental problems" (LeLe 2007: 1106).

DEALING WITH CLIMATE CHANGE

In spite of mounting evidence that fossil fuels are the major factor in global warming, many major corporations and some governments, especially in the US, have resisted taking action to limit fossil-fuel emissions.

Take, for example, the 1997 Kyoto Protocol, a major effort to deal with climate change due to carbon emissions (Rhomberg 2012b). Ratifying nations would have been required by 2012 to reduce their emissions to 5% below what they were in 1990. The agreement created ceilings for the carbon emissions of developed countries, but none for developing countries, especially China and India. Many nations ratified the Kyoto Protocol, but it required that countries that were responsible for a total of 55% of the emissions be signatories; it did not reach the required percentage. Especially notable is the fact that the US did not ratify the Kyoto Protocol and in 2001 it was finally rejected by President George W. Bush. Arguments against the treaty were that it was based on questionable science, it would hurt the American economy, and that it was not fair and would not be successful because the rapidly developing nations, especially China (and India), were not restricted in terms of their emissions. In spite of the failure to ratify the Kyoto Protocol, many believe that something like it will need to be negotiated (Christoff and Eckersley 2013). After all, the evidence on global climate change, especially global warming, is even clearer and stronger today than it was in the late 1990s. In fact, the actual global warming that has taken place since the 1990s is worse than the worst predictions made at the time.

There are signs that the reluctance of developed nations, especially the US, and their political and corporate leaders, is giving way to the increasingly clear reality that global warming is here and its adverse effects are already being felt. For example, in an early effort in 2007, ten large corporations joined many environmental groups and called for "federal law to slow, stop and reverse the growth" of global-warming emissions "over the shortest period of time reasonably achievable" (Ball 2007: A1, A17). Increasingly, corporations are producing sustainability reports and emission reduction targets, and participating in discussions on climate change. Of course, a cynic might wonder what took corporate leaders and politicians so long to realize what was abundantly obvious not only to scientists but to increasing numbers of laypeople. Furthermore, there is the suspicion that sensing that change was coming, corporations simply acted so that they would be included in the deliberations and could limit the costs to them. In many cases, it appears that corporations are jumping on the ecological bandwagon largely because it is good public relations (this is known as "greenwashing"). This is supported by the fact that, as of 2012, few global corporations made meaningful efforts to curb their greenhouse gas emissions. The Carbon Disclosure Project, which is a group that provides investors with information on environmental risks among the world's largest corporations, released a 2012 report that found only 20% of its 379 corporations set emission targets beyond 2020 (Barringer 2012). On average, companies strived to reduce their emissions by only 1%, which was "well below the level of ambition needed," according to the report. Furthermore, some of these corporations sense that there is money to be made in clean-energy technologies and they want a piece of the action. For example, some corporations have invested heavily in wind, hydroelectric, and nuclear power and they would gain business if there are cuts in those power sources that emit large amounts of carbon dioxide (Strassel 2007: A10). Furthermore, various industries are jockeying for position in order to force others to absorb the costs associated with change. For example, the auto industry wants the oil industry to produce more low-carbon alternatives and the latter, for its part, wants the auto industry to produce more efficient automobiles.

As of this writing, the most recent global meeting on climate change took place at the Rio+20 conference in 2012. Given the widespread acknowledgement of global warming and the increasing need for climate governance, participants and movement activists hoped that the meeting would be a turning point in the development of global environmental governance (Christoff and Eckersley 2013). However, little was accomplished at the meeting. While attendance more than doubled from the 1992 Earth Summit, there were not as many heads of state in attendance. For example, Barack Obama, Germany's Angela Merkel, and the UK's David Cameron were absent from the conference.

Rio+20 failed to achieve any significant political commitments or new institutions that could oversee their development. Instead, national governments simply reaffirmed previous commitments and the vague principles which underpinned them. One of the few positive outcomes was the creation of a working group to establish a set of Sustainable Development Goals, analogous to the UN's Millennium Development Goals. But advocates wanted to see more institutional support to govern climate change, such as stronger environmental authority granted to the UN or the development of a World Environment Organization (WEO) (analogous to the WTO), but neither garnered adequate support. As a result, the conference was heavily criticized by environmental and anti-poverty NGOs, with participating governments admitting to the meeting's failures.

The Rio+20 meetings also reflected a long-standing tension between many developed and developing nations. For example, while the US wants to see developing countries, especially China (and India), limit its emissions, China (and other developing countries) tends to take the view that many of today's problems are a result of what the developed countries have done, and are doing, to the environment. At Rio+20, they would not agree to any framework that placed any "conditionalities" on their own development. Furthermore, it is China's view that it is now its time to develop, to catch up, and in order to do so, it must both industrialize further and develop more of a consumer society (including many more highly polluting private automobiles). The result, of course, would be a great increase in both China's absolute and relative contribution to global pollution. Indeed, China is already the largest producer of greenhouse gases. This is largely traceable to China's extremely rapid industrial development and the fact that almost 70% of that nation's energy comes from coal-fired power plants, many with poor and outmoded devices to limit pollution. Thus, the US wants to see limits on China before it reaches this point, but for its part, China is determined to develop economically.

Another complicating factor in dealing with climate change is the uneven trade-offs in proposed solutions. When certain locales or groups adopt practices to reduce risk in climate change, these changes can lead to greater risks for others globally. For example, creating carbon sinks might displace peasant subsistence communities from forests; or geo-engineering solutions might unexpectedly alter multiple fisheries and farm ecologies; or just investing in water desalination could consume more fossil fuels and create further carbon emissions and drought problems.

CARBON TAX

Carbon tax: a tax applied to fossil fuels (e.g. oil, coal, and natural gas) used to curb carbon emissions.

Another proposal for helping to reduce the emission of greenhouse gases is the **carbon tax**. Businesses would pay a tax based on the amount of their carbon emissions from the use of fossil fuels (e.g. oil, coal, and natural gas). The idea is that the economic costs involved in paying the tax would motivate them to modify their production processes in order to reduce emissions and therefore the taxes they would need to pay. Many economists agree that a carbon tax would actually be the simplest and most effective way to reduce greenhouse emissions (Tyson 2013). For example, the US Congressional Budget Office estimated that a $20 tax on a ton of carbon dioxide, which would add about 15 cents to the cost of a gallon of gasoline, would reduce emissions by 8% and create as much as $1.2 trillion in government revenues over ten years, which could then be spent on further environmental programs. The ideal scheme would be a global carbon tax so that all nations of the world would participate. Clearly, the effectiveness of the system would be reduced if some areas of the world participated and others did not. However, the participation of any nations, especially major polluters such as the US and China, would help to reduce global carbon emissions and thereby ultimately global warming.

CAP-AND-TRADE

Cap-and-trade: a system that limits the total carbon emissions allowed, where companies buy permits in order to allow them to produce additional emissions with prices set by the market.

An alternative to the carbon tax is a system of **cap-and-trade** (Goulder and Schein 2013). In this system, there is a limit placed on total carbon emissions allowed, and then companies buy permits in order to allow them to produce additional emissions. The permits are bought and sold in the marketplace, allowing the market, rather than regulators, to set the price of carbon. According to the logic of cap-and-trade, companies then have an incentive to pollute less so they have to buy fewer permits. As a result, investments in better technology are rewarded economically, perhaps even allowing companies to sell the permits they no longer need. The system is more complicated than a carbon tax, but has had greater political success. One reason for this is that politicians view cap-and-trade as more palatable to voters and businesses that fear new taxes (Galbraith 2013). So while some countries, like Japan, Switzerland, and Ireland, have carbon taxes (with South Africa set to introduce a carbon tax in 2015), the larger EU has a system of cap-and-trade, and Australia is moving from a carbon tax to a cap-and-trade system largely for political reasons.

Despite the political success of the cap-and-trade system, the actual workings of these carbon markets have been riddled with problems and are highly controversial. After a great start, where the European system of cap-and-trade went from a market value of $15 billion in 2005 to $144 billion in 2009 (thus making it more expensive to emit greenhouse gases), prices in carbon markets around the world stagnated for several years (Gronewold 2011). Trading declined and prices on carbon emissions dropped, thereby weakening its incentive structure for polluting less. The system was further hurt by widespread fraud. As a result, Europe more recently voted to decrease the number of permits available, a tactic they delayed during the Great Recession (Reed 2013). However, many environmental groups point to the fact that, under this system, companies are still allowed to emit greenhouse gases and that such systems are not nearly sufficient for curbing greenhouse gas emissions at rates necessary to slow global warming. Nonetheless, as countries around the world continue to experiment with carbon taxes and cap-and-trade, the world's two largest polluters – China and the US – have adopted neither system and made no significant steps toward curbing their emissions.

CARBON NEUTRAL

The most ambitious goal in cutting emissions would be for a country to go carbon neutral, where their carbon emissions are equal to (or less than) the amount of those emissions that are absorbed by the natural environment. Some ways in which a country might achieve **carbon neutrality** include switching to renewable energies, collecting industrial pollutants or methane produced by industrial farming, or buying carbon offsets (purchasing forests that capture emissions from other sources). The difficulty of actually reducing carbon emissions is reflected in the case of Norway, which announced in 2007 that it would be "carbon neutral" by 2050. By early 2008 the Norwegian government announced that the date for carbon neutrality had been moved up two decades to a startling 2030. However, it turns out that these gains are the result not so much of reducing carbon emissions in Norway, but by canceling them out by, for example, "planting trees or cleaning up a polluting factory in a country far away" (Rosenthal 2008b: A6). This kind of accounting sleight of hand is allowable under the environmental accounting policy of the UN. Even with its limitations, Norway's methods of dealing with carbon emissions are costly and few other nations can afford it (Norway is awash with oil income). More importantly, it is not sustainable since there are just not enough trees to plant and factories to clean up in the less developed world to compensate for carbon emissions in developed (and some developing) countries. Critics of Norway and other countries engaging in these practices argue that they conceal the fact that much more needs to be done at home to cut carbon emissions (e.g. cutbacks in its heavy industries). More recently, Norway has sought to reduce its emissions by 40%. This goes significantly further than the EU, which has sought to reduce emissions by 20% (Kanter 2009).

> **Carbon neutrality**: a scenario where carbon emissions are equal to (or less than) the amount of those emissions that are absorbed by the natural environment.

ALTERNATIVE FUELS AND POWER SOURCES

The global problems associated with the extraordinary use, especially in the US, of gasoline to power automobiles has finally led to the beginnings of a serious effort to find alternatives to it, especially in the US, the world leader in automobile and gasoline use.

Hybrid technology

One development of note is the increasing importance of hybrid automobiles that derive at least part of their power from electricity. With future sources of oil dwindling, demand rising, and growing concern about global warming, we will see more and more efforts to create alternatives to the gasoline-powered automobile. Cars that plug into an electrical outlet and run entirely on electric power are also increasingly available. For example, the Chevrolet Volt (sold as the Holden Volt in Australia and New Zealand, or the Vauxhall Ampera in Great Britain and Opel Ampera in Europe) runs purely on an electric battery until the battery is drained, at which point it can draw its power from a gasoline engine.

Ethanol

There is also growing interest in alternative fuels to gasoline, with great attention focused on ethanol. The major current source of ethanol is corn, especially in the US, but it can be made from other agricultural products. For example, ethanol can be made from cellulosic sources such as switchgrass or wood chips, and Brazilian ethanol made from sugar requires less energy than ethanol made from corn (Wald 2013). Ethanol, however, is a third less efficient than gasoline.

Ethanol drew so much attention in recent years because it promised to help with various global problems, including dependence on oil produced and controlled elsewhere in the world, and carbon dioxide emissions. The expectations placed on ethanol and other biofuels were so high in the US that the government provided subsidies to spur more ethanol production. The Environmental Protection Agency (EPA) set quotas on the percentages of cellulosic fuel to be integrated in gasoline. They were increased each year from 2010 until 2012. However, there have been many problems associated with ethanol, and because of insufficient production and supply of various biofuels, a federal court threw out the EPA quota in 2013 (Wald 2013). The US has also ended many of its subsidies on ethanol and many ethanol plants in the US have closed down in recent years.

The global problems with ethanol are significant. First, the growing interest in ethanol has driven up corn prices and this threatens American exports of corn to many parts of the world. Second, it is also a threat in other parts of world, such as Mexico and Guatemala, where there is great reliance on corn for food staples like tortillas. Because of globalization, Mexico has, as we have seen (see Chapter 6), grown increasingly reliant on American corn and is therefore directly affected by its increase in price. Furthermore, because there is a global market for corn, the price of Mexican corn has risen as well.

Concern has also surfaced recently that biofuels such as ethanol may exacerbate the problem of greenhouse gas emissions rather than reduce them. While biofuels on their own produce fewer such emissions than fossil fuels, they cause *more* when we adopt a broader view. It has been known for quite some time that the refining and transportation of these fuels produce carbon emissions. What is new is the realization that in order to produce biofuels, rainforests, grasslands, and other natural ecosystems are reduced or destroyed and that the burning or plowing of those systems releases greenhouse gases. Further, the problem is also exacerbated because natural ecosystems act like sponges in absorbing carbon emissions. Still further, the cropland that replaces these natural systems absorbs much less carbon.

The global reverberations associated with producing biofuels can eventually be immense. Already, as the US devotes more farm land to producing corn, countries like Brazil are responding by producing more soybeans to compensate for the decline in American production of that crop. This leads to more deforestation in Brazil to create new farm land and that, in turn, leads as we saw above to more carbon emissions and less ability to absorb them. Sugar cane seems to offer some hope because it requires little energy to grow and it can easily be made into fuel. A better possibility would be agricultural waste products because they would not require more farm land in order to produce fuel (Rosenthal 2008c: A9).

Other problems associated with ethanol are becoming increasingly clear. For example, as more land is devoted to the crops needed to produce it, less is devoted to growing food. This serves to increase food prices not only for Guatemala and its corn, but around the world (Rosenthal 2013). Another problem is that factories that produce ethanol use huge amounts of water and, as is discussed above, water is itself an increasingly endangered resource.

Palm oil

The difficulties involved in finding alternatives to fossil-based (coal, oil) sources of energy are also manifest in the case of palm oil. Not long ago the Netherlands hit upon the idea of using biofuel (especially palm oil) in its electrical plants as a way of moving toward greener, more sustainable, energy. Some plants created generators that ran exclusively on palm oil. The government provided massive subsidies and the Netherlands became Europe's leading importer of palm oil. However, the need to provide the Netherlands with palm oil led to the decimation of rainforests, to massive deforestation, in places like Indonesia and Malaysia. Between 1990 and 2010, Indonesia lost 20% of its rainforests, mostly to deforestation for palm oil plantations (Schonhardt 2013). In addition, there was a tendency in those locales to use too much potentially destructive fertilizer to produce the palm oil. Furthermore, to create new plantations, peatland was drained and burned leading to massive carbon emissions – just what the Dutch sought to reduce in the first place by moving to palm oil. A realization dawned on some that a broader, global view on this was required. A focus on the Netherlands, or Europe more generally (where biofuel is more of an alternative to diesel fuel for automobiles), ignores the impact elsewhere in the world of changes made there. Global problems resulting from carbon emissions are not solved by simply transferring such emissions from one region to another. At the minimum, to provide a clearer accounting, some urge that nations like the Netherlands take into account *all* of the emissions resulting from such changes. As a result, European countries have moved away from the extensive use of palm oil and Norway offered to pay Indonesia up to $1 billion toward halting its deforestation (Schonhardt 2013).

Solar power

A better alternative source of energy is solar power. One of its attractions is that it produces no greenhouse gases. Another, especially in warmer climes, is that it produces its maximum energy just when it is needed. That is, it produces the most energy on hot, sunny days and those are the times of the greatest demand for energy to run air conditioners. Some technologies needed to use solar energy are able to store it (in batteries or even in molten salt!) and are therefore able to operate at night and on cloudy days. Solar power remains more expensive than using fossil fuels, but the difference continues to decrease as demand for energy increases, the supply of fossil fuels decreases, and the costs of solar energy decline (as technologies improve and economies of scale kick in). Indeed, local governments and utilities (especially in Europe) are sometimes paying homeowners for producing electricity from solar panels installed on their homes.

A TECHNOLOGICAL FIX?

Talk of increased use of solar power is related to the growing interest these days in a "technological fix" for at least some global environmental problems such as global warming. There is a longstanding attraction to finding technological solutions to all social problems. To many, finding new technologies seems far easier and less painful than the much harder task of getting large numbers of people to change longstanding behaviors. That is, people tend to be loath to change their consumption patterns and thus prefer the hope of technological fixes to the ecological problems they play a large role in causing. Furthermore, many industries have a vested interest in people continuing to consume at high levels. Thus, a major cause of global warming is the ever-increasing burning of fossil fuels, but innumerable industries and people are wedded to it and many people in other parts of the world would dearly like to do more of it. This is especially the case with the use in highly developed countries of gasoline in automobiles, the increasing number of people in countries like China and India that can now afford them, and the large numbers in less developed countries who would dearly love to drive automobiles. In the face of this huge and growing demand, it is unlikely that calls to cut back on gasoline use are going to be heeded (although the Great Recession did force people to cut back). Hence the attraction of the search for a technological fix that will solve the problems caused by the burning of gasoline and, more generally, fossil fuels. With such a fix, production and consumption throughout the world can not only continue, but expand further.

Enter "geoengineering" and a series of relatively new proposals for dealing with global ecological problems while leaving untouched and unaddressed the underlying and growing causes of global warming (Hamilton 2013). Among the ideas being discussed are "injecting chemicals into the upper atmosphere to cool the poles, or blocking sunlight by making clouds more reflective or stationing mirrors in space" (Dean 2007: A11). Scientific support for these possibilities has been muted for several reasons: there is fear that talk of such solutions would encourage people to continue, if not increase, their use of fossil fuels; there is great fear that even if some of the proposals do work, they might have a series of unanticipated consequences that will pose as great, or greater, problems than the problems they are designed to help deal with; these innovations in geoengineering are untried, incredibly difficult, and likely to be extraordinarily expensive; and there are many other climate-related problems (e.g. the increasing acidity of the oceans) which would be unaffected by global climate changes produced by such technologies. Undertaking such projects would require truly global efforts and a massively funded global governance structure. The hope here is that already functioning global governance that "regulate the use of radio frequencies, organize air traffic control, track space" (Dean 2007: A11) will be a model for what is needed to deal with global climate problems.

While geoengineering technologies are little more than vague ideas at this point and a long way from anything approaching functionality, a leading expert in the area predicted that within two centuries the earth will be "an artifact," that is, it will be a product of human design and geoengineering. Already underway are efforts to respond to the adverse effects of global warming on agriculture and crops. This involves new aspects of the "green revolution" such as the creation of crops, through selective breeding and genetic engineering, that can survive in warmer climates, that can use increased salinity rather than being destroyed by it, that are not desiccated by droughts, and that can even thrive while submerged under water (Weiss 2007: A6). Less dramatic responses include reducing plowing and tilling (reduces evaporation and amount of carbon dioxide released), reducing the amount of fertilizer used (fertilizer produces nitrous oxide which is far more harmful to the atmosphere than carbon dioxide), the planting of shade trees, and the addition of fruit trees better able to survive climate change than subsistence crops.

There is even a "doomsday vault" in a Norwegian mountainside which is being stocked by seeds from around the world (Rimmer 2012). The idea is that in the event of dramatic and unexpected climate changes, we cannot know in advance which seeds will survive and thrive. Even in worst-case scenarios, the hope is that some of these seeds stored in the Norwegian vault will be the ones that save humanity from starvation.

ECONOMIC ISSUES

Long-term solutions, and even very short-term solutions, to environmental problems in general, and the problems of climate change in particular, are likely to be hugely, if not monumentally, expensive. The kinds of advanced scientific efforts outlined above will cost huge sums to just research, let alone to implement. Even less innovative changes such as more wind turbines, solar panels, reforestation, retooling large industries, building power plants able to recapture carbon dioxide, and, most controversially, lots more nuclear power plants, involve unimaginable costs. Furthermore, these efforts need to be undertaken globally and that would involve many nations without the resources to do much, if anything, about these problems. Even in the highly developed countries, it is not clear that people understand the costs involved in these efforts, let alone being willing to pay for them. This is especially the case in the United States which lags behind Europe in implementing and paying for even the most rudimentary of these changes. Germany, for example, is the European leader in the use of wind and solar power and the US lags far behind it in this. And, of course, continuing concerns about economic growth make it even less likely that such massive, and hugely expensive, programs will be undertaken.

OPPOSING ENVIRONMENTALISM

While it seems like an unmitigated good, it is not unusual for there to be opposition to environmentalism. Most generally those interested in economic development have little patience for environmentalists, especially when environmental concerns slow down, or stop, such development. An interesting example of this involves efforts by the World Wildlife Fund (WWF), beginning in 2003, to create parks and reserves in Brazil in a program known as Amazon Region Protected Areas (Rohter 2007a: A4). A great concern there is the limiting of further deforestation. As discussed above, the Amazon has already been deforested to a great degree. The Amazon forest was, and is, important to the world for its uncountable trees that absorb enormous quantities of carbon dioxide. That capacity has declined dramatically and, instead, decaying plant life in the Amazon is contributing heavily to the production of carbon dioxide and therefore to global warming. As of this writing, over 20% of the Amazon rainforest has been deforested and scientists fear that further deforestation could have far-reaching ecological effects (both locally and globally). The goal of WWF is to protect not only the trees in Brazil but also its biodiversity. However, some businessmen have reacted negatively to this for two basic reasons. First, it is seen as impeding their ability to develop the region and its natural resources and thereby to increase their business and profits. Second, it is seen as, itself, a kind of colonialism and perhaps a precursor to the re-emergence of more traditional kind of colonialism (see Chapter 3), in which foreign (especially American) entrepreneurs come in to develop the area, perhaps preceded by the military. The WWF denies such interests and associations and says that it is simply seeking to protect land that the Brazilian government has failed to protect.

FROM LIGHTNESS TO HEAVINESS IN ENVIRONMENTAL FLOWS

The environmental flows described above are literally gases and liquids that flow throughout the world. Greenhouse gases (e.g. carbon dioxide) that contribute to global warming may the lightest of all. But other flows, including polluted waterways (that might lead to the Pacific Trash Vortex), toxic chemicals, or the rising oceans, also move freely across space. But as these light (or even weightless) flows continue accumulating, their effects become very heavy indeed. In other words, it may not be possible to lower greenhouse gases in a significant way, humans will be unable to move water out of the rising oceans, and the dramatic loss in biodiversity cannot be reversed. Depleted forests, fresh water supplies, fisheries, arable farmland, and other natural resources might not be replaced on reasonable time scales. By acknowledging such heavy effects, the dramatic need for implementing some combination of the solutions described above is underscored.

COLLAPSE

This chapter has highlighted many of the world's most pressing environmental problems, with climate change being the direst situation. It has also highlighted the dramatic failures, thus far, in dealing with these problems. In light of this, it is worth considering the findings of Jared Diamond's popular book – *Collapse* – about societal collapse and the role of environmental factors in that collapse (2006). He concludes that not all civilizations that collapsed in the past have had environmental causes, but at least some have. For example, the Norse of Greenland cut down all their trees, thus making it difficult to build houses or boats (deforestation was the most important of several causes of their collapse). One factor in collapse due to environmental causes is the amount and type of damage that people inadvertently inflict on their environment. Damage will depend, in part, on what people do and in part on the degree of fragility or resilience of the environment (e.g. its ability to restore itself). Another factor affecting degree of damage is the way in which different societies respond to these environmental problems. For example, historically those societies (e.g. Highland New Guinea) that developed sound forest management policies and procedures continue to survive, while others that did not (e.g. Easter Island) collapsed.

What is unique about the global era is the fact that unlike in the past societies are not likely to collapse in isolation from others (as Easter Island did). On the one hand, globalization can be a cause of optimism in the sense that other parts of the world will be alerted to dangers elsewhere long before the dangers are critical to them. Those in other parts of the world can, therefore, act to ward off or reduce the problem and help their societies avoid collapse. On the other hand, global interconnectedness means that ecological problems in one part of the world are likely to affect others, perhaps the entire planet. Thus, profligate use of fossil fuels (especially oil) by the US has played a huge role in the global warming that is threatening large portions of the globe. Similarly, the emergence of China as an economic superpower has also earned it the dubious position of being the leading contributor to global warming and therefore a considerable threat to the ecology of the world. The nature of the problem makes it impossible for significant ecological problems, including collapse, to be isolated to one locale in the global age.

CHAPTER SUMMARY

This chapter examines the detrimental impact of negative global flows on the environment. The most developed countries are disproportionately responsible for the current environmental problems. These countries are also better equipped to deal with these problems.

Today's global environmental flows and problems are closely connected to modernization, or the supposedly evolutionary process that moved humankind from agricultural and premodern societies into the modern era, brought about by wide-scale rational planning. Among other changes, modernization reflected an anthropocentric worldview, where humans were seen as the center of the natural order of the world and inevitably came to dominate and subjugate the non-human world. Through the application of science and technology, humans have created countless new chemicals and altered ecosystems for their own development. There was little consciousness of the human impacts of these activities until the 1960s and 1970s, when scientists, some business groups, and new environmental activists began documenting the relationship between modernization, economic growth, and the environment.

Today, neoliberals and environmentalists debate the impact of free trade on the environment. Environmentalists argue that environmental issues should be given priority over economic issues. Free trade, through its emphasis on the expansion of manufacturing, is associated with environmental damage. For their part, neoliberals see the efforts of the environmentalists as serious impediments to trade. Some seek to integrate these approaches. For instance, ecological economists see globalization as a process that can both protect and enhance the environment.

The most pressing global environmental problem is climate change. The science of climate change, which is no longer under dispute, shows that greenhouse gases trap sunlight and heat in the earth's atmosphere, and contribute greatly to global warming. In turn, this process causes the melting of land-based and glacial ice with potentially catastrophic effects. Apart from the possibility of substantial flooding, global warming threatens ecosystems and fresh water supplies, which will both diminish biodiversity and human access to water. The destruction of the water ecosystem may lead to the creation of climate refugees, people who are forced to migrate due to the effects of climate change. Global warming also poses a threat to the global food supply, human health, and national security.

Another major environmental problem is the destruction of natural habitats, particularly through deforestation. Industrial fishing has contributed to a significant destruction of marine life and ecosystems. Pollution through toxic chemicals has had a long-term impact on the environment. The use of persistent organic pollutants (POP) has led to significant industrial pollution. Population growth and the attendant increase in consumption intensify ecological problems. The global flow of waste is another major concern, with e-waste often being dumped in developing countries.

Degradation of the environment has elicited significant global responses. One approach is that of sustainable development, which seeks to chart a middle path between economic growth and a sustainable environment. The relationship between globalization and sustainability is multidimensional – it involves economic, political, and technological aspects.

Various efforts are underway to deal with climate change. However, these are countered by strong resistance on the part of governments and corporations. For instance, the Kyoto Protocol, aimed at a reduction of global carbon emissions, failed to take off, especially because it was not ratified by the US. More recently, the Rio+20 conference in 2012 failed to achieve commitments to curbing greenhouse gas emissions or develop the political framework necessary to develop such policies in the future.

There are significant challenges involved in implementing various measures (e.g. carbon tax, cap-and-trade, or carbon neutrality) to deal with environmental problems. It is also difficult to find alternatives to fossil fuels. For instance, the use of ethanol as an alternative to gasoline has an attendant set of problems – it is less efficient and it has led to an escalation in the price of corn (which currently serves as a major source of ethanol). Although biofuels themselves produce lower emissions, their extraction and transport contribute significantly to total emissions.

Previous experience in dealing with environmental issues indicates that a global view of the problem is required. A focus on specific regions, such as Europe, overlooks impacts in other regions. Instead of dealing with the causes of global warming, there is some interest in "technological fixes" such as geoengineering.

The relationship between environmental damage and societal collapse is examined in this chapter. It is argued that, unlike in the past, global interconnectedness ensures that damage to nature will not be confined to isolated geographical areas.

DISCUSSION QUESTIONS

1. In what ways are global environmental problems a result of modernization?

2. Outline as many connections as possible among the world's leading environmental problems.

3. Examine the influence of various consumption practices on environmental degradation.

4. Examine the role of global corporations in causing and alleviating environmental problems.

5. Do you think that the world may someday "collapse" because of accelerating environmental problems? Why? Why not?

6. In what ways can global flows positively affect the environment?

7. Analyze the various global responses to environmental degradation. Develop an argument for why one of those responses is the best way forward.

8. Examine the feasibility of sustainable development as a global project.

9. Are environmental problems likely to bring the world's nations together or drive them apart?

ADDITIONAL READINGS ··

Zygmunt Bauman. *Liquid Fear*. Cambridge: Polity, 2006.

Jared Diamond. *Collapse: How Societies Choose to Fail or Succeed*. New York: Penguin, 2006.

Peter Christoff and Robyn Eckersley. *Globalization and the Environment*. New York: Rowman and Littlefield, 2013.

Arjen Y. Hoekstra and Ashok K. Chapagain. *Globalization of Water: Sharing the Planet's Freshwater Resources*. Oxford: Blackwell, 2008.

Rachel Carson. *Silent Spring*. Boston: Houghton Mifflin, 1962.

David Held, Angus Hervey, and Marika Theros, eds. *The Governance of Climate Change: Science, Economics, Politics, and Ethics*. Malden, MA: Polity Press, 2011.

Simone Borghesi and Alessandro Vercelli. *Global Sustainability: Social and Environmental Conditions*. New York: Palgrave Macmillan, 2008.

Jacob Park, Ken Conca, and Matthias Finger, eds. *The Crisis of Global Environmental Governance: Towards a New Political Economy of Sustainability*. New York: Routledge, 2008.

NOTES ··

1 This is not the first time we have faced such crises. On the ecological crisis associated with the Dark Ages, see Chew (2002).

2 However, hurricanes themselves tend to spawn tornados, especially in coastal areas.

3 The East Coast of the US is strongly, perhaps increasingly, affected by hurricanes which tend to spin off tornados.

4 Fish and other seafood perform other functions such as keeping the oceans clean.

5 www.pops.int; David Downie (2007: 953–5).

6 The report was a product of its time (the then existence of many communist regimes), and its authors wanted its ideas to apply to both market-oriented and centrally planned nations. While there are few centrally planned nations today (Cuba is one lingering exception), the report's point about sustainability's applicability to developed and developing countries is as relevant, or more relevant, than ever.

NEGATIVE GLOBAL FLOWS AND PROCESSES

DANGEROUS IMPORTS, DISEASES, CRIME, TERRORISM, WAR

Globalization: A Basic Text, Second Edition. George Ritzer and Paul Dean.
© 2015 John Wiley & Sons, Ltd. Published 2015 by John Wiley & Sons, Ltd.

The previous chapter on environmental problems began with, and was informed by, Zygmunt Bauman's (2006: 96) concept of negative globalization. That idea is even more relevant to this chapter since he enumerates a number of issues under that heading that will be of concern to us here. While there are many negative flows that could concern us in this chapter, the discussion will be limited to the global flows associated with dangerous imports, borderless diseases, crime, terrorism, and war.

While we recognize these negative flows, and agree with Bauman on the idea of increasing global liquidity, he goes too far with the idea of negative globalization, or at least farther than we are prepared to go. That is, in his view "ours is a wholly *negative* globalization: unchecked, unsupplemented and uncompensated for by a 'positive' counterpart which is still a distant prospect at best, though according to some prognoses already a forlorn chance" (Bauman 2006: 96). While there are certainly many negative aspects, flows, and processes associated with globalization, we would not accept the view that globalization is wholly negative. A discussion of the problems associated with globalization and of the kind offered in both this chapter and the preceding one should not blind us to its positive side (e.g. the flow of life-saving pharmaceuticals, medical personnel to check the outbreak of a new pandemic, or global movements that promote human rights around the world).

Another key point is that the issue of what is regarded as positive or negative about globalization often depends on one's perspective and position.[1] Thus, while most of us would agree that terrorism is a negative process, those who are involved in, and support it, disagree. To take another example, some in the US see neoliberalism as a good thing (Hackworth 2012), but there is no shortage of others (including Bauman and these authors) who see it as creating problems for large parts of the world[2] and therefore, from that perspective, an example of negative globalization. This general orientation applies to the examples of negative globalization discussed throughout this chapter. That is, while many, perhaps most, would agree with this characterization, others would adopt a more positive view toward them.

Finally, it needs to be pointed out that negative globalization does not merely involve negative flows and processes, but also structures whose effects at least some would regard as largely, if not totally, negative. Thus, for those (the vast majority of people in the world) who take a negative view of terrorism, the cellular organization of al-Qaeda would be considered a negative structure; if one thinks of neoliberalism as a negative global process, then the structures associated with it, such as the IMF and the World Bank, would be seen as negative structures. Of course, as was pointed out early in this book, the distinction between structure and process is, in many ways, a false one. Among the many reasons for this argument is that any structure is made up of a series of processes and those processes are affected by, and affect, a series of larger processes.

It is also worth noting that negative global flows of various kinds lead to global counter-reactions; to global efforts, both processes and structures, to deal with those flows. In terms of processes, one example is the development of increasingly sophisticated, often continuous, global surveillance techniques to deal, among other things, with terrorism (Bergesen 2012; Lyons 2004; Schmitt 2013). As to structures, the World Social Forum is the broadest example of a structure created to centralize efforts to deal with the negative flows associated with globalization, especially those associated with neoliberal globalization (Kohler 2012).

DANGEROUS IMPORTS

The flow of all sorts of products from every corner of the world has made it near-impossible to know precisely the true nature of the products entering a country. From the food we eat to everyday household products, globalization has facilitated flows of many things, including those that are dangerous in various ways.

FOOD

Over the last several decades, food exports and imports have increased dramatically and even products produced locally contain ingredients from many parts of the world. Take the case of Sara Lee's Soft&Smooth Whole Grain White bread which includes the following ingredients (with the nations supplying each indicated): guar gum – India; calcium propionate – Netherlands; honey – China, Vietnam, Brazil, Uruguay, India, Canada, Mexico, Argentina; flour enrichments – China; beta-carotene – Switzerland; vitamin D3 – China; wheat gluten – France, Poland, Russia, Netherlands, Australia (Schoenfeld 2007: B9). The greater the use of global ingredients, the greater the difficulty in ensuring that no contaminants find their way into finished products. Further, when finished products include numerous ingredients from many different locales throughout the world, it becomes difficult, if not impossible, to locate the source of the contamination. Thus, if, for example, Sara Lee's bread were to make people sick, there are many potential sources of the contamination. Thus involved here are *both* a global value chain involving the ingredients in various foods *and* the possibility, because the chain is so long and diverse, of the spread of contaminants associated with at least some of the ingredients.

Furthermore, many of the ingredients come from nations whose food safety standards are not likely to equal those in the US and other nations in the North. This issue has gained much notoriety lately in the case of Chinese imports (Wu and Chen 2013), as the quantity and diversity of products imported from China into many nations (especially the US) have exploded in the past two decades. For example, the US imports 70% of its apple juice, 43% of its processed mushrooms, and 22% of its frozen spinach from China; overall food imports from China increased from 453.6 million pounds in 1990 to 3,867.3 million pounds in 2010 (Food and Water Watch 2011). However, food production in China has weak regulations and enforcement, and outcries over problems associated with them have increased proportionately with this explosion in food imports (Assmann 2013). The worst scandals were from an industrial chemical, melamine, that was added to pet food (4,000 pets died from ingesting the food), as well as milk, candy, hot cocoa, and infant formula. Other food problems include industrial pollution that spills into waterways that irrigate crops, illegal use of antibiotics in honey, and illegal veterinary drugs used in hogs and other livestock.

In some cases, consumers are helpless since food labels do not always offer sufficient information on where such ingredients come from. While the US passed more requirements for Country of Origin Labeling (COOL) in 2009 (for beef, poultry, lamb, goat, some nuts, fresh and some frozen fruits and vegetables, and ginseng), there are still many loopholes and the food industry continues aggressively to fight the law. For example, any foods that are roasted, cooked, smoked, or cured are exempt from labeling (because most nuts are roasted, they, too, are excluded from labeling requirements). Any foods combined with another ingredient are also exempt. Because so many foods are highly processed and have long lists of ingredients, they escape labeling.

While we focus on Chinese imports, it is important to remember that many other countries have been, and still are, involved in the global exportation of dangerous foods. For example, rice imported into the US from the Czech Republic, Bhutan, Italy, India, and Thailand (in addition to China and Taiwan) have all been found to have dangerously high levels of lead (Jaslow 2013). The Swiss company Nestlé was guilty of aggressively exporting baby formula to the South, especially Africa, even though it had adverse effects on infants. Among other things, the water needed to mix the formula could well have been contaminated and the formula replaced nutritious breast milk.

CHEMICALS

A wide range of chemicals flow from Chinese manufacturers (there are estimated to be about 80,000 of them) that are neither certified nor inspected. Leveraging ties with local governments, they often avoid governmental regulation (Guizhen et al. 2014). A large number of Chinese companies manufacture chemicals as raw materials that end up in many pharmaceuticals. There have been various scandals associated with them including unauthorized production (counterfeiting), mislabeling, patent violations, selling to illegal steroid laboratories in the US, selling substandard materials, and selling mislabeled pharmaceuticals that proved poisonous and killed and injured hundreds of people in Haiti and Panama (Chinese authorities took no action against the companies involved) (Bogdanich, Hooker, and Lehren 2007: A1, A10). In spite of all this, there is little oversight or control by regulatory agencies in or over China. The potential for these sorts of problems has been increased with the increasingly long and complex supply chains that accompany globalization. For its part, the US, specifically the Food and Drug Administration (FDA), lacks the resources to oversee all but a few (about 20) of the legal (about 700) Chinese firms, let alone the illegal firms, manufacturing drug products for the US market.

Again, China is certainly not the only source of dangerous chemicals and the products that contain them. For example, American companies have exported pharmaceuticals to other countries that were banned in the US.

FISH

In 2013, for the first time, the majority of fish eaten by people was raised on fish farms rather than being caught in the natural environment. Farmed fish has now surpassed beef production (Leisher 2013). Much of this fish comes from China, which is the leading exporter of seafood. For example, 78% of tilapia consumed in the US and 67% of cod come from China (Food and Water Watch 2011). Much of the seafood is produced off-shore, but it is also produced "on land, in lakes, ponds, rivers and reservoirs, or in huge rectangular fish ponds dug into the earth" (Barboza 2007b: A10). China has huge factory-like aquaculture farms that make it the world's biggest producer of farmed fish (overall it produces 62% of the world's farmed fish). Water contaminated by industrial waste and agricultural runoff (including pesticides) finds its way into these bodies of water and contaminates the seafood with pesticides, drugs, lead, heavy metals, and so on. Furthermore, in order to keep the fish alive in the huge breeding pools needed to supply gigantic fish farms, the fish are sometimes treated with antibiotics. Products with traces of the latter, as well as those found to have traces of chemicals and pesticides, are banned from the US because they are considered harmful to consumers.

Then, there is the huge Xulong factory in Taishan, China with, among other things, a roasting oven the size of a football field. Although the factory appears to have made major efforts to provide clean seafood, its seafood has been barred from entry into the US on many occasions by the FDA because it comes from seas that have been fouled by Chinese factories and that are loaded with chemicals and pesticides, some of them carcinogens. While overall China accounted for approximately 22% of seafood imports to the US, 60% of the seafood denied entry into the US comes from China.

This is a huge problem for the US (and other nations such as those of the EU) which imports 80% of its seafood and, like other nations, finds the stock of wild seafood dwindling. It is potentially also a huge problem for China (and its consumers) and its $35 billion aquaculture industry. It is not only the leading exporter of seafood to the US, but also of garlic and apple juice concentrate, and China is of growing importance in the export to the US of processed vegetables, frozen food, and food ingredients.

As in the case of pharmaceuticals, the FDA is active in refusing the importation of tainted food, but it is ill prepared for the explosion of imports in this area and thus samples only a small portion of the food imported into the US. For example, the FDA inspects less than 2% of the food imported from China and rarely inspects production facilities there. Between June 2009 and June 2010, the FDA conducted only 13 food inspections in China (Food and Water Watch 2011). In terms of the perspective taken in this book, the FDA is a woefully inadequate structure in the face of the flood of imported food. Even so, the Chinese claim that the barriers that do exist to its products are a result of **trade protectionism** in the US and they have accused the US of raising its standards in certain areas and of acting "indiscriminately."

> **Trade protectionism:** Policy of systematic government intervention in foreign trade with the objective of encouraging domestic production.

BORDERLESS DISEASES

While borderless diseases have become much more common in recent years, they are not a new phenomenon (Ali 2012). Diseases such as the plague, malaria (see Figure 12.1 for a map showing the areas of the globe at high risk for malaria, 2010; while the risk of malaria has shrunk dramatically, several regions remain at high risk for the disease and that risk may increase with global warming), tuberculosis (TB), and sexually transmitted infections (STIs) of various types have long spread globally. A specific example of the latter is syphilis which now is spreading mainly throughout a number of less developed countries. However, the roots of the disease were probably in Europe and it was spread by European colonialism and military exploits. In fact, for many, the disease was closely associated with French soldiers and came to be known in some parts of the world as the "French Disease."

Then there is the increasing prevalence of other borderless diseases, many of them relatively new, such as Bovine Spongiform Encephalopathy (BSE) (or "Mad Cow Disease," a disease often found in cattle that can cause a brain disease, Creutzfeldt-Jakob Disease, in humans – outbreaks of this disease in cattle in, for example, Great Britain have led to periodic halts in the exportation of beef [Ong 2007]), swine and avian flu, Ebola virus, HIV/AIDS, and the chikungunya virus. The nature of these diseases and their spread either in fact (HIV/AIDS [Whiteside 2012]), or merely (so far) as a frightening possibility (avian flu), tell us a great deal about the nature and reality of globalization in the twenty-first

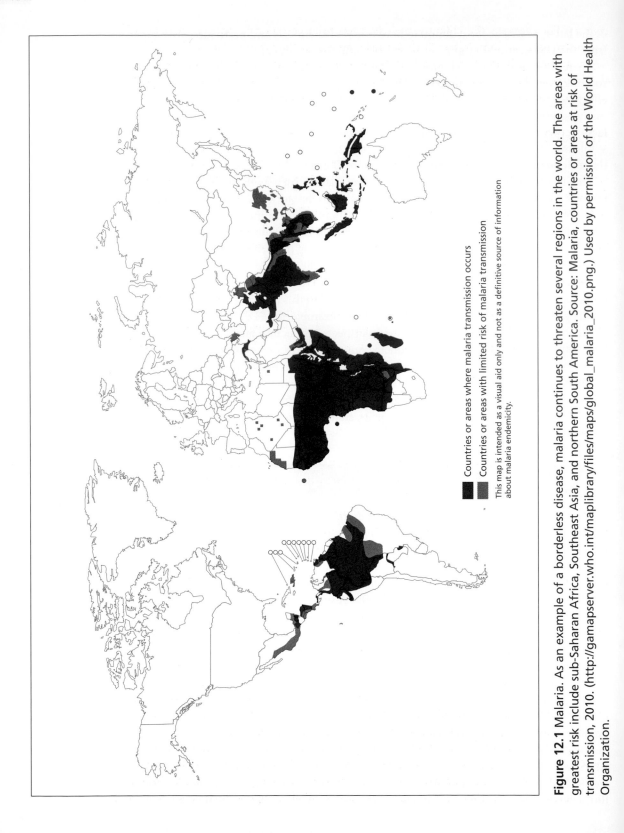

Figure 12.1 Malaria. As an example of a borderless disease, malaria continues to threaten several regions in the world. The areas with greatest risk include sub-Saharan Africa, Southeast Asia, and northern South America. Source: Malaria, countries or areas at risk of transmission, 2010. (http://gamapserver.who.int/maplibrary/files/maps/global_malaria_2010.png.) Used by permission of the World Health Organization.

■ Countries or areas where malaria transmission occurs

■ Countries or areas with limited risk of malaria transmission

This map is intended as a visual aid only and not as a definitive source of information about malaria endemicity.

century. For example, the chikungunya virus has been common in parts of Africa and Southeast Asia, but only in late 2013 did cases appear in the Western Hemisphere. They began appearing in the Caribbean Islands and quickly spread. The pathogens that cause these diseases flow, or have the potential to flow, readily throughout the globe and it is very difficult, if not impossible, to erect barriers to many, if not any, of them.

HIV/AIDS

HIV/AIDS spreads in various ways (e.g. blood transfusions), but it is its spread through sexual human contact (as an STI) that is especially relevant in the context of this book (Whiteside 2012). The globalization of the disease is a result of the increasingly heightened flow, movement, of people throughout much of the world. Unlike the other diseases to be discussed below, HIV/AIDS cannot be contracted through casual contact with people who have the disease. Thus, passengers on an international flight will not contract AIDS simply because they sit next to, or converse with, a fellow passenger with the disease.

The spread of AIDS is closely linked with globalization, especially the increased global mobility associated with tourism (including, and perhaps especially, sex tourism), the greater migration rates of workers, increased authorized and unauthorized immigration, much greater rates of commercial and business travel, the movements (sometimes on a mass basis) of refugees, military interventions and the movement of military personnel, and so on.

People who have the disease can travel great distances over a period of years without knowing they have it and therefore have the ability to transmit the disease to many others in a number of widely scattered locales. Thus, when those with HIV/AIDS have unprotected sexual contact with people in other countries, they are likely to transmit the disease to at least some of them. Similarly, those without the disease can travel to nations where HIV/AIDS is prevalent, contract it, and then bring it back to their home country. In either case, the disease moves from region to region, country to country, and ultimately globally, carried by human vectors.

More and more people, especially in the South, are contracting the disease, but it is initially largely symptomless. In the early stages of the disease people move freely around their communities, cities, countries, continents, and in some cases the world, carrying it with them. For example, in Africa one well-known way in which the disease has spread across the continent is through truck drivers who work their way from country to country. If they have the disease, they may infect those who live in areas that were to that point in time free of the disease.

In fact, no area of the world has been more devastated by AIDS than Africa, with some nations having infection rates approaching 30% of the adult population. The disease, as well as the many burdens associated with it, is having an adverse effect on all aspects of social and economic life throughout Africa. Some even predict the failure of at least some African states and their complete economic collapse as a result of the spread of the disease. The economies of many African nations have already contracted as average life expectancy declines and it becomes harder to find healthy adults to perform basic work-related tasks.

The greater prevalence of AIDS in Africa is just one example of the greater vulnerability of the world's have-nots to this and many other borderless diseases. This is not just a question of economic marginality, but also social and political marginality. Compounding the problem is the fact that it is precisely this *most* vulnerable population that is also *least* likely to have access to the high-quality health care and the very expensive drugs that can slow the disease for years, or even decades.

FLU

Flu may be the disease most adept at eluding borders (Ali 2012). For many years (beginning in the late 1990s), there has been fear of a pandemic of "avian flu" (H5N1) that, because of globalization, could perhaps spread faster and affect more people (and kill them) and more parts of the world than the Spanish flu pandemic of 1918. It is hard to know exactly how many people were killed worldwide by the Spanish flu pandemic (somewhere between 20 million and more than 100 million), but we do know that about a half million Americans died from the disease; more than a quarter of the American population was made ill by it (Kolata 1999). The World Bank estimates that a severe outbreak of influenza could cost the global economy as much as $3 trillion (Robbins 2012).

The worst recent flu outbreak came in a different strain of the disease, "swine flu" (H1N1), which emerged in Mexico in March 2009 and it quickly proved to be far more infectious than avian flu. Avian flu has not been, and may never be, transmissible from human to human, but swine flu quickly demonstrated that it was being transmitted in that way. It is that which makes it potentially far more dangerous than avian flu has proven to be. That danger is greatly enhanced by the fact that we live in the global age. Many people travel great distances very quickly and this gives them the ability to spread the flu throughout the world in a relatively short period of time. However, it is also the case, as will be discussed below, that the ability to deal with such a pandemic has also been enhanced as a result of globalization (for example, global monitoring and the ability to get health workers and pharmaceuticals rapidly to the site of an outbreak).

The outbreak of swine flu in Mexico demonstrates these global realities. For one thing, the disease quickly spread throughout much of the world (initially to the US, Canada, Europe, Israel, and New Zealand). Much of the early spread was traceable to those who had recently visited Mexico and apparently contracted the disease there. When they returned home they appeared to pass the disease on to at least some others (school mates, family members). Its spread to the US made it the first health pandemic there in 40 years. President Obama had declared it a national emergency. After the virus was later contained, US officials did however note that the virus probably could have been detected earlier if they had better cooperated with Mexico (McNeil, Jr 2010).

As the disease spread, in April 2009, WHO raised its alert level to 5 (human–human spread in at least two countries) and, in June 2009, raised it to its highest level – 6 (such spread in one more country) – a pandemic. Throughout the period when the disease was spreading, WHO officials were also able to quickly address rumors and misinformation that could have negatively impacted public health efforts (McNeil, Jr 2010). The involvement and reaction of WHO reflects the other side of globalization as global responses to the outbreak are mobilized. The optimum scenario would have been containment in a small area in Mexico, but it had spread globally before Mexico recognized that it was a new strain of flu. Once the flu had migrated to so many different countries, it became almost impossible to contain and the focus shifted to limiting the number affected and to treating those found to have the disease (with anti-viral medications). A global effort was also mounted to create a vaccine to help prevent the disease before the next flu season. This flu did not rapidly mutate, which is a worst-case scenario during such an outbreak, and it was ultimately contained in late 2009.

While it was not an overwhelming concern in the spread of H1N1 flu, it is worth noting that global limitations on the ability to produce and distribute the vaccine make it likely that at best only a small proportion of the global population will be able to get the vaccine. Furthermore, that ability, like much else associated with globalization (see Chapters 13 and 14), will be affected by global inequality. The wealthy North is likely to get much more of needed vaccines, while the poorer South is apt to receive relatively little. It should come as no surprise that, in fact, vaccines are often needed much more in the South where the population is likely to be less healthy and therefore less likely to be able to survive the flu.

More recently, fears about avian bird flu have resurfaced. As of early 2014, a newer strand of the bird flu (H7N9) infected more than 300 people in China. Approximately 25% of people contracting the disease died (McNeil, Jr 2014). A WHO official referred to it as "unusually dangerous," and it has spread to at least one other country (Feng and Grady 2013). An individual in Taiwan, who traveled regularly to China for work, contracted the disease. Furthermore, an even newer strain (H10N8) has emerged. Although it has only been confirmed in two people, it demonstrates further mutation. It is these kinds of rapid mutations that, when combined with global travel and industrial farming practices (Wallace 2009), can lead to further pandemics. As of now, there is no evidence that the disease can be transmitted from human to human (people contract it when coming in contact with infected poultry), but the possibility of such mutations in the future could pose significant global risks.

EBOLA VIRUS

Ebola hemorrhagic fever is a viral disease that was first identified in Sudan and Zaire (now the Congo) in 1976.[3] Other outbreaks of the disease have occurred in Africa in the intervening years including in southern Sudan in 2004, the Congo in 2007, Uganda in 2012, and Guinea, Liberia, and Sierra Leone in 2014. The disease is highly virulent, killing between 50 and 90% of those who contract it. It is not spread by casual contact, but rather through direct contact with the blood, body fluids, and tissues of those infected with the disease. Thus far, the spread of the disease has been highly limited. This is at least in part a result of global responses to any reported outbreak. Health officials rush to the affected area and seek to contain it by ministering to the sick and by restricting contact with those outside the affected area. However, the US and international community were highly criticized for their slow response to the 2014 outbreak in west Africa.

TROPICAL DISEASES IN EUROPE

The increase in tropical diseases in Europe indicates not only the importance of borderless diseases, but also that the impact of such diseases is not restricted to the South. It is related to another global problem – global warming (see Chapter 11). One of the consequences of global warming is the increased ability of disease-bearing vectors (e.g. mosquitoes) from the hot tropical areas to survive in areas (like Europe) that are heating up as a result of global warming. According to a WHO official: "This is the first case of an epidemic of a tropical disease in a developed, European country.... Climate change creates conditions that make it easier for this mosquito to survive and it opens the door to diseases that didn't exist here previously. This is a real issue. Now, today. It is not something a crazy environmentalist is warning about" (quoted in Rosenthal 2007: 21).

For example, tiger mosquitoes arrived in Italy about a decade ago from Albania in shipments of tires. Since then the mosquito has spread throughout southern Europe and even into Switzerland and France. These mosquitoes spread a tropical disease, chikungunya (a relative of dengue fever usually found in the Indian Ocean area), by drinking the blood of a person infected by the disease and then passing it on to those the mosquitoes subsequently bite. In August, 2007, there was an outbreak of the disease (about 100 people contracted it) in a small village (2,000 residents) in northern Italy; it was traced to the visit of an infected person from India. Presumably, that person was bitten by a tiger mosquito and the disease was off and running. Victims often had fevers of 104 degrees and some continued to experience symptoms (e.g. arthritis) long after they contracted the disease. The outbreak waned as the weather grew colder. More recently, Chagas, a deadly blood parasite, made its way to Spain from Latin America (McNeil, Jr 2011). Other tropical diseases becoming more common in Europe include worm infestations, food parasites, and fly-transmitted infections – diseases that are likely to grow as travel between tropical locations and Europe increases and as Europe gets warmer through human-induced climate change.

CHIKUNGUNYA VIRUS

The chikungunya virus is spread by mosquitoes and causes fever and debilitating joint pain. The disease has long been found in parts of Africa and Southeast Asia, but in early 2014, it spread rapidly throughout the Caribbean. In a period of only two months, approximately 3,700 people contracted the disease (Robles 2014). From a global perspective, the most alarming issue with this spread is that the Caribbean is a major tourist destination, attracting over 2 million tourists per year. This poses great risks of spreading the disease to other areas (especially into Central and South American regions where mosquitos flourish). As a result, many countries issued travel warnings to the region, including Saint Martin/St. Maarten, Dominica, Guadeloupe, Martinique, Saint-Barthélemy, and the British Virgin Islands (*CBC News* 2014). The disease could, therefore, have disastrous effects on the local economy that depends on tourists. In response to this, local authorities have conducted insecticide fogging across entire islands and gone house-to-house to remove areas where the mosquitoes might breed.

CRIME

The sheer quantity of global, or cross-border crime (Karstedt 2012a; McCulloch and Pickering 2012) has increased in concert with the growth of globalization. While there is, as we will see, much more to the issue of crime in the global age than this, the fact is that globalization makes more cross-border crime possible than ever before. Since there have been nation-states, and even before, there has been international crime that flowed across broad areas of the world. However, today there seems to be far more of such crime, much of it associated with the general propensity for all sorts of things, including crime, to flow more freely in the global age.

In addition, and perhaps because of the increase in global criminal flows, much more public and government attention than ever before seems to be devoted to these crimes. Attention to, as well as action against, crime flows more easily globally with the crimes themselves. This growth is largely traceable to increasing concern with drugs in the US in the late 1960s and early 1970s, as well as Western European interest in terrorism traceable to roughly the same period.

Drugs and terrorism (we also discuss terrorism separately from crime in the following section) now top the list of global concerns as far as crime is concerned, but others include stolen property, counterfeiting, human trafficking, fraud and cybercrime, commercialized sex, extortion and racketeering, money laundering, and corruption (Albanese 2011). Especially notable is the role of globalization in changes in existing forms of crime (e.g. terrorism) and in the development of new forms of crime (cybercrime).[4] All of these involve flows of all sorts – drugs, money, human victims (e.g. people who are sex trafficked [see Chapter 10]), human perpetrators (e.g. terrorists), as well as the various illegal sorts of things that flow through the worldwide web (e.g. child pornography, laundered funds, the spread of computer viruses).

These illegal flows have been aided by the decline of the nation-state and its increasing inability to stem, let alone halt, these flows. Furthermore, global criminal cartels are structures that have come into existence to better expedite illegal flows and to increase the profits that can be derived from them. In fact, a recent book, *McMafia*, attributes much of their success to increasingly sophisticated organizational methods (e.g. economies of scale, global partnerships, the opening of new markets) that are copied from leading legitimate businesses such as McDonald's (Glenny 2008). New technologies have been employed to make at least some criminal flows more successful (e.g. even going so far as the use of a primitive submarine to transport drugs). And then there is the Internet, the very nature of which makes a number of illegal flows much easier (e.g. of pornography, Internet scams) and is largely impervious to efforts at control by individual nation-states.

The growth in global crime has been met, of course, by "the growing importance of the international component of policing and the policing component of international relations" (Andreas and Nadelmann 2006: 6).[5] Thus, this seems like a simple story of increases in global crime being met by increasing global policing. However, the story, as in all stories that relate to crime and efforts to control it, is far more complex than that.

Crime is always a matter of social definition or social construction (Brownstein 1996; Goode and Ben-Yehuda 1994; Roberts and Chen 2013). That is, few acts everywhere and at all times are crimes; they need to be *defined* as such by large numbers of people. Very often, that which was at one time "normal" comes to be defined as deviant. One famous example is that of cocaine which was a legal substance (small amounts of it were found in Coca-Cola – that's how the famous soda pop got its name – until 1929), but came to be defined as illegal. However, it is rarely the case that large numbers of people come to define something as deviant on their own. This is even truer of something coming to be defined as illegal, i.e. against the law, since that requires the action of government officials. In fact, for some act or product to come to be defined as both deviant and illegal, the actions of so-called "moral entrepreneurs" are almost always required. Moral entrepreneurs are individuals or groups of individuals who come to define an act as a moral outrage and lead a campaign to have it defined as deviant and to have it made illegal and therefore subject to legal enforcement (Becker 1963). Drugs are a good example of this, especially globally, since moral entrepreneurs located especially in the US have taken it upon themselves to have them defined as illegal and their use as deviant. They have done so even though the use of many of these drugs (e.g. marijuana) is common and accepted not only in many societies throughout the world, but also among a large portion of the American population.

This relates to the point that while the power of nation-states has generally declined in the global age, it continues to matter greatly in what comes to be *defined* as a global form of deviance and crime. In the era of globalization, it is the nation-states of Western Europe and the US that have played, by far, the central role in this; it is *their* sense of morality and *their* norms of behavior that have come to be disseminated throughout much of the world: "To an extent virtually unprecedented in world history, a few European states and the United States proved successful in proselytizing to diverse societies around the world, in shaping the moral views of substantial sectors of elite opinion outside their borders, and in imposing their norms on foreign governments" (Andreas and Nadelmann 2006: 20). While there have been a number of such efforts to define acts as deviant and illegal, they are certainly not always, and perhaps not even frequently, successful. This, of course, is reflected in the continuation, perhaps expansion, of the global drug trade in spite of great efforts by the US and other nation-states to at least slow it down.

Related to the point that crime must be defined as such, there is also significant overlap and interconnection between licit and illicit activities (Hall 2013). For example, China's growth as the industrial center of many transnational corporations has been paralleled with the growth of a huge market in counterfeit goods. The counterfeit goods even may find their way to legitimate retailers in European, North American, or Japanese markets. Some cities like London function not only as global financial centers in the legitimate economy, but are also hubs for money laundering and the financing of terrorists (Unger and Rawlings 2008). Sometimes large transnational corporations are directly involved in criminal activity (e.g. Wal-Mart's bribing of Mexican officials to accelerate expansion there), but they also frequently have connections to illicit criminal organizations. These indirect linkages bind licit and illicit economies in ways that make them difficult to disentangle, and therefore, the boundaries between positive and negative globalizations are unclear.

Much of the publicity about drugs, including the ways in which they are implicated in globalization, involves cocaine and heroin. Thus, great attention is devoted to, for example, the growing of poppies in Afghanistan and drug production in Guatemala and the ways in which drugs from those areas, and many others, make their way around the world.

A relatively new global drug is methamphetamine (meth), made easily and cheaply in home-based "cooking facilities" from the main ingredient in cough medicine, pseudoephedrine (Weinsheit and White 2009). Once largely an American phenomenon, the production and use of methamphetamine is beginning to expand globally. For example, it is a growing problem in Afghanistan, where opium use has also increased (Ahmed 2013).

Free-trade zones are structures that expedite the flow of illegal products; they are efficient transit points (there are no tariffs and there is minimal oversight over most of these zones since goods do not officially enter the country in which the zone exists) for all sorts of legal (and illegal) products moving throughout the world (Pasko 2012). A raid on a free-trade zone in Dubai revealed the role they play in the global distribution of counterfeit drugs for a wide range of serious health problems (Bogdanich 2007: A1, A6). In this case, the fake drugs traveled from China, to Hong Kong, through Dubai, and then to Great Britain, the Bahamas, and ultimately to an Internet seller who marketed them to Americans as Canadian drugs. Ports in rapidly developing cities like Karachi, Pakistan, also become important way stations for the flows of illicit goods (see Chapter 13). Such shipments are difficult to intercept and it is even more difficult to find out where the products have been manufactured.

Global flows of crime, and especially drugs, have proved particularly difficult to fight (Roberts and Chen 2013). There are several aspects of crime and drugs that help account for this lack of success: the crimes "require limited and readily available resources," they need "no particular expertise to commit," they "are easily concealed," they are "unlikely to be reported to the authorities," and they are "those for which the consumer demand is substantial, resilient, and not readily substituted for by alternative activities or products" (Andreas and Nadelmann 2006: 22).

However, it would be wrong to judge global efforts to control drugs, as well as other illegal substances and activities, as complete failures. The fact is that while drugs continue to flow readily throughout the world for the reasons suggested above, the US has had considerable success in internationalizing its views, laws, procedures, and efforts at enforcement:

> Foreign governments have changed their own laws and enforcement methods and signed extradition, mutual legal assistance, and other law enforcement treaties demanded by US authorities. Beginning with the US prohibitionist approach to drug control during the first decades of the twentieth century, foreign governments have followed in the footsteps of the United States, adopting US-style investigative techniques, creating specialized drug enforcement agencies, stationing law enforcement representatives abroad, and enacting conspiracy statutes, asset forfeiture laws, and checks and bans on drug-related money laundering. Pressures to cooperate in US drug trafficking investigations were largely responsible for instigating changes, beginning in the 1970s, in financial secrecy laws to authorize greater assistance to US (and other foreign) law enforcement authorities. (Andreas and Nadelmann 2006: 107)

Drugs were not the first form of global crime that the US took the lead in countering and in influencing other nations in the world to work against. Its influence "was readily apparent during the first decades of the century in shaping foreign and international approaches to white slavery, during the cold war era with respect to export controls on weapons and sophisticated technology, and starting in the mid-1980s with respect to the regulation of securities markets (in particular the criminalization of insider trading)" (Andreas and Nadelmann 2006: 107).

Since 9/11, there has been a dramatic erosion of various distinctions in the world of crime (and elsewhere) that had existed for decades, if not centuries. For example, the distinction between law enforcement and intelligence operations has eroded as authorities seek to gain intelligence on potential terrorists in order to forestall further terrorist attacks and to catch or kill people defined as terrorists. Then there is the related fact that border control, especially between the US and Mexico, has increasingly become a matter of surveillance along the border, and in immigrant communities in the US, in order to better enforce the laws against undocumented immigrants. In the process, many immigrants have been defined as criminals, apprehended, and then returned to Mexico. It is important to note the selectivity involved in all of this since far less attention is devoted to surveillance on the much longer border with Canada and those who do cross that border without authorization are much less likely to be defined, or apprehended, as criminals.

In Europe, a similar, although not as extreme, toughening of border controls with, and surveillance of, non-EU states occurred while internal to the EU, border controls and surveillance were relaxed. Border law enforcement within the EU became "more domesticated through greater homogenization of criminal justice norms and procedures and the regularization of law enforcement contacts and information exchange among member states" (Andreas and Nadelmann 2006: 186). Of great importance was the formation of Europol which allowed better and increased communication and cooperation among national police agencies.

The globalization of policing did not occur simply as a consequence of September 11, but rather was well underway as a result of a variety of forces before that event occurred. However, the globalization of policing did change after 9/11. For example, we have witnessed an accelerating decline in the distinction between law enforcement and security (in the US, the Patriot Act [Uniting and Strengthening America by Providing Appropriate Tools Required to Intercept and Obstruct Terrorism Act], signed into law on October 26, 2001, played a key role in this by, for example, extending concern to domestic terrorism). For another, the need to deal with global issues relating to terrorism has come into conflict with the desire to keep borders open and free in order to facilitate international economic transactions.

While global crime control has improved in various ways, there are also a variety of downsides associated with these efforts. For one thing, there is great fear of threats to democracy posed by these efforts. Crime control efforts are not always as transparent as they might be and the officials involved often need to be more accountable. There is great fear of the threats to civil and human rights posed by these new policing methods and practices (e.g. laws that are more invasive, more intrusive surveillance technologies).

For another, there is the collateral damage associated with greater global law enforcement efforts by nation-states. Greater border and immigration controls have led to more daring and dangerous efforts to cross borders that are leading to more deaths in the process. The global anti-drug campaign has led to mass incarceration, especially women of color (Pasko 2012). In the developing world, marginalized women have often turned to low-level drug trafficking (as "mules" who smuggle drugs in or on their bodies) as a matter of economic survival. With a lack of legitimate economic alternatives, poor social supports brought about by neoliberal globalization (see Chapter 4), and the increased policing of drugs, the number of imprisoned female drug offenders in the world has tripled since the 1980s. For these reasons, some commentators argue that efforts by the US (and other nations) to deal with trafficking in women and children "has been far more focused on criminalizing the traffic than helping to protect the human rights of those being trafficked" (Andreas and Nadelmann 2006: 251).

Finally, the attention and money devoted to international crime and its control has tended to distract attention, and to take money away, from efforts to deal with a wide range of fundamental issues within nation-states including the welfare of large portions of society.

TERRORISM

There is a tendency to discuss crime and terrorism as distinct phenomena, but they overlap to some degree (Karstedt 2012a; White 2013). In fact, we have already had some things to say about terrorism under the heading of crime. One example, of many, is involvement of the Taliban (linked to the terrorist organization, al-Qaeda) in Afghanistan in poppy growing and the opium business. Another example is Hezbollah's (a militant Shiite group in Lebanon) involvement in drug trafficking (Hernández 2013). Hezbollah began doing business with Los Zetas, recently considered one of the strongest (and most brutal) Mexican drug cartels; their partnership represented the "convergence between transnational drug trafficking and international terrorism" (Hernández 2013: 47). The further blurring of these criminal enterprises with licit activity was made clear when the US Treasury shut down the Lebanese

Canadian Bank for their involvement with money laundering in connection to these criminal networks. Furthermore, both crime and terrorism are global in character and have been aided by various aspects of globalization. For example, both the operations of terrorist groups like al-Qaeda and Hezbollah and the global distribution of narcotics are aided by modern means of global transportation and communication. And the global mass media fan the interest in, even hysteria about, these (and many other) problems. However, the relationship between terrorism and crime is only one of many involved in trying to get a handle on terrorism, as well as its relationship to globalization.

Objectively, terrorism can be defined as actions that cause "deaths, serious bodily injuries, and serious damage to public or private property, places, facilities, or other systems" and are aimed at intimidating citizens, governments, or international organizations (Bergesen 2012; Rehman 2007: 1137). However, terrorism tends to be an idea that those in power seek to impose on those who are not in power. Thus, the US (and many other nation-states) labels al-Qaeda a terrorist organization, but resists the label itself even though it has engaged in actions ("state terrorism") that have at least some similarities with those of al-Qaeda (e.g. missile strikes from unmanned drones in Afghanistan, Pakistan, and Niger that kill innocent citizens). Similarly, Israel labels Hamas and Hezbollah as terrorist organizations, but refuses the label for itself even though in the 2006 war against Hezbollah it destroyed much infrastructure (and killed many people) in Lebanon that had little or nothing to do with Hezbollah. Furthermore, a recent study found that governments are more likely to label organizations as "terrorist" if they have a different ideology from the state (Beck and Miner 2013). In other words, governments do not identify a group as terrorist simply because it targets their citizens and threatens national security, but also because the "terrorist" organization exhibits different values and beliefs about the world from them.

A key distinction, alluded to above, is between "terrorism from above" and "terrorism from below" (Martin 2012). Both forms involve violence against non-military targets and citizens, but the former involves stateless organizations or "dissidents" (such as al-Qaeda or Hamas) while the latter is undertaken by the state (such as Israel). Both forms are increasingly global as witnessed by al-Qaeda's 9/11 attacks on the US and US missile and bombing attacks on Iraq at the beginning of the war in 2003 that destroyed non-military targets either intentionally or because they involved collateral damage associated with the attacks on the main targets. The initial US attack was labeled "shock and awe" because it was designed to intimidate *both* the Iraqi government and its citizens. And both forms of terrorism are political in that al-Qaeda was attacking, at least in part, the American government and its policies, while the US was seeking, and achieved, "regime change" in Iraq.

Terrorism, or even international terrorism, is certainly not new, but there does seem to be something different about its most recent and most important manifestations. First, the types of organizations that practice terrorism beyond domestic boundaries have changed (Martin 2012). From the 1960s until the early 1980s, the primary groups engaging in terrorism across state borders were leftist "solidarity" groups. For example, Western European groups attacked important symbols in solidarity with marginalized groups in other countries. In the US, the radical leftist Weather Underground directed their bombings and arson in support of the Viet Cong during the Vietnam War. Few leftist terror groups remain today, and those that do (the Fuerzas Armadas Revolucionarias de Colombia [FARC] in Colombia), do not typically practice international terrorism. While there have been some other groups (e.g. ethnic-based groups, Palestinian nationalist groups such as Hamas) practicing international terrorism, the main type of organizations practicing terrorism beyond state boundaries are religious extremists, such as al-Qaeda (although these groups are not mutually exclusive).

A second important change in terrorism is the terrorist organizations' global aspirations and reach. For example, traditional militant Islamic groups (e.g. Hamas) have focused on capturing state power and revolutionizing national societies via the state (Kevin McDonald 2012). Even if nationalist groups, such as Hezbollah, engage in terrorism in nearby countries, it is in the service of nationalist projects (Barnard 2013). Al-Qaeda has actually criticized leaders of Hamas for their focus on national issues. Al-Qaeda's leaders only care about local/ national conflicts to the degree that they are manifestations of a global struggle. They have set up local affiliates in regions around the world in efforts to spread their global ideology. Certainly earlier terrorist organizations (e.g. Irgun and its efforts to oust the British and to foster the emergence of an independent Israel) had global aspirations and reach. For example, Jewish terrorists sought to bring their grievances to the attention of a global audience. However, while al-Qaeda achieved its status as today's paradigmatic terrorist organization through its attacks on American and Western interests in various places throughout the world, the Irgun restricted itself to actions in and around the future territory of Israel. Thus, for example, it did not launch attacks in Great Britain, but limited itself to attacks in its homeland (most famously the 1946 bombing of the King David hotel in Jerusalem which killed and injured a number of British soldiers, officials, and citizens).

Thus, while earlier terrorist groups operated, largely because they had little choice, in and around their home territory, today's terrorist groups are much freer to launch, and much more interested in launching, attacks far from home (indeed, they may not have a "home" in a conventional sense). Furthermore, their attacks often take place in global cities (New York, Washington, London, Madrid) and are at least some of the time aimed at highly symbolic, even iconic (see Chapter 13), targets (World Trade Center, London Underground, Madrid train, a failed bombing attempt in New York Times Square in 2010, the bombing at the 2013 Boston Marathon was "inspired" by al-Qaeda) which, if they are successfully attacked, will guarantee great media attention throughout the world.

Another distinguishing characteristic of today's terrorist groups is their greatly enhanced ability to get their message across, often almost instantaneously, to a global audience (Espeseth et al. 2013). Certainly earlier terrorist groups sought to do this, but they had far fewer means at their disposal to accomplish this. They could, by their actions, garner headlines around the world (e.g. the King David hotel bombing), but they had little or no control over the messages that were communicated to others – those messages were controlled by the international media. However, while today's terrorist groups welcome the attention of the global media, they also have more direct means of getting their message across to large numbers of people throughout the world *and* in precisely the way they want it stated and framed. Thus, al-Qaeda uses self-produced videotapes that are broadcast over major media outlets and posted on its websites to communicate directly with a global audience. Al-Qaeda even has its own magazine, where, amongst other things, it provides directions on building bombs and celebrated the bombing at the 2013 Boston Marathon (Killough and Cruickshank 2013). Pro al-Qaeda bloggers also communicate their messages over the Internet. Thus, the more recent terrorist groups are distinguished by their increasingly sophisticated use of global communication channels unavailable to earlier terrorist organizations, as well as their ability to completely control the content of those messages.

There are several other characteristics of the new, global age that aid today's terrorists. First, global transportation systems make it easier for individual terrorists to move around the world in order to plan and carry out terrorist acts (this was abundantly clear in the actions and activities of the terrorists both prior to, and during, the 9/11 attacks) (Szyliowicz 2013). Second, more porous national borders, and the growing inability of nations to control their borders, also make it easier for terrorists to move about relatively freely (although greater vigilance in the US and elsewhere appears to have thwarted further terrorist attacks, at least as of this writing). Third, the reactions against globalization have produced and solidified broad political alliances that are ready audiences for the ideas and actions of terrorist groups. For example, there are at least some in much of the Islamic world sympathetic to, or at least tolerant of, the ideas and actions of al-Qaeda because of global actions taken against them, real and perceived, by the West, especially the US. An even larger audience for al-Qaeda is the millions, if not billions, of people throughout the world who feel that they have been left out of, or disadvantaged by, globalization. Finally, earlier forms of terrorism, especially during the heyday of the Soviet Union and its efforts to expand globally, tended to be more narrowly ideological (e.g. socialism, communism). Today's terrorists are based on broader appeals to ethnicity and/or to a wider set of grievances against the process of globalization.

The weapons at the disposal of recent terrorist organizations are also a reflection and a part of the global age. The most obvious example is al-Qaeda's use of jetliners in the 9/11 attacks. Further, there is the rather ready global flow of weapons that can be used by terrorists. However, the great fear here is the global flow of knowledge about chemical and biological weapons, and especially about nuclear technology, and the ability of terrorist groups to make use of that knowledge. In an example of terrorism from above, the Syrian government used chemical weapons on its own people in 2013. Over 1,000 people were killed, including hundreds of children.

While it is not as powerful as it once was, the most well-known (or notorious) global terrorist organization today is al-Qaeda. It is believed to be organized on the basis of largely independent cells throughout the world, some of them so-called "sleeper cells" that have lain dormant and undercover for years. It can be seen as being structured as a global secret "franchise" system (versus McDonald's highly public franchise system) (Hubbard 2014; Mendelsohn 2011). But this franchise system has become increasingly decentralized, and with the death of Osama bin Laden in 2011, lacks a unifying figure. It is held together by a loose ideology, but al-Qaeda affiliates are now more likely to differ in how they interpret that ideology and implement it within their terrorist activities. This was illustrated in early 2014 when Ayman al-Zawahiri, the leader of al-Qaeda, ordered a local group – Islamic State in Iraq and Syria (ISIS) – to pull out of Syria because of in-fighting with rebel allies. In an unprecedented public display of breaking ranks, the ISIS leader stated they would stay in Syria "as long as we have a vein that pumps and an eye that blinks." This does not mean that al-Qaeda has abandoned entirely any hierarchical structure, but that it is more diffuse today.

While its global structure is changing, al-Qaeda remains the most significant terrorist threat. Their areas of rapid growth are now focused in countries far away from Afghanistan and Pakistan – countries like Algeria, Libya, Yemen, Syria, and Iraq – which are less politically stable and have ungoverned territories. Sometimes these new groups (e.g. ISIS) may focus more on local struggles and are not as loyal to a single leader, but they are essential for the continuation of its terrorist network. They help to recruit new members and even work to recruit Americans and Europeans who travel to areas of conflict, such as the Syrian civil war (Schmidt and Schmitt 2014). As such, they continue to plan out attacks both locally and abroad on Western targets.

Karin Knorr Cetina (2005: 215) has offered considerable insight into global terrorist organizations by considering them as examples of "complex global microstructures" with four basic characteristics. First, they are, as was mentioned in Chapter 1, and consistent with one of the major orientations of this book, *light*. By this, Knorr Cetina (2005: 215) means

> that mechanisms and structures involved suggest a reversal of the historical trend toward formal, rationalized (bureaucratic organizational) structures … while microstructures are on some level organized or coordinated systems, the coordinating elements involved are not the kind we associate with formal authority, complex hierarchies, rationalized procedure or deep institutional structure.

Instead they utilize methods of coordination that are more like those people use on a daily basis in face-to-face relationships. Even so, they are able to hold together systems and relationships that stretch over great geographic distances.

Second, terrorist microstructures are effective even though they do not employ the rationalized structures, especially heavy bureaucracies, we usually associate with effectiveness in the modern world. They achieve this effectiveness in several ways including augmenting and amplifying their effect by using such technologies as hijacked airplanes and the media (especially the Internet), by "outsourcing" support functions and keeping them distinct from the internal structure, and by keeping regulations to a minimum in order to maximize adaptability to large developments. They rely on both a cellular structure as well as linkages built on diaspora (in this case, the Arab diaspora; see Chapter 10).

Third, while complex global microstructures are networks through which various things, especially people, flow, there is more to them than that including, in al-Qaeda's case, its "Islamist religious representations, its family structure and its self-reproducing mechanism" (Knorr Cetina 2005: 216). Thus, it is not just relational connectivity that holds these microstructures together; they are far richer and more textured than that.

Finally, such microstructures are not only organizationally, but also temporally, complex. The key point here is that organizations increase in complexity when they exist both spatially and temporally (Giddens 1990; Harvey 1989). That is, they not only have a spatial existence (although, by design, it is hard to pin down exactly where al-Qaeda is physically), but they have succeeded in continuing to exist over time, and the combination of the two forms of existence, spatial and temporal, gives them greater complexity. It is the global stream of developments over time stemming from al-Qaeda (e.g. terrorist attacks, threats via the media, etc.) that have made it more successful than terrorist groups that are more locked into a given local or national context and have failed to maintain an existence over time. Also important in holding the widely dispersed members of al-Qaeda together from a temporal point of view is a close linkage between the situation the group faces at the moment and the past as it exists in "collective memory" (Halbwachs 1992). Al-Qaeda is also held together by a belief in a future desired state such as a successful *jihad* or achieving personal paradise. These perspectives and beliefs help to account for the patience and persistence of al-Qaeda and the long-term planning that must go into some of its terrorist activities.

More threatening than this unusual network of people is the transformation of al-Qaeda into more of an ideology ("Qaedaism") than a cellular organization of people (McDonald 2012). What is ominous about this, at least from the point of view of the West (and promising from the perspective of al-Qaeda), is that ideas flow around the world far more easily than people and it is nearly impossible to set up effective barriers to the flow of ideas. If large numbers of people can be converted to Qaedaism simply by the dissemination, and power, of its ideas, then it has great possibilities to expand and become an even more important global force in the future.

Of course, the fact that contemporary terrorism is much more globalized means that the efforts to respond to, and deal with, it must also be increasingly global. Hence, the US has, for example, undertaken, on its own and in conjunction with other nation-states, overt and covert steps around the world to combat terrorism. Well known are American actions in Iraq and Afghanistan, but the US has also engaged in actions elsewhere such as launching air attacks in Somalia and Niger against suspected al-Qaeda hideouts and centers.

There have also been more multilateral efforts to cope with terrorism such as internationally binding agreements on preventing and dealing with offenses on airplanes, the hijacking of airplanes, and airport violence (Nagan and Haddad 2012). There have been agreements to deal with terrorism at sea and terrorist acts committed against platforms at sea, especially oil platforms. Among the other agreements are those that deal with hostage-taking and nuclear terrorism. There have also been a number of more regional agreements on terrorism. However, there is as yet no comprehensive, universal treaty that deals with all forms and aspects of terrorism.

Both terrorism and the reactions against it raise issues of *human rights* (see Chapter 5) which involve "entitlements of individuals to life, security, and well-being" (Turner 2007a: 591). Clearly, by their actions, terrorists deprive people of their human rights, in some cases their lives. However, the actions against terrorism, especially the US "war on terrorism," has led to many complaints that the war is violating people's human rights in various ways including causing their deaths (e.g. bombings in Pakistan or Yemen), the incarceration of many suspected terrorists in camps like those in Guantánamo Bay, Cuba, for many years without any due process, the use of torture (e.g. "waterboarding"[6]) in an effort to extract confessions from accused terrorists (Otterman 2007), and the use of drones for "targeted killings" of people without trial (i.e. extrajudicial killings).

On the one hand it is clear that the 9/11 attacks on the World Trade Center deprived many victims and their families of their human rights and in a particularly deadly and gruesome way. While we must not lose sight of that, much of the attention in recent years has been focused on human rights abuses related to the war on terror. There is, for example, the case of Nabil Hadjarab, an Algerian who grew up in France and who was held in Guantánamo Bay for 11 years without ever being charged with a crime. Hadjarab was living in an Algerian guesthouse in Kabul, Afghanistan, in 2011. After 9/11 happened, the US government began offering cash payments to anyone who could provide suspicious Arabs, and Hadjarab was sold to the United States government for $5,000. In January 2002, he was first held in a makeshift prison at Bagram Air Base in Afghanistan:

> "As one of the first prisoners, there were no walls, only razor-wire cages. In the bitter cold, Nabil was forced to sleep on concrete floors without cover. Food and water were scarce. To and from his frequent interrogations, Nabil was beaten by United States soldiers and dragged up and down concrete stairs. Other prisoners died." (Grisham 2013)

The US had no hard evidence linking Hadjarab to al-Qaeda, the Taliban, or any criminal activity. Nonetheless, he was eventually transferred to Guantánamo Bay in February 2002.

There, he experienced "sleep deprivation, sensory deprivation, temperature extremes, prolonged isolation, lack of access to sunlight, almost no recreation and limited medical care," and was not permitted family visitors for the entirety of his 11-year incarceration. In 2007, a review board assembled by the Bush administration recommended his release, but no release was given. In 2009, another review board under Obama recommended his transfer, but no transfer was made. When he went on a hunger strike in 2013, he was force-fed through a tube. Hadjarab was never charged with a crime. Finally, in late 2013, he was transferred to Algeria, although, as of this writing, his fate remains unclear.

More generally, there is the danger that terrorism leads nation-states to reactions that threaten their very legitimacy. For example, the US has jeopardized not only its objective in the "war on terror" (which is not a "true" war), but its overall legitimacy by, for example, "its lawless behavior at its penal colonies" (e.g. Guantánamo Bay) (Bobbitt 2008: 17). More generally, there is the danger, perhaps already the reality, that nation-states employ tactics "that are indistinguishable from those of terrorists" (Bobbitt 2008: 45). As a result, at least in part, of such behavior, the US government has weakened its ability to convince American (and even more, global) public opinion of the justness of its cause and this, in turn, has adversely affected its ability to pursue legal objectives.

WAR

In spite of its great importance, war has not received a great deal of attention in globalization studies (Mabee 2012). However, it clearly deserves more attention and not only because of its great social and political importance. It is also a realm that well illustrates the basic ideas about globalization that orient this book. While it seems like a dysfunctional way to make such linkages, there is a long line of work in the social sciences that analyzes the functions of social conflict (Coser 1956; Simmel 1908/1955), including warfare.

For much of human history – until recently – nations have usually been engaged in war in some capacity, whether preparing for war, in the midst of war, or recovering from its aftermath (Nester 2010). States had more commonly used violence, or the threat of it, against other states. These internationally based geopolitical conflicts have lessened in the contemporary era as many nations experience longer periods of peace. So one thing that is new about war during this period of globalization is that it is more often "instigated by rogue states, militant ideologies, transnational terrorist groups, revolutionary movements, voracious, ruthless economic interests, and environmental collapse" (Nester 2010: 2). Few contemporary wars have involved the world's wealthy countries, but when they do, it is usually a rich country attacking a poorer one (e.g. the US attacking North Korea, North Vietnam, or Afghanistan [Atwood 2010]). They are increasingly targeted toward al-Qaeda and other terrorist organizations and rogue states (e.g. the threat of war against North Korea). The prospect of environmental catastrophes brought on by global climate change (see Chapter 11) will likely be an increasingly important motivation for war going into the future.

Experts are now distinguishing between "new" and "old" wars (Kaldor 2013). The "old" wars between nation-states, which battle by inflicting as much damage on their enemy as possible, are now being replaced by a form of organized violence that includes a mixture of war, organized crime, and wide-scale human rights violations. The actors in the "new" wars are fought "on the basis of seemingly traditional identities – nation, tribe, religion" – but become entangled in war through new global processes (Kaldor 2013: 71). In the context of globalization, which purports to link all social and cultural groups in a universalizing process, these identities get mobilized as responses to their exclusion from, or rejection of, these processes. Consider the violence waged by al-Qaeda against the West. In their global struggle, they emphasize the need for a militant ideology, based on a specific interpretation of Islam, and the need to reject the continued global spread of American or Western values. The newness is not the fact that their religion serves as a call to arms but that it happens in the context of a globalizing ideological force, and that the response must be globally, and not nationally, focused.

Another dimension of these wars is that they are fought using the weapons, networks, and other resources of transnational criminal groups that profit from wars. These range from private contractors for government militaries (e.g. the infamous Blackwater group hired by the US military to fight in Iraq) to networks dealing in the illegal arms trade. Through many of these emerging networks, both public and private actors systematically commit human rights abuses that are ignored, or even endorsed by, the state. In new wars, organizations tend to enlist a broader network in waging war. This might involve, for example, global actors (e.g. the US or al-Qaeda) enlisting local organizations (local rebel groups) to carry out their fighting in pursuit of mutual interests. Again, this is very different from the military of one nation actively fighting the military of another nation through traditional means of warfare.

Even seemingly local wars are shaped by globalization in profound ways.[7] This can be seen in all of the types of processes we have associated with globalization. The numerous *relations* that exist among the different regions of the world mean that a war in one is likely to involve others. For example, the 1991 invasion of Kuwait by Iraq led to a coalition of armed forces led by the US that pushed the Iraqi army back across its borders and liberated Kuwait from Iraqi occupation. Many of the countries involved in the military coalition were involved in relations with Kuwait because it is a major oil producer. The Iraqi invasion of Kuwait was seen by them as not only a threat to relations with Kuwait, but all other oil-producing nations in the region.

This, of course, is intimately related to the global *flow* of oil. The developed nations, and even almost all less developed nations, are highly dependent on a steady flow of oil. The invasion of Iraq in 1991 demonstrated once again that many nations, especially the US which is most dependent on that oil, are willing to go to war to keep the oil flowing. Flows of arms (Chivers 2008: A5) and material, to say nothing of troops, were also necessary to conduct the war.

People are involved in various *networks* and some of those networks (e.g. among those involved in the oil business) were disrupted by the invasion of Kuwait. Furthermore, existing networks were revived and new ones created in order to mount opposition to the Iraqi invasion. Propaganda networks around the world were ramped up to create and solidify opposition to that invasion. Intelligence and military networks were also revived, or created anew, in order to make the ultimate invasion possible.

And, of course, what all of this demonstrates is that more and more social structures and social institutions are *interconnected* on a global basis (Nester 2010). Various governments and government agencies needed to be interconnected in order to mount the invasion of Iraq. And that invasion reverberated throughout various social institutions in many of the world's nation-states. For example, it became the focal concern of the global media. Even families in many parts of the world were affected as sons and daughters, fathers and mothers went off to war.

Overall, is it possible to determine whether globalization makes war less or more likely? There are those who argue that the increasing economic bonds that accompany globalization are likely to mean a reduction in the likelihood of war (Friedman 2005; Schneider 2007). That is, nation-states are unlikely to sacrifice valuable economic relationships by going to war with one another. On the other hand, the economic gains of war may seem so great that nations may be more likely to engage in warfare, no matter what the consequences for their relationships with other nation-states. Then there is the huge global market for, and flow of, weapons of all sorts, new and used. Such a huge market serves to make such weapons increasingly inexpensive and they can be acquired easily and quickly. Overall, "one in every twenty dollars spent worldwide feeds the military" (Nester 2010: 58).

Another factor making war more likely in the age of globalization is time and space compression, both of which make it easier to engage in warfare with other countries. Militaries can be mobilized rapidly (the Israeli military is a model in this regard) and they can be moved across great distances more quickly and easily (as in the case of the coalition of military forces involved in the first war against Iraq following its invasion of Kuwait). Furthermore, new global technologies make it possible to wage wars thousands of miles away without ever leaving home (Sheehan 2011). An example is the employment in Pakistan and Yemen of those drones equipped with missiles that are controlled remotely by military technicians in the US using computers and video monitors (see section on drones below).

At the same time, there have been steps taken in the global community to limit the likelihood of war (Nester 2010). The mere fact that these countries have become interdependent has made them acknowledge common interests and develop common rules around mutually destructive violence. Two of the most important attempts in this process were first the League of Nations and later the United Nations. It should come as no surprise, then, that wars recently have been brought about by organizations *not* involved in these global communities (e.g. terrorist organizations, rogue states). Overall, the best we can do is to say that globalization has an ambiguous relationship with the likelihood of international warfare.

What we can say unambiguously is that in various ways globalization is changing, and will continue to change, the nature of warfare (Kaldor 2013). To take one example, the decline of the nation-state and the increasing importance of state-less societies are causing the US to rethink its basic doctrines about warfare. Instead of traditional combat operations such as ground operations with major armies facing off against one another, some within the American military are arguing for the need to engage, instead, in long-lasting stability operations. In fact, that is what the US military is doing in the war on terror. With the increasing number of fragile, weak, or even state-less societies, the view is emerging that a major task for the military in the future will be nation-building rather than war-making.

GLOBAL MILITARY STRUCTURES

Many international military organizations and alliances have been formed over the centuries, but the most important and most global of such organizations, at least until the end of the Cold War, was the North Atlantic Treaty Organization (NATO). NATO was formed in 1949 as a reaction against the growing threat of the Soviet Union and its allies (Whitefield 2012). In response, the latter formed the Warsaw Pact in 1955. While the Warsaw Pact lasted only until 1991, NATO continues to exist. There are currently 28 nations in NATO, mostly in Western Europe, but also including Canada, Iceland, and the US. (NATO has been dominated by the US since its inception.) A number of former Soviet-bloc nations (e.g. Albania) and others (e.g. Croatia) have joined NATO in recent years and Macedonia has been invited to join (although there is resistance to at least some of them within NATO, especially by Greece).

NATO was engaged in military operations in Kosovo in 1999 and in the Libyan Civil War in 2011, has been engaged in the Gulf of Aden against Somali pirates since 2009, and has been fighting in Afghanistan against the Taliban and al-Qaeda since 2006 (it is scheduled to pull its troops from Afghanistan in late 2014).[8] It remains a strong multilateral military force today, although the United States has always held disproportionate power over its decision-making.

DRONES AND OTHER TECHNOLOGY

One of the things that makes war today increasingly likely to be global is the existence of advanced information and communications technologies (ICTs) such as computers and advanced weaponry (Sheehan 2011). Of course, it is the developed countries, especially the US, that are likely to have the ability to afford, to have access to, and to use, these technologies. But, even the least developed countries are implicated in this, at least in the sense that the technologies are likely to be used against them. Thus, the US uses its satellites to keep track of developments in some of the world's least developed countries (Afghanistan, Somalia), as well as to guide the use of military technology in them.

Drones are easily the most rapidly growing and controversial military technology (Gregory 2011; Hall and Coyne 2013; Whetham 2013). Also known as unmanned aerial vehicles (UAVs), drones are controlled remotely and are used for military purposes in surveillance and combat (although their non-military uses are rapidly expanding as well). As of this writing, the heaviest use of drones was by the US military in its war on terror in Pakistan, which has been the site of several hundred drone strikes since 2008 (Walsh 2013). For example, a missile from an American drone killed Hakimullah Mehsud, leader of the Taliban in Pakistan. The US has also actively deployed drones in Afghanistan, although civilian deaths from drones in late 2013 sparked a significant backlash from President Hamid Karzai (Nordland 2013). But the US has expanded its military drone use around the world. American officials have deployed drones to Yemen and Mali, where they work with French commanders to fight terrorism, including al-Qaeda and its offshoots, in northern Africa (Schmitt 2013). Drones fly surveillance missions (Soderlund 2013) there of ten hours or more and gather intelligence in a region where al-Qaeda presence is growing.

American officials report that the advantages of drones include their accuracy and reduced risk to its military personnel, making them more effective in warfare. But critics, including Ben Emmerson, the UN special rapporteur on counter-terrorism and human rights, note that many civilian casualties have resulted from seemingly "accurate" drone strikes. For example, the first known drone strike in Yemen that was authorized by President Obama resulted in the deaths of 14 women and 21 children (Mothana 2012). While the Obama administration defends its drone usage, it was concerned about the bad public image that civilian deaths caused. As a result, it then redefined a "militant" as any male of military age, which allowed them to count fewer civilians in death tolls from their drone strikes. This subtle redefinition allows the US military to claim fewer civilian deaths in its official estimates. Critics further note that the deaths – especially the deaths from drone strikes of innocent civilians – are likely to help terror organizations to recruit participants and perpetuate war (Boyle 2013). Indeed, in Pakistan, where drone strikes are most frequent, thousands of citizens recently protested

American drone strikes and vowed to disrupt NATO efforts there in order to thwart future attacks (Masood and Mehsud 2013). One recent study also found that drone strikes have no impact on al-Qaeda's ability to produce propaganda, suggesting that they have little effect on disrupting their organizational capacity (Smith and Walsh 2013). Not only do drones lead to civilian deaths, but they can lead to an emotional disengagement from war, which desensitizes people to the death and destruction that war entails. Drone pilots sit behind computer screens, as if playing a video game, but unleash real weapons and violence on the military targets, and on the civilians that are nearby or subject to errant missiles and bombs. It is important to remember that technologies do not act of their own accord. People and social organizations are needed to bring such technologies into existence, to decide how they are to be used, and then to use them in that way.

Until recently, unmanned military drones have largely been produced by the US. This technological superiority has given it important advantages in war, and this will continue for some time. But other countries, such as Pakistan, are producing drones, although they have much more limited range and may not yet be able to carry military weapons (Associated Press 2013). There is even increasing evidence that terrorist organizations, such as Hezbollah, have built drones and are exploring their purposes for terrorist activities (Kershner 2013). As other nations and terrorist networks continue to develop their military technology, drones will be an increasing global dimension of war, like the advanced communication and information technologies that underpin all globalizing military systems.

INFORMATION WAR

The new, advanced technologies have made possible both traditional warfare and the more recent "information war" or "infowar" (Lawson 2013; Pötzsch Forthcoming; Tumber and Webster 2007). This new information technology is deeply implicated in the new advanced weaponry employed in contemporary wars. For example, the "smart missiles" employed by the US in the second Iraq war required advanced information technology so that they could be targeted to hit very minute and precise targets with a high degree of accuracy (although, these weapons, like virtually all weapons, were not immune from missing their targets and causing collateral damage). Not only do these weapons depend on advanced information technologies, but so do many other aspects of contemporary warfare such as surveillance (by satellites, airplanes, drones, and so on) as well as the "command and control" needed to run a modern military operation.

We are moving from a world dominated by *heavy* "industrial war" (e.g. that was waged during WW II) to one that is best seen as *light* "information war." *Industrial war* generally involved sovereign nation-states, the homeland deeply supported it, it was fought over territory, involved the mobilization of a large portion of the population and led to mass casualties, was largely symmetrical in that massed armies confronted one another, witnessed the media harnessed in support of the war effort, and provided the media with only a very limited view of what was taking place on the battlefield.

In contrast, **information war** involves information permeating all aspects of war, involves all sorts of new technologies (digital soldiers, drones, computer-driven weapons, etc.), is massively asymmetrical in that only the most advanced nations, especially the US, have access to these technologies, involves relatively small numbers of troops (many of whom are better thought of as "knowledge warriors"), is less oriented to gaining territory, involves only a small portion of the population, and is likely to be a war of short duration.

Information war: Information and information technology increasingly permeating warfare perpetrated by developed countries.

Modern global warfare also increasingly involves a battle over information among and between various representatives of the media in the nation-states involved. Most generally, there is the battle among media giants to be the first to announce, and even show, an important event. For example, in the Middle East there is a rivalry between Western media giants versus Arab competitors. Thus, when Saddam Hussein was hanged in 2006, there was great competition to see who would be the first to announce, and show, the hanging (the Arab media companies won this one).

In addition, the combatants involved in war seek to use these media outlets to get their messages across and to further their interests. Thus, these media outlets are dominated by the "talking heads" representing the various interests involved. Increasingly, this war over the ability to influence global public opinion is a very important, even integral, part of the war itself. If public opinion in a given country turns against a particular war (as it did in the US in the case of the second war in Iraq), it is very difficult for that country to continue the war (but not impossible, as again is illustrated by the second Iraq War and America's continued involvement in it in spite of public opinion strongly against the war), at least for very long. Thus, the national and international competition among the media, and among the various spokespeople who appear on them, are an integral, even often decisive, aspect of modern global warfare.

Then there is the fact that reporters from a large number of global media descend on a war zone to report on it. Thus, lots of reports are filed and many of them are in conflict with one another. These reports may reflect differences among reporters in experience and access, but they also may reflect differences in the ideological and political orientations of the specific media that they represent.

The military seeks to affect the information war in various ways. It issues news releases and holds press conferences designed to give reporters, and indirectly the global public, the information and perspective of that military and its government. The military also employs its own public relations officers to get its messages across more directly. And the military seeks to control what the reporters get to see. For example, in the war in Iraq only a select few reporters were allowed by the military to be "embedded" with the troops and therefore were the only ones who had direct knowledge of front-line battles (of course, even their view of those battles was restricted and what they saw was limited to a small number of those battles). Other reporters had to rely on the reports of those embedded in writing their own stories.

An information war was waged in Syria in August 2013. It was alleged that the Syrian government used chemical weapons against its own people, but the Syrian government claimed they were used by rebel forces. While a UN report indicated the Syrian government was involved, its ally, Russia, cited "the report of a Lebanese-born nun who, from a hotel room in Geneva, did her own analysis of videos of the scene at Ghouta [the Damascus suburb where the attacks occurred] and declared them fake" (Bohlen 2013). Syria also attempted to control the flow of information by controlling journalists themselves; 16 foreign journalists and 60 Syrian journalists were either detained, kidnapped, or missing at the time. In some cases, NGOs and other advocates have led the way in on-the-ground reporting. For example, Human Rights Watch found evidence of the Syrian government's involvement in the attack; the information was later corroborated by US intelligence (Entous et al. 2013). The struggle reflects a global effort at both uncovering and shaping public perception of the event, ultimately shaping military and political interventions.

A major development from the point of view of the globalization of war (and much else) is the ability of the Internet and social media to disseminate alternative perspectives directly to large numbers of people throughout the world. Thus even though the global media giants are more powerful than ever, there is at the same time increased democratization of media communication with the result that many more voices are heard, and perspectives available, to global consumers of information than ever before. Thus, during the Arab Spring, thousands of people used Twitter, Facebook, and blogs to disseminate information that was otherwise censored by governments or not covered by mainstream media. This is another demonstration of the democratization of information dissemination in the age of the Internet. At the same time, governments and their militaries have also sought to use social media to influence public opinion covertly, thus complicating this seeming democratization of information technologies (Lawson 2013).

Also of note here is the fact that because of the increasing sophistication of the global media, people around the globe are able to listen to and actually see war-related events in real time. Thus, they are able to form their own views on these events more directly, less shaped by the views of media representatives and spokespeople for various perspectives.

What all of the above indicate is an increasing profusion of global sources of information on war (and much else) and, as a result, it is increasingly difficult for any one nation or military to control that information. That means that the information will be carried on many fronts at the same time and that there is likely to be no single or clear winner in these media battles.

While this means less ability on anyone's part to control media messages, it also means that the profusion of different messages is likely to lead to much greater ambiguity, ambivalence, and confusion in the minds of the public. This might make it more difficult for a given nation to undertake a war or carry one out for any lengthy period of time. This is complicated by a virtual "blizzard" of information that overwhelms even the most attentive students of world affairs.

Often used in this context is Joseph Nye's (2005) distinction between "soft" and "hard" war (Price 2012). The information war is usually seen as soft (that is, "hard" military technology is *not* employed), whereas an actual military engagement is seen as hard (involving the use of such "hard" technologies). However, because military hardware is increasingly dependent on information technology, it is more and more difficult to make such a clear distinction. Hard military war is increasingly influenced by various media (employing soft technologies) that are more important in deciding whether a war begins and even the outcome of a war.

Overall, the public is less personally involved, less personally touched, by information war than they were by industrial war. For example, far fewer fight (compare the millions of troops involved in WW II to the hundreds of thousands involved in the Iraq war) and there are fewer casualties and therefore fewer families are personally touched by war. Less directly involved and affected, the population, especially of the developed nations waging the war (often in distant lands), is much more dependent on second-hand, media-based, rather than personal (e.g. letters from loved ones at the front), information for learning about what is taking place.

CYBERWAR

The increasing importance of computers and the Internet has had, as we have seen in various places in this book, many implications for globalization. One of the potentially most important and devastating is the possibility of cyberwar (Singer and Friedman 2014).

Indeed, this is not just a possibility, but has already occurred, most notably in the case of Iran in 2006–2011 (Sanger 2012). The US National Security Agency (NSA) and Israeli military, in a project code named Olympic Games, wrote a computer worm that was aimed at disrupting Iran's nuclear enrichment program. The computer worm was designed to make centrifuges, vital to nuclear enrichment, spin too fast or too slow, causing some of them to explode. In 2008, centrifuges began failing at Natanz, Iran's most important nuclear facility, but the code was designed to make the breakdowns appear like random accidents, with different code causing different disruptions. When President Obama took office in 2009, he was briefed about the program under way and advised that continuing the secret cyberattack could mean the difference between war and peace. The US decided to continue the program, and in 2010, it targeted a critical set of centrifuges. The subsequent cyberattack took out over 1,000 centrifuges (approximately 20% of Iran's nuclear capacity), but the worm had already escaped into the public Internet and was replicating quickly. Computer engineers in the public observed the worm, calling it Stuxnet, and the story eventually made its way into the mainstream press. Iran then became aware of the cyberwar underway and took measures to defend the plant against the attacks. In 2011, the US and Israeli governments claimed major setbacks for Iran's nuclear program but the actual effect is disputed.

There are currently not only national efforts to figure out how to carry out, or respond to, such attacks, but also a kind of "arms race" involving China, Russia, and the US, all of which are seeking to develop more powerful "information-warfare programs." More recently, China has been "mounting attacks on United States government computer systems and defense contractors in a systematic effort to steal intellectual property and gain strategic advantage" (*New York Times* 2013). These attacks range from the theft of industrial technology for economic gain to stealing secrets on military intelligence and planning (Hannas et al. 2013). Military targets might include access to military strategy, diplomatic negotiations, and weaponized technology. The continued "arms race" and centrality of computer networks in the digital age raises the possibility of far more devastating attacks in the future.

THE IMPACT OF NEGATIVE GLOBAL FLOWS ON INDIVIDUALS

All of the negative flows discussed above, indeed all of the analyses offered throughout virtually this entire book, deal in general and abstract terms with large-scale aspects of globalization. This is to a large degree because globalization itself is large in scale, general, and abstract (although an effort has been made throughout this book to concretize it). However, it is also the case that globalization in general, as well as the various negative flows discussed in this chapter, has a wide range of very profound effects on individuals (Lemert and Elliott 2006).

Clearly, each of the major negative flows discussed above have profoundly adverse effects on individuals: people are victimized, even killed, as a result of global crime; citizens pay the costs resulting from corruption on a global level; innocent people, like those in the Twin Towers, in the subway systems in London and Madrid, and in Bali, Indonesia are the victims, often the intended victims, of terrorists; and it is certainly the case that large numbers of innocent civilians die, and have their lives destroyed, by war.

We can also look at this in another way by thinking about the individual implications of the various insecurities iterated by the United Nations Development Report[9]: financial volatility and economic insecurity, job and income insecurity, health insecurity, cultural insecurity, personal insecurity, environmental insecurity, and political and community insecurity. While all of these insecurities exist globally, nationally, and in other large-scale collectivities of one kind or another, they are also certainly manifest at the individual level. Individuals suffer in global economic crises; in global wars; and from fear of such things as contracting AIDS, hostile neighbors, identity theft, the effects of global warming, and being caught up in the turmoil associated with a failed or failing state.

Along these lines, Lemert and Elliott (2006) have gone so far as to argue that globalization[10] is toxic to individuals and their emotional lives. The authors see a variety of personal problems resulting from globalization such as hyperindividualism, privatization, and the decreasing solidity and durability of personal identity (although they recognize that globalization also brings with it the possibility of more open and flexible selves). Overall, they conclude that people are being emotionally damaged (Walker 2008) by the new "globalized individualism" and by globalization in general, at least its negative aspects.

CHAPTER SUMMARY

This chapter analyzes negative global flows and processes such as dangerous imports, borderless diseases, cross-border crime, terrorism, and war. With globalization, such flows can move across borders with ease and at great speed. Negative globalization comprises not only flows and processes, but also structures. Negative flows also induce global counter-reactions.

Global value chains involve the importation of both products and product ingredients. The length and multiplicity of these chains leave them vulnerable to the spread of contaminants along their entire length and breadth. Further, the complexity of the chain often makes it difficult to locate the source of contamination.

The transmission of diseases across borders is not a novel phenomenon. However, it has become much more common in recent years. The spread of such diseases indicates the difficulty involved in checking the flow of disease-causing pathogens across borders. This global spread is particularly influenced by the increasing mobility of people. For instance, AIDS travels from one region to the other through human vectors. The situation calls for an appropriately global response. It is often the most vulnerable populations that bear the burden of such diseases, for instance the high incidence of AIDS cases in regions across Africa. This segment of the global population is also least likely to have access to the expensive health care required to combat such diseases. Globalization also contributes to the spread of diseases in other ways. For instance, global warming has resulted in the spread of tropical diseases to what is now a warmer Europe.

The magnitude and volume of cross-border crime has increased with globalization. Correspondingly, global attention to this flow has also increased. Cross-border crime involves flows of drugs, money, victims, perpetrators, as well as illegal commodities, through physical as well as virtual (Internet-based) channels. The decline in the regulatory powers of the nation-state translates into an increasing inability to check such flows. However, the adoption of the latest technologies, as well as sophisticated organizational methods based on legitimate businesses models, is helping to improve the ability to deal with global crime.

Despite its decline, the nation-state retains the power to define global forms of deviance and crime (for instance the categorization of marijuana as illegal and harmful in the US and

Europe). In the era of globalization, the nation-states of Western Europe and the US disseminated their sense of morality and norms of behavior to the rest of the world. The growth of global crime has led to a selective tightening of border controls in the US and Europe. However, more stringent measures of global crime control have given rise to concerns about the violation of human rights as well as the threats posed to democracy.

Crime and terrorism are closely related, often through financial linkages. Terrorism is defined as actions that cause "deaths, serious bodily injuries, and serious damage to public or private property, places, facilities, or other systems" and are aimed at intimating citizens, governments, or international organizations. There is a need to distinguish terrorism from below (undertaken by stateless organizations such as al-Qaeda) from terrorism from above (i.e. practiced by the state). Terrorist activities are expanding in terms of their global aspirations and reach. Terrorist groups are no longer restricted to their home territory and can strike anywhere in the world. They also have access to sophisticated technology that enables them to transmit their messages to a global audience. As a result, the counter-reaction to terrorism is also increasingly global. However, in launching such an offensive, nation-states often resort to tactics that resemble those of the terrorists they seek to combat.

Warfare is increasingly influenced by globalization. Global interconnectedness implies that a war in a region is no longer an isolated phenomenon and will involve other regions, often quite distant, directly or indirectly. In fact, this interconnectedness is interpreted by some as an indication that the incidence of war might decline with globalization. However, the economic gains of war and easy access to weapons in the global era might actually lead to an increase in warfare. Drones are becoming an increasingly common technology deployed in war and will continue to shape warfare far into the future. Further, advanced technologies make new forms of warfare, including information war and cyberwar, possible. This involves information permeating all aspects of war and warfare that increasingly takes place through the Internet.

DISCUSSION QUESTIONS

1. Discuss the role of structures in perpetuating negative globalization.

2. What actions can be taken by nation-states to deal with dangerous imports?

3. What actions can be taken globally to deal with borderless diseases?

4. Examine the global flows of crime. What is the role of the nation-state and international agencies in dealing with such flows?

5. Discuss the concepts of terrorism from above and below. What is the relationship between these two types of terrorism in the context of globalization?

6. Examine the impact of global media flows on warfare in the current global age.

7. Discuss the role of drones in modern warfare and how they will likely shape war in the future.

ADDITIONAL READINGS ·······································

Maj-Lis Follér and Håkan Thörn, eds. *The Politics of AIDS: Globalization, the State and Civil Society*. New York: Palgrave Macmillan, 2008.

Gina Kolata. *Flu: The Story of the Great Influenza Pandemic of 1918 and the Search for the Virus That Caused It*. New York: Touchstone, 1999.

Kathryn Farr. *Sex Trafficking: The Global Market in Women and Children*. New York: Worth, 2005.

William Nestor. *Globalization, War, and Peace in the Twenty-First Century*. New York: Palgrave Macmillan, 2010.

Mary Kaldor. *New and Old Wars: Organised Violence in a Global Era*. Malden, MA: Polity Press, 2013.

Vidyamali Samarasignhe. *Female Sex Trafficking*. New York: Routledge, 2012.

Carolyn Nordstrom. *Global Outlaws: Crime, Money, and Power in the Contemporary World*. Berkeley: University of California Press, 2007.

Gus Martin. *Understanding Terrorism: Challenges, Perspectives, and Issues*, 4th edn. Thousand Oaks, CA: Sage, 2012.

Philip Bobbitt. *Terror and Consent: The Wars for the Twenty-First Century*. New York: Knopf, 2008.

Tarak Barkawi. *Globalization and War*. Lanham, MD: Rowman and Littlefield, 2007.

Jude McCulloch and Sharon Pickering, eds. *Borders and Crime: Pre-Crime, Mobility, and Serious Harm in an Age of Globalization*. New York: Palgrave Macmillan, 2012.

NOTES ·······································

1 However, we might all agree that certain global problems, borderless diseases to take one example, are negative.

2 As well as being a major cause of the global recession.

3 www.who.int/csr/disease/ebola/en/.

4 See for example, "Arresting Transnational Crime," a special issue of the electronic journal, *Global Issues*, 6, 2 (August 2001).

5 However, in spite of this growth, most policing remains within nation-states and is generally insulated from international relations and foreign affairs.

6 Waterboarding involves pouring water over an inclined prisoner's face to create the feeling of suffocation.

7 As well as conceptions, even erroneous conceptions, of globalization. See Roxborough (2002: 339–59).

8 www.nato.int.

9 United Nations Development Programme, *United Nations Development Report* 1999.

10 Unfortunately, it is *not* at all clear from their analysis that globalization is the cause of these difficulties.

GLOBAL INEQUALITIES I

CLASS AND RURAL–URBAN INEQUALITIES

Globalization: A Basic Text, Second Edition. George Ritzer and Paul Dean.
© 2015 John Wiley & Sons, Ltd. Published 2015 by John Wiley & Sons, Ltd.

Given the great importance of inequality in the world today, we will devote two chapters to the issue of inequality and its relationship to globalization. In this chapter we will discuss class inequality among societies throughout the world (Galbraith 2012; Sernau 2014), as well as how that inequality relates to the rural–urban differentiation. In the following chapter, the focus will shift to the relationship between globalization and inequality based on race, ethnicity, gender, and sexuality.

The first part of this chapter is based on the premise that one of the most pressing problems, if not *the* most pressing problem, in the world today is the great economic inequalities that exist among and between societies. These inequalities not only raise enormous moral and ethical concerns (for example, how can we live with the fact that so few are so rich and so many are so poor?), but they also represent a major source of instability and conflict in many areas of the world. Inequality among societies is not only a problem in itself, but there is also the issue of whether or not globalization contributes to greater and greater inequality in the world or, conversely, whether it represents the great hope for reducing much of that inequality.

On the one hand, there are those who argue that globalization, especially economic globalization, is a major contributor to global inequality (Korzeniewicz and Moran 2010). One version of this argument is that economic globalization, at least as it exists today, is capitalistic in nature and, as Marx argued over a century ago, capitalism is an economic system that is characterized by great inequalities and the exploitation of the "have nots" by the "haves" (Marx 1867/1967). Immanuel Wallerstein (1974) has extended this argument, as discussed previously (see Chapter 3), to a global level by differentiating primarily between the "core" and the "periphery" in the capitalist "world system." His key point is that there is great inequality between these two global areas[1] and the wealthy and powerful core countries (such as the US, the nation-states in the EU) grow ever-wealthier by exploiting at ever-higher levels impoverished peripheral countries (especially most countries in Africa and Latin America). This distinction is most often referred to in this book as the North–South divide. There are many other ways of thinking about global inequality, including many other Marxian positions on it (see, for example, Chapter 4), but few observers would argue with the point that there is enormous inequality in the world today. There is also little debate over the fact that inequality exists, at least in part, because some groups and/or geographic areas are exploiting others.

On the other hand, there are other thinkers, most notably many of the neoliberals discussed in Chapter 4, who would certainly admit that there is inequality in the world today, but who would argue that such global inequality is declining and will decline further as economic globalization progresses. A global free-market, with increasingly free flows of products and money, is seen as enriching everyone, at least in the "long run."[2] This is based on the general premise that a free and open global market will lead to great growth in the global economy and that all will benefit from such growth. Consistent with this perspective is Thomas Friedman's notion, discussed in Chapter 4, that globalization is leading to a "flat world" and a flat world means the elimination of barriers to participation in the global economy (as well as other aspects of globalization). With such barriers minimized or eliminated, more and more people can participate in, and profit from, the global economy thereby greatly reducing, if not ultimately eliminating, inequality. A flat world is, to a large extent, an equal world, or at least one where everyone, everywhere has an equal chance to succeed. Put another way, and in terms central to this book, in a flat world, money and economic success are free to flow everywhere in the world; they would no longer be limited largely to the North and small pockets in the South.

Whatever position one takes on this issue, all would agree that economic globalization is related to global inequality (and equality). However, it is important to remember that there is much more to globalization than economics, and many other aspects of the broad process of globalization (many will be discussed in Chapter 14) relate to the issue of inequality.

Given these general views on globalization and its relationship to inequality, it is not immediately obvious how the other major topic to be covered in this chapter – rural–urban differences – relates to inequality, globalization, and the relationship between them. While there is much more to the rural–urban issue than its relationship to inequality, inequality is central to it in various ways. For one thing, there is great inequality throughout the world between urban and rural areas. In the main, it is the urban areas (especially in the North) that are the centers of wealth, and most of the major cities (although there are great exceptions such as Karachi, Pakistan; see below) have grown wealthier as economic globalization has grown and expanded. However, there is also great inequality among the world's great cities, for example between New York and Karachi. Yet, the far greater inequality is that which exists between urban and rural areas throughout the world. (However, there are exceptions such as rural America, especially with its large government subsidies and high commodity prices until quite recently, which is far better off economically than most other rural areas, although it is characterized by great poverty, as well [Harrington 1997].) For these and other reasons, it makes sense to discuss the rural–urban issue in a chapter that is also concerned with global economic inequality. However, the reader should bear in mind that there is much else that is important about the rural–urban issue from a global perspective than inequality. For example, political power tends to rest in the world's major cities and not in other cities, let alone rural areas.

The rural–urban issue also relates to globalization in more general ways. For one thing, a small number of the world's cities (e.g. New York, London, Tokyo) are so central to globalization that they are called "global" (or "world") cities. Many global processes originate and flow through these cities. In addition, rural areas are more and more global in nature as the ability to sell agricultural products and livestock is increasingly determined by a global market. In whatever ways they are involved in globalization, rural areas are much more likely than cities to be part of the hinterland and therefore excluded from, or of secondary importance in, global processes.

CLASS INEQUALITY

Derived from the classic work of Max Weber, **social class** relates to social rankings made on the basis of economic factors such as occupation, wealth, and income. There is a hierarchy of social classes all over the world, although what it takes (in terms of income, wealth, etc.) to be included in a specific social class varies greatly from society to society and from one time to another. In any case, there is almost always a hierarchy of social classes with the most common being some sort of distinction between upper, middle, and working classes. This most often plays itself out within nation-states, but it is also possible to delineate global differences, and potential class conflicts, on the basis of economics. Thus, for example, more of those in the upper classes are to be found today in North America, Europe, and increasingly Asia, while a disproportionate number of those in the lower classes are in Africa and South America.

> **Social class:** Social rankings made on the basis of economic factors such as occupation, wealth, and income.

The issue of class inequality among and between areas of the world (especially North and South) would seem to require little or no discussion. Even a casual examination of global realities makes it clear that such inequalities exist and that they are extraordinarily dramatic and disturbing. Billions of people live in global poverty amidst a time of abundant wealth. While globalization has linked countries from around the world into a global economy, many nations or even many people within rich nations have not benefited from this tremendous creation of wealth. Although this profound inequality seems indisputable, we will see in this chapter that there is, in fact, an important debate over the issue of global inequality.

Also, from a global perspective, many readers might not be familiar with the relationship between the global North and South, and how it shapes global economic inequality. Finally, a discussion of the less well-off in the world, especially the most impoverished people in the world, is also needed.

INEQUALITY IN THE WORLD SYSTEM

In Chapter 3, we discussed world-systems theory as an early theory of globalization that relates to an important perspective on development (Wallerstein 1974, 2004). It is necessary to return to world-systems theory now in relation to global economic inequality. As we noted earlier, world-systems theory envisions a world divided between the core, periphery, and semi-periphery. The core includes the wealthiest industrialized countries with strong state institutions (referred to in this text as the global North), such as Western European countries, the US, Australia, and Japan. The periphery includes the least developed countries with weak state institutions (referred to in this text as the global South), including most of Africa, and parts of Asia (e.g. Indonesia, Vietnam, Afghanistan), the Middle East (e.g. Iran, Syria), and South America (e.g. Peru, Bolivia). The semi-periphery includes intermediate countries with developing economies, including much of Eastern Europe, Thailand, India, China, South Africa, Brazil, and Argentina.

The world-systems perspective focuses on understanding these global economic inequalities in a broad historical context and examining the interrelationship of the core, periphery, and semi-periphery (Reifer 2012). First, it explains the development and level of wealth of individual countries and regions by situating them in the context of the world capitalist system. The earlier a country became integrated in the capitalist world economy, the more rapidly it accumulated wealth (although this also meant inequality increased more rapidly *within* those countries). Positions within the world economy were largely determined by 1640 with European countries at the top. This is not to say that countries have not changed positions (e.g China and India have moved from the periphery to the semi-periphery in recent years), but the emphasis is on the role of history and the timing of a country's integration into the global economy as necessary for understanding their position within it today.

Second, world-systems theory posits that we cannot understand an individual nation's wealth today by understanding development processes that have only occurred within that country. Instead, we must understand a nation's position in the world system by its current relationship to other countries in the core, periphery, and semi-periphery. For example, consider the many nations that were brought (or forced) into the capitalist world system through colonization. As a British colony, much of India's natural resources and foods were sent back to England. When droughts hit India in the late 1800s, millions of Indians died because the majority of their food was being redirected from its own people to Britain as the colonizing power (Davis 2002). In other colonized countries around the world, gold, timber, and other natural resources were extracted from those colonized countries (i.e. the periphery) for the benefit of the colonizers (i.e. the core). When the US abducted people from territories throughout Africa and made them slaves, not only did it help the US to accumulate more wealth, it also removed people of prime working age and fertility from their home countries, thus compromising for generations their ability to develop their home countries. If these countries had been independent of their colonizers, they could have benefited from their own resources and labor, and could have ultimately been more economically developed today.

While colonial systems have largely disappeared, this power relationship continues through global financial institutions. The World Bank and IMF, which are disproportionately controlled by rich core countries, make loans to countries in the periphery and semi-periphery. They set the terms of global loans and terms of repayment. For example, the IMF has made loans to countries in the periphery where 90% of the loan must be spent on infrastructure projects carried out by US corporations (e.g. Halliburton, Bechtel), thus ensuring financial rewards flow back to wealthy countries.

In each of the examples above, it is the core nations that benefit most from their position of power within the world system. They largely control the world economy and keep resources and cheap labor flowing from the periphery to the core. This enables them to stay wealthy atop the global class pyramid. With their intermediate position, the semi-periphery benefits from their power over the periphery but is exploited by their weaker position relative to the core. Inevitably, this power relationship leads to conflicts between the core and periphery. The semi-periphery also mediates and lessens these conflicts, helping to reinforce global economic inequalities. In sum, periphery countries do not stay poor only because of their own failed policies or bad decisions, but also because they are made poor (and stay poor) because of the policies and practices of wealthier countries. We can, therefore, only fully understand a country's economic development today – or the resulting economic inequality relative to the rest of the world – by understanding their relationship to other countries in the world system.

"THE BOTTOM BILLION"

As illustrated by world-systems theory, the most common way of looking at economic inequality in the world (indeed the way we introduced the issue in this chapter) is to focus on the differences between the North and the South, core and periphery, or between the developed and less developed areas of the world. However, Paul Collier (2007, 2012) argues that in making that gross distinction we ignore the poorest people in the world, what he calls "the bottom billion." There is certainly great inequality between the North and the South, but a focus on that relationship tends to obscure the full extent of global inequality. The latter is clear when we look at the bottom billion and compare them, at least implicitly, to the rich and the super-rich in the world, most of whom are in the North.

The vast majority (70%) of the people in the bottom billion, as well as the countries in which they live, are in Africa. Among the other countries that contain large numbers of the bottom billion are Haiti, Bolivia, Laos, North Korea, and Yemen. Wherever they live, the bottom billion have incomes of only about a fifth of those in other developing countries and their situation will only grow worse unless there are dramatic changes in the near future.

They also have many other serious problems such as low life expectancy (about 50 years whereas the average is 67 in other developing nations), high infant mortality (14% of the children of the bottom billion die before their fifth birthday versus 4% in other developing countries), and they are more likely to show symptoms of malnutrition (36% as opposed to 20% in other developing countries). Perhaps of greatest importance is the fact that their situation has grown worse in recent years and they have fallen further behind those in not only the developed countries but the other less developed countries, as well.

Collier argues that there are four "traps" that differentiate the nation-states (and failed states) that contain most of the bottom billion from other nation-states and that disproportionately account for the impoverishment of the bottom billion.

Conflict trap

Conflict trap: Nation-state confronted with either continuing civil wars or frequent violent coups d'état.

The first is what Collier calls the **conflict trap**. A state involved in a conflict trap is confronted with either continuing civil wars or frequent violent coups d'état. Various African countries (most notably Rwanda, Congo, and Sudan) have experienced wrenching civil wars in recent years. Coups d'état have been common, as well, in countries such as Congo, Niger, Mali, and Ivory Coast. In addition, various African nations have experienced a number of failed coup attempts that can also be quite disruptive. A nation caught in continuing rounds of violent conflict, coups, coup attempts, and counter-coups is likely to suffer economically and to see large portions of its population plunged into poverty and, perhaps, into the bottom billion.

The contrast, of course, is to the North where violent conflicts within states are rare and coups d'état are even rarer. Thus, Northern states and their citizens live in much more stable and peaceful conditions and can, as a result, concentrate on that which enhances their economics and their economic well-being.

Natural resources trap

Natural resources trap: Limiting economic development because of excessive dependence on abundant natural resources.

The world's poorest countries also fall into the **natural resources trap**. Ironically, these countries are often rich in at least some natural resources, but dependence on those resources, and the wealth they provide, militates against broader economic development. The focus on natural resources makes it less likely that there will be sufficient attention to other forms of production. The result is that these other types of production tend to decline leading to a wide range of shortages. For example, in Nigeria in the 1970s, oil became a valuable export and the focus of national attention. Other resources such as peanuts and cocoa came to be seen as less- or un-profitable crops and, as a result, their production declined precipitously as did the income from them. It is also the case that the availability of these crops as a source of food for the local population declined.

The market for natural resources is also very volatile with the result that periods of boom are followed by busts that hurt the economy, especially those in it who are the poorest members of society. During boom times public spending is largely devoted to the profitable exports and other interests and concerns founder. Further, the periodic extremes of boom and bust, as well as their consequences, become increasingly difficult for the government to manage and it grows increasingly ineffective at more and more levels. Cycles of booms and busts also make it more difficult for the electorate to determine whether or not the government is doing a good job. A relatively small number of people grow increasing wealthy (thereby increasing inequality *within* the country) because they benefit the most from a poor nation's exports, especially during boom periods. As a result, they tend to grow more powerful and their power, and their desire to maintain and extend that power, serves to undermine democratic governments and the chances that democracy can succeed.

The resource trap may also come to affect adversely other countries where relatively few of the bottom billion reside. They include the now oil-rich nations in the Arab world, Russia, and others. Russia, given the great economic disparity between its developed areas in the western part of the country and its less developed areas in the east, undoubtedly contains some of the bottom billion, but there are relatively few of them in the Arab oil states. Nevertheless, even those states may become so dependent on oil as a source of wealth that they fail to diversify and to find alternate sources of income and wealth. Many nations in the Arab world seem to have come to this realization in recent years and we are seeing much more diversification there (the United Arab Emirates, especially Dubai, is a notable example, although Dubai experienced hard times in the Great Recession), perhaps in part because they are awash in oil money and are desperate to find new ways to spend and invest it. There is, as yet, little evidence that Russia is diversifying in this way and it remains in the natural resource trap which may well hurt the country when the oil begins to run out.

Trap of being landlocked with bad neighbors

The third trap is being *landlocked with bad neighbors*. Being landlocked does not in itself necessarily lead to poverty. Switzerland is a landlocked country (Luxemburg is another), but it and its people are extraordinarily well-off economically. However, overall, the fact is that almost 40% of the poorest billion live in landlocked countries, and the overwhelming majority of them are in Africa.

One problem faced by these landlocked countries is the unavailability of transportation to the coast (and the high cost when it is available), needed so that a country can export its products. Internally, many African nations lack adequate roads, railroad systems, river boats, and the like and, in fact, in many cases the infrastructure is deteriorating further rather than improving. If a landlocked country's neighbors are similarly lacking in a transportation infrastructure to the coast, and this is often the case in Africa (and *not*, for example, in the wealthy countries surrounding Switzerland such as Germany, France, and Italy), this creates huge, if not insurmountable, impediments to being involved in the export business and to reaping the income to be derived from it.

It is also the case that a landlocked nation does better when its neighbor is successful economically and can therefore serve as a market for its products. While Switzerland is surrounded by successful countries and markets, Uganda (to take one example in Africa) "has Kenya, which has been stagnant for nearly three decades; Rwanda, which had a genocide; Somalia, which completely collapsed; the Democratic Republic of the Congo, the history of which was sufficiently catastrophic for it to change its name from Zaire; and finally Tanzania, which invaded it" (Collier 2007: 55).

Some landlocked African countries do overcome such disadvantages and barriers, but those seem to be countries (e.g. Botswana) with enormous, well-managed resources. However, in many cases, landlocked African countries lack such enormous resources, manage them poorly, *and* they have "bad" or problematic neighbors. Such neighbors can impede or block shipment of the landlocked country's products, can have serious internal problems of their own (some of which may spill over) such as growing slowly if at all, may have weak economies, and have weak or even non-existent governments ("failed states" such as Somalia).

Bad governance trap

The final trap discussed by Collier is *bad governance in a small country*. A bad government with bad policies can not only inhibit an economy from growing, but it can literally destroy the economy. One example is the government of Robert Mugabe in Zimbabwe which came to power in 1980. In spite of disastrous inflation in the early twenty-first century which decimated the economy and the society as a whole, Mugabe clung to power, and even vowed to remain in power for the rest of his life (at the age of 89, he won the 2013 election over rival Morgan Tsvangirai).

In a disputed election in 2008, Mugabe had been involved in a run-off election (after questionable, likely fraudulent, vote-counting by his government in the first round of the election) against Tsvangirai. Eager to remain in power, Mugabe had his thugs attack and even kill supporters of Tsvangirai in an effort to prevent them from voting or to intimidate them into voting for him. Mugabe's supporters also hounded and harassed Tsvangirai himself and at several points during the campaign he was imprisoned for brief periods of time. In order to protect his supporters, Tsvangirai finally withdrew from the run-off and, in order to protect himself, took refuge in the Dutch embassy. Mugabe "won" the election. Millions of people fled Zimbabwe, many crossing the border into South Africa without authorization. This led to protests, riots, and even violence against these immigrants in South Africa. Mugabe's second win over Tsvangirai in 2013 was also challenged by American officials, who cited "substantial electoral irregularities reported by domestic and regional observers" (Polgreen 2013).

While the trap of bad government can be disastrous and can be difficult to escape, it is possible for a country to recover from a bad government. The most notable example in recent history, although in a large not a small country, has been the remarkable economic turnaround in China after the death of Mao Zedong in 1976 and the economic reforms then undertaken by Deng Xiaoping. Mao had engaged in a series of disastrous policies such as the infamous "Great Leap Forward" in which he attempted to force China to make a rapid transition from a farm-based to an industrial economy. The policy was highly disruptive and extremely unsuccessful. In fact, it led to great failures on the farms and to a famine in China. It took decades for the Chinese economy to recover from this misguided policy and others promulgated by Mao and his supporters.

Breaking out of these four "traps" is difficult for the countries that contain the vast majority of the bottom billion. They are precisely the countries that have great difficulty breaking into the global market for trade, in attracting capital investment, and they are the ones that are highly likely to experience a brain drain (see Chapter 10) that leads to the emigration of the very people who can help them to develop economically.

As useful as Collier's work is in bringing the bottom billion to our attention, his work does tend to blame the victim for its problems. While the countries in which most of the bottom billion live are certainly at fault, we cannot ignore the role played by the North. As stipulated from a world-systems perspective, core countries have made and kept the bottom billion poor through imperialism and colonialism (see also Chapter 3) as well as contemporaneously in terms of, to take only one example, the structural adjustment (see Chapter 4) programs associated with the IMF (see Chapter 6).

GROWING GLOBAL INEQUALITY IN HEALTH AND HEALTH CARE

While globalization has been associated with increased aggregate life expectancy throughout the world, it also has tended to widen global disparities in life span and in health (Hashemian and Yach 2007; Johns et al. 2013; Vogli et al. 2014). For example, in 2013, the World Health Organization (WHO) found that the widening gap between the world's rich and poor continues to increase differences in life expectancy. Economic inequality drives many of these health disparities.

Those in poor nations tend to have poorer health as a result of limited access to health services, education, sanitation, adequate nutrition, and housing. Conversely, poor health tends to limit economic growth in those nations mainly by adversely affecting productivity. Developing countries have a disproportionate share of mortality and morbidity, much of which could be prevented inexpensively and treated effectively if the money was available. Ninety percent of the total burden of disease in the world is concentrated in low- and middle-income countries which, in turn, account for only 10% of health-care expenditures. Similarly, only 10% of research money in the US is devoted to the health problems that account for 90% of the global disease burden. Furthermore, developing countries have lower levels of education, which lessens the likelihood of knowing about preventive strategies and of obtaining knowledge about how to control one's own health (Rinaldo and Ferraro 2012). As a result of such disparities, there is a 19-year gap in life expectancy between high- and low-income countries. Those improvements that we have seen in the developing world tend to be in those less developed countries – e.g. Brazil, Egypt, Malaysia – that are more deeply involved than the rest in the globalization process. However, for most of the rest, especially the least developed countries, globalization has brought with it a decline in economic growth, an increase in poverty, and, as a result, a decline in health.

Developing countries in the South also suffer disproportionately from hunger and malnutrition (Serra-Majem and Ngo 2012). There are roughly 850 million people there affected by these problems and "19 countries suffer from levels of hunger that are either 'alarming' or 'extremely alarming'" (von Grebmer et al. 2013). The causes include inadequate or almost totally unavailable food supplies, a lack of assured and continual access to food, as well as poor and unbalanced diets. This is especially important for children who are likely to die young from malnutrition. Furthermore, those underweight children that survive are, when they become adults, likely to be less physically and intellectually productive and to suffer more chronic illnesses and disabilities. This carries on inter-generationally as the ability of such adults to provide adequate nutrition for their children is compromised. An increase in obesity among other segments of the poor in less developed countries is now being added to the problems associated with being underweight. Developing countries therefore now increasingly suffer from a "double nutritional burden" – those who do not have enough to eat *and* those who eat too much, especially of the wrong kinds of food (e.g. that which is high in fat and cholesterol).

Finally, poorer countries are less likely to provide extensive health care for their populations. Low-income countries tend to have fewer hospitals, less research capacity on health and disease, and fewer people covered by medical insurance programs. These problems can be addressed through economic growth when national governments prioritize spending on health care. For example, the WHO reported that in just four years, China added 172 million previously uninsured people to its health coverage programs. Coverage in rural areas, where poverty is especially high, increased from 10% to 97%. From 2009 to 2013, the Chinese government built 2,400 county-level hospitals and more than 40,000 grassroots medical facilities, dramatically expanding health coverage. This can be contrasted with India, which, despite its significant growth, has done little to extend health coverage to its poor.

It is also worth noting that a society's wealth does not always correspond to health coverage or better health outcomes. For example, the US spends the most in the world on health care, but it ranks significantly lower than other developed countries on a number of public health indicators. Americans tend to live shorter lives, are more likely to experience violent deaths, are more likely to be obese, and have many higher disease rates. Unlike all other developed countries in the world, many of its citizens (especially Americans with low incomes) do not have health coverage. While the number of uninsured Americans decreased dramatically with so-called "Obamacare" (or the Affordable Care Act), many remain uninsured: when the law went into effect, the percentage of uninsured Americans fell from 18% to 14.7% (Levey 2014). For a developed country, it is also one of the most economically unequal countries. Research shows that the more unequal the country, the lower the health of its overall population (Pickett and Wilkinson 2011). With a highly inefficient private health insurance system, Americans pay more money for lower quality health care.

GLOBAL DIGITAL DIVIDE

The rapid global diffusion of digital technology, at a faster pace than any previous technology, led many observers to proclaim the liberating potential of technology and its potentials for helping to alleviate a great number of inequalities (in accessing information and education, greater government transparency, and so on). However, not only have these potentials not been realized, there is evidence to suggest that the global digital divide has increased (Drori 2012b). On the one hand, those in poor countries are often not able to afford, or even to have the electricity needed to run, a computer to give them Internet access (Wakefield 2013). On the other hand, the lack of advanced technology, especially when it is so abundant in the North, means that the South continues to fall further and further behind the North economically; that global inequality is increasing.

There is great inequality in the world in terms of access to (in people's ability to get their hands on the technology), and use of (once people gain access, their ability to operate the technology), the Internet, as well as, of course, computers, to say nothing of other digital technologies. Most computers are in the developed countries, the less developed countries have relatively few computers and the gap is not narrowing appreciably. As a result, the number of online users in the South is negligible. The International Telecommunications Union found that, in 2012, the percentage of individuals using the Internet remained very low in many developing countries, such as Ethiopia (1.5%), Tanzania (4.0%), Cambodia (4.9%), Iraq (7.1%), Haiti (9.8%), and Nicaragua (13.%). This is compared with the world's most developed countries, whose Internet usage was usually above 80%, including the US (81.0%), Australia (82.4%), Germany (84.0%), Finland (91.0%), Denmark (93.0%), and Sweden (95.0%). In addition, the vast majority of Internet hosts are in the North and, once again, there is little representation of such hosts in less developed countries. The main barriers to global equality in Internet access and use are the lack of infrastructure within less developed countries and the low incomes in those areas that make digital technologies, and therefore access to the Internet, prohibitively expensive for most in those areas. However, all of these aspects of Internet use are not only unequally distributed among nations of the world, but they are also unequally distributed within nations, even the most highly developed nations, with the poor (including immigrants from the South) having far less access than the middle class and the rich.

Language represents another source of inequality on the Internet (Warschauer 2012). The vast majority (over 80%) of webpages on the Internet are in English and less than 1% are in languages other than English – German, Japanese, French, Spanish, and Swedish. Clearly those who do not speak any of these languages (the overwhelming majority in the South) are at a huge disadvantage on the Internet and may even find the Internet totally inaccessible because of the language barrier.

E-WASTE AND INEQUALITY

Another dimension of global economic inequality in this realm involves e-waste, or electronic waste (e.g. old computers), that is laced with all sorts of hazardous and toxic materials (see, also, Chapter 11) (Lawhon 2013). In spite of the 1992 Basel Convention designed to regulate the traffic in hazardous waste and to bar its shipment from developed to less developed countries, such shipments continue to occur even though they are illegal (three countries – Haiti, Afghanistan, and the US – have yet to ratify the treaty). The reason is that developed countries much prefer to ship the hazardous material out of their domains and away from their populations. Further, it is much cheaper to have e-waste processed in less developed countries than in developed ones (in one estimate the cost is $2,500 per ton in developed countries versus as little as $3 per ton in less developed countries). The hazardous work involved in extracting useful parts and metals from old computer technology provides income for large numbers in the less developed world (Drori 2006). However, the income is very low and those who do such work are likely to become ill, at least in the long run, from exposure to dangerous elements and components. The income earned will do little to improve the economic situation in the less developed world and the negative health effects will only increase the gap between rich and poor countries, at least in terms of health issues.

IS GLOBAL ECONOMIC INEQUALITY INCREASING OR DECREASING?

The idea that the world is a highly unequal place would seem to be incontrovertible. A bit less incontrovertible, but no less intuitively obvious, or seemingly so, is that the world is growing *increasingly unequal*. Many of those who accept the latter view also tend to accept the idea that globalization is the root cause of this increasing inequality, but this is a topic of much debate within globalization studies (Milanovic 2013).

Within this debate, some argue that globalization is increasing global inequality (Korzeniewicz and Moran 2007; Milanovic 2012), while others contend that it is decreasing such inequality (Chotikapanich et al. 2012; Firebaugh and Goesling 2007). It also involves, as we will see below, an important methodological issue and debate (Babones 2007). And it is a theoretical issue, as well, pitting, at least in one view, (world) system theory against modernization theory (see below) (Korzeniewicz and Moran 2007).

Glenn Firebaugh and Brian Goesling (2007) are major proponents of the idea that global inequality is decreasing. They discuss three forms of global inequality – income, health, and education – although their focus is on the former which is clearly closely tied to our main concern here with global economic inequality.[3] While they examine several competing explanations of both increasing and declining global income inequality, their preferred position is that the major factor is the spread of industrialization that leads to the modernization of poorer regions of the world. The resulting economic gains there lead, in turn, to an overall reduction in global income inequality as those regions draw closer to more affluent areas in terms of economic well-being.

This view is based on several methodological positions, including measuring national income on the basis of "purchasing power parity" (PPP) as opposed to the measure based on "official exchange rates" (FX) preferred by Korzeniewicz and Moran, the major proponents of the idea that global economic inequality is increasing (see also Milanovic 2005).[4] Purchasing power parity takes some independent phenomenon and then compares the cost of it in the countries being measured. The most famous example of this is the *Economist* magazine's Big Mac Index which compares currencies in terms of the cost of a Big Mac in various countries. Studies using official exchange rates (FX) do not make this correction and simply employ official exchange rates in assessing and comparing national income.

In terms of the future, Firebaugh and Goesling foresee in the short run a further decline in global income inequality in the early twenty-first century. This is traceable mainly to the fact that while poor countries will experience an increase in their working-age populations, rich countries will witness a relative decline in such workers and a significant expansion in the elderly population which has moved beyond its working years, or is likely to be employed more marginally than in its prime. While those of working age will earn incomes in poor countries, the elderly in the rich countries will either earn little (compared to their prior incomes) or will not earn any income at all; in fact, they are likely be an ever-greater drain on national resources.

A second factor in the decline in global income inequality is the continued growth and expansion of Asian economies, especially China and, to a lesser extent, India. Because so many people live in those two countries (about 2.6 billion), their income gains will have a profound overall effect on the income of "poor" countries thereby significantly reducing the gap between rich and poor. However, in the longer term, the average income in Asia will come to exceed the world average. The economic growth of China and India will make them, especially China, economic superpowers. They will join the club of rich nations and they, along with the already rich nations, will exacerbate global income inequality.

Korzeniewicz and Moran focus their attention more narrowly on economic inequality and report the differences between their conclusions on this issue (using FX-based data) versus those of Firebaugh and Goesling (using PPP-based data). While there are obviously technical issues involved here in the use of the two types of data (Atkinson and Brandolini 2013; Milanovic 2012), Korzeniewicz and Moran choose to focus on theoretical differences in the two ways of thinking. They argue that Firebaugh and Goesling are interested in "differences between populations in their relative access to welfare," whereas they focus on "relations between populations" (Korzeniewicz and Moran 2007: 567). Firebaugh and Goesling are seen, given the centrality they accord to industrialization, as employing modernization theory (Inkeles 1974) which leads to a focus on individual nations and the degree to which they have, or have not, modernized or industrialized. In contrast, Korzeniewicz and Moran adopt a more systemic – especially world-system – approach that leads to a focus on overall patterns of global interaction (e.g. the integration of labor markets on a global scale). On a more technical note, recent revisions to PPP data suggest that global income inequality has actually increased in more recent years (Milanovic 2012).

Korzeniewicz and Moran compare the economics of Simon Kuznets (Kuznets 1940; Morrisson and Murtin 2013) which is in tune with a modernization approach, to that of Joseph Schumpeter (see Chapter 7) which is more in line with their (world) system approach. Kuznets's work, especially the Kuznets curve, is consistent with a modernization approach. While it sees early development leading to increasing inequality, development eventually leads to less inequality, more equality, in the developing nation. However, what most interests Korzeniewicz and Moran about Kuznets's work is his view that newly developing countries do not necessarily follow the pattern of those that have already developed; they do not necessarily modernize in the same way as did developed countries.

Schumpeter's thinking on "creative destruction" leads to a view of constant change rather than one of modern equilibrium (Schumpeter 1976: 81–7). In fact, Korzeniewicz and Moran argue that combining the insights of Kuznets and Schumpeter leads to a perspective on the world involving a "constant drive toward rising inequality." However, how that plays out in specific nations depends on the actions of various institutions. Their key point, however, is that as relational systems, institutions (e.g. the World Bank) have often served to reduce inequality within high-income nations while increasing between-nation inequality through the exclusion of poorer nations. Such a systemic, institutional approach seems to imply that the best we can hope for in the future is *not* less inequality, but merely a different global reconfiguration of inequality. A significant decline, let alone disappearance, of such inequality would require a substantial transformation of the institutional processes that have characterized the development of the world economy over the last 200 years. Korzeniewicz and Moran do not foresee such a dramatic change, although it is clear that, from a political point of view, they would like to see it happen because only such a change promises a decline in global economic inequality; a more equal world.

RURAL–URBAN INEQUALITY

We turn now to the second major topic in this chapter – the rural–urban relationship, with particular attention to how it relates to global inequality. As we will see, there are important linkages between the two issues, but there is also much more to the relationship between rural and urban, especially as it relates to globalization.

RURAL

In conceiving of the rural from the point of view of globalization, we are generally thinking of agricultural[5] areas in the South. While it is true that there are agricultural areas in the North (e.g. the American Midwest), they are comparatively inconsequential (although not economically) in comparison to the size and local importance of agricultural areas in the South. That being said, it is the case that agricultural areas in the North are, as we will see, profoundly implicated in, and affected by, globalization, although that impact is in many ways more negative than positive.

The South encompasses over 5 billion people and has been seen as being in the "vortex of globalization" (McMichael 2007a: 216–38). This is not the first time the South has played a central role in global relations, especially global agriculture. For example, the British outsourced[6] agricultural production to it (e.g. to India) during the height of their empire. However, contemporary globalization has profoundly affected and altered North–South relationships in agriculture and much else.

Relations of agricultural production

The first of these transformations involve the new *relations of agricultural production*. The crucial development here is the rise of global agribusiness dominated by the North in general, and the US in particular. Also of great importance is the factory farm, with the same points of origin. Both global agribusiness and the factory farm involve new relations of agricultural production (e.g. between global corporations and local farms) compared to relations that existed in and between local, more traditional farms.

Most generally, these new relations of agricultural production have come to be defined by the "law of comparative advantage." In practice, this has come to mean that the South produces what are for it non-traditional products (e.g. flowers, fruit, vegetables, shrimp), for which it comes to have a comparative advantage, and it exports those products to the North. This means that Southern countries are producing and consuming less of their own traditional products, including those that have been the staples of their diet. Instead, they are increasingly coming to consume cheap (sometimes, but often not, cheaper) industrialized food imports from the North (the latter are subject to both great fluctuations in availability depending on the global market for such products and to even greater price fluctuations). These imports not only serve to replace traditional staples, but also to displace large numbers of local farmers who are either forced off the farm or into different types of farming.

For example, thanks, in the opinion of many, to NAFTA, Mexico's inexpensive, traditional, locally grown and produced white maize Mexican tortilla has been replaced to a large degree by yellow corn tortillas mass-produced at perhaps triple the price by agribusinesses in the American Midwest (see Chapter 6). This constitutes a whole new relation of production, in this case between Mexico and the US, which is leading to changes in social class and dietary relationships not only between the US and Mexico, but also for many nations throughout the world.

The US, its agricultural model, and its emphasis on commercial mono-crops and capital-/energy-intensive agriculture are often accorded responsibility (and the blame) for most of these changes. The US model has transformed the rural landscape not only in the South, but throughout much of the world. Indeed, post-WW II Europe was one of the early targets of this transformation through the Marshall Plan. Later, agribusiness disseminated this model to other countries around the globe. It was also fostered by the "green revolution"[7] which, among other things, led to the decline of traditional mixed crops and their replacement by capital-intensive hybrids of wheat, corn, and rice.

Also involved in this is the development and exportation of US-style consumption patterns, in this case of food. This has led to global convergence on a diet that includes a narrowing base of staple grains; increased consumption of animal protein, edible oils, and salt and sugar; and a decline in dietary fiber. Such a diet has contributed, among other things, to a rise in such diseases as diabetes as well as to the global epidemic of obesity (Hashemian and Yach 2007; Popkin and Slining 2013). In fact, in recent years obesity has come to be as common throughout the world as malnutrition (Rinaldo and Ferraro 2012). Even in places like Crete, renowned for its healthy "Mediterranean diet," the expansion of American-style fast food has led to greater obesity and other health problems, even, and most disturbingly, among children (Rosenthal 2008d: A1, A12).

Another US-based development (although the UK is also a huge player in this) – the supermarket revolution – has also played a key role here. It has obviously centralized food processing and retailing, but it has also exerted increasing control over farmers, ranchers, and so on. (The same could be said about the fast-food chain revolution [Ritzer 2012; Schlosser 2005].) However, these farmers and ranchers rarely have binding contracts, are rewarded only if they meet centrally defined quality standards, and have tended to face declining prices for their products because virtually all of the power in this relationship rests with the great supermarket chains. The creation of both public and private standards for things like food quality and packaging are central not only to increasing global inequality (the North tends to set the standards that the South must follow), but also to homogenization of both food production (e.g. industrial agriculture, factory farms) and food consumption (less grain, more animal protein).

Overall, the South is enveloped by new relations of production which, among other things, mean the displacement of local farmers, the transformation of many who remain from being producers of local staples to producers of non-traditional exports for which there is a global demand (e.g. flowers, more exotic fruits and vegetables), involvement in global specialized commodity chains, and so on.

Relations of social production

A second area of concern is **relations of social production**, or how populations survive within international and national institutions that govern material conditions and opportunities to earn a livelihood. Overall, a broad change is occurring in the shift from local solutions of problems relating to food issues to those solutions being put in the hands of global processes of social reproduction. Most generally, commercial agriculture replaces local provisioning. Agricultural markets come to respond to global demand, rather than to local needs, with the result that hunger and deprivation may well increase in local areas. Declining income in less developed rural areas leads people to need to supplement their incomes through off-farm sources such as working on neighboring farms, taking jobs in rural industries/*maquilas*, or relying on remittances from family members who have moved elsewhere, perhaps in the North.

> **Relations of social production:** Processes through which populations survive within institutions that govern material conditions.

These changes in the South have not eliminated poverty and hunger, but have led to a change from poverty/hunger amidst scarcity to poverty/hunger amidst abundance. Neoliberal philosophies and policies, including free trade, serve to advantage the North and its enormous agribusinesses (and supermarkets). In the meantime, rural economies everywhere are in depression and crisis with low prices, declining public supports, rural exodus, increases in rural suicides, and so on. The rural South has been forced to open its farm sectors to the global market (while the North retains huge farm subsidies and trade barriers). The removal of subsidies and barriers, and increasing openness to the global market, has led to declining prices and less income for Southern farmers. De-agrarianization and de-peasantization have been accompanied by the rise of rural industrialization, beginning with export-processing zones.

Mexico's 1965 Border Industrial Program was a key development, leading to the creation of a series of *maquiladoras* designed to compete with the rising economies of East Asia. This sparked the revolutionary movement of low-wage factories and manufacturing jobs from the North to the South. By the early twenty-first century there were 70 million *maquila* jobs in existence, but most who work in those settings take home only about a third of a living wage. As a result, they are forced to supplement their incomes in various ways and, thereby, in a sense, subsidize the factories and their work. But the *maquilas*, themselves, are now being undercut by the increasing importance of low-wage Chinese, and more recently Vietnamese, manufacturing (even the Chinese are now sending work to Vietnam), making even those settings increasingly tenuous in the "race to the bottom" (see Chapter 7).

Relations of resistance

Relations of resistance: Movements opposed to exploitative global practices.

The third issue of concern is "**relations of resistance**." This includes a wide range of consumer (focusing, for example, on issues of food safety), farmer (impact of globalization on rural–urban distribution), farm worker (human rights, pesticide use, worker safety), farmer/peasant (protection of their way of life), and indigenous peasant (fighting for regional, cultural autonomy) movements. Also of importance are the Slow Food Movement (see Chapter 2), land-rights activists, the occupation of land en masse, as well as the transnational peasant movement, Via Campesina, involving nearly 150 farm organizations from 70 countries and millions of farm families. The latter does not reject modernity, but is seeking an alternative to it that involves credit, land, fair prices, and rules of fair trade. Overall, it can be argued that food is the core of the new relations of resistance to globalization around the world.

In spite of a generally bleak picture, there is hope for the future of rural agricultural life. Agricultural life is resilient and capable of taking on new forms. (In fact, agriculture in the US and elsewhere experienced an unusual period of great and increasing prosperity because of the global boom in food prices in 2008 [Streitfeld 2008: 1–16], although that was ended by the Great Recession). At the same time, there are social and environmental limits to the corporate globalization of agriculture. Once these limits are reached, it will be possible to envision a new, robust form of agriculture dedicated to social and ecological sustainability. This holds out the promise (hope?) of a renewal and a revaluing of agrarian life. It also holds out hope of greater economic equality between rural and urban areas, as well as between the South and the North. However, such a change may require the kinds of larger, systemic changes discussed by Korzeniewicz and Moran.

URBAN

The world has always been predominantly rural, but some time between 2000 and 2010 a "watershed in human history" occurred as for "the first time the urban population of the earth" outnumbered the rural (Davis 2007: 1). (Figure 13.1 shows the world's largest cities in 2014.) However, cities have been central to both scholarly and popular discourse on globalization from the beginning of interest in it as a topic and a phenomenon (Timberlake and Ma 2007). Cities were seen as "cosmopolitan" (Alarcón 2012; Beck 2007; Short 2013), and therefore inherently global, because they encompassed a range of cultures, ethnicities, languages, and consumer products. Cities also exerted a powerful influence (cultural, political, and economic) over surrounding areas. The many city-based organizations were also linked, through elaborate networks, to organizations in other cities throughout the home country and the world. The system of national and global cities was hierarchical with substantial flows of people, information, and objects moving both up and down the hierarchy.

The most important of the world's cities are *global cities* (Sassen 1991), with only New York, London, and Tokyo usually included in that elite category. It is no coincidence that the world's most important stock exchanges are located in those cities. More generally, those cities tend to be chosen by many organizations as sites for key offices through which they

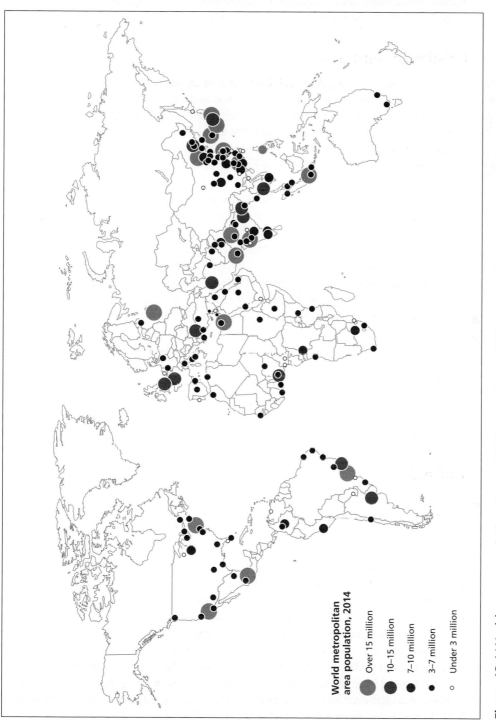

Figure 13.1 World metro population. The world's largest cities in 2014. Source: data from Demographia World Urban Areas, 10th annual edition, May 2014 Revision. Table 1.

exert great control over the world's political economy and, in the process, accrue great riches to themselves and the denizens of those cities.

Global cities

The idea of a global, or a world, city has a long history, but it has exploded as a topic of interest in the study of globalization since the publication of Saskia Sassen's *The Global City: New York, London, and Tokyo* (1991). She, and many others, have continued to work on the topic in the intervening years and to advance our thinking on global cities (Abrahamson 2004; Brenner and Keil 2006; Bulkeley et al. 2013; Hudson 2010; Marcuse and van Kempen 2000; Sassen 2012c; Timberlake and Ma 2007). Sassen clearly embeds her notion of **global cities** in the process of globalization and focuses on economic, especially capitalistic, globalization. In this context, she privileges the three cities mentioned above on the basis of their place in the new world economy. Specifically, they are the key locations for leading industries and marketplaces, the centers of the production and creation of innovative, cutting-edge financial services, the homes of new financial, legal, and accountancy products, and the settings from which businesses and organizations exercise global command and control.

> **Global cities:** Key cities in the global, especially capitalist, economy.

To Sassen, and others, a key point is that global cities are central nodes in a new international division of labor. Of great importance are the linkages among and between these global cities and the flows among and between them. In many ways the global cities have more in common with one another than with the smaller cities and the hinterlands within their own country. They are also more integrated into the global economy than those in hinterlands.

More recently, Saskia Sassen has argued that the economies in global cities are also becoming the primary geopolitical units (Sassen 2012a). She argues that geopolitics will be determined less by the US and China, than by the approximately 20 top strategic worldwide urban networks. According to Sassen, this future will be heavily influenced by firm-to-firm relationships in the global economy that capitalize on specialized niches in their respective global cities. She argues that these "geopolitical urban vectors" form the infrastructure for the global economy, with global cities serving as the axes around which regional economies are organized. As such, state-to-state transactions will become less important than transactions between these "urban vectors." In the next decade, the most significant urban vectors will be as follows.

- Washington, New York, and Chicago. "These cities are becoming more important geopolitically than the United States is as a country" (Sassen 2012b).
- Beijing, Hong Kong, and Shanghai. While Beijing is the center of power in China, Shanghai is the primary financial and industrial center.
- Berlin and Frankfurt. These German cities are the geopolitical center of the European Union.
- Istanbul and Ankara. While Istanbul continues to be considered the gateway between the East and West, Ankara plays a jointly critical role in regional geopolitics.
- São Paulo, Rio de Janeiro, and Brasília. These cities are the driving force behind Brazil as another rising global power.
- Cairo and Beirut. These cities are redefining the relationship between the Middle East and the world, including Beirut's deep global politico-economic networks.

- Geneva, Vienna, and Nairobi. "These cities have the critical mass and mix of institutions long devoted to social questions and justice for the powerless, with Nairobi's habitat increasingly important in a rapidly urbanizing world and a powerful new leadership. All three cities – long overshadowed by global finance and mega-militaries – could emerge as crucial actors in making a global commons, which will be important for the global economy." (Sassen 2012b: 8)

However, others have a much more expansive sense of what constitutes such cities and recognize that the number of such cities is likely to grow in the future. Many have come to prefer the far broader notion of *world cities* to the highly limited, and limiting, notion of global cities (Beckfield and Alderson 2006: Lin 2012).

World cities

John Friedmann's work on world cities pre-dates that of Sassen and offers such a more expansive view of these cities (for a representation of different mappings of world cities, see Figure 13.2). While Friedmann's (1986) early work on world cities ranked cities on the basis of mostly economic criteria (the degree to which major financial institutions make the city their home base; the degree to which MNCs are headquartered there; the degree to which other international institutions are based there; the speed with which the business service sector there is growing; importance as a center of manufacturing[8]; the degree to which it is an important transportation hub; the city's population size), his more recent work used a broader set of criteria.

The focus in Friedmann's (1995) newer system is the global reach of the organizations found in these cities (their geographic scale and their intensity). There are four types of global reach, or what Friedmann calls "global articulations." It is interesting that at the top of his list is "global financial articulations" leading Friedmann to privilege the same three cities categorized by Sassen's early work on global cities. Also of interest is the fact that the second category, "Multinational Articulations" is also based explicitly on economic criteria. However, even the other categories are shaped by economic factors.

Global Financial Articulations: New York, London, Tokyo
Multinational Articulations: Miami, Los Angeles, Frankfurt, Amsterdam, Singapore
Important National Articulations: Paris, Zurich, Madrid, Mexico City, Sao Paulo, Seoul, Sydney
Subnational/Regional Articulations: Osaka-Kobe, San Francisco, Seattle, Houston, Chicago, Boston, Vancouver, Toronto, Montreal, Hong Kong, Milan, Lyon, Barcelona, Munich, Dusseldorf

This differentiation reflects important changes in world cities. An interesting example of this is the place of Tokyo in global financial articulations. Tokyo is already the financial capital of Asia, but it is being pressed by other cities such as Hong Kong and Singapore, as well as Mumbai (formerly Bombay) (Alberts 2010; Fackler 2007b). Tokyo's goal is not only to attract more foreign investors and investment, but also to lure more finance professionals from the West to come to work in Tokyo. Behind this is a realization that Japan, like the US, is losing its preeminence as a manufacturing power and needs to find alternative sources of income and wealth. The US and Great Britain long recognized this and moved aggressively

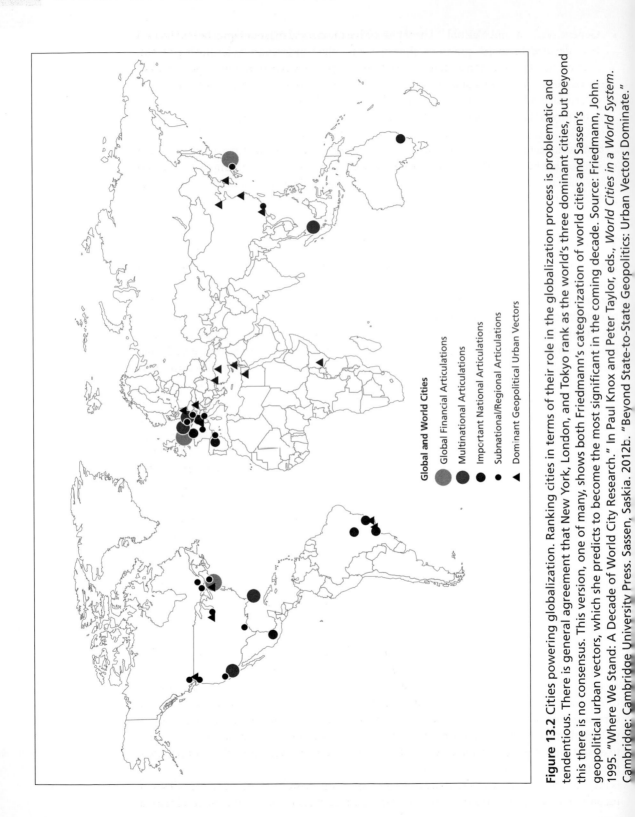

Figure 13.2 Cities powering globalization. Ranking cities in terms of their role in the globalization process is problematic and tendentious. There is general agreement that New York, London, and Tokyo rank as the world's three dominant cities, but beyond this there is no consensus. This version, one of many, shows both Friedmann's categorization of world cities and Sassen's geopolitical urban vectors, which she predicts to become the most significant in the coming decade. Source: Friedmann, John. 1995. "Where We Stand: A Decade of World City Research." In Paul Knox and Peter Taylor, eds., *World Cities in a World System.* Cambridge: Cambridge University Press. Sassen, Saskia. 2012b. "Beyond State-to-State Geopolitics: Urban Vectors Dominate."

Global and World Cities

○ Global Financial Articulations
● Multinational Articulations
● Important National Articulations
• Subnational/Regional Articulations
▲ Dominant Geopolitical Urban Vectors

into activities like finance (as well as many other business services), but Japan lagged behind in this area. There remain serious barriers in Japan to such expansion including high taxes, an onerous regulatory system, bureaucratization, comparative lack of English-speakers, and the need for more modern and upscale buildings and facilities (e.g. health clubs) to house those they hope to attract to work and to do business in Japan.

A more recent index was created in a collaboration between *Foreign Policy* magazine, consulting firm A.T. Kearney, and the Chicago Council on Global Affairs (2010). Their list of global cities was ranked by a broader set of criteria, including business activity, human capital, information exchange, cultural experience, and political engagement. Their top ten cities were (in descending order) New York, London, Tokyo, Paris, Hong Kong, Chicago, Los Angeles, Singapore, Sydney, and Seoul.

Also indicative of the rapidly changing nature of the world is the relative absence of Chinese cities as compared with the rest of the world. This will likely not be the case for long. For example, *Foreign Policy* and the McKinsey Global Institute (2012) ranked "the most dynamic cities of 2025" using a much more basic set of criteria (based solely on projections for population growth and GDP per capita growth). Six of the top ten cities are in China. The ranking (in descending order) is Shanghai, Beijing, Tianjin, São Paulo, Guangzhou, Shenzen, New York, Chongqing, Moscow, and Tokyo. Chinese cities will become increasingly important (and powerful) in the global economy and among world cities more generally. This leads to the key point that global changes, especially in the economy, are so rapid that changes in the world cities and their ordering are likely to occur with great frequency and rapidity.

The categorization of cities in these ways clearly conveys a sense of hierarchization, and therefore inequality (see below), among them (Beaverstock et al. 2002). However, as Friedmann notes, there are other important inequalities to take into consideration. For one thing, as one descends this list of cities, and the countries in which they exist, we encounter more and more deprived, marginal, even subsistence economies in which people in general fare far worse than those in the world cities at the top of the list. For another, there are many other cities, even large cities, in the world that are not listed in any of these iterations and their economies are likely to be in even worse shape. Furthermore, even the global cities are likely to have internal inequalities with the well-to-do living in elite areas of the cities, while the poor might live in inner-city ghettos (more the America pattern) or in suburban squatter housing (more the European and Latin American pattern). The key cities are much more tied into the world economy than the hinterlands with the result that those who live in the latter are more likely to be isolated from that economy and therefore less likely to be well-off than those who reside in the cities.

Why are global/world cities still important in a supposedly flat world of computer-enhanced telecommunications? Since everyone can, at least theoretically, have access to this system from anywhere, the world's great cities should cease to be so important. However, contradicting the flat-world thesis once again, these cities remain important. The cities are, in effect, "hills," if not "mountains," that are yet another factor (see above on economic inequality) giving the lie to the idea of a flat world. In fact, beyond their continued centrality in the global economy, these cities tend to be the centers for the various aspects of the telecommunications industry, as well as the places where the most important innovations take place.

Increasingly, global/world cities can be seen, following Castells (2000), as key nodes in a variety of networks and flows. In fact, leaders in those cities compete to make their city a central node in one or more flows and networks. For example, one type of flow is that of people, especially airline passengers. Cities compete with each other to become hubs for airlines, that is, central nodes where many flights connect and through which many passengers flow (see Figure 1.1). It is relatively easy to quantify the number of passengers passing through such nodes and thereby to determine whether a city has been successful in becoming a central node, at least in this particular flow (Choi, Barnett, and Bum-Soo 2006; Sassen 2012a). This means, of course, that locales (e.g. airport hubs) remain important, even in a world increasingly dominated by networks and flows.

Some have argued that the global, or world, city network is of such great importance that it can be equated with globalization (Timberlake and Ma 2007: 254–71). While it is clear that cities, especially global/world cities, are important in globalization, this is clearly a bit of hyperbole, especially given the many different aspects of globalization discussed throughout this book.

A major empirical study of the world-city system demonstrated that there is a fairly strong hierarchy among world cities and a small number of them have a monopoly on power and prestige (Alderson and Beckfield 2004). At the top in this study were the cities most often identified as world cities – New York, London, and Tokyo. However, this research indicated that Tokyo may be more powerful than is usually thought and Paris may need to be considered as being in the first rank of world cities. There is also a strong relationship between the power and the prestige of a world city; that is, cities with power also tend to rank high in prestige. World cities tend be differentiated between "core" and "peripheral" cities, with the former being far more central to the global system. There is also a strong relationship between the position of world cities and the nation-states in which they exist in terms of the degree to which both exist in the core or in the periphery of the world system.

Megacities (and beyond)

Megacities:
Cities with a population greater than 10 million people.

Megacities are defined as cities with continuous urban development and a population greater than 10 million people. Of course, at least some of the global and world cities discussed above meet that criterion (e.g. New York, Tokyo), but what is striking is the large and growing number of cities in the South that can be defined as megacities. The largest is Jakarta with 26.7 million inhabitants as of 2013, but others of note are Seoul (22.9 million), Delhi (22.8 million), Shanghai (21.8 million), and Manila (21.2 million). And these cities are expected to grow dramatically in the coming years with, for example, Shanghai reaching a population of 31 million by 2025 (Foreign Policy and McKinsey Global Institute 2012).

Such population concentrations bring with them enormous problems associated with the large number of very poor people who will be living in these cities, especially in the third world. Indeed many of those problems already exist as we will soon discuss in the case of Karachi. More generally, Mike Davis (2007: 19) envisions a planet of urban slums that are a far cry from what the visionaries had in mind for the development of cities:

> the cities of the future, rather than being made out of glass and steel as envisioned by earlier generations of urbanists, are instead largely constructed out of crude brick, straw, recycled plastic, cement blocks and scrap wood. Instead of cities of light soaring toward heaven, much of the twenty-first-century urban world squats in squalor, surrounded by pollution, excrement, and decay.

Of course, these megacities, even the most blighted of them, will have wealthy residents as well, and thus they will be (and are) sites of some of the most profound inequalities in the world.

One other point about not only megacities, but also global and world cities, is worth mentioning. That is the growth of the **megalopolis**, or a long chain of interconnected cities with the potentiality of becoming one huge city. There has long been talk, and we are closer to the reality, of a megalopolis that runs from Boston through New York to Washington, DC and another that stretches from San Diego to San Francisco (and perhaps ultimately to Seattle, or even Vancouver). However, of greatest interest here are the emerging megalopolises in the South. For example, the megalopolis that has Lagos as its fulcrum will likely stretch along the Gulf of Guinea from Benin City to Accra; by 2020 it will have a population of about 60 million people (roughly the size of the East Coast of the US). However, "it probably will also be the biggest single footprint of urban poverty on earth" (Davis 2007: 6). Poverty, however, is not the only problem that tends to be centered in the megacity and in cities in general.

> **Megalopolis:** A long chain of interconnected cities with the potentiality of becoming one huge city.

CITIES: THE MAIN LOCUS OF GLOBAL PROBLEMS

While global or world cities are generally rich, powerful, prestigious, and the main beneficiaries of globalization (for example, the income and other benefits derived from being at the heart of global financial flows), it is also the case that cities, including the global or world cities, are especially hard hit by a wide range of global problems. Among other things, it is the world's cities that have been the targets of major terrorist attacks; the destination for large numbers of immigrants, many of them without authorization, who are impoverished and in need of public assistance; the settings where large numbers of those affected by global health problems are likely to end up in search of medical help, and so on. Thus, according to Bauman (2003: 101), "cities have become dumping grounds for globally forgotten problems."

In spite of their global nature and source, dealing with these problems becomes a local city problem; it is a political problem for the city. This represents a huge difficulty for city officials who often lack the economic resources to even begin to deal with many of these problems. Furthermore, since the sources are global, whatever city officials seek to do is doomed to failure. Thus, for example, the Mayor of London is helpless in dealing with the roots of terrorism in the tribal territories of Pakistan, the global epidemic of HIV/AIDS, or the air pollution being generated in nearby cities on the Continent. To quote Bauman (2003: 102) again: "Local politics – and particularly urban politics – has become hopelessly overloaded." While all large cities face great, perhaps overwhelming problems, it is the large and impoverished cities in the South that are the most affected by such problems. We see almost all of these problems in Karachi.

Karachi, Pakistan

Karachi is not on the list of world cities, but it is enormous; with 20.9 million people, it is currently the world's seventh-largest city. In fact, it is the fastest-growing megacity in the world (between 2000 and 2010, it grew by more than 80%). There were 9.8 million residents in Karachi in 1998; by 2020 it is projected that it will have 27.5 million inhabitants. No city has ever grown at such a rapid pace in the world. As a context for this growth, Karachi had only 1 million inhabitants in 1950. With a population density of 67,300 people per square mile, it is one of the most densely populated cities in the world (by comparison, the New York metro area has a population density of 4,600 people per square mile).

Based on size alone, one might think of Karachi as a world city, but it is a backwater economically and in many other ways; it is one of the main examples of a city that is overwhelmed by its slums (Davis 2007). Among its more appalling characteristics are:

- a deteriorating infrastructure that was built for a much smaller population;
- city services, including power, that are unreliable if not non-existent for many;
- massive slums;
- clean drinking water that is difficult to obtain and costly;
- enormous growth, but growth that is largely unplanned and building that is uncontrolled;
- ubiquitous garbage that is a source of work and income for many (pickers who "work" in dumps);
- enormous traffic jams and a cacophony of noises produced by them and other factors that is sometimes overwhelming;
- economic activity that takes place mainly on the streets;
- worsening air pollution;
- gang violence;
- one of the world's largest populations of street children (1.2–1.5 million);
- a murder rate 25% higher than in any other megacity in the world;
- a ranking of sixth "least-liveable" city in the world by *The Economist*.

The plight of street children in Karachi is especially bad. It is estimated that "90 percent of Karachi street children regularly sniff glue or other solvents and about 85 percent to 90 percent are survivors of physical or sexual abuse" (Jilani 2013). Chemicals (e.g. toluene and benzene) in the glue often lead to self-mutilation, aggression, and deliriousness, but the glue is used because it is easily obtained and numbs users to a horrible reality. Because of the glue, many children die from Sudden Sniffing Death Syndrome.

Nevertheless, Karachi remains a lure for those outside the city who are impressed with what new residents can acquire there compared to what can be acquired in rural Pakistan. In other words, rural Pakistan is even poorer than Karachi. Thus, more, hundreds of thousands more, people come every year to Karachi and as the numbers swell, living conditions grow harsher.

Surprisingly, some observers see Karachi as offering a positive model; a demonstration of how millions of people survive through constant improvisation. With few regular jobs available, one such improvisation involves setting up informal businesses that sell anything and everything along almost every street to take advantage of traffic jams and any other selling opportunity that might come along.

Interestingly, although it is a city that is largely excluded from most global flows, or at least most beneficial flows, Karachi, and Pakistan more generally, is the object (e.g. flows of drugs and crime) and the source of many negative global flows (see Chapters 11 and 12). In terms of the latter, it is the breeding ground for the Taliban and other terrorist organizations. The ranks of unemployed youth – about 33% of whom are illiterate – provide a large pool of vulnerable and uneducated recruits for their criminal networks. The security of food, shelter, and community are attractive to such destitute individuals that might ultimately end up as part of the global flows of crime or terrorism. In addition, the city's ports have become important way stations for global flows of narcotics and weapons smuggling. Aside from negative global flows, Karachi exists largely outside the process of globalization, at least its most beneficial aspects. While it remains as Pakistan's financial center and is home to much of its industry, it lacks all of the advanced productive service functions associated with a world city (Qutub 2005). Indeed, economic globalization (including trade liberalization) and economic migration have arguably had a negative impact on Pakistan's human development and well-being (Hussain et al. 2010). In particular, the limited degree to which Karachi, and Pakistan more generally, has become integrated within the global economy has also brought significant income inequality.

CHAPTER SUMMARY

Global class inequality is a major source of instability and conflict. This chapter analyzes economic inequality among societies as well as some of the ways in which it is manifest in rural and urban areas.

One of the most important theories of global economic inequality is world-systems theory. By dividing the world into core, periphery, and semi-periphery – and looking at their interrelationships – world-systems theory explains how economic inequalities were created and continue to be reproduced today. In particular, resources and cheap labor flow from the periphery to the core, enriching the core countries and maintaining the periphery's weaker state of development.

Paul Collier focuses on the poorest billion people, nearly 70% of whom reside in Africa. The nation-states that contain the bottom billion are confronted with four traps – a conflict trap (unstable political problems with continuing rounds of violent conflict), natural resources trap (heavy dependence on natural resources, which impedes broader economic development), the trap of being landlocked with bad neighbors (who impede transport of exports), and the bad governance trap (bad policies which can inhibit or destroy the economy).

Although there has been an increase in aggregate global life expectancy, disparities in terms of health are growing. The declining access of the global poor to health services and nutrition leads to a decline in productivity levels. They are also affected disproportionately by various diseases, hunger, and malnutrition. Developing countries face a "double nutrition burden" involving both those who do not have adequate access to food as well as those who have access to too much unhealthy food (relatively inexpensive food that is high in fat, cholesterol, and sugar). This contributes to the increasing cost of dealing with chronic diseases in developing countries.

There also exists a significant global digital divide with the poor lacking access not only to computers and the Internet, but also to basic infrastructure such as electricity. This contributes to a widening economic divide between the North and the South. Language represents another barrier for the poor in the South, since 80% of the content on the Internet is in English.

Debates over the relationship between globalization and global inequality persist. Firebaugh and Goesling suggest that the gains from modernization in developing countries have led to a reduction in income and health inequality. They also foresee a further decline in global economic inequality due to the economic renaissance of Asia. Korzeniewicz and Moran reach a rather different conclusion using a theoretical approach based on the world-systems approach. They argue that the world experiences a "constant drive towards increasing inequality."

The chapter also explores the rural–urban differentiation and its relationship to globalization. The term rural refers primarily to agricultural areas. Globalization has deeply altered

North–South relations in agriculture. For instance, the relations of agricultural production have been altered due to the rise of global agribusiness and factory farms. In this scenario, the South produces non-traditional products for export, and becomes increasingly dependent on industrialized food exports from the North. Consequently, this leads to a replacement of the staple diet as well as the displacement of local farmers. As commercial agriculture replaces local provisioning, the relations of social production are also altered. Rural economies are exposed to low prices and mass migration. However, there also emerge global relations of resistance through a broad range of farmer, consumer, farm-worker, and indigenous movements.

Sassen uses the concept of global cities to describe the three urban centers of New York, London, and Tokyo as economic centers that exert control over the world's political economy. A broader view of world cities is offered by John Friedmann. World cities are categorized as such based on the global reach of organizations found in them. Not only are there inequalities between these cities, there also exist inequalities within each city. Alternatively, following Castells, these cities can be seen as important nodes in a variety of global networks.

Although cities are major beneficiaries of globalization, they are also the most severely affected by global problems. Therefore the city faces unique political problems, wherein it is often fruitlessly seeking to deal locally with global problems.

DISCUSSION QUESTIONS

1. Examine the four "traps" that confront the bottom billion. How does globalization affect these "traps"? To what degree does such a focus blame the bottom billion for their problems?

2. Compare and contrast the ways in which world-systems theory and the idea of the "bottom billion" explain global economic inequality.

3. Examine the trend toward inequality within nations in the context of globalization. Compare and contrast the two perspectives on inequality discussed in the chapter.

4. Examine the gap between rural and urban areas across the globe. How is that gap affected by global flows?

5. Discuss the impact of global flows on the agricultural sector.

6. Compare Karachi, Pakistan to the global cities.

ADDITIONAL READINGS

Immanuel Wallerstein. *The Modern World-System: Capitalist Agriculture and the Origins of the European World-Economy in the 16th Century*. New York: Academic Press, 1974.

Salvatore Babones and Christopher Chase-Dunn, eds. *Routledge International Handbook of World-Systems Analysis*. New York: Routledge, 2012.

James Galbraith. *Inequality and Instability: A Study of the World Economy Just Before the Crisis*. New York: Oxford University Press, 2012.

Paul Collier. *The Bottom Billion: Why the Poorest Countries Are Failing and What Can Be Done About It*. New York: Oxford University Press, 2007.

Gili S. Drori. *Global E-Litism: Digital Technology, Social Inequality, and Transnationality*. New York: Worth, 2006.

Mike Davis. *Planet of Slums*. London: Verso, 2007.

Saskia Sassen. *The Global City: New York, London, and Tokyo*. Princeton: Princeton University Press, 1991.

Saskia Sassen. *Cities in a World Economy*, 4th edn. Thousand Oaks, CA: Sage, 2012.

Scott Sernau. *Social Inequality in a Global Age*, 4th edn. Thousand Oaks, CA: Sage, 2014.

NOTES ···

1 There is a third area, the semi-periphery, but that will not concern us here.

2 Famously, Lord John Maynard Keynes (1935), a major economist and key figure at Bretton Woods, argued that "In the long run we are all dead."

3 For an analysis and critique of Firebaugh's focus on income inequality, see Nell (2005).

4 Korzeniewicz and Moran (2007: 565–92); Babones (2007) supports their methodological position.

5 There are, of course, non-agricultural rural areas (e.g. small towns, factories in small towns), but they are of relatively minor significance, at least in this context.

6 See Ritzer and Lair (2007).

7 A post-WW II revolution in agriculture brought about by research, new technologies, new farming methods, and the like.

8 This would seem now to be an increasingly dated criterion, especially in the North.

GLOBAL INEQUALITIES II

INEQUALITIES OF RACE, ETHNICITY, GENDER, AND SEXUALITY[1]

Globalization: A Basic Text, Second Edition. George Ritzer and Paul Dean.
© 2015 John Wiley & Sons, Ltd. Published 2015 by John Wiley & Sons, Ltd.

This chapter will examine a wide range of relationships that can be subsumed under the heading of global majority–minority relations (Chapman and Werthheimer 1990; Yetman 1991). The focus will be on the problems and difficulties experienced by minority groups, but it will be presented in the context of the fact that many of those difficulties are traceable to the thoughts (e.g. prejudice) and, more importantly, the actions (e.g. discrimination) of the majority group (Jackson 2007). The majority–minority relationships to be covered here are *dominant and subordinate races and ethnic groups, male dominance over females*, and *heterosexual dominance of homosexuals and lesbians*. This builds upon two other dimensions of majority–minority relations that have been discussed in the last chapter and various other places in this book, the *power of the upper social classes over those lower in the stratification system* and the *power and control of the North over the South*. In all cases, although to varying degrees, those in a dominant group or category are not only superordinate, but also prone to taking actions that exploit and, in many cases, injure, if not at times destroy, members of subordinate groups.

Since we will deal with an array of minority groups in this chapter, it is important to point out that many of their experiences and problems overlap and intersect in various ways. Thus, they need to be examined in the context of the key concept of **intersectionality**, or the idea that members of any given minority group are affected by the nature of their position in other arrangements of social inequality (Chow et al. 2011; Collins 2000).[2] This concept was developed, at least initially, to deal with the situation confronting women as a minority group, but it can be extended to all minority groups. Minority-group members are seen as being enmeshed in a "matrix of oppression" that involves their gender, race, ethnic group, sexual orientation, age, social class, and the part of the globe (North or South) in which they live. All of these variables can be seen as "vectors of oppression" and minority-group members are likely to be affected by many of them. Furthermore, the experience of a member of any given minority group is not simply additive, but the disadvantages change, as do their effects, as the number of minority statuses occupied, and vectors of oppression experienced, multiply. Thus, for example, one of the most disadvantaged groups of people in the world is composed of those who occupy simultaneously the following categories – a female, black, Ibo (an African tribe found primarily in Nigeria), working-class, lesbian, adolescent from the global South. Conversely, an example of one of the most advantaged groups of people in the world would be a male, white, Anglo-Saxon, upper-class, heterosexual, adult from the global North.

Inter-sectionality: Members of any minority group are affected by their position in other arrangements of social inequality.

DEFINING MAJORITY–MINORITY RELATIONS

What encompasses all of these categories and groups is the broad distinction between majority and minority groups. All of those in the second set of categories mentioned above (male, white, Anglo-Saxon, upper-class, heterosexual, adult from the global North), alone or, more extremely, in combination with one another, are in the majority group, while those in the first set (female, black, Ibo, lower-class, homosexual, adolescent from the global South) are in the minority group. What most interests us here is the nature of majority and minority groups *and* the ways in which they relate to one another in a global context. However, the distinction between majority and minority raises a number of questions: How you might ask, can, for example, the white race be a majority group when it is by a wide margin outnumbered in the world by those in the other races? Or, how can women be a minority when they outnumber men? The answers lie in the sociological definitions of majority and minority, definitions which do *not* rely on the numerical size of a group. The classic example of this is apartheid South Africa where the whites were vastly outnumbered by blacks, but it was the whites who set up and controlled a system that oppressed blacks.

Rather than numbers, the definitions of majority and minority rely on money, prestige, and power (or, as the classic social theorist Max Weber [1921/1968] put it, class, status, and power). A **minority group** is in a subordinate position in wealth, power, and/or prestige (status), while a **majority group** is in a superordinate position in wealth, power, and/or prestige (status).[3] Thus, it is a concern for superordination/subordination that runs through our discussion of the various minority groups in this chapter.

In more general terms, we are interested in social stratification and the relationship between majority and minority groups within stratified systems. This relationship is part of a general tendency to create hierarchies as, for example, among races (Bashi and McDaniel 1997), and ethnic groups (Noel 1968). The nature of these hierarchies varies from society to society and from one time to another. As a result of this, of great interest and importance is the relationship, especially superordination–subordination, between, for example, races and ethnic groups within given societies (e.g. whites and blacks in apartheid-era South Africa and after), between areas of the world dominated by different racial and ethnic groups (North–South), and over time (e.g. the relationship among Ibos and other tribes – Yoruba and Hausa – in Nigeria, or between the Tutsi and Hutu in Burundi, over the years). From a racial perspective, of concern globally is the changing relationship between North America and Europe dominated (although this is changing) by whites, Africa by blacks, and Asia by Asians. From an ethnic perspective, Huntington's thinking on civilizations (see Chapter 8) is highly relevant since it is based on cultural (the heart of ethnicity), rather than racial, differences. Of greatest relevance in that context is, as we have seen, the super-ordination of (ethnic) whites in the West and the subordination of all other ethnic groups. Contemporary challenges to that hierarchy are leading to economic conflict between the West (US and Europe) and Asia and, at least from Huntington's perspective, the potential for bloody conflict between the West and the Islamic world (Muslims would be an ethnic group from this perspective).

A concern with majority–minority relations, with stratification, inherently involves an interest in conflict, if not violence (Collins 1975). That is, all majority/minority relations are fraught with at least the potential for conflict because of the interest of members of the majority group in maintaining or enhancing their privileged position and that of minority-group members in improving theirs (or, at least, preventing it from declining any further). As a general rule, these conflicts, potential or real, are resolved in favor of the majority group because it has far greater resources (money, power) than the minority group. At times, potential conflict becomes real and even descends into violence (e.g. ethnic conflict between Tutsis and Hutus in Burundi and among various ethnic groups in the former Yugoslavia; see below).

Most work on majority–minority relations has dealt with them within the context of a specific nation-state (for example, South Africa, Brazil, or the US[4]), but our focus is on those relations in a global context. In fact, all of the minority (and majority) groups have been represented, at least implicitly, in many of the preceding chapters. They are often represented most generally by the North–South distinction that runs through the book. As a general rule, it could be argued that the North is characterized by more majority-group members, while the South has more minority-group members.[5] Furthermore, it has

Minority group:
A group of people in a subordinate position in wealth, power, and/or prestige (status).

Majority group:
A group of people in a superordinate position in wealth, power, and/or prestige (status).

long been the case, and it continues to this day, that the North has dominated, controlled, exploited, and oppressed the South.

Beyond the overriding distinction between North and South, there are many examples from preceding chapters that relate to majority–minority relations. One specific example (Chapter 10) concerns migration. People in the majority categories are more likely to be able to move freely, while those in minority categories are more likely to be either immobile, forced to move, or not given authorization when migrating. Further, it is those in the latter categories who are more likely to be moving, when they can, from South to North (as well as South to South). Those in the former categories are highly unlikely to move from the North to the South. Another example from an earlier chapter (13) relates to the bottom billion. Most of the bottom billion are in the South and greatly overrepresented in the bottom billion are those in most of the other minority groups. In contrast, few from the bottom billion are in the North where we tend to find more members of several of the majority groups.

Historically, many of the processes discussed in Chapter 3 can be said to have had much the same kind of relationship to majority–minority relations. This is clearly true of imperialism, colonialism, development, Westernization, and Americanization. That is, all of these processes tended to be creations of majority groups and to work to their advantage and to the disadvantage of minority groups. Indeed, these processes often involved the *creation* of a minority group (e.g. Indians after the British colonized India) to control and oppress. It is also often argued that neoliberalism, especially neoliberal economics, helps those in the advantaged categories and hurts, often badly, those in the disadvantaged categories (although defenders of neoliberalism suggest it helps all groups). Also relevant in this context is Edward Said's (1979/1994; see also Said [1993]) work (to be discussed in more detail in the Appendix) on Orientalism. **Orientalism** was (and still is, to some degree[6]) a set of ideas and texts produced in the West that served as the basis to dominate, control, and exploit the Orient (the East) (Munif 2012).

> **Orientalism**: Ideas, texts produced in the West the basis of the domination, control, exploitation of the East.

Another way to think of majority–minority relations and their relationship to globalization is to return to our definition of globalization in Chapter 1 and its major dimensions. First, it could be argued that those in the minority categories are far less likely to participate in the globe's positive flows of, for example, money, commodities, food, health care, technologies, and the like. Conversely, those in the majority categories are likely to be in the thick of these flows, both as creators and recipients.

Of course, the opposite is the case for negative flows (Chapter 12). Those in minority groups are more likely to be on the receiving end of such negative flows as borderless diseases, crime, corruption, war, and most environmental problems. Those in the majority groups certainly cannot completely avoid these negative flows, but they are far better able to insulate and protect themselves from them. Furthermore, those in majority groups often initiate negative flows (armaments, global warming) that have profoundly negative effects on minority groups.

Paul Gilroy's (1993) *The Black Atlantic: Modernity and Double Consciousness* is an important example of work on majority–minority relations that stresses global flows. As the title makes clear, Gilroy is particularly interested in race. In studying race, he moves away from a focus on races within the context of structures (such as the state[7]) and instead examines the flows that relate to blacks involved in the Atlantic region: "I have settled on an image of ships across the spaces between Europe, America, Africa and the Caribbean as a central organizing symbol…. The image of a ship … in motion …" (Gilroy 1993: 4). This allows him to encompass not only the flow of slaves on the "middle passage," the later return of some blacks to Africa, as well as the circulation of activists, ideas, books, works of art, etc., that relate to blacks and race relations. All are seen as involved in "displacements, migrations, and journeys" (Gilroy 1993: 111), as flowing across the Black Atlantic. Similarly, Gilroy (1993: 218) argues for the need to move away from a focus on national boundaries and in the direction of "the web of diaspora identities and concerns that I have labeled the Black Atlantic." In these ways, Gilroy offers a fluid sense of race instead of hard-and-fast definitions of race (and ethnicity).

This brings us to the other key component of our definition of globalization – structures that inhibit and expedite flows. Another way of discussing the advantages of the majority groups is to say that they are better able than minority groups to create barriers between themselves and various negative flows. These barriers can include border controls in the nation-states dominated by advantaged groups, local actions such as creating gated communities patrolled by guards, and even individual actions such as having alarm systems in one's home. Those in minority categories can afford few, if any, of these kinds of protective barriers.

Then there are structures that expedite flows. On the one hand, those in advantaged groups are able to create structures that greatly enhance positive or protective flows. For example, in advantaged locales, the police and medical systems allow personnel to flow easily and quickly through well-established structures (e.g. 911 phone calls leading to a series of actions resulting in help arriving quickly, elderly people with medical alert buttons and the expensive contact networks associated with them that allow such people to summon help even if they can't get to a phone). Clearly, those in disadvantaged categories have little or no access to such structures and therefore to the positive flows expedited by them.

On the other hand, there are a number of structures that expedite various negative flows and those structures are more likely to dump into, and to be found in, areas dominated by minority groups. For example, a variety of illegal structures allow the relatively free flow of weapons into and through areas dominated by minority groups. On the other hand, there are much stronger structures in place that prevent their flow into advantaged areas dominated by majority groups. To take another, much more specific example, people in disadvantaged categories are more likely to live in close proximity to disease vectors (malaria-bearing mosquitoes, pigs carrying swine flu), with the result that they are at greater risk of contracting various diseases, including malaria and swine flu. In contrast, majority-group members are far more likely to live in a world where they are more protected, or even widely separated, from mosquitoes carrying disease or live pigs, to say nothing of the sources of many other diseases.

There is another way of discussing all of this that relates to other distinctions made in Chapter 1. For one thing, minority statuses relating to race, ethnicity, gender, class, sexual orientation, age, and living in the South are likely, in and of themselves, to serve as "subtle" barriers that impede many positive flows. People in those categories are not likely to participate, or at least participate equally, in those flows. For example, there are no physical barriers, no walls, between Muslims and Christians in Europe, or Hispanics and Anglos in the US, but the mere fact of being a Muslim or a Hispanic, or being perceived as one, serves as a barrier to all sorts of things for members of these minority groups.

Yet another way of getting at this is to say that those in these minority groups are more likely to be "heavy" and therefore less likely to be able to be part of, to avail themselves of, positive flows. Being defined in any of these categories, and defining oneself in such categories, serves to make one heavy. At one level, there is a heaviness associated with the mere fact of being a member of certain races (blacks), ethnic groups (Hispanic Americans), a given gender (i.e. women), classes (lower), sexual orientation categories (homosexual), age groups (children), and global areas (South). At another level, this heaviness often prevents those in these categories from being able to acquire the various things (e.g. education, training, wealth) that are likely to make them "lighter."

THE SOCIAL CONSTRUCTION OF RACE, ETHNICITY, GENDER, AND SEXUALITY

We tend to think of most, if not all, of the categories being discussed here, either majority or minority, as being objective in the sense that they are based on such seemingly objective, phenotypic characteristics as the color of one's skin, sex, or age. However, the fact is that *all* majority and minority statuses are products of social interaction; in other words, the categories are defined differently by different cultures and social groups struggling with each other to shape what they mean and how they should be interpreted. This means that since they are socially constructed, majority–minority statuses also differ – because those definitions vary – over time and from one locale to another. In this way, the social definitions are not based in immutable, objective traits. But just because they are not objective categories does not mean that they do not have powerful effects on people's lives. This is based on one of the classic arguments in social theory: "If [people] define situations as real, they are real in their consequences" (Thomas and Thomas 1928: 572). This not only points to the importance of social definitions, but also to the fact that "erroneous" social definitions can and do have powerful consequences. For example, a white defined as black, or a black defined as white, will be profoundly affected by that definition, whatever the "objective" reality.

There is nothing intrinsic about, for example, any racial or ethnic group that makes it distinct from any other; race and ethnicity are dynamic, fluid categories that are socially defined. What *is* different about races and ethnic groups is the basis for the social definitions, but those differences do not determine whether one is considered a member of a given racial or ethnic group. Thus, it is *not* the color of her skin that makes a person black or white. Someone defined by others, or who defines herself, as black in the US might be considered, and consider herself, white in Peru. So while it is true that people have different skin colors, the concept of race comes from the meaning that societies ascribe to that skin color. The same can be said of ethnic groups. In Great Britain, for example, whether one is considered Jewish or Italian relates, as well, to definitions of others and to self-definitions.

Race: Defined based on meanings attached to physical or biological characteristics.

If both involve definitions, what serves to differentiate a race from an ethnic group? The lines are not clear because races (e.g. whites) are often considered ethnic groups (e.g. "white ethnics" [Greeley 1976]) and ethnic groups are often considered races (Jews, most notoriously in Nazi Germany and in the effort to destroy them in the Holocaust, are frequently thought of as a race). However, the basic difference is that while a **race** is generally defined as the differentiation of people into groups based on a set of meanings attached to some *physical* or *biological* characteristic, an **ethnic group** is defined as a group that shares some *cultural* characteristic (e.g. religious beliefs and practices, what they eat, how they dress). In the American context, whites, blacks, American Indians, Asian and Pacific Islanders, and Hispanics are usually considered to be races (the main basis for the definition is physical), while Italians, Jews, Poles, and White Anglo-Saxon Protestants are considered ethnic groups (mainly on the basis of cultural characteristics).

Ethnic group: Social group defined on the basis of some cultural characteristic(s).

Thus, race and ethnicity are social constructions and social creations. For example, the "invention" of race as an ideological concept dates back to the Enlightenment and to the emergence of modern society (Winant 2001: 290). The concept of race has been used to refer to inherent biological differences between human groups and to justify the associated ideas of racial superiority and inferiority. In the nineteenth and early twentieth centuries, ideas about race were supplemented with "science" and allegedly fixed biological characteristics of groups were used to justify scientifically the unequal distribution of wealth, power, prestige, access to resources, and life chances.

Even though "biological" or "scientific" racism continues to exist, a new type of racism, more based on social and cultural factors, such as religion, language, and national origin, is more prevalent today. In other words, **racism**, as an ideological construct, has been transformed in the second half of the twentieth century in that ideas of cultural superiority have increasingly replaced those associated with biological superiority. Further, racism is now more a matter of *hegemony* than physical domination (e.g. by the state). That is, one race now subordinates another more on the basis of dominant ideas (especially about cultural differences) and the fact that hegemonic racist ideas come to "operate as a taken-for-granted, almost unconscious common sense" (Winant 2001: 293) in the minds of the individuals who accept them.

> **Racism:** Belief in the inherent superiority of one racial group and the inferiority of others.

The emerging emphasis on culture in the understanding of race has led that concept to increasingly resemble that of "ethnicity." *Ethnicity* can be broadly defined as a set of common characteristics of social groups that include language, religion, traditions, and cultural practices. Since different cultural characteristics are almost always associated with racial groups and cultural discrimination is central to racial discrimination, it is increasingly difficult to differentiate between racism and ethnicism (as a result, we will deal with them together below, at least in part).

Racism and ethnicism serve similar functions in social discrimination; both define the Other as inherently different from, and inferior to, the dominant group in society. Therefore, racism and ethnicism are often accompanied by xenophobia which, etymologically, translates as "the fear caused by strangers." **Xenophobia** involves the beliefs, attitudes, and prejudices that reject, exclude, and vilify groups that are outsiders or foreigners to the dominant social group. Xenophobia sometimes leads to violence. Racism/ethnicism and xenophobia take forms as diverse as murder, physical attacks, hate speech, denial of entry to stores, restaurants, clubs, and denial of access to employment.

> **Xenophobia:** Beliefs, attitudes, and prejudices that reject, exclude, and vilify groups made up of outsiders or foreigners.

Turning to gender and its meaning as being socially constructed, we need to distinguish conceptually gender from sex. **Sex** refers to the physical differences between males and females.[8] This includes differences in genitalia, chromosomes (XX/XY), and hormones. **Gender**, however, is, like race and ethnicity (and class for that matter), a matter of social definition and social distinction (Bourdieu 1984). It refers to the different meanings, which vary across time and place, that people attribute to men and women. For example, when someone is physically born as a female (i.e. their sex), people then start to place expectations on how that person might dress or behave, what kinds of college major they might want, or what type of occupation they might pursue (i.e. their gender). While conceptions of sex have remained the same across time, conceptions of gender have varied tremendously across time and cultures (some cultures even have more than masculine or feminine genders; cultures have had up to five or more different gender categories). Also like race and class, gender involves more than simply making distinctions. Gender distinctions are used to organize the social world and to affect, often adversely, women.

> **Sex:** Physical differences between males and females.

> **Gender:** Differences between males and females based on social definition and distinction.

These distinctions are made even though there are great similarities between men and women and great variations exist within both (Hess and Marx Ferree 1987). Of greatest interest from the point of view of this chapter is the way gender differences are used to advantage men and disadvantage women not only within nation-states, but also globally. Most extremely, definitions of gender employed by men often lead to acts of violence (beatings, rape, even murder) against women.

Finally, social definitions are deeply implicated in the distinctions around sexuality. There are no incontrovertible physical signs that one is homosexual, heterosexual, or bisexual, so inclusion in those categories depends on how society defines the categories, and perhaps ultimately on one's self-identity as being heterosexual, lesbian, gay, or bisexual. Until very recently, identifying as bi- or homosexual had very negative consequences for those individuals, but there are signs of improvement in many places – but certainly not all – throughout the world. For example, in early 2014, President Goodluck Jonathan of Nigeria instituted a law that criminalized homosexuality. Offenders now can be stoned to death for being gay (Nossiter 2014). That being homosexual is a matter of social definition is clearly manifest in the fact that many homosexuals, much more so in the past than today (although that varies by areas of the world), were "in the closet." If they were successful in concealing their homosexuality, they were not defined, at least by heterosexuals, as being homosexuals.

RACE AND ETHNICITY

Perhaps the most important similarity between racial and ethnic groups from the perspective of this analysis is the way in which they relate to the majority–minority issue. That is, some racial and ethnic groups tend to be minorities in many different societies around the world, while others tend to be in the majority. This is clearest in the case of the white–black distinction where whites are disproportionately in the majority and blacks are disproportionately in the minority. This is true within many societies, although not all (in most African societies blacks are the majority group). However, what is most important for our purposes is the global picture and global relationships. At the global level, whites are disproportionately in the dominant North, while blacks are primarily in the South (although this is changing with South-to-North migration). As a result, according to Winant (2004: 131): "Globalization is a re-racialization of the world. What have come to be called 'North–South' issues are also deeply racial issues. The disparities … between the (largely white and wealthy) global North and the (largely dark-skinned and poor) global South have always possessed a racial character." The key issue from the point of view of globalization is the nature of the relationship, of the flows and barriers, between predominantly white and black areas of the world and more generally between different areas dominated by different races.

Historically, most work on the issue of race and ethnicity has focused on particular nation-states and what transpires within them. This is particularly true of the US, largely because of its unique history both in terms of race and ethnicity. In terms of race it is, of course, the history of slavery and the continuing legacy of that system and its impact on black Americans. In terms of ethnicity, it is the history of massive immigration to the US, especially in the late nineteenth and early twentieth centuries. Many ethnic groups from Europe made their way to the US. Some of these groups (e.g. the Irish and Italians) were not considered "white" at the time, but a different race. Over time, they became assimilated into the white race and were then viewed as different ethnic groups (illustrating the changing social construction of racial categories). Of course, other racial groups, especially Asians and, more recently, large numbers of Hispanics, have also immigrated to the US. For the most part, these groups are still considered separate races. Thus, the US was, at least until recently, a uniquely multi-racial and multi-ethnic society. This has changed as many other societies, for example those in Europe, have become much more multi-racial (as a result largely of South-to-North migration from Africa) and multi-ethnic (mostly as a result of both South-to-North [e.g. from Turkey] and North-to-North [from Eastern Europe] migration).

Of course, other societies have been in the forefront of discussions of race and ethnicity. In terms of race, South Africa was long a focus of attention (Dunbar Moodie 1975; Dunbar Moodie and Ndatshe 1994) because of its system of *apartheid*, a formal system of "separate development" for whites and blacks (the vast majority of the South African population is, and was, black) that served to perpetuate both white privilege and power and black subordination and weakness. Apartheid was formally abolished in 1991, but its history and legacy continues to be important in analyses and discussions of race in South Africa. While whites continue to be the statistical minority, they are considered the majority in terms of power relations and privilege.

Brazil is another nation-state that gets much attention in discussions of race (Degler 1971/1986), largely because of the more harmonious relationship between the races there than in the US (but as we will see below, racial inequalities still persist there as well). There is also a much more fluid definition of race in Brazil than in the US. People in Brazil think about race much more on a continuum, and someone who is considered black in the US would not necessarily be considered black in Brazil.

The issue of racism (Law 2012) can be seen in an 1876 statement by an Australian writer defending the efforts to destroy native peoples of New Zealand, Australia, and Tasmania: "When exterminating the inferior Australian and Maori races ... the world is better for it.... [By] protecting the propagation of the imprudent, the diseased, the defective, the criminal ... we tend to destroy the human race" (Hartwig 1972: 16). It should be noted that while there are physical differences between the majority-group whites and the minority-group natives (e.g. the Maori in New Zealand), the main argument is that these groups, like all races, are distinguished on the basis of social definitions. Thus, this makes it clear that on the basis of a social definition (that is, as we've seen, always ambiguous and open to debate), at least some members of the white majority were willing to take harsh actions against the minority race, even going so far as exterminating the minority race in the geographic area in question. It is also important to note that this is not merely an historical issue. While the rhetoric is toned down today, Maoris continue to be a minority group in contemporary New Zealand and they face racism in various ways and areas of life.

To further complicate matters, there are important differences within racial groups. For example, in central Africa, there is a history of great conflict between two tribes – the Hutu and Tutsi. The Tutsi tend to be very tall (over six feet) and the Hutu very short (little more than four feet). Thus, in this context it is height that is the major criterion for distinguishing among groups. More recently, tensions have flared in the new fledgling nation of South Sudan (it declared its independence from Sudan in 2011). One major dispute has erupted between the Dinka Ngok farmers and cattle-herding Misseriya Arab tribesmen over land. As a result of similar conflicts, fighting between government and rebel forces left thousands of people dead in late 2013, with another 60,000 people seeking refuge with

UN peace-keeping forces (Kulish 2013). These conflicts are best understood as ethnic conflicts, which will be explored further below.

However, while discussions of various societies throughout the world in terms of their distinctive patterns of racial (and ethnic) relations is important, far more important from the perspective of globalization is a focus on global flows and barriers. Of special importance in this context is the global flow of *people* from various racial and ethnic groups as well as the global flow of *ideas* such as *racism* (a belief, such as Orientalism, in the inherent superiority or one racial group and the inferiority of others), **pluralism** (the idea that different races and ethnic groups can live together; they can co-exist), or *resistance* (the idea that racial and ethnic minorities must resist discrimination and its deleterious effects).

> **Pluralism:**
> The idea and fact that different races and ethnic groups can live together, can co-exist.

In terms of ethnicity, it is closely related to the idea, and status, of the nation-state. More specifically, the idea of a "nation" is linked to the concept of ethnicity. Take, for example, the definition[9] of a nation as "a human grouping who share a conviction of being ancestrally related" (Connor 2007: 3142).[10] This also can be seen as a definition of ethnicity, or is at least pretty close to such a definition (see above). Both ethnic groups and nations can be seen in Benedict Anderson's (1991) terms as "imagined communities" (see Chapter 5). Thus, the idea of the nation-state involves a fusion of a given nation, or ethnic group, with a state apparatus within a given territory and its borders. However, a nation has never been coterminous with territorial boundaries and that is even less true today in the era of globalization and global migration. A number of different ethnic groups always reside within given national borders. That is, no territory is ever totally homogeneous (in spite of efforts such as those associated with ethnic cleansing; see below). In addition, ethnic groups exist in a number of nation-states. A good example is the Kurds who lack a nation-state of their own, but are spread out among a number of nation-states, especially Iran, Iraq, Syria, and Turkey (the general area is often referred to as Kurdistan). These realities are greatly increased in the global age as more ethnic groups are being found within many national borders and ethnic groups are moving in great numbers to nation-states in which they heretofore have been only minor presences. This movement (detailed, at least in part, in Chapter 10) has served to erode the meaning of the nation-state since there is no longer, if there ever was, a dominant nation (or ethnic group) within many nation-states, or at least the nature of the dominant group is changing dramatically. For example, the US, always associated with white ethnics, is changing dramatically and the forecasts are that whites will be in the minority in the US by 2043 (Yen 2012). Similar trends are being seen throughout the EU.

Take, for example, the case of Albanian Muslims in Italy. Tens of thousands of Albanians, many of them Muslims, migrated to Italy in the 1990s with the fall of Albania's communist regime (Donadio 2008a: A11). As in many other places in the world, anti-immigrant feelings are high in Italy with many seen as criminals; there is at least some violence against them. However, some Albanians are settling into life in Italy and becoming integral to various industries, such as winemaking. What is interesting about the latter is that while many Albanian Muslims are working in Italian vineyards planting and pruning grape vines and picking grapes, observant Muslims are forbidden from drinking alcoholic beverages. Thus, Albanian Muslims who are teetotalers and wine-loving Italian Christians are living, still somewhat uncomfortably, side-by-side in at least some parts of Italy. There is hope that ethnic relations in Italy (and elsewhere) will grow more harmonious in the future as more majority- and minority-group children attend school together.

Such changes are, of course, related to the much discussed porosity of the nation-state. The fact is that even if a nation-state wanted to remain closed to the influx of unwanted ethnic groups, it would find it difficult to do so.

This is also closely related to the issue of *nationalism* in the global era (Delanty and O'Mahony 2002; Gellner 1983; Greenfeld 2012; Kastoryano 2013). Political definitions of nationalism predominated prior to the global age. That is, nationalism focused on the state and the actions the latter could take to bring state and nation in alignment with one another and to protect both. While such nationalism continues to exist today, globalization has brought with it much more of a focus on cultural nationalism. That is, the focus is more on culture, nation, and ethnicity wherever it may exist in the world. Thus, in whatever nation-state individuals may reside, their nationalism is oriented to their ethnic group wherever in the world it may reside. Thus, wherever Jews, Muslims, Hispanics, or Italians live, their nationalistic feelings may well be more oriented toward their ethnic group (or nation) than to the nation-state in which they happen to be. In the case of the specific example discussed above, Albanian Muslims in Italy are more likely to see themselves as Albanian Muslims than as Italians, at least for another generation or two.

This, of course, is the basis of one of today's great global tensions. That is, do people owe their greatest allegiance to their ethnic group/nation or to the nation-state of which they are citizens, or at least in which they reside? The unwillingness, or the failure, of many Hispanics in the US to learn English has raised the issue for some of whether they owe more allegiance to the US or to the global community of Hispanics. Then there is the case of Muslims, especially in Europe, and whether they are more committed to the European nation in which they live or to the global community of Muslims. This issue is of great concern these days given the conflict between Europe (and the West) and Islamic militants associated with, for example, al-Qaeda and the Taliban. The question is: Do Muslims in Europe identify more with the nation-state in which they live or with Muslims in general? If it is the latter, the issue then becomes whether that identification extends to sympathy for militant Islam and whether that sympathy could turn into overt action in the state, or global area (the West), in which they live.

ETHNIC CONFLICT AND GENOCIDE

Greater ethnic diversity within many nation-states has increased the possibility of ethnic conflict within their confines. Of course, such ethnic conflict is not new. Among the most notable examples have been conflicts between Turks and Armenians in Turkey, Germans (especially Nazis) and Jews in Germany, Tamils and Sinhalese in Sri Lanka, the Tutsi and Hutu in Burundi, and the conflict between various ethnic groups – Slovenes, Croatians, Serbs, Bosnians, Montenegrins, Macedonians, and Albanians – after the breakup of Yugoslavia in 1991. However, today with more members of ethnic groups in more and more countries, there is the potential for a great increase in the number, if not the intensity, of ethnic conflicts.

Historically, efforts to "deal" with ethnic minorities have occurred within nation-states or other delimited territories. The most extreme cases involve extermination or genocide. **Genocide** was defined in 1948 by the United Nations Convention on the Prevention and Punishment of the Crime of Genocide as "acts committed with the intent to destroy, in whole or in part, a national, ethnic, racial, or religious group" (cited in Karstedt 2012b). This was prompted by the Nazi Holocaust committed primarily, but not exclusively, against Jews. At first, the Holocaust occurred within the confines of Germany, but later spread to the European countries allied with, or conquered by, Germany. It was in that sense global and it would have undoubtedly become far more global had the Nazis achieved their goal of world

Genocide: Acts committed with the intent to destroy a national, ethnic, racial, or religious group.

conquest. For example, had the Nazis succeeded in conquering the US, we would have undoubtedly seen the genocide of American Jews. A later example of a more global genocide was the mass killings during the Stalin era that extended throughout the then-vast Soviet Empire. In the main, though, genocide continues to be practiced within nation-states (e.g. the murder of millions by the Khmer Rouge in Cambodia in the mid- to late 1970s).

However, it is important to point out that the global age brings with it at least the possibility of even more global genocide. That is, genocide could become another of the negative flows discussed in Chapter 12. In the global age, one can imagine a scenario whereby genocide that takes place in one part of the world eventually makes its way, flows, to other parts of the world. This might be a far-fetched scenario (a "Mad Max" scenario of the kind discussed in Chapter 15), but it is more likely because of globalization, of proliferating and accelerating global flows, as well as the increased inability of nation-states to block many of these flows.

One of the processes of greatest concern in the context of ethnicity and globalization is ethnic cleansing. Ethnic cleansing can be seen as, at least in part, a specific example of another way of dealing with ethnic minorities – *expulsion*. Expulsion can take two forms (Eaton Simpson and Yinger 1985). First, it can be direct with minority ethnic groups forcibly ejected by the majority through military and other government action. Second, such a minority group can leave "voluntarily" because it is being harassed, discriminated against, and persecuted. Of course, in the real world these two forms of expulsion occur in concert with one another. Thus, many of those involved in diasporas of one kind or another have often experienced both forms of expulsion. This is particularly true of Jews who have often moved both because they have been forcibly ejected (e.g. by the Romans from Jerusalem in the second century AD) and voluntarily (those German Jews who left before the Holocaust because of harassment or who left both Czarist Russia and the Stalinist Soviet Union for similar reasons).

> **Ethnic cleansing:** Forcibly removing people of another ethnic group.

Ethnic cleansing (Ahmed 1995; Oberschall 2012) is defined in terms similar to that of expulsion as "various policies of forcibly removing people of another ethnic[11] group" (Sekulic 2007). Of course, Nazi actions against Jews fit the definition of ethnic cleansing, but ethnic cleansing achieved more recent notoriety during the wars that were associated with the dissolution of Yugoslavia in 1991 (for a map of this area see Figure 14.1). Many of the ethnic groups that dominated various regions (e.g. Croatia) sought to create areas that were ethnically homogeneous and they did this by expelling and even killing (this is genocide rather than expulsion) members of other ethnic groups. For example, Croatians were expelled from parts of Croatia inhabited by Serbs. Bosnia, which declared independence in 1992, was composed of three major ethnic groups – Slavic Muslims (the largest single group), Serbs, and Croats. Ethnic cleansing took the form of Serbian armed forces creating ethnically homogeneous enclaves by forcibly removing the other ethnic groups, especially Muslims.

GLOBALIZATION AND RACE RELATIONS IN THE US

Globalization has aggravated race relations in many developed countries, particularly in the US where race relations have long been fraught with difficulties. To take two examples, the outsourcing/flexibilization of production and the facilitation of labor migration have helped to transform the nature of racism in the US (and elsewhere). Whereas earlier forms of racism were more based in the political economy and the history of slavery and segregation in

Figure 14.1 Serbia and its neighbors. The still-evolving political geography of the former Yugoslavia and Albania. Landlocked, dominantly Muslim Kosovo remains a challenge. Source: de Blij, Harm J. 2008. *Power of Place: Geography, Destiny, and Globalization's Rough Landscape*. Chapter 9: Promise and Peril in the Provinces, p. 220. © 2008 Oxford University Press. Used by permission.

the US, newer forms of racism stem more from the restructuring of economic production due to the forces of global capitalism.

As we saw in Chapter 7, US corporations have been outsourcing millions of jobs, many of which provided the livelihood for African Americans. Outsourcing is but one of the factors involved in the loss of these jobs which is also traceable to plant closings, layoffs, and the introduction of new production technologies (Bernard and Jensen 2007). The loss of these jobs has affected the African American community disproportionately, especially those who worked in large numbers in the factories of Detroit, St. Louis, Chicago, Baltimore, Pittsburgh, and other industrial cities.

Highly desirable manufacturing jobs have tended to be replaced by low-wage, low-skill, service-sector jobs that typically provide few, if any, benefits and involve more exploitative working conditions. African Americans tend to hold positions in the lower reaches of the service sector – in retail, food service, janitorial and housekeeping, and low-level health delivery.

Immigration is another major global factor that has served to adversely affect race relations in the US. Globalization has, at least in most observers' eyes, increased inequality among and between countries and, therefore, intensified the movement of labor across borders. While migration of skilled labor is a small part of global immigration streams, cross-border mobility of less-skilled or unskilled workers constitutes the most significant portion of labor migration. About 1.8 million documented and undocumented immigrants enter the US each year. Between the 1950s and the early 1990s, the proportion of immigrants coming from less developed countries in Asia and Latin America rose from 30 to 75% (Lerman and Schmidt 1999).

As a result of massive international migration, most developed, industrialized societies have become, or are becoming, increasingly diverse in terms of their racial and ethnic composition. The rapid influx of ethnic and racial groups in host societies tends to lead to racism and xenophobia. Many migrants are exposed to discrimination, exploitation, exclusion, even violence. Unauthorized migrants are particularly vulnerable to racist and xenophobic hostility. Because many acts directed against them are largely invisible, unauthorized migrants are reluctant to seek protection or legal aid.

Racism and xenophobia are often found among the lower/working classes of the host countries; they are more likely to believe they are losing jobs to immigrants. For example, most African Americans believe that their situation is worse today than it was five or even ten years ago and nearly half of them also say immigrants, specifically Hispanics, reduce job opportunities for African Americans (Morin 2008).

Latinos are the largest minority group in the US, constituting 17% of the population (over 53 million people). In 2011, 36% of all Hispanics in the US were foreign born (*UPI* 2013: August 10). In terms of national origin, the Hispanic population is highly diverse – 65% of Hispanics are from Mexico; 9.4% from Puerto Rico; 3.8% from El Salvador; 3.6% from Cuba; and 3.0% from the Dominican Republic. The remainder come from other Central and South American countries and other regions, including Spain.

Hispanics have among the highest rates of poverty, unemployment, and occupational segregation in the US. Although Hispanic national groups have varied occupational patterns, they all find themselves segregated occupationally. They face barriers in upward mobility through employment because of language deficiencies, lack of formal education, mismatch in work skills, and discrimination. As a result, they tend to be mired in occupations that require little education and little cultural capital, and therefore pay lower wages (Motel and Patten 2013).

In the past, Hispanics were concentrated occupationally in manufacturing; however that has changed dramatically with the restructuring of production. Today, Hispanics tend to be in low-paying, non-professional, service occupations such as household/ground/building cleaning, construction, and food preparation and serving (Motel and Patten 2013).

Hispanics contend that they face discrimination in the workplace and in schools. According to a 2002 national survey, 45% of Hispanics report being treated with less respect because of their race or ethnic background (Pew Hispanic Center/Kaiser Family Foundation 2002: 78). Forty-one percent of Hispanics report that at least occasionally they receive poorer service than other people at restaurants or stores, and 30% report that at least at times they are called derogatory names or insulted because of their race or ethnicity. They also report their physical appearance and language as the main reasons for discrimination or unfair treatment.

Asian Americans constitute the third-largest minority group in the US, comprising 5.6% of the total population, and at a 46% population growth rate, were the fastest-growing minority group from 2000 to 2010 (Pew Research Center 2012). The largest sub-groups are Chinese (23.2%), Filipino (19.7%), Indian (18.4%), Vietnamese (10.0%), Korean (9.9%), and Japanese (7.5%). Asian Americans are often considered a "model minority" because, despite experiencing severe prejudice and discrimination in the past, they are now doing better than other minorities on most socioeconomic measures. Yet, the model minority concept – or myth – overlooks the socioeconomic backgrounds of Asian immigrants over time and the incredible diversity among Asian Americans. For example, early Asian immigrants tended to have higher educational backgrounds, better English language skills, and more wealth than other immigrant groups. As a result, Asian immigrants started their lives in the US in a higher class position. Over time (and especially more recently), however, more Asian immigrants came to the US from poorer class backgrounds. While Asian Americans, on average, still tend to do better economically than other racial groups (including whites), there are now great discrepancies between and within Asian sub-groups. For instance, Vietnamese Americans are, overall, worse off economically than Japanese Americans, and there are high levels of income inequality within both groups as well.

The global production system's exploitative conditions are also found in the US. There are hundreds of sweatshops in New York City alone, in which recent immigrants work for minimal wages. Working conditions in these sweatshops have many similarities to those in China or the Philippines; workers labor up to seven days a week, 16 hours a day with no overtime pay. Workers may go weeks without being paid (Ong 1991).

While recent Asian immigrants, especially those who are undocumented, experience economic and social hardships, Asian Americans indicate lower levels of discrimination than other minority groups. They also experience less occupational and residential segregation than other minority groups, and have higher educational and income levels.

Arab Americans, especially immigrants from the Arab world, have suffered from increased levels of discrimination since the terrorist attacks on September 11, 2001. There have been increased reports of hate crimes against Arab Americans and their property. Arab Americans experience discrimination in employment, are denied service in businesses, and face physical and verbal abuse in schools and universities (*ADC Fact Sheet: The Condition of Arab Americans Post-9/11* 2007).

GLOBALIZATION AND RACE RELATIONS IN EUROPE

The picture of globalization and race relations in Europe is complex. While a few European countries, such as the UK, France, and the Netherlands, have been somewhat ethnically and racially diverse for some time due to their colonial history, they, and many other European countries, experienced a substantial influx of various ethnic and racial immigrant groups in the second half of the twentieth century and the early twenty-first century.

In the post-WW II period, the shortage of labor forced Western Europe – particularly West Germany, France, Switzerland, and the UK – to recruit labor from abroad. Between the 1950s and 1970s, millions of immigrant workers moved to Europe, from the poorer countries of southern and Eastern Europe, Turkey, and the former colonies in Africa and Asia. The migrant laborers were referred to as "guestworkers" based on the assumption (hope?) that they would return to their home countries at the end of their work period.

Beginning in the 1980s, Europe witnessed a second major influx of immigrants due to the collapse of the Soviet bloc, the fragmentation of the former Yugoslavia, and political and economic crises in the Middle East, Africa, and Asia. These global upheavals led massive numbers of people to emigrate to Europe.

It is estimated that, as of 2012, there are approximately 33 million immigrants living in Europe today (European Commission 2013). The countries that received the most immigrants in 2011 were the United Kingdom (566,000), Germany (489,400), Spain (457,600), Italy (385,800), and France (267,400). The population of Switzerland, which is a much smaller country, is comprised of 27% immigrants. There are also great variations in the nationalities of the immigrant populations across European countries. The migration patterns in any given country in Europe depend on its colonial history, its proximity to the European Union's external borders, the effect of its migration policies, and the needs of its economy. For instance, while Germany and Austria receive most of their immigrants from Eastern Europe and Turkey, Scandinavian countries tend to receive citizens fleeing from Iraq, Afghanistan, and Somalia (they are more often escaping warfare or persecution in their home countries). In southern Europe, Greece receives immigrants from neighboring countries; Spain from Morocco and Latin America; Italy from Albania (see above), Morocco, sub-Saharan Africa, and the Indies; and Portugal from Cape Verde, Brazil, and Angola (Breem and Thierry 2004).

The rapid transformation of the ethnic and racial composition of Europe's population due to the influx of large numbers of immigrants has resulted in an increase in racial and ethnic discrimination and violence. There is considerable variation across countries and among various migrant populations within European countries. Undocumented migrants, asylum seekers, Roma people, Jews, and Muslims are among the most vulnerable to discrimination in employment, housing, education, health care, access to goods and services, and the media. They are also more likely to be victims of racial profiling, racist violence, and racially motivated crime.

Discrimination in employment and in commercial transactions is a routine aspect of the immigrant experience (Dancygier and Laitin 2014). Immigrants in Europe, in accord with the experiences of immigrants around the globe, face discrimination through denial of access to jobs, skipped promotions, and harassment at work. Ethnic minorities face further discrimination in housing, access to health services and education, and access to vital social services (Kahanec et al. 2013). Immigrants, such as those in the UK, are more likely to live in areas with the highest rates of unemployment, have a household income of less than half the national average, suffer from more health problems, and have higher rates of infant mortality (RAXEN National Focal Point for United Kingdom 2005).

In addition to economic and social discrimination, immigrants experience more direct and extreme forms of hostility such as racist violence and crime. For example, in Portugal, 15% of immigrants were "reported to be victims of at least one episode of violence during the last year" (Dias et al. 2013: 119). In most European countries, propaganda, hate speech, or incitement to hatred or violence are not uncommon. No country in Europe is immune to this. In fact, in the last few years, there has been a significant increase in acts of violence against immigrants all across Europe. The countries in the EU with the greatest problems in this regard are Germany, Sweden, and the UK. Jews, Muslims, people of North African/Arab origin, and Roma people are the main victims. One example occurred in Italy in 2008 when a young black man from Burkina Faso in Africa was killed, apparently for stealing a package of cookies (and perhaps some money). The father-and-son owners of the shop were accused of beating him to death with a metal rod. During the assault, the attackers shouted "dirty black." This was only the latest in a series of attacks on blacks and other minorities in Italy. The President of Italy urged the state to work together with the Catholic Church "to overcome racism." The Parliament debated what Italian newspapers heatedly called a "racism emergency." A church official spoke out against "discrimination, xenophobia and racism" toward immigrants in Italy. All of this is in the context of a significant rise in the flow of immigrants into Italy. Some groups want to erect more barriers to immigration, but the church official quoted above said that such barriers were causing an "erosion of humanitarian standards" (quoted in Donadio 2008b: A5).

Perpetrators of violence and criminal acts against immigrants are typically unemployed young males with below average education. Ill-treatment, brutality, and verbal abuse by the police toward minorities and migrants are also not uncommon (European Monitoring Center on Racism and Xenophobia 2002). However, negative attitudes toward migrant and minority populations are not restricted to young males (and the police). In a 2002 study in the UK, only 31% of the population accepted the view that discrimination against minority groups should be outlawed, only 16% of the population accepted people from Muslim countries without restrictions, 47% of the population believed that the presence of ethnic minorities increased unemployment. Overall, 33% of the population agreed with the statement that "legally established immigrants from outside the European Union should be sent back to their country of origin if they are unemployed" (RAXEN National Focal Point for United Kingdom 2005).

Global migration has become a key focus of extreme right-wing and xenophobically oriented political groups and parties across Europe. Right-wing populism that feeds ultra-nationalist political parties has been gaining influence in a number of countries including Germany, Austria, Switzerland, the Netherlands, and Denmark (see Chapter 10). Several of the wealthier countries are also concerned about the strain placed on their generous welfare systems, sparking intense debates about immigration restriction (Eddy 2014). In 2014, Swiss voters approved quotas on immigrants. In Germany, political groups, such as skinheads and neo-Nazis which support National Socialism (Nazism) and are nationalistic, anti-Semitic, and xenophobic, constitute a significant part of the voter demographic of extreme right-wing political parties. The German National Democratic Party, Union of German People, and the Republicans openly denounce multiculturalism, ethnic pluralism, and immigration. Recent immigrants – foreign nationals and asylum seekers – have replaced Jews as the major victims of racist violence in Germany. Today, "non-German looking" people, mainly Turkish nationals, people of African origin, Romany people, and Vietnamese nationals, are particularly vulnerable to violence in Germany (RAXEN National Focal Point for Germany 2005). Global conflicts are another cause of the rise of racial and ethnic violence in Europe. The continuing Israeli/Palestinian conflict, the wars in Iraq and Afghanistan, and the terrorist attacks of September 11 have had a direct impact on the increase of local violence in European countries. Islamophobia and discrimination against Muslim populations since September 11 have been on the rise across Europe. Reports indicate numerous incidents of attacks on mosques, restaurants, businesses, graves, as well as physical attacks on Muslim immigrants. Muslim immigrants are not the only victims of

Islamophobia. For instance, as a result of France's colonial history, the great majority of the Muslim population in France is from Maghreb (Algeria, Morocco, Tunisia), and even though Maghrebi people are French citizens, segments of the public continue to consider them immigrants even after four generations of living in France. Social and cultural exclusion of Muslim citizens has significant implications for their economic status. Discrimination is pervasive in hiring, in the workplace, and in housing in France (Open Society Institute EU Monitoring and Advocacy Program 2007). It is claimed that on the basis of their names Muslims are frequently discriminated against in gaining access to certain professional positions. They suffer disproportionately from unemployment and they have less access to full-time, long-term employment. Muslim citizens typically occupy the least qualified professional positions and are underrepresented in executive positions.

French riots and protests

Riots broke out in the Paris suburbs of Argenteuil in 2005 and in Villiers-le-Bel in 2007, and have been followed by non-violent protests in more recent years. The riots occurred in areas dominated by the working and lower classes associated with large immigrant groups, especially Arab and African populations (Sciolino 2007b: A8). The riots revealed to the world the fact that racism, long most associated with the US, was also a French, if not a global, problem. In fact, racism in France is much more blatant now than it is in the US and Great Britain (which has also witnessed the development and emergence of a major race problem). For example, in 2013, France's black justice minister was taunted by a group of middle-class children (surrounded by their parents) waving "banana skins and [shouting] obscenity-laced chants about monkeys" (Ramdani 2013a). It resembles the racism in those countries of decades ago. Among other things, at the behest of landlords, French real estate agents seek out white-only tenants, *patisseries* sell cakes covered in chocolate called *tête de nègre* (head of a Negro), TV programs are peopled predominantly by white actors and actresses, and women from Africa and Asia are seen in the wealthy areas of town as workers (e.g. as "nannies") accompanying well-dressed children to and from school. Racial and ethnic minorities in France primarily work, if they work, in low-paid manual jobs that are likely to involve cleaning, pushing, serving, digging, or carrying. They are crucial to the health service since they perform virtually all of the "dirty work" (Ritzer 1972: 275) associated with it.

Minorities are almost totally absent among the elites in almost every walk of life in France. Its far-right National Front party has also gained supporters with its anti-immigration agenda in recent years (Ramdani 2013b). While the French electorate has not elected (so far) far-right politicians such as Jean-Marie Le Pen to its top positions (although Le Pen does hold a seat in the European Parliament), many of France's politicians, as well as its public philosophers, have moved in the direction of right-wing ideas leading to what some have called the "Le-Penization" of France (Murray 2006). Even its more recent socialist government, under President François Hollande, has cracked down on undocumented immigrants. Its interior minister, Manuel Valls, "has been a strong proponent in particular of deporting the Roma" (Rubin 2013). In 2013, when France deported a 19-year-old Armenian student and a 15-year-old Roma girl from Kosovo – she was removed from a school bus and put in a police car in front of her classmates – the nation was shocked and the event sparked protests calling for the resignation of Valls. But despite the protests, polls show that a majority of French citizens support expelling at least the Roma, who are stereotyped as petty criminals and pickpockets.

Racial (and ethnic) minorities in France experience a variety of other problems. They generally are housed in government-run "projects," many built in the 1960s, in the suburbs where unemployment can be as high as 40%. These are not American-style suburbs with well-manicured lawns, but dull expanses of concrete and asphalt. The suburbs are generally isolated from the city center and it takes a great deal of time and several changes of buses and/or trains to get there. Jobs are few in the suburbs, especially since many factories have been shuttered as a result of globalization and operations have been moved to places like Tunisia, Slovakia, and Southeast Asia. The result is poverty and hopelessness, especially among the young who represented the vast majority of the rioters in the Paris suburbs. There is great tension with the police who are apt to harass minority-group members, address them impolitely, call them names, treat them brutally, and on occasion kill them.

These riots and protests can be seen as being linked to globalization, especially the large-scale migration of people associated with it. Thus, the rioting by the minorities outside Paris can be seen as both resistance to the way they are treated in France and more generally to the negative effects and consequences of globalization. In any case, it is clear that the riots would never have occurred were it not for globalization, in particular large-scale South-to-North migration.

THE LATIN AMERICANIZATION OF RACE RELATIONS

One key dimension of the social construction of race is that conceptions of race vary across place and time (i.e. they are not a fixed and essential category). For example, the US has historically viewed race through a black-white paradigm, but in other areas (e.g. Japan, Turkmenistan, or Cambodia) race is important but "black" is not a meaningful category and "blackness" is not an issue (Law 2012). Throughout Latin America, race is seen on a continuum.

From a global perspective, it is particularly interesting to see the global flows of cultural ideas about race. For example, the historical black-white paradigm found in the US and other countries is being transformed into a "multi-racial" paradigm (Bowman and Betancur 2010). In particular, race relations in the US (and other countries) look increasingly like those found in Latin America (Bonilla-Silva 2013; Bonilla-Silva and Dietrich 2008). This is shaping race relations in new and important ways.

Bonilla-Silva (2013) outlines the central features of race in Latin America. First, almost all Latin American nations, with some exceptions, are "thoroughly racially mixed." Despite this racial mixing and widespread beliefs that racism does not exist in Latin America, whites remain the dominant group. In Latin America's racial hierarchy, Indian and black groups are at the bottom, but there are also intermediate groups of "browns," "pardos," or "mestizos." Even within racial strata, there are internal divisions based on a variety of factors, including "skin tone, phenotype, hair texture, eye color, culture and education, and class" (Bonilla-Silva 2013: 230). This reflects the idea of pigmentocracy or colorism, where for example, darker skinned members of a group are more discriminated against than lighter skinned members. This can even be seen in families, where racial mixing can be undertaken with the goal of becoming more and more white. Finally, despite all these important racial influences, Latin Americans tend not to identify themselves through racial categories, but instead emphasize their nationality (e.g. Brazilian or Puerto Rican). There is a myth throughout much of Latin America that its nations have moved beyond race by achieving national unity.

Bonilla-Silva explains why these ideas are flowing to other parts of the world – especially the United States – resulting in the "Latin Americanization of race." As noted above and in Chapter 10, mass migration from Latin America to other nations (largely the US) is rapidly changing social demographics. In the US, 37% of the population is now made up of racial minorities. Between 2000 and 2011, the Hispanic population alone increased from 35.2 million to 51.9 million (a 47.5% increase) (Motel and Patten 2013). Second, race relations themselves have become more globalized. According to Bonilla-Silva (2013: 232), "the once almost all-white Western nations have now 'interiorized the other.' The new world system need for capital accumulation has led to the incorporation of 'dark' foreigners as 'guest workers' and even as permanent workers." Now in both US and European countries, the darkest-skinned members of racial groups have been shaped into a highly oppressed underclass within this emerging racial structure. Coupled with the unique racial histories and ideologies of these receiving countries, racial hierarchies are subtly forming into multiple hierarchical levels but they are still very powerful.

The outcome of this Latin Americanization of race is new tripartite systems of race that are replacing the previous black-white paradigms in some nations. This is most evident in the US. At the top of this three-tiered racial hierarchy are "whites" (including traditionally defined whites, new whites such as Russians, assimilated white Hispanics, some light-skinned multi-racials, assimilated urban Native Americans, and a few people of Asian origin). The middle group are the "honorary whites" (including light-skinned Latinos, Japanese Americans, Korean Americans, Asian Indians, Chinese Americans, Middle Eastern Americans, and most multi-racials), with the group of "collective blacks" at the bottom (including Vietnamese Americans, Filipino Americans, Hmong Americans, dark-skinned Latinos, blacks, new West Indian and African immigrants, and Native Americans on reservations). In this system, not only does the hierarchy reflect a continuum of racial advantages, but the intermediate group (i.e. "honorary whites") serves as a buffer in racial conflicts wherein that group is discriminated against by whites but also discriminates against the "collective blacks" below them, with contradictory interests in preserving the new racial order.

Some evidence suggests this structure of Latin American race relations has been developing for some time in the US. Several social and economic indicators reflect the better outcomes for groups in the category of "whites," followed by "honorary whites," with "collective blacks" having the poorest outcomes. For example, this is true for average income and levels of residential segregation. Looking just at Mexican immigrants, "complexion appeared to play a role in the likelihood of owning a home, having a bank account, and occupational status" (Dávila et al. 2011). This hierarchy is also true for racial attitudes, where people across the hierarchy have the most favorable attitudes for groups in the "white" category, then the "honorary whites," with the least favorable attitudes (or the most negative stereotypes) about "collective blacks." In addition, when whites interact outside their own racial group, they are more likely to have friends and to marry members of the "honorary whites" than the more socially distant "collective blacks."

GENDER

Recent analyses of globalization demonstrate that gender is critical in terms of globalization's effects on human groups. Globalization reinforces preexisting gender structures, barriers, and relationships, only now on a global scale (Everett and Charlton

2014; Runyan 2012). Therefore, any analysis of globalization that does not take gender into consideration is deficient.

Mainstream perspectives on, and theories of, globalization in sociology, economics, international relations (and many other fields, see Appendix) often claim to be gender-neutral or gender-blind. Leaving the gendered effects of globalization aside, mainstream theories (e.g. neoliberal theories) imply that global processes have similar effects on men and women. Women's experiences and voices, especially those in the developing world, are frequently not taken into account. However, gender is a critical aspect of globalization, especially global capitalist processes and relations.

Feminists' interest in the gendered processes of global capitalism found their way into development studies, critiques of neoliberalism, international relations, international political economy, and transnational networking. Numerous feminist accounts of global processes have analyzed the gendered effects of globalization, which shape gendered ideologies, institutions, hierarchies, and inequality structures. Specifically highlighting the experiences of poor third-world women, these works reveal that the most devastating effects of globalization fall on women (see, for example, Figure 14.2 which shows the risks of maternal mortality in countries around the globe). Such perspectives, which consider how gender intersects with class, nation, race, and other structures, also reflect an intersectional perspective (Collins 2000; Runyan 2012) that is important in analyses of globalization.

GENDER AND THE ECONOMY

As noted throughout this book, a central feature of globalization is the transformation of the global economy. From the 1970s on, production has been reorganized through global production systems. To cut labor costs, MNCs shifted production to low-wage economies. The effects have been significant for the labor force both in developed and developing countries. In developed countries, low-income part-time and temporary jobs replaced middle-income manufacturing jobs. Developing countries have seen a growth in low-paying, informal, and temporary jobs as their economies have shifted from nationalized industries and public sectors to export-oriented production. Women are found disproportionately in all these types of jobs in both developed and less developed countries.

The major changes in production systems in developing countries have been spurred on through structural adjustment programs (see Chapters 4 and 6), which have been imposed on developing countries as the path to economic development. Although these policies have had adverse effects across many different groups, their impact on women's labor and well-being has been especially negative, with an expansion of female labor-intensive production (Berik 2000; Cagatay and Ozler 1995; Elson 1995; Runyan 2012).

Within the last two decades, women's labor-force participation in paid employment has increased dramatically around the globe. Since the late 1970s and early 1980s, there has been a notable increase in women's labor-force participation rates in the Americas and Western Europe. Even though there are significant variations within and across regions, women's labor-force participation has also risen substantially in sub-Saharan Africa, North Africa, Eastern Europe, Southeast Asia, and East Asia over this period (Cagatay and Ozler 1995; Heintz 2006; Moghadam 1999). While the progress in women's employment status is linked, at least in part, to gender equality movements, the key factor in this change appears to be the better integration of an increasing number of areas into the world economy.

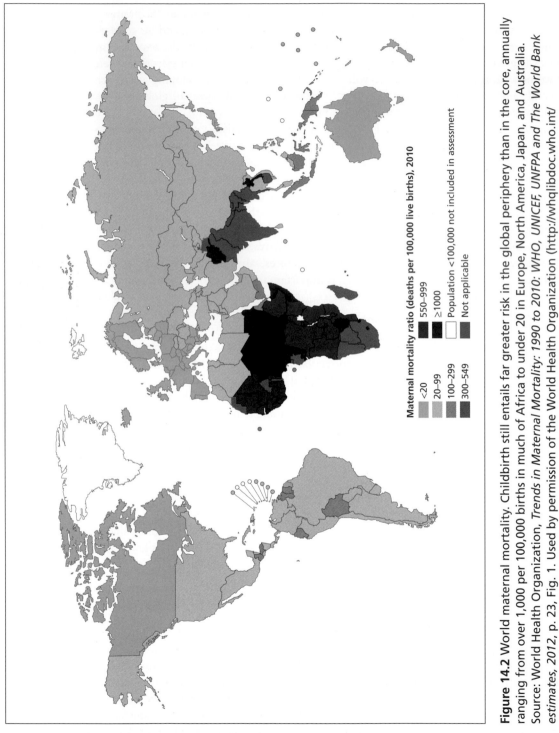

Figure 14.2 World maternal mortality. Childbirth still entails far greater risk in the global periphery than in the core, annually ranging from over 1,000 per 100,000 births in much of Africa to under 20 in Europe, North America, Japan, and Australia. Source: World Health Organization, *Trends in Maternal Mortality: 1990 to 2010: WHO, UNICEF, UNFPA and The World Bank estimates, 2012*, p. 23, Fig. 1. Used by permission of the World Health Organization (http://whqlibdoc.who.int/publications/2012/9789241503631_eng.pdf?ua=1).

The greater involvement of women in the global paid-labor market is observable in all productive sectors and in a variety of occupations and professions in the service sector. Women are increasingly employed in public service and are more likely to work as teachers and university professors; as nurses and doctors in state hospitals; and as workers and administrators in government offices (Moghadam 1999). Women are also concentrated in professional services such as law, banking, accounting, computing, and architecture. Women predominate in such office jobs as data entry, airline booking, credit-cards, word-processing, and telecommunications (Freeman 2001; Gaio 1995; Pearson 2000). There has also been a significant increase in the informal as well as the formal employment of women. Women's labor migration to work as nannies, domestics, nurses, waitresses, and sex workers (Williams 2012) constitutes a significant proportion of the international informal labor force (and of human trafficking; see Chapter 10). Beyond services, women are heavily employed in agriculture, as well as in the labor-intensive manufacture of products such as garments, sportswear, and electronics.

The increasing participation of women in both the global formal and informal paid labor force has been termed the **feminization of labor** (Richer 2012; Standing 1989). This refers to the rise of female labor participation in all sectors and the movement of women into jobs traditionally held by men. This global trend has occurred in both developing and developed countries. In many developed countries, educated middle-class women have made inroads in professional and managerial employment, resulting in a decline in the differences between male and female labor participation rates. The feminization of labor has also taken place in the developing world.

> **Feminization of labor:** Increasing participation of women in the global formal and informal paid-labor force.

The feminization of labor in the developing economies is often accompanied by the *feminization of poverty* (Chant 2012) and by *female proletarianization*. In many of those economies, women's increased participation in paid employment is caused mainly by the shift from import substitution to export-oriented manufacturing (Cagatay and Ozler 1995; Joekes 1987; Standing 1989; Standing 1999). Globally, more women are being drawn into labor-intensive and low-paying industries such as textiles, apparel, leather products, food processing, and electronics. For instance, women represented more than half of the workforce in electronics production in Hong Kong, Macau, Singapore, Taiwan, the Czech Republic, Malaysia, Indonesia, Puerto Rico, Slovenia, Cuba, the Philippines, Thailand, and Sri Lanka (Ferus-Comelo 2006).

Jobs in these industries are characterized by the flexible use of labor, high turnover rates, part-time and temporary employment, and a lack of security and benefits. Women are preferred in these industries because they will typically work for lower wages and they are seen as easier for male employers and managers to supervise. They are not only considered to be more docile, but also to have greater patience and more dexterity than men in performing standardized and repetitive work (Elson and Pearson 1981). Female employment is also characterized by poorer working conditions, more compulsory overtime with no extra pay, and more dangerous working conditions.

A great deal of attention has been focused on the relationship between globalization and the place of women in the local, regional (Bose and Acosta-Belen 1995), and global economy. Of particular importance, at least from the perspective of globalization, is the place of women in what has been called the "global assembly line in which research and management are controlled by the core and developed countries while assembly line work is relegated to semiperiphery or periphery nations that occupy less privileged positions in the global economy" (Ward 1990: 1). Clearly, women are much more likely to be employed in the latter than in the higher-level positions in the core.

Jane Collins (2003) has done an ethnography of part of this global assembly line involving the headquarters of a global apparel firm in New Jersey, a knitting mill in the southern part of Virginia, and two apparel factories in Aguascalientes in Mexico. Work in this industry is highly gendered and is dominated by females. It is of particular interest in this book, given its focus on global flows, especially its concern with the "flow of resources and power between these sites" (Collins 2003: ix). It is also of interest because wherever she looked in the world, Collins found an increasing McDonaldization (see Chapter 8) of work, especially reliance on Taylorism to measure, control, and de-skill work dominated by females. Workers, especially in Mexico, had their positions weakened vis-à-vis their employers because of subcontracting (workers have no contact with their employers and little knowledge of the firm) and the casualization of work. These contributed to the fact the female Mexican workers had no way to present grievances about their work situation or to act collectively against their employer.

As we saw in Chapter 4, Export Processing Zones (EPZs) are special industrial areas, often in developing countries, designed to draw foreign companies and capital investment. EPZs offer multinational companies incentives including exemption from labor and environmental regulations, taxes, tariffs, and quotas. EPZs are characteristically unstable as they are likely to move time and again to countries where labor is cheaper and more compliant. A wide range of products are produced in EPZs including tennis rackets in St. Vincent (Caribbean), furniture in Mauritius, and jewelry in Thailand. However, EPZs mainly focus on the production of textiles, clothing, and electronics for the mass market. Again, women are preferred in these production sites because they are considered more meticulous, disciplined, and compliant than men, and therefore, among other things, less likely to unionize.

It is often suggested that EPZs reduce poverty and unemployment and, as a result, facilitate the economic development of the host countries. While some development can occur, especially if countries can shift to more advanced manufacturing over time, it does come with some serious costs. Working conditions are brutal in most EPZs, where violence and abuse are daily routines. A work day may consist of long shifts with unpaid overtime, non-payment for workers on sick leave, insufficient health and safety measures, monitored access to bathrooms, sexual harassment, physical abuse, and in some cases forced consumption of amphetamines to ensure efficiency. Working conditions are particularly hard on women, especially those who are pregnant and with infants. In some EPZs, corporations require pregnancy testing as a condition for employment and for maintaining a job. Gender bias can also intersect with age discrimination. EPZs tend to hire mostly young and single women; women over 25 years of age are usually not hired since they are seen to be more likely to bear children (Pun 1995).

While women's labor-force participation has increased in almost all regions, the most significant increase in female employment in developing countries has been in informal sectors of the economy (Moghadam 1999). Two-thirds of female labor-force participation in developing countries is concentrated in the informal economy; in sub-Saharan Africa the proportion is as high as 84%.[12] Informal employment includes temporary work without fixed employers, paid employment from home, domestic work for households (Parreñas 2001), and industrial work for sub-contractors. Informal sectors are characterized by low pay and a lack of secure contracts, worker benefits, or social protection. Workers in the informal economy do not have wage agreements, employment contracts, regular working hours, and health insurance or unemployment benefits. They typically earn below legal minimum wage and are often not paid on time.

While greater informal employment characterizes both the male and female labor force globally, women and men are concentrated in different types of informal work. Men are concentrated mainly in informal wage and agricultural employment, while women are typically concentrated in non-agricultural employment, domestic work, and unpaid work in family enterprises. Compared to men's informal employment, women's employment is much more likely to have lower hourly wages and less stability.

The trend toward flexibilization and decentralization in production has contributed significantly to the rise in informal female employment in developing countries. In order to reduce labor costs, most MNCs establish sub-contracting networks with local manufacturers employing low-paid workers, mostly women, who can be terminated quickly and easily (Pyle and Ward 2003). In these production networks women are more likely to work in small workshops or from home.

Traditional gender roles and ideas about femininity encourage home-based work. Gendered ideas relating to the division of labor assign reproductive work to women and productive work to men. As a result, the "real" work of women is considered care-giving and homemaking as mothers, wives, and daughters, rather than as wage earners. Since the increase in female labor participation is almost never accompanied by a decrease in their domestic workload, many women accept the lower wages and less formal working arrangements of home-based work in order to be able to continue to carry out household responsibilities.

The global economy creates jobs not only in developing economies, but also in the developed world. The advanced corporate economic centers, especially world and global cities (see Chapter 13), require large amounts of low wage labor to maintain the operation of their offices and the lifestyles of entrepreneurs, managers, and professionals associated with them. The state-of-the art offices of MNCs' headquarters require clerical, cleaning, and repair workers, truckers to bring their software, copying paper, office furniture, and even toilet paper (Sassen 2004). Furthermore, provisioning and cleaning offices, child care, caring for the elderly and for homes is done by others. The vast majority of these tasks are performed by immigrants, primarily women, from third-world countries (Acker 2004: 34).

The feminization of wage labor in the global economy has contributed to the increase in female migration. As Ehrenreich and Hochschild (2002: 2) put it, "Women are on the move as never before in history." Much of this involves women from the South moving, with or without authorization, to the North to handle women's work (as, for example, nannies [Cheever 2002], maids [Ehrenreich 2002], and sex workers [Williams 2012]) historically performed by women from the North. Nine of the largest immigrant-exporting countries are China, India, Indonesia, Myanmar, Pakistan, the Philippines, Sri Lanka, Thailand, and Bangladesh. This immigration serves to enrich the North and to enhance the already elevated lifestyle in the North. Intensifying the feminization of migration, domestic work has grown on a local and global scale and is now considered the largest labor market for women worldwide.

Since most female migration takes place in undocumented and informal ways, women laborers face the worst forms of discrimination, exploitation, and abuse. They can be held as debt hostages by the recruitment agencies for their transportation and placement fees, locked up in the houses of their employers, treated inhumanely, and sometimes even murdered. An increasing number of migrant women are victims of sexual abuse, sex-trafficking, and prostitution.

GLOBAL CARE CHAINS

Arlie Hochschild (2000) argues that migration of domestic workers is part of a **global care chain**, involving a series of personal relationships between people across the globe based on the paid or unpaid work of caring (see Chapter 7) (Yeates 2012). Care includes social, health, and sexual care services, and usually involves menial tasks such as cooking, cleaning, and ironing. In global care chains, women supply their own care labor to the employer while consuming other women's care labor, both paid and unpaid. Migrant domestic workers often rely on female relatives, neighbors, and daughters as well as paid domestic workers for the care of their children. For instance, while a mother works as a nanny in a developed country, her young children may be cared for by an older daughter or by a nanny who migrated from some even less developed country. On one end of the chain is a woman in the North pursuing professional employment and finding herself unable to fulfill her duties within the family. On the other is a domestic worker's oldest daughter taking over her mother's familial duties.

Referred to not only as *the global care chain*, but also the *international transfer of caretaking*, *global nanny chain*, and *racial division of reproductive labor*, the transfer of reproductive labor from women in advanced economies to those in developing economies points to a paradoxical situation in women's empowerment through participation in the labor force. While women in the North are able to undertake careers, they tend to pass their household duties and reproductive labor on to low-wage immigrant workers. Rather than pushing for a redistribution of household responsibilities among family members, women as employers maintain the gender division of labor by transferring the most devalued work to disadvantaged women. As a result, the worth of reproductive labor (and of women) declines even further (Parreñas 2001). In this sense, women's labor-force participation does not necessarily result in a change in traditional gender roles, but rather in the greater exploitation of immigrant women by middle- and upper-class women.

The provision of reproductive labor by migrant domestic workers is not new. It has been obtained by class-privileged women for centuries. However, the flow of reproductive labor has increased due to globalization and the growth of the global economy. There is a substantial and increasing demand for migrant domestic workers in the North and the bulk of the supply comes from the South.

MAIL-ORDER BRIDES

The relative lack of power and economic opportunity of women is also illustrated by the rapid rise of the mail-order bride industry. Largely because of the Internet, the mail-order bride business has become a multi-million-dollar global industry (Sarker et al. 2013). The mail-order bride industry more than doubled between 1999 and 2007, when 16,500 marriages were arranged through such services (Wayne 2011). Men, usually in the global North, pay several thousands of dollars to acquire wives who are usually much younger than them, and who come from developing countries. Some women enter the market for mail-order brides willingly because they see the US and other developed countries as desirable places to live. However, many women advertised as mail-order brides are trafficked (see also Chapter 10). These human-trafficking victims come mostly from the Philippines, Laos, Myanmar, Vietnam, Thailand, and the former Soviet Union.

The mail-order bride industry is a segmented market much like any other. For example, Thai women are often promoted as sex workers, while Filipina women are advertised as helpers and wives. Hand-In-Hand is one business that provides mail-order brides, and their website appeals to men who are looking for docile and obedient wives:

> Hand-In-Hand's website trumpets the fact that its females are "unspoiled by feminism." … "You take a beautiful woman from the Czech Republic and you bring her into your home, she does all your cooking and cleaning and ironing," he says. "At the end of the day, the service is free." Hand-In-Hand estimates the potential savings of a homemaking wife at $150 per week. (Wayne 2011)

Clearly, women here are treated as objects to be bought and used by men. For trafficked women, they may be forced into sex or domestic work through this industry with no hope of escape.

SEXUALITY

Sexual minorities represent a diverse group of people, whose identities are conceived on a spectrum including lesbian, gay, bisexual, transgender, and queer and/or questioning (LGBTQ) peoples. Like race, ethnicity, and gender, conceptions of sexuality are also socially constructed. For example, homosexuality depends on how a society defines sex and gender (Ryan 2012). In most Western cultures, the idea of two genders, which are each representative of a specific sex, presumes homosexuality to be between two men or two women. Some other cultures, however, have conceptions of a third gender category, which is neither man nor woman. One example is the Samoan *Fa'afafine*, who are people whose sex is male, but who behave, dress, work, and are treated in most respects as social women. It is important to note that they are not considered to be masculine, feminine, or transgender; they are considered to be an entirely different gender (there is no equivalent to this in western cultures). In Samoan culture, if men have sex with a *Fa'afafine* (who is biologically a male), they are not considered homosexual because the sexual relationship is with someone of a different gender. Not only do many westerners have a difficult time understanding the concept of a third gender (e.g. *Fa'afafine*), they are likely to perceive this to be a homosexual relationship.

There is a tremendous degree of global variation in the rights between majority (i.e. heterosexual) and minority (i.e. LGBTQ) populations (Lind 2010). For example, in most countries, homosexual partners are not legally allowed to marry. As of early 2014, only 17 countries had marriage equality, including Argentina, England/Wales, New Zealand, South Africa, Belgium, France, Norway, Spain, Brazil, Iceland, Portugal, Sweden, Canada, the Netherlands, Scotland, Uruguay, and Denmark (plus some jurisdictions in Mexico and the US). Fewer countries (14) permitted homosexual parents to adopt children, despite the fact that not a "single peer-reviewed study has ever shown significant harm to children of same-sex parents as opposed to opposite-sex parents (with the exception of added societal discrimination having nothing to do with the parents themselves)" (Ryan 2012).

A particularly striking form of inequality includes national laws that make homosexuality itself illegal (Figure 14.3 shows which countries have made homosexual acts illegal, including places that have made it punishable by death). For example, homosexual sex has been illegal in Nigeria since it was under colonial rule by the British, but a 2014 law promoted more convictions and covered more homosexual activities. Now people can receive

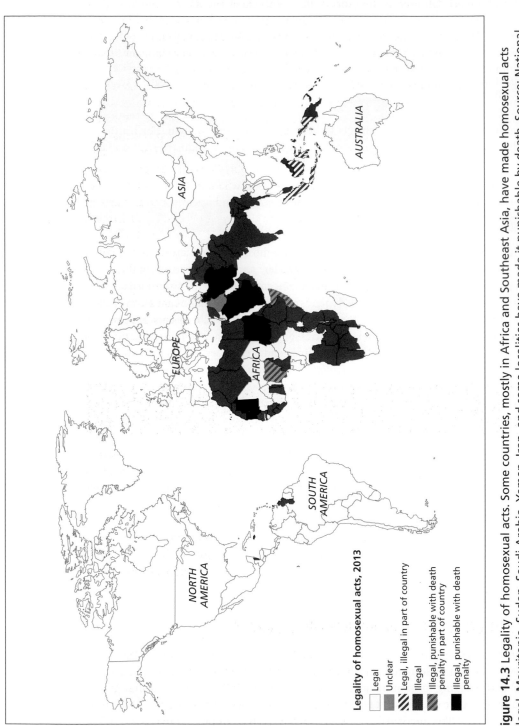

Figure 14.3 Legality of homosexual acts. Some countries, mostly in Africa and Southeast Asia, have made homosexual acts illegal. Mauritania, Sudan, Saudi Arabia, Yemen, Iran, and some localities have made it punishable by death. Source: National Geographic Staff/National Geographic Creative. Image 1916761, Legality of Homosexual Acts, 2013. Data from International Lesbian, Gay, Bisexual, Trans and Intersex Association.

ten years in jail for "directly or indirectly" making a "public show" of homosexual relationships (Nossiter 2014). Of course, the penalty for homosexual sex itself is much higher: being stoned to death. In fact, Amnesty International reports that homosexuality has been criminalized in 38 of 54 African countries, and is punishable by death in four of them. The problem exists far beyond African countries, with violent clashes over gay rights in Russia, Ukraine, and many other countries around the world (Schmemann 2014).

Another key issue from the perspective of this book is the barriers that are erected both within their home country, as well as between countries, and the ways in which those barriers inhibit or cause a global flow of sexual minorities. Barriers at home (e.g. to equal opportunity at work, to same-sex marriages), as well as more extreme problems (e.g. physical assaults on, even murders of, sexual minorities), can force sexual minorities into seeking a better life elsewhere in the world. They are not only "pushed" by problems at home (e.g. Nigeria, Russia), but they can also be pulled elsewhere in the world by better conditions (e.g. more opportunities to work and marry; large and open [especially urban] sexual minority groups accepted by the majority group). Other aspects of globalization such as inexpensive air travel and the Internet have made it easier for sexual minorities to communicate and to be with those who share their orientation and life-style. Globalization has also contributed to the rise of gay and lesbian global social movements (Parker et al. 2014) and to the increasing acceptance in large parts of the world of same-sex sexual relationships (Frank and McEneaney 1999). Yet, while it could be argued that globalization has aided sexual minorities, globalization has also aided the spread of forms of prejudice and discrimination against them (e.g. homophobia [Binnie 2004: 77]); globalization has not been an unmitigated good as far as sexual minorities are concerned.

RESPONDING TO AND RESISTING GLOBAL MINORITY STATUS: THE CASE OF WOMEN

While the next chapter will deal with responses, and resistance, to globalization, especially its negative consequences, we have already dealt with some of these issues in Chapter 11 on responses to global environmental problems. We will follow that precedent in this chapter and close it by dealing with the way one minority group, women, has responded to globalization (Moghadam 2013). We choose to focus on women in part because we lack the space to deal with all the minorities discussed in this chapter and because it is women who have mobilized the broadest and most successful resistance to the problems they face throughout the world as a result of globalization (see Figure 14.4, which shows the global spread of the enfranchisement of women over time).

THE INTERNATIONAL WOMEN'S MOVEMENT

The International Women's Movement has a long history traceable back to the late 1800s (Rupp 1997), and its greatest triumphs have related to the increasingly global acquisition of the rights of suffrage (Ramirez, Soysal, and Shanahan 1997). However, it has grown dramatically in recent years both because of problems created for women by globalization and because of the increased ability to create a global women's movement. A key event was the United Nations International Women's Year in 1975 and four world conferences – Mexico City (1975), Copenhagen (1980), Nairobi (1985), and Beijing (1995)

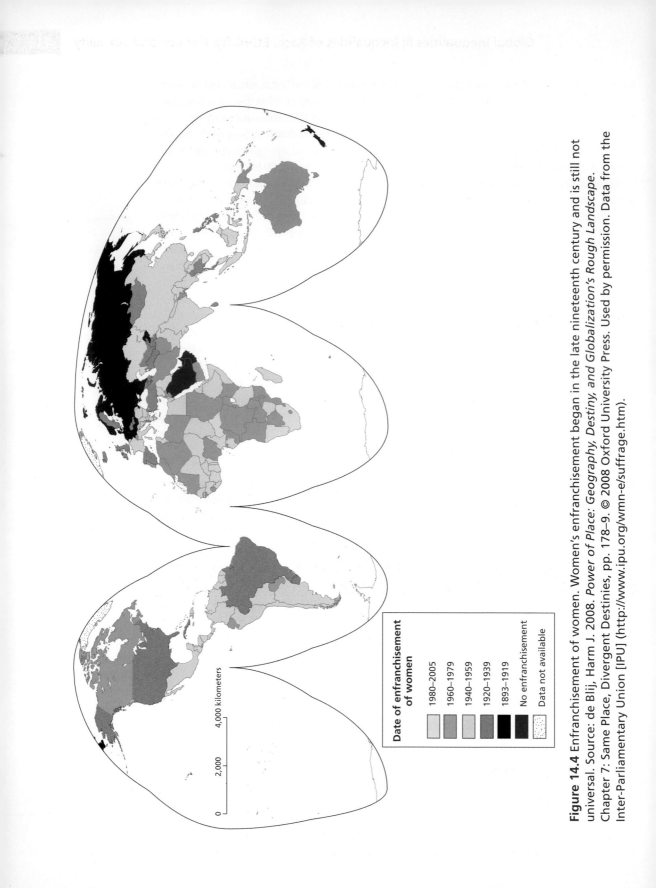

Figure 14.4 Enfranchisement of women. Women's enfranchisement began in the late nineteenth century and is still not universal. Source: de Blij, Harm J. 2008. *Power of Place: Geography, Destiny, and Globalization's Rough Landscape.* Chapter 7: Same Place, Divergent Destinies, pp. 178–9. © 2008 Oxford University Press. Used by permission. Data from the Inter-Parliamentary Union [IPU] (http://www.ipu.org/wmn-e/suffrage.htm).

(Alter Chen 1995). (Snyder [2006] sees the UN as an "unlikely godmother" of the women's movement.) Personal networks throughout the globe emerged from these meetings and the Internet has greatly increased the ability of women to interact and to mobilize on a global basis (Moghadam 2013). A variety of specific issues were the focus of the UN meetings, as well as the larger global movement that developed, including human rights (Yuval-Davis 2006), economic concerns, health-care issues, and violence against women. Later, concern came to focus on the adverse effects of global capitalism (e.g. increased global trafficking in women), the lack of a voice in global civil society, the growth of antifeminist fundamentalist movements (e.g. the Taliban), and the HIV/AIDS epidemic. More positively, the global women's movement has come to focus on issues of global justice for women and other minorities. It has come to have a strong impact on the UN and has helped to create strong linkages between the UN, national governments, and NGOs (George 2007).

LOCAL RESPONSES TO GLOBAL PROBLEMS

Women throughout the world have not only been involved in the global women's movement, but they have responded at local and regional levels to a variety of problems caused there by globalization.[13] They interact and organize across borders and at transnational and global levels to deal with common problems caused by globalization. They also localize global political activities undertaken by the women's movement, global human rights groups, etc., and they organize against global activities (e.g. militarism) and use global organizations (such as the UN and INGOs) to help in local and regional activities (Naples and Desai 2002b). While these and other global linkages are important, it is also the case that many of the activities undertaken by women have been primarily or exclusively local in nature (Basu 1995). Nevertheless, many of these actions have had a profound effect globally. Even with all the local variations, Marx Ferree and Tripp (2006: viii) argue that feminism needs to be seen as "a truly global phenomenon."

CHAPTER SUMMARY

This chapter examines the relations between a variety of global majority and minority groups. A key concept in this analysis is intersectionality, the idea that members of any given minority group are affected by the nature of their positions in other forms of social inequality simultaneously.

Categorization as a majority or minority group concerns relations of superordination and subordination, rather than numbers. Thus a minority group is in a subordinate position in wealth, power, and (or) privilege, while a majority group is in a superordinate position on these variables. Majority–minority relations are fraught with the potential for conflict, which may descend into violence. As a general rule, it may be argued that the North is characterized by more majority-group members, while the South has more minority-group members. Processes such as imperialism, colonialism, development, Westernization, Americanization, and neoliberalism often involve the creation of minority groups to control and oppress.

Minority groups are more likely to be affected by negative flows. Meanwhile, those in the majority groups are likely to be involved in positive flows, both as creators as well as recipients. They are also better able to create protective barriers between themselves and negative flows. Minority statuses relating to race, ethnicity, gender, class, sexual orientation, and living in the South serve, in themselves, as subtler barriers to positive flows.

All majority and minority statuses involve social definition. As a result these statuses tend to differ, with variations in social definition from one locale to another and over time. For instance, there is nothing intrinsically distinctive about any racial or ethnic group that distinguishes it from others – these are fluid categories that are socially constructed.

Ethnicity is closely related to the idea of a nation-state. The idea of the nation-state involves a fusion of a given nation, or ethnic group, with a state apparatus within a given territory and its borders. However, a nation has never been coterminous with territorial boundaries and this is more evident in the era of globalization and global migration. Due to the movements of ethnic groups nation-states are becoming increasingly porous. Political definitions of nationalism have given way to a focus on cultural nationalism. While some argue that globalization poses a threat to ethnic identities, they may in fact be reinforced by resistance to global pressures toward homogenization of identity. Indeed, globalization and the creation of ethnicity may be seen as a part of the same modern process. Greater ethnic diversity within a nation-state has increased the possibility of ethnic conflict within their confines. Various methods may be adopted to "deal" with ethnic minorities in nation-states or other delimited areas. The most extreme involve genocide.

Racism is defined as the belief that one racial group is superior and another is inferior. Racial minorities are sometimes seen as sub-human and destructive of not only human values but human life. Globalization has aggravated race relations in many developed countries. As a result of massive international migration, most developed industrial societies have become increasingly diverse in terms of racial and ethnic composition. This rapid influx can lead to racism and xenophobia. The Latin Americanization of race relations refers to the tripartite system of racial hierarchy (of whites, honorary whites, and collective blacks) that has flowed from Latin America to other countries (especially the US).

Globalization reinforces gender structures, barriers, and relationships. A key aspect of globalization has been the transformation of the nature of economic activity. Women are found disproportionately in low-paying, part-time, and temporary jobs in both developed and less developed countries. The increasing participation of women in both the formal and informal paid-labor force has been termed feminization of the labor force. In developing economies, this may be accompanied by the feminization of poverty as well as female proletarianization. It is also accompanied by an increase in female migration. A large part of this migration takes place in illegal and informal ways, leaving female laborers vulnerable to discrimination, exploitation, and abuse.

Sexual minorities experience much discrimination, such as homosexuals being denied the right to marry in many countries throughout the world. They also face barriers both within their home country, as well as between countries. These barriers may inhibit or cause a global flow of sexual minorities. Globalization has also contributed to the rise of gay and lesbian global movements, but it has also aided the spread of forms of prejudice and discrimination against them.

The global and local women's movement is a prime example of successful resistance to some of the excesses of globalization.

DISCUSSION QUESTIONS

1. Discuss the concept of intersectionality with respect to global flows and structures.

2. Examine the social construction of "majority" and "minority" and the ways those constructs effect immigration.

3. Examine the impact of global flows on ethnicity and nationality.

4. Analyze the impact of global flows and structures on gendered social relations, particularly in the global South.

5. Examine the impact of global flows on race relations.

6. Can the success of the women's movement be a model for other minority groups seeking to combat the negative effects of globalization?

ADDITIONAL READINGS ···

Howard Winant. *The World is a Ghetto: Race and Democracy since World War II*. New York: Basic Books, 2001.

Howard Winant. *The New Politics of Race: Globalism, Difference, Justice*. Minneapolis: University of Minnesota Press, 2004.

Paul Gilroy. *The Black Atlantic: Modernity and Double Consciousness*. Cambridge, MA: Harvard University Press, 1993.

Carl Degler. *Neither Black Nor White: Slavery and Race Relations in Brazil and the United States*. Madison: University of Wisconsin, 1971/1986.

Rebecca King-O'Riain, Stephen Small, Minelle Mahtani, Miri Song, and Paul Spickard, eds. *Global Mixed Race*. New York: NYU Press, 2014.

Ernest Gellner. *Nations and Nationalism*. Oxford: Blackwell, 1983.

Chow, Esther Ngan-Ling, Marcia Texler Segal, and Tan Lin, eds. *Analyzing Gender, Intersectionality, and Multiple Inequalities: Global-Transnational and Local Contexts*. Cambridge, MA: Emerald, 2011.

Rhacel Salazar Parreñas. *Servants of Globalization: Women, Migration and Domestic Work*. Stanford, CA: Stanford University Press, 2001.

Barbara Ehrenreich and Arlie Hochschild, eds. *Global Woman: Nannies, Maids and Sex Workers in the New Economy*. New York: Henry Holt, 2002.

Shirin M. Rai and Georgina Waylen, eds. *New Frontiers in Feminist Political Economy*. New York: Routledge, 2014.

Dennis Altman. *Global Sex*. Chicago: University of Chicago Press, 2001.

Jon Binnie. *The Globalization of Sexuality*. London: Sage, 2004.

Amy Lind. *Development, Sexual Rights and Global Governance*. New York: Routledge, 2010.

Leila J. Rupp. *Worlds of Women: The Making of an International Women's Movement*. Princeton: Princeton University Press, 1997.

Nancy A. Naples and Manisha Desai, eds. *Women's Activism and Globalization: Linking Local Struggles and Transnational Politics*. New York: Routledge, 2002.

NOTES

1   Thank you to Zeynep Atalay for her significant contributions to this chapter.
2   For a somewhat similar view, see Gilroy (1993: 32), as well as Winant (2004: 135).
3   Actually, majority–minority status is not necessarily defined by all three of these dimensions; a higher ranking in only one (or two) could be enough to accord a group majority status and, by implication, make another a minority group.
4   Howard Winant (2001) analyzes these three cases, as well as that of Europe.
5   Winant (2001: xiv) sees the North–South distinction as the same as that between white- and dark-skinned.
6   Huntington is sometimes viewed as an Orientalist, especially for his negative views of Islam.
7   He identifies with W. E. B. Du Bois, who Gilroy (1993: 127) sees "in explicit opposition to a mode of analysis premised on the fixity of the modern nation-state as a receptacle of black culture."
8   Although, social definitions are involved here, as well.
9   This is but one of five definitions of nation offered by Cox (2007) – essentialist, subjectivist, inventions, imagined (see below), and discursive formations.
10 A somewhat more expansive definition is offered by Cerny (2007: 853–8): "a social group that is linked th[r]ough common descent, culture, language, or territorial contiguity."
11 Such expulsion can occur on other bases, as well, such as religion, politics, and ideology.
12 ICFTU – International Confederation of Free Trade Unions, 2004: "The Informal Economy: Women on the Frontline." Trade Union World Briefing, No. 2, March 2.
13 For many examples, see Naples and Desai (2002a).

DEALING WITH, RESISTING, AND THE FUTURES OF, GLOBALIZATION

Globalization: A Basic Text, Second Edition. George Ritzer and Paul Dean.
© 2015 John Wiley & Sons, Ltd. Published 2015 by John Wiley & Sons, Ltd.

The reader should find several things jarring about the title of this final chapter. First, there appears to be a lot going on, seemingly too much, in one chapter. Having devoted 14 chapters to discussing numerous aspects of globalization, it would seem to require perhaps an equal number of chapters to discuss adequately all aspects of just the first two topics in the title – the ways in which globalization is dealt with and resisted (although some aspects of both have been touched on earlier; see especially the last sections of Chapters 11 and 14). Then there is the future of globalization which would require another large number of chapters discussing the future of all the issues discussed previously. However, we clearly cannot offer yet another 30, or even 15, chapters; we will need to be content with this one chapter which can do little more than give a sense of the way people and collectivities have dealt with, resisted, and sought to shape globalization, and offer a few broad brush strokes on the future of globalization.

In addition, the first part of the title of this chapter seems to imply that there is a broad consensus that globalization is problematic and, as such, needs to be dealt with and/or to be resisted. While there are many throughout the world who *do* see globalization in this way, many others are quite content with it, and there are even some who extol its virtues (see Chapter 2). Thus, the title and focus of this chapter should *not* be interpreted to mean that there is universal consensus that globalization is problematic.

Another prefatory remark is needed. As we have seen throughout this book, and pointed out on several occasions, there is no one globalization, there are many globalization*s*. Thus, there is no single phenomenon, no single globalization, to be dealt with; to be resisted. Almost everyone would want to deal with or resist the globalization of crime, but most would be quite happy to see further globalization of the distribution of pharmaceuticals, for example, the "cocktail" needed to treat AIDS. Within the economy, there are huge differences in the way people respond to great concentrations of wealth in comparison to the ever-escalating ability to distribute goods and services globally. The former may need to be dealt with or resisted, but most would want to see the latter encouraged further. Thus, as we discuss various coping mechanisms in this chapter, we need to keep in mind which globalization, or which aspect of it, is being dealt with and/or resisted.

The same point applies to the third topic of this chapter – the future of globalization – there is *no* single future for globalization. Because there are many globalization*s*, there are many futures. While we will need to make do with a few generalizations about the future of globalization and of a few of the globalization*s*, the reader also should keep this in mind.

DEALING WITH GLOBALIZATION

Given limited space, this section will only cover dealing with the economy, the polity, and health care.

DEALING WITH THE GLOBAL ECONOMY

From the perspective of that which needs to be responded to, no issue gets more attention, undoubtedly mainly because of the profound economic inequality in the world, than the economy. This is especially true today as many around the world attempt to deal with the profound economic disruptions caused by the Great Recession. We examine three broad ways of responding to/resisting economic globalization.

Protectionism

Trade exists, of course, within nations (among individuals, companies, and so on) but it is of particular interest here because it occurs globally, and at an accelerating rate in the era of globalization. There has been a general consensus that the free flow of global trade benefits the nations engaged in it. Yet trade, especially free trade, has its critics and there are those who seek to restrict trade through barriers – protectionism – of one sort or another (Mann and Pluck 2007).

Protectionism, or more specifically trade protectionism, is "a policy of systematic government intervention in foreign trade with the objective of encouraging domestic production. This encouragement involves giving preferential treatment to domestic producers and discriminating against foreign competitors" (McAleese 2007). There are various ways to protect and encourage domestic production including tariffs and quotas on foreign imports. Domestic production can be helped more directly through export subsidies (widely used in American agriculture) and more indirectly by such policies as tax relief to producers. Protectionism has existed since the mercantilist era (1500–1800), as well as the early days of the Industrial Revolution, and has been practiced by almost every nation (Chorev 2007). It reached something of a peak following the onset of the Depression in 1929. However, following the end of WW II, and as a result of GATT (1947), and later the founding of the European Economic Union (1958), the tide began to shift away from trade protectionism and toward trade liberalization (Tan 2007). This led the way toward the great expansion of foreign trade and investment.

> **Protectionism:** Government intervention in order to encourage domestic production.

A broad consensus emerged that protectionism did not work, but nonetheless it continued to be practiced by many nations and in various economic sectors. Trade protection continued to co-exist – *very* uncomfortably – with trade liberalization. In spite of its rhetoric of trade liberalization, the United States, among others, was often accused of practicing protectionism (especially in agriculture). And, the US, in turn, often accused many other nations, most notably China and Japan, of continuing to engage in protectionism.

Many reasons have been put forth in defense of a protectionist policy, some as early as the pioneering work of Adam Smith (1953). Smith argued that it was legitimate to protect a nation's important defense industries, to impose a tax on foreign imports, to retaliate against a country imposing a tax on a given nation's exports, and to use protectionism to ease the transition to a more liberal trading position. Other reasons that have emerged to legitimate protectionism include assisting in the birth of new industries (as the EU did in the case of Airbus), protecting such new industries as they develop, as well as more generally protecting new economies. In spite of these and other rationales, there was, given the ascendancy of neoliberal economics, a decline in both the belief in, and the practice of, trade protectionism (at least until very recently). Nevertheless, various forms of protectionism remained in place and have been resurrected in various parts of the world, especially in the South, from time to time when the adverse effects of the global neoliberal economy took center stage.

Trade protectionism declined because of a perception that its negative effects outweighed the benefits. First, those industries that receive protection tend, over time, to grow increasingly inefficient. They seem to require the competition brought about by free trade to hone their operations. It clearly is not in a nation's interest to support inefficient industries, at least in the long run. Second, protectionism not only discourages imports, but also exports because the tariffs on imported components raise the cost of production to industries in the nation engaging in protectionism. This leads to increases in prices and tends to make a protectionist nation's exports less competitive, especially compared to those of nations without the kinds of trade barriers that tend to raise costs. Third, the protected industries have little interest in, and motivation for, innovation; their protected position makes innovation unnecessary. Fourth, protectionism tends to lead, especially in developing nations (but not, historically, in the US), to a focus on manufacturing with the result that agriculture is adversely affected, or at least not similarly advantaged. Such countries are highly dependent on their agriculture for subsistence and its decline can have disastrous consequences for the population as a whole.

Interestingly, those nations that have restricted imports (engaged in protectionism) tended to suffer more from protectionism than those countries (the "victims" of protectionism) that were impeded from exporting to those nations. Thus, the US, for example, would gain more from eliminating its protective agricultural policies than would those nations that would then be freer to export their products to the US.

While trade liberalization became dominant, especially in the hegemonic neoliberal perspective, there continued to be pressures toward protectionism. On the one hand, developed nations often wanted trade protection because of fear that inexpensive imports from less developed countries would destroy domestic industries. On the other hand, less developed countries often complained about continuing trade barriers in developed nations and about pressures on them (but *not* developed countries) by the IMF and the World Bank to liberalize – and rapidly – much of their economies. Furthermore, less developed countries often felt that as a result of trade liberalization they were engaged with other less developed nations in a "race to the bottom" (see Chapter 7) in which they competed with one another to produce more at lower cost for the developed world. Instead of their standard of living improving as a result of trade liberalization, they frequently found that it was at best stable and more likely in decline. In spite of these, and other, issues, the trend for many years after the end of WW II was certainly in the direction of trade liberalization. However, there were critics who argued that trade liberalization really didn't offer the benefits it was supposed to have and that it disproportionately helped the developed rather than the less developed nations. Some, especially in the South, saw trade liberalization as part of neoliberal economics designed to help the richer nations at their expense. In spite of such arguments and views, there were few in those days anywhere in the world who would have argued for a resurrection of full-scale trade barriers.

There are a large number of factors that explain periodically renewed calls for increased protectionism (Reuveny and Thompson 2001). For example: shocks to the economic system, a long-term shift from one system to another (from agrarian to industrial), the preferences of voters and the politicians they elect, the use of protection to further a nation's foreign policy objectives and the interests of one's allies, the absence of a free-trade ideology and the persistence of an ideology favoring protectionism, reciprocity because of protectionism practiced by another nation, and so on. These and other factors continued to foster protectionism, but they were subordinated, at least at the time, to the global triumph (not without deep and continuing resistance) of neoliberalism and trade liberalization. Nonetheless, resentment of trade liberalization, as well as the ways in which it seemed to benefit the rich nations and disadvantage the poor, continued to stimulate efforts at protectionism, especially in less developed nations. For their part, the rich nations generally wished to retain their positions and were often hostile to the advantages (e.g. lower wages) industries in less developed nations had over their own industries. Thus, there were pressures in *both* developed and less developed nations to retain, or re-impose, trade barriers even in a global economy increasingly characterized by trade liberalization.

The onset of the Great Recession led to a widespread questioning of the neoliberal model of free and unregulated trade. As in the Great Recession (see Chapter 6), there was a resurgence of interest in protectionism as a way of warding off the worst effects of the recession. Thus President Barack Obama's 2009 stimulus plan involved a "buy American" provision. That is, public works and building projects that used funds derived from the plan were to use goods and materials, including iron and steel, made in the US. Similar positions were being taken elsewhere in the world. How far various nations move in the direction of greater protectionism depends to a large degree on how long the recession lasts and how deep it gets. Whatever happens, the increased use of protectionism fits with the general orientation of this book because protectionism is being used as a *barrier* in an attempt to ward off the worst effects of the *negative flows* associated with a deep global recession.

Fair trade

Taken to its logical extreme, trade protectionism implies a rejection of the global economy, especially in its neoliberal form. However, there are less extreme ways of dealing with inequities in the global economy and one of them is "fair trade" (Brown 2013; Lyon and Moberg 2010; Nicholls and Opal 2005; Raynolds, Murray, and Wilkinson 2007; Stehr 2008) which stands in opposition to the "free trade" that is at the heart of neoliberalism.

Fair trade is defined by the International Fair Trade Association as a "concern for the social, economic and environmental well-being of marginalized small producers" (Andrew Downie 2007: C1–C5). In contrast to the purely utilitarian orientation of neoliberalism, fair trade is oriented toward a more *moral* and *equitable* global economic system.[1] It is concerned with:

> **Fair trade:** Concern for the social, economic, and environmental well-being of marginalized small producers.

- creating direct relationships between producers, usually in the South, and consumers, ordinarily in the North;
- "establishing more just prices"; price should not be set simply by the "free" market, but by what is just as far as producers, and the social and ecological environment in which they live and work, are concerned; price is not to be set by the "market" but negotiated openly, transparently, and equally by producers and those who seek to acquire what they produce; each should seek to understand and accommodate the other's needs;
- protecting producers, especially farmers, from dramatic swings in prices for their products;
- providing work for those, especially in the South, who are economically disadvantaged;
- protecting workers' rights, including the right to unionize;
- providing work that is safe and not exploitative of women and children;
- engaging in environmentally sound practices; in sustainable production;
- being sure that that which is produced is healthy to consume;
- educating consumers and employing them to put pressure on producers to engage in fair trade practices.

While other parts of the developed world, especially Europe, have been great supporters of fair trade for some time, there are signs that interest in fair trade is finally growing in the US, as well. For example, in 2004 only 12% of Americans said they were aware of fair trade, but this number grew to 27% in 2006 and 34% by 2011. In countries where fair trade is most common (e.g. the UK, Germany), 90% of consumers recognize the Fairtrade logo. Chains such as Dunkin' Donuts and Starbucks are buying more fair trade coffee (as of 2013, 8.4% of Starbucks' coffee was Fairtrade certified) and warehouse chains like Costco are stocking their shelves with more of it. Fair trade coffee imports into Canada and the US grew 18% from 2011 to 2012, with larger increases in many western European countries. Worldwide it is estimated that $5 billion euros were spent on certified Fairtrade products in 2011. A few markets are now becoming dominated by fair trade goods; for example, in Switzerland, 55% of all bananas sold are certified Fairtrade, and in the UK, 42% of all bagged sugar meets fair trade standards.

Fair trade coffee serves to benefit approximately 7 million people in the developing world, where they get at least $1.40 per pound of coffee ($1.70 if it is also certified organic), plus a premium of 20 cents per pound that goes toward communities projects (building schools, health clinics, improving productivity and quality, etc.). Conventional coffee growers are subject to world market prices, which can go as low as $0.45 per pound (in 2013, they averaged $1.10 per pound). In order to qualify for the fair trade designation, a farmer must follow many rules on pesticide use, farming techniques, recycling, democratically run workplaces, etc.

Fair trade is the popular term for the more formal idea of "alternative trade schemes" (McMichael 2007b). Such schemes have a long history going back to WW II. They were built on the base of the sending of aid by England's Oxfam to areas in Europe overrun by the Nazis. Faith-based organizations emerged out of this to import handicrafts from Eastern Europe, and later from less developed areas, to be sold directly to consumers in nonprofit (e.g. church-based) shops. In the 1970s organizations like Traidcraft emerged. Traidcraft used "mail order and other social networking devices to connect producers in lesser-developed countries directly with conscientious consumers in the developed world" (Carducci 2007). Interest in them has expanded dramatically since the 1980s and 1990s with the growth of, and reactions against, neoliberal economic globalization.

There are several global organizations involved in the fair trade movement, including the World Fair Trade Organization and the Fairtrade Labeling Organization (FLO)[2] formed in 1997 on the base of three organizations that had been involved in the European market.

> The FLO's goal is to educate consumers to use their purchasing power as a weapon against the abuses of the corporate system. The certification of fair trade practices, via a guaranteed superior (world) price, includes demands for representative associations of producers or workers to monitor labor conditions, protect worker rights, prohibit child and forced labor, promote safe and healthy working conditions, and sustain communities and environments. (McMichael 2007b: 34)

Thus, for example, a Chilean involved in growing bananas acquired FLO registration by "eliminating herbicide use, reducing chemical fertilizers, building democratic union procedures, raising wages, and establishing a fund, or 'social premium,' set aside for community projects such as housing improvement, electrification, and environmental monitoring" (McMichael 2007b: 34).

Many products have become the focus of fair trade interest and concern, including coffee (Bacon et al. 2008; Brown 2013; Howard and Jaffee 2013; Jaffee 2007), bananas (Moberg 2014), cotton, wine (Moseley 2008), tea (Dolan 2008: 305–18), and chocolate. An interesting fair trade case involves Cadbury Schweppes, the world's largest confectioner in terms of sales, and the supplier of all of the cocoa for its British operations, as well as for 70% of its worldwide operations (*Economist* 2008: January 31 ["Cocoa Farming: Fair Enough?"]). Instead of working with Fairtrade, the company set up its own "Cadbury Cocoa Partnership" with a fund of $87 million to be spent in the ensuing ten years. While Fairtrade emphasizes setting a fair price for a product like cocoa, Cadbury argues that price was not the issue (the chocolate involved from Ghana trades at about 10% above the average world price). Rather, the key problem, at least from its perspective, was the level of cocoa productivity in Ghana. Yields had dropped to 40% and the future looked bleak for cocoa production because farmers' children were less likely than their parents to want to go into the industry. To deal with this, and broader social issues, the Cadbury Cocoa Partnership sought to:

- teach Ghanaian farmers how to increase yields by using fertilizers and by working more collaboratively with one another;
- find additional sources of income for Ghanaian farmers from growing red peppers and mangoes below cocoa trees and coconuts that can grow above them;
- commission the construction of 850 water wells to free women and children from water-fetching chores and allow them to do other tasks, and to invest in schools, teachers, and libraries.

Fairtrade welcomed Cadbury's efforts, but guardedly: "We welcome Cadbury's initiative to support Ghanaian cocoa farmers and their communities, and we will be looking to the company to ensure that principles of sustainable production and fair trade are embedded in the initiative" (*Economist* 2008: January 31 ["Cocoa Farming: Fair Enough?"]). In other words, what Cadbury had done was acceptable to Fairtrade, but it didn't go nearly far enough in supporting the broader principles of the fair trade movement. In fact, Cadbury's initiative helped the farmers, was a good step for Cadbury's from a public relations point of view, and it seemed to support fair trade without signing on to all of Fairtrade's rules. As such, it can be seen as "Fairtrade lite" (*Economist* 2008: January 31 ["Cocoa Farming: Fair Enough?"]).

In general, it does not seem likely that any corporation will go much further than this, at least on its own and without external pressure. This is where organizations like Fairtrade, as well as groups organized and inspired by them (e.g. of farmers, consumers, etc.), have a role, undoubtedly a key role, in fair trade.

However, there are limits to, and problems, with fair trade: there are questions as to whether a fair trade system can really supply a mass global market (e.g. for coffee); it is difficult to see how fair trade can be used in the far more globally significant area of mass-manufactured products; and while fair trade has made inroads among "enlightened" consumers in the developed world, it may be harder to get producers (and consumers) in the lesser developed world, given far more pressing problems, to buy into it.

Helping the "bottom billion"

In Chapter 13 we discussed the bottom billion in the world. It is clear that if any population needs economic assistance, if any global economic problem needs to be dealt with, it is this one. There are several areas in which things can be done to improve the situation facing the bottom billion in the global age.

The first is aid. In 2012, the most generous countries, in terms of foreign aid as a percentage of Gross National Income (GNI), were Luxembourg (1.0%), Sweden (0.99%), Norway (0.93%), Denmark (0.84%), the Netherlands (0.71%), the United Kingdom (0.56%), Finland (0.53%), and Ireland (0.48%). Globally, countries gave 4% less in grants and loans for developing countries, compared to the previous year. In 2012, the US gave less than 0.2% of GNI for foreign aid. While this represented $30 billion, it was also a decline from the previous year, and was a much smaller percentage than almost all other developed countries.

In any case, Collier is not optimistic about aid – even if it is doubled – for a variety of reasons including the fact that:

- while some aid will help, the effect tends to diminish as aid increases;
- the bureaucracies involved do not function well and tend to interfere with one another;
- aid money tends to flow into dysfunctional areas such as the military;
- it can even make the conflict trap (on this and other traps, see Chapter 13) worse by stimulating civil wars by making the capture of the government more valuable;
- it has little effect on the natural resources trap;
- in terms of the trap of being landlocked, it has failed to do what is perhaps of greatest importance in dealing with this trap – improved transportation links to the coast;
- aid to deal with the trap of bad governance has the greatest potential to help, although it too has often failed.

In spite of all this, it is possible that aid could help but only in concert with other actions from the developed countries, especially the G8.

Military intervention can be useful in restoring order, maintaining peace after a conflict ends, and preventing later military coups. While external military intervention can be helpful (but certainly not always), the militaries in the world's poorest countries often make matters worse. For example, once in power through a coup, the military can demand (extort) huge sums of money.

Also of use are changes in laws and charters. Changes are needed in the laws of developed countries in order to better prevent their companies and banks from engaging in exploitative and corrupt practices (e.g. bribes) that adversely affect the bottom billion. International norms, standards, and codes which were largely developed in and for the developed countries need to be adapted and modified (e.g. emphasizing greater transparency) to fit the needs of the bottom billion.

The marginalization of less developed nations can be reversed through trade policy. One course of action is the reduction and elimination of trade barriers (see above) in both developed countries (in part at least through unreciprocated barrier reduction within the WTO) and those that contain most of the bottom billion. The latter would need at least temporary trade protection until they were more competitive economically. However, when goods from free trade are made cheaper because employers can evade social and environmental regulations (e.g. workplace safety standards, taxes to fund education and other social programs) of developing countries, this can simultaneously hurt those in the bottom billion.

It is interesting to note that Collier is *not* a big fan of fair trade. He sees it as a kind of "charity" to, for example, coffee growers in less developed countries. He sees it as even less beneficial than straight aid because higher fair trade prices tend to keep people involved in what they have always done – that is, in this case, producing coffee. The problem is a lack of diversification for the least developed countries, and fair trade serves to reinforce a single-minded focus on producing that which has served to lock such countries into poverty.

DEALING WITH POLITICAL GLOBALIZATION

As was the case with economic issues, there is a near-endless array of things that can be done to deal with global political problems. Space constraints will limit us to the issues of account-ability and transparency, as well as special attention to Transparency International (TI).

Accountability

In a world of increasingly global organizations, especially in this case political organiza-tions, the issue of accountability (or lack thereof) is increasingly important (Germain 2004; Moghadam 2013). On the one hand, all political organizations, including the nation-state, need to be held more accountable for their actions. On the other hand, the decline of the nation-state has freed various organizations (including political organizations) from the constraints of being embedded in it. With the nation-state of declining importance, or out of the picture, the issue arises of to whom or to what they are to be held accountable politi-cally (and in many other ways). Furthermore, there is the more practical problem of whether there is any way that political organizations can be held accountable. One route to ensuring accountability is to have enhanced surveillance over such organizations in order to be sure they operate not only in accord with their own rules and regulations, but also international norms about how such organizations should behave. Another route involves having more organizations and individuals involved in what these political organizations do and involved in a greater dialogue and reciprocity with those who have a stake – the stakeholders – in political organizations.

Transparency

Organizations of all types including, and perhaps especially, political organizations (including nation-states), are generally inclined to secrecy on many matters and this means that much of what they do is *not* transparent. Contemporary examples include the lack of transpar-ency by Iran in terms of its nuclear weapons program, as well as by the US and Israel (which has never publicly revealed that it has a nuclear weapons program that has produced a number of nuclear weapons) over whether they have plans to attack Iran should it be shown to be getting close to obtaining nuclear weapons.

While much political secrecy remains, and this is also the case for many other types of organizations, one recent book on the topic concludes that transparency is growing. However, at the same time, it argues that transparency "is still surrounded by an ocean of opacity" (Holzner and Holzner 2006: 336). Implied here is an historical and ongoing dialec-tic between transparency[3] and secrecy (the deliberate withholding of information), as well as opacity (an absence of information) (Gupta 2012). However, there is also a grand narra-tive offered describing a long-term increase in transparency. Three cases are compared – the United States, the European Union (with particular attention to the very different examples of Sweden and Greece), and Japan. Health care and the business world are two of the major contexts in which the dialectic is examined. Overall, while there are important differences, there is a general trend over time in the direction of greater transparency.

Some of the most interesting discussions deal with case studies – such as the Holocaust, WW II crimes, the Tuskegee syphilis study, and so on – that tend to show the deleterious effects of government secrecy. They also show the movement over time toward more open acknowledgment and discussion of these cases as well as the ways in which they, and innumerable other heinous crimes, were greatly aided by the secrecy and opacity that surrounded them.

A variety of developments have aided in increased transparency including transnational justice systems and movements, international tribunals, civil society, and more specifically Transparency International.

Transparency International (TI)

TI is an INGO founded in 1993 by Peter Eigen, who had become frustrated with his work at the World Bank. He felt he had been forbidden from addressing the issue of corruption in many nations throughout the world because it would adversely affect the image of the World Bank. As a result, at least in part, of this, Eigen left the World Bank and created TI, headquartered in Berlin, which now has about 90 national chapters.[4] It focuses on combating corruption, especially by pushing for greater transparency (Florini 2007). Along these lines in 1995 TI created the Corruption Perceptions Index (CPI). It is based on, and brings together, a number of studies of the perceptions of experts on corruption in their countries. Countries obtain scores ranging from zero (extreme corruption) to 100 (no corruption). In 2013, the most corrupt countries were Afghanistan (8), North Korea (8), Somalia (8), Sudan (11), South Sudan (14), Libya (15), and Iraq (16). The least corrupt countries were Denmark (91), New Zealand (91), Finland (89), Sweden (89), Norway (86), Singapore (86), Switzerland (85), and the Netherlands (83). Some other countries of interest include Japan (74), the US (73), Brazil (42), China (40), and India (36).

Later, TI created the Bribe Payers Index in order to get at the propensity of companies from developed countries to bribe public officials in emerging market economies such as Brazil, Mexico, and Russia. Out of 25 countries ranked in 2011, the Netherlands and Switzerland were the least prone to such bribery, the US ranked in the middle at #10 (again this contradicts the argument made in Chapter 12 that the US is a paragon of virtue as far as corruption is concerned), and Russia was the most bribe-prone nation. The idea behind the publication of such indices is that greater public transparency about the breadth and depth of bribery and other forms of corruption will lead to increased concern about them and that, in turn, will lead to efforts to reduce them and their deleterious effects.

TI has been involved in other activities as well. It publishes *National Integrity Systems: The TI Source Book* (translated into many languages), offering local activists practical strategies for dealing with corruption and for developing greater transparency. It was also instrumental in negotiating an agreement among global banks to combat money laundering, providing small sums of money to those fighting corruption in less developed countries, as well as efforts to combat corruption and bribes that lead to environmental destruction (e.g. through deforestation). Overall, TI seeks a world free of corruption and with far greater transparency. However, there are various barriers to the latter with a notable one being the global concern over terrorism that is leading to greater secrecy and opacity and these, in turn, tend to feed greater corruption.

DEALING WITH GLOBAL HEALTH ISSUES

Dealing with global health problems has been the focus of the UN's World Health Organization (WHO) (Hall 2012). While there were a number of precursors, WHO was founded in 1948 and is composed of almost 200 member states. It has three main goals: "First, it develops global norms and technical standards in virtually every health field. Second, it provides technical advice to governments and nongovernmental organizations (NGOs) to enable them to deal with transborder health risks. Third, it promotes international cooperation on health" (Buse 2007: 1277).

WHO has had some important successes such as its Global Outbreak Alert and Response Network which was key in preventing the spread of SARS during the 2003 outbreak in Asia, as well as its role in the creation, also in 2003, of the Framework Convention on Tobacco Control. However, WHO has come under severe criticism on various grounds (poor leadership, being overly bureaucratized, corruption) and it has been poorly funded.

Most observers agree that there needs to be a new approach to global governance and health. WHO is no longer the major player it once was. Other organizations have become increasingly important, especially the Melinda and Bill Gates Foundation. WHO's annual budget for 2014–2015 was approved for less than $4 billion per year, while the Gates Foundation will spend many times that amount during that period.

WHO focuses on various tasks. Among other things, it "gives advice on policies, evaluates treatments – especially for poor countries – maintains a network of laboratories and sends teams to fight outbreaks of disease, like avian flu or Ebola" (McNeil 2008: A6). However, WHO spends relatively little on research on disease. Especially notable is its lack of investment in research on diseases that affect the South. In contrast, the Gates Foundation has invested heavily in such research.

In fact, there is growing tension and outright conflict between WHO and the Gates Foundation as the latter takes the lead in various health-related projects and, as a result, garners global headlines. For example, there is some feeling that the Gates Foundation is seeking to supplant WHO. More specifically, WHO officials have criticized the secrecy (the lack of transparency) that characterizes Gates Foundation activities. Until recently there has been no monitoring of private organizations such as the Gates Foundation. Another area of complaint is over the assessment of the efficacy of various treatments and in ranking various countries' health systems. These activities are seen at the heart of what WHO does, but the Gates Foundation has recently entered this domain by giving a $105 million grant to the University of Washington to create the Institute for Health Metrics and Evaluation.

The Gates Foundation is certainly not the only NGO involved in health-related work around the world. Among the others is the Bloomberg Philanthropies sponsored by the wealthy (former) Mayor of New York City, Michael Bloomberg. However, it is not in conflict with WHO (perhaps because it is much smaller and has a much less ambitious agenda than the Gates Foundation), but rather works with it, in particular on a global antismoking project to which it contributed $2 million (McNeil 2008: A6). The project collected data on global smoking (and tobacco chewing), cigarette taxes collected, and antismoking programs. It found that poor and middle-income countries collect infinitely more in cigarette taxes than they invest in programs to combat smoking. To combat smoking, the report suggested "raising cigarette taxes, banning smoking in public places, enforcing laws against giving or advertising tobacco to children, monitoring tobacco use, warning people about the dangers and offering free or inexpensive help to smokers trying to quit" (McNeil 2008: A6).

A concerted global approach (or approaches) is needed which operates under the assumption that health is a human right. It is clear that in the area of health, and much else, both the risks and the potential gains from globalization are great.

ALTER-GLOBALIZATIONS

Globalization, or rather globalizations, has/have created enemies and people have sought to reshape it/them for innumerable reasons. One broad view on this is that resistance has arisen because globalization has not delivered on its promises for much of the world (Cohen 2006). It has served to raise the expectations of many, but not afforded them the where-withal even to begin to fulfill those expectations. Billions throughout the world, especially the "bottom billion," continue to lack the infrastructure – schools, roads, Internet access – needed to start to move toward fulfilling those expectations. Worse, they often lack the bare necessities needed to survive – food, water, shelter, safety, and so on.

In addition, Daniel Cohen argues that the less developed world has, in effect, been disenfranchised. In those cases where parts of that world have been able to obtain Northern innovations – telephone, television, Internet – they often find themselves feeling as if these technologies have been imposed on them; that they have no role in the creation of these technologies. A more just world would be one in which people from every part of the globe contribute to these developments as well as to human destiny in general.

Thus, globalization produces critics, opponents, and "enemies" and it is they who are most likely to resist globalization. Cohen, for example, identifies two broad enemies of globalization. The first is the enemies of Westernization (he identifies the "mullahs" of the world with this position and therefore with Huntington's thinking on the war of civilizations; see Chapter 3). The second is those who are opposed to capitalism and who see much of globalization as motivated by, and advancing, capitalism (this is in tune with the kind of global class struggle discussed by Marx and various Marxists). To Cohen, both sets of enemies are unified in the view that a world that they do not want (Western or capitalistic) is being imposed on them.

Cohen's argument is a useful beginning, but it is limited in several ways. Most importantly, he makes the mistake of reducing globalization to economic and geo-political globalization; as we know, there are many globalizations. The latter leads us to the realization that there are also many other types of enemies of other kinds of globalization (e.g. Slow Food's opposition to global fast food), and they engage in a wide range of actions designed to resist them. Restricting our sense of globalization limits much else about our understanding of this process, including the myriad forms taken by resistance to it.

While globalization is seemingly omnipresent, resistance to it has grown dramatically in recent years and in some cases (e.g. the World Social Forum) it, too, has become globalized. A wide variety of specific aspects of globalization have become the focus of resistance movements. These include the exploitation of indigenous labor by MNCs, the adverse effect on the environment of actions taken in the developed world (e.g. global warming), the threats posed by global culture to indigenous culture, and so on (Kahn and Kellner 2007).

Resistance, like globalization itself, must be seen as being highly complex, contradictory, and ambiguous, ranging from the radically progressive (the positions taken by the World Social Forum and its participants) to the reactionary and conservative (including frontier-style self-determination, isolationism, fundamentalism, neo-fascism, and ultra-nationalism).

In addition to making immediate gains, the resistance movement could constitute the beginning of a global civil society, of a new public sphere, that might uphold such progressive values as autonomy, democracy, peace, ecological sustainability, and social justice. While the forces that resist globalization have tended to portray globalization in a negative light (as, for example, being top-down, neoliberal capitalism, imperialism, and terror war; involving the McDonaldization of the planet, creating disequilibrating social changes, and so on), they are themselves products of globalization that often survive by using such globe-straddling technologies as the Internet.

As discussed in Chapter 2 there is some debate over what to call the groups that resist globalization. Historically, they have been seen as constituting the anti-globalization movement, but as we saw above and previously, the problem with that label is that the resistance groups themselves are often global in scope and their orientations and actions make them very much a part of globalization. For another thing, the movement is not, as we have seen, opposed to all aspects of globalization; to all globalizations. It is opposed to *some* varieties of globalization (e.g. neoliberal economic globalization) and not to others (e.g. the global spread of human rights in the political realm).

As a result, it is better to think of these resistance movements as part of globalization from below[5] and as such they stand in opposition to globalization from above (see Chapter 2). The latter would include the globalizing efforts of neoliberal economic systems, of MNCs, of aggressively expanding nation-states, of large and proselytizing religions, of McWorld, and the like. These efforts involve globalization from above since they emanate from powerful entities and are imposed on those with less or little power (they involve grobalization; see Chapter 8).

The heart of the resistance to globalization lies in individuals, groups, and organizations that we associate with globalization from below. They arise among those who are, or feel they are, wronged or oppressed by globalization from above (e.g. the Zapatistas [Gilman-Opalsky 2008] in Chiapas, Mexico) or by organizations supported more by those who come from the same social classes as those involved in globalization from above (e.g. the many members of an INGO like The Rainforest Alliance or Greenpeace), but which seek to represent the interests of those who are adversely affected by it. Their actions often translate into opposition to neoliberal globalization, or the "Washington consensus." They also involve opposition to globalization, especially economic globalization, stemming from the West in general, and the US in particular. And there is opposition to the main IGOs involved in globalization – the World Bank, the IMF, WTO – as well as more regional efforts such as NAFTA. More positively, the movement seeks a more democratic process of globalization; one that actively involves those from "below." It also seeks greater justice in globalization – a fairer and more just process of globalization; it is the global justice movement (Brooks 2008; Moghadam 2013).

While the above emphasizes globally active groups and organizations, globalization from below also occurs at various other levels (Langman 2012; Mittelman 2004). Individuals can take an array of actions that serve to resist the aspects of globalization that they oppose. Examples include José Bové and his actions in France against the expansion of McDonald's, individuals refusing to buy global products (e.g. Coca-Cola), refusing to have coffee in global chains of coffee shops (e.g. Starbucks), or refusing to shop in Wal-Mart because its ruthless commitment to low prices often translates into low-wage work in the South (the latter is one of the "high costs of low price"[6]). There are also small, more locally active, grass roots groups that oppose globalization, or at least some aspects of it. These may develop into the kind of globally active groups and organizations discussed above, but they also can remain wholly local phenomena (see below).

As mentioned above, while we often associate globalization from below with the left, there are less visible, more right-wing elements involved in this movement. First, there are groups (e.g. Scottish National Party[7]) that represent a kind of "frontier" mentality emphasizing self-determination and that, as a result, oppose global efforts to limit their freedom or to impinge on their territory. Second, there are other groups (e.g. America First Party[8]) that can be thought of as isolationists and that seek to protect the borders of their nation and to limit its (and their) involvement in global processes. Third, there are religious fundamentalists (e.g. the Taliban) who seek a return to at least their vision of a pure version of their religion and to resist global processes that they think are a threat to that purity. And there is an array of other groups and organizations that would fit into this category including those with ultra-nationalist and neo-fascist orientations.

Today, globalization from below includes many individuals, groups, social movements (Langman 2012; Jackie Smith 2008), and issues from every part of the world. Many have ties to one another, but they are generally very weak ties (although "weak ties" can be quite strong and very useful [Granovetter 1973]), and overall they form a very loose system. It is a highly fluid system and is continually changing its style, messages, and constituencies.

Of great and growing importance today is the technopolitics of global resistance, especially use of the Internet. These are new terrains for political struggle and places where new voices can be heard. Use of these technologies tends to be highly democratic and generally decommodified. They create domains where campaigns can be waged against global corporations. Wholly or primarily web-based forms of resistance include McSpotlight, the Clean Clothes Campaign, and the paradigmatic globalization from below activities in Seattle in 1999.[9] Mention should also be made in this context of the "hacktivists" (see Chapter 9) who can create, and have created, havoc on the Internet and perhaps one day will cause a "digital Pearl Harbor."

There are several theories that relate to this resistance, many of which have been covered at one or more points in this book. They include Karl Polanyi's ideas on counter-movements; Antonio Gramsci's thinking on hegemony/counter-hegemony; and Michael Hardt and Antonio Negri's on empire/multitude. While they all are of use in thinking about resistance, they have all been found wanting as complete explanations of this resistance for one reason or another. There are those who see the need for more complex and critical theories of global resistance. Furthermore, such theories need to avoid the extremes of "globophobia" (see Chapter 2) (Watts 2012).

Perhaps the best term applied to all of this, one we have used on several occasions throughout this book, is *alter-globalization*. It reflects, once again, the fact that many of these groups are themselves global in nature and that they are not opposed to globalization per se, but rather the way it (e.g. neoliberalism) is practiced today. Thus, while all such efforts might resist a certain form of globalization, they do not reject it outright. Instead, they seek to steer it in one way or another; they want to influence how these global processes unfold.

LOCAL RESISTANCE

The actions of local groups or communities face severe limitations in terms of their chances of having an impact on globalization from above. Their major problem is that while they are largely local in nature, the problems they are confronting (e.g. global warming) are often global in scope and have their sources perhaps halfway around the world. There is little or no way in which such groups, acting alone and in isolation, can have much of an impact on such global issues (although alliances among a number of them would fare better [Saguier 2007]).

One example of resistance undertaken by a small, local community (Hall and Fenelon 2008) involves the Amungme and Kamoro peoples of Papua, Indonesia, and their resistance to the world's largest gold and copper mine, Freeport McMoRan Copper & Gold (Abrash 2001). Before Freeport arrived in 1967, the two peoples had been involved in a subsistence economy based on agriculture, fishing, hunting, and the use of products derived from the forest. Freeport displaced many of these people and forced them to resettle elsewhere. The company seized and despoiled their land and resources. There is also evidence of torture, rape, disappearance, and even murder. The company has also admitted to paying "military and police officers to oversee security operations, despite accusations that the Indonesian military has been linked to human rights abuses against local Papuans" (Schonhardt 2011). Adding to the disruptions caused by the company itself, thousands of migrants found their way there in search of the jobs created in and around the mine and they brought with them different customs and ways of life. Freeport, and all the developments in and around it, disrupted what the locals considered a harmonious relationship among people, the environment, and their ancestral spirits. Amungme consider at least part of the area being mined to be sacred.

Local protests began soon after the arrival of Freeport in 1967. Among the mechanisms employed by the locals were the positioning of the Amungme's "taboo sticks" around a Freeport base camp, public demonstrations, sit-ins, and attempts at open dialogue with the company. Some modest concessions were made (e.g. Freeport agreed to construct schools and clinics), but the fundamental problems remained. In 1996 the Amungme brought two civil suits against Freeport in US federal and state courts. They also have appealed to, among others, the US government, the Indonesian government, and even directly to the shareholders of the company. There have been additional concessions by the company over time (e.g. job training, scholarships, land payments, and support for local businesses). Overall, however, these changes brought about by local resistance have not, at least until now, led to fundamental changes in activities undertaken by Freeport that are destructive to the local community. In the main, the most important players in this – the company and the government of Indonesia (as well as the US government) – have been largely unresponsive to local needs and interests.

A SOCIAL MOVEMENT?

Donatella della Porta, along with several colleagues, studied two specific Italian protests against globalization (della Porta et al. 2006). One was protests against the G8 meeting in Genoa in July 2001 and the other involved protests during the European Social Forum in Florence in November 2002. The study examined the characteristics of the protesters, the networks of the organizations involved and their activities, and the relationship between those involved in the protests and their larger environment.

The key issue addressed in this study is whether the various groups involved in protests, and more generally in globalization from below, are sufficiently organized and integrated to be considered a global social movement (Jackie Smith 2008). A social movement has the following characteristics: "networks of groups and activists, with an emerging identity, involved in conflictual issues, using mainly unconventional forms of participation" (della Porta et al. 2006: 234). The authors conclude that the groups *do* constitute a social movement. A loose network of formal and informal organizations and groups has been sustained over time. This allows the authors to conclude that these disparate groups and organizations do form a global, or at least a transnational, movement in opposition to globalization from above. Two facts are crucial to this conclusion. First, there are frequent overlaps among individuals and organizations in various anti-globalization campaigns. Second, the interactions among the individuals and groups have intensified over time. Thus, the authors conclude: "the results of our research seem to indicate that a movement on global justice is truly in the making" (della Porta et al. 2006: 233).

They also conclude that these are not only social movements, but that they are also global in nature. First, large numbers of those involved *identify* themselves with a movement that is critical of the process of globalization (or at least globalization from above), define themselves as global citizens, know about global developments, and express a sense of solidarity with the deprived in the world, especially in the South. Second, they engage in unconventional *action* (e.g. street protests), and such action is increasingly aimed at global targets. Third, they have developed a global *organizational structure*, especially via the Internet. Fourth, their *definition of the conflict* is that it is global in scope.

The heart of these movements is *protest* and it is based on three logics. First, protest has at least the potential to cause *material damage* and merely this threat, let alone whatever damage may actually be caused, has great symbolic value. Second, protests require great *numbers* of people to participate. When the numbers are there, this demonstrates not only the strength of, but also the extent of the danger posed by, these movements to those in power. Finally, there is the logic of *witnessing* in that those involved engage in acts – e.g. civil disobedience – that constitute potential risks to them – they are putting their bodies, even their lives, on the line.

These social movements involve flexible organizational forms and are involved in networks linked to a number of other networks. This looseness leads to the use of another term associated with globalization from below, *movement of movements*, which has come to be employed by a number of observers and analysts.

MORE FORMAL SOCIAL MOVEMENTS

Those who resist globalization often use globally similar "philosophical, bureaucratic, and technological defenses" (Niezen 2004: 170). As a result, "over the long term they homogenize societies even further through globally similar struggles for recognition and self-determination. Both the ills and the remedies of modernity are rapidly becoming part of every cultural community. The cumulative effect of such global transformations has already been a reduction of possibilities for the expression of collective character" (Niezen 2004: 170). The paradox here is that those who resist globalization may use techniques that serve to make them increasingly integral to that process. While this is less likely to be the case with highly local and informal social movements, it is much more likely for formal social movements, including those involved in globalization from below.

TRANSNATIONAL SOCIAL MOVEMENTS

One form that such resistance may take is transnational social movements, such as the labor movement (Bieler, Lindberg, and Pillay 2008; Evans 2005; Timms 2012), that are "counter-hegemonic" in the sense that they oppose neoliberal globalization.

Labor movements[10]

The modern labor movement is traceable to the nineteenth century and the development of industrialization. It was clear from the beginning, at least in Europe, that labor needed to operate transnationally (Cornfield 1997) in order to deal with industries that were operating in that manner. The early movement in Europe included not only unions, but also left-wing political parties (both communist and socialist), cooperatives, and so on. An early example (1864–1872) of a transnational labor movement was the International Working Men's Association, or the First International, aimed at supporting strikes, educating workers and the larger public, lobbying governments in the interest of workers and unions, and supporting political and organizing campaigns. The personal and intellectual force behind the First International was Karl Marx. His well-known phrase, "Workers of the World, Unite," was an inspiration to the First International and innumerable related movements (Marx and Engels 1848/2000). The point was that the workers of the world had far more interests in common than they did with capitalists in their own country. Furthermore, in order to succeed against the international capitalist system, they had to organize and one way to do that was to form labor unions.

The First International collapsed, primarily because of internal differences, but was succeeded by the Second International (1889–1915) which was more organized on the basis of alliances among socialist parties. However, their international efforts were rendered ineffective by the strengthening of nation-states and national borders (as well as of nationalism).[11] This International came to an end as European nations plunged into WW I (a war that also ended an early period of economic globalization). The International had sought to prevent that war through a global appeal to workers not to go to war and kill workers from other parts of the world. However, workers (and others) were led to do just that because the International's efforts were trumped by increasing nationalism. Led by the communists in the Soviet Union who had come to power in 1917, a Third International came into existence in 1919 (lasting until 1943). In response, the Western, more anti-communist (and -socialist), International Labor Organization (ILO) was formed in 1920 in order to improve the conditions of at least some workers so that they would not be drawn to leftwing unions and political movements. International labor efforts that followed the end of WW II were divided between pro-communist and pro-capitalist labor organizations. Most unions in the West, especially in the US, tended to support capitalism and oppose left-wing unionization, while communist unions there and in the East supported left-wing unions and the actions of the Soviet Union.

In the latter part of the twentieth century, labor unions throughout much of the world weakened and, of course, the Soviet Union and much of global communism collapsed. By the 1980s, the once powerful unions in, for example, Great Britain and the US saw neoliberal globalization as a threat to the jobs of their members and tended to fight a rear-guard action against it.

The dominant view today is that labor unions in general are of declining importance and this is seen as especially the case in relationship to globalization. That is, they are seen as more-or-less helpless in comparison to the power of MNCs and global financial institutions (e.g. WTO, IMF). However, there are those who see examples of success throughout the world in organizing against global processes and who believe that unions can play a significant role in ameliorating the excesses of neoliberal globalization and in furthering the interests of workers throughout much of the world.[12]

A hopeful sign for those who believe unions should and can perform such a role was an international conference in New York City in 2006 entitled "Global Companies–Global

Unions–Global Research–Global Campaigns." As the title makes abundantly (and repeatedly) clear, globalization was front and center at this meeting, as it was in the remarks of the Secretary-Treasurer of the AFL-CIO:

> Brothers and Sisters, I like the theme of this conference because it lays out the challenges before us in almost biblical terms – global companies begat global problems for workers – global problems begat the need for global unions – and if global unions want to truly match the might and power of global corporations we have to undertake global research and global campaigns. (Bronfenbrenner 2007: 1)

The problem for more integrated and powerful unions with a global reach is the opposition of MNCs, neoliberal states, as well as various IGOs (WTO, World Bank, IMF) that are tightly linked to neoliberalism.

There are some examples of successful global union actions such as the 1986 global boycott (it occurred in a dozen countries) of the oil companies, especially Royal Dutch/Shell, operating in then-apartheid South Africa. The boycott involved unions and other organizations from the US and South Africa (unions from other countries came to participate in various ways). There have been, and are, other transnational efforts by unions, but Bronfenbrenner concludes that two decades after the Shell campaign:

> the world's largest corporations wield more power and are more globally connected and less fettered by global union solidarity. . . . Now the challenges are greater. Where before transnational corporations seemed at least somewhat bounded by loyalty to industry or country, today the largest of these firms increasingly supersede most government authority and are constrained only by the interests of their biggest investors, lenders, and shareholders. (Bronfenbrenner 2007: 4)

Nevertheless, there have been a number of recent transnational (but not global) campaigns involving labor unions including those involving Malaysian workers and a Danish NGO (dominated by its labor movement); Caribbean unions of banana workers and European and North American NGOs and the IUF (Internal Union of Foodworkers); as well as a number of cross-border operations in Europe. Labor unions are increasingly framing workplace issues as human rights issues, seeking to curb the assault on workers' rights (Kang 2012).

While these efforts remain meager, at least in comparison to the success of global neoliberal capitalism, an area of greater global success has been in the creation of international labor standards, primarily through the efforts of the International Labor Organization (ILO). It has passed almost 200 conventions dealing with such issues as "safety and health at work, working hours, holidays with pay, minimum wage, social security," and so on, although ratification (and enforcement) of these conventions has been uneven among nation-states and support seemed to be declining as neoliberal globalization grew more powerful and influential (Maupain 2007). However, these conventions have influenced legislation and practice in many nations.

Social movements and the boomerang pattern

Another dimension of global movements is the formation of transnational advocacy networks and a "boomerang pattern" for bringing about change. In *Activists Beyond Borders*, Keck and Sikkink (1998) describe how local movements build transnational relationships to promote change within local settings. They note that in some countries (in the global South), domestic governments themselves are not responsive to the needs of their citizens. Specifically, domestic NGOs and social movements might have little access to state institutions to protect human rights, indigenous rights, or the environment. In these cases, one option for "domestic NGOs [is to] bypass their state and directly search out international allies to try to bring pressure on their states from outside" (Keck and Sikkink 1998: 12). They might reach out to NGOs in the North and provide information about what is happening in their country. Through this network, NGOs in the North pressure their own states (and possibly a third party like an Intergovernmental Organization), who in turn pressure the government that has blocked access in the original country. This forms a boomerang pattern when the original NGOs reach out to potential international allies, and the movement activity comes back to the home country in the form of international pressure.

The same pattern has been observed in the global justice movement targeting MNCs (Dale 2011; Seidman 2007). For example, workers' rights groups in Indonesia have documented human rights abuses committed by Nike contractors there. Their local rights groups could make appeals to the company itself or to the Indonesian government, but the government and company are often not responsive, or the country might lack the laws protecting workers there. Without sufficient channels to address their problems domestically, they reach out to workers' rights and human rights groups in the North, showing them the conditions in which they must work. Groups in the North then can make appeals to consumers to boycott Nike products, or to shareholders who might be concerned about Nike's corporate image being tarnished, thereby putting pressure on the company to adopt more socially responsible business practices back in Indonesia. If this transnational network is effective, it can lead to change in Indonesia. Much like the process described above focusing on Third World governments, this process does not focus directly on the employer (i.e. the Nike contractor) but they are the ultimate target in this transnational boomerang pattern.

WORLD SOCIAL FORUM

An especially significant development in global social movements broadly (and the global justice movement in particular) is the World Social Forum. Emerging from the origins of the alter-globalization movement at the WTO meetings in Seattle in late November 1999, as well as ensuing protests in Washington, DC (April 2000), Prague (September 2000), and Genoa (July 2001), the World Social Forum (WSF) (Fisher and Ponniah 2003; Kohler 2012; Sen et al. 2004), held its first meeting in January, 2001, in Porto Alegre, Brazil.

The WSF was also formed as a reaction against the World Economic Forum. A key overall focus was the lack of democracy in global economic and political affairs. It was born of the idea that more needed to be done about this problem, and others, than protests. That is, there was a need for more positive and concrete proposals to deal with such issues (especially greater democracy [Smith and Karides 2008]) as well as a forum in which they could be generated. Its slogan has been "Another World Is Possible" (Kohler 2012). That is, there must be, and there is, an alternative to the neoliberalism (Peter Smith 2008) that dominates the world economically and politically. While the slogan is powerful, as yet the WSF has not gone much beyond it to produce actions that actually help make that world a reality.

The initial meeting of the WSF in Porto Alegre, Brazil (Byrd 2005), drew about 5,000 participants, and the number of participants grew to 100,000 at the 2004 meetings in Mumbai, India, and in 2005 in Porto Alegre. In 2006 the meeting was decentralized and held on three continents and many local, national, and regional meetings have developed. Recent locations of the WSF included Dakar, Senegal in 2011, a return to Porto Alegre in 2012, and Tunis, Tunisia in 2013.

The WSF is, by design, not a political movement or an actor, but merely an arena in which like-minded people can exchange ideas on global issues. The very diversity of those involved in the WSF makes the development of concrete political proposals, let alone actions, difficult. The WSF continues to struggle with this issue and its identity and role in globalization.

WSF was formed initially and in large part on the basis of cyberactivism. The WSF is a huge social network and it should come as no surprise that cyberactivism (as well as the WSF) is based on the "cultural logic of networking" including: the creation of horizontal ties and connections among diverse and autonomous elements; the free and open communication of information among and between those elements; coordination among the elements that is decentralized and involves directly democratic decision-making; and networking that is self-directed (Juris 2005).

CYBERACTIVISM

While cyberactivism has been involved in all the examples above, a more specific case of the power of cyberactivism involves a series of events following the 1997 Asian financial crisis, specifically in Indonesia where anger over the crisis was aimed at ethnic Chinese (Ong 2003). By May 1998, Chinese stores in Indonesia had been looted and burned and Chinese residents had been attacked and women raped. Vigilante groups were reported to have hunted Chinese, killed them, and paraded about with the victims' heads on the ends of spikes. The police were reported to have looked on. There has been a long history of anti-Chinese feeling in Indonesia and the government, as well as the international community, has been seen by Chinese in Indonesia and around the world as having done little or nothing to help the victims of anti-Chinese violence.

Beginning in August 1998, rallies against the violence against Chinese residents in Indonesia were held in many cities in the US, as well as in Canada, Australia, and Asia. These protests were made possible and coordinated through the creation of a website – Global Huaren (Global Chinese People) – and the formation of the World Huaren Federation.

There are something like 50 million people with Chinese ancestry in the Chinese diaspora and they are scattered throughout well over 100 countries in the world. And a large number of them are users of computers with access to the Internet. Their great numbers and their high level of computer literacy make them an ideal group to form a cyberpublic such as that involved in Global Huaren.

What Global Huaren did was, in effect, to create a global Chinese public where one did not exist before. Further, Global Huaren became an interesting global watchdog for Chinese interests. It was a disembedded[13] organization, that is, it was not embedded in any particular geographic location; it existed solely on the Internet; it was a "virtual organization." Yet, another way of saying this is that it was a *placeless* organization. That is, it existed in no single place; it had no headquarters. We are likely to see more such global organizations as access to the Internet continues to proliferate.

While one cannot quarrel with the objectives of Global Huaren, it should be noted that the Internet can easily be used to create, with only a few keystrokes, a global movement with nefarious objectives. Further, even if the objectives are high-minded, the information that is disseminated can be confusing and it can have a series of unanticipated consequences.

Resistance to globalization, or to some aspect of it (as in the case of ethnic Chinese being blamed for the economic crisis in Indonesia), can be largely or totally virtual, or it can take quite material forms as it did in the riots outside Paris (see Chapter 14) and in individual pronouncements and actions.

THE FRENCH ALTERNATIVE

There is a widely shared view that French society as a whole, in contrast to the rioters discussed in Chapter 14, has taken the lead in resisting globalization. This has been exemplified by, among others, the early French reaction to Coca-Cola (and "coca-colonization" [Kuisel 1993]; see Chapter 3) after WW II, a French government official describing the opening of Euro Disney outside Paris as a "cultural Chernobyl,"[14] and the actions of José Bové against McDonald's in France (Morse 2002).

While there is a strong element of truth in this, in *The French Challenge: Adapting to Globalization*, Philip H. Gordon and Sophie Meunier (2001) argue that the story of the relationship between France and globalization is far more complex. In fact, they point out that France has adapted in various ways, especially economically, to globalization. And they were writing before the presidential elections of Nicolas Sarkozy in 2007 and François Hollande in 2012. Sarkozy and Hollande have continued reforms that further integrate France in processes of globalization.

In spite of this, Gordon and Meunier enumerate some of the reasons why globalization also represents such a challenge to France. First, France has been devoted to state control over much of what transpires in the country and globalization clearly poses a threat to such state control. Second, the French are strongly attached to their culture and identity and they see both as threatened by globalization, especially Americanization, which many in France more or less equate (erroneously) with globalization. Third, with its strong roots in the Enlightenment, France is committed to rationality, but globalization is seen as a messy process that threatens rational order. Fourth, France has continued to have global aspirations long after many other European countries (e.g. Great Britain) gave them up. However, a global world, especially one dominated by the US, threatens France's exalted vision of itself in the world. Finally, the French are generally satisfied with the quality of their lives and see little reason to have this threatened by globalization, especially neoliberal reforms, or perhaps anything else. The French are legendarily conservative, especially on quality-of-life issues.

Within the economy (e.g. privatization, stock market development, global industries, economic openness, etc.), France's adaptation to globalization has been quite far-reaching and it has adapted quite well to it. However, France has adapted less well culturally as it has sought to defend its distinctive cultural, linguistic, and culinary traditions. Yet, globalization should not necessarily be seen as an enemy of these traditions, but can also be seen, and serve, as a way in which all of them can be disseminated more broadly throughout the world.

Overall, the French can be seen as resisting the idea that a one-size-fits-all model of globalization (e.g. neoliberalism) is inevitable throughout the world. It is not necessarily the case that more globalization is better for everyone. The French have accepted globalization, especially in the economy, but in other areas (especially culture) their approach has been much more measured. In all areas they have sought not simply to succumb to, but to manage, globalization (*mondialization maîtrisée*). Included under this heading are efforts to preserve the state, a commitment to the European Union as a way of limiting American-led globalization, the use of trade policy to limit the negative effects of neoliberal economic globalization, and the development of a foreign policy that emphasizes a multi-polar world to counter American political and military hegemony (although this relationship has become less clear in recent years). In terms of the latter, France was notable in its opposition to, and lack of participation in, the American-led war in Iraq.

IS THE RESISTANCE TO GLOBALIZATION SIGNIFICANT?

While the resistance by France is notable, and resistance globally is generally strong and diverse, such resistance is to a large extent dismissed by the supporters of globalization and believers in its continued, if not inevitable, expansion. For example, in dismissing the opposition to globalization, de la Dehesa (2006: 182) offers two "empirical truths":

> The first is that those minorities, who are adversely affected by a phenomenon, or those who choose to protest, generally have the loudest voice, while those who benefit tend to remain silent. The second is that it is mainly the best-organized groups – those that exert most pressure on decision-makers – that lead the debate. This often leaves less organized but majority groups out of the picture.

In other words, the opponents of globalization are dismissed as being a small number of well-organized loudmouths while the supporters represent a less well-organized "silent majority." Readers might keep this critique in mind as they think about this chapter and review in their minds the various forms of coping, opposition, and resistance to globalization discussed previously.

THE FUTURES OF GLOBALIZATION

We close this book with a brief discussion of the future of globalization (Adam 2012; Zedillo 2007), although as the heading makes clear, we are talking about a complex scenario that involves multiple futures for multiple globalizations (Turner 2007b). To put it another way, since there is no single globalization, there can be no single future for it. But just as in the preceding sections of this chapter where we have only been able to discuss a few of the methods of dealing with and resisting globalization, we can only touch on a few aspects of the future of globalization, or a few of the futures of a few globalizations. It would simply be impossible to offer an overview of the future of economic, political, educational, religious, sport, urban–rural, and demographic, to mention just a few, globalizations. Complicating matters is the fact that each of these broad areas encompasses a number of more specific globalizations. For example under the heading of the economy, we could discuss the future of neoliberal economies, MNCs, the labor movement, consumption, and of the economies of China, India, the US, EU, and on and on.

It is also worth noting that while the social sciences are pretty good at analyzing the past and even the present, their prognostications about the future are notoriously weak. The history of social thought is littered with wrong-headed (Marx on the collapse of capitalism, at least so far) and sometimes downright ridiculous (Auguste Comte on the coming of a new positivistic religion of which he would be supreme pontiff) predictions for the future. Given this history, this book will offer no bold predictions about the futures of globalizations, but rather will be content with some ruminations about, and some sketchy scenarios on, them.

Seemingly the most obvious conclusion to be drawn from all that has gone before in this book, and all that has happened globally in at least the late twentieth and early twenty-first century, is that both globalization in general, and at least most globalizations, will continue and most likely grow and expand. This prediction seems safest within the economy which has globalized faster and farther than any other aspect of the social world.

However, various experts on the economy are not prepared to guarantee its future globalization. Jeffry Frieden points strongly to the fact that the previous epoch of economic globalization died with the outbreak of WW I. He is quite aware that globalization, especially economic globalization, did re-emerge and grow enormously in the last half of the twentieth and into the early years of the twenty-first century. And while this new phase of globalization has been extraordinarily powerful, Frieden does not believe that its future is necessarily assured (Frieden 2006). The major impediments, in his view, are political in nature and are likely to come from two sources. On the one hand, supporters of globalization and its markets want to gain greater control over it and its vagaries and difficulties through better forms of global governance. On the other hand, critics of globalization see more the need for greater accountability (see above) through the creation of various political institutions that can exercise greater control over those markets. Both of these involve external oversight, if not control, over the global economy, and, at least from a neoliberal perspective, such external direction could spell the death knell for an economy which, from that perspective, operates best when it is left to its own devices.

However, the major threat to globalization appears to stem from the economy itself. As long as the state of global economy is good, globalization is likely to thrive. However, economic catastrophes have in the past threatened and, in the case of the Great Depression, all but destroyed globalization. That threat is clearly with us again as the recent great global financial, credit, banking, and economic crisis dramatically affected the world economy. If the future of economic globalization is not assured, then it seems even more likely that one cannot unequivocally forecast continued growth and expansion of globalization more generally.

A grim, but slightly more optimistic, economic scenario is offered by Immanuel Wallerstein (2005), noted for the creation of world-systems theory (see Chapters 3 and 13), who looks at the future of the global economy in terms of three related issues.

First, can every part of the world in the not-too-distant future achieve the standard of living (as well as similar cultural and political institutions) of the most economically advanced and progressive nations in the world (e.g. Denmark)? That is, will we see economic and social equality in the future? Wallerstein responds in the negative. For one thing, he argues that the history of the world has always involved increases rather than decreases in inequality. For another, if a few countries and their industries can no longer monopolize productive activity, "the *raison d'être* of a capitalist world-economy will be undermined" (Wallerstein 2005: 1268). The assumption is that capitalism cannot and will not permit its basic reason for being, and the inequality that underlies it, to be threatened.

Second, can the currently highly unequal world persist pretty much as it is? Wallerstein says no for two basic reasons. First, the ability of capitalism to accumulate capital is declining and this is weakening the political structures that are based on such accumulation.

This is related to the second point and that is that the weakened states will increasingly be unable to control the rise of the "dangerous classes." Already, Wallerstein sees "spreading anarchy" in the twenty-first century.

Third, what alternatives present themselves? Wallerstein foresees the likelihood of the collapse of the current world-system, but what will replace it cannot be discerned with any great precision, although the possibility of the development of less developed countries is more likely than ever before. Wallerstein sees more hope in social movements (e.g. those associated with the World Social Forum) than with the actions of nation-states. He sees these movements as best advised to push decommodification.[15] Such a process runs counter to the objectives of neoliberalism and it can provide the base for an alternative political system.

Given the fact that Wallerstein is a Marxist, he can't help but offer some hope for the future in a decommodified economy that would be the basis for a different political system. However, since commodities lie at the base of the modern economy, it is not at all clear what kind of an economy a decommodified economy would be and whatever it is, whether it has any chance of success.

A "MAD MAX" SCENARIO

At the most extreme, one observer foresees a global future that he calls a "Mad Max" scenario (Turner 2007b). This refers to a series of movies that dealt with an apocalyptic vision of the future with people thrown back into primitive and extremely violent ways of life (the fourth movie in the series is scheduled to be released in 2015). In fact, it could be argued that we are already beginning to see anticipations of this on the streets of cities in Iraq, Afghanistan, Pakistan, Somalia, and so on. It could be that it is states without governments, non-states, such as Somalia, that offer the most extreme examples of the Mad Max scenario, where such a world is closest to, if not already, a reality.

The Mad Max scenario is made more likely, for larger portions of the global population, by a variety of ongoing trends:

- ever-accelerating crises in the capitalist economy;
- dramatically rising oil prices (while they have dropped recently, they seem sure to rise again soon given limitations on supply) will contribute, among things, to higher prices of food, food shortages (already a "silent tsunami" affecting perhaps 100 million people [Sullivan 2008: A1, A13]), and riots, because of the increased cost of producing and transporting food of all sorts;
- increasingly short supplies of oil will not only lead to higher prices, but battles and perhaps outright warfare over the declining number of functioning oil wells, oil reserves, and, perhaps, oil-producing countries;
- population growth in less developed areas[16] will lead to pitched battles over food that is available only in limited quantities;
- declining supplies of fresh water will lead to similar battles between the water "haves" and the water "have-nots";
- rising sea water will displace large numbers of people from islands and coastal areas (i.e. climate refugees), with those from the latter moving inland where they will come into conflict with residents unwilling to give up, or even share, their territory;
- nuclear exchanges that could lead to larger nuclear wars and possibly "nuclear winter." Among the most likely nuclear combatants today are Israel and Iran, India and Pakistan;

- the collapse of a nuclear power (Pakistan would seem most likely) could lead to a series of events through which nuclear weapons would fall into the hands of rogues, or terrorists;
- even the explosion in a major Northern city of a "dirty bomb" packed in suitcase would devastate that city, primarily through the creation of high levels of radiation that linger for a long period of time making at least part of the city uninhabitable;
- the detonation of such a suitcase bomb would lead to retaliation, likely involving nuclear weapons, against the presumed perpetrators.

There is no end to such bleak, Mad Max scenarios; there are undoubtedly many more that are not listed and have yet to be imagined. Any one of them, let alone some combination of them, has the potential to put an end to this era of globalization in the same way that previous cataclysms – WW I and the Great Depression – ended an earlier global age.

CHAPTER SUMMARY

Globalization is not a single phenomenon, rather there are many globalizations. While some need to be resisted, others are welcome and should be encouraged. There are bound to be multiple futures for multiple globalizations.

There are at least three approaches to global economic resistance. Trade protectionism involves systematic government intervention in foreign trade through, for example, tariffs and non tariff barriers, in order to encourage domestic producers and deter their foreign competitors. Although there exists a widespread consensus regarding its inefficiency, protectionism is still popular since it shields the domestic economy from systemic shocks.

"Fair Trade" is a different approach to economic globalization, which emerged as a counter to neoliberal "free trade" principles. Fair trade aims at a more moral and equitable global economic system in which, for instance, price is not to be set by the market, instead it is to be negotiated transparently by both producers and consumers. While it is popular among consumers in the North, it has met only limited acceptance among producers. Its ability to supply a mass market or its applicability to manufactured products is also doubted.

The third form of resistance to economic globalization relates to helping the "bottom billion." Increasing aid is only one of the many measures that are required. International norms and standards can be adapted to the needs of the bottom billion. The reduction of trade barriers would also reduce the economic marginalization of these people and their nations.

Increased accountability and transparency are key issues in dealing with political globalization. All political organizations, at different levels, should be more accountable for their actions; they are now surrounded by an "ocean of opacity." Increased transparency has been aided by various mechanisms such as transnational justice systems, international tribunals, civil society, and Transparency International.

Global health issues are being dealt with by major transnational organizations such as the World Health Organization (WHO) as well as more private initiatives such as the Gates Foundation. While WHO has had some important success, it has also been criticized for poor leadership and inadequate funding.

Like globalization itself, resistance to globalization is multiple, complex, contradictory, and ambiguous. This movement also holds the potential of emerging as the new public sphere, which might uphold progressive values such as autonomy, democracy, peace, ecological sustainability, and social justice. These forces of resistance are themselves products of globalization and can be seen as "globalization from below" and a form of "alter-globalization." The impetus for such movements comes from individuals, groups, and organizations which are, or perceive themselves to be, oppressed by globalization from above (neoliberal economic systems, aggressively expanding nations and corporations). They seek a more democratic process of globalization. However, globalization from below also involves less visible, more right-wing elements, such as America's First Party and the Taliban.

Those who resist globalizations may use techniques that make them an integral part of the process. For example, the international labor movement has met with limited successes, such as the creation of international labor standards. Domestic NGOs in the South, which resist globalization from above, might rely on transnational partners to put pressure on governments and MNCs in their homes countries through a "boomerang pattern." The World Social Forum (WSF) is centered on addressing the lack of democracy in economic and political affairs. However, the diversity of elements involved in the WSF hinders the development of concrete political proposals. A significant influence on the WSF has been that of cyberactivism, which is based on the "cultural logic of networking." Apart from "virtual movements" such as the Global Huaren, positive resistance can take more material forms, as in the case of the French alternative.

Since there is no single globalization, the future is also multidimensional. Some foresee the continuing expansion of globalization both in general as well as in more specific globalizations. Others have a far more pessimistic vision of "Mad Max" scenarios that could well end the current era of globalization.

DISCUSSION QUESTIONS

1. Discuss the contradictory and ambiguous nature of the resistance to globalization.

2. Examine the three approaches to economic global resistance.

3. Examine the concepts of accountability and transparency with respect to political globalization.

4. What strategies have local organizations adopted to shape how global processes affect them?

5. What is *your ideal vision* of the future of globalization?

6. In contrast to your ideal vision, what do you think is the *most likely future* of globalization?

ADDITIONAL READINGS

Alex Nicholls and Charlotte Opal. *Fair Trade: Market-Driven Ethical Consumption.* London: Sage, 2005.

Keith Brown. *Buying into Fair Trade: Culture, Morality, Consumption.* New York: New York University Press, 2013.

Laura Raynolds, Douglas Murray, and John Wilkinson. *Fair Trade: The Challenges of Transforming Globalization*. New York: Routledge, 2007.

Nico Stehr. *Moral Markets: How Knowledge and Affluence Change Consumers and Products*. Boulder, CO: Paradigm, 2008.

Sarah Lyon and Mark Moberg, eds. *Fair Trade and Social Justice: Global Ethnographies*. New York: New York University Press, 2010.

Daniel Jaffee. *Brewing Justice: Fair Trade Coffee, Sustainability and Survival*. Berkeley: University of California Press, 2007.

Margaret Keck and Kathryn Sikkink. *Activists Beyond Borders*. Ithaca, NY: Cornell University Press, 1998.

John Dale. *Free Burma: Transnational Legal Action and Corporate Accountability*. Minneapolis, MN: University of Minnesota Press, 2011.

Daniel Cohen. *Globalization and Its Enemies*. Cambridge, MA: MIT Press, 2006.

Donatella della Porta, Massimiliano Andretta, Lorenzo Mosca, and Herbert Reiter. *Globalization from Below: Transnational Activists and Protest Networks*. Minneapolis: University of Minnesota Press, 2006.

Valentine Moghadam. *Globalization and Social Movements*, 2nd edn. Lanham, MD: Rowman and Littlefield, 2013.

Kate Bronfenbrenner, ed. *Global Unions: Challenging Transnational Capital Through Cross-Border Campaigns*. Ithaca, NY: ILR Press, 2007.

Susan Kang. *Human Rights and Labor Solidarity: Trade Unions in the Global Economy*. Philadelphia, PA: University of Pennsylvania Press, 2012.

Jackie Smith and Marina Karides. *Global Democracy and the World Social Forums*. Boulder, CO: Paradigm, 2008.

NOTES

1 Some would say that neoliberalism has a moral base that sees the majority benefiting from an open market, others see it as being proudly amoral, and still others view it as immoral.

2 Other organizations involved in international fair trade are the Network of European Worldshops (NEWS), European Fair Trade Association (EFTA), Fair Trade Federation (FTF; in the US and Canada), and Slow Food.

3 See also Florini (2007).

4 www.transparency.org.

5 As we will see below, another term suggested for these movements is "movement of movements." The World Social Forum has come to be seen as the embodiment of this idea.

6 www.walmartmovie.com.

7 Thanks to Professor Robert J. Antonio for this example.

8 www.americafirstparty.org.

9 www.indymedia.org.

10 The brief history to follow is based on O'Brien (2007); Munck and Waterman (1999); Munck (2002b); Munck (2004).

11 As we have seen many times in this book, in more recent years nation-states have weakened considerably.

12 See, for example, Bronfenbrenner (2007).

13 This is another concept associated with the work of Anthony Giddens.

14 www.time.com/time/europe/etan/disney.html.

15 That is, to a world where goods and services are not transformed into products that are produced and consumed in an environment designed to maximize profit.

16 In contrast, population growth in developed areas will be negligible or non-existent. A birth rate of 2.1 is generally considered "replacement rate", but in southern and Eastern Europe it has dropped below 1.3. See Shorto (2008: 34 ff.).

APPENDIX

DISCIPLINARY APPROACHES TO GLOBALIZATION

....

Anthropology
Sociology
Political Science
Economics
Geography
Psychology
Literary Criticism (Postcolonial)
Other Fields

....

Globalization: A Basic Text, Second Edition. George Ritzer and Paul Dean.
© 2015 John Wiley & Sons, Ltd. Published 2015 by John Wiley & Sons, Ltd.

This Appendix offers a brief overview of the approach(es) to globalization taken in a number of the social sciences (as well as in literary theory). While we will treat the disciplines separately below, there are those who move back and forth between two or more disciplines quite comfortably and to good effect.[1]

ANTHROPOLOGY

A defining characteristic of the anthropological approach to globalization is its focus on culture (Friedman 1994: 67–7; Nordstrom 2007: 144). When anthropologists examine other spheres of the social world, they tend to look at them through the prism of culture (e.g. the political culture of a given society). Anthropologists, following the "Western model" (Hill and Baba 2006), have tended to see culture as tied to a particular place, or territory (e.g. a small tribe or a community). In the global age, many have come to recognize that culture has, at least to some degree, been torn from locale; it has been deterritorialized.[2] However, most anthropologists recognize that deterritorialized culture tends to be reinserted somewhere, perhaps in many places, although usually as a culture that is less stable than it had been in the past (Inda and Rosaldo 2008a: 3–46; Nordstrom 2004: 13). In reterritorializing culture in this way, anthropologists are able to return to their traditional concern with place-based culture, albeit with a sense of how that culture is involved in, and affected by, global processes. Mundane examples of this anthropological approach are found in studies of fast-food restaurants in various locales (Caldwell 2004; Ritzer 2012; Watson 1997: 1–38) and Coca-Cola in Trinidad.[3]

While culture (and meaning) go to the heart of anthropology, it may well be that the defining characteristic of the anthropological approach to globalization stems from the discipline's methodological commitment to ethnographic research, or fieldwork (Ferguson 2006: 3). This allows anthropologists to study the experiences of people in the locales they are studying. "What anthropology offers that is often lacking in other disciplines is a concrete attentiveness to *human agency*, to the *practices of everyday life*, in short, to how *subjects mediate the process of globalization*" (Inda and Rosaldo 2008a: 7, italics added).

In the past, and to some extent to this day, anthropologists have tended to do their ethnographic research in a single locale (or at least in one at a time). However in a world characterized by global flows, "*ethnography must be able to follow the question*" and the questions of interest to many ethnographers "can't be encompassed by studying a single site" (Nordstrom 2004: 13). Thus, anthropology, as well as its basic methods (especially ethnography), is being radically altered because of the fluid nature of the increasingly globalized world.[4]

SOCIOLOGY

Some social sciences focus on specific social structures and social institutions. Political science focuses on political entities, especially the nation-state; economics focuses on the economy. Sociology (Martin, Metzger, and Pierre 2006: 499–521; Sassen 2007b) also deals with these structures and institutions; there is a political sociology, an economic sociology, as well as others (e.g. sociology of religion, sociology of the family). Culture is also one of their major concerns in sociology (Best 2008). Sociology is concerned with both macro-level phenomena (social structures and social institutions associated with the state, the economy, etc.) and micro-level phenomena (thought, action, and interaction), as well as with the myriad interrelationships among and between them (Ritzer 1981). Sociology's strength is in offering the widest possible view of globalization (as well as of the social world), but the other fields offer more depth in their contributions. Thus, for example, anthropologists[5] offer far more in-depth analyses of culture in general, as well as specific cultures, than do sociologists.

Globalization has called into question macro-sociology's focus, influenced by Durkheim's focus on social facts, on society. A more complete approach to globalization would require utilization of an "integrated sociological paradigm" (Ritzer 1981) involving the examination of the relationship (both positive and negative) among and between various "levels" of social reality: of globalization as the largest-scale macroscopic social process and structure that is affecting and being affected by all other levels within the social world; how globalization is affecting and being affected by large-scale *social structures* such as the nation-state and by *culture* in its broadest sense; how at the micro-level the things that almost all of us do, and think about, have been, and are being, affected by and affecting globalization.

POLITICAL SCIENCE

Historically, political scientists have been led to focus on nation-states and their interrelationships, as well as the ways in which they relate to globalization.

International Relations (IR) focuses on the relations among and between the nation-states of the world (Clark 2007: 664–6). They are viewed as distinct actors in the world, occupying well-defined territories, and as sovereign within their own borders. There is also an emphasis on a distinct and well-defined inter-state system. The orientation and plight of International Relations is clear in a fascinating essay which argues that the focus of most globalization theories is misguided (Rosenberg 2005: 2–74). Rosenberg argues that such theories may have enjoyed a boom in the 1990s but they are now, in his view, moribund. Instead, he argues for a renewed focus on nation-states and their interrelationship, specifically from a Marxian perspective and its focal concern with capitalism. Rosenberg is making this case from the point of view of International Relations and seeking the renaissance of a field that has tended to be eclipsed by a variety of globalization theories that see the nation-state as eroding, or even disappearing.[6]

Within IR, *political realism* (Keohane and Nye 2000) begins with the premise that international politics is based on power, organized violence, and ultimately war. It assumes that nation-states are the predominant actors on the global stage; act as coherent units in the global arena, that force is not only a usable, but also an effective, method by which nation-states wield power on the global stage; and that military issues are of utmost importance in world politics.

Complex interdependence sees nation-states relating to one another through multiple channels; formally and informally; through normal channels and so-called "back channels." Where complex interdependence differs from realism is in the importance accorded to these informal channels where, for example, entities (e.g. MNCs) other than the state connect societies to one another. There is no clear hierarchy of interstate relationships and it is certainly not the case that military issues always, or even often, predominate. Coalitions arise within and between nation-states on these issues. Conflict may or may not arise and, if conflict arises, it varies greatly in terms of degree of intensity. Complex interdependence tends to lead to the decline in, or even the disappearance of, the use of military force by one nation-state against other(s) within a given region or alliance, although military action may continue to occur outside that region or bloc. While international organizations have only a minor role to play in the realist view of the world, they play an expanded role from the perspective of complex interdependence. Such organizations bring together representatives from various countries, set agendas, serve as catalysts for the formation of coalitions, serve as arenas from which political initiatives arise, and are helpful to weak states in playing a larger role in the international arena. Thus, the complex interdependence perspective continues to focus on relationships among nation-states, but takes a much wider and broader view of the nature of those relationships.

There are also a variety of positions within political science that are at variance with IR and its derivatives and that offer fundamental challenges to it. Among these are Marxist/ radical and social constructionist perspectives on international relations. There are also a wide range of other scholars associated with IPE (international political economy) that challenge IR. Among them are Philip Cerny (1995, 2003: 153–75), Robert W. Cox (1971: 554–84), Stephen R. Gill (Gill and Law 1989: 475–99), Richard Higgott (Brassett and Higgott 2003: 29–55), and James Mittelman (2002: 3–23), as well as Susan Strange (see Chapter 5). Roger Tooze summarizes Susan Strange's distinctive contributions as a focus on power, an analysis of the disastrous separation of economics and politics, and the state-centrism (of IR, for example) which ignores other entities with political and economic power, especially the corporation (Tooze 2000: 1–10).

ECONOMICS

Economics is primarily concerned with "systems of money-coordinated exchange and wage-based production." While in its early years it had more of a large-scale institutional focus, in the last century it has become increasingly dominated by the "use of mathematical models and quantitative data to explore *markets*, i.e. the aggregate outcomes of individual actors' decisions to buy and sell various *commodities*" (Reay 2008). This is clearly represented in the dominant approach in the field – *microeconomics*. However, there is a huge gap between the large-scale issues of concern in globalization and the micro-level foci of microeconomics. It is *macroeconomics* that is better suited to the study of globalization since it involves the aggregation of micro-level data to deal with large-scale phenomena such as geographic regions or nation-states.

On the issue of globalization,[7] economists are primarily concerned with the relationships among various markets. These markets exist generally within nation-states which are the major sources of data for economic research of this type. The relative absence of global-level data is a limitation of economic work in this area. Thus, global studies in economics are basically studies of inter-national economic relationships. Specifically, economists study the relationship between various national *markets*, including those for commodities, labor (Choi and Greenaway 2001), and capital. This leads to a focus on "[t]rade in goods and services [commodities], international migration [labor], and international capital flows" (O'Rourke 2007: 357–63). Among the other issues of concern to economists are the flows of technologies across national borders and foreign investment by MNCs. In sum: "Economic globalization constitutes integration of national economies into the international economy through trade, direct foreign investment (by corporations and multinationals), short-term capital flows, international flows of workers and humanity generally, and flows of technology" (Bhagwati 2004: 3).

For each of their focal concerns, economists are much concerned with the degree of integration of international markets. This leads to a focus, consistent (at least in part[8]) with the basic orientation of this book, on cross-border *flows* of commodities, people, and capital. Economic integration is measured by the size of these flows or by prices. The larger the size of each of the flows and the more equal prices are for commodities, for labor (Haskel 2001: 25–36) (people), and for capital (e.g. interest rates), the more integrated economies are into the global economy.

Economists tend to be supporters of capitalism (according to one noted economist, Jeffrey Sachs [1997], "Global capitalism is surely the most promising institutional arrangement for worldwide prosperity that history has ever seen") and the market. They may find flaws in the way capitalism and its markets operate, but this is likely to lead them to seek to reform the markets and not to overhaul or to replace them. One flaw recognized by economists is inequalities in global markets (Hunter Wade 2004: 567–89). The main cause of this inequality is *not* seen as the market, but rather is traceable to fundamental differences in the nature of the societies themselves that are either winners or losers (de la Dehesa 2006: x–xi). It is not the global market that is the problem for the losers, but rather the losing societies themselves and their lack of credible social institutions. Further, the answer to their problems is for them to be more open to the market, especially the global market.

However, the traditional economic approaches to globalization have their critics within economics (Hunter Wade 2003: 621–44, 2004: 567–89; Rodrik 1997). In a series of books, Joseph Stiglitz (2002, 2006) has critiqued mainstream economics and its neoliberal orientation (for more on Stiglitz see Chapter 6). For example: "The neo-liberal approach relies on strong theoretical assumptions about the efficiency and completeness of markets which … are unlikely to hold in developed countries, let alone developing countries" (Stiglitz and Charlton 2005: 89). Rather than leaving things to the operation of the free market, there is a need for the developed countries, and the international organizations that they dominate (e.g. the WTO), to help developing countries rather than abandon them to their fate in the global marketplace (of course, developing nations must also play a role by undertaking various internal reforms).

Economists and the field of economics have played a disproportionately large role in the contemporary view of globalization, both for public officials and laypersons. At its extreme, they have led to the view that globalization *is* economic globalization. For example, de la Dehesa (2006: 1) defines globalization as "a dynamic process of liberalization, openness, and international integration across a wide range of markets, from labor to goods and from services to capital and technology."

GEOGRAPHY

Geography encompasses the "study of social relationships and the spatial structures that underpin those relations" (Jackson 2000: 753–4), as well as the study of "spatial differentiation and organization of human activity and its interrelationships with the physical environment" (Johnston 2000: 353–60).

Geography relates to globalization in at least four ways (Taylor, Watts, and Johnston 2002a: 1–17). First, the field was global long before laypeople and scholars began thinking about globalization, let alone possessing such a concept. This experience equips geographers to look at developments in the global age from the point of view of a geohistorical perspective. Early geographers were involved in geopolitics and their ideas shaped the geopolitics of nation-states. The 1960s and 1970s saw a rebirth of interest in the field of geography in global studies. This took the form of interest in the global environment and environmental problems, the global reach of multinational corporations, and the problem of global inequality. Second, geographers are well positioned to identify basic differences in spatial arrangements between today's globalized world and various points in the past. One such distinction, created by Manuel Castells (1996), is the difference between earlier "spaces of places" and today's "spaces of flows." Third, geographers are concerned with the "spatial distribution of things global" (Taylor, Watts, and Johnston 2002a: 3). Of particular importance here is the study of various geographic inequalities that result from globalization. Fourth, a geographic approach involves the study of the reactions to globalization. This can involve resistance to globalization based on place as well as a cosmopolitanism that rejects any given place and embraces the globe as a whole.

Globalization has made necessary a *remapping* of the world focusing on "new divisions of labor, an enhanced role for finance, and new possibilities of control through communication and computing-technology innovations" (Taylor, Watts, and Johnston 2002b: 448), the "promotion of markets as resource allocators in an increasingly deregulated world" (Taylor, Watts, and Johnston 2002b: 448), the changing role and functions of the nation-state, the development of new civil societies that straddle at least part of the globe, the focus on the environment that transcends geographic boundaries (including those of the nation-state), a questioning of modernity and the idea of progress associated with it, the rise of information technology leading to the "end of geography" and to domains that cannot be mapped geographically, that in a sense have no geography.[9]

While social geographers retain a traditional interest in such issues as spatiality and mapping, the difference between them and other social scientists, especially sociologists, seems to have narrowed considerably. This is particularly clear in the work of a leading social geographer, David Harvey, and a leading sociologist, Anthony Giddens. Harvey (1989) is very interested in sociological issues and is best known in this area for his work on time-space compression. One of the many influences on Giddens's (1990) thinking was geography in general, and social geography in particular, and his best-known contribution in this area is time-space distanciation (see Chapter 9).

More generally, the field has become increasingly multidisciplinary, transdisciplinary, perhaps even postdisciplinary. As a result, geographers are now "engaged with an astonishing range of issues across the whole field of the humanities, social sciences and the sciences (so much so that these distinctions are themselves increasingly seen as problematic and even counter-productive)" (Johnston et al. 2000: vii). Thus, for example, if one looks at the list of global issues of concern to social geographers, it is not much different from a similar list in sociology (see Herod 2009).

PSYCHOLOGY

Given its micro-level focus, psychology has not often addressed such a macro-level issue as globalization. However, it is clear that globalization has a wide-ranging set of effects and some psychologists have recognized the need for the field to address the psychological impact and effects of globalization. For example, Arnett (2002) looks at the issue of identity[10] (defined as the way in which people think about themselves in relationship to the social environment in which they live) and how it relates to globalization. He identifies four key issues under the heading of identity and globalization. The first is bicultural identity. In this case, people's identity is divided between the local community and a sense of their place in the global culture and world. That is, people can be seen as developing an identity that is a hybrid composed of both local and global elements. While such bicultural identities are particularly true for immigrants, large numbers of those who continue to live in the same place have developed such identities (just living near to immigrant groups may lead to bicultural identities). Those with bicultural identities may be deeply immersed in the local culture (e.g. eat local foods in local establishments), but also actively engaged in the global culture (e.g. eat "global foods" in Pizza Hut). They may have little trouble living in these two worlds and in identifying with both of them simultaneously.

The second is identity confusion. As a result of globalization, people may identify with neither the global nor the local; they simply may be confused about their identities. They may not truly understand the new global culture; it may seem too different, too foreign. Their moorings in traditional local culture may also be loosened by global culture and their increasing awareness of it. The local may seem increasingly irrelevant to, and out of touch with, the new global world. In the end, they may not feel part of either the global or the local. Those who are likely to be most confused about their identity are those who grow up in cultures that are very different from, and at odds with, the new and emerging global culture. Identity confusion can have a variety of deleterious effects on the psychological functioning and behavior of individuals leading to mental problems (e.g. depression), behavioral problems (drug abuse), and even suicide. In fact, as we saw in Chapter 12 one analysis recently concluded that globalization creates a "toxic world" for individuals and their emotional lives (Lemert and Elliott 2006).

Third is self-selected cultures. People may create their own cultures with which they identify. This is often a reaction against the seemingly homogeneous global culture, but it does not constitute a return to the local culture; it involves the creation of a new culture and therefore something new with which to identify. Identification with a variety of alter-globalization movements would be a good example of this. Then there is the creation of groups that revive past local practices (Bak 1997) with which people can identify.

Finally, there is emerging adulthood. More people throughout the world may find their search for identity stretching into their adult years. Such an extension is made possible by globalization, especially by the economic advances associated with globalization in the North that make it possible for young people to devote more time to a search for identity while they earn little or no income. On the other hand, the longer search for identity made possible by globalization increases the ways in which it disrupts traditional identities, and creates numerous possibilities for new identities.

The above has dealt with the impact of globalization on the psychology of individuals, but it would also be worth exploring the ways in which individual psychology, and changes in it, affect globalization.

LITERARY CRITICISM (POSTCOLONIAL)

Literary theory involves, as its name suggests, studying, thinking, and theorizing that takes as its focus some body of literature. In the case of globalization, the most relevant body of literary theory involves the study of literature that was produced in, or is about, the experience of people who once lived in areas that were colonized, usually by the major Western powers (especially Great Britain). This literature is usually categorized under the heading of postcolonialism. "The term postcolonialism designates a systematic discourse dedicated to investigating, analyzing, and deconstructing structures of knowledge, ideologies, power relations, and social identities that have been authored by and authorized by the imperial West in ruling and representing the non-West over the past 500 years" (Xie 2007: 986–90).

Edward Said's (1979/1994)[11] *Orientalism* is "the founding document of postcolonial thought" (Acocella 2008: 68–9). While it was not written with the idea of globalization in mind, and was written before the current era of globalization, it has powerful implications for contemporary thinking on globalization.[12]

Orientalism has several interrelated meanings for Said. First it is an area of academic interest (a discipline) with schools of "Oriental Studies." Thus, "the Orient was a scholar's word" (Said 1979/1994: 92). Second, it is a "style of thought based upon an ontological and epistemological distinction made between 'the Orient' and (most of the time) 'the Occident'" (Said 1979/1994: 2). Third, and perhaps most importantly, Orientalism is a Western discourse "for dominating, restructuring, and having authority over the Orient" (Said 1979/1994: 3). It was the basis for the ways in which European culture "was able to manage – and even produce – the Orient politically, sociologically, militarily, ideologically, scientifically, and imaginatively" (Said 1979/1994: 3).

Orientalism was (and still is) a diverse cultural enterprise that included, among other things:

> The imagination itself, the whole of India and the Levant, the Biblical texts and the Biblical lands, the spice trade, colonial armies and the long tradition of colonial administrators, a formidable scholarly corpus, innumerable Oriental 'experts' and 'hands', an Oriental professoriate, a complex array of 'Oriental' ideas (Oriental despotism, Oriental splendor, cruelty, sensuality), many Eastern sects, philosophies and wisdoms domesticated for local European use. (Said 1979/1994: 4)

In spite of this diversity, and although it is far more than just ideas/discourse, Orientalism is primarily a set of ideas expressed in a specific discourse. Following Foucault (and Nietzsche), knowledge cannot be divorced from power and it was to a large degree as a result of Orientalism that Europe and the West more generally were able to exercise power over the East. To get at Orientalism as ideas/discourse, Said (1979/1994: 23) examines a variety of "texts" including not only scholarly works on the topic, "but also works of literature, political tracts, journalistic texts, travel books, religious and philological studies." The Orient that emerges from these texts "is less a place than a *topos*, a set of references, a congeries of characteristics, that seems to have its origin in a quotation, or a fragment of a text, or a citation from someone's work on the Orient, or some bit of previous imagining, or an amalgam of all of these" (Said 1979/1994: 177). The ideas associated with Orientalism are largely repeatedly reproduced fictions (although they are not totally false) that are rarely, if ever, based on observation, let alone careful empirical study.

Said's basic problem with Orientalism, aside from its disastrous effects on those labeled Orientals, is that it is an idea characterized by biases, ignorance, lack of knowledge, stereotypes, standardized views, and fictions. Orientalism reflects the power of the West and has little to do with the realities of life in the Orient. Negative stereotypes of Orientals abounded and they were shaped by Westerners' stereotypes of themselves. Westerners produced biased and limited "texts" about the Orient and it was those texts, and not life as it really existed in the Orient, which came to be considered the basis of the "truth" about the Orient.

There are a variety of intellectual problems with Orientalism that result from it "disregarding, essentializing, denuding the humanity of another culture" (Said 1979/1994: 108). People in the Orient were not discussed in individual or humanistic terms, but rather in collective or abstract terms. Furthermore, the view of the Orient has remained more or less the same in terms of both time and place for those in the West who think about, analyze, manage, and seek to subdue, it. It is as if nothing has changed, or will ever change, in the Orient. More generally, Said (1979/1994: 109) argues that: "The West is the spectator, the judge and jury, of every facet of Oriental behavior." Knowledge of the Orient, often unchanged over great stretches of time, was accumulated in the West and this was closely related to the accumulation of both the people and territories of the Orient by the West.

Said (1979/1994: 261) reserves his most scathing indictment for Orientalism as it relates to Islam. It is characterized by its "retrogressive position when compared with the other human sciences (and even with the other branches of Orientalism), its general methodological and ideological backwardness, and its comparative insularity from developments both in the other humanities and in the real world of historical, economic, social and political circumstances."

OTHER FIELDS

There are various other fields that deal with, or at least touch on, globalization. For example, a number of philosophers have dealt with the issue of justice in the global age (Pogge 2001). Another group of philosophers addresses the various challenges facing globalization (Hicks and Shannon 2007). One deals with the "horrors of globalization" (Santilli 2007) from the point of view of postmodern philosophy and especially the postmodern social theory of Zygmunt Bauman whose work on liquid modernity plays, as we saw in the first chapter, a key role in the shaping of this book. Of course, there is much more to the philosophy of globalization than the issue of justice. For example, Nancy (2007) critically analyzes globalization as a closed process and contrasts it to the more open and creative process of what in France is called *mondialization*.

The field of history, like many other fields (e.g. sociology, political science, especially International Relations), has focused on the nation-state or even smaller units of analysis. It has tended not to examine the larger process of globalization. Jerry Bentley calls for both historicizing globalization and globalizing history (Bentley 2004). It is likely that history, like many other fields, will move more in the direction of the study of globalization.

ADDITIONAL READINGS

Jonathan Xavier Inda and Renato Rosaldo, eds. *The Anthropology of Globalization: A Reader*, 2nd edn. Oxford: Blackwell, 2008.

Saskia Sassen. *A Sociology of Globalization*. New York: W.W. Norton and Company, 2007.

Keri E. Iyall Smith. *Sociology of Globalization: Culture, Economies, and Politics*. Boulder, CO: Westview Press, 2012.

Guillermo de la Dehesa. *Winners and Losers in Globalization*. Oxford: Blackwell, 2006.

Guillermo de la Dehesa. *What Do We Know About Globalization? Issues of Poverty and Income Distribution*. Oxford: Blackwell, 2007.

Andrew Herod. *Geographies of Globalization*. Oxford: Wiley-Blackwell, 2009.

R. J. Johnston, Peter J. Taylor, and Michael J. Watts, eds. *Geographies of Global Change: Remapping the World*. Oxford: Blackwell, 2002.

Jeffrey Jensen Arnett. "The Psychology of Globalization." *American Psychologist*, October, 2002: 774–83.

Edward W. Said. *Orientalism*. New York: Vintage Books, 1979/1994.

Thomas W. Pogge. ed. *Global Justice*. Oxford: Blackwell, 2001.

Jerry H. Bentley. "Globalizing History and Historicizing Globalization." *Globalizations* 1, 1, 2004: 69–81.

NOTES

1 For example, Canclini (1995) integrates perspectives and insights from anthropology and sociology.

2 Tomlinson (1999); Inda and Rosaldo (2008a: 13); Nordstrom (2004: 12).

3 Miller (2005: 66–7). This is a quite telling argument and reflects the bias of anthropologists toward what has been termed "glocalization" and against "grobalization" (see Chapter 8).

4 For a critique of anthropological approaches to globalization, see Edelman and Haugerud (2005: 22).

5 Interestingly, Inda and Rosaldo (2008b: 7) offer a view of an anthropological approach to globalization that is not much different from the sociological perspective offered here: "to focus at once on the large-scale processes (or flows of subjects and objects) through which the world is becoming increasingly, albeit unevenly, interconnected and how subjects respond to these processes in culturally specific ways."

6 For an analysis of Rosenberg's argument, see Axford (2007).

7 For overviews of the work of economists on various issues relating to globalization, see de la Dehesa (2006, 2007).

8 However, as is made clear in Chapter 1, we do not assume that global flows necessarily lead to increased integration; they can lead to disintegration, as well, as occurred with the start of WW I and could occur again in the Great Recession.

9 Nevertheless, there are those who argue that we are witnessing the emergence of a geography of information technology, especially cyberspace, see Kitchin and Dodge (2002: 340–54).

10 Those in many other fields (e.g. anthropology, sociology) are interested in identity (and its relationship to globalization), although they may define it differently.

11 Among other key figures are Homi Bhabha (1994) and Gayatri Chakravory Spivak (1987, 1999).

12 See also Said (1993).

GLOSSARY

Americanization is the import by non-Americans of products, images, technologies, practices, and behavior that are closely associated with America/Americans.

Americanization without America is a phenomenon where a nation-state can be Americanized by the spread of increasingly universal consumer capitalism without necessarily being affected by America per se.

Anthropocene is a potential new geological era characterized by several accelerating human-made ecological changes, including mass extinctions, global warming, and oceanic changes, that are far-reaching and in many cases permanent.

Asylum seekers are refugees who seek to remain in the country to which they flee.

Autarky is the turn inward of a nation-state in order to create as much economic self-sufficiency as possible.

Brain drain is the systematic loss by a given nation-state of people highly prized elsewhere in the world because of their great intellect and advanced training and education; those who have much intellectual capital.

Brain gain refers to the possibility that nation-states, especially those that are developed, could be net gainers acquiring more people with an increased knowledge base than they lose.

Cap-and-trade is a system that limits the total carbon emissions allowed, where companies buy permits in order to allow them to produce additional emissions with prices set by the market.

Carbon neutrality is a scenario where carbon emissions are equal to (or less than) the amount of those emissions that are absorbed by the natural environment.

Carbon tax is a tax applied to fossil fuels (e.g. oil, coal, and natural gas) used to curb carbon emissions.

Civil society is process through which individuals negotiate, argue, struggle against, or agree with each other and with the centers of political and economic authority.

Climate refugees are people displaced by environmental changes brought about by climate change, such as rising sea levels, drought, and increased exposure to hurricanes and floods.

Colonialism entails the creation by the colonial power of an administrative apparatus in the country (or geographic area) that has been colonized in order to run its internal affairs, including its settlements.

Globalization: A Basic Text, Second Edition. George Ritzer and Paul Dean.
© 2015 John Wiley & Sons, Ltd. Published 2015 by John Wiley & Sons, Ltd.

Conflict trap is a situation wherein a nation-state is confronted with either continuing civil wars or frequent violent *coups d'état*.

Conflicting flows are those transplanetary processes that conflict with one another (and with much else).

Creolization involves a combination of languages and cultures that were previously unintelligible to one another.

Cultural convergence is when cultures are subject to many of the same global flows and tend to grow more alike.

Cultural differentialism involves barriers that prevent flows that serve to make cultures more alike; cultures tend to remain stubbornly different from one another.

Cultural globalization involves cultural influences that exist at a global level, between and among various nations.

Cultural hybridization is the mixing of cultures and the integration of the global and the local leading to unique combinations.

Cultural imperialism indicates that one or more cultures impose themselves, more or less consciously, on other cultures thereby destroying local culture, in whole, or in part.

Dependency theory is a body of work critical of the development project. It emphasizes that the development project contributed not to the development of the nation-states of the South, but more to a decline in their independence and to an increase in their dependence on the countries of the North, especially the US. Underdevelopment is not an aberrant condition, or one caused by the less developed nations themselves, but it is built into the development project itself (as well as into global capitalism).

Deregulation is the commitment by nation-states to limit or eliminate restraints on the free market and free trade.

Deterritorialization is the declining significance of the geographic location in which culture exists.

Development is a "project" that was primarily concerned with the economic development of specific nation-states, usually those that were not regarded as sufficiently developed economically.

Diaspora is the large-scale dispersal, dislocation, and deterritorialization of a population.

Double movement is the coexistence of the expansion of the laissez-faire market and the reaction against it.

Easternization involves the economic and cultural influences of the East on the West. It includes a wide array of phenomena that are Eastern in origin and that are increasingly visible in the West such as Eastern business practices (Toyotism), yoga, a "Zen" outlook on life, various beliefs (e.g. reincarnation), vegetarianism, and Eastern music.

Ecological economics is a field of economic theory that considers the ecological carrying capacity of the earth thus integrating economic theory with environmental knowledge.

Economic globalization is the most well-known form of globalization and refers to growing economic linkages at the global level.

Ecotourism involves efforts to allow tourists to experience natural environments while doing little or no harm to them.

Empire involves global dominance without a nation-state at its center; decentered global dominance.

Ethnic cleansing involves various policies oriented to forcibly removing people of another ethnic group.

Ethnic group is a social group defined on the basis of some cultural characteristic(s).

Ethnoscapes involve the actual movement, as well as fantasies about moving, of mobile groups and individuals (tourists, refugees, guest workers).

Ethnotourism involves efforts by tourists to experience the way other people live, often people very different from the tourists.

Export Processing Zone (EPZ) is an independent area controlled by corporations and free of national control; it is denationalized.

Fair trade is defined as a concern for the social, economic, and environmental well-being of marginalized small producers.

Family reunification migrants are individuals whose family ties motivate them to migrate internationally.

Feminization of labor involves the increasing participation of women in both the global formal and informal paid-labor force.

Financescapes involve the processes by which huge sums of money move through nation-states and around the world at great speed through commodity speculations, currency markets, and national stock exchanges.

Flows involve the movement of people, things, information, and places due, in part, to the increasing porosity of global barriers.

Forced migrants include refugees and asylum seekers who are forced to leave their home country.

Foreign Direct Investment (FDI) is investment by a firm in one nation-state in a firm in another nation-state with the intention of gaining control over it.

Free market is one which is allowed to operate free of any impediments, especially those imposed by the nation-state and other political entities.

Free-market capitalism is the creation of an open domestic economy governed by policies such as the deregulation of the economy (particularly the capital markets), lowering or elimination of tariffs on imported goods, elimination of restrictions on foreign investment, dropping of trade quotas, elimination of domestic monopolies, opening of industries and stock and bond markets to direct foreign investment and ownership, and the opening of banking and telecommunications to private ownership and to competition.

Gaseousness involves hyper-mobility of people, things, information, and places in the global age.

Gender refers to differences between males and females that are based on social definition and distinction.

Genocide is defined as acts committed with the intent to destroy, in whole or in part, a national, ethnic, racial, or religious group.

Global care chains involve a series of personal relationships between people across the globe based on the paid or unpaid work of caring.

Global cities are the key cities in the global, especially capitalist, economy.

Global civil society is a global, non-governmental, pluralistic form of society composed of interlinked social processes and oriented to civility.

Global commodity chains combine value-adding chains and the global organization of industries, while according a central place to the growing importance of the sellers of global products.

Global value chains emphasize the relative value of those economic activities that are required to bring a good or service from conception, to the various phases of production (involving a combination of physical transformation and the input of various producer services), to delivery to final consumers, and to final disposal after use.

Globalists take the position that there is such a thing as globalization and it encompasses virtually the entirety of the globe.

Globality is the omnipresence of the process of globalization.

Globalization is a transplanetary process or set of processes involving increasing liquidity and growing multidirectional flows of people, objects, places, and information as well as the structures they encounter and create that are barriers to, or expedite, those flows.

Globalization from above is a process that is created and controlled by centralized and powerful actors, such as wealthy elites or MNCs (especially in the North), and imposed on broader society.

Globalization from below takes the form of marginalized groups and social movements that struggle to make globalization benefit more people and for global processes to be more democratic.

Globaphilia is an emphasis on the positive aspects of globalization, with the expectation that it would result in greater economic success and the spread of democracy.

Globaphobia is an emphasis on the negative aspects of globalization, especially for the less well-off portions of the global population.

Glocalization is the interpenetration of the global and the local resulting in unique outcomes in different geographic areas.

Graduated sovereignty involves the phenomenon wherein instead of governing the entire geographic area of the nation-state, the national government retains full control in some areas, but surrenders various degrees of control in others to corporations and other entities.

Greenfield investment involves the building of totally new corporate facilities in another country.

Grobalization is the imperialistic ambitions of nation-states, corporations, organizations, and the like and their desire, indeed need, to impose themselves on various geographic areas throughout the world.

Growth triangles are largely autonomous domains linking contiguous areas of neighboring countries allowing for the exploitation of complementary resources that exist in the border areas between countries.

Highly skilled migrants are workers with special qualifications (e.g. managers, executives, professionals, technicians) who migrate for better economic opportunities.

Human trafficking is the recruitment and movement of people through force or coercion, for purposes of sexual exploitation or forced labor.

Hybridization involves a process in which external flows interact with internal flows producing a unique cultural hybrid that combines elements of the two.

Hyperconsumption involves buying more than one can afford.

Hyperdebt involves owing more than one will be able to pay back.

Ideology is a system of widely shared ideas, patterned beliefs, guiding norms and values, and ideals accepted as truth by some group.

Ideoscapes involve flows of images that are primarily political in nature, produced either by nation-states in line with their ideology, or as counter-ideologies produced by movements that seek to contest those in power.

Imagined community is the idea that a nation exists primarily as a set of ideas that exist in people's minds.

Imperialism involves methods employed by one nation-state to gain control (sometimes through territorial conquest) of another country (or geographic area) and then to exercise control, especially political, economic, and military, over that country (or geographic area), and perhaps many other countries.

Industrial upgrading involves processes through which economic actors – nations, firms and even workers – move from low-value to relatively high-value activities in global production networks.

Information war reflects the fact that information and information technology is increasingly permeating all aspects of warfare perpetrated by developed countries.

Interconnected flows are global flows that do not occur in isolation from one another; many different flows interconnect at various points and times.

Intergovernmental Organizations (IGOs) are organizations such as the UN that are international in scope.

International migrants are people who live in a country where they were not born and have important social ties to that country.

International Non-Governmental Organizations (INGOs) are international not-for-profit organizations that perform public functions but are not established or run by nation-states.

International production networks involve the networks of producers involved in the process of producing a finished product.

Intersectionality is the idea that members of any given minority group are affected by the nature of their position in other arrangements of social inequality.

Irregular migrants are migrants that enter, or stay in, a country without proper documentation.

Isomorphism is the idea that a series of global models in a variety of different domains – politics, business, education, family, religion, and so on – has led to a great uniformity throughout the world.

Laissez faire refers to policies that involve non-intervention of the nation-state in matters concerning the market, trade, or the economy more generally.

Leapfrogging involves developing nations bypassing earlier technologies, enabling those nations to adopt more advanced technologies.

Limited government involves the idea that no government or government agency can do things as well as the market. This renders a government less able, or unable, to intervene in the market.

Liquidity is the increasing ease of movement, the mobility, of people, things, information, and places in the global age.

Majority group is a group of people in a superordinate position in wealth, power, and/or prestige (status).

Market fundamentalism is the idea that markets will take care of all our needs.

McDonaldization is the process by which the principles of the fast-food restaurant are coming to dominate more and more sectors of American society, as well as the rest of the world.

Media imperialism is the theory that Western (especially US) media, and the technologies associated with it, dominate less developed nations and their cultures.

Mediascapes involve both the electronic capability to produce and transmit information around the world as well as the images of the world that these media create and disseminate.

Megacities are defined as cities with a population greater than 10 million people.

Megalopolis is a long chain of interconnected cities with the potentiality of becoming one huge city.

Metaphors involve the use of one term to better help us understand another term.

Minority group is a group of people in a subordinate position in wealth, power, and/or prestige (status).

Modernization is the belief of an evolutionary process that moved humankind from agricultural and pre-modern societies into the modern era, brought about by the reality of wide-scale rational planning.

Multidirectional flows involve all sorts of things flowing in every conceivable direction among various points in the world.

Multinational corporation (MNC) is a corporation that operates in more than two countries.

Nation is a social group that is linked through common descent, culture, language, or territorial contiguity.

Nation-state integrates sub-groups that define themselves as a nation with the organizational structure that constitutes the state.

National identity is a fluid and dynamic form of collective identity, founded upon a community's subjective belief that the members of the community share a set of characteristics that make them different from other groups.

Nationalism is a doctrine and (or) political movement that seek to make the nation the basis of a political structure, especially a state.

Natural resources trap involves the limiting of economic development as a result of excessive dependence on abundant natural resources.

Neoliberalism is the theory (as well as an ideology) that involves a combination of the liberal commitment to individual liberty with neoclassical economics devoted to the free market and opposed to state intervention in that market. Entrepreneurs are to be liberated, markets and trade are to be free, states are to be supportive of this and to keep interventions to a minimum, and there are to be strong property rights.

Non-people are those who occupy positions that lead them to be devoid of distinctive content (at least in those positions); for example, employees associated with non-places such as telemarketers (who may be virtually anywhere in the world) who interact with all customers in much the same way relying heavily on scripts.

Non-places are settings that are largely devoid of distinctive content.

Non-services are services that are largely devoid of distinctive content such as those provided by ATMs (the services provided are identical; the customer does all the work involved in obtaining the services) as opposed to those offered by human bank tellers.

Non-things are objects that are largely devoid of distinctive content such as chain-store products and credit cards (there is little to distinguish one credit card from the billions of others, all of which work in exactly the same way for all who use them anywhere in the world).

Nothing involves (largely) empty social forms; forms largely devoid of distinctive content.

Offshore outsourcing involves the transfer of work to companies in other countries in exchange for money.

Orientalism involves a set of ideas and texts produced in the West that are the basis of the domination, control, and exploitation of the East.

Outsourcing involves the transfer of activities once performed by an entity to a business (or businesses) in exchange for money.

Pluralism is the idea and fact that different races and ethnic groups can live together; they can co-exist.

Political globalization involves political relations that exist at a global level, including, but not restricted to, inter-national relations.

Portfolio investment is the purchase of equities in companies in other countries for financial gain, not control.

Postcolonialism relates to various developments that take place in a former colony after the colonizing power departs.

Precariat includes the growing number of part-time workers, temporary workers, and others living precariously without stable jobs, occupational identities, or social protections as a result of neoliberalism.

Prosumers are those who simultaneously produce what they consume.

Protectionism is government intervention in order to encourage domestic production.

Race is defined based on meanings attached to physical or biological characteristics.

Race to the bottom is the phenomenon whereby countries are involved in a downward spiral of competitiveness as a result of undercutting prices, lowering wages, making working conditions poorer, lengthening hours of work, and increasing pressure on and demands of workers.

Racism is the belief in the inherent superiority of one racial group and the inferiority of others.

Refugees are those who are forced to leave their homeland, or who leave involuntarily, because they fear for their safety.

Reification is the idea that people come to accord social processes a reality of their own and come to feel that even though they created – and in fact *are* in many ways – those processes, there is nothing they can do about them.

Relations of resistance involve a wide range of consumer, farmer, farm worker, farmer/peasant, and indigenous peasant movements opposed to exploitative global practices.

Relations of social production involve the processes through which populations survive within international and national institutions that govern material conditions and opportunities to earn a livelihood.

Remittances are monetary transactions by which successful migrants send money back to their country of origin for the care and support of various family members.

Return migrants are people who, after spending time in their destination country, go back to their home country.

Reverse flows are processes which, while flowing in one direction, act back on their source.

Sex refers to the physical differences between males and females.

Skeptics contend that there is no such thing as globalization because vast portions of the globe, and a significant portion of the world's population, are wholly, or in significant part, outside of, and even actively excluded from, the processes generally associated with it.

Social class relates to social rankings made on the basis of economic factors such as income and overall wealth.

Solidity refers to the fact that people, things, information, and places "harden" over time and therefore have limited mobility.

Something involves [largely] full social forms; forms rich in distinctive content.

Sovereign wealth funds are funds controlled by nation-states (not corporations or individual investors) and that often invest in other countries.

State is an organizational structure with relatively autonomous office-holders outside other socioeconomic hierarchies, with its own rules and resources increasingly coming from taxes rather than from feudal, personal, or religious obligations.

Structural adjustment involves the conditions of economic "restructuring" that are imposed by organizations such as the World Bank and the IMF on borrowing nations. Receiving nations are expected, among other things, to put into place tight monetary and fiscal policies, to liberalize financial markets and trade, to privatize, and to deregulate.

Structures involve encompassing sets of processes of "congealed flows" that may either impede or block flows or serve to expedite and channel them.

Supply chains involve value-adding activities in the production process. The chain begins with raw materials and follows the value-adding process through a variety of inputs and outputs and ultimately to a finished product.

Sustainable development involves economic and environmental changes that meet the needs of the present, especially of the world's poor, without jeopardizing the needs of the future.

Technoscapes are the fluid, global configurations of high and low, mechanical and informational, technology and the wide range of material that now moves freely and quickly around the globe and across borders.

Temporary labor migrants are guest workers and overseas contract workers that move to a country for a limited amount of time.

Time-space compression involves the shrinking of space, and the reduction of the time required by a wide range of processes, brought about by changes in transportation and communication technologies advanced mainly by capitalist corporations.

Time-space distanciation is the stretching of social relations across space and time, which is brought about by technological change.

Tourists are people who move about the world because they *want to* (and because they are "light").

Trade protectionism is a policy of systematic government intervention in foreign trade with the objective of encouraging domestic production. This encouragement involves giving preferential treatment to domestic producers and discriminating against foreign competitors.

Trade-Related Aspects of International Property Rights (TRIPS) is an agreement negotiated through the WTO to protect the interests of those individuals, organizations, and states that create ideas.

Trade-Related Investment Measures (TRIMs) is a WTO agreement on a range of operating or performance measures that host-country governments impose on foreign firms to keep them from having a distorting effect on trade in goods and services.

Transnationalism involves processes that interconnect individuals and social groups across specific geo-political borders.

Transnationality is the rise of new communities and formation of new social identities and relations that cannot be defined through the traditional reference point of nation-states.

Vagabonds are people who, if they are able to move at all, are likely to be doing so because they are forced to (e.g. forced to migrate to escape poverty [and to find work], by war, because of discrimination).

Westernization refers to the economic, political, and cultural influence of the West on the rest of the world. The concept is often held to be coterminous with globalization, although it is a unidirectional flow as opposed to the multidirectional flows characteristic of globalization. It is also tied closely to the notions and earlier periods of Western imperialism and colonialism.

World culture involves the spread of global models leading to global convergence.

World-systems theory envisions a world divided mainly between the *core* and the *periphery* with the nation-states associated with the latter being dependent on, and exploited by, the core nation-states.

Xenophobia involves the beliefs, attitudes, and prejudices that reject, exclude, and vilify groups that are outsiders or foreigners to the dominant social group.

REFERENCES

Aalbers, Manuel. 2013. "Neoliberalism is Dead … Long Live Neoliberalism." *International Journal of Urban and Regional Research* 37 (3): 1083–1090.

Abbott, Kenneth. 2012. "Organisation for Economic Co-Operation and Development." In George Ritzer, ed., *Wiley-Blackwell Encyclopedia of Globalization*. Oxford: Wiley-Blackwell.

Abrahamson, Mark. 2004. *Global Cities*. New York: Oxford University Press.

Abrash, Abigail. 2001. "The Amungae, Kamoro & Freeport: How Indigenous Papuans Have Resisted the World's Largest Gold and Copper Mine." *Cultural Survival Quarterly* 25 (1): 38–44.

Abrutyn, Seth. 2012. "Religions, Global." In George Ritzer, ed., *Wiley-Blackwell Encyclopedia of Globalization*. Oxford: Wiley-Blackwell.

Acker, Joan. 2004. "Gender, Capitalism and Globalization." *Critical Sociology* 30 (1): 17–41.

Acocella, Joan. 2008. "A Better Place." *New Yorker* February 4.

Adam, Barbara. 2012. "Future, Globalization and the." In George Ritzer, ed., *Wiley-Blackwell Encyclopedia of Globalization*. Oxford: Wiley-Blackwell.

ADC Fact Sheet: The Condition of Arab Americans Post-9/11. 2007. American-Arab Anti-Discrimination Committee.

Ahmed, Akbar S. 1995. "'Ethnic Cleansing': A Metaphor for Our Time?" *Ethnic and Racial Studies* 18 (1): 1–25.

Ahmed, Azam. 2013. "The Other Big Afghan Crisis, the Growing Army of Addicts." *New York Times* November 2.

Alarcón, Antonio V. Menéndez. 2012. "Cosmopolitanism." In George Ritzer, ed., *Wiley-Blackwell Encyclopedia of Globalization*. Oxford: Wiley-Blackwell.

Albanese, Jay. 2011. *Transnational Crime and the 21st Century: Criminal Enterprise, Corruption, and Opportunity*. New York: Oxford University Press.

Alberts, Hana. 2010. "Asia's Up and Coming Financial Centers." *Forbes* July 13.

Albrow, Martin. 1996. *The Global Age*. Cambridge, UK: Polity Press.

Alderson, Arthur S., and Jason Beckfield. 2004. "Power and Position in the World City System." *American Journal of Sociology*, 109 (4): 811–851.

Alexander, Anne, and Miriyam Aouragh. 2014. "Egypt's Unfinished Revolution: the Role of the Media Revisited." *International Journal of Communication* 8: 890–915.

Alexander, Jeffrey C. 2006a. "Global Civil Society." *Theory, Culture & Society* 23: 521–524.

Alexander, Jeffrey C. 2006b. *The Civil Sphere*. Oxford: Oxford University Press.

Alexander, Jeffrey C. 2010. "Power, Politics, and the Civil Sphere." In Kevin Leicht and J. Craig Jenkins, eds., *Handbook of Politics: State and Society in Global Perspective*. New York: Springer.

Ali, S. Harris. 2012. "Borderless Diseases." In George Ritzer, ed., *Wiley-Blackwell Encyclopedia of Globalization*. Oxford: Wiley-Blackwell.

Alter Chen, Martha. 1995. "Engendering World Conference: The International Women's Movement and the United Nations." *Third World Quarterly* 16 (3): 477–494.

Altman, Daniel. 2007. *Connected: 24 Hours in the Global Economy*. New York: Farrar, Straus and Giroux.

Alvarez, Lizette. 2006a. "A Growing Stream of Illegal Immigrants Choose to Remain Despite the Risks." *New York Times* December 20.

Alvarez, Lizette. 2006b. "Fear and Hope in Immigrant's Furtive Existence." *New York Times* December 20.

Alves, Ruben. 1969. *Theology of Hope*. Cleveland: Corpus Books.

American Academy of Pediatrics. 2012. "AAP Makes Recommendations to Reduce Children's Exposure to Pesticides." Press Release November 26.

Anderson, Benedict. 1991. *Imagined Communities: Reflections on the Origin and Spread of Nationalism*. Revised edn. London: Verso.

Anderson, Benedict. 2006. *Imagined Communities: Reflections on the Origin and Spread of Nationalism*. New edn. London: Verso.

Anderson, David M., and Neil Carrier. 2006. "'Flowers of Paradise' or 'Polluting the Nation': Contested Narratives of Khat Consumption." In John Brewer and Frank Trentmann, eds., *Consuming Cultures, Global Perspectives: Historical Trajectories, Transnational Exchanges*. Oxford: Berg.

Andreas, Peter, and Ethan Nadelmann. 2006. *Policing the Globe: Criminalization and Crime Control in International Relations*. Oxford: Oxford University Press.

Andrews, David. 2012. "Disneyization." In George Ritzer, ed., *Wiley-Blackwell Encyclopedia of Globalization*. Oxford: Wiley-Blackwell.

Andrews, David, and Ron Mower. 2012. "Sport." In George Ritzer, ed., *Wiley-Blackwell Encyclopedia of Globalization*. Oxford: Wiley-Blackwell.

Andrews, David, and George Ritzer. 2007. "The Grobal in the Sporting Glocal." In Richard Giulianotti and Roland Robertson, eds., *Globalization and Sport*. Oxford: Blackwell.

Aneesh, A. 2012. "Negotiating Globalization: Men and Women of India's Call Centers." *Journal of Social Issues* 68 (3): 514–533.

Ang, Ien. 1985. *Watching Dallas: Soap Opera and the Melodramatic Imagination*. London: Routledge.

Anner, Mark, and Peter Evans. 2004. "Building Bridges Across a Double-Divide: Alliances between US and Latin American Labor and NGOs." *Development in Practice* 14 (1–2): 34–47.

Antonio, Robert J. 1991. "Postmodern Storytelling vs. Pragmatic Truth-Seeking." *Sociological Theory* 9: 154–163.

Antonio, Robert J. 2007. "The Cultural Construction of Neoliberal Globalization." In George Ritzer, ed., *Blackwell Companion to Globalization*. Oxford: Blackwell.

Apostolopoulos, Yiorgos, Stella Leivadi, and Andrew Yiannakis, eds. 2013. *The Sociology of Tourism: Theoretical and Empirical Investigations*. New York: Routledge.

Appadurai, Arjun. 1996. *Modernity at Large: Cultural Dimensions of Globalization*. Minneapolis: University of Minnesota Press.

Arjomand, Said. 2007. "Islam." In Jan Aart Scholte and Roland Robertson, eds., *Encyclopedia of Globalization*. New York: MTM Publishing.

Armstrong, Karen. 1996. *Jerusalem: One City, Three Faiths*. New York: Ballantine Books.

Arnett, Jeffrey. 2002. "The Psychology of Globalization." *American Psychologist* 57 (10): 774–783.

"Arresting Transnational Crime." 2001. A special issue of the electronic journal, *Global Issues* 6 (2): 774–883.

Arrighi, Giovanni. 2007. *Adam Smith in Beijing: Lineages of the Twenty-First Century*. London: Verso.

Arrighi, Giovanni, Beverly J. Silver, and Benjamin D. Brewer. 2007. "Industrial Convergence and the Persistence of the North–South Divide." In J. Timmons Roberts and Amy Bellone Hite, eds., *The Globalization and Development Reader*. Oxford: Blackwell.

Arviddson, Adam. 2012. "Brands." In George Ritzer, ed., *Wiley-Blackwell Encyclopedia of Globalization*. Oxford: Wiley-Blackwell.

Ashcroft, Bill. 2012a. "Colonialism." In George Ritzer, ed., *Wiley-Blackwell Encyclopedia of Globalization*. Oxford: Wiley-Blackwell.

Ashcroft, Bill. 2012b. "Postcolonialism." In George Ritzer, ed., *Wiley-Blackwell Encyclopedia of Globalization*. Oxford: Wiley-Blackwell.

Ashcroft, Bill, Gareth Griffiths, and Helen Tiffin. 1998. *Post-Colonial Studies: The Key Concepts*. New York: Routledge.

Ashcroft, Bill, Gareth Griffiths, and Helen Tiffin, eds. 2006. *The Post-Colonial Reader*. 2nd edn. New York: Routledge.

Assmann, Stephanie. 2013. "Reassessing Food Safety, Risk, and Globalization in China and Japan: An Overview of Emerging Research Trends." *Food, Culture, and Society: An International Journal of Multidisciplinary Research* 16 (1): 7–19.

Associated Press. 2013. "Pakistan: Domestic Drones Ready." *New York Times* November 25.

Atkinson, Anthony, and Andrea Brandolini. 2013. "On Analyzing the World Distribution of Income." *The World Bank Economic Review* 24 (1): 1–37.

Atwood, Paul. 2010. *War and Empire: The American Way of Life*. New York: Pluto Press.

Auge, Marc. 1995. *Non-Places: An Introduction to an Anthropology of Supermodernity*. London: Verso.

Axford, Barrie. 2007. "In at the Death? Reflections on Justin Rosenberg's 'Post-Mortem' on Globalization." *Globalizations* 4 (2): 171–191.

Ayanso, Anteneh, Danny I. Cho, and Kaveepan Lertwachara. 2014. "Information and Communications Technology Development and the Digital Divide: A Global and Regional Assessment." *Information Technology for Development* 20 (1): 60–77.

Babb, Sarah L. 2001. *Managing Mexico: Economists from Nationalism to Neoliberalism*. Princeton, NJ: Princeton University Press.

Babb, Sarah. 2005. "The Social Consequences of Structural Adjustment: Recent Evidence and Current Debates." *Annual Review of Sociology* 31: 199–222.

Babb, Sarah. 2007. "Embeddedness, Inflation, and International Regimes: The IMF in the Early Postwar Period." *American Journal of Sociology* 113: 128–164.

Babones, Salvatore. 2007. "Studying Globalization: Methodological Issues." In George Ritzer, ed., *Blackwell Companion to Globalization*. Oxford: Blackwell.

Bacon, Christopher M., V. Ernesto Mendez, Maria E. Flores Gomez, Douglas Stuart, and Sandro R. Diaz Flores. 2008. "Are Sustainable Coffee Certifications Enough to Secure Farmer Livelihoods? The Millennium Development Goals and Nicaragua's Fair Trade Cooperatives." *Globalizations* 5 (2): 259–264.

Badenhausen, Kurt. 2012. "David Beckham Departs MLS After Earning $255 Million." *Forbes* November 30.

Bair, Jennifer, and Gary Gereffi. 2003. "Upgrading, Uneven Development, and Jobs in the North American Apparel Industry." *Global Networks* 3 (2): 143–169.

Bajaj, Vikas. 2011. "Wal-Mart Debates Rages in India." *New York Times* December 5.

Bajaj, Vikas. 2012a. "Tata Motors Finds Success in Jaguar Land Rover." *New York Times* August 30.

Bajaj, Vikas. 2012b. "India Unit of Wal-Mart Suspends Employees." *New York Times* November 3.

Bajaj, Vikas, and Julia Werdigier. 2011. "BP to Pay $7.2 Billion for Stake in Oil Fields in India." *New York Times* February 21.

Bak, Sangmee. 1997. "McDonald's in Seoul: Food Choices, Identity and Nationalism." In James L. Watson, ed., *Golden Arches East: McDonald's in East Asia*. Cambridge, MA: Harvard University Press.

Bale, John. 1994. *The Global Sports Arena: Athletic Migration in an Interdependent World*. London: Frank Cass.

Bales, Kevin, Laurel Fletcher, and Eric Stever. 2004. *Hidden Slaves: Forced Labor in the United States*. Berkeley, CA: Human Rights Center.

Ball, James, Julian Borger, and Glenn Greenwald. 2013. "Revealed: How US and UK Spy Agencies Defeat Internet Privacy and Security." *The Guardian* September 5.

Ball, Jeffrey. 2007. "In Climate Controversy, Industry Cedes Ground." *Wall Street Journal* January 23.

Barber, Benjamin R. 1995. *Jihad vs. McWorld*. New York: Times Books.

Barber, Benjamin R. 2007. *Consumed: How Markets Corrupt Children, Infantilize Adults, and Swallow Citizens Whole*. New York: W.W. Norton.

Barboza, David. 2007a. "Blazing a Paper Trail in China." *New York Times* January 16.

Barboza, David. 2007b. "China's Seafood Industry: Dirty Water, Dangerous Fish." *New York Times* December 15.

Barboza, David, and Charles Duhigg. 2012. "China Contractor Again Faces Labor Issue on iPhones." *New York Times* September 10.

Barnard, Anne. 2013. "Pressed on Syria, Hezbollah Leader Urges Focus on Israel." *New York Times* August 2.

Barringer, Felicity. 2012. "Racing Up (and Down) the Performance Index." *New York Times* January 27.

Basch, L. G., N. Glick Schiller, and C. Blanc-Szanton. 1994. *Nations Unbound: Transnational Projects, Post-Colonial Predicaments, and Deterritorialized Nation-States*. Langhorne, PA: Gordon and Breach.

Bashi, Vilna, and Antonio McDaniel. 1997. "A Theory of Immigration and Racial Stratification." *Journal of Black Studies* 27: 668–682.

Basu, Amrita, ed. 1995. *The Challenge of Local Feminisms: Women's Movements in Global Perspective*. Boulder, CO: Westview Press.

Batista, Juliana. 2012. "General Agreement on Trade in Services." In George Ritzer, ed., *Wiley-Blackwell Encyclopedia of Globalization*. Oxford: Wiley-Blackwell.

Bauman, Zygmunt. 1989. *Modernity and the Holocaust*. Ithaca, NY: Cornell University Press.

Bauman, Zygmunt. 1992. *Intimations of Postmodernity*. London: Routledge.

Bauman, Zygmunt. 1993. *Postmodern Ethics*. Oxford: Basil Blackwell.

Bauman, Zygmunt. 1998. *Globalization: The Human Consequences*. New York: Columbia University Press.

Bauman, Zygmunt. 2000. *Liquid Modernity*. Cambridge: Polity.

Bauman, Zygmunt. 2003. *Liquid Love*. Cambridge: Polity.

Bauman, Zygmunt. 2005. *Liquid Life*. Cambridge: Polity.

Bauman, Zygmunt. 2006. *Liquid Fear*. Cambridge: Polity.

Bauman, Zygmunt. 2011. *Culture in a Liquid Modern World*. Malden, MA: Polity Press.

BBC. 2013. "China Smartphone Users Swell Internet Users." *BBC News* July 17.

Beaverstock, J. V., M. A. Doel, P. J. Hubbard, and P. J. Taylor. 2002. "Attending to the World: Competition, Cooperation and Connectivity in the World City Network." *Global Networks* 2 (2): 111–132.

Beck, Colin, and Emily Miner. 2013. "Who Gets Designated a Terrorist and Why?" *Social Forces* 91 (3): 837–872.

Beck, Ulrich. 1992. *Risk Society: Towards a New Modernity*. London: Sage.

Beck, Ulrich. 2007. "Cosmopolitanism: A Critical Theory for the Twenty-first Century." In George Ritzer, ed., *Blackwell Companion to Globalization*. Oxford: Blackwell.

Beck, Ulrich, Natan Sznaider, and Rainer Winter, eds. 2003. *Global America? The Cultural Consequences of Globalization*. Liverpool: Liverpool University Press.

Becker, Howard. 1963. *Outsiders: Studies in the Sociology of Deviance*. New York: Free Press.

Beckfield, Jason, and Arthur S. Alderson. 2006. "Whither the Parallel Paths? The Future of Scholarship on the World City System." *American Journal of Sociology* 112 (3): 895–904.

Bedirhanoglu, Nazan. 2012. "Trade-Related Intellectual Property Rights." In George Ritzer, ed., *Wiley-Blackwell Encyclopedia of Globalization*. Oxford: Wiley-Blackwell.

Beer, David, and Roger Burrows. 2007. "Sociology and, of and in Web 2.0: Some Initial Considerations." *Sociological Research Online* 12 (5). http://www.socresonline.org.uk/12/5/17.html (last accessed August 17, 2014).

Beer, Todd. 2012. "Global Warming." In George Ritzer, ed., *Wiley-Blackwell Encyclopedia of Globalization*. Oxford: Wiley-Blackwell.

Beland, Daniel. 2008. *States of Global Insecurity: Policy, Politics and Society*. New York: Worth.

Ben-Sasson, Haim H., ed. 1976. *A History of the Jewish People*. London: Weidenfeld and Nicolson.

Bentley, Jerry H. 2004. "Globalizing History and Historicizing Globalization." *Globalizations* 1 (1): 69–81.

Berberoglu, Berch. 2003. *Globalization of Capital and the Nation-State: Imperialism, Class Struggle, and the State in the Age of Global Capitalism*. Lanham, MD: Rowman & Littlefield.

Berger, Peter, and Thomas Luckmann. 1967. *The Social Construction of Reality*. Garden City, NY: Anchor Books.

Bergesen, Albert. 2012. "Terrorism." In George Ritzer, ed., *Wiley-Blackwell Encyclopedia of Globalization*. Oxford: Wiley-Blackwell.

Berggren, D. Jason, and Nicol C. Rae. 2007. "George W. Bush, Religion and European Anti-Americanism." In Brendon O'Connor, ed., *Anti-Americanism: History, Causes, and Themes, Vol. 1: Causes and Sources*. Oxford: Greenwood World Publishing.

Berik, Gunseli. 2000. "Mature Export-Led Growth and Gender Wage Inequality in Taiwan." *Feminist Economics* 6 (3): 1–26.

Bernard, A., and B. Jensen. 2007. "Firm Structure, Multinationals, and Manufacturing Plant Deaths." *The Review of Economics and Statistics* 89 (2): 193–204.

Bernstein, Nina. 2006. "A Climate of Fear as Immigration Agents Raid New York Farms." *New York Times* December 24.

Bernstein, Nina, and Elizabeth Dwoskin. 2007. "For Many Brazilians Here Illegally, the Promised Land Has Lost Its Promise." *New York Times* December 4.

Besant, Alexander. 2012. "Greece Completes Border Wall to Keep out Immigrants." *Global Post* December 17.

Best, Steven. 2008. "The Cultural Turn." In George Ritzer, ed., *The Blackwell Encyclopedia of Sociology Online*. Oxford: Blackwell.

Bestor, Theodore C. 2005. "How Sushi Went Global." In James L. Watson and Melissa L. Caldwell, eds., *The Cultural Politics of Food and Eating: A Reader*. Oxford: Blackwell.

Beyer, Peter. 1994. *Religion and Globalization*. London: Sage.

Bhabha, Homi. 1994. *The Location of Culture*. London: Routledge.

Bhagwati, Jagdish. 2004. *In Defense of Globalization*. New York: Oxford University Press.

Bieler, Andreas, Ingemar Lindberg, and Devan Pillay, eds. 2008. *Labour and the Challenges of Globalization: What Prospects for Transnational Solidarity?* Ann Arbor, MI: Pluto Press.

Bielsa, Esperança. 2008. "The Pivotal Role of News Agencies in the Context of Globalization: A Historical Approach." *Global Networks* 8 (3): 347–366.

Bilefsky, Dan. 2007. "Spain Says Adios Siesta and Hola Viagra." *New York Times* February 11.

Bilefsky, Dan, and Nicholas Wood. 2007. "Euro-Wary Slovenians Already Miss Their Tolar." *New York Times* January 3.

Binnie, Jon. 2004. *The Globalization of Sexuality*. London: Sage.

Birdsall, William. 2012. "Web 2.0." In George Ritzer, ed., *Wiley-Blackwell Encyclopedia of Globalization*. Oxford: Wiley-Blackwell.

Bislev, Sven, Dorte Salskov-Iversen, and Hans Krause Hansen. 2002. "The Global Diffusion of Managerialism: Transnational Discourse Communities at Work." *Global Society* 16 (2): 199–212.

Blackman, Michael. 2008. "Warmth for Americans in Once Hostile Tehran." *New York Times* February 13.

Blake, Andrew. 2004. "Americanisation and Popular Music in Britain." In Neil Campbell, Jude Davies, and George McKay, eds., *Issues in Americanisation and Culture*. Edinburgh: Edinburgh University Press.

Blau, Judith. 2012. "Human Rights." In George Ritzer, ed., *Wiley-Blackwell Encyclopedia of Globalization*. Oxford: Wiley-Blackwell.

Bloomberg News. 2013. "China Scrap Cooper Imports Curbed by Custom Rules, Price." *Bloomberg* May 16.

Blow, Charles. 2013. "Border Surge Meets Bluster Surge." *New York Times* June 21.

Blum, Douglas W., ed. 2008. *Russia and Globalization: Identity, Security, and Society in an Era of Change*. Washington, DC: Johns Hopkins University.

Blumenfeld, Warren. 2013. "Conservative Commentators Further Racialize Immigration Debate." *Huffington Post* April 26.

Blumenthal, Ralph. 2000. "In Texas, Weighing Life with a Fence." *New York Times* January 13.

Boahene, Kofi. 2013. "How African Doctors Can Cure Medical 'Brain Drain.'" *CNN* April 16.

Boas, Morten, and Kathleen M. Jennings. 2007. "'Failed States' and 'State Failure': Threats or Opportunities?" *Globalizations* 4 (4): 475–485.

Bobbitt, Philip. 2008. *Terror and Consent: The Wars for the Twenty-First Century*. New York: Knopf.

Bogdanich, Walt. 2007. "Free Trade Zones Ease Passage of Counterfeit Drugs to US." *New York Times* December 17.

Bogdanich, Walt, Jake Hooker, and Andrew W. Lehren. 2007. "Chinese Chemicals Flow Unchecked to Market." *New York Times* October 31.

Bohlen, Celestine. 2013. "In Syria, Advocates Step in to Sift for Truth." *New York Times* September 27.

Boisvert, Mathieu. 2007. "Pilgrimage." In Jan Aart Scholte and Roland Robertson, eds., *Encyclopedia of Globalization*. New York: MTM Publishing.

Boli, John, and Frank Lechner. 2009. "Globalization Theory." In Bryan Turner, ed., *The New Blackwell Companion to Social Theory*. Oxford: Blackwell.

Boli, John, and Velina Petrova, 2007. "Globalization Today." In George Ritzer, ed., *Blackwell Companion to Globalization*. Oxford: Blackwell.

Boli, John, and George M. Thomas. 1997. "World Culture in the World Polity: A Century of International Non-Governmental Organization." *American Sociological Review* 62 (2): 171–190.

Bonanno, Alessandro, and Robert Antonio. 2012. "Multinational Corporations." In George Ritzer, ed., *Wiley-Blackwell Encyclopedia of Globalization*. Oxford: Wiley-Blackwell.

Bond, Michael. 2000. "The Backlash against NGOs." *Prospect* April. www.prospectmagazine.co.uk.

Bonilla-Silva, Eduardo. 2013. *Racism Without Racists: Color-Blind Racism and the Persistence of Racial Inequality in the United States*. 4th edn. New York: Rowman & Littlefield.

Bonilla-Silva, Eduardo, and David Dietrich. 2008. "The Latin Americanization of Racial Stratification in the United States." In Ronald Hall, ed., *Racism in the 21st Century*. New York: Springer.

Bordo, Michael D., and Barry Eichengreen, eds. 1993. *A Retrospective on the Bretton Woods System*. Chicago: University of Chicago Press.

Bose, Christine E., and Edna Acosta-Belen, eds. 1995. *Women in the Latin American Development Process*. Philadelphia: Temple University Press.

Bose, Nandita. 2013. "Held Up by Red Tape and Graft." *New York Times* May 6.

Boughton, James. 2007. "Bretton Woods System." In Jan Aart Scholte and Roland Robertson, eds., *Encyclopedia of Globalization*. New York: MTM Publishing.

Bourdieu, Pierre. 1984. *Distinction: A Social Critique of the Judgment of Taste*. Cambridge, MA: Harvard University Press.

Bovet, Christian. 2007. "Satellites." In Jan Aart Scholte and Roland Robertson, eds., *Encyclopedia of Globalization*. New York: MTM Publishing.

Bowman, Phillip, and John Betancur. 2010. "Sustainable Diversity and Inequality: Race in the USA and Beyond." In M. Janssens, M. Bechtoldt, A. de Rujiter, D. Pinelli, G. Prarolo, and V. Stenius, eds., *The Sustainability of Cultural Diversity: Nations, Cities and Organizations*. Northampton, MA: Edward Elgar Publishing.

Boyd, Danah, and Nicole Ellison. 2007. "Social Network Sites: Definition, History, and Scholarship." *Journal of Computer-Mediated Communication* 13 (1): 210–230.

Boykoff, Maxwell, and Jules Boykoff. 2004. "Balance as Bias: Global Warming and the US Prestige Press." *Global Environmental Change* 14: 125–136.

Boyle, Michael. 2013. "The Costs and Consequences of Drone Warfare." *International Affairs* 89 (1): 1–29.

Bozkurt, Umut. 2012. "Westernization." In George Ritzer, ed., *Wiley-Blackwell Encyclopedia of Globalization*. Oxford: Wiley-Blackwell.

Bradlow, Daniel D. 2007. "World Bank Group." In Jan Aart Scholte and Roland Robertson, eds., *Encyclopedia of Globalization*. New York: MTM Publishing.

Bradsher, Keith. 2008a. "Inflation in Asia Begins to Sting US Consumers." *New York Times* April 8.

Bradsher, Keith. 2008b. "Throughout Asia, Exporters Brace for Tremors from a US Pullback." *New York Times* January 25.

Bradsher, Keith. 2011. "GM Plans to Develop Electric Cars with China." *New York Times* September 20.

Brändle, Gaspar, and J. Michael Ryan. 2012. "Consumption." In George Ritzer, ed., *Wiley-Blackwell Encyclopedia of Globalization*. Oxford: Wiley-Blackwell.

Brandt, Loren, and Thomas G. Rawski, eds. 2008. *China's Great Economic Transformation*. Cambridge: Cambridge University Press.

Brassett, James, and Richard Higgott. 2003. "Building the Normative Dimension(s) of a Global Polity." *Review of International Studies* 29 (S1): 29–55.

Braziel, Jana Evans. 2008. *Diaspora: An Introduction*. Oxford: Blackwell.

Breem, Yves, and Xavier Thierry. 2004. *Immigration in Europe and Development Levels of the Source Countries: What Are the Associations?* Second Conference of the EAPS Working Group on International Migration in Europe.

Brenner, Neil, and Roger Keil, eds. 2006. *The Global Cities Reader*. New York: Routledge.

Brewer, Anthony. 2012. "Imperialism." In George Ritzer, ed., *Wiley-Blackwell Encyclopedia of Globalization*. Oxford: Wiley-Blackwell.

Brewer, John, and Frank Trentmann. 2006. "Introduction: Space, Time and Value in Consuming Cultures." In John Brewer and Frank Trentmann, eds., *Consuming Cultures, Global Perspectives: Historical Trajectories, Transnational Exchanges*. Oxford: Berg.

Broad, Robin. 2004. "The Washington Consensus Meets the Global Backlash: Shifting Debates and Policies." *Globalizations* 1 (2): 129–154.

Bronfenbrenner, Kate, ed. 2007. *Global Unions: Challenging Transnational Capital through Cross-Border Campaigns*. Ithaca, NY: ILR Press.

Brooks, Thom, ed. 2008. *The Global Justice Reader*. Oxford: Blackwell.

Brothers, Caroline. 2008. "Unwilling New Frontier for Migrants: 3 Greek Isles." *New York Times* January 3.

Brown, Keith. 2013. *Buying into Fair Trade: Culture, Morality, Consumption*. New York: New York University Press.

Brown, Oli. 2008. *Migration and Climate Change*. Geneva, Switzerland: International Organization for Migration.

Brown, Richard Harvey. 1989. *A Poetic for Sociology: Toward a Logic of Discovery for the Human Sciences*. Chicago: University of Chicago Press.

Brownstein, Henry. 1996. *The Rise and Fall of a Violent Crime Wave: Crack Cocaine and the Construction of a Social Crime Problem*. New York: Criminal Justice Press.

Brulle, Robert, Jason Carmichael, and J. Craig Jenkins. 2012. "Shifting Public Opinion on Climate Change: An Empirical Assessment of Factors Influencing Concern Over Climate Change in the U.S., 2002–2010." *Climate Change* 114 (2): 169–188.

Bruneau, Michel. 1995. *Diasporas*. Montpellier: GIP Reclus.

Bryman, Alan. 2004. *The Disneyization of Society*. London: Sage.

Brysk, Alison. 2013. *Human Rights and Private Wrongs*. New York: Routledge.

Buchanan, Pat. 2011. *Suicide of a Superpower: Will America Survive to 2025?* New York: Thomas Dunne Books.

Bulkeley, Harriet, JoAnn Carmin, Vanesa Broto, Gareth Edwards, and Sara Fuller. 2013. "Climate Justice and Global Cities: Mapping the Emerging Discourses." *Global Environmental Change* 23 (5): 914–925.

Buse, Kent. 2007. "World Health Organization." In Jan Aart Scholte and Roland Robertson, eds., *Encyclopedia of Globalization*. New York: MTM Publishing.

Business Standard. 2013. August 28. "Malaysia to Begin Crackdown on Illegal Immigrants on Sunday."

Butler, K. D. 2001. "Defining Diaspora, Refining a Discourse." *Diaspora* 10 (2): 198–219.

Byrd, Scott. 2005. "The Porto Alegre Consensus: Theorizing the Forum Movement." *Globalizations* 2 (1): 151–163.

Cagatay, Nilufer, and Sule Ozler. 1995. "Feminization of the Labor Force: The Effect of Long Term Development and Structural Adjustment." *World Development* 23 (11): 1883–1894.

Caldwell, Melissa L. 2004. "Domesticating the French Fry: McDonald's and Consumerism in Moscow." *Journal of Consumer Culture* 4 (1): 5–26.

Caldwell, Melissa L., and Eriberto P. Lozada, Jr, 2007. "The Fate of the Local." In George Ritzer, ed., *Blackwell Companion to Globalization*. Oxford: Blackwell.

Calmes, Jackie, and Stephen Castle. 2013. "G8 Meeting Ends with Cordial Stalemate on Syria." *New York Times* June 18.

Campbell, Colin. 2007. *The Easternization of the West: A Thematic Account of Cultural Change in the Modern Era*. Boulder, CO: Paradigm Publishers.

Campbell, Colin. 2012. "Easternization." In George Ritzer, ed., *Wiley-Blackwell Encyclopedia of Globalization*. Oxford: Wiley-Blackwell.

Campbell, John L., and Ove K. Pederson, eds. 2001. *The Rise of Neoliberalism and Institutional Analysis*. Princeton: Princeton University Press.

Campbell, Neil. 2003. *Landscapes of Americanisation*. Derby: University of Derby.

Campbell, Neil. 2004. "Landscapes of Americanisation in Britain: Learning from the 1950s." In Neil Campbell, Jude Davies, and George McKay, eds., *Issues in Americanisation and Culture*. Edinburgh: Edinburgh University Press.

Campbell, Neil. 2012. "Americanization." In George Ritzer, ed., *Wiley-Blackwell Encyclopedia of Globalization*. Oxford: Wiley-Blackwell.

Campbell, Neil, Jude Davies, and George McKay, eds. 2004. *Issues in Americanisation and Culture*. Edinburgh: Edinburgh University Press.

Canclini, Nestor Garcia. 1995. *Hybrid Cultures: Strategies for Entering and Leaving Modernity*. Minneapolis: University of Minnesota Press.

Cardoso, Fernando Henrique. 1972. "Dependency and Development in Latin America." *New Left Review* 74.

Cardoso, Fernando Henrique, and E. Faletto. 1979. *Dependency and Development in Latin America*. Berkeley, CA: University of California Press.

Carducci, Vince. 2007. "Fair Trade." In George Ritzer, ed., *Blackwell Encyclopedia of Sociology Online*. Oxford: Wiley-Blackwell.

Carson, Rachel. 1962. *Silent Spring*. Boston: Houghton Mifflin.

Cartier, Carolyn. 2001. *Globalizing South China*. Oxford: Blackwell.

Casanova, Jose. 1997. "Globalizing Catholicism and the Return to a 'Universal' Church." In Susan Hoeber Rudolph and James Piscatori, eds., *Transnational Religion and Fading States*. Boulder, CO: Westview Press.

Castells, Manuel. 1996. *The Rise of the Network Society*. Oxford: Blackwell.

Castells, Manuel. 2000. *The Rise of the Network Society*. New edn. Oxford: Blackwell.

Castle, Stephen. 2008. "For Global Trade Talks, the Stakes Have Risen." *New York Times* July 19.

Castle, Stephen. 2013. "British Government Moves to Toughen Rules on Immigrants." *New York Times* May 8.

Castle, Stephen, and Judy Dempsey. 2011. "Spain Gets Approval to Keep Romanians Out." *New York Times* August 11.

Cavanagh, John, and Robin Broad. 2007. "Washington Consensus." In Jan Aart Scholte and Roland Robertson, eds., *Encyclopedia of Globalization*. New York: MTM Publishing.

Cave, Damien. 2011. "Crossing Over, and Over." *New York Times* October 2.

CBS News. 2013. December 1. "Amazon Unveils Futuristic Plan: Delivery by Drone."

CBC News. 2014. February 13. "Chikungunya Travel Health Warning for Caribbean Expands."

Ceaser, James. 2003. "A Genealogy of Anti-Americanism." *The Public Interest* Summer, 2003.

Cerny, Philip G. 1995. "Globalization and the Changing Logic of Collective Action." *International Organization* 49 (4): 595–625.

Cerny, Philip G. 2003. "Globalization at the Micro Level: The Uneven Pluralization of World Politics." In Axel Hülsemeyer, ed., *Globalization in the 21st Century: Convergence and Divergence*. London: Palgrave.

Cerny, Philip G. 2007. "Nation-State." In Jan Aart Scholte and Roland Robertson, eds., *Encyclopedia of Globalization*. New York: MTM Publishing.

Chakraborty, Barnini. 2013. "With Farm Bill Defeat, Americans on Hook for $147M a Year to Brazilian Cotton Farmers." *Fox News.com* June 21.

Chanda, Nayan. 2007. *Bound Together: How Traders, Preachers, Adventurers, and Warriors Shaped Globalization*. New Haven: Yale University Press.

Chang, Kenneth. 2013. "Privately Finances Spaceship Roars Closer to Space." *New York Times* April 29.

Chant, Sylvia. 2012. "Feminization of Poverty." In George Ritzer, ed., *Wiley-Blackwell Encyclopedia of Globalization*. Oxford: Wiley-Blackwell.

Chapman, J., and A. Werthheimer, eds. 1990. *Majorities and Minorities*. New York: New York University Press.

Charron, Andrea, and Jane Boulden. 2012. "United Nations." In George Ritzer, ed., *Wiley-Blackwell Encyclopedia of Globalization*. Oxford: Wiley-Blackwell.

Chatterjee, Deen K., ed. 2008. *Democracy in a Global World: Human Rights and Political Participation in the 21st Century*. Lanham: Rowman & Littlefield.

Cheever, Susan. 2002. "The Nanny Dilemma." In Barbara Ehrenreich and Arlie Hochschild, eds., *Global Woman: Nannies, Maids and Sex Workers in the New Economy*. New York: Henry Holt.

Chew, Sing C. 2002. "Globalisation, Ecological Crisis, and Dark Ages." *Global Society* 16 (4): 333–356.

Chiang, Chi-Chen. 2012a. "Trade-Related Investment Measures." In George Ritzer, ed., *Wiley-Blackwell Encyclopedia of Globalization*. Oxford: Wiley-Blackwell.

Chiang, Chi-Chen. 2012b. "Group of Thirty." In George Ritzer, ed., *Wiley-Blackwell Encyclopedia of Globalization*. Oxford: Wiley-Blackwell.

Chilcote, Ronald H. 2000. "Introduction." In Ronald H. Chilcote, ed., *Imperialism: Theoretical Directions*. Amherst, NY: Humanity Books.

Chivers, C. V. 2008. "US Position Complicates Global Effort to Curb Illicit Arms." *New York Times* July 19.

Choi, E. Kwan, and David Greenway, eds. 2001. *Globalization and Labor Markets*. Oxford: Blackwell.

Choi, Junho H., George A. Barnett, and Chon Bum-Soo. 2006. "Comparing World City Networks: A Network Analysis of Internet Backbone and Air Transport Intercity Linkages." *Global Networks* 6 (1): 81–99.

Chomsky, Noam. 2003. *Hegemony or Survival: America's Quest for Global Dominance*. New York: Metropolitan Books.

Chomsky, Noam. 2013. *Power Systems: Conversations on Global Democratic Uprisings and the New Challenges to U.S. Empire*. New York: Metropolitan Books.

Chorev, Nitsan. 2007. *Remaking U.S. Trade Policy: From Protectionism to Globalization*. Ithaca, NY: Cornell University Press.

Chotikapanich, Duangkamon, William Griffiths, D. S. Prasado Rao, and Vicar Valencia. 2012. "Global Income Distributions and Inequality, 1993 and 2000: Incorporating Country-Level Inequality Modeled with Beta Distributions." *The Review of Economics and Statistics* 94 (1): 52–73.

Chow, Esther Ngan-Ling, Marcia Texler Segal, and Tan Lin, eds. 2011. *Analyzing Gender, Intersectionality, and Multiple Inequalities: Global-Transnational and Local Contexts*. Cambridge, MA: Emerald.

Christen, Marius, and Stephan Schmidt. 2012. "A Formal Framework for Conceptions of Sustainability – a Theoretical Contribution to the Discourse of Sustainable Development." *Sustainable Development* 20 (6): 400–410.

Christoff, Peter, and Robyn Eckersley. 2013. *Globalization and the Environment*. New York: Rowman & Littlefield.

Chua, Vincent, and Ern Ser Tan. 2012. "National Identity." In George Ritzer, ed., *Wiley-Blackwell Encyclopedia of Globalization*. Oxford: Wiley-Blackwell.

Chun, Allen. 2012. "Ethnoscapes." In George Ritzer, ed., *Wiley-Blackwell Encyclopedia of Globalization*. Oxford: Wiley-Blackwell.

Ciolek, T. Matthew. 2007. "Trade Routes." In Jan Aart Scholte and Roland Robertson, eds., *Encyclopedia of Globalization*. New York: MTM Publishing.

Clark, Ian. 2007. "International Relations." In Jan Aart Scholte and Roland Robertson, eds., *Encyclopedia of Globalization*. New York: MTM Publishing.

Clark, Nicola. 2013. "French Air Traffic Controllers Plan Strike Over Pan-European Plan." *New York Times* June 10.

Clavé, Salvatore Anton. 2007. *The Global Theme Park Industry*. Cambridge, MA: CABI.

Clegg, Stewart. 2012. "Management, Global Models." In George Ritzer, ed., *Wiley-Blackwell Encyclopedia of Globalization*. Oxford: Wiley-Blackwell.

Clegg, Stewart, and Chris Carter. 2007. "The Sociology of Global Organizations." In George Ritzer, ed., *Blackwell Companion to Globalization*. Oxford: Blackwell.

Cliff, S., and S. Carter, eds. 1998. *Tourism and Sex: Culture, Commerce and Coercion*. London: Pinter.

Clifford, James. 1994. "Diasporas." *Cultural Anthropology* 9 (3): 302–338.

Clifford, Stephanie, and Liz Alderman. 2011. "American Retailers Try Again in Europe." *New York Times* June 15.

Cohen, Daniel. 2006. *Globalization and Its Enemies*. Cambridge, MA: MIT Press.

Cohen, Phil. 1999. "Rethinking the Diasporama." *Patterns of Prejudice* 33 (1): 3–22.

Cohen, Robin, ed. 1995. *The Cambridge Survey of World Migration*. Cambridge: Cambridge University Press.

Cohen, Robin. 2007. "Creolization and Cultural Globalization: The Soft Sounds of Fugitive Power." *Globalizations* 4 (3): 369–384.

Coleman, John A., S. J. 2007. "Roman Catholic Church." In Jan Aart Scholte and Roland Robertson, eds., *Encyclopedia of Globalization*. New York: MTM Publishing.

Collier, Paul. 2007. *The Bottom Billion: Why the Poorest Countries Are Failing and What Can Be Done About It*. New York: Oxford University Press.

Collier, Paul. 2012. "Bottom Billion." In George Ritzer, ed., *Wiley-Blackwell Encyclopedia of Globalization*. Oxford: Wiley-Blackwell.

Collins, Jane L. 2003. *Threads: Gender, Labor, and Power in the Global Apparel Industry*. Chicago: University of Chicago Press.

Collins, Michael. 2012. "Group of 77." In George Ritzer, ed., *Wiley-Blackwell Encyclopedia of Globalization*. Oxford: Wiley-Blackwell.

Collins, Patricia Hill. 2000. *Black Feminist Thought: Knowledge, Consciousness and the Politics of Empowerment*. New York: Routledge.

Collins, Patricia Hill. 2012. "Social Inequality, Power, and Politics: Intersectionality and American Pragmatism in Dialogue. *The Journal of Speculative Philosophy* 26 (2): 442–457.

Collins, Randall. 1975. *Conflict Sociology: Toward an Explanatory Science*. New York: Academic Press.

Collins Rudolph, John. 2007. "The Warming of Greenland." *New York Times* January 16.

Conca, Ken. 2006. *Governing Water: Contentious Transnational Political and Global Institution Building*. Cambridge, MA: MIT Press.

Conca, Ken. 2007. "Water." In Jan Aart Scholte and Roland Robertson, eds., *Encyclopedia of Globalization*. New York: MTM Publishing.

Conley, Tom. 2002. "Globalisation as Constraint and Opportunity: Reconceptualising Policy Capacity in Australia." *Global Society* 16 (4): 378–399.

Connell, R. W., and June Crawford. 2005. "The Global Connections of Intellectual Workers." *International Sociology* 20 (1): 5–26.

Connor, Walker. 2007. "Nation-state." In George Ritzer, ed., *The Blackwell Encyclopedia of Sociology*. Oxford: Blackwell.

Cooper, Andrew F., Christopher W. Hughes, and Philippe De Lombaerde, eds. 2008. *Regionalisation and Global Governance: The Taming of Globalisation?* New York: Routledge.

Cornfield, Daniel B. 1997. "Labor Transnationalism?" *Work and Occupations* 24: 278–287.

Correa, Carlos. 2000. *Intellectual Property Rights: The TRIPS Agreement and Policy Options*. London: Zed.

Coser, Lewis. 1956. *The Functions of Social Conflict*. New York: Free Press.

Cowen, Tyler. 2002. *Creative Destruction*. Princeton: Princeton University Press.

Cox, Lloyd. 2007. "Nation-state and Nationalism." In George Ritzer, ed., *The Blackwell Encyclopedia of Sociology*. Oxford: Blackwell.

Cox, Robert W. 1971. "Labor and Transnational Relations." *International Organization* 25 (3): 554–584.

Cox, Robert, and Albert Schilthuis. 2012. "Governance." In George Ritzer, ed., *Wiley-Blackwell Encyclopedia of Globalization*. Oxford: Wiley-Blackwell.

Crack, Angela M. 2007. "Transcending Borders? Reassessing Public Spheres in a Networked World." *Globalizations* 4 (3): 341–354.

Crouch, Colin. 2011. *The Strange Non-Death of Neo-Liberalism*. Malden, MA: Polity Press.

Cunningham, Carolyn, ed. 2012. *Social Networking and Impression Management: Self-Presentation in the Digital Age*. Lanham, MD: Lexington.

Cvetkovich, Ann, and Douglas Kellner. 1997. *Articulating the Global and the Local: Globalization and Cultural Studies*. Boulder, CO: Westview Press.

Da Costa, Dia, and Philip McMichael. 2007. "The Poverty of the Global Order." *Globalizations* 4 (4): 588–602.

Dale, John. 2011. *Free Burma: Transnational Legal Action and Corporate Accountability*. Minneapolis, MN: University of Minnesota Press.

Daley, Suzanne. 2011. "Swedes Begin to Question Liberal Migration Tenets." *New York Times* February 26.

Dallek, Robert. 2007. *Nixon and Kissinger: Partners in Power*. New York: Harper Perennial.

Daly, Herman, and Joshua Farley. 2011. *Ecological Economics: Principles and Applications*. 2nd edn. Washington, DC: Island Press.

Dancygier, Rafaela, and David Laitin. 2014 "Immigration into Europe: Economic Discrimination, Violence, and Public Policy." *Annual Review of Political Science* 17: 43–64.

Darcy, Jane. 2004. "The Disneyfication of the European Fairy Tale." In Neil Campbell, Jude Davies, and George McKay, eds., *Issues in Americanisation and Culture*. Edinburgh: Edinburgh University Press.

Dauvergne, Peter. 2008. *Shadows of Consumption: Consequences for the Global Environment*. Cambridge, MA: MIT Press.

Dávila, Alberto, Marie Mora, and Sue Stockly. 2011. "Does *Mestizaje* Matter in the US? Economic Stratification of Mexican Immigrants." *American Economic Review* 101 (3): 593–597.

Davis, Mike. 2002. *Late Victorian Holocausts: El Niño Famines and the Making of the Third World*. Brooklyn, NY: Verso.

Davis, Mike. 2007. *Planet of Slums*. London: Verso.

de Blij, Harm J. 2008. *Power of Place: Geography, Destiny, and Globalization's Rough Landscape*. New York: Oxford University Press.

de Blij, Harm J., and Roger Downs. 2007. *College Atlas of the World*. Washington, DC: National Geographic Society.

de Grazia, Victoria. 2005. *Irresistible Empire: America's Advance through 20th-Century Europe*. Cambridge, MA: The Belknap Press of Harvard University Press.

de la Dehesa, Guillermo. 2006. *Winners and Losers in Globalization*. Oxford: Blackwell.

de la Dehesa, Guillermo. 2007. *What Do We Know About Globalization? Issues of Poverty and Income Distribution*. Oxford: Blackwell.

de Sousa Santos, Boaventura. 2006. "Globalizations." *Theory, Culture & Society* 2–3 (23): 393–399.

Dean, Cornelia. 2007. "Experts Discuss Engineering Feats, Like Space Mirrors, to Slow Climate Change." *New York Times* November 10.

Dean, Paul, and George Ritzer. 2012. "Globalization." In George Ritzer, ed., *Wiley-Blackwell Encyclopedia of Globalization*. Oxford: Wiley-Blackwell.

DeBord, Guy. 1967/1994. *The Society of the Spectacle*. New York: Zone Books.

Degler, Carl. 1971/1986. *Neither Black Nor White: Slavery and Race Relations in Brazil and the United States*. Madison: University of Wisconsin.

Delanty, Gerard. 2003. "Consumption, Modernity and Japanese Cultural Identity: The Limits of Americanisation?" In Ulrich Beck, Natan Sznaider, and Rainer Winter, eds., *Global America? The Cultural Consequences of Globalization*. Liverpool: Liverpool University Press.

Delanty, Gerard, and Patrick O'Mahony. 2002. *Nationalism and Social Theory: Modernity and the Recalcitrance of the Nation*. London: Sage.

della Porta, Donatella, Massimiliano Andretta, Lorenzo Mosca, and Herbert Reiter. 2006. *Globalization from Below: Transnational Activists and Protest Networks*. Minneapolis: University of Minnesota Press.

Demsteader, Christine. 2010. "Fifth of Swedish Population Foreign." *The Local* January 29.

Denyer, Simon, and Rama Lakshmi. 2012. "Satisfying India's Thirst for Power Could Be Nation's Biggest Challenge." *Washington Post* August 22.

DeParle, Jason. 2007a. "A Western Union Empire Moves Migrant Cash Home." *New York Times* November 22.

DeParle, Jason. 2007b. "A Good Provider Is One Who Leaves." *New York Times Magazine* April 22.

DeParle, Jason. 2008. "World Banker and His Cash Return Home." *New York Times* March 17.

Derudder, Ben, Michael Hoyler, Peter J. Taylor, and Frank Witlox. 2012. *International Handbook on Globalization and World Cities*. Northampton, MA: Edward Elgar Publishing.

Deutsch, Claudia H. 2007. "For Fiji Water, a Big List of Green Goals." *New York Times* November 7.

Dezalay, Yves. 1990. "The *Big Bang* and the Law: The Internationalization and Restructuring of the Legal Field." In Mike Featherstone, ed., *Global Culture: Nationalism, Globalization and Modernity*. London: Sage.

Diamond, Jared. 2006. *Collapse: How Societies Choose to Fail or Succeed*. New York: Penguin.

Diamond, Jared. 2008. "What's Your Consumption Factor?" *New York Times* January 2.

Dias, Sónia, Sílvia Fraga, and Henrique Barros. 2013. "Interpersonal Violence Among Immigrants in Portugal." *Journal of Immigrant and Minority Health* 15 (1): 119–124.

Dicken, Peter. 2007. *Global Shift: Mapping the Changing Contours of the World Economy*. 5th edn. New York: Guilford Press.

Diez-Nicolas, Juan. 2002. "Two Contradictory Hypotheses on Globalization: Societal Convergence or Civilization Differentiation and Clash." *Contemporary Sociology* 1: 465–493.

DiMaggio, Paul J., and Walter W. Powell. 1983. "'The Iron Cage Revisited:' Institutional Isomorphism and Collective Rationality in Organizational Fields." *American Sociological Review* 48: 147–160.

Dinham, Barbara. 1993. *The Pesticide Hazard: A Global Health and Environmental Audit*. London: Zed.

Dinham, Barbara. 2007. "Pesticides." In Jan Aart Scholte and Roland Robertson, eds., *Encyclopedia of Globalization*. New York: MTM Publishing.

Dixon, Hugo. 2013. "Returning Some Power to EU Members." *New York Times* July 21.

Docquier, Frédéric, and Hillel Rapoport. 2012. "Globalization, Brain Drain, and Development." *Journal of Economic Literature* 50 (3): 681–730.

Dolan, Catherine. 2008. "In the Mists of Development: Fairtrade in Kenyan Tea Fields." *Globalizations* 5 (2): 305–318.

Dollar, David, and Art Kraay. 2002. "Growth is Good for the Poor." *Journal of Economic Growth* 7 (3): 195–225.

Domhoff, William. 2009. *Who Rules America? Challenges to Corporate and Class Dominance*. 6th edn. McGraw-Hill.

Dominelli, Lena. 2010. "Globalization, Contemporary Challenges, and Social Work Practice." *International Social Work* 53 (5): 599–612.

Donadio, Rachel. 2008a. "Albanians Adjust to Italy, in Unlikeliest of Places." *New York Times* October 3.

Donadio, Rachel. 2008b. "Italy's Attacks on Migrants Fuel Debate on Racism." *New York Times* October 13.

Donnelly, Jack. 2013. *International Human Rights*. Boulder, CO: Westview Press.

Dossani, Rafiq. 2008. *India Arriving: How this Economic Powerhouse is Redefining Global Business*. New York: AMACOM/American Management Association.

Downie, Andrew. 2007. "Fair Trade in Bloom." *New York Times* October 2.

Downie, David. 2007. "Persistent Organic Pollutants." In Jan Aart Scholte and Roland Robertson, eds., *Encyclopedia of Globalization*. New York: MTM Publishing.

Drane, John. 2008. *After McDonaldization: Mission, Ministry, and Christian Discipleship in an Age of Uncertainty*. Grand Rapids, MI: Baker Academic.

Drane, John. 2012. *The McDonaldization of the Church: Consumer Culture and the Church's Future*. Macon, GA: Smyth & Helwys Publishing.

Drori, Gili S. 2006. *Global E-Litism: Digital Technology, Social Inequality, and Transnationality*. New York: Worth.

Drori, Gili S. 2012a. "Science." In George Ritzer, ed., *Wiley-Blackwell Encyclopedia of Globalization*. Oxford: Wiley-Blackwell.

Drori, Gili S. 2012b. "Digital Divide." In George Ritzer, ed., *Wiley-Blackwell Encyclopedia of Globalization*. Oxford: Wiley-Blackwell.

Dufoix, Stephane. 2007. "Diasporas." In Jan Aart Scholte and Roland Robertson, eds., *Encyclopedia of Globalization*. New York: MTM Publishing.

Dube, Godwin, and Joseph Rukema. 2013. "Intracontinental Brain Drain and African Migrant Social Science Scholars in South Africa." *International Journal of Sociology* 43 (1): 68–78.

Dugger, Celia W. 2007. "World Bank Neglects African Agriculture, Study Says." *New York Times* October 15.

Duhamel, Georges. 1931. *America the Menace: Scenes from the Life of the Future*. Boston: Houghton Mifflin.

Duhigg, Charles, and Keith Bradsher. 2012. "How the US Lost Out on iPhone Work." *New York Times* January 21.

Duignan, Peter, and Lewis Gann. 1992. *The Rebirth of the West: The Americanization of the Democratic World*. Oxford: Blackwell.

Dunbar Moodie, T. 1975. *The Rise of Afrikanerdom: Power, Apartheid, and the Afrikaner Civil Religion*. Berkeley, CA: University of California Press.

Dunbar Moodie, T., and Vivienne Ndatshe. 1994. *Going for Gold: Men, Mines, and Migration*. Berkeley, CA: University of California Press.

Dustin, Donna. 2007. *The McDonaldization of Social Work*. Burlington, VT: Ashgate.

Dyb, Kari, and Susan Halford. 2009. "Placing Globalizing Technologies: Telemedicine and the Making of Difference." *Sociology* 43 (2): 232–249.

Dyreson, Mark. 2013. "The Republic of Consumption at the Olympic Games: Globalization, Americanization, and Californization." *Journal of Global History* 8 (2): 256–278.

Easterly, William. 2006a. "Chapter 2: Freedom versus Collectivism in Foreign Aid." *Economic Freedom of the World: 2006 Annual Report*.

Easterly, William. 2006b. *The White Man's Burden: Why the West's Efforts to Aid the Rest Have Done So Much Ill and So Little Good*. New York: Penguin.

Eaton Simpson, George, and J. Milton Yinger. 1985. *Racial and Cultural Minorities: An Analysis of Prejudice and Discrimination*. 5th edn. New York: Plenum.

Eberly, Don. 2008. *The Rise of Global Civil Society: Building Communities and Nations from the Bottom Up*. New York: Encounter Books.

Economist. 2006. January 12. "Genghis the Globalizer."

Economist. 2006. March 10. "DP World Agree to Divest Its American Ports."

Economist. 2007. October 11. "Adding Sugar."

Economist. 2008. January 3. "Keep Out."

Economist. 2008. January 3. "Of Bedsheets and Bison Grass Vodka."

Economist. 2008. January 3. "Open Up."

Economist. 2008. January 3. "Send Me a Number."

Economist. 2008. January 24. "Hocking the Rock."

Economist. 2008. January 31. "Cocoa Farming: Fair Enough?"

Economist. 2008. February 7. "Of Internet Cafes and Power Cuts."

Economist. 2008. March 6. "An Unreliable Ally."

Economist. 2008. March 6. "The Decoupling Debate."

Economist. 2008. March 27. "Selling Rhythm to the World."

Economist 2011. January 18. "The End of the End of History."

Economist 2013. March 16. "A Tale of Two Traders: Business People from Lebanon Fare Better Abroad than at Home."

Economist 2013. April 21 "How Does China Censor the Internet?"

Eddy, Melissa. 2014. "Swiss Voters Narrowly Approve Curbs on Immigration." *New York Times* February 9.

Edelman, Marc, and Angelique Haugerud, eds. 2005. *The Anthropology of Development: From Classical Political Economy to Contemporary Neoliberalism*. Oxford: Blackwell.

Edwards, Paige. 2012. "Global Sushi: Eating and Identity." *Perspectives on Global Development and Technology* 11 (1): 211–225.

Ehrenreich, Barbara. 2002. "Maid to Order." In Barbara Ehrenreich and Arlie Hochschild, eds., *Global Woman: Nannies, Maids and Sex Workers in the New Economy*. New York: Henry Holt.

Ehrenreich, Barbara, and Arlie Hochschild. 2002. "Introduction." In Barbara Ehrenreich and Arlie Hochschild, eds., *Global Woman: Nannies, Maids and Sex Workers in the New Economy*. New York: Henry Holt.

Einhorn, Bruce. 2013. "China Tries Even Harder to Censor the Internet." *Bloomberg Businessweek* September 12.

Eisenberg, Anne. 2013. "Microsatellites: What Big Eyes They Have." *New York Times* August 10.

Elasser, Shuan, and Riley Dunlap. 2013. "Leading Voices in the Denier Choir: Conservative Columnists' Dismissal of Global Warming and Denigration of Climate Science." *American Behavioral Scientist* 57 (6): 754–776.

Elger, Tony, and Chris Smith. 1994. *Global Japanization: The Transnational Transformation of the Labor Process*. London; New York: Routledge.

Elliott, Jennifer. 2012. *An Introduction to Sustainable Development*. New York: Routledge.

Elson, Diane. 1995. "Gender Awareness in Modeling Structural Adjustment." *World Development* 23 (11): 1851–1868.

Elson, Diane, and Ruth Pearson. 1981. "Nimble Fingers Make Cheap Workers: An Analysis of Women's Employment in Third World Export Manufacturing." *Feminist Review* 7: 87–107.

Emanuel, Rahm, and Luis Gutierrez. 2013. "Priced out of Citizenship." *New York Times* April 3.

Encyclopaedia Britannica. 2007. *Encyclopaedia Britannica Book of the Year 2007*. Chicago: Encyclopaedia Britannica.

Entous, Adam, Nour Malas, and Rima Abushakra. 2013. "As Syrian Chemical Attack Loomed, Missteps Doomed Civilians." *Wall Street Journal* November 22.

Eriksen, Thomas Hylland. 2007. "Steps to an Ecology of Transnational Sports." In Richard Giulianotti and Roland Robertson, eds., *Globalization and Sport*. Oxford: Blackwell.

Erlanger, Steven. 2011. "Amid Rise of Multiculturalism, Dutch Confront Their Questions of Identity." *New York Times* August 13.

Erlanger, Steven. 2013. "Muslim Woman Suffers Miscarriage After Attack in France." *New York Times* June 18.

Esmer, Yilmaz. 2006. "Globalization, 'McDonaldization' and Values: Quo Vadis?" *Comparative Sociology* 5 (2–3): 183–202.

Espeseth, Craig, Jessica Gibson, Andy Jones, and Seymour Goodman. 2013. "Terrorist Use of Communication Technology and Social Networks." In U. F. Aydoğdu, ed., *Technological Dimensions of Defence Against Terrorism*. Fairfax, VA: IOS Press.

Euronews. 2013. "Number of Refugees Worldwide at a 14-year High." *Euronews* June 19.

European Commission. 2013. "Migration and Migrant Population Statistics" Statistics Explained (data from May 2014). http://epp.eurostat.ec.europa.eu/statistics_explained/index.php/Migration_and_migrant_population_statistics# (last accessed August 17, 2014).

European Monitoring Center on Racism and Xenophobia. 2002. *Racism and Xenophobia in the EU Member States: Trends, Developments and Good Practice 2002, Annual Report – Part 2*. http://fra.europa.eu/sites/default/files/fra_uploads/131-AR_02_part2_EN.pdf (last accessed August 17, 2014).

Evans, Peter. 2005. "Counterhegemonic Globalization: Transnational Social Movements in the Contemporary Global Political Economy." In Thomas Janoski, Robert R. Alford, Alexander M. Hicks, and Mildred A. Schwartz, eds., *The Handbook of Political Sociology: States, Civil Societies, and Globalization*. Cambridge: Cambridge University Press.

Everett, Jana, and Sue Ellen Charlton. 2014. *Women Navigating Globalization: Feminist Approaches to Development*. Lanham, MD: Rowman & Littlefield.

Ewing, Jack. 2013. "Euro Zone Crisis Has Increased IMF's Power." *New York Times* April 17.

Fackler, Martin. 2007a. "A Japanese Export: Talent." *New York Times* May 24.

Fackler, Martin. 2007b. "Tokyo Seeking a Top Niche in Global Finance." *New York Times* November 16.

Faiola, Anthony. 2007. "Ancient Temples Face Modern Assault." *Washington Post* February 6.

Fairclough, Gordon. 2006. "As Barriers Fall in Auto Business, China Jumps in." *Wall Street Journal* November 7.

Fairlie, Robert. 2012. *Immigrant Entrepreneurs, Small Business Owners, and their Access to Financial Capital*. Washington, DC: US Small Business Administration.

Faist, Thomas. 2012. "Migrants." In George Ritzer, ed., *Wiley-Blackwell Encyclopedia of Globalization*. Oxford: Wiley-Blackwell.

Fanon, Frantz. 1968. *The Wretched of the Earth*. New York: Grove Press.

Farr, Kathryn. 2005. *Sex Trafficking: The Global Market in Women and Children*. New York: Worth.

Farr, Kathryn. 2013. "Human Trafficking." In Steven J. Gold and Stephanie J. Nawyn, eds., *The Routledge International Handbook of Migration Studies*. New York: Routledge.

Fassin, Didier. 2008. "Compassion and Repression: The Moral Economy of Immigration Policies in France." In Jonathan Xavier Inda and Renato Rosaldo, eds., *The Anthropology of Globalization: A Reader*. 2nd edn. Oxford: Blackwell.

Featherstone, Mike. 1995. *Undoing Culture: Globalization, Postmodernism and Identity*. London: Sage.

Feng, Bree, and Denise Grady. 2013. "As Bird Flu Spreads to Taiwan, Government Acts to Prepare." *New York Times* April 24.

Ferguson, James. 2006. *Global Shadows: Africa in the Neoliberal World*. Durham: Duke University Press.

Ferguson, Niall. 2004. *Colossus: The Rise and Fall of the American Empire*. New York: Penguin.

Ferguson, Niall. 2008. "War Plans." *New York Times Review of Books* April 13.

Ferguson, Niall. 2012. *Civilization: The West and the Rest*. New York: Penguin.

Fernie, John. 2012. "Wal-Mart(ization)." In George Ritzer, ed., *Wiley-Blackwell Encyclopedia of Globalization*. Oxford: Wiley-Blackwell.

Ferus-Comelo, Anibel. 2006. "Double Jeopardy: Gender Migration in Electronics Manufacturing." In Ted Smith, David A. Sonnefield, and David Naguib. eds., *Challenging the Chip*. Philadelphia: Temple University Press.

Fiddian-Qasmiyeh, Elena. 2012. "Diaspora." In George Ritzer, ed., *Wiley-Blackwell Encyclopedia of Globalization*. Oxford: Wiley-Blackwell.

Firebaugh, Glenn, and Brian Goesling. 2007. "Globalization and Global Inequalities: Recent Trends." In George Ritzer, ed., *Blackwell Companion to Globalization*. Oxford: Blackwell.

Fischer, Stanley. 2003. "Globalization and Its Challenges." *American Economic Review* 93 (2): 1–30.

Fisher, Ian. 2007. "For African Migrants, Europe Becomes Further Away." *New York Times* August 26.

Fisher, Max. 2013. "Israel's Brain Drain Crisis." *Washington Post* October 15.

Fisher, William F., and Thomas Ponniah. 2003. *Another World Is Possible: Popular Alternatives to Globalization at the World Social Forum*. London: Zed Books.

Flanigan, James. 2008. "Passports Essential for the M.B.A.'s." *New York Times* February 21.

Fletcher, Thomas. 2011. "The Making of English Cricket Cultures: Empire, Globalization, and Post-Colonialism." *Sport in Society* 14 (1): 17–36.

Florini, Ann. 2007. "Transparency." In Jan Aart Scholte and Roland Robertson, eds., *Encyclopedia of Globalization*. New York: MTM Publishing.

Fludernik, Monika. 2003. "The Diasporic Imaginary: Postcolonial Reconfigurations in the Context of Multiculturalism." In *Diaspora and Multiculturalism: Common Traditions and New Developments*. Amsterdam; New York: Rodopi.

Food and Agriculture Organization (FAO). 2012. *The State of World Fisheries and Aquaculture*. Washington, DC: FAO.

Food and Water Watch. 2011. *A Decade of Dangerous Food Imports from China*. Washington, DC: Food and Water Watch.

Foran, John, and Richard Widick. 2013. "Break Barriers to Climate Justice." *Contexts* 12 (2): 34–39.

Foreign Policy, A.T. Kearney, and the Chicago Council on Global Affairs. 2010. "The Global Cities Index 2010." *Foreign Policy* August 16.

Foreign Policy and Fund for Peace. 2013. "Failed States, 2012 Edition." http://www.foreignpolicy.com/failed_states_index_2012_interactive (last accessed August 17, 2014).

Foreign Policy and McKinsey Global Institute. 2012. "The Most Dynamic Cities of 2025." *Foreign Policy* August 13.

Fortune. 2013. "Global 500." http://money.cnn.com/magazines/fortune/global500/2012/ (last accessed August 17, 2014).

Foster, Robert. 2012. "Coca-Globalization." In George Ritzer, ed., *Wiley-Blackwell Encyclopedia of Globalization*. Oxford: Wiley-Blackwell.

Fourcade-Gourinchas, Marion, and Sarah Babb. 2002. "The Rebirth of the Liberal Creed: Paths to Neoliberalism in Four Countries." *American Journal of Sociology* 108 (3): 533–579.

Frank, Andre Gunder. 1969. "The Development of Underdevelopment." *Monthly Review* 18 (4).

Frank, David John, and Elizabeth H. McEneaney. 1999. "The Individualization of Society and the Liberalization of State Policies on Same Sex Sexual Relations, 1984–1995." *Social Forces* 77: 911–944.

Frazer, Garth. 2008. "Used Clothing Donations and Apparel Production in Africa." *The Economic Journal* 118 (532): 1764–1784.

Frederick, Scott. 2013. "The Key to Making Telemedicine Work." *Health Management Technology* April 1.

Frederickson, Caroline, and Vania Leveille. 2007. *"Eradicating Slavery: Preventing the Abuse, Exploitation, and Trafficking of Domestic Workers by Foreign Diplomats and Ensuring Diplomat Accountability."* ACLU Statement to the House Foreign Affairs Committee. Washington, DC, October 18.

Freeman, Carla. 2001. "Is Local: Global as Feminine: Masculine? Rethinking the Gender of Globalization." *Signs: Journal of Women in Culture and Society* 26 (4): 1007–1037.

French, Howard W. 2008. "Great Firewall of China Faces Online Rebels." *New York Times* February 4.

Frieden, Jeffry A. 2006. *Global Capitalism: Its Fall and Rise in the Twentieth Century*. New York: W.W. Norton.

Friedman, Jonathan. 1994. *Culture Identity and Global Processes*. London: Sage.

Friedman, Milton. 2002. *Capitalism and Freedom*. Chicago: University of Chicago Press.

Friedman, Thomas. 1999. *The Lexus and the Olive Tree*. New York: Farrar, Straus, Giroux.

Friedman, Thomas. 2005. *The World is Flat: A Brief History of the Twenty-first Century*. New York: Farrar, Strauss, Giroux.

Friedman, Thomas. 2007. *The World is Flat 3.0: A Brief History of the Twenty-First Century*. New York: Picador.

Friedman, Thomas. 2012. *The Lexus and the Olive Tree: Understanding Globalization*. Revised and updated edn. New York: Picador.

Friedmann, John. 1986. "The World City Hypothesis." *Development and Change* 17 (1): 69–83.

Friedmann, John. 1995. "Where We Stand: A Decade of World City Research." In Paul Knox and Peter Taylor, eds., *World Cities in a World System*. Cambridge: Cambridge University Press.

Fukuyama, Francis. 1989. "The End of History?" *The National Interest* 16: 3–18.

Fukuyama, Francis. 1992. *The End of History and the Last Man*. New York: Free Press.

Fukuyama, Francis. 2011. "US Democracy Has Little to Teach China." *Financial Times* January 17.

Gaio, Fatima Janine. 1995. "Women in Software Programming: The Experience in Brazil." In Swasti Mitter and Sheila Rowbotham, eds., *Women Encounter Technology*. London: Routledge.

Galbraith, James. 2012. *Inequality and Instability: A Study of the World Economy Just Before the Crisis*. New York: Oxford University Press.

Galbraith, Kate. 2013. "A Carbon Tax by any Other Name." *New York Times* July 24.

Galli, Anya, and Piergiorgio Degliesposti. 2012. "Slow Food Movement." In George Ritzer, ed., *Wiley-Blackwell Encyclopedia of Globalization*. Oxford: Wiley-Blackwell.

Gangopadhyay, Abhrajit, and Jason Ng. 2013. "Malaysia Launches Immigration Operation to Deport Illegal Workers." *Wall Street Journal* September 1.

Gareau, Brian. 2013. *From Precaution to Profit: Contemporary Challenges to Environmental Protection in the Montreal Protocol*. New Haven, CT: Yale University Press.

Garrett, William R. 2007. "Christianity." In Jan Aart Scholte and Roland Robertson, ed., *Encyclopedia of Globalization*. New York: MTM Publishing.

Gassert, F., M. Luck, M. Landis, P. Reig, and T. Shiao. 2013. "Aqueduct Global Maps 2.0." Working Paper. Washington, DC: World Resources Institute. http://www.wri.org/publication/aqueduct-global-maps-20 (last accessed August 17, 2014).

Gelernter, Lior, and Motti Regev. 2010. "Internet and Globalization." In Bryan Turner, ed., *The Routledge Handbook of Globalization Studies*. New York: Routledge.

Gellner, Ernest. 1983. *Nations and Nationalism*. Oxford: Blackwell.

Gentleman, Amelia. 2008. "India Nurtures Business of Surrogate Motherhood." *New York Times* March 10.

George, Kimberly. 2007. "Women's Movements." In Jan Aart Scholte and Roland Robertson, eds., *Encyclopedia of Globalization*. New York: MTM Publishing.

Gereffi, Gary. 2005. "The Global Economy: Organization, Governance, and Development." In Neil Smelser and Richard Swedberg, eds., *Handbook of Economic Sociology*. Princeton: Princeton University Press.

Gereffi, Gary. 2012. "Value Chains." In George Ritzer, ed., *Wiley-Blackwell Encyclopedia of Globalization.*. Oxford: Wiley-Blackwell.

Gereffi, Gary, and Miguel Korzeniewicz, eds. 1994. *Commodity Chains and Global Capitalism*. Westport, CT: Praeger.

Germain, Randall D. 2004. "Globalising Accountability within the International Organisation of Credit: Financial Governance and the Public Sphere." *Global Society* 18 (3): 217–242.

Gibbon, Edward. 1998. *The History of the Decline and Fall of the Roman Empire*. London: Wordsworth.

Giddens, Anthony. 1984. *The Constitution of Society: Outline of the Theory of Structuration*. Berkeley, CA: University of California Press.

Giddens, Anthony. 1990. *The Consequences of Modernity*. Stanford: Stanford University Press.

Giddens, Anthony. 1994. *Beyond Left and Right*. Cambridge: Polity Press.

Gilbert, Christopher L., and David Vines, eds. 2000. *The World Bank: Structure and Policies*. Cambridge: Cambridge University Press.

Gill, Stephen R., and David Law. 1989. "Global Hegemony and the Structural Power of Capital." *International Studies Quarterly* 33 (4): 475–499.

Gillis, Justin. 2013a. "By 2047, Coldest Years May Be Warmer Than Hottest in Past, Scientists Say." *New York Times* October 9.

Gillis, Justin. 2013b. "Climate Change Seen Posing Risk to Food Supplies." *New York Times* November 1.

Gillis, Justin. 2014. "Panel's Warning on Climate Risk: The Worst Is Yet to Come." *New York Times* March 31.

Gilman-Opalsky, Richard. 2008. *Unbounded Publics: Transgressive Public Spheres, Zapatismo, and Political Theory*. Lanham, MD: Lexington Books.

Gilpin, Robert. 2001. *Global Political Economy*. Princeton: Princeton University Press.

Gilroy, Paul. 1993. *The Black Atlantic: Modernity and Double Consciousness*. Cambridge, MA: Harvard University Press.

Giulianotti, Richard, and Roland Robertson. 2004. "The Globalization of Football: A Study in the Glocalization of the 'Serious Life.'" *British Journal of Sociology* 55: 545–568.

Giulianotti, Richard, and Roland Robertson. 2007. "Recovering the Social: Globalization, Football and Transnationalism." In Richard Giulianotti and Roland Robertson, eds., *Globalization and Sport*. Oxford: Blackwell.

Giulianotti, Richard, and Roland Robertson. 2012. "Glocalization." In George Ritzer, ed., *Wiley-Blackwell Encyclopedia of Globalization*. Oxford: Wiley-Blackwell.

Givens, Jennifer, and Andrew Jorgenson. 2013. "Individual Environmental Concern in the World Polity: A Multilevel Analysis." *Social Science Research* 42 (2): 418–443.

Gjelten, Tom. 2012. "Shutdowns Counter the Idea of a World Wide Web." *NPR* December 1.

Gladwell, Malcolm. 2010. "Small Change: Why the Revolution Will Not Be Tweeted." *The New Yorker* October 4.

Glancy, Mark. 2013. *Hollywood and the Americanization of Britain from the 1920s to the Present*. London: I.B. Tauris.

Glantz, M. 1977. *Desertification*. Boulder, CO: Westview.

Glassner, Barry. 2000. *Culture of Fear: Why Americans Are Afraid of the Wrong Things*. New York: Basic Books.

Glenny, Misha. 2008. *McMafia: A Journey Through the Global Criminal Underworld*. New York: Knopf.

Goffman, Erving. 1961. *Encounters: Two Studies in Sociology of Interaction*. Indianapolis: Bobbs-Merrill.

Gokariksel, Banu, and Katharine Mitchell. 2005. "Veiling, Secularism, and the Neoliberal Subject: National Narratives and Supranational Desires in Turkey and France." *Global Networks* 5 (2): 147–165.

Gold, Steven, and Stephanie Nawyn, eds. 2013. *The Routledge International Handbook of Migration Studies*. New York: Routledge.

Goldberg, Harvey E. 2007. "Judaism." In Jan Aart Scholte and Roland Robertson, eds., *Encyclopedia of Globalization*. New York: MTM Publishing.

Goldburg, Rebecca J. 2008. "Aquaculture, Trade, and Fisheries Linkages: Unexpected Synergies." *Globalizations* 5 (2): 183–194.

Goldman, Robert, and Stephen Papson. 1998. *Nike Culture*. London: Sage.

Gonsalves, Ralph E. 2004. "Foreword." In Gordon Myers, *Banana Wars: The Price of Free Trade*. London: Zed Books.

Goode, Erich, and Nachman Ben-Yehuda. 1994. *Moral Panics*. Oxford: Blackwell.

Goodman, Douglas. 2007. "Globalization and Consumer Culture." In George Ritzer, ed., *Blackwell Companion to Globalization*. Oxford: Blackwell.

Goodman, Peter S. 2008a. "A Fresh Look at the Apostle of Free Markets." *New York Times* April 13.

Goodman, Peter S. 2008b. "Trading Partners Fear U.S. Consumers Won't Continue Free-Spending Ways." *New York Times* January 25.

Goodman, Peter S., and Louise Story. 2008. "Foreigners Buy Stakes in the US at a Record Pace." *New York Times* January 20.

Gordon, Philip H., and Sophie Meunier. 2001. *The French Challenge: Adapting to Globalization.* Washington, DC: Brookings Institution Press.

Gordon, Jr, R. G., ed. 2007. *Ethnologue: Languages of the World.* Dallas: SIL International.

Gotham, Kevin. 2006. "The Secondary Circuit of Capital Reconsidered: Globalization and the US Real Estate Sector." *American Journal of Sociology* 112: 231–275.

Goulder, Lawrence, and Andrew Schein. 2013. "Carbon Taxes vs. Cap and Trade: A Critical Review." NBER Working Paper No. 19338.

Grainge, Paul. 2004. "Global Media and Resonant Americanisation." In Neil Campbell, Jude Davies, and George McKay, eds., *Issues in Americanisation and Culture.* Edinburgh: Edinburgh University Press.

Grainger, Alan. 2012. "Environmental Globalization." In George Ritzer, ed., *Wiley-Blackwell Encyclopedia of Globalization.* Oxford: Wiley-Blackwell.

Grainger, Andrew David. 2008. *The Browning of the All Blacks: Pacific Peoples, Rugby, and the Cultural Politics of Identity in New Zealand.* PhD dissertation, University of Maryland, College Park, MD.

Grainger, Andrew, and Steven Jackson. 2005. "'I'm Afraid of Americans': New Zealand's Cultural Resistance to Violence in 'Globally' Produced Sports Advertising." In Steven J. Jackson and David A. Andrews, eds., *Sport, Culture and Advertising: Identities, Commodities and the Politics of Representation.* London; New York: Routledge.

Gramsci, Antonio. 1992. *Prison Notebooks.* New York: Columbia University Press.

Granovetter, Mark. 1973. "The Strength of Weak Ties." *American Journal of Sociology* 78: 1360–1380.

Gray, John. 2000. *False Dawn: The Delusions of Global Capitalism.* New York: New Press.

Greeley, Andrew. 1976. "The Ethnic Miracle." *The Public Interest* 45: 20–36.

Greenfeld, Liah. 2012. "Nationalism." In George Ritzer, ed., *Wiley-Blackwell Encyclopedia of Globalization.* Oxford: Wiley-Blackwell.

Greenhouse, Steven, and Stephanie Clifford. 2013. "A Respite in Efforts by Wal-Mart in New York." *New York Times* March 6.

Greenstone, Michael, and Adam Looney. 2010. *Ten Economic Facts about Immigration.* Washington, DC: Brookings Institution.

Gregory, Derek. 2011. "From a View to a Kill Drones and Late Modern War." *Theory, Culture & Society* 28 (7–8): 188–215.

Grimal, Henri. 1978. *Decolonization: The British, Dutch, and Belgian Empires, 1919–1963.* London: Routledge.

Grimwade, Nigel Stewart. 2007. "Trade-Related Investment Measures." In Jan Aart Scholte and Roland Robertson, eds., *Encyclopedia of Globalization.* New York: MTM Publishing.

Grisham, John. 2013. "After Guantánamo, Another Injustice." *New York Times* August 10.

Gronewold, Nathanial. 2011. "After Explosive Growth, Global Carbon Markets Stall and Begin to Shrink." *New York Times* June 2.

Gross, Daniel. 2008. "The US Economy Faces the Guillotine." *Newsweek* February 4.

Grynbaum, Michael M. 2008. "Investors See Recession, and Market Drops." *New York Times* January 18.

Gruzd, Anatoliy, Barry Wellman, and Yuri Takhteyev. 2011. "Imagining Twitter as an Imagined Community." *American Behavioral Scientist* 57 (8): 1294–1318.

Guhathakurta, Subhrajit, David Jacobson, and Nicholas C. DelSordi. 2007. "The End of Globalization? The Implications of Migration for State, Society and Economy." In George Ritzer, ed., *Blackwell Companion to Globalization.* Oxford: Blackwell.

Guibernau, Montserrat. 2007. "National Identity." In Jan Aart Scholte and Roland Robertson, eds., *Encyclopedia of Globalization.* New York: MTM Publishing.

Guillen, Mario F. 2001. "Is Globalization Civilizing, Destructive or Feeble? A Critique of Five Key Debates in the Social Science Literature." *Annual Review of Sociology* 27: 235–260.

Guillory, Sean. 2013. "Corruption, Not Migrants, Is Russia's Problem." *The Nation* August 20.

Guizhen, He, Lei Zhang, Arthur Mol, Tieyu Wang, and Yonglong Lu. 2014. "Why Small and Medium Chemical Companies Continue to Pose Severe Environmental Risks in Rural China." *Environmental Pollution* 185: 158–167.

Gunewardena, Nandini, and Mark Schuller, eds. 2008. *Capitalizing on Catastrophe: Neoliberal Strategies in Disaster Reconstruction*. Lanham, MD: AltaMira Press.

Gupta, Aarti. 2012. "Transparency." In George Ritzer, ed., *Wiley-Blackwell Encyclopedia of Globalization*. Oxford: Wiley-Blackwell.

Gutterplan, D. D. 2013. "Vying for a Spot on the World's A List." *New York Times* April 12.

Guttman, Allen. 2002. *The Olympics: A History of the Modern Games*. 2nd edn. Champaign, IL: University of Illinois Press.

Guttman, Allen. 2007. "Olympic Games." In Jan Aart Scholte and Roland Robertson, eds., *Encyclopedia of Globalization*. New York: MTM Publishing.

Hackworth, Jason. 2012. *Faith Based: Religious Neoliberalism and the Politics of Welfare in the United States*. Athens, GA: University of Georgia Press.

Halbwachs, Maurice. 1992. *On Collective Memory*. Chicago: University of Chicago Press.

Hale, Galina, and Bart Hobijn. 2011. "The US Content of 'Made in China.'" Federal Reserve Bank of San Francisco. August 8.

Hale, Thomas. 2011. "Citizen Submission Process of the North American Commission for Environmental Cooperation." In Thomas Hale and David Held, eds., *Handbook of Transnational Governance: Institutions and Innovations*. Malden, MA: Polity Press.

Hale, Thomas, and David Held, eds. 2011. *Handbook of Transnational Governance: Institutions and Innovations*. Malden, MA: Polity Press.

Hall, Abigail, and Christopher Coyne. 2013. "The Political Economy of Drones." *Defence and Peace Economics* 1–16.

Hall, Derek. 2007. "Double Movement." In Jan Aart Scholte and Roland Robertson, eds., *Encyclopedia of Globalization*. New York: MTM Publishing.

Hall, Jason. 2012. "World Health Organization." In George Ritzer, ed., *Wiley-Blackwell Encyclopedia of Globalization*. Oxford: Wiley-Blackwell.

Hall, Marc. 2013. "EU Debates Biopiracy Law to Protect Indigenous People." *The Guardian* May 1.

Hall, Thomas D., and James V. Fenelon. 2008. "Indigenous Movements and Globalization: What is Different? What is the Same?" *Globalizations* 5 (1): 1–11.

Hall, Tim. 2013. "Geographies of the Illicit: Globalization and Organized Crime." *Progress in Human Geography* 37 (3): 366–385.

Hamdan, Sara. 2012. "Local Projects Replace Global Investments in Mideast." *New York Times* June 6.

Hamilton, Clive. 2013. "Geoengineering: Our Last Hope, or a False Promise?" *New York Times* May 26.

Hannas, William, James Mulvenon, and Anna Puglisi. 2013. *Chinese Industrial Espionage: Technology Acquisition and Military Modernisation*. New York: Routledge.

Hannerz, Ulf. 1987. "The World in Creolisation." *Africa* 57: 546–559.

Harding, H. 1993. "The Concept of 'Greater China': Themes and Variations." *The China Quarterly* 136: 660–686.

Harding, James. 2008. *Alpha Dogs: The Americans Who Turned Political Spin into a Global Business*. New York: Farrar, Straus, and Giroux.

Hardt, Michael, and Antonio Negri. 2000. *Empire*. Cambridge, MA: Harvard University Press.

Hardt, Michael, and Antonio Negri. 2004. *Multitude*. New York: Penguin Press.

Harrington, Michael. 1997. *The Other America: Poverty in the United States*. New York: Scribner.

Hartwig, M. C. 1972. "Aborigines and Racism: An Historical Perspective." In F. S. Stevens, ed., *Racism: The Australian Experience*, Vol. 2. New York: Taplinger.

Harvey, David. 1989. *The Condition of Postmodernity: An Enquiry into the Origins of Cultural Change*. Oxford: Blackwell.

Harvey, David. 2003. *The New Imperialism*. Oxford: Oxford University Press.

Harvey, David. 2005. *A Brief History of Neoliberalism*. Oxford: Oxford University Press.

Harvey, David. 2006. *Spaces of Global Capitalism: Towards a Theory of Uneven Geographical Development*. London: Verso.

Harvey, David. 2011. "The Rise of Neoliberalism and the Riddle of Capital." In Sasha Lilley, ed., *Capital and its Discontents: Conversations with Radical Thinkers in a Time of Tumult*. Oakland: Fernwood Publishing.

Harwood, John. 2010. "Obama's Balancing Act on US Trade Policies." *New York Times* February 7.

Hashemian, Farnoosh, and Derek Yach. 2007. "Public Health in a Globalizing World: Challenges and Opportunities." In George Ritzer, ed., *Blackwell Companion to Globalization*. Oxford: Blackwell.

Haskel, Jonathan E. 2001. "Trade and Labor Approaches to Wage Inequality." In E. Kwan Choi and David Greenway, eds., *Globalization and Labor Markets*. Oxford: Blackwell.

Hassler, Markus. 2003. "The Global Clothing Production System: Commodity Chains and Business Networks." *Global Networks* 3 (4): 513–532.

Hayes, Dennis, and Robin Wynyard, eds. 2002. *The McDonaldization of Higher Education*. Westport, CT: Bergin and Garvey.

Hayman, P. A., and John Williams. 2006. "Westphalian Sovereignty: Rights, Intervention, Meaning and Context." *Global Society* 20 (4): 521–541.

Headley, John M. 2008. *The Europeanization of the World: On the Origins of Human Rights and Democracy*. Princeton: Princeton University Press.

Headley, John M. 2012. "Europeanization." In George Ritzer, ed., *Wiley-Blackwell Encyclopedia of Globalization*. Oxford: Wiley-Blackwell.

Hebdige, Dick. 1988. *Hiding in the Light: On Images and Things*. London: Routledge.

Heintz, James. 2006. "*Globalization, Economic Policy and Employment: Poverty and Gender Implications*." Employment Strategy Unit, International Labor Organization

Held, David. 2005. "At the Global Crossroads: The End of the Washington Consensus and the Rise of Global Social Democracy?" *Globalizations* 2 (1): 95–113.

Held, David, and Anthony McGrew. 2000. "The Great Globalization Debate: An Introduction." In David Held and Anthony McGrew, eds., *The Global Transformations Reader: An Introduction to the Globalization Debate*. Cambridge: Polity.

Held, David, Anthony McGrew, David Goldblatt, and Jonathan Perraton. 1999. *Global Transformations: Politics, Economics and Culture*. Cambridge and Palo Alto: Polity and Stanford University Press.

Hernández, Joel. 2013. "Terrorism, Drug Trafficking, and the Globalization of Supply." *Perspectives on Terrorism* 7 (4): 41–61.

Herod, Andrew. 2009. *Geographies of Globalization*. Oxford: Wiley-Blackwell.

Hess, Beth B., and Myra Marx Ferree. 1987. "Introduction." In Beth B. Hess and Myra Marx Ferree, eds., *Analyzing Gender: A Handbook of Social Research*. Beverly Hills, CA: Sage.

Hicks, Steven V., and Daniel E. Shannon, eds. 2007. *The Challenges of Globalization: Rethinking Nature, Culture, and Freedom*. Oxford: Blackwell.

Higgins, Andrew. 2013. "Danish Opponent of Islam Is Attacked, and Muslims Defend his Right to Speak." *New York Times* February 27.

Higgins, Andrew. 2014. "Populists' Rise in Europe Vote Shakes Leaders." *New York Times* May 26.

Higo, Masa. 2012. "Group of 8." In George Ritzer, ed., *Wiley-Blackwell Encyclopedia of Globalization*. Oxford: Wiley-Blackwell.

Hill, Carol E., and Marietta L. Baba, eds. 2006. *The Globalization of Anthropology*. American Anthropological Association NAPA Bulletin.

Hirst, Paul, and Grahame Thompson. 1999. *Globalization in Question*. Cambridge: Polity.

Hirst, Paul, Grahame Thompson, and Simon Bromley. 2009. *Globalization in Question*. 3rd edn. Malden, MA: Polity Press.

Ho, Karen. 2005. "Situating Global Capitalisms: A View from Wall Street Investment Banks." *Cultural Anthropology* 20 (1): 68–96.

Hobsbawm, Eric. 2012. *Nations and Nationalism since 1780: Programme, Myth, Reality*. 2nd edn. New York: Cambridge University Press.

Hobson, J. A. 1902/1905/1938. *Imperialism: An Empirical Study*. London: George Allen and Unwin Limited.

Hochschild, Arlie. 2000. "Global Care Chains and Emotional Surplus Value." In W. Hutton and Anthony Giddens, eds., *On the Edge: Living with Global Capitalism*. London: Jonathan Cape.

Hodson, Joel. 2001. "'Intercourse in Every Direction': America as Global Phenomenon." *Global Networks* 1 (1): 79–87.

Hoefer, Michael, Nancy Rytina, and Brian Baker. 2012. *Estimates of the Unauthorized Immigrant Population Residing in the United States: January 2011*. Washington, DC: Office of Immigration Statistics.

Hoekstra, Arjen Y. 2012. "Water." In George Ritzer, ed., *Wiley-Blackwell Encyclopedia of Globalization*. Oxford: Wiley-Blackwell.

Hoekstra, Arjen Y., and Ashok K. Chapagain. 2008. *Globalization of Water: Sharing the Planet's Freshwater Resources*. Oxford: Blackwell.

Hoffman, Andy, and Tara Perkins. 2011. "China's Sovereign Wealth Fund Sets Up Shop in Toronto." *The Globe and Mail* January 12.

Hoffman, Stanley. 2002. "Clash of Globalizations." *Foreign Affairs* 81 (4): 104–115.

Hollander, Paul. 1992. *Anti-Americanism: Critiques at Home and Abroad, 1965–1990*. New York: Oxford University Press.

Holson, Laura M., and Steven Lee Myers. 2006. "The Russians Are Filming! The Russians Are Filming!" *New York Times* July 16.

Holt, Douglas. 2004. *How Brands Become Icons: Principles of Cultural Branding*. Cambridge, MA: Harvard Business School.

Holton, Robert. 2007. "Networks." In Jan Aart Scholte and Roland Robertson, eds., *Encyclopedia of Globalization*. New York: MTM Publishing.

Holzner, Burkart, and Leslie Holzner. 2006. *Transparency in Global Change: The Vanguard of the Open Society*. Pittsburgh: University of Pittsburgh Press.

Hooper, David, E. Carol Adair, Bradley J. Cardinale et al. 2012. "A Global Synthesis Reveals Biodiversity Loss as a Major Driver of Ecosystem Change." *Nature* 486: 105–108.

Horwitz, Betty. 2011. *The Transformation of the Organization of American States: A Multilateral Framework for Regional Governance*. New York: Anthem Press.

House, Robert. 2007. "General Agreement on Tariffs and Trade." In Jan Aart Scholte and Roland Robertson, eds., *Encyclopedia of Globalization*. New York: MTM Publishing.

Howard, Philip, and Daniel Jaffee. 2013. "Tensions Between Firm Size and Sustainability Goals: Fair Trade Coffee in the United States." *Sustainability* 5 (1): 72–89.

Hsu, Spencer. 2010. "Work to Cease on 'Virtual Fence' Along US-Mexico Border." *The Washington Post* March 16.

Hubbard, Ben. 2014. "The Franchising of Al Qaeda." *New York Times* January 25.

Hudec, Robert. 1975. *The GATT Legal System and World Trade Diplomacy*. New York: Praeger.

Hudson, Cheryl. 2007. "American Popular Culture and Anti-Americanism." In Brendon O'Connor, ed., *Anti-Americanism: History, Causes, and Themes, Vol. 1: Causes and Sources*. Oxford: Greenwood World Publishing.

Hudson, Chris. 2010. "Global Cities." In Bryan Turner, ed., *The Routledge Handbook of Globalization Studies*. New York: Routledge.

Hunter Wade, Robert. 2003. "'What Strategies Are Viable for Developing Countries Today'? The World Trade Organization and the Shrinking of 'Development Space.'" *Review of International Political Economy* 10 (4): 621–624.

Hunter Wade, Robert. 2004. "Is Globalization Reducing Poverty and Inequality?" *World Development* 32 (4).

Huntington, Samuel P. 2004. "The Hispanic Challenge." *Foreign Policy* (March/April).

Huntington, Samuel P. 2011. *The Clash of Civilizations and the Remaking of the World Order*. New York: Simon and Schuster.

Hurdle, Jon. 2013. "Taking a Harder Look at Fracking and Health." *New York Times* January 21.

Hussain, Adnan, Sadaf Majeed, Sulaiman Muhammad, and Irfan Lal. 2010. "Impact of Globalization on HDI (Human Development Index): Case Study of Pakistan." *European Journal of Social Sciences* 13 (1): 46.

Inda, Jonathan Xavier, and Renato Rosaldo. 2008a. "Tracking Global Flows." In Jonathan Xavier Inda and Renato Rosaldo, eds., *The Anthropology of Globalization: A Reader*. 2nd edn. Oxford: Blackwell.

Inda, Jonathan Xavier, and Renato Rosaldo, eds. 2008b. *The Anthropology of Globalization: A Reader*. 2nd edn. Oxford: Blackwell.

Inkeles, Alex. 1974. *Becoming Modern*. Cambridge, MA: Harvard University Press.

Intergovernmental Panel on Climate Change. 2013. *Climate Change 2013: The Physical Science Basis*. Cambridge, MA: Cambridge University Press.

International Labor Organization. 2012. *ILO 2012 Global Estimate of Forced Labor*. Geneva, Switzerland: ILO.

International Organization of Motor Vehicle Manufacturers. n.d. "2012 Production Statistics." http://www.oica.net/category/production-statistics/2012-statistics/ (last accessed August 17, 2014).

International Telecommunication Union. 2014. *ICT Facts and Figures 2014*. Geneva, Switzerland: International Telecommunication Union.

Isikoff, Michael, and David Corn. 2006. *Hubris: The Inside Story of Spin, Scandal and the Selling of the Iraq War*. New York: Crown.

Jackson, Peter. 2000. "Social Geography." In R. J. Johnston, Derek Gregory, Geraldine Pratt, and Michael Watts, eds., *The Dictionary of Human Geography*. 4th edn. Oxford: Blackwell.

Jackson, Shirley. 2007. "Majorities." In George Ritzer, ed., *The Blackwell Encyclopedia of Sociology*. Oxford: Blackwell.

Jacobs, Andrew. 2013. "Behind Cry for Help from China Labor Camp." *New York Times* June 11.

Jaffee, Daniel. 2007. *Brewing Justice: Fair Trade Coffee, Sustainability and Survival*. Berkeley, CA: University of California Press.

Jakobi, Anja. 2012. "Human Trafficking." In George Ritzer, ed., *Wiley-Blackwell Encyclopedia of Globalization*. Oxford: Wiley-Blackwell.

James, Harold. 2001. *The End of Globalization: Lessons from the Great Depression*. Cambridge, MA: Harvard University Press.

Janmohamed, Abdul R. 2006. "The Economy of Manichean Allegory." In Bill Ashcroft, Gareth Griffiths, and Helen Tiffin, eds., *The Post-Colonial Reader*. 2nd edn. New York: Routledge.

Jaslow, Ryan. 2013. "Imported Rice May Contain Dangerously High Lead Levels." *CBS News* April 11.

Jenkins, Philip. 2002. *The Next Christendom: The Coming of Global Christianity*. Oxford: Oxford University Press.

Jessop, Bob. 2012. "Neoliberalism." In George Ritzer, ed., *Wiley-Blackwell Encyclopedia of Globalization*. Oxford: Wiley-Blackwell.

Jilani, Seema. 2013. "Saving Karachi's Street Children, One Goal at a Time." *New York Times* February 12.

Joekes, Susan P. 1987. *Women in the World Economy: An INSTRAW Study*. New York: Oxford University Press.

Joffe-Walt, Chana. 2010. "Why US Taxpayers are Paying Brazilian Cotton Growers." *NPR Planet Money* November 9.

Johns, Nicole, Krycia Cowling, and Emmanuela Gakidou. 2013. "The Wealth (and Health) of Nations: A Cross-Country Analysis of the Relation between Wealth and Inequality in Disease Burden Estimation." *Lancet* 381: S66.

Jolly, David. 2011. "Dutch Court Acquits Anti-Islam Politician." *New York Times* June 23.

Jolly, David. 2012. "OECD Sees Euro Zone Crisis Hurting World Recovery." *New York Times* May 12.

Jolly, David. 2013a. "Pacific Tuna Stocks Have Plummeted, Scientists Warn." *New York Times* January 10.

Jolly, David. 2013b. "France Upholds Ban on Hydraulic Fracturing." *New York Times* October 11.

Johnston, Ron. 2000. "Human Geography." In R. J. Johnston, Derek Gregory, Geraldine Pratt, and Michael Watts, eds., *The Dictionary of Human Geography*. 4th edn. Oxford: Blackwell.

Johnston, R. J., Derek Gregory, Geraldine Pratt, and Michael Watts. 2000. "Preface to the Fourth Edition." In R. J. Johnston, Derek Gregory, Geraldine Pratt, and Michael Watts, eds., *The Dictionary of Human Geography*. 4th edn. Oxford: Blackwell.

Jurgenson, Nathan. 2012. "Twitter Revolution." In George Ritzer, ed., *Wiley-Blackwell Encyclopedia of Globalization*. Oxford: Wiley-Blackwell.

Juris, Jeffrey. 2005. "The New Digital Media and Activist Networking within Anti-Corporate Globalization Movements." *Annals* 597: 189–208.

Juris, Jeffrey S. 2008. "The New Digital Media and Activist Networking within Anti-Corporate Globalization Movements." In Jonathan Xavier Inda and Renato Rosaldo, eds., *The Anthropology of Globalization: A Reader*. 2nd edn. Oxford: Blackwell.

Kahanec, Martin, Anna Myung-Hee Kim, and Klaus Zimmermann. 2013. "Pitfalls of Immigrant Inclusion into the European Welfare State." *International Journal of Manpower* 34 (1): 39–55.

Kahn, Joseph, and Mark Landler. 2007. "China Grabs West's Smoke-Spewing Factories." *New York Times* December 21.

Kahn, Richard. 2012. "Globophilia." In George Ritzer, ed., *Wiley-Blackwell Encyclopedia of Globalization*. Oxford: Wiley-Blackwell.

Kahn, Richard, and Douglas Kellner. 2007. "Resisting Globalization." In George Ritzer, ed., *Blackwell Companion to Globalization*. Oxford: Blackwell.

Kai, Saritha. 2007. "Grandma Cooks, They Deliver." *New York Times* May 29.

Kaldor, Mary. 2003. *Global Civil Society: An Answer to War*. London: Polity.

Kaldor, Mary. 2007. "Civil Society." In Jan Aart Scholte and Roland Robertson, eds., *Encyclopedia of Globalization*. New York: MTM Publishing.

Kaldor, Mary. 2013. *New and Old Wars: Organised Violence in a Global Era*. Malden, MA: Polity Press.

Kaldor, Mary, Henrietta Moore, and Sabine Selchow, eds. 2012. *Global Civil Society 2012: Ten Years of Critical Reflection*. New York: Palgrave Macmillan.

Kamau, Evanson, and Gerd Winter, eds. 2013. *Common Pools of Genetic Resources: Equity and Innovation in International Biodiversity Law*. New York: Routledge.

Kang, Susan. 2012. *Human Rights and Labor Solidarity: Trade Unions in the Global Economy*. Philadelphia, PA: University of Pennsylvania Press.

Kanter, James. 2009. "Norway Pledges 40 Percent Emissions Cut." *New York Times* October 9.

Kanter, James. 2013. "Grind of Euro Crisis Wears Down Support for Union, Poll Finds." *New York Times* May 13.

Karstedt, Susanne. 2012a. "Crime." In George Ritzer, ed., *Wiley-Blackwell Encyclopedia of Globalization*. Oxford: Wiley-Blackwell.

Karstedt, Susanne. 2012b. "Genocide." In George Ritzer, ed., *Wiley-Blackwell Encyclopedia of Globalization*. Oxford: Wiley-Blackwell.

Kastoryano, Riva, ed. 2013. *Turkey between Nationalism and Globalization*. New York: Routledge.

Kaufman, Jason, and Orlando Patterson. 2005. "Cross-National Cultural Diffusion: The Global Spread of Cricket." *American Sociological Review* 70: 82–110.

Kay, Tamara. 2012. "North American Free Trade Agreement." In George Ritzer, ed., *Wiley-Blackwell Encyclopedia of Globalization*. Oxford: Wiley-Blackwell.

Keane, John. 2003. *Global Civil Society*. Cambridge: Cambridge University Press.

Keck, Margaret, and Kathryn Sikkink. 1998. *Activists beyond Borders*. Ithaca, NY: Cornell University Press.

Keen, Andrew. 2007. *The Cult of the Amateur: How Today's Internet is Killing Our Culture*. New York: Doubleday.

Kellner, Douglas. 2002. "Theorizing Globalization." *Sociological Theory* 20 (3): 285–305.

Kellner, Douglas, and Clayton Pierce. 2007. "Media and Globalization." In George Ritzer, ed., *Blackwell Companion to Globalization*. Oxford: Blackwell.

Kellogg, Paul. 2012. "Civil Society." In George Ritzer, ed., *Wiley-Blackwell Encyclopedia of Globalization*. Oxford: Wiley-Blackwell.

Kelly, William W. 2007. "Is Baseball a Global Sport? America's 'National Pastime' as a Global Field and International Sport." In Richard Giulianotti and Roland Robertson, eds., *Globalization and Sport*. Oxford: Blackwell.

Kennedy, J. Michael. 2012. "For Illegal Immigrants, Greek Border Offers a Back Door to Europe." *New York Times* July 14.

Kenny, Charles. 2012. "Why More Immigration, Not Less, is Key to US Economic Growth." *Bloomberg Businessweek* October 28.

Keohane, Robert O., and Joseph S. Nye. 2000. *Power and Independence*. 3rd edn. New York: Addison-Wesley.

Kershner, Isabel. 2013. "Israel Shoots Down Drone Possibly Sent by Hezbollah." *New York Times* April 25.

Keynes, John Maynard. 1935. *The General Theory of Employment, Interest and Money*. New York: Harcourt Brace.

Khanna, Parag. 2008a. *The Second World: Empires and Influence in the New Global Order*. New York: Random House.

Khanna, Parag. 2008b. "Waving Goodbye to Hegemony." *New York Times Magazine* January 27.

Khatchadourian, Raffi. 2007. "Neptune's Navy." *New Yorker* November 5.

Kick, Edward. 2012. "Dependency Theory." In George Ritzer, ed., *Wiley-Blackwell Encyclopedia of Globalization*. Oxford: Wiley-Blackwell.

Kiely, Ray. 2012. "Development." In George Ritzer, ed., *Wiley-Blackwell Encyclopedia of Globalization*. Oxford: Wiley-Blackwell.

Killick, Tony. 2007. "Structural Adjustment Programs." In Jan Aart Scholte and Roland Robertson, eds., *Encyclopedia of Globalization*. New York: MTM Publishing.

Killough, Ashley, and Paul Cruickshank. 2013. "Al-Qaeda Magazine Encourages Boston-Style Bombings." *CNN* May 30.

Kim, Samuel S. 2000. *Korea's Globalization*. New York: Cambridge University Press.

Kirton, John. 2007. "Group of Eight." In Jan Aart Scholte and Roland Robertson, eds., *Encyclopedia of Globalization*. New York: MTM Publishing.

Kirton, John, Joseph Daniels, and Andreas Freytag, eds. 2001. *Guiding Global Order: G8 Governance in the Twenty-First Century*. Aldershot, UK: Ashgate.

Kitchin, Rob, and Martin Dodge. 2002. "The Emerging Geographies of Cyberspace." In R. J. Johnston, Peter J. Taylor, and Michael J. Watts, eds., *Geographies of Global Change: Remapping the World*. Oxford: Blackwell.

Kitroeff, Natalie. 2013. "Immigrants Pay Lower Fees to Send Money Home, Helping to Ease Poverty." *New York Times* April 27.

Kivisto, Peter. 2012. "Time-Space Compression." In George Ritzer, ed., *Wiley-Blackwell Encyclopedia of Globalization*. Oxford: Wiley-Blackwell.

Klein, Naomi. 2009. *No Logo: Taking Aim at the Brand Bullies*. Toronto: Vintage, Canada.

Klein, Naomi. 2007. *The Shock Doctrine: The Rise of Disaster Capitalism*. New York: Metropolitan Books.

Kletzer, Lori G. 2007. "Trade-Related Job Loss and Wage Insurance: A Synthetic Review." In David Greenway, ed., *Adjusting to Globalization*. Oxford: Blackwell.

Knörr, Jacqueline. 2012. "Creolization." In George Ritzer, ed., *Wiley-Blackwell Encyclopedia of Globalization*. Oxford: Wiley-Blackwell.

Knorr Cetina, Karin. 2005. "Complex Global Microstructures: The New Terrorist Societies." *Theory, Culture & Society* 22 (5): 213–234.

Knorr Cetina, Karin. 2012. "Financial Markets." In George Ritzer, ed., *Wiley-Blackwell Encyclopedia of Globalization*. Oxford: Wiley-Blackwell.

Knorr Cetina, Karin, and Urs Bruegger. 2002. "Global Microstructures: The Virtual Societies of Financial Markets." *American Journal of Sociology* 107 (4): 905–950.

Kohler, Kristopher. 2012. "World Social Forum." In George Ritzer, ed., *Wiley-Blackwell Encyclopedia of Globalization*. Oxford: Wiley-Blackwell.

Kolata, Gina. 1999. *Flu: The Story of the Great Influenza Pandemic of 1918 and the Search for the Virus That Caused It*. New York: Touchstone.

Kornprobst, Markus, Vincent Pouliot, Nisha Shah, and Ruben Zaiotti, eds. 2008. *Metaphors of Globalization: Mirrors, Magicians and Mutinies*. Basingstoke: Palgrave Macmillan.

Korzeniewicz, Roberto Patricio, and Timothy Patrick Moran. 2007. "World Inequality in the Twenty-First Century: Patterns and Tendencies." In George Ritzer, ed., *Blackwell Companion to Globalization*. Oxford: Blackwell.

Korzeniewicz, Roberto Patriciio, and Timothy Patrick Moran. 2010. "Rethinking Inequality from a World-Historical Perspective." In Christian Suter, ed., *Inequality Beyond Globalization: Economic Changes, Social Transformations, and the Dynamics of Inequality*. Piscataway, NJ: Transaction Publishers.

Krauss, Clifford. 2007. "Oil-Rich Nations Use More Energy, Cutting Exports." *New York Times* December 9.

Krauss, Clifford. 2008. "Commodities' Relentless Surge." *New York Times* January 15.

Krings, Matthias, and Onookome Okome, eds. 2013. *Global Nollywood: The Transnational Dimensions of an African Video Film Industry*. Bloomington, IN: Indiana University Press.

Krisher, Tom. 2013. "US to Sell 30 Million Shares of GM Stock in Aim to Wind Down Bailout Ownership Stake." *Huffington Post* June 5.

Krishnaswamy, Revathi, and John C. Hawley, eds. 2008. *The Postcolonial and the Global*. Minneapolis: University of Minnesota Press.

Kritz, Mary M. 2008. "International Migration." In George Ritzer, ed., *Blackwell Encyclopedia of Sociology Online*. Oxford: Blackwell.

Kroen, Sheryl. 2006. "Negotiations with the American Way: The Consumer and the Social Contract in Post-war Europe." In John Brewer and Frank Trentmann, eds., *Consuming Cultures, Global Perspectives: Historical Trajectories, Transnational Exchanges*. Oxford: Berg.

Kroes, Rob, Robert W. Rydell, D. F. J. Bosscher, and John F. Sears. 1993. *Cultural Transmissions and Receptions: American Mass Culture in Europe*. Amsterdam: VU Press.

Krueger, Anne. 2000. *The WTO as an International Organization*. Chicago: University of Chicago Press.

Krueger, Anne. 2012. "World Trade Organization." In George Ritzer, ed., *Wiley-Blackwell Encyclopedia of Globalization*. Oxford: Wiley-Blackwell.

Kuipers, Giselinde. 2012. "Mediascapes." In George Ritzer, ed., *Wiley-Blackwell Encyclopedia of Globalization*. Oxford: Wiley-Blackwell.

Kuisel, Richard F. 1993. *Seducing the French: The Dilemma of Americanization*. Berkeley, CA: University of California Press.

Kuisel, Richard F. 2003. "Debating Americanization: The Case of France." In Ulrich Beck, Natan Sznaider, and Rainer Winter, eds., *Global America? The Cultural Consequences of Globalization*. Liverpool: Liverpool University Press.

Kukreja, Sunil. 2012. "Neoconservatism." In George Ritzer, ed., *Wiley-Blackwell Encyclopedia of Globalization*. Oxford: Wiley-Blackwell.

Kulish, Nicholas. 2013. "South Sudan's President Condemns Ethnic Killings." *New York Times* December 25.

Kuznets, Simon. 1940. "Economic Growth and Income Inequality." *American Economic Review* 30: 257–271.

Labban, Mazen. 2012. "Oil (Petroleum)." In George Ritzer, ed., *Wiley-Blackwell Encyclopedia of Globalization*. Oxford: Wiley-Blackwell.

LaFraniere, Sharon. 2008. "Europe Takes Africa's Fish, and Migrants Follow." *New York Times* January 14.

Laguerre, M. S. 2002. *Virtual Diasporas: A New Frontier of National Security*. The Nautilus Project on Virtual Diasporas.

Lakoff, Andrew. 2008. "Diagnostic Liquidity: Mental Illness and the Global Trade in DNA." In Jonathan Xavier Inda and Renato Rosaldo, eds., *The Anthropology of Globalization: A Reader*. 2nd edn. Oxford: Blackwell.

Landler, Mark. 2008. "At a Tipping Point." *New York Times* October 1.

Langman, Lauren. 2012. "Globalization from Below." In George Ritzer, ed., *Wiley-Blackwell Encyclopedia of Globalization*. Oxford: Wiley-Blackwell.

Lapidus, I. M. 1988. *A History of Islamic Societies*. Cambridge: Cambridge University Press.

Law, Ian. 2012. "Racism." In George Ritzer, ed., *Wiley-Blackwell Encyclopedia of Globalization*. Oxford: Wiley-Blackwell.

Lawhon, Mary. 2013. "Dumping Ground or Country-in-transition? Discourses of e-Waste in South Africa." *Environment and Planning C: Government and Policy* 31 (4): 700–715.

Lawson, Sean. 2013. "The US Military's Social Media Civil War: Technology as Antagonism in Discourses of Information-Age Conflict." *Cambridge Review of International Affairs* DOI: 10.1080/09557571.2012.734787.

Lechner, Frank. 2007. "Imagined Communities in the Global Game: Soccer and the Development of Dutch National Identity." In Richard Giulianotti and Roland Robertson, eds., *Globalization and Sport*. Oxford: Blackwell.

Lechner, Frank. 2012. *The Netherlands: Globalization and National Identity*. New York: Routledge.

Lechner, Frank, and John Boli. 2005. *World Culture: Origins and Consequences*. Oxford: Blackwell.

Lee, Susan Hagood. 2012a. "International Monetary Fund." In George Ritzer, ed., *Wiley-Blackwell Encyclopedia of Globalization*. Oxford: Wiley-Blackwell.

Lee, Susan Hagood. 2012b. "World Bank." In George Ritzer, ed., *Wiley-Blackwell Encyclopedia of Globalization*. Oxford: Wiley-Blackwell.

Lee, Susan Hagood. 2012c. "Sex Trafficking." In George Ritzer, ed., *Wiley-Blackwell Encyclopedia of Globalization*. Oxford: Wiley-Blackwell.

Leifer, Michael. 1989. *ASEAN and the Security of Southeast Asia*. London: Routledge.

Leisher, Craig. 2013. "Mileston Looms for Farm-Raised Fish." *New York Times* January 24.

LeLe, Sharachchandra. 2007. "Sustainability." In Jan Aart Scholte and Roland Robertson, eds., *Encyclopedia of Globalization*. New York: MTM Publishing.

Lelyveld, Michael. 2013. "China's Economy Slows Oil Growth." *Radio Free Asia* May 27.

Lemert, Charles, and Anthony Elliott. 2006. *Deadly Worlds: The Emotional Costs of Globalization*. Lanham, MD: Rowman & Littlefield.

Lenin, Vladimir. 1917/1939. *Imperialism: The Highest Stage of Capitalism*. New York: International Publishers.

Leonhardt, David. 2011. "Gene Sperling 101." *New York Times* January 5. http://economix.blogs. nytimes.com/2011/01/05/gene-sperling-101/ (last accessed August 17, 2014).

Lerman, Robert, and Stephanie Schmidt. 1999. "*An Overview of Economic, Social, and Demographic Trends Affecting the US Labor Market*." Washington, DC: The Urban Institute.

Leung Louis. 2011. "Loneliness, Social Support, and Preference for Online Social Interaction: the Mediating Effects of Identity Experimentation Online Among Children and Adolescents." *Chinese Journal of Communication* 4 (4): 381–399.

Levey, Noam. 2014. "Number of Americans without Health Insurance Reaches New Low." *LA Times* April 7.

Levy, Daniel, and Natan Sznaider. 2006. "Sovereignty Transformed: A Sociology of Human Rights." *British Journal of Sociology* 57 (4): 657–676.

Lewin, Tamar. 2008. "Universities Rush to Set Up Outposts Abroad." *New York Times* February 10.

Li, Rebecca S. K. 2002. "Alternative Routes to State Breakdown: Toward an Integrated Model of Territorial Disintegration." *Sociological Theory* 20 (1): 1–20.

Lie, John. 1995. "From International Migration to Transnational Diaspora." *Contemporary Sociology* 24 (4): 303–306.

Liftin, Karen T. 2007. "Ozone Depletion." In Jan Aart Scholte and Roland Robertson, eds., *Encyclopedia of Globalization*. New York: MTM Publishing.

Lim, Hyun-Chin. 2012. "World Economic Forum." In George Ritzer, ed., *Wiley-Blackwell Encyclopedia of Globalization*. Oxford: Wiley-Blackwell.

Lin, Jan. 2012. "World Cities." In George Ritzer, ed., *Wiley-Blackwell Encyclopedia of Globalization*. Oxford: Wiley-Blackwell.

Lind, Amy. 2010. *Development, Sexual Rights and Global Governance*. New York: Routledge.

Linn, James, and Debra Rose Wilson. 2012. "Health." In George Ritzer, ed., *Wiley-Blackwell Encyclopedia of Globalization*. Oxford: Wiley-Blackwell.

Lipschutz, Ronnie D. 2007. "The Historical and Structural Origins of Global Civil Society." *Globalizations* 4 (2): 304–308.

Lipton, Eric, Nicola Clark, and Andrew Lehren. 2011. "Diplomats Help Push Sales of Jetliners on the Global Market." *New York Times* January 2.

Lipton, Eric, and Michael Moss. 2012. "Housing Agency's Flaws Revealed by Storm." *New York Times* December 9.

Lowenhaupt Tsing, Anna. 2005. *Friction: An Ethnography of Global Connection*. Princeton: Princeton University Press.

Lowrey, Annie. 2013. "IMF Concedes Major Missteps in Bailout of Greece." *New York Times* June 5.

Lyon, Sarah, and Mark Moberg, eds. 2010. *Fair Trade and Social Justice: Global Ethnographies*. New York: New York University Press.

Lyons, David. 2004. "Globalizing Surveillance: Comparative and Sociological Perspectives." *International Sociology* 12 (2): 135–149.

Mabee, Bryan. 2012. "War." In George Ritzer, ed., *Wiley-Blackwell Encyclopedia of Globalization*. Oxford: Wiley-Blackwell.

Macdonald, L., and Ruckert, A., eds. 2009. *Post-Neoliberalism in the Americas*. Basingstoke: Palgrave Macmillan.

MacFarquhar, Neil. 2007. "To Muslim Girls, Scouts Offer a Chance to Fit In." *New York Times* November 28.

Mackey, Robert, and Andrew Roth. 2013. "New Pussy Riot Video Asks Where Russia's Oil Wealth Goes." *New York Times* July 16.

Macpherson, Crawford B. 1962. *The Political Theory of Possessive Individualism*. Oxford: Clarendon Press.

Madan, T. N. 2007. "Hinduism." In Jan Aart Scholte and Roland Robertson, eds., *Encyclopedia of Globalization*. New York: MTM Publishing.

Maguire, Joseph, and David Stead. 1998. "Border Crossing: Soccer Labour Migration and the European Union." *International Review for the Sociology of Sport* 33: 59–73.

Mahr, Krista. 2009. "Top 10 Heros: 2. Neda Agha-Soltan." December 8. http://content.time.com/time/specials/packages/article/0,28804,1945379_1944701_1944705,00.html (last accessed August 17, 2014).

Makan, Ajay. 2013. "Gulf Oil Producers Benefit from Falling Iran Sales." *Financial Times* July 23.

Malkin, Elisabeth. 2007. "Thousands in Mexico City Protest Rising Food Prices." *New York Times* February 1.

Mallén, Patricia Rey. 2013. "Remittances Worldwide Increase in 2013, Except for Mexico; Is the US Crisis Hurting Mexican Economy?" *International Business Times* October 11.

Mann, Catherine L., and Katharine Pluck. 2007. "Trade." In Jan Aart Scholte and Roland Robertson, eds., *Encyclopedia of Globalization*. New York: MTM Publishing.

Mann, Michael. 2007. "Has Globalization Ended the Rise and the Rise of the Nation-State?" *Review of International Political Economy* 4 (3): 472–496.

Marcano, Arturo, and David Fidler. 2012. "Ballplayer: Pelotero – Major League Baseball, Human Rights, and the Globalization of Baseball." *Insights* 16 (26).

Marcuse, Herbert. 2006. *One-Dimensional Man: Studies in the Ideology of Advanced Industrial Society*. London: Routledge.

Marcuse, Peter, and Ronald van Kempen, eds. 2000. *Globalizing Cities: A New Spatial Order?* Oxford: Blackwell.

Markoff, John. 2007. "Imperialism." In Jan Aart Scholte and Roland Robertson, eds., *Encyclopedia of Globalization*. New York: MTM Publishing.

Marling, William. 2006. *How American is Globalization?* Baltimore: Johns Hopkins University Press.

Marranchi, Gabriele. 2004. "Multiculturalism, Islam, and the Clash of Civilizations Theory: Rethinking Islamophobia." *Culture and Religion* 5 (1): 105–117.

Martens, Kerstin. 2001. "Non-Governmental Organisations as Corporatist Mediator: An Analysis of NGOs in the UNESCO System." *Global Society* 15 (4): 388–404.

Martin, David. 2002. *Pentecostalism: The World Their Parish.* Oxford: Blackwell.

Martin, Dominique, Jean-Luc Metzger, and Philippe Pierre. 2006. "The Sociology of Globalization: Theoretical and Methodological Reflections." *International Sociology* 21: 499–521.

Martin, Gus. 2012. *Understanding Terrorism: Challenges, Perspectives, and Issues.* 4th edn. Thousand Oaks, CA: Sage.

Martínez, Airín. 2012. "Ideoscapes." In George Ritzer, ed., *Wiley-Blackwell Encyclopedia of Globalization.* Oxford: Wiley-Blackwell.

Marx Ferree, Myra, and Aili Mari Tripp. 2006. "Preface." In Myra Marx Ferree and Aili Mari Tripp, eds., *Global Feminism: Transnational Women's Activism, Organizing, and Human Rights.* New York: New York University Press.

Marx, Emanuel. 2008. "Hashish Smuggling by Bedouin in the South of Israel." In Dina Siegel and Hans Nelen, eds., *Organized Crime: Culture, Markets and Policies.* New York: Springer.

Marx, Karl, and Friedrich Engels. 1848/2000. "The Communist Manifesto." In David McLellan ed., *Karl Marx: Selected Writings.* 2nd edn. Oxford; New York: Oxford University Press, 2000.

Marx, Karl. 1867/1967. *Capital: A Critique of Political Economy*, Vol. 1. New York: International Publishers.

Mason, Charles. 2012. "Organization of the Petroleum Exporting Countries." In George Ritzer, ed., *Wiley-Blackwell Encyclopedia of Globalization.* Oxford: Wiley-Blackwell.

Masood, Salman, and Ihsanullah Tipu Mehsud. 2013. "Thousands in Pakistan Protest American Drone Strikes." *New York Times* November 23.

Mathews, Jessica. 1997. "Power Shift." *Foreign Affairs* 76 (1): 50–66.

Matthews, Lee. 2013. "Cryptolocker Malware Masterminds Make Around $30 Million in Ransom in 30 Days." *Geek.com* December 19. http://www.geek.com/news/cryptolocker-malware-master minds-make-around-30-million-in-ransom-in-100-days-1580168/ (last accessed August 17, 2014).

Matthews, Michael. 2012. "iPhone Smuggling into China?" *Forbes* March 5.

Maupain, Francis. 2007. "Labor Standards." In Jan Aart Scholte and Roland Robertson, eds., *Encyclopedia of Globalization.* New York: MTM Publishing.

May, Christopher. 2002. "Unacceptable Costs: The Consequences of Making Knowledge Property in a Global Society." *Global Society* 16: 123–144.

Mazzetti, Mark. 2010. "US Expands Role of Diplomats in Spying." *New York Times* November 28.

McAleese, Dermot. 2007. "Trade Protectionism." In Jan Aart Scholte and Roland Robertson, eds., *Encyclopedia of Globalization.* New York: MTM Publishing.

McAuliffe, Cameron. 2007. "A Home Far Away? Religious Identity and Transnational Relations in the Iranian Diaspora." *Global Networks* 7 (3): 307–327.

McCannell, Dean. 1989. *The Tourist: A New Theory of the Leisure Class.* 2nd edn. New York: Schocken.

McChesney, Robert. 1999. "The New Global Media." *The Nation* November 29.

McCreary, Edward A. 1962. *The Americanization of Europe: The Impact of Americans and American Business on the Uncommon Market.* Garden City, NY: Doubleday.

McCulloch, Jude, and Sharon Pickering, eds. 2012. *Borders and Crime: Pre-Crime, Mobility, and Serious Harm in an Age of Globalization.* New York: Palgrave Macmillan.

McDonald, Kevin. 2012. "Qaedaism." In George Ritzer, ed., *Wiley-Blackwell Encyclopedia of Globalization.* Oxford: Wiley-Blackwell.

McDonald, Mark. 2012. "Girl Guides Change Oath to Delete God and the Queen." *International Herald Tribune* July 8.

McGeehan, Patrick. 2007. "Chain Stores Make a Push Beyond Manhattan." *New York Times* January 14.

McKinley, Jr, James C. 2007a. "Cost of Corn Soars, Mexico to Set Price Limits." *New York Times* January 19.

McKinley, Jr, James C. 2007b. "Despite Crackdown, Migrants Stream into South Mexico." *New York Times* January 28.

McKinley, Jr, James C. 2008. "Mexican Farmers Protest End of Corn-Import Taxes." *New York Times* February 1.

McLuhan, Marshall, and Quentin Fiore. 2005. *The Medium is the Massage*. Corte Madera, CA: Gingko Press.

McMichael, Philip. 2007a. "Globalization and the Agrarian World." In George Ritzer, ed., *Blackwell Companion to Globalization*. Oxford: Blackwell.

McMichael, Philip. 2007b. "Alternative Trade Schemes." In Jan Aart Scholte and Roland Robertson, eds., *Encyclopedia of Globalization*. New York: MTM Publishing.

McMichael, Philip. 2008. *Development and Social Change: A Global Perspective*. 4th edn. Thousand Oaks, CA: Pine Forge Press.

McNeil, Jr, Donald G. 2008. "W.H.O. Official Complains of Gates Foundation Dominance in Malaria Research." *New York Times* February 16.

McNeil, Jr, Donald G. 2010. "US Reaction to Swing Flu: Apt and Lucky." *New York Times* January 1.

McNeil, Jr, Donald G. 2011. "Europe: Increase in Tropical Diseases is Aided by Migration and Weak Economies." *New York Times* August 1.

McNeil, Jr, Donald G. 2014. "Cases of New Deadly Bird Flu Surge in China, Experts Say." *New York Times* February 4.

Mele, Vincenzo. 2012. "Technoscapes." In George Ritzer, ed., *Wiley-Blackwell Encyclopedia of Globalization*. Oxford: Wiley-Blackwell.

Mendelsohn, Barak. 2011. "Al-Qaeda's Franchising Strategy." *Survival: Global Politics and Strategy* 53 (3): 29–50.

Meunier, Sophie. 2013. "The Dog That Did Not Bark: Anti-Americanism and the 2008 Financial Crisis in Europe." *Review of International Political Economy* 20 (1): 1–25.

Meyer, Birgit, and Peter Geschiere, eds. 2003. *Globalization and Identity: Dialectics of Flow and Closure*. Oxford: Blackwell.

Meyer, John W. 1980. "The World Polity and the Authority of the Nation-State." In A. J. Bergesen, ed., *Studies of the Modern World-System*. New York: Academic Press.

Meyer, John W., John Boli, George M. Thomas, and Francisco O. Ramirez. 1997. "World Society and the Nation-State." *American Journal of Sociology* 103: 144–181.

Meyfroidt, Patrick. 2012. "Deforestation." In George Ritzer, ed., *Wiley-Blackwell Encyclopedia of Globalization*. Oxford: Wiley-Blackwell.

Milanovic, Branko. 2005. *Worlds Apart: Measuring International and Global Inequality*. Princeton, NJ: Princeton University Press.

Milanovic, Branko. 2012. "Global Inequality Recalculated and Updated: The Effect of New PPP Estimates on Global Inequality and 2005 Estimates." *The Journal of Economic Inequality* 10 (1): 1–18.

Milanovic, Branko. 2013. "Global Income Inequality in Numbers: In History and Now." *Global Policy* 4 (2): 198–208.

Miller, Daniel. 2005. "Coca-Cola: A Black Sweet Drink from Trinidad." In James L. Watson and Melissa L. Caldwell, eds., *The Cultural Politics of Food and Eating: A Reader*. Oxford: Blackwell.

Miller, Toby, Nitin Govil, John McMurria, Ting Wang, and Richard Maxwell. 2005. *Global Hollywood 2*. London: British Film Institute.

Misra, Kavita. 2008. "Politico-moral Transactions in Indian AIDS Service: Confidentiality, Rights, and New Modalities of Governance." In Jonathan Xavier Inda and Renato Rosaldo, eds., *The Anthropology of Globalization: A Reader*. 2nd edn. Oxford: Blackwell.

Mitchell, Douglas, and Selin Yildiz Nielsen. 2012. "Internationalization and Globalization in Higher Education." In Hector Cuadra-Montiel, ed., *Globalization–Education and Management Agendas*. New York: InTech.

Mittelman, James H. 2002. "Making Globalization Work for the Have Nots." *International Journal on World Peace* 19 (2): 3–25.

Mittelman, James H. 2004. "Globalization Debates: Bringing in Microencounters." *Globalizations* 1 (1): 24–37.

Moberg, Mark. 2014. "Certification and Neoliberal Governance: Moral Economies of Fair Trade in the Eastern Caribbean." *American Anthropologist* 116 (1): 8–22.

Moghadam, Valentine. 1999. "Gender and Globalization: Female Labor and Women's Mobilization." *Journal of World-Systems Research* 5 (2): 367–388.

Moghadam, Valentine. 2007. "Gender and the Global Economy." In J. Timmons Roberts and Amy Bellone Hite, eds., *The Globalization and Development Reader*. Oxford: Blackwell.

Moghadam, Valentine. 2013. *Globalization and Social Movements: Islamism, Feminism, and the Global Justice Movement*. 2nd edn. Lanham, MD: Rowman & Littlefield.

Mohammadi, Ali. 2003. *Iran Encountering Globalization: Problems and Prospects*. New York: Routledge Curzon.

Mooallem, Jon. 2008. "The Afterlife of Cellphones." *New York Times Magazine* January 13.

Moores, Shaun. 1995. "TV Discourse and 'Time-Space Distanciation': On Mediated Interaction Modern Society." *Time and Society* 4 (3): 329–344.

Moran, Theodore. 2012. "Foreign Direct Investment." In George Ritzer, ed., *Wiley-Blackwell Encyclopedia of Globalization*. Oxford: Wiley-Blackwell.

Morawska, Eva. 2007. "Transnationalism." In Mary C. Waters and Reed Ueda, eds., *The New Americans: A Guide to Immigration Since 1965*. Cambridge, MA: Harvard University Press.

Morgan, Iwan. 2007. "The Washington Consensus and Anti-Americanism." In Brendon O'Connor, ed., *Anti-Americanism: History, Causes, and Themes, Vol. 1: Causes and Sources*. Oxford: Greenwood World Publishing.

Morin, Richard. 2008. "Do Blacks and Hispanics Get Along?" Washington, DC: Pew Research Center.

Morley, David, and Kevin Robins. 2013. *Spaces of Identity: Global Media, Electronic Landscapes and Cultural Boundaries*. New York: Routledge.

Morrisson, Christian, and Fabrice Murtin. 2013. "The Kuznets Curve of Human Capital Inequality: 1870–2010." *Journal of Economic Inequality* 11 (3): 283–301.

Morse, David. 2002. "Striking the Golden Arches: French Farmers Protest McD's Globalization." In George Ritzer, ed., *McDonaldization: The Reader*. Thousand Oaks, CA: Pine Forge Press.

Moseley, William G. 2008. "Fair Trade Wine: South Africa's Post-Apartheid Vineyards and the Global Economy." *Globalizations* 5 (2): 291–304.

Moses, Jonathon W. 2006. *International Migration: Globalization's Last Frontier*. London: Zed Books.

Motel, Seth, and Eileen Patten. 2013. "Statistical Portrait of Hispanics in the United States, 2011." Washington, DC: Pew Research Center.

Mothana, Ibrahim. 2012. "How Drones Help Al Qaeda." *New York Times* June 13.

Munck, Ronaldo. 2002a. "Globalization and Democracy: A New Great Transformation." *Annals* 581: 10–21.

Munck, Ronaldo. 2002b. *Globalisation and Labour: The New "Great Transformation."* London: Zed Books.

Munck, Ronaldo, ed. 2004. *Labour and Globalisation: Results and Prospects*. Liverpool: Liverpool University Press.

Munck, Ronaldo. 2006. "Globalization and Contestation: A Polanyian Problematic." *Globalizations* 3 (2): 175–186.

Munck, Ronaldo, and Peter Waterman. 1999. *Labour Worldwide in the Era of Globalization: Alternative Union Models in the New World Order*. New York: St. Martin's Press.

Mungiu-Pippidi, Alina, and Igor Munteanu. 2009. "Moldova's 'Twitter Revolution'." *Journal of Democracy* 20 (3): 136–142.

Munif, Yasser. 2012. "Orientalism." In George Ritzer, ed., *Wiley-Blackwell Encyclopedia of Globalization*. Oxford: Wiley-Blackwell.

Munton, Don, and Ken Wilkening. 2007. "Acid Rain." In Jan Aart Scholte and Roland Robertson, eds., *Encyclopedia of Globalization*. New York: MTM Publishing.

Murray, Graham. 2006. "France: The Riots and the Republic." *Race and Class* 47: 26–45.

Murray, Rachel. 2004. *Human Rights in Africa: From the OAU to the African Union*. Cambridge: Cambridge University Press.

Mustafa, Fahad. 2013. "Cricket and Globalization: Global Processes and the Imperial Game." *Journal of Global History* 8 (2): 318–341.

Mydans, Seth. 2007. "A Growing Source of Fear for Migrants in Malaysia." *New York Times* December 10.

Myers, Gordon. 2004. *Banana Wars: The Price of Free Trade*. London: Zed Books.

Myers, Norman. 2005. "Environmental Refugees: An Emergent Security Issue." 13th Economic Forum, Prague, May 2005.

Nagan, Winston, and Aitza Haddad. 2012. "War on Terror, International Law on." In George Ritzer, ed., *Wiley-Blackwell Encyclopedia of Globalization*. Oxford: Wiley-Blackwell.

Naim, Moisés. 2002. "Missing Links: Anti-Americanisms." *Foreign Policy* 128.

Najam, Adil. 2007. "Earth Summit." In Jan Aart Scholte and Roland Robertson, eds., *Encyclopedia of Globalization*. New York: MTM Publishing.

Nancy, Jean-Luc. 2007. *The Creation of the World or Globalization*. Albany: State University Press of New York.

Naples, Nancy A., and Manisha Desai, eds. 2002a. *Women's Activism and Globalization: Linking Local Struggles and Transnational Politics*. New York: Routledge.

Naples, Nancy A., and Manisha Desai. 2002b. "Women's Local and Transnational Responses: An Introduction to the Volume." In Nancy A. Naples and Manisha Desai, eds., *Women's Activism and Globalization: Linking Local Struggles and Transnational Politics*. New York: Routledge.

Napoli, Philip, and Jonathan Obar. 2013. *Mobile Leapfrogging and Digital Divide Policy*. Washington, DC: New America Foundation.

Navarro, Mireya. 2006a. "For Divided Family, Border is Sorrowful Barrier." *New York Times* December 21.

Navarro, Mireya. 2006b. "Traditional Round Trip for Workers is Becoming a One-Way Migration North." *New York Times* December 21.

Nederveen Pieterse, Jan. 2004. "Neoliberal Empire." *Theory, Culture & Society* 21: 119–140.

Nederveen Pieterse, Jan. 2009. *Globalization and Culture: Global Mélange*. 2nd edn. Lanham, MD: Romwan & Littlefield.

Nederveen Pieterse, Jan. 2012. "Periodizing Globalization: Histories of Globalization." *New Global Studies* 6 (2): 1–25.

Nell, Philip. 2005. "Review Article: Global Inequality Revisited." *Global Society* 19 (3): 317–327.

Nelson, Barbara. 2013. "Cinematic Memory and the Americanization of the Holocaust." *Romanian Journal of English Studies* 9 (1): 138–146.

Nesadurai, Helen E. S. 2003. *Globalisation, Domestic Policies and Regionalism: ASEAN Free Trade Area*. London: Routledge.

Nesadurai, Helen E. S. 2007. "Association of Southeast Asian Nations." In Jan Aart Scholte and Roland Robertson, eds., *Encyclopedia of Globalization*. New York: MTM Publishing.

Nester, William. 2010. *Globalization, War, and Peace in the Twenty-First Century*. New York: Palgrave Macmillan.

Netting, Nancy. 2010. "Marital Ideoscapes in 21st-Century India: Creative Combinations of Love and Responsibility." *Journal of Family Issues* 31 (6): 707–726.

New York Times. 2008. March 7. "Britain to Issue Identity Cards for Foreigners in November."

New York Times. 2010. December 12. "When Fish and Farmland Are Scarce: Yemen and the Horn of Africa."

New York Times. 2013. May 7. "China and Cyberwar."

Nicholls, Alex, and Charlotte Opal. 2005. *Fair Trade: Market-Driven Ethical Consumption*. London: Sage.

Niezen, Ronald. 2004. *A World beyond Difference: Cultural Identity in the Age of Globalization.* Oxford: Blackwell.

Nguyen, Lisa, Steven Ropers, Esther Nderitu, Anneke Zuyderduin, Sam Luboga, and May Hagopian. 2008. "Intent to Migrate Among Nursing Students in Uganda: Measures of the Brain Drain in the Next Generation of Health Professionals." *Human Resources for Health* 6 (5).

Nkrumah, Kwame. 1965. *Neo-Colonialism: The Last Stage of Imperialism.* Atlantic Islands, NJ: Humanities Press International.

Noel, Donald L. 1968. "A Theory of the Origin of Ethnic Stratification." *Social Problems* 16 (2): 157–172.

Norberg, Johan. 2003. *In Defense of Global Capitalism.* Washington, DC: Cato Institute.

Nordland, Rod. 2013. "Afghan Leader Lashes Out at US Allies After NATO Drone Strike." *New York Times* November 28.

Nordstrom, Carolyn. 2004. *Shadows of War: Violence, Power, and International Profiteering in the Twenty-First Century.* Berkeley, CA: University of California Press.

Nordstrom, Carolyn. 2007. *Global Outlaws: Crime, Money, and Power in the Contemporary World.* Berkeley, CA: University of California Press.

Nordstrom, Carolyn. 2010. "Women, Economy, War." *International Review of the Red Cross* 92 (877): 161–176.

Northedge, F. S. 1989. *The League of Nations: Its Life and Times.* Leicester, UK: Leicester University Press.

Nossiter, Adam. 2014. "Nigeria Tries to 'Sanitize' Itself of Gays." *New York Times* February 8.

Nye, Joseph S. 2005. *Soft Power: The Means to Success in World Politics.* New York: Public Affairs.

O'Brien, Robert. 2007. "Labor Movements." In Jan Aart Scholte and Roland Robertson, eds., *Encyclopedia of Globalization.* New York: MTM Publishing.

O'Connor, Brendon. 2007a. "Introduction: Causes and Sources of Anti-Americanism." In Brendon O'Connor, ed., *Anti-Americanism: History, Causes, and Themes, Vol. 1: Causes and Sources.* Oxford: Greenwood World Publishing.

O'Connor, Brendon. 2007b. "What is Anti-Americanism?" In Brendon O'Connor, ed., *Anti-Americanism: History, Causes, and Themes, Vol. 1: Causes and Sources.* Oxford: Greenwood World Publishing.

O'Connor, Brendon. 2012. "Anti-Americanism." In George Ritzer, ed., *Wiley-Blackwell Encyclopedia of Globalization.* Oxford: Wiley-Blackwell.

O'Rourke, Kevin H. 2007. "Economic Globalization." In Jan Aart Scholte and Roland Robertson, eds., *Encyclopedia of Globalization.* New York: MTM Publishing.

Oberschall, Tony. 2012. "Ethnic Cleansing." In George Ritzer, ed., *Wiley-Blackwell Encyclopedia of Globalization.* Oxford: Wiley-Blackwell.

Ohmae, Kenichi. 1996. *The End of the Nation-State: The Rise of Regional Economies.* New York: Free Press.

Oiarzabal, Pedro, and Ulf-Dietrich Reips. 2012. "Migration and Diaspora in the Age of Information and Communication Technologies." *Journal of Ethnic and Migration Studies* 38 (9): 1333–1338.

Ong, Aihwa. 1991. "The Gender and Politics of Postmodernity." *Annual Review of Anthropology* 20: 279–309.

Ong, Aihwa. 2003. "Cyberpublics and Diaspora Politics among Transnational Chinese." *Interventions* 5 (1): 82–100.

Ong, Aihwa. 2006a. "Mutations in Citizenship." *Theory, Culture & Society* 23: 499–505.

Ong, Aihwa. 2006b. *Neoliberalism as Exception: Mutations in Citizenship and Sovereignty.* Durham, NC: Duke University Press.

Ong, Paul. 2007. "Bovine Spongiform Encephalopathy." In Jan Aart Scholte and Roland Robertson, eds., *Encyclopedia of Globalization.* New York: MTM Publishing.

Onishi, Norimitsu. 2008. "In Japan, Buddhism, Long the Religion of Funerals, May Itself Be Dying Out." *New York Times* July 14.

Open Society Institute EU Monitoring and Advocacy Program. 2007. *Muslims in the EU: France*. Budapest: Open Society Institute.

Oreskes, Naomi. 2004. "Beyond the Ivory Tower: The Scientific Consensus on Climate Change." *Science* 306 (5702): 1686.

Orr, Martin. 2012. "Great Recession." In George Ritzer, ed., *Wiley-Blackwell Encyclopedia of Globalization*. Oxford: Wiley-Blackwell.

Ortiz, Renato. 2006. "Mundialization/Globalization." *Theory, Culture & Society* 23: 401–403.

Ostrower, Gary. 2012. "League of Nations." In George Ritzer, ed., *Wiley-Blackwell Encyclopedia of Globalization*. Oxford: Wiley-Blackwell.

Otero, Gerardo. 2011. "Neoliberal Globalization, NAFTA, and Migration: Mexico's Loss of Food and Labor Sovereignty." *Journal of Poverty* 15 (4): 384–402.

Otterman, Michael. 2007. *American Torture: From the Cold War to Abu Ghraib and Beyond*. Ann Arbor, MI: Pluto Press.

Ougaard, Morton. 2007. "Organization for Economic Co-operation and Development." In Jan Aart Scholte and Roland Robertson, eds., *Encyclopedia of Globalization*. New York: MTM Publishing.

Paletta, Damian, Keith Johnson, and Sudeep Reddy. 2012. "Obama Blocks Chinese Firms from Windfarm Projects." *Wall Street Journal* September 28.

Panitch, Leo, Sam Gindin, and James Parisot. 2013. "American Empire, Global Crisis, and the Rise of China: An Interview with Leo Panitch and Sam Gindin." *International Critical Thought* 3 (2): 139–245.

Park, Jacob, Ken Conca, and Matthias Finger, eds. 2008. *The Crisis of Global Environmental Governance: Towards a New Political Economy of Sustainability*. New York: Routledge.

Parker, Richard, Jonathan Garcia, and Miguel Muñoz-Laboy. 2014. "Sexual Social Movements and Communities." In Deborah Tolman, Lisa Diamond, José Bauermeister, William George, James Pfaus, and Monique Ward, eds., *APA Handbook of Sexuality and Psychology, Vol. 2: Contextual Approaches*. Washington, DC: American Psychological Association.

Parreñas, Rhacel S. 2001. *Servants of Globalization: Women, Migration, and Domestic Work*. Stanford, CA: Stanford University Press.

Pasko, Lisa. 2012. "Drug Trafficking." In George Ritzer, ed., *Wiley-Blackwell Encyclopedia of Globalization*. Oxford: Wiley-Blackwell.

Passel, Jeffrey, and D'Vera Cohn. 2012. "Unauthorized Immigrants: 11.1 Million in 2011." Washington, DC: Pew Research Center. http://www.pewhispanic.org/2012/12/06/unauthorized-immigrants-11-1-million-in-2011/ (last accessed August 17, 2014).

Paul, Cuckoo. 2013. "Ratan Tata Flies AirAsia's Tony Fernandes to Meet Aviation Minister Ajit Singh." *Forbes India* July 2.

Pearce, Robert. 2007. "Transnational Corporation." In Jan Aart Scholte and Roland Robertson, eds., *Encyclopedia of Globalization*. New York: MTM Publishing.

Pearson, Richard. 2012. "Protecting Many Species to Help Our Own." *New York Times* June 1.

Pearson, Ruth. 2000. "Moving the Goalposts: Gender and Globalization in the Twenty-First Century." *Gender and Development* 8 (1): 10–18.

Peck, Jamie. 2010. *Constructions of Neoliberal Reason*. New York: Oxford University Press.

Peck, Jamie, Nick Theodore, and Neil Brenner. 2009. "Postneoliberalism and its Malcontents." *Antipode* 41 (S1): 94–116.

Peet, Richard. 2003. *Unholy Trinity: The IMF, World Bank, and the World Trade Organization*. New York: Zed Books.

Pelikan, Jaroslav. 1971. *The Christian Tradition*, Vol. 1: *The Emergence of the Catholic Tradition (100–600)*. Chicago: University of Chicago Press.

Pelikan, Jaroslav. 1974. *The Christian Tradition*, Vol. 2: *The Spirit of Eastern Christendom (600–1700)*. Chicago: University of Chicago Press.

Penney, Joel. 2011. "KEVIN07: Cool Politics, Consumer Citizenship, and the Specter of 'Americanization' in Australia." *Communication, Culture, and Critique* 4 (10): 78–96.

Perlez, Jane, David Sanger, and Eric Schmitt. 2010. "Nuclear Fuel Memos Expose Wary Dance with Pakistan." *New York Times* November 30.

Persaud, Randolph B. 2007. "North–South Relations." In Jan Aart Scholte and Roland Robertson, eds., *Encyclopedia of Globalization*. New York: MTM Publishing.

Peters, Rudolph. 1979. *Islam and Colonialism: The Doctrine of Jihad in Modern History*. Hague: Mouton.

Peters, Tom, and Robert Waterman. 1988. *In Search of Excellence*. New York: Harper and Row.

Pew Forum. 2012. "The Global Religious Landscape: A Report on the Size and Distribution of the World's Major Religious Groups as of 2010 – Hindus." Washington, DC: Pew Research Center. December 18.

Pew Hispanic Center/Kaiser Family Foundation. 2002. *2002 National Survey of Latinos*. Washington, DC: Pew Hispanic Center/Menlo Park, CA: Kaiser Family Foundation. http://pewhispanic.org/files/reports/15.pdf (last accessed August 17, 2014).

Pew Research Center. n.d. "Global Indicators Database: Opinion of the United States." http://www.pewglobal.org/database/indicator/1/survey/all/ (last accessed August 17, 2014).

Pew Research Center. 2012. *The Rise of Asian Americans*. Washington, DC: Pew Research Center.

Pfanner, Eric. 2012. "Drafters of Communications Treaty are Split on Issue of Internet Governance." *New York Times* December 6.

Phillips, Nicola. 2007. "Organization of American States." In Jan Aart Scholte and Roland Robertson, eds., *Encyclopedia of Globalization*. New York: MTM Publishing.

Pickard, Victor. 2012. "Indymedia." In George Ritzer, ed., *Wiley-Blackwell Encyclopedia of Globalization*. Oxford: Wiley-Blackwell.

Pickett, Kate, and Richard Wilkinson. 2011. *The Spirit Level: Why Greater Equality Makes Societies Stronger*. New York: Bloomsbury Press.

Pieke, Frank N., Nicholas Van Hear, and Anna Lindley. 2007. "Beyond Control? The Mechanics and Dynamics of 'Informal' Remittances between Europe and Africa." *Global Networks* 7 (3): 348–366.

Pirages, Dennis. 2007. "Oil Industry." In Jan Aart Scholte and Roland Robertson, eds., *Encyclopedia of Globalization*. New York: MTM Publishing.

Platt, Kevin Holden. 2013. "China's Venetian Quandary: Chinese Artists." *New York Times* June 11.

Plehwe, Dieter. 2007. "A Global Knowledge Bank? The World Bank and Bottom-Up Efforts to Reinforce Neoliberal Development Perspectives in the Post-Washington Consensus Era." *Globalizations* 4 (4): 514–528.

Plehwe, Dieter. 2010. "The Making of a Comprehensive Transnational Discourse Community." In Marie-Laure Djelic and Sigrid Quack, eds., *Transnational Community: Shaping Global Economic Governance*. New York: Cambridge University Press.

Pogge, Thomas W., ed. 2001. *Global Justice*. Oxford: Blackwell.

Polanyi, Karl. 1944. *The Great Transformation: The Political and Economic Origins of Our Time*. Boston: Beacon Press.

Polgreen, Lydia. 2012. "Angola Fund Set to Invest Oil Revenue in Businesses." *New York Times* October 17.

Polgreen, Lydia. 2013. "Mugabe Wins Again in Zimbabwe, Leaving Rival Greatly Weakened." *New York Times* August 3.

Polillo, Simone, and Mauro F. Guillen. 2005. "Globalization Pressures and the State: The Worldwide Spread of Central Bank Independence." *American Journal of Sociology* 110 (6): 1764–1802.

Popkin, B., and M. Slining. 2013. "New Dynamics in Global Obesity Facing Low and Middle Income Countries." *Obesity Review* 14 (S2): 11–20.

Portes, Alejandro. 2001a. "Introduction: The Debates and Significance of Immigrant Transnationalism." *Global Networks* 1 (3).

Portes, Alejandro, ed. 2001b. "New Research and Theory on Immigrant Transnationalism." *Global Networks* 1 (3).

Pötzsch, Holger. Forthcoming. "The Emergence of iWar: Changing Practices and Perceptions of Military Engagement in a Digital Era." *New Media and Society*.

Powell, Jason. 2012a. "Financescapes." In George Ritzer, ed., *Wiley-Blackwell Encyclopedia of Globalization*. Oxford: Wiley-Blackwell.

Powell, Jason. 2012b. "Internet." In George Ritzer, ed., *Wiley-Blackwell Encyclopedia of Globalization*. Oxford: Wiley-Blackwell.

Preston, Julia. 2006. "Low-Wage Workers from Mexico Dominate Latest Great Wave of Immigrants." *New York Times* December 19.

Preston, Julia. 2011. "Some Cheer Border Fence as Others Ponder the Cost." *New York Times* October 19.

Preston, Julia. 2013. "Number of Illegal Immigrants in US May be on Rise Again, Estimates Say." *New York Times* September 23.

Price, Monroe. 2012. "Iran and the Soft War." *International Journal of Communication* 6: 19: 2397–2415.

Pun, Nagi. 1995. "Theoretical Discussions on the Impact of Industrial Restructuring in Asia." In *Silk and Steel: Asia Women Workers Confront Challenges of Industrial Restructuring*. Hong Kong: CAW.

Pyle, Jean. 2006. "Globalization, Transnational Migration, and Gendered Care Work: Introduction." *Globalizations* 3 (3): 283–295.

Pyle, Jean L., and Kathryn B. Ward. 2003. "Recasting Our Understanding of Gender and Work during Global Restructuring." *International Sociology* 18 (3): 461–489.

Qutub, Syed Ayub. 2005. "Karachi – A Case of Asymmetric Inclusion in the Current Globalization?" In Harry W. Richardson and Chang-Hee C. Bae, *Globalization and Urban Development*. Berlin: Springer.

Ram, Uri. 2008. *The Globalization of Israel*. New York: Routledge.

Ram, Uri. 2009. "Tensions in the 'Jewish Democracy': The Constitutional Challenge of the Palestinian Citizens in Israel." *Constellations* 16 (3): 523–536.

Ramdani, Nabila. 2013a. "France Must Follow the Example Shown by a More Racially Tolerant Britain." *The Guardian* November 9.

Ramdani, Nabila. 2013b. "Immigrants are Scapegoats." *New York Times* December 1.

Ramirez, Francisco. 2012. "Education." In George Ritzer, ed., *Wiley-Blackwell Encyclopedia of Globalization*. Oxford: Wiley-Blackwell.

Ramirez, Francisco O., Yasemin Soysal, and Suzanne Shanahan. 1997. "The Changing Logic of Political Citizenship: Cross-National Acquisition of Women's Suffrage Rights, 1890–1990." *American Sociological Review* 62: 735–745.

Rampell, Catherine. 2013. "Immigration and Entrepreneurship." *New York Times* July 1.

Randall, Tom. 2013. "Highest and Cheapest Gas Prices by Country." *Bloomberg News* February 13.

Rangnekar, Dwijen. 2007. "Trade-Related Intellectual Property Rights." In Jan Aart Scholte and Roland Robertson, eds., *Encyclopedia of Globalization*. New York: MTM Publishing.

Rao, Sujata. 2013. "Sovereign Wealth Funds to Hit Record $5.6 trln by Year End-Study." *Reuters* March 12.

Rapoza, Kenneth. 2013. "The Dying Business of Email Spam." *Forbes* January 21.

Ratha, Dilip, and Sanket Mohapatra. 2012. "Remittances and Development." In George Ritzer, ed., *Wiley-Blackwell Encyclopedia of Globalization*. Oxford: Wiley-Blackwell.

RAXEN National Focal Point for Germany: European Forum for Migration Studies. 2005. *National Analytical Study on Racist Violence and Crime: Germany*. European Monitoring Center on Racism and Xenophobia. http://infoportal.fra.europa.eu/InfoPortal/publicationsFrontEndAccess.do?id=8779 (last accessed August 17, 2014).

RAXEN National Focal Point for United Kingdom. 2005. *National Analytical Study on Racist Violence and Crime: United Kingdom*. European Monitoring Center on Racism and Xenophobia. http://info portal.fra.europa.eu/InfoPortal/publicationsFrontEndAccess.do?id=8790 (last accessed August 17, 2014).

Ray, Larry. 2012. "Communism." In George Ritzer, ed., *Wiley-Blackwell Encyclopedia of Globalization*. Oxford: Wiley-Blackwell.

Ray, Manashi. 2012. "Brain Drain." In George Ritzer, ed., *Wiley-Blackwell Encyclopedia of Globalization*. Oxford: Wiley-Blackwell.

Raynolds, Laura T., Douglas L. Murray, and John Wilkinson, eds. 2007. *Fair Trade: The Challenges of Transforming Globalization*. New York: Routledge.

Reay, Michael. 2008. "Economics." In George Ritzer, ed., *The Blackwell Encyclopedia of Sociology Online*. Oxford: Blackwell.

Redclift, Michael, and Graham Woodgate. 2013. "Sustainable Development and Nature: The Social and the Material." *Sustainable Development* 21 (2): 92–100.

Reed, Stanley. 2013. "After Failed Attempt in April, Europe Approves Emission Trading System." *New York Times* July 3.

Rehman, Javaid. 2007. "Terrorism." In Jan Aart Scholte and Roland Robertson, eds., *Encyclopedia of Globalization*. New York: MTM Publishing.

Reifer, Tom. 2012. "World Systems Analysis." In George Ritzer, ed., *Wiley-Blackwell Encyclopedia of Globalization*. Oxford: Wiley-Blackwell.

Reuters. 2012. "Japanese Engineers Find New Life in China." *New York Times* April 17.

Reuveny, Rafael, and William R. Thompson. 2001. "Explaining Protectionism: 17 Perspectives and One Common Denominator." *Global Society* 15 (3): 229–249.

Rhomberg, Markus. 2012a. "Media Convergence." In George Ritzer, ed., *Wiley-Blackwell Encyclopedia of Globalization*. Oxford: Wiley-Blackwell.

Rhomberg, Markus. 2012b. "Kyoto Protocol." In George Ritzer, ed., *Wiley-Blackwell Encyclopedia of Globalization*. Oxford: Wiley-Blackwell.

Ricardo, David. 1817/1971. *On the Principles of Political Economy and Taxation*. Harmondsworth, UK: Penguin.

Richer, Zach. 2012. "Feminization of Labor." In George Ritzer, ed., *Wiley-Blackwell Encyclopedia of Globalization*. Oxford: Wiley-Blackwell.

Richmond, Anthony H. 2007. "Asylum Seekers." In Jan Aart Scholte and Roland Robertson, eds., *Encyclopedia of Globalization*. New York: MTM Publishing.

Riera-Crichton, Daniel. 2012. "Euro Crisis." In George Ritzer, ed., *Wiley-Blackwell Encyclopedia of Sociology*. Oxford: Wiley-Blackwell.

Rimmer, Matthew. 2012. "The Doomsday Vault: Seed Banks, Food Security and Climate Change." In Matthew Rimmer and Alison McLennan, eds., *Intellectual Property and Emerging Technologies: The New Biology*. Northampton, MA: Edward Elgar.

Rinaldo, Lindsay, and Kenneth Ferraro. 2012. "Inequality, Health." In George Ritzer, ed., *Wiley-Blackwell Encyclopedia of Globalization*. Oxford: Wiley-Blackwell.

Risen, James. 2012. "A Military and Intelligence Clash Over Spy Satellites." *New York Times* April 19.

Ritzer, George. 1972. *Working: Conflict and Change*. New York: Appleton-Century-Crofts.

Ritzer, George. 1975. "Professionalization, Bureaucratization, and Rationalization: The Views of Max Weber." *Social Forces* (June): 627–634.

Ritzer, George. 1981. *Toward an Integrated Sociological Paradigm: The Search for an Exemplar and an Image of the Subject Matter*. Boston: Allyn and Bacon.

Ritzer, George. 1991. *Metatheorizing in Sociology*. Lexington, MA: Lexington Books.

Ritzer, George. 1995. *Expressing America: A Critique of the Global Credit Card Society*. Thousand Oaks, CA: Pine Forge Press.

Ritzer, George. 1997a. *Postmodern Social Theory*. New York: McGraw-Hill.

Ritzer, George. 1997b. *The McDonaldization Thesis*. London: Sage.

Ritzer, George. 2001. "Hyperrationality: An Extension of Weberian and Neo-Weberian Theory." In George Ritzer, *Explorations in Social Theory*. London: Sage.

Ritzer, George, ed. 2006. *McDonaldization: The Reader*. 2nd edn. Thousand Oaks, CA: Pine Forge Press.

Ritzer, George. 2007. *The Globalization of Nothing*. 2nd edn. Thousand Oaks, CA: Pine Forge Press.

Ritzer, George. 2008a. *Classical Sociological Theory*. 5th edn. New York: McGraw-Hill.

Ritzer, George. 2008b. *Modern Sociological Theory*. 7th edn. New York: McGraw-Hill.

Ritzer, George. 2008c. *Sociological Theory*. 7th edn. New York: McGraw-Hill.

Ritzer, George. 2009. *Enchanting a Disenchanted World*. 3rd edn. Thousand Oaks, CA: Pine Forge Press.

Ritzer, George. 2012. *The McDonaldization of Society*. 20th anniversary edn. Thousand Oaks, CA: Pine Forge Press.

Ritzer, George. 2014. "Prosumption: Evolution, Revolution, or Eternal Return of the Same?" *Journal of Consumer Culture* 14 (1): 3–24.

Ritzer, George, and Zeynep Atalay, eds. 2010. *Readings in Globalization: Key Concepts and Major Debates*. Oxford: Blackwell.

Ritzer, George, Paul Dean, and Nathan Jurgenson. 2012. "The Coming of Age of the Prosumer." *American Behavioral Scientist* 56 (4): 379–398.

Ritzer, George, and Nathan Jurgenson. 2010. "Production, Consumption, Prosumption: The Nature of Capitalism in the Age of the Digital 'Prosumer.'" *Journal of Consumer Culture* 10 (1): 13–36.

Ritzer, George, and Craig Lair. 2007. "Outsourcing: Globalization and Beyond." In George Ritzer, ed., *Blackwell Companion to Globalization*. Oxford: Blackwell.

Ritzer, George, and Allan Liska. 1997. "McDisneyization and Post-Tourism: Complementary Perspectives on Contemporary Tourism." In Chris Rojek and John Urry, eds., *Touring Cultures: Transformations in Travel and Theory*. London: Routledge.

Ritzer, George, Wendy Weidenhoft, and Douglas Goodman. 2001. "Theories of Consumption." In George Ritzer and Barry Smart, eds., *Handbook of Social Theory*. London: Sage.

Rivoli, Pietra. 2009. *The Travels of a T-Shirt in the Global Economy: An Economist Examines the Markets, Power, and Politics of World Trade*. 2nd edn. Hoboken, NJ: John Wiley & Sons, Inc.

Rizvi, Fazal. 2012. "Bollywood." In George Ritzer, ed., *Wiley-Blackwell Encyclopedia of Globalization*. Oxford: Wiley-Blackwell.

Roache, Shaun. 2012. "China's Impact on World Commodity Markets." International Monetary Fund Working Paper WP/12/115.

Robbins, Jim. 2012. "The Ecology of Disease." *New York Times* July 14.

Roberts, Bryan, and Yu Chen. 2013. "Drugs, Violence, and the State." *Annual Review of Sociology* 39: 105–125.

Robertson, Roland. 1990. "Mapping the Global Condition: Globalization as the Central Concept." In Mike Featherstone, ed., *Global Culture: Nationalism, Globalization and Modernity*. London: Sage.

Robertson, Roland. 1992. *Globalization: Social Theory and Global Culture*. London: Sage.

Robertson, Roland. 2001. "Globalization Theory 2000 Plus: Major Problematics." In George Ritzer and Barry Smart, eds., *Handbook of Social Theory*. London: Sage.

Robertson, Roland. 2003. "Afterword. Rethinking Americanization." In Ulrich Beck, Natan Sznaider, and Rainer Winter, eds., *Global America? The Cultural Consequences of Globalization*. Liverpool: Liverpool University Press.

Robertson, Roland, and David Inglis. 2004. "The Global Animus: In the Tracks of World Consciousness." *Globalizations* 1 (1): 38–49.

Robinson, Lillian. 2007. "Sex Tourism." In Jan Aart Scholte and Roland Robertson, eds., *Encyclopedia of Globalization*. New York: MTM Publishing.

Robinson, William I. 2007. "Transnationality." In Jan Aart Scholte and Roland Robertson, eds., *Encyclopedia of Globalization*. New York: MTM Publishing.

Robles, Frances. 2014. "Virus Advances Through East Caribbean." *New York Times* February 8.

Rodrik, Dani. 1997. *Has Globalization Gone Too Far?* Washington, DC: Institute for International Economics.

Roett, Riordan, ed. 1999. *Mercosur: Regional Integration and World Markets*. Boulder, CO: Lynne Rienner.

Roett, Riordan. 2012. "Mercosur." In George Ritzer, ed., *Wiley-Blackwell Encyclopedia of Globalization*. Oxford: Wiley-Blackwell.

Rogers, Phil. 2013. "Commissioner Envisions True World Series." *Chicago Tribune* March 9.

Rohter, Larry. 2007a. "In the Amazon: Conservation or Colonialism?" *New York Times* July 27.

Rohter, Larry. 2007b. "Venezuela Wants Trade Group to Embrace Anti-Imperialism." *New York Times* January 19.

Rojek, Chris. 2003. *Stuart Hall*. Cambridge, UK: Polity.

Rootes, Christopher, ed. 1999. *Environmental Movements: Local, National and Global*. London: Routledge.

Rosenau, James N. 2002. "Governance in a New Global Order." In David Held and Anthony McGrew, eds., *Governing Globalization: Power, Authority and Global Governance*. London: Polity.

Rosenau, James N., and Ernst-Otto Czempiel, eds. 1992. *Governance without Government: Order and Change in World Politics*. Cambridge: Cambridge University Press.

Rosenberg, Julius. 2005. "Globalization Theory: A Post Mortem." *International Politics* 42: 2–74.

Rosenthal, Elisabeth. 2007. "As Earth Warms Up, Virus From Tropics Moves to Italy." *New York Times* December 23.

Rosenthal, Elisabeth. 2008a. "In Europe, the Catch of the Day Is Often Illegal." *New York Times* January 15.

Rosenthal, Elisabeth. 2008b. "Lofty Pledge to Cut Emissions Comes With Caveat in Norway." *New York Times* March 22.

Rosenthal, Elisabeth. 2008c. "Studies Call Biofuels a Greenhouse Threat." *New York Times* February 8.

Rosenthal, Elisabeth. 2008d. "Fast Food Hits Mediterranean; Diet Succumbs." *New York Times* September 24.

Rosenthal, Elisabeth. 2011. "Another Side of Tilapia, the Perfect Factory Fish." *New York Times* May 2.

Rosenthal, Elisabeth. 2013. "As Biofuel Demand Grows, So Do Guatemala's Hunger Pangs." *New York Times* January 5.

Rosenthal, Joel T. 2007. "Voyages of Discovery." In Jan Aart Scholte and Roland Robertson, eds., *Encyclopedia of Globalization*. New York: MTM Publishing.

Rothenberg-Aalami, Jessica. 2004. "Coming Full Circle? Forging Missing Links Along Nike's Integrated Production Networks." *Global Networks* 4 (4): 335–354.

Roxborough, Ian. 2002. "Globalization, Unreason and the Dilemmas of American Military Strategy." *International Sociology* 17 (3): 339–359.

Rubin, Alissa. 2013. "Protests After France Expels 2 Immigrant Students." *New York Times* October 17.

Rugman, Alan. 2012. *The End of Globalization*. New York: Random House.

Rumford, Chris. 2002. *The European Union: A Political Sociology*. Oxford: Blackwell.

Rumford, Chris. 2007a. "Does Europe Have Cosmopolitan Borders?" *Globalizations* 4 (3): 327–339.

Rumford, Chris. 2007b "European Union." In Jan Aart Scholte and Roland Robertson, eds., *Encyclopedia of Globalization*. New York: MTM Publishing.

Rumford, Chris. 2007c. "More than a Game: Globalization and the Post-Westernization of World Cricket." In Richard Giulianotti and Roland Robertson, eds., *Globalization and Sport*. Oxford: Blackwell.

Rumford, Chris, and Stephen Wagg, eds. 2010. *Cricket and Globalization*. Newcastle upon Tyne, UK: Cambridge Scholars Publishing.

Runyan, Anne Sisson. 2012. "Gender." In George Ritzer, ed., *Wiley-Blackwell Encyclopedia of Globalization*. Oxford: Wiley-Blackwell.

Rushe, Dominic. 2013. "Zuckerberg: US 'Blew it' on NSA Surveillance." *The Guardian* September 11.

Rupp, Leila J. 1997. *Worlds of Women: The Making of an International Women's Movement*. Princeton: Princeton University Press.

Ryan, J. Michael. 2007. "Grobalization." In George Ritzer, ed., *Encyclopedia of Sociology*. Oxford: Blackwell.

Ryan, J. Michael. 2012. "Homosexuality." In George Ritzer, ed., *Wiley-Blackwell Encyclopedia of Globalization*. Oxford: Wiley-Blackwell.

Ryoko, Yamamoto. 2012. "Immigrants, Undocumented." In George Ritzer, ed., *Wiley-Blackwell Encyclopedia of Globalization*. Oxford: Wiley-Blackwell.

Sachs, Jeffrey. 1997. "The Limits of Convergence." *Economist* June 14.

Sader, Emir. 2009. "Postneoliberalism in Latin America." *Development Dialogue* 51: 171–179.

Saeed, Amir. 2007. "Media, Racism and Islamophobia: The Representation of Islam and Muslims in the Media." *Sociology Compass* 1 (2): 443–462.

Safran, William. 1991. "Diasporas in Modern Societies." *Diaspora* 1 (1): 83–99.

Saggi, Kamal, and Halis Yildiz. 2011. "Bilateral Trade Agreements and the Feasibility of Multilateral Free Trade." *Review of International Economics* 19 (2): 356–373.

Saguier, Marcelo I. 2007. "The Hemispheric Social Alliance and the Free Trade Area of the Americas Process: The Challenges and Opportunities of Transnational Coalitions Against Neo-liberalism." *Globalizations* 4 (2): 251–265.

Said, Edward W. 1979/1994. *Orientalism*. New York: Vintage Books.

Said, Edward W. 1993. *Culture and Imperialism*. New York: Knopf.

Salaff, Janet W. 2013. "Return Migration." In Steven J. Gold and Stephanie J. Nawyn, eds., *The Routledge International Handbook of Migration Studies*. New York: Routledge.

Sanger, David. 2012. "Obama Order Sped Up Wave of Cyberattacks Against Iran." *New York Times* June 1.

Sanger, David, and William Broad. 2013. "Iran is Seen Advancing Nuclear Bid." *New York Times* May 22.

Santilli, Paul. 2007. "Culture, Evil and Horror." In Steven V. Hicks and Daniel E. Shannon, eds., *The Challenges of Globalization: Rethinking Nature, Culture, and Freedom*. Oxford: Blackwell.

Santos, Fernanda. 2013. "Judge Finds Violations of Rights by Sheriff." *New York Times* May 24.

Santos, Fernanda, and Rebekah Zemansky. 2013. "Arizona Desert Swallows Migrants on Riskier Paths." *New York Times* May 20.

Sarker, Suprateek, Suranjan Chakrobaorty, Patriya Silpakit Tansuhaf, Mark Mulder, and Kivilcim Dogerlioglu-Demir. 2013. "The 'Mail-Order Bride' (MOB) Phenomenon in the Cyberworld: An Interpretive Investigation." *ACM Transactions on Management Information Systems* 4 (3).

Sarroub, Loukia K. 2005. *All American Yemeni Girls: Being Muslim in a Public School*. Philadelphia: University of Pennsylvania Press.

Sassatelli, Roberta. 2008. "Consumer Society." In George Ritzer, ed., *The Blackwell Encyclopedia of Sociology Online*. Oxford: Blackwell.

Sassen, Saskia. 1991. *The Global City: New York, London, and Tokyo*. Princeton: Princeton University Press.

Sassen, Saskia. 2004. "Local Actors in Global Politics." *Current Sociology* 52 (4): 469–470.

Sassen, Saskia. 2007a. "Migration." In Jan Aart Scholte and Roland Robertson, eds., *Encyclopedia of Globalization*. New York: MTM Publishing.

Sassen, Saskia. 2007b. *A Sociology of Globalization*. New York: W.W. Norton.

Sassen, Saskia. 2012a. *Cities in a World Economy*. 4th edn. Thousand Oaks, CA: Sage.

Sassen, Saskia. 2012b. "Beyond State-to-State Geopolitics: Urban Vectors Dominate." *2012 Global Cities Index*. A.T. Kearney.

Sassen, Saskia. 2012c. "Cities." In George Ritzer, ed., *Wiley-Blackwell Encyclopedia of Globalization*. Oxford: Wiley-Blackwell.

Sassen, Saskia. 2013. "The Global City: Strategic Site/New Frontier." In Engin Isin, ed., *Democracy, Citizenship, and the Global City*. New York: Routledge.

Savage, Charlie. 2013. "Soldier Admits Providing Files to Wikileaks." *New York Times* February 28.

Savage, Charlie, and Scott Shane. 2013. "Secret Court Rebuked NSA on Surveillance." *New York Times* August 21.

Saxenian, Annalee. 2006. *The New Argonauts: Regional Advantage in a Global Economy*. Cambridge, MA: Harvard University Press.

Sayers, Janet, and Margot Edwards. 2004. "The Brawn-Drain? Issues for the Professional Sports Worker." In Paul Spoonley, Ann Dupuis, and Anne de Bruin, eds., *Work and Working in Twenty-First Century New Zealand*. Palmerston North, NZ: Dunmore Press.

Schabas, William, and Yvonne McDermott. 2012. "International Criminal Courts." In George Ritzer, ed., *Wiley-Blackwell Encyclopedia of Globalization*. Oxford: Wiley-Blackwell.

Schejter, Amit, and Noam Tirosh. 2012. "Social Media New and Old in the Al-'Arakeeb Conflict: A Case Study." *The Information Society* 28: 304–315.

Schlosser, Eric. 2005. *Fast Food Nation*. New York: Harper Perennial.

Schmalzbauer, Leah. 2008. "Family Divided: The Class Formation of Honduran Transnational Families." *Global Networks* 8 (3): 329–346.

Schmeman, Serge. 2014. "Tussling Over Ukraine; Gains and Grave Setbacks for Gay Rights." *New York Times* February 28.

Schmidt, Michael, and Eric Schmitt. 2014. "Syria Militants Said to Recruit Americans to Attack US." *New York Times* January 9.

Schmidt, Volker. 2012. "Modernization." In George Ritzer, ed., *Wiley-Blackwell Encyclopedia of Globalization*. Oxford: Wiley-Blackwell.

Schmitt, Eric. 2013. "Drones in Niger Reflect New US Tack on Terrorism." *New York Times* July 10.

Schneider, Gerald. 2007. "War in the Era of Globalization." In George Ritzer, ed., *Blackwell Companion to Globalization*. Oxford: Blackwell.

Schoenfeld, Amy. 2007. "A Multinational Loaf." *New York Times* June 16.

Scholte, Jan Aart. 2004. "Globalization Studies: Past and Future: A Dialogue of Diversity." *Globalizations* 1 (1): 102–110.

Scholte, Jan Aart. 2005. *Globalization: A Critical Introduction*. 2nd edn. New York: Palgrave.

Schonberger, Richard J. 1982. *Japanese Manufacturing Techniques*. New York: Free Press.

Schonhardt, Sara. 2011. "Gunmen Attack Helicopter Carrying Mine Workers in Indonesia." *New York Times* December 17.

Schonhardt, Sara. 2013. "In Indonesia, Environmentalists See a Disaster in the Making." *New York Times* October 11.

Schumpeter, Joseph A. 1976. *Capitalism, Socialism and Democracy*. 5th edn. London: George Allen and Unwin.

Schwarzenbach, René, Thomas Egli, Thomas B. Hofstetter, Urs von Gunten, and Bernhard Wehrli. 2010. "Global Water Pollution and Human Health." *Annual Review of Environment and Resources* 35: 109–136.

Sciolino, Elaine. 2007a. "Megastores on March, Paris Takes to Barricades." *New York Times* January 31.

Sciolino, Elaine. 2007b. "Sarkozy Pledges Crackdown on Rioters." *New York Times* November 29.

Seabrook, John. 2008. "American Scrap: An Old-School Industry Globalizes." *New Yorker* January 14.

Seckinelgin, Hakan. 2002. "Civil Society as a Metaphor for Western Liberalism." *Global Society* 16 (4): 357–376.

Seelye, Katharine. 2010. "Boy Scouts Seek a Way to Rebuild Ranks." *New York Times* July 30.

Segato, Rita. 2007. "Liberation Theology." In Jan Aart Scholte and Roland Robertson, eds., *Encyclopedia of Globalization*. New York: MTM Publishing.

Seidman, Gay. 2007. *Beyond the Boycott: Labor Rights, Human Rights, and Transnational Activism*. New York: Russell Sage Foundation.

Seidman, Steven. 1991. "The End of Sociological Theory: The Postmodern Hope." *Sociological Theory* 9: 131–146.

Sekulic, Dusko. 2007. "Ethnic Cleansing." In George Ritzer, ed., *The Blackwell Encyclopedia of Sociology*. Oxford: Blackwell.

Sen, Amartya. 2002. "How to Judge Globalism." *The American Prospect* 13 (1).

Sen, Jai, Anita Anand, Arturo Escobar, and Peter Waterman, eds. 2004. *World Social Forum: Challenging Empires*. New Delhi: Viveka Foundation.

Sengupta, Somini. 2008. "Thirsting for Energy in India's Boomtowns and Beyond." *New York Times* March 2.

Sernau, Scott. 2014. *Social Inequality in a Global Age*. 4th edn. Thousand Oaks, CA: Sage.

Serra-Majem, Luis, and Joy Ngo. 2012. "Undernutrition." In George Ritzer, ed., *Wiley-Blackwell Encyclopedia of Globalization*. Oxford: Wiley-Blackwell.

Serra, Narcís, and Joseph E. Stiglitz, eds. 2008. *The Washington Consensus Reconsidered: Towards a New Global Governance.* New York: Oxford University Press.

Servan-Schreiber, J.-J. 1968. *The American Challenge.* New York: Atheneum.

Shamir, Ronen. 2005. "Without Borders? Notes on Globalization as a Mobility Regime." *Sociological Theory* 23 (2): 197–217.

Shane, Scott. 2010. "Keeping Secrets WikiSafe." *New York Times* December 11.

Shane, Scott, and Michael Gordon. 2008. "Dissident's Tale of Epic Escape from Iran's Vise." *New York Times* July 13.

Sheehan, Michael. 2011. "The Changing Character of War." In John Baylis, Steve Smith, and Patricia Owens, eds., *The Globalization of World Politics.* 5th edn. New York: Oxford University Press.

Sheffer, Gabriel. 2013. "The Historical, Cultural, Social, and Political Backgrounds of Ethno-National Diasporas." In Steven J. Gold and Stephanie J. Nawyn, eds., *The Routledge International Handbook of Migration Studies.* New York: Routledge.

Shelley, Louise. 2010. *Human Trafficking: A Global Perspective.* New York: Cambridge University Press.

Short, John. 2013. *Global Metropolitan: Globalization Cities in a Capitalist World.* New York: Routledge.

Shorto, Russell. 2008. "No Babies?" *New York Times Magazine* June 29.

Sifry, Micah. 2011. *Wikileaks and the Age of Transparency.* New York: OR Books.

Silver-Greenberg, Jessica. 2012. "New Rules for Money Transfers, but Few Limits." *New York Times* June 1.

Simmel, Georg. 1908/1955. *Conflict and the Web of Group Affiliations.* New York: Free Press.

Singer, Barnett. 2013. *The Americanization of France: Searching for Happiness after the Algerian War.* Lanham, MD: Rowman & Littlefield.

Singer, P. W., and Allan Friedman. 2014. *Cybersecurity and Cyberwar: What Everyone Needs to Know.* New York: Oxford University Press.

Singh, Robert. 2006. "Are We All Americans Now? Explaining Anti-Americanisms." In Brendan O'Connor and Martin Griffiths, eds., *The Rise of Anti-Americanism.* New York: Routledge.

Singh, Robert. 2007. "Guns, Capital Punishment and Anti-Americanism." In Brendon O'Connor, ed., *Anti-Americanism: History, Causes, and Themes,* Vol. 1: *Causes and Sources.* Oxford: Greenwood World Publishing.

Singh Grewal, David. 2008. *Network Power: The Social Dynamics of Globalization.* New Haven: Yale University Press.

Singh, J. P. 2010. *United Nations Education, Scientific, and Cultural Organization (UNESCO): Creating Norms for a Complex World.* New York: Taylor & Francis.

Sklair, Leslie. 2002. *Globalization: Capitalism and Its Alternatives.* Oxford: Oxford University Press.

Sklair, Leslie. 2009. "The Transnational Capitalist Class and the Politics of Capitalist Globalization." In Samir Dasgupta and Jan Nederveen Pieterse, eds., *Politics of Globalization,* Thousand Oaks, CA: Sage.

Sklair, Leslie. 2012. "Transnational Capitalist Class." In George Ritzer, ed., *Wiley-Blackwell Encyclopedia of Globalization.* Oxford: Wiley-Blackwell.

Smart, Barry. 2007. "Not Playing Around: Global Capitalism, Modern Sport and Consumer Culture." In Richard Giulianotti and Roland Robertson, eds., *Globalization and Sport.* Oxford: Blackwell.

Smith, Adam. 1776/1977. *An Inquiry into the Nature and Causes of the Wealth of Nations.* Chicago: University of Chicago Press.

Smith, Adam. 1953. *The Wealth of Nations.* Chicago: Henry Regnery.

Smith, Jackie. 2001. "Globalizing Resistance: The Battle of Seattle and the Future of Social Movements." *Mobilization* 6: 1–20.

Smith, Jackie. 2008. *Social Movements for Global Democracy.* Baltimore: Johns Hopkins University Press.

Smith, Jackie, and Dawn West. 2005. "The Uneven Geography of Global Civil Society." *Social Forces* 84: 621–652.

Smith, Jackie, and Marina Karides. 2008. *Global Democracy and the World Social Forums.* Boulder, CO: Paradigm Publishers.

Smith, Megan, and James Walsh. 2013. "Do Drone Strikes Degrade Al Qaeda? Evidence From Propaganda Output." *Terrorism and Political Violence* 25 (2): 311–327.

Smith, Peter. 2008. "Going Global: The Transnational Politics of the Dalit Movement." *Globalizations* 5 (1): 13–33.

Snyder, Margaret. 2006. "Unlikely Godmother: The UN and the Global Women's Movement." In Myra Marx Ferree and Aili Mari Tripp, eds., *Global Feminism: Transnational Women's Activism, Organizing, and Human Rights*. New York: New York University Press.

So, Alvin. 2012. "Political Globalization." In George Ritzer, ed., *Wiley-Blackwell Encyclopedia of Globalization*. Oxford: Wiley-Blackwell.

Soderlund, Gretchen. 2013. "Introduction to 'Charting, Tracking, and Mapping: New Technologies, Labor, and Surveillance." *Social Semiotics* 23 (2): 163–172.

Soderquist, Don. 2005. *The Wal-Mart Way: The Inside Story of the Success of the World's Largest Company*. Nashville, TN: Thomas Nelson.

Soederberg, Susanne. 2007. "Taming Corporations or Buttressing Market-Led Development?: A Critical Assessment of the Global Compact." *Globalizations* 4 (4): 500–513.

Sorensen, Georg. 2007. "Sovereignty." In Jan Aart Scholte and Roland Robertson, eds., *Encyclopedia of Globalization*. New York: MTM Publishing.

Soros, George. 2000. *Open Society: Reforming Global Capitalism*. New York: Public Affairs.

Sovereign Wealth Fund Institute. 2013. "Fund Rankings, Updated July 2013." http://www.swfinstitute. org/fund-rankings/ (last accessed August 17, 2014).

Sparks, Colin. 2007. *Globalization, Development and the Mass Media*. London: Sage.

Sparshott, Jeffrey, and Erik Holm. 2012. "End of a Bailout: US Sells Last AIG Shares." *WSJ* December 11.

Spivak, Gayatri Chakravory. 1987. *In Other Worlds: Essays in Cultural Politics*. New York: Routledge.

Spivak, Gayatri Chakravory. 1999. *A Critique of Postcolonial Reason: Toward a History of the Vanishing Present*. Cambridge, MA: Harvard University Press.

St. John, Allen. 2013. "Why 'Breaking Bad' is the Best Show Ever and Why that Matters." *Forbes* September 16.

Standing, Guy. 1989. "Global Feminization through Flexible Labor." *World Development* 17: 1077–1095.

Standing, Guy. 1999. "Global Feminization through Flexible Labor: A Theme Revisited." *World Development* 27 (3): 583–602.

Standing, Guy. 2011a. *The Precariat: The Dangerous New Class*. New York: Bloomsbury.

Standing, Guy. 2011b. "Who Will Be a Voice for the Emerging Precariat?" *The Guardian* June 1.

Starbucks. 2012. "Starbucks Company Profile." http://www.starbucks.com/assets/9a6616b98dc64271 ac8c910fbee47884.pdf (last accessed August 17, 2014).

Steger, Manfred B. 2007. "Globalization and Ideology." In George Ritzer, ed., *Blackwell Companion to Globalization*. Oxford: Blackwell.

Stehr, N. 2008. *Moral Markets: How Knowledge and Affluence Change Consumers and Products*. Boulder, CO: Paradigm.

Steingart, Gabor. 2008. *The War for Wealth: The True Story of Globalization or Why the Flat World is Broken*. New York: McGraw-Hill.

Steinmetz, George. 2012. "Geopolitics." In George Ritzer, ed., *Wiley-Blackwell Encyclopedia of Globalization*. Oxford: Wiley-Blackwell.

Stelter, Brian. 2013. "Al Jazeera America Shifts Focus to US News." *New York Times* May 26.

Stempel, Jonathan, and Nate Raymond. 2013. "Citigroup Arbitration Win in $4 Billion Abu Dhabi Case Upheld." *Reuters* March 4.

Stiglitz, Joseph E. 2002. *Globalization and Its Discontents*. New York: W.W. Norton.

Stiglitz, Joseph E. 2006. *Making Globalization Work*. New York: W.W. Norton.

Stiglitz, Joseph E. 2010. *The Stiglitz Report: Reforming the International Monetary and Financial Systems in the Wake of the Global Crisis*. New York: New Press.

Stiglitz, Joseph E., and Andrew Charlton. 2005. *Fair Trade for All: How Trade Can Promote Development*. Oxford: Oxford University Press.

Stockhammer, Philipp, ed. 2012. *Conceptualizing Cultural Hybridization: A Transdisciplinary Approach*. New York: Springer.

Strange, Susan. 1996. *The Retreat of the State: The Diffusion of Power in the World Economy*. Cambridge: Cambridge University Press.

Strange, Susan. 1999. "The Westfailure System." *Review of International Studies* 25 (3): 345–354.

Strassel, Kimberly A. 2007. "If the Cap Fits." *Wall Street Journal* January 26.

Streitfeld, David. 2008. "A Global Need for Grain That Farmers Can't Fill." *New York Times* March 19.

Struck, Doug. 2007a. "At the Poles, Melting Occurring at Alarming Rate." *Washington Post* October 22.

Struck, Doug. 2007b. "Warming will Exacerbate Global Water Conflicts." *Washington Post* August 20.

Suarez-Orozco, Marcelo M., and Carolyn Smith. 2007. "Learning in the Global Era." In Marcelo M. Suarez-Orozco, ed., *Learning in the Global Era: International Perspectives on Globalization and Education*. Berkeley, CA: University of California Press.

Subramanian, Ramesh. 2012. "Computer Viruses." In George Ritzer, ed., *Wiley-Blackwell Encyclopedia of Globalization*. Oxford: Wiley-Blackwell.

Süderbaum, Fedrik. 2012. "African Union." In George Ritzer, ed., *Wiley-Blackwell Encyclopedia of Globalization*. Oxford: Wiley-Blackwell.

Sullivan, Kevin. 2008. "Food Crisis Is Depicted as 'Silent Tsunami.'" *Washington Post* April 28.

Sznaider, Natan. 2003. "The Americanisation of Memory: The Case of the Holocaust." In Ulrich Beck, Natan Sznaider, and Rainer Winter, eds., *Global America? The Cultural Consequences of Globalization*. Liverpool: Liverpool University Press.

Szyliowicz, Joseph. 2013. "Transportation Technology and its Effects on the Speed, Distance, and Magnitude of Terrorist Attacks." In U. F. Aydoğdu, ed., *Technological Dimensions of Defence Against Terrorism*. Fairfax, VA: IOS Press.

Tan, Celine. 2007. "Liberalization." In Jan Aart Scholte and Roland Robertson, eds., *Encyclopedia of Globalization*. New York: MTM Publishing.

Tapscott, Don, and Anthony D. Williams. 2006. *Wikinomics: How Mass Collaboration Changes Everything*. New York: Portfolio.

Taylor, Ian. 2003. "The United Nations Conference on Trade and Development." *New Political Economy* 8 (3): 409–418.

Taylor, J. L. 2007. "Buddhism." In Jan Aart Scholte and Roland Robertson, eds., *Encyclopedia of Globalization*. New York: MTM Publishing.

Taylor, Jerome. 2012. "Wikileaks is Back – Without Assange, but with a Cache of Syrian Emails." *The Independent* July 5.

Taylor, Peter J., Michael J. Watts, and R. J. Johnston. 2002a. "Geography/Globalization." In R. J. Johnston, Peter J. Taylor, and Michael J. Watts, eds., *Geographies of Global Change: Remapping the World*. Oxford: Blackwell.

Taylor, Peter J., Michael J. Watts, and R. J. Johnston. 2002b. "Remapping the World: What Sort of Map? What Sort of World?" In R. J. Johnston, Peter J. Taylor, and Michael J. Watts, eds., *Geographies of Global Change: Remapping the World*. Oxford: Blackwell.

Telecompaper. 2013. "Bangladesh Nearing 100 Mln Mobile Subs." May 2.

Teune, Henry. 2002. "Global Democracy." *Annals* 581: 22–34.

The Associated Press. 2009. "Eurozone Unemployment Reaches 15 Million." *CBC News* July 2.

The Local. 2013. April 25. "Sweden's 'Racist Sniper' Felled for Further Crimes."

Therborn, Goran. 2000. "Globalizations: Dimensions, Historical Waves, Regional Effects, Normative Governance." *International Sociology* 15: 151–179.

Thomas, George M. 2007. "Globalization: The Major Players." In George Ritzer, ed., *Blackwell Companion to Globalization*. Oxford: Blackwell.

Thomas, June. 2012. "Why Don't Brits Watch Breaking Bad?" *Slate* July 18.

Thomas, Jr, Landon. 2008. "Cash-Rich, Publicity-Shy." *New York Times* February 28.

Thomas, William I., and Dorothy Thomas. 1928. *The Child in America: Behavior Problems and Programs*. New York: Knopf.

Thompson, Ginger. 2008. "Fewer People are Entering US Illegally, Report Says." *New York Times* October 3.

Timberlake, Michael, and Xiulian Ma. 2007. "Cities and Globalization." In George Ritzer, ed., *Blackwell Companion to Globalization*. Oxford: Blackwell.

Timms, Jill. 2012. "Labor Movements." In George Ritzer, ed., *Wiley-Blackwell Encyclopedia of Globalization*. Oxford: Wiley-Blackwell.

Tocqueville, Alexis de. 1825–1840/1969. *Democracy in America*. Garden City, NY: Doubleday.

Tomlinson, John. 1999. *Globalization and Culture*. Chicago: University of Chicago Press.

Tomlinson, John. 2007. "Cultural Globalization." In George Ritzer, ed., *Blackwell Companion to Globalization*. Oxford: Blackwell.

Tomlinson, John. 2012. "Cultural Globalization." In George Ritzer, ed., *Wiley-Blackwell Encyclopedia of Globalization*. Oxford: Wiley-Blackwell.

Tonkiss, Fran. 2012. "Economic Globalization." In George Ritzer, ed., *Wiley-Blackwell Encyclopedia of Globalization*. Oxford: Wiley-Blackwell.

Tooze, Roger. 2000. "Susan Strange, Academic International Relations and the Study of International Political Economy." *New Political Economy* 5 (2): 1–10.

Townsend, Mark. 2011. "Sex Trafficking in the UK: One Woman's Horrific Story of Kidnap, Rape, Beatings, and Prostitution." *The Guardian* February 5.

Tsatsou, Panayiota. 2009. "Reconceptualising 'Time' and 'Space' in the Era of Electronic Media and Communications." *PLATFORM: Journal of Media and Communication* 1: 11–32.

Tsing, Anna. 2000. "The Global Situation." *Cultural Anthropology* 15 (3): 327–360.

Tsingou, Eleni. 2007. "Group of Thirty." In Jan Aart Scholte and Roland Robertson, eds., *Encyclopedia of Globalization*. New York: MTM Publishing.

Tuathail, Gearoid Ó, Simon Dalby, and Paul Routledge, eds. 1998. *The Geopolitics Reader*. London: Routledge.

Tumber, Howard, and Frank Webster. 2007. "Globalization and Information and Communications Technologies: The Case of War." In George Ritzer, ed., *Blackwell Companion to Globalization*. Oxford: Blackwell.

Tunstall, Jeremy. 1977. *The Media Are American: Anglo-American Media in the World*. New York: Columbia University Press.

Tunstall, Jeremy. 2008. *The Media Were American: U.S. Mass Media in Decline*. Oxford: Oxford University Press.

Turner, Bryan S. 1993. "Outline of a General Theory of Human Rights." *Sociology* 27 (3): 489–512.

Turner, Bryan S. 2007a. "Human Rights." In Jan Aart Scholte and Roland Robertson, eds., *Encyclopedia of Globalization*. New York: MTM Publishing.

Turner, Bryan. 2007b. "The Futures of Globalization." In George Ritzer, ed., *Blackwell Companion to Globalization*. Oxford: Blackwell.

Turner, Rachel S., and Andrew Gamble. 2007. "Neoliberalism." In Jan Aart Scholte and Roland Robertson, eds., *Encyclopedia of Globalization*. New York: MTM Publishing.

2002 National Survey of Latinos. Pew Hispanic Center/Kaiser Family Foundation.

Tyson, Laura. 2013. "The Myriad Benefits of a Carbon Tax." *New York Times* June 28.

Unger, Brigitte, and Gregory Rawlings. 2008. "Competing for Criminal Money." *Global Business and Economics Review* 10: 331–352.

UNICEF and the UNESCO Institute for Statistics. 2012. *Global Initiative on Out-of-School Children*. UNICEF: New York.

United Nations Development Programme, 1999. *United Nations Development Report 1999*. Oxford: Oxford University Press.

United Nations Office on Drugs and Crime (UNODC). 2012. *Global Report on Trafficking in Persons*. New York: United Nations.

United Nations. 2012. "Composition of the Secretariat: Staff Demographics." http://www.un.org/ga/search/view_doc.asp?symbol=A/67/329 (last accessed August 17, 2014).

United Nations. 2013a. *World Economic Situation and Prospects 2013*. New York: United Nations.

United Nations. 2013b. "Number of International Migrants Rises Above 232 Million." UN Department of Economic and Social Affairs. http://www.un.org/en/development/desa/news/population/number-of-international-migrants-rises.html (last accessed August 17, 2014)

UPI. 2013. January 9. "China 2012 Trade Surplus Surges to $231B."

UPI. 2013. August 10. "53 Million Hispanics Constitute 17 Percent of US Population."

Urry, John. 2002. *The Tourist Gaze*. 2nd edn. London: Sage.

Urry, John. 2009. "Mobilities and Social Theory." In Bryan Turner, ed., *The New Blackwell Companion to Social Theory*. Oxford: Blackwell.

US Census Bureau. 2013. "US Trade in Goods and Services – Balance of Payments (BOP) Basis." http://www.census.gov/foreign-trade/statistics/historical/gands.pdf (last accessed August 17, 2014).

Valdes, Gustavo. 2013. "Undocumented Immigrant Population on the Rise in the US." *CNN* September 25.

Vertigans, Stephen, and Philip W. Sutton. 2002. "Globalisation Theory and Islamic Practice." *Global Society* 16 (1): 31–46.

Vertovec, Steven. 1999. "Conceiving and Researching Transnationalism." *Ethnic and Racial Studies* 22 (2): 447–462.

Vertovec, Steven. 2004. "Cheap Calls: The Social Glue of Migrant Transnationalism." *Global Networks* 4 (2): 219–224.

Veseth, Michael. 2005. *Globaloney: Unraveling the Myths of Globalization*. Lanham, MD: Rowman & Littlefield.

Villagran, Lauren. 2013. "Slow US Growth, Zero Immigration, Hurt Remittances to Mexico." *CBS SmartPlanet* February 27.

Vlasic, Bill. 2013. "Chinese Creating New Auto Niche Within Detroit." *New York Times* May 21.

Vogel, Ann. 2006. "Who's Making Global Civil Society? Philanthropy and US Empire in World Society." *British Journal of Sociology* 57: 635–655.

Vogli, Robert De, Anne Kouvonen, Makro Elovainio, and Michael Marmot. 2014. "Economic Globalization, Inequality, and Body Mass Index: A Cross-National Analysis of 127 Countries." *Critical Public Health* 24 (1): 7–21.

Von Grebmer, Klaus, Derek Headey, Tolulope Olofinbyi et al. 2013. *2013 Global Hunger Index*. Washington, DC: International Food Policy Research Institute.

Vora, Shivani. 2013. "India's Tata Group Maps US Expansion." *New York Times* April 18.

Wagner, Gernot, and Martin Weitzman. 2013. "Inconvenient Uncertainties." *New York Times* October 10.

Wakefield, Kelly. 2013. "Global Digital Divide: Inequality and Internet Access." *Geography Review* 26 (4): 10–13.

Wald, Matthew. 2013. "Court Overturns EPA's Biofuels Mandate." *New York Times* January 25.

Walker, Carl. 2008. *Depression and Globalization: The Politics of Mental Health in the 21st Century*. New York: Springer.

Walker, Gordon. 2012. *Environmental Justice: Concepts, Evidence, and Politics*. New York: Routledge.

Wallace, Robert. 2009. "Breeding Influenza: The Political Virology of Offshore Farming." *Antipode* 41 (5): 916–951.

Wallerstein, Immanuel. 1974. *The Modern World-System: Capitalist Agriculture and the Origins of the European World-Economy in the 16th Century*. New York: Academic Press.

Wallerstein, Immanuel. 1992. "America and the World: Today, Yesterday and Tomorrow." *Theory and Society* 21 (1): 1–28.

Wallerstein, Immanuel. 2004. *World-Systems Analysis: An Introduction*. Durham, NC: Duke University Press.

Wallerstein, Immanuel. 2005. "After Developmentalism and Globalization, What?" *Social Forces* 83 (3): 1263–1278.

Walsh, Declan. 2013. "In a Surprise, Pakistan Says Fewer Civilians Died by Drones." *New York Times* October 30.

Walsh, Dylan. 2012. "The Budding Health Care Costs of Climate Change." *New York Times* December 10.

Wang, Xia. 2012. "Undocumented Immigrants as Perceived Criminal Threat: A Test of the Minority Threat Perspective." *Criminology* 50 (3): 743–776.

Ward, Kathryn. 1990. "Introduction and Overview." In Kathryn Ward, ed., *Women Workers and Global Restructuring*. Ithaca, NY: ILR Press.

Warf, Barney. 2008. *Time-Space Compression: Historical Geographies*. New York: Routledge.

Warkentin, Craig. 2007. "Nongovernmental Organizations." In Jan Aart Scholte and Roland Robertson, eds., *Encyclopedia of Globalization*. New York: MTM Publishing.

Warschauer, Mark. 2012. "Language and the Digital Divide." In Carol Chapelle, ed., *Wiley-Blackwell Encyclopedia of Applied Linguistics*. Oxford: Wiley-Blackwell.

Waruingi, Macharia, Kerrie Downing, Isaac Amos et al. 2013. "Globalization of Health Care: Designing, Developing and Implementing a Just World Class Health System in a Frontier Market." *The Journal of Global Healthcare Systems* 3 (2): 3–23.

Watling, Les, and Gilles Boeuf. 2013. "Deep Sea Plunder and Ruin." *New York Times* October 2.

Watson, Iain. 2001. "Politics, Resistance to Neoliberalism and the Ambiguities of Globalisation." *Global Society* 15: 201–218.

Watson, James L., ed. 1997. *Golden Arches East: McDonald's in East Asia*. Cambridge, MA: Harvard University Press.

Watts, Michael. 2012. "Globophobia." In George Ritzer, ed., *Wiley-Blackwell Encyclopedia of Globalization*. Oxford: Wiley-Blackwell.

Wax, Emily. 2007. "An Ancient Indian Craft Left in Tatters." *Washington Post* June 6.

Wayne, Teddy. 2011. "The Mail-Order-Bride Trade is Flourishing." *Business Week* January 6.

Weaver, Adam. 2012. "Tourism." In George Ritzer, ed., *Wiley-Blackwell Encyclopedia of Globalization*. Oxford: Wiley-Blackwell.

Weber, Max. 1904–1905/1958. *The Protestant Ethic and the Spirit of Capitalism*. New York: Scribner's.

Weber, Max. 1921/1968. *Economy and Society*. 3 vols. Totowa, NJ: Bedminster Press.

Weber, Max. 1927/1981. *General Economic History*. New Brunswick, NJ: Transaction Books.

Weinsheit, Ralph, and William White. 2009. *Methamphetamine: Its History, Pharmacology, and Treatment*. Center City, MN: Hazelden.

Weisman, Steven R. 2007a. "Cracks in the Financial Foundation." *New York Times* May 23.

Weisman, Steven R. 2007b. "I.M.F. Faces A Question of Identity." *New York Times* September 28.

Weisman, Steven R. 2007c. "Oil Producers See the World and Buy It Up." *New York Times* November 28.

Weiss, Linda. 1998. *The Myth of the Powerless State*. Ithaca, NY: Cornell University Press.

Weiss, Rick. 2007. "Facing a Threat to Farming and Food Supply." *Washington Post* November 19.

Weiss, Thomas G., David P. Forsythe, and Roger A. Coate. 2004. *The United Nations and Changing World Politics*. 4th edn. Boulder, CO: Westview Press.

Weiss, Thomas G., and Danielle Zach. 2007. "United Nations Organization." In Jan Aart Scholte and Roland Robertson, eds., *Encyclopedia of Globalization*. New York: MTM Publishing.

Werdigier, Julia. 2008a. "Government to Control Struggling British Bank." *New York Times* February 18.

Werdigier, Julia. 2008b. "Debt-Gorged British Start to Worry That the Party is Ending." *New York Times* March 22.

Westbrook, David A. 2006. "The Globalization of American Law." *Theory, Culture & Society* 23 (2–3): 526–528.

Western Union. 2013. "Global Organization." http://corporate.westernunion.com/Global_Organization.html (last accessed August 17, 2014).

Wherry, Frederick F. 2008. *Global Markets and Local Crafts: Thailand and Costa Rica Compared*. Baltimore: Johns Hopkins University Press.

Whetham, David. 2013. "Killer Drones: The Moral Ups and Downs." *The RUSI Journal* 158 (3): 22–32.

White, Jonathan. 2013. *Terrorism and Homeland Security*. 8th edn. Belmont, CA: Wadsworth.

White, Russell. 2004. "Sign of a Black Planet: Hip-hop and Globalization." In Neil Campbell, Jude Davies, and George McKay, eds., *Issues in Americanisation and Culture*. Edinburgh: Edinburgh University Press.

White, Thomas, and Jon Mark Yeats. 2011. *Franchising McChurch: Feeding our Obsession with Easy Christianity*. Colorado Springs, CO: David C. Cook.

Whitefield, Kristi. 2012. "North Atlantic Treaty Organization." In George Ritzer, ed., *Wiley-Blackwell Encyclopedia of Globalization*. Oxford: Wiley-Blackwell.

Whiteside, Alan. 2012. "AIDS." In George Ritzer, ed., *Wiley-Blackwell Encyclopedia of Globalization*. Oxford: Wiley-Blackwell.

Wiggershaus, Rolf. 1994. *The Frankfurt School: Its History, Theories, and Political Significance*. Cambridge, MA: MIT Press.

Wilk, Richard. 2006. "Consumer Culture and Extractive Industry on the Margins of the World System." In John Brewer and Frank Trentmann, eds., *Consuming Cultures, Global Perspectives: Historical Trajectories, Transnational Exchanges*. Oxford: Berg.

Wilkinson, Ray. 2006. "The Biggest Failure: A New Approach to Help the World's Internally Displaced People." *Refugees* 4: 4–19.

Williams, Erica. 2012. "Sex Work." In George Ritzer, ed., *Wiley-Blackwell Encyclopedia of Globalization*. Oxford: Wiley-Blackwell.

Williams, Francis. 1962. *The American Invasion*. New York: Crown.

Williams, Marc. 2007. "United Nations Conference on Trade and Development." In Jan Aart Scholte and Roland Robertson, eds., *Encyclopedia of Globalization*. New York: MTM Publishing.

Williams, Patrick, and Laura Chrisman. 1994a. *Colonial Discourse and Post-Colonial Theory: A Reader*. New York: Columbia University Press.

Williams, Patrick, and Laura Chrisman. 1994b. "Introduction." In Patrick Williams and Laura Chrisman, *Colonial Discourse and Post-Colonial Theory: A Reader*. New York: Columbia University Press.

Williamson, John. 1990a. *The Progress of Policy Reform in Latin America*. Policy Analysis in International Economics, no. 28. Washington, DC: Institute of International Economics.

Williamson, John. 1990b. "What Washington Means by Policy Reform." In John Williamson, ed., *Latin American Adjustment: How Much Has Happened?* Washington, DC: Institute for Internal Economics.

Williamson, John. 1993. "Democracy and the 'Washington Consensus.'" *World Development* 21 (8): 1329–1336.

Winant, Howard. 2001. *The World is a Ghetto: Race and Democracy since World War II*. New York: Basic Books.

Winant, Howard. 2004. *The New Politics of Race: Globalism, Difference, Justice*. Minneapolis: University of Minnesota Press.

Wolf, Martin. 2005. *Why Globalization Works*. New Haven: Yale University Press.

Wood, David Murakami. 2012. "Globalization and Surveillance." In Kirstie Ball, Kevin Haggerty, and David Lyon, eds., *The Routledge Handbook of Surveillance Studies*. New York: Routledge.

World Bank. 2013. "Developing Countries to Receive Over $410 Billion in Remittances in 2013, Says World Bank." http://www.worldbank.org/en/news/press-release/2013/10/02/developing-countries-remittances-2013-world-bank (last accessed August 17, 2014).

World Commission on Environment and Development. 1987. *Our Common Future*. New York: Oxford University Press.

World Economic Forum. 2012. "World Economic Forum Annual Meeting 2012 The Great Transformation: Shaping New Models." http://www.weforum.org/reports/world-economic-forum-annual-meeting-2012-great-transformation-shaping-new-models (last accessed August 17, 2014).

World Health Organization. 2012. *Trends in Maternal Mortality: 1990 to 2010: WHO, UNICEF, UNFPA and The World Bank Estimates*. Geneva: World Health Organization.

World Trade Organization. 2013. "Understanding the WTO: The Organization, Members and Observers." http://www.wto.org/english/thewto_e/whatis_e/tif_e/org6_e.htm (last accessed August 17, 2014).

Wu, Yongning, and Yan Chen. 2013. "Food Safety in China." *Journal of Epidemiology and Community Health* 67: 478–479.

Wyatt, Edward. 2013. "Senators Question Chinese Takeover of Smithfield." *New York Times* July 10.

Wyatt, Edward. 2014. "US to Cede Oversight of Addresses on Internet." *New York Times* March 14.

Xie, Shaobo. 2007. "Postcolonialism." In Jan Aart Scholte and Roland Robertson, eds., *Encyclopedia of Globalization*. New York: MTM Publishing.

Yagatich, William. 2012. "Wikileaks." In George Ritzer, ed., *Wiley-Blackwell Encyclopedia of Globalization*. Oxford: Wiley-Blackwell.

Yang, M. M.-h. 1996. "Mass Media and Transnational Subjectivity in Shanghai: Notes on (Re)cosmopolitanism in a Chinese Metropolis." In Aihwa Ong and Donald Nonini, eds., *Ungrounded Empires: The Cultural Politics of Modern Chinese Transnationalism*. New York: Routledge.

Yearley, Steve. 2007. "Globalization and the Environment." In George Ritzer, ed., *Blackwell Companion to Globalization*. Oxford: Blackwell.

Yeates, Nicola. 2012. "Global Care Chains: State of the Art Review and Future Directions." *Global Networks: A Journal of Transnational Affairs* 12 (2): 135–154.

Yen, Hope. 2012. "White Population to Lose Majority Status in 2043." *Boston Globe* December 13.

Yergin, Daniel, and Joseph Stanislaw. 1998. *The Commanding Heights: The Battle for the World Economy*. New York: Touchstone.

Yetman, Norman R., ed. 1991. *Majority and Minority: The Dynamics of Race and Ethnicity in American Life*. 5th edn. Boston: Allyn and Bacon.

Yuan, Li. 2006. "Big Phone Firms Delve Undersea for Asian Growth." *Wall Street Journal* December 18.

Yuval-Davis, Nira. 2006. "Human/Women's Rights and Feminist Transversal Politics." In Myra Marx Ferree and Aili Mari Tripp, eds., *Global Feminism: Transnational Women's Activism, Organizing, and Human Rights*. New York: New York University Press.

Zakaria, Fareed. 2008. *The Post-American World*. New York: W.W. Norton.

Zakaria, Fareed. 2011. *The Post American World: Release 2.0*. New York: W.W. Norton.

Zedillo, Ernesto, ed. 2007. *The Future of Globalization: Explorations in Light of Recent Turbulence*. New York: Routledge.

Zhang, Yin, and Louis Leung. Forthcoming. "A Review of Social Networking Service (SNS) Research in Communication Journals from 2006 to 2011." *New Media and Society*.

Zhou, Moming. 2013. "World Energy Consumption to Increase 56% by 2040." *Bloomberg News* July 25.

Zhu, Tao, David Phipps, Adam Pridgen, Jedidiah Crandall, and Dan Wallach. 2013. "The Velocity of Censorship: High-Fidelity Detection of Microblog Post Deletions." Paper presented at 22nd USENIX Security Symposium in Washington, DC, August 2013.

INDEX

Page references in *italics* refer to Figures